# Flood De

# Flood Defence Law

*by*
**William Howarth**

**Shaw & Sons**

*Published by*
Shaw & Sons Limited
Shaway House
21 Bourne Park
Bourne Road
Crayford
Kent DA1 4BZ

www.shaws.co.uk

© Shaw & Sons Limited 2002

Published July 2002

ISBN 0 7219 1610 4

A CIP catalogue record for this book is available from the British Library

No part of this publication may be reproduced or transmitted in any form without the written permission of the copyright holder

*Cover design and Thames Barrier photograph by Roy Sands, Bexleyheath, Kent*

*Main cover photograph reproduced by kind permission of the Environment Agency*

*Printed and bound in Great Britain by Bell & Bain Limited, Glasgow*

# SUMMARY OF CONTENTS

The Author
Table of Contents
Preface
Acknowledgements
Table of Statutes
Table of Statutory Instruments
Table of European Secondary Legislation
Table of Cases

Chapter 1 – INTRODUCTION AND BACKGROUND

Chapter 2 – PRIVATE RIGHTS AND DUTIES

Chapter 3 – INSTITUTIONAL RESPONSIBILITIES

Chapter 4 – OPERATIONAL AND REGULATORY POWERS

Chapter 5 – COAST PROTECTION

Chapter 6 – FUNDING

Chapter 7 – SEWERAGE AND WATER SUPPLY

Chapter 8 – PUBLIC HEALTH, HIGHWAYS AND RESERVOIRS

Chapter 9 – PLANNING

Chapter 10 – ENVIRONMENTAL AND ECOLOGICAL IMPACTS

Chapter 11 – INFORMATION, WARNINGS AND INSURANCE

Chapter 12 – SUSTAINABILITY

Bibliography

Index

# THE AUTHOR

**William Howarth** is Professor of Environmental Law at the University of Kent at Canterbury and the author of several books, including *Wisdom's Law of Watercourses* and, with Donald McGillivray, *Water Pollution and Water Quality Law*, both published by Shaw & Sons. He has also written reports and numerous articles in academic journals on diverse aspects of water and environmental law. He is the General Editor of the journal *Water Law* and has acted as an advisor on water and fisheries legislation to governments and regulatory bodies at national and international levels.

# TABLE OF CONTENTS

Summary of Contents ........................................................................... v
The Author ........................................................................................... vi
Preface ................................................................................................. xv
Acknowledgements ............................................................................. xix
Table of Statutes ................................................................................. xxiii
Table of Statutory Instruments ........................................................... xli
Table of European Secondary Legislation ......................................... xliv
Table of Cases ..................................................................................... xlv

**Chapter 1 – INTRODUCTION AND BACKGROUND** ............... 1
  1.1 OBJECTIVES ............................................................................. 1
  1.2 WATER QUANTITY AND WATER QUALITY ..................... 4
  1.3 THE MEANING AND CAUSES OF 'FLOODING' ................. 5
  1.4 THE EXTENT OF THE HAZARD ........................................... 8
  1.5 RISK ........................................................................................... 10
  1.6 CLIMATE CHANGE ................................................................. 13
  1.7 THE PRECAUTIONARY PRINCIPLE .................................... 17
  1.8 EXTREME FLOODING EVENTS ........................................... 19
      1.8.1 The East Coast Flood 1953 ............................................. 19
      1.8.2 The Easter Floods 1998 .................................................. 23
      1.8.3 The Autumn Floods 2000 ............................................... 25
  1.9 HISTORICAL DEVELOPMENT OF THE LAW ..................... 27
      1.9.1 Early Legislation ............................................................. 28
      1.9.2 The Royal Commission .................................................. 30
      1.9.3 Modern Legislation ........................................................ 32
  1.10 LAYOUT OF THE WORK ...................................................... 34

**Chapter 2 – PRIVATE RIGHTS AND DUTIES** ........................... 37
  2.1 INTRODUCTION ...................................................................... 37
  2.2 RIPARIAN RIGHTS .................................................................. 39
  2.3 WATERCOURSES AND OTHER WATERS ........................... 41
  2.4 RIPARIAN DRAINAGE RIGHTS AND DUTIES ................... 44
      2.4.1 The Discharge of Floodwater to Watercourses ............. 44
      2.4.2 Alleviating Flooding from Watercourses ...................... 46
      2.4.3 Maintaining the Channel of a Watercourse ................... 52
      2.4.4 Maintenance: The Traditional Approach ....................... 54
      2.4.5 Maintenance: The Modern Approach ............................ 56
      2.4.6 Easements concerning Maintenance .............................. 58
  2.5 RIGHTS BETWEEN LANDOWNERS IN NUISANCE ........... 60
      2.5.1 Land Drainage Rights between Landowners ................ 62
      2.5.2 The Mining Cases .......................................................... 66
      2.5.3 The Culverting Cases ..................................................... 71
  2.6 RIGHTS OF SUPPORT ............................................................. 77

| | |
|---|---|
| 2.7 LAND EROSION | 79 |
| 2.8 NUISANCE AND NEGLIGENCE | 81 |
| 2.9 CIVIL LIABILITY OF PUBLIC BODIES | 86 |

**Chapter 3 – INSTITUTIONAL RESPONSIBILITIES** ............................ 92
- 3.1 INTRODUCTION .......................................................................... 92
- 3.2 DEPARTMENT FOR ENVIRONMENT, FOOD AND RURAL AFFAIRS .................................................................................. 95
  - 3.2.1 Administrative Background ................................................. 95
  - 3.2.2 Overall Policy Objectives .................................................... 97
  - 3.2.3 Flood Warning Systems ....................................................... 97
  - 3.2.4 Encouraging Sound and Sustainable Measures ..................... 98
  - 3.2.5 Technical and Indicative Standards ...................................... 99
  - 3.2.6 Guidance on Priorities for Grant Funding .......................... 100
  - 3.2.7 Guidance on Environmental Matters .................................. 101
  - 3.2.8 Guidance on Climate Change ............................................. 102
  - 3.2.9 Discouragement of Inappropriate Development ................. 103
  - 3.2.10 Research and Development ............................................... 103
  - 3.2.11 Sponsorship of the Environment Agency .......................... 103
  - 3.2.12 High Level Targets ............................................................ 104
  - 3.2.13 Statutory Functions ........................................................... 107
  - 3.2.14 Environment Act 1995 ...................................................... 108
  - 3.2.15 Water Resources Act 1991 ................................................ 109
  - 3.2.16 Land Drainage Act 1991 ................................................... 110
  - 3.2.17 Coast Protection Act 1949 ................................................ 112
- 3.3 THE NATIONAL ASSEMBLY FOR WALES ............................ 112
- 3.4 THE ENVIRONMENT AGENCY ................................................ 114
  - 3.4.1 Introduction ....................................................................... 114
  - 3.4.2 The Principal Aim and Objectives ...................................... 116
  - 3.4.3 The Costs and Benefits Duty .............................................. 119
  - 3.4.4 Organisation and Staffing ................................................... 120
  - 3.4.5 Regional Flood Defence Committees ................................. 121
  - 3.4.6 Local Flood Defence Committees ...................................... 123
  - 3.4.7 The Flood Defence Function .............................................. 124
  - 3.4.8 Main River Functions ........................................................ 127
  - 3.4.9 Transfer of Functions and Arrangements with Other Authorities ......................................................................... 131
  - 3.4.10 Flood Defence Byelaws ..................................................... 132
  - 3.4.11 Powers of Entry ................................................................. 134
  - 3.4.12 Incidental Functions .......................................................... 135
- 3.5 INTERNAL DRAINAGE BOARDS ............................................ 136
  - 3.5.1 Introduction ....................................................................... 136
  - 3.5.2 Composition and Constitution ............................................ 138
  - 3.5.3 Boundaries and Reorganisation .......................................... 139
  - 3.5.4 Supervisory Role of Internal Drainage Boards ................... 142
  - 3.5.5 Supervisory Role of the Environment Agency ................... 142
  - 3.5.6 Relationships with Other Operating Authorities ................ 144
  - 3.5.7 Byelaws ............................................................................. 145
  - 3.5.8 Powers of Entry ................................................................. 146

| | |
|---|---|
| 3.6 LOCAL AUTHORITIES | 148 |
| 3.6.1 Introduction | 148 |
| 3.6.2 Supervision by the Agency | 149 |
| 3.6.3 Arrangements with Other Persons | 150 |
| 3.6.4 Powers of Entry and Byelaws | 150 |
| 3.7 LONDON | 150 |
| 3.7.1 Administrative Arrangements | 150 |
| 3.7.2 The Thames Barrier | 152 |
| 3.8 ASSESSMENT OF FLOOD DEFENCE ADMINISTRATION | 154 |
| **Chapter 4 – OPERATIONAL AND REGULATORY POWERS** | 159 |
| 4.1 INTRODUCTION | 159 |
| 4.2 THE MINISTERS | 159 |
| 4.3 THE ENVIRONMENT AGENCY: OPERATIONAL POWERS | 160 |
| 4.3.1 General Flood Defence Works Powers | 160 |
| 4.3.2 Compensation | 165 |
| 4.3.3 Compulsory Works Orders | 171 |
| 4.3.4 Power to Dispose of Spoil | 172 |
| 4.3.5 Powers concerning Schemes for Small Areas | 176 |
| 4.3.6 Powers under Agreements | 176 |
| 4.3.7 Powers arising from Default | 177 |
| 4.4 THE ENVIRONMENT AGENCY: REGULATORY POWERS | 178 |
| 4.4.1 Controls over Structures in Main Rivers | 178 |
| 4.4.2 Obstructions in Ordinary Watercourses | 180 |
| 4.4.3 Culverting Policy | 180 |
| 4.4.4 Powers concerning Repairs to Watercourses | 181 |
| 4.4.5 Powers to Maintain the Flow of a Watercourse | 182 |
| 4.4.6 Supervision of Internal Drainage Boards | 183 |
| 4.4.7 Concurrent Powers | 183 |
| 4.4.8 Supervision of Local Authorities | 184 |
| 4.4.9 Commutation of Obligations | 185 |
| 4.4.10 Powers to Vary Awards | 186 |
| 4.4.11 Powers to Vary Navigation Rights | 187 |
| 4.5 OPERATIONAL AND REGULATORY POWERS: INTERNAL DRAINAGE BOARDS AND LOCAL AUTHORITIES | 187 |
| 4.6 OPERATIONAL POWERS: INTERNAL DRAINAGE BOARDS AND LOCAL AUTHORITIES | 188 |
| 4.6.1 General Flood Defence Works Powers | 188 |
| 4.6.2 Power to Dispose of Spoil | 190 |
| 4.6.3 Drainage of Small Areas (by Local Authorities) | 191 |
| 4.6.4 Works by Arrangement | 192 |
| 4.7 REGULATORY POWERS: INTERNAL DRAINAGE BOARDS AND LOCAL AUTHORITIES | 193 |
| 4.7.1 Works to Maintain Watercourses | 193 |
| 4.7.2 Enforcement of Repair Obligations (by Internal Drainage Boards) | 194 |
| 4.7.3 Prohibition of Obstructions in Watercourses (by Internal Drainage Boards) | 195 |

4.8 POWERS OF LANDHOLDERS ............................................................. 196
    4.8.1 Authorisation of Landowners to Carry Out Works ............ 196
    4.8.2 Orders Requiring Cleansing of Ditches ................................ 197
4.9 PRIVATE AND LOCAL LEGISLATION ........................................ 199

## Chapter 5 – COAST PROTECTION .................................................... 204

5.1 INTRODUCTION ............................................................................... 204
5.2 IMPLICATIONS OF COAST PROTECTION–FLOOD DEFENCE DISTINCTION ........................................................................................ 206
5.3 COMMON LAW AND COAST PROTECTION ............................ 209
5.4 THE COAST PROTECTION ACT 1949 ........................................ 213
    5.4.1 Coast Protection Authorities and Boards ............................ 213
    5.4.2 Powers of Coast Protection Authorities .............................. 214
    5.4.3 General Coast Protection Work ............................................ 218
    5.4.4 Works Schemes ........................................................................ 218
    5.4.5 Coast Protection Charges ....................................................... 220
    5.4.6 Maintenance and Repair of Works ....................................... 222
    5.4.7 Compulsory Acquisition of Land .......................................... 224
    5.4.8 Compensation ........................................................................... 225
    5.4.9 Subsisting Obligations ............................................................ 229
    5.4.10 Consents and Notification concerning Works ................... 230
    5.4.11 Prohibition of Excavations .................................................. 232
    5.4.12 Powers of Entry ..................................................................... 234
    5.4.13 Default Powers of the Minister ........................................... 235
    5.4.14 Grants and Contributions towards Expenses .................... 236
5.5 POLICY AND SHORELINE MANAGEMENT PLANS .............. 237

## Chapter 6 – FUNDING ............................................................................ 239

6.1 INTRODUCTION ............................................................................... 239
    6.1.1 An Outline of Funding Arrangements ................................. 239
    6.1.2 Allocation of Costs .................................................................. 243
    6.1.3 The Flood Defence Funding Review .................................... 245
6.2 CENTRAL GOVERNMENT FUNDING ........................................ 248
6.3 THE ENVIRONMENT AGENCY .................................................... 251
    6.3.1 General Funding Position ...................................................... 251
    6.3.2 Grants to the Environment Agency ...................................... 254
    6.3.3 Grants for Flood Warning Systems ...................................... 255
    6.3.4 Other Grants for Flood Defence Purposes .......................... 256
    6.3.5 Levies on Local Authorities .................................................. 257
    6.3.6 Contributions from Internal Drainage Boards .................... 259
    6.3.7 Contributions to Internal Drainage Boards ......................... 260
    6.3.8 Contributions where the Agency is the Internal Drainage Board .................................................................................. 260
    6.3.9 General Drainage Charges ..................................................... 261
    6.3.10 Special Drainage Charges .................................................... 263
6.4 INTERNAL DRAINAGE BOARDS ................................................ 264
    6.4.1 General Funding Position ...................................................... 264
    6.4.2 Grants to Drainage Bodies .................................................... 264

## Table of Contents

- 6.4.3 Raising the Expenses of Internal Drainage Boards ............. 265
- 6.4.4 Levying and Assessment of Drainage Rates ....................... 267
- 6.4.5 Adjustment of Annual Values .............................................. 269
- 6.4.6 Appeals against Determinations of Annual Value and Drainage Rates ................................................................... 270
- 6.4.7 Differential Drainage Rates ................................................. 271
- 6.4.8 Exemption from Drainage Rates ......................................... 273
- 6.4.9 Special Levies ..................................................................... 274
- 6.4.10 Borrowing Powers ............................................................. 275
- 6.4.11 Local Authority Contributions to Drainage Expenses ....... 275
- 6.5 LOCAL AUTHORITIES AND LAND DRAINAGE FINANCE ... 276
- 6.6 FUNDING OF COAST PROTECTION WORKS ......................... 277

### Chapter 7 – SEWERAGE AND WATER SUPPLY ............................. 278
- 7.1 INTRODUCTION ........................................................................... 278
- 7.2 SEWERAGE RESPONSIBILITIES ............................................... 279
- 7.3 THE DEFINITIONS OF 'SEWER' AND 'DRAIN' ....................... 281
- 7.4 THE FUNCTIONAL DEFINITION OF 'PUBLIC SEWER' ......... 284
  - 7.4.1 Purpose of Construction ...................................................... 284
  - 7.4.2 Changes in Use .................................................................... 287
  - 7.4.3 The Significance of Culverting ........................................... 289
  - 7.4.4 The 'Proper Outfall' Requirement ....................................... 290
- 7.5 SEWER MAPS ................................................................................ 293
- 7.6 THE VESTING OF SEWERS IN SEWERAGE UNDERTAKERS . 295
- 7.7 STATUTORY PROVISIONS ON SEWERS AND FLOODING .. 299
  - 7.7.1 Customer Service Standards ................................................ 299
  - 7.7.2 Discharges from Sewers ...................................................... 301
- 7.8 CIVIL LIABILITY OF SEWERAGE UNDERTAKERS: THE TRADITIONAL APPROACH ........................................................ 304
- 7.9 SEWAGE FLOODING AND HUMAN RIGHTS ......................... 306
  - 7.9.1 The Facts of the *Marcic* Case ............................................. 307
  - 7.9.2 Determining Priorities for Sewerage Improvements ........... 308
  - 7.9.3 The Common Law Claim .................................................... 310
  - 7.9.4 The Human Rights Issues .................................................... 312
  - 7.9.5 The High Court's Approach to Human Rights .................... 314
  - 7.9.6 The Court of Appeal's Approach to Human Rights ............. 317
  - 7.9.7 Compensation for Human Rights Contraventions ............... 319
  - 7.9.8 Implications of the Marcic Decision ................................... 321
- 7.10 WATER SUPPLY .......................................................................... 322
- 7.11 STATUTORY LIABILITY FOR ESCAPE OF WATER ............. 323
- 7.12 CIVIL LIABILITY FOR WATER SUPPLY SYSTEMS ............. 325

### Chapter 8 – PUBLIC HEALTH, HIGHWAYS AND RESERVOIRS ... 328
- 8.1 INTRODUCTION ........................................................................... 328
- 8.2 PUBLIC HEALTH .......................................................................... 328
  - 8.2.1 Statutory Nuisances ............................................................. 328
  - 8.2.2 Powers concerning Ponds and Ditches ................................ 330
  - 8.2.3 Culverting of Watercourses ................................................. 331

## 8.3 HIGHWAY DRAINAGE ... 333
- 8.3.1 Highways and Highway Authorities ... 333
- 8.3.2 Highway Drains ... 334
- 8.3.3 Highway Drainage Operations ... 337
- 8.3.4 The Power to Fill in Roadside Ditches ... 341
- 8.3.5 Protection of Highways against Hazards of Nature ... 342
- 8.3.6 Diversion of Watercourses ... 343
- 8.3.7 Agreements with Sewerage Undertakers ... 344
- 8.3.8 Responsibilities for Roadside Ditches ... 345

## 8.4 RESERVOIR SAFETY ... 347
- 8.4.1 Introduction ... 347
- 8.4.2 Large Raised Reservoirs ... 348
- 8.4.3 Registration of Reservoirs by Local Authorities ... 348
- 8.4.4 Qualifications of Engineers ... 349
- 8.4.5 Certification of Reservoirs ... 349
- 8.4.6 Periodic Inspections ... 350
- 8.4.7 Discontinuance or Abandonment ... 352
- 8.4.8 Enforcement Powers ... 353
- 8.4.9 Criminal and Civil Liability ... 354

# Chapter 9 – PLANNING ... 356
## 9.1 INTRODUCTION ... 356
## 9.2 THE ADMINISTRATION OF PLANNING LAW ... 357
## 9.3 DEVELOPMENT PLANNING ... 358
## 9.4 DEVELOPMENT CONTROL ... 360
## 9.5 PLANNING CONDITIONS AND OBLIGATIONS ... 364
## 9.6 THE PLANNING ROLE OF THE ENVIRONMENT AGENCY ... 368
## 9.7 PLANNING GUIDANCE ... 372
## 9.8 DEVELOPMENT AND FLOOD RISK ... 373
- 9.8.1 Sustainable Development and the Precautionary Principle ... 374
- 9.8.2 Flood Risk as a Material Consideration ... 375
- 9.8.3 The Sequential Test ... 377
- 9.8.4 Previously Developed Land and Housing Provision ... 379
- 9.8.5 Integration of Plans ... 380
- 9.8.6 Sustainable Drainage Systems ... 381
- 9.8.7 Regional Planning ... 382
- 9.8.8 Development Plans ... 383
- 9.8.9 Development Control ... 385
- 9.8.10 Developer Contributions ... 386
- 9.8.11 Application and Consultation Procedures ... 387

## 9.9 COASTAL PLANNING ... 390
## 9.10 NATURE CONSERVATION ... 392
## 9.11 HOUSING ... 393
## 9.12 CONTAMINATED LAND ... 394
## 9.13 OTHER PLANNING POLICIES ... 395
## 9.14 ENVIRONMENTAL IMPACT ASSESSMENT ... 395
- 9.14.1 The Environmental Impact Assessment Directive ... 397

## Table of Contents

  9.14.2 The Amending Directive .................................................... 400
  9.14.3 The Environmental Impact Assessment Regulations ........ 400
  9.14.4 The Land Drainage Improvement Works Regulations ...... 402
  9.14.5 Strategic Environmental Assessment ................................ 404
 9.15 BUILDING CONTROL .............................................................. 406

### Chapter 10 – ENVIRONMENTAL AND ECOLOGICAL IMPACTS .. 408
 10.1 INTRODUCTION ...................................................................... 408
 10.2 GENERAL DUTIES OF THE ENVIRONMENT AGENCY ....... 409
  10.2.1 Duties concerning sites of special interest ......................... 412
  10.2.2 Codes of Practice ............................................................... 414
 10.3 GENERAL DUTIES OF INTERNAL DRAINAGE BOARDS
   AND LOCAL AUTHORITIES ............................................. 418
  10.3.1 Duties concerning sites of special scientific interest ......... 420
  10.3.2 Ministerial Directions and Codes of Practice ................... 421
 10.4 DUTIES UNDER NATURE CONSERVATION
   LEGISLATION ....................................................................... 422
  10.4.1 Notification and Protection of sites of special scientific
    interest ................................................................................ 423
  10.4.2 Conservation Duties on Public Authorities ....................... 426
  10.4.3 Authorisation of Operations by Public Authorities ........... 428
  10.4.4 Management Schemes and Notices ................................... 429
  10.4.5 Compulsory Acquisition and Restoration ......................... 430
  10.4.6 Duties concerning Biological Diversity and Ramsar Sites ... 430
 10.5 EUROPEAN COMMUNITY CONSERVATION
   LEGISLATION ....................................................................... 431
  10.5.1 The Wild Birds Directive ................................................... 432
  10.5.2 The Habitats Directive ....................................................... 434
 10.6 THE HABITATS REGULATIONS 1994 .................................... 435
  10.6.1 General Duties and Powers ................................................ 436
  10.6.2 Site Selection ..................................................................... 437
  10.6.3 Management of Sites ......................................................... 438
  10.6.4 Special Nature Conservation Orders ................................. 440
  10.6.5 Adaptation of Planning and Other Controls ..................... 441
  10.6.6 Assessment of Implications for European Sites ................ 442
  10.6.7 Review of Existing Decisions ............................................ 442
  10.6.8 Planning Permissions: Review, Revocation and
    Compensation ..................................................................... 443
  10.6.9 General Development Orders ............................................ 445
  10.6.10 Application of Assessment and Review Requirements ... 445
 10.7 WATER LEVEL MANAGEMENT PLANS ............................... 447

### Chapter 11 – INFORMATION, WARNINGS AND INSURANCE ....... 449
 11.1 INTRODUCTION ...................................................................... 449
 11.2 INFORMATION ACCESS ......................................................... 450
  11.2.1 General Provisions ............................................................ 450
  11.2.2 Environment Agency Information ..................................... 452

11.3 ENVIRONMENT AGENCY FLOOD WARNINGS ............ 454
    11.3.1 Flood Warning Systems .......................................... 454
    11.3.2 The Flood Warning Direction ................................ 455
    11.3.3 Environment Agency Flood Warning Practice ........ 457
    11.3.4 Emergency Response Obligations .......................... 459
    11.3.5 Negligence and Flood Warnings ............................ 462
11.4 OTHER KINDS OF FLOOD WARNING ............................ 466
    11.4.1 Warnings of the Propensity of Land to Flood ......... 466
    11.4.2 Warnings of Flood Hazards to Highway Users ....... 469
    11.4.3 Occupiers' Liability ................................................ 472
    11.4.4 Disclosure in Property Transactions ...................... 476
11.5 FLOODING INSURANCE ................................................... 478
    11.5.1 General Considerations concerning Insurance ....... 478
    11.5.2 Legal Aspects of Flood Insurance .......................... 480
    11.5.3 The Meaning of 'Flood' .......................................... 481
    11.5.4 Availability of Flood Insurance .............................. 484

**Chapter 12 – SUSTAINABILITY** ........................................................ 487
12.1 INTRODUCTION ................................................................ 487
12.2 SUSTAINABLE LAND DRAINAGE .................................. 489
12.3 LEGAL IMPLICATIONS OF SUSTAINABLE DRAINAGE ..... 492
    12.3.1 Categorisation Issues ............................................. 493
    12.3.2 Sewerage Adoption Implications ........................... 494
    12.3.3 Local Authority and Highway Drain Adoption ...... 496
    12.3.4 Environment Agency Involvement ........................ 497
    12.3.5 Private Responsibilities .......................................... 499
12.4 DRAINAGE OF UNDEVELOPED LAND .......................... 501
12.5 SUSTAINABLE FLOOD DEFENCE .................................. 504
12.6 SUSTAINABLE COAST DEFENCE .................................. 507
12.7 THE COST OF SUSTAINABILITY ................................... 510

**BIBLIOGRAPHY** ............................................................................... 515
    BOOKS AND ARTICLES ........................................................ 515
    OFFICIAL PUBLICATIONS AND PUBLICATIONS BY PUBLIC
        BODIES ................................................................................. 520
        Government Publications .................................................. 520
        Departmental Publications ................................................ 520
        Welsh Office and National Assembly for Wales Publications ...... 525
        Parliamentary Committee Reports ................................... 525
        English Nature and Countryside Council for Wales Publications . 526
        Environment Agency Publications .................................. 526
        Miscellaneous Official Publications ................................ 527
        European Commission Publications ................................ 527

**INDEX** .............................................................................................. 529

# PREFACE

The thought of writing a book on flood defence law came as a direct result of the floods that affected England and Wales in the autumn of 2000. Night after night, television news reports showed alarming pictures of people being rescued by the emergency services or saddening accounts of families wading through water trying to salvage what little they could from their inundated homes. The floods persisted for week after week and wrecked businesses, incapacitated farms and destroyed homes without discrimination. The financial cost was estimated at £1 billion, but this figure completely fails to take account of the human misery that was inflicted. In some instances, families were forced to evacuate their homes several times. In many cases the work required to repair the damage is still not completed, so that a significant number of families remain in temporary accommodation a year or more afterwards. The human impacts of the flooding are enormous but impossible to quantify.

Following the immediate feeling of empathy towards the flood victims, the second response of many was the need to understand and interpret the events that were appearing on their television screens. Previously, there had been a widespread and 'comfortable' belief that hazards of nature had been placed at a 'safe distance' by infrastructure with the capacity to withstand them. The United Kingdom, in particular, is normally regarded as outside those regions that suffer significant earthquakes, hurricanes and other extreme climatic phenomena. Flooding, previously at least, was popularly assumed to have been effectively 'prevented' by adequate defences capable of containing rivers within their banks and the sea within its proper limits. Despite these general preconceptions, the reality proved to be different. The Autumn 2000 floods shocked many who had assumed that flooding on this scale could never happen and caused much rethinking about our vulnerability to natural hazards.

An aspect of the new anxiety about flooding was the common reflex reaction that 'someone must be to blame' and a local-to-global search for culprits was seized upon by the media. Remarkably, 'nature' seemed to appear nowhere on the list of suspects or at least seemed markedly less satisfactory as a target for blame than the various human agencies and individuals that were lined up for scrutiny. However much flooding may have been an adversity of life to which past generations were reconciled, the new climate of opinion seems to be one of public intolerance and unwillingness to accept that natural hazards cannot be withstood. The widely held view that flooding somehow represents a human failing did not appear to be greatly shaken by many interpretations of the events of Autumn 2000.

When it comes to allocating blame, law has an unrivalled vantage point. The language of rights and duties is sharply honed by legislation and case law to identify blame wherever this is remotely possible. Recognising this, the most surprising feature of flood defence law is the general reluctance of the law to impose criminal culpability or civil liability in relation to flooding damage. There is no criminal offence of causing flooding and the possibilities for enforcement of private duties to prevent flooding are quite limited. Public bodies with responsibility for flood defence are given extensive *powers* but comparatively few *duties*. As compared with the law on water quality, for example, the law on excess water quantity shows an underlying appreciation that the problem of preventing damage from the extremes of nature is one which human beings are ultimately unable to prevent. The counterpart of this is that legal obligations are cautiously formulated to avoid imposing liabilities for matters which are beyond human control or to place public bodies under an obligation to prevent flooding incidents which cannot reasonably be prevented.

Fundamentally, this is a book about the *balance* which is drawn between those circumstances where flooding is properly recognised to be attributable to some kind of human failing, for which liability of some kind may be found, and those situations where flooding is recognised to occur without human fault, most frequently as a result of nature. Over time, the potential for human liability has increased markedly, with a corresponding reduction in the role of nature, but the fact that flooding has occurred still provides no basis for the inference that someone must be legally liable. Nature remains a powerful force in shaping the law of flood defence, however different this may be from public preconceptions.

The book is written in the hope that it will provide a useful account of the law on all aspects of flooding and flood defence which will be of value to all who are involved with the subject. This is no small challenge. Flooding is a matter of concern to policymakers, in central and local government; legal practitioners, working with environmental and water-related agencies and organisations, or in private practice; engineers and environmental professionals, engaged to plan, undertake or evaluate flood-defence projects; and individuals who are the unfortunate recipients of floodwater. Each kind of reader will have his or her own particular interests and concerns, and it is hoped that the work is sufficiently comprehensive and accessible to address these.

In addition, it is hoped that the book will provide a useful discussion of the broader policy background to the law and the research sources that have

*Preface* xvii

informed present understanding. Clearly, the floods of Autumn 2000 have given new prominence to an issue of significant public concern, but they have not yet prompted the kind of fundamental reassessment of the organisational structures and legal mechanisms which may be warranted. If, as is being predicted, flood events are likely to become more common in the future, the adequacy of the existing mechanisms for alleviating flooding are likely to come under ever more intense scrutiny in the years ahead. How are increasing public expectations of safety from flooding to be reconciled against the natural inevitability of flooding and the impossibility of totally preventing it at any realistic level of economic and environmental cost? It is hoped that some parts of this work will make a useful contribution to this debate.

The law is generally stated on the basis of sources available on 1 January 2002. However, some changes have been introduced at proof stage and these have allowed reference to be made to the Court of Appeal decision in *Peter Marcic* v *Thames Water Utilities Ltd* ([2002] EWCA 65) in section 7.9 and for brief coverage to be given of the Department for Environment, Food and Rural Affairs and National Assembly for Wales consultation document, *The Flood and Coastal Defence Funding Review* (2002), in section 6.1.3.

# ACKNOWLEDGEMENTS

As the end product of my researches into flood defence law, this book owes a considerable debt of gratitude to a range of people who have provided support, offered comments and advice, and generally saved me from a range of misconceptions and simple errors. With the usual author's disclaimer, that I am entirely responsible for any mistakes that remain, thanks must be offered to all the following for their help, with sincere apologies if there is anyone who has been overlooked.

Invaluable comments on the whole or large parts of the draft manuscript were provided by distinguished experts who were able to offer insightful guidance from a range of perspectives. Julie Gledhill, Senior Legal Adviser, North East Region of the Environment Agency, offered observations on the text from the perspective of someone in the front line as regards the practicalities of flood defence law. Geoffrey Gibbs, Regional Flood Defence Regulation Engineer, Southern Region of the Environment Agency, commented from the outlook of an experienced flood defence engineer. David Wilkinson, University of Keele, provided some valuable academic feedback and drew helpful attention to a range of points on which some 'second thought' was needed. Conor Linehan, Barrister, looked at the work from a practitioner's perspective and provided me with important guidance on presentation of some issues. Thankfully, none of the expert readers were deeply critical of the earlier draft but it was, nonetheless, comforting to have the benefit of this range of experience and wisdom to provide reassurance that I was not significantly 'off track' on any of the main issues.

Some chapters were read and constructively commented on by experts in particular fields. David Withrington, English Nature, suggested some significant improvements in the chapter on environmental and ecological impacts. Wendy Le Las, Planning Consultant, gave useful guidance on some points arising in the planning chapter. Graham Johnson and Peter Spillett, Thames Water, offered helpful advice and invaluable commentary on the chapter on sewerage and water supply issues.

In addition, a large number of people provided help on particular points or assistance in locating obscure sources of information: Jenny Bough, Imperial College at Wye; Monica Henry, Judy Johnson, David Richardson and Pat Thorne, Flood Management Division, Department for Environment, Food and Rural Affairs; Cathie Jackson, Cardiff Law Resources Centre; Peter Martin, Binnie, Black and Veatch; Jane Milne, Association of British

Insurers; Mari Momii, Research Student at the University of Kent at Canterbury; Richard Nunn, Environment Agency; Adrian Nuttall, Environment Agency; Jayne Smith, Solicitor with German and Soar; Peter Stuttard, Countryside Council for Wales; and Huw Williams, Environment Agency.

A general thanks is due to the Institution of Civil Engineers, and particularly John Bircumshaw, who have organised a number of seminars and workshops on flood defence law over the years to which I have been pleased to contribute. The points raised in discussion at these sessions were always pertinent and instructive and they have done much to shape my thinking about the practicalities of flood alleviation and the problems encountered by those at the 'work face' of the subject. More recently, it has been most instructive to be a member of the Institution of Civil Engineers' Working Group on Flooding Issues and I was grateful for the opportunity to participate in discussions of the key issues with a panel of people incorporating a broad range of expertise.

Closer to home, it is important to recognise the invaluable support for research that has been provided by the University of Kent at Canterbury. My colleagues in Kent Law School have been tremendously supportive of my research efforts and have enhanced my thinking on a range of legal subjects by the diverse and stimulating range of perspectives that they are invariably able to offer on any legal topic. Particular thanks are due to Nick Jackson and John Wightman for help on specific property law and civil law issues, and former colleague Donald McGillivray who greatly influenced my thinking on flood defence, particularly whilst we collaborated in producing the Institution of Civil Engineers publication *Land Drainage and Flood Defence Responsibilities* (3rd ed. 1996). The supportive research facilities provided by the University's Templeman Library were outstanding in all respects, and particular thanks are due to Sarah Carter, Jane Venis and Angela Faunch who were extremely helpful in responding to my enquiries for obscure cases and publications. In addition, the administrative staff of the Law School were invariably helpful in providing a combination of secretarial support and good humour, with particular thanks to Liz Cable.

Finally, this project would never have seen the light of day without the support of two key people. Crispin Williams of Shaw & Sons saw the importance of the project from the outset and provided constant support and patience (particularly about the late submission of a manuscript which was about twice as long as we had originally agreed). Carol Sturgeon was absolutely wonderful in her encouragement of the project over the months that I completely neglected my share of the domestic duties. Her willingness to point out my numerous typographical and stylistic errors was invaluable, but her ability to keep flood defence law in balance with the rest of my life was more important still.

To all these people, I am profoundly grateful.

**William Howarth**
*University of Kent at Canterbury*

# TABLE OF STATUTES

Acquisition of Land Act 1981 ............................................................. 189, 224
Agriculture Act 1970
    Part V ............................................................................................................ 33
Agriculture Act 1986
    s 18 .............................................................................................................. 511
Agriculture (Miscellaneous Provisions) Act 1968
    Part IV ........................................................................................................... 33
Airports Act 1986
    Part V .......................................................................................................... 426
Allotments Act 1922 .............................................................................................. 262
Ancient Monuments and Archaeological Areas Act 1979 .................................... 412
Bill of Sewers 1531 (A General Act concerning Commissions of Sewers to be directed in all Parts within this Realm 1531 (23 Hen.8 c.5)) ......................... 29, 31
Building Act 1984 ................................................................................................ 406
    s 1 ............................................................................................................... 406
Christchurch District Drainage Act 1951 ............................................................. 467
Chronically Sick and Disabled Persons Act 1970 ................................................ 410
Civil Defence Act 1948 ........................................................................................ 462
Civil Defence in Peacetime Act 1986 ................................................................... 462
Civil Liability (Contribution) Act 1978
    s 1(1) ............................................................................................................ 84
    s 2(1) ............................................................................................................ 84
Coast Protection Act 1947 .................................................................................... 113
    s 2 ................................................................................................................ 114
    s 5(4) ........................................................................................................... 114
    s 8(4) ........................................................................................................... 114
    s 17 .............................................................................................................. 114
    s 18(2) ......................................................................................................... 114
    s 21 .............................................................................................................. 277
Coast Protection Act 1949 ...... 2, 96, 108, 116, 148, 161, 208–210, 212–238, 416, 436
    Part I ................................................................................................... 112, 213
    Part II ......................................................................................................... 232
    s 1(1), (2) ................................................................................................... 214
    s 2 ................................................................................................................ 112
        (1), (2) ................................................................................................. 214
        (5) ....................................................................................................... 214
    s 4 ....................................................................................................... 215, 237
        (3) ....................................................................................................... 224
    s 5 ................................................................................................................ 218
        (4) ....................................................................................................... 112
    s 6 ................................................................................................................ 229
        (1), (2) ................................................................................................. 219
        (3) ................................................................................................ 112, 219
    s 7 ........................................................................................................ 237, 247
        (1) ................................................................................................ 219, 221
        (2) ....................................................................................................... 221
        (3) ................................................................................................ 220, 221
        (4), (5) ................................................................................................ 221
        (6) ................................................................................................ 112, 221
        (7) ....................................................................................................... 221

*Coast Protection Act 1949 (cont.)*

| | |
|---|---|
| s 8 | 237 |
| (1) | 219 |
| (4) | 112 |
| (5), (6) | 219 |
| s 9 | 237 |
| (1)–(3) | 220 |
| (4) | 218 |
| s 10 | 219, 237 |
| (1) | 221 |
| (2) | 221, 222 |
| (3) | 221 |
| (5) | 221 |
| s 11 | 219, 237 |
| s 12 | 223 |
| s 13 | 230 |
| (1)–(6) | 223 |
| s 14 | 112, 222, 224, 237 |
| s 15 | 210 |
| (1)–(3) | 230 |
| (4) | 112, 230 |
| (5) | 230 |
| s 16(1) | 230 |
| (2)–(4) | 231 |
| (5) | 230 |
| s 17(1), (2) | 231 |
| (3) | 232 |
| (4), (5) | 112, 232 |
| (6) | 231 |
| (7), (8) | 232 |
| s 18 | 211 |
| (1)–(3) | 232 |
| (4) | 112 |
| (5)–(8) | 233 |
| s 19 | 235 |
| (1)–(3) | 226 |
| s 20 | 112 |
| (1), (2) | 236 |
| (4)–(6) | 237 |
| s 21 | 112, 236 |
| s 22 | 225 |
| s 23 | 218 |
| s 24(1) | 226 |
| s 25(1)–(3) | 235 |
| (5), (6) | 235 |
| (9) | 235 |
| s 26 | 225 |
| (4) | 235 |
| (7), (8) | 235 |
| s 27 | 225 |
| s 28 | 112 |
| (1) | 223 |
| (2) | 235 |

*Coast Protection Act 1949 (cont.)*
- s 29 ............................................................................................... 216, 220
  - (1), (2) ................................................................................................. 236
- s 31(1) ................................................................................................... 213
- s 32(2) ........................................................................................... 224, 235
  - (5) ........................................................................................................ 114
- s 43 ............................................................................... 230, 231, 233, 235
- s 46(1) ................................................................................................... 236
- s 49(1) ............................................................... 205, 206, 213, 215, 218, 230
  - (2) ............................................................................................... 213, 232
- Sch 1 ...................................................................................................... 214
- Sch 2, Part II ......................................................................................... 232
- Sch 4 .............................................................................................. 213, 232

Commission of Sewers Shall be Granted 1427 (6 Hen VI c.5) ................. 29
Compulsory Purchase Act 1965 ............................................................. 302
Compulsory Purchase Act 1991 ............................................................. 302
Countryside Act 1968
- s 11 ........................................................................................................ 451
- s 15 ................................................................................... 424, 429, 430

Countryside Act 1981 ........................................................................... 409
Countryside and Rights of Way Act 2000 ....................... 409, 413, 414
- Part III ................................................................................................... 422
- s 74(1), (2) ............................................................................................ 431

Criminal Damage Act 1971 ...................................................................... 5
Derby Corporation Act 1901
- s 109 ...................................................................................................... 306
- s 113 ...................................................................................................... 306

Drainage Rates Act 1958 ......................................................................... 33
Drainage Rates Act 1962 ......................................................................... 33
Drainage Rates Act 1963 ......................................................................... 33
Electricity Act 1989
- s 6 .......................................................................................................... 426

Enclosure Act 1800 ................................................................................. 336
Environment Act 1995 ...................................... 33, 34, 111, 394, 409, 422
- Part I ............................................................................................. 115, 121
- s 1(2)(a) ................................................................................................ 108
  - (b) ....................................................................................................... 120
  - (5) ....................................................................................................... 115
- s 2(1) .................................................................................................... 115
  - (a) ............................................................................................... 132, 368
- s 4 ....................................................................................... 119, 410, 411
  - (1) ............................................................................................... 116, 117
  - (2) ........................................................................................... 108, 116–118
  - (3) ........................................................................................... 108, 117, 450
  - (4) ....................................................................................................... 117
- s 6 .......................................................................................................... 397
  - (1) ............................................................................................... 410, 413
  - (4) ............................................................................................... 124, 452
- s 7 ....................................................................................... 397, 410, 413
  - (1) ....................................................................................................... 116
    - (a) ..................................................................................................... 411
    - (b) ..................................................................................................... 410
    - (c) ..................................................................................................... 411
  - (2)–(6) ................................................................................................. 412

*Environment Act 1995 (cont.)*
- s 8(1)–(4) ............ 413
- s 9 ............ 416
  - (1)–(4) ............ 415
- s 10(1), (2) ............ 135
- s 11 ............ 113, 121
- s 12 ............ 120
- s 14 ............ 122
- s 15(1) ............ 123
  - (a) ............ 108
  - (5) ............ 123
  - (6) ............ 122
- ss 16, 17 ............ 123
- s 18 ............ 124
- s 20 ............ 265
- s 36(1) ............ 265
- s 37(1) ............ 135, 172
  - (a) ............ 396, 450
- s 39 ............ 116, 410
  - (1), (2) ............ 119
- s 40 ............ 162, 415, 455, 456
  - (1), (2), (8) ............ 108
- s 41(5)–(7) ............ 254
- s 42(7), (8) ............ 254
- s 43 ............ 254
- s 44(4) ............ 253
- s 46(1), (3), (4) ............ 252
- s 47 ............ 251, 455
- ss 48–50 ............ 251
- s 51(1)–(3) ............ 450
- s 52 ............ 450
- s 54 ............ 135
- s 56(1) ............ 108, 117, 119
- s 100 ............ 1, 116
- s 101 ............ 116, 255
  - (2) ............ 265
- s 108 ............ 134
- Sch 1, para 6 ............ 120
- Sch 4 ............ 122
  - para 12 ............ 122
- Sch 5 ............ 123, 124
- Sch 22
  - para 147 ............ 179
  - para 156 ............ 456
  - para 165 ............ 134
  - para 190 ............ 132
  - para 192 ............ 195

Environmental Protection Act 1990
- Part II ............ 172
- Part IIIA ............ 394
- Part III ............ 55, 172, 190, 328
- s 33(1)(c) ............ 5
- s 79(1) ............ 328
  - (h) ............ 56, 329
  - (7)(a) ............ 328

*Environmental Protection Act 1990 (cont.)*
    s 80(1) .................................................................................................... 328
        (4) ..................................................................................................... 328
        (6) ..................................................................................................... 329
Food and Environment Protection Act 1985
    Part II ..................................................................................................... 173
Freedom of Information Act 2000 ............................................................. 451, 452
General Rate Act 1967
    s 26(4) ..................................................................................................... 262
    s 88(5) ..................................................................................................... 270
Government of Wales Act 1994 ........................................................................ 205
Government of Wales Act 1998
    Part I ........................................................................................................ 113
    ss 21, 22 ................................................................................................... 113
    s 29 .......................................................................................................... 113
    ss 90–96 ................................................................................................... 113
    s 106 ........................................................................................................ 113
    s 147 ........................................................................................................ 113
    Sch 2 ........................................................................................................ 113
Greater London Authority Act 1999
    Sch 29, para 16 ....................................................................................... 460
Highways Act 1835
    s 67 .................................................................................... 335, 339, 345
Highways Act 1959
    s 44 .......................................................................................................... 470
Highways Act 1980 .......................................................................................... 91
    Part XI ..................................................................................................... 296
    s 1 ............................................................................................................ 334
    s 38 ................................................................................................. 333, 367
    s 41 ................................................................................... 90, 337, 341, 470
    s 47 .......................................................................................................... 346
    s 58 .......................................................................................................... 341
        (1) ....................................................................................................... 90
    s 72 .......................................................................................................... 346
    s 100 .............................................................................................. 335, 339, 346
        (1) ............................................................................................... 337, 340
        (2) ............................................................................................... 302, 338, 340
        (3) ............................................................................................... 338, 340, 342
        (4) ............................................................................................... 339, 340, 342
        (5) ............................................................................................... 340, 342
        (6) ..................................................................................................... 340
        (6A), (6B) ........................................................................................... 340
        (7) ..................................................................................................... 340
        (8) ..................................................................................................... 338
        (9) ............................................................................................... 297, 334, 336, 497
    s 101(1), (2) ............................................................................................. 342
        (6) ..................................................................................................... 342
    s 102 ........................................................................................................ 342
    s 103(1) ................................................................................................... 343
        (3) ..................................................................................................... 339
    s 108–110 ................................................................................................ 343
    s 250 ........................................................................................................ 342
    s 263(1) ................................................................................................... 334
    s 264(1), (2) ............................................................................................. 334

*Highways Act 1980 (cont.)*
- s 291 .... 340
- s 299 .... 338, 340
- s 308 .... 338
- s 328(1), (2) .... 333
- s 329(1) .... 333, 337, 343
- s 335 .... 334
- s 339 .... 181, 185
  - (1)–(3) .... 338, 342, 344
- Sch 1
  - Part I .... 343
  - Part III .... 343

Highways (Miscellaneous Provisions) Act 1961
- s 1 .... 341

Human Rights Act 1998 .... 307, 308, 312–315, 317, 320, 321, 512
- s 6(1) .... 312, 314
  - (2)(a) .... 314
  - (3) .... 312
  - (6) .... 314
- Sch 1, Part 1
  - art 1 .... 313, 319, 512, 514
  - art 6 .... 357, 514
  - art 8 .... 313, 319

Lancashire County Council (Drainage) Act 1921 .... 30
Land Drainage Act 1861 .... 29, 30
Land Drainage Act 1918 .... 30
Land Drainage Act 1926 .... 30
Land Drainage Act 1930 .... 32, 33, 50, 128, 136, 138, 154, 162, 185, 199, 200, 212
- s 4(1)(b) .... 139
- s 38(1) .... 173
- s 62(2) .... 167
- s 81 .... 173

Land Drainage Act 1961 .... 33
Land Drainage Act 1976 .... 33, 34, 206, 414
- s 6 .... 137
- s 7(4) .... 138
- s 33 .... 174
- s 45(2), (3) .... 257
- s 46(5), (7), (8) .... 258
- s 116(1) .... 150

Land Drainage Act 1991 .... 33, 34, 96, 114, 116, 134, 342, 344, 409, 436, 496
- Part I .... 138
- Part II .... 137, 138, 148
- Part IV, Ch II .... 265, 271
- Part IVA .... 418
- Part V .... 148
- s 1(1) .... 139
  - (2)(a) .... 142
  - (3) .... 138
  - (4) .... 110, 138
  - (5) .... 139
- s 2 .... 110, 121, 141
  - (7) .... 141
- s 3 .... 110, 121, 138, 141, 260

## Land Drainage Act 1991 (cont.)

- s 4 .................................................................. 110, 121, 142, 260
- s 5 .................................................................. 110, 121, 142
- s 6 .................................................................. 121
- s 7 .................................................................. 121
  - (1)–(5) .................................................................. 143, 183
  - (6) .................................................................. 183
- s 8 .................................................................. 121, 143, 177, 184
- s 9 .................................................................. 111, 121
  - (1) .................................................................. 143, 177
  - (2)–(6) .................................................................. 143, 178
- s 10 .................................................................. 111, 144, 151
- s 11 .................................................................. 144, 190
  - (1) .................................................................. 177
  - (2) .................................................................. 177
    - (a) .................................................................. 162
- s 14 .................................................................. 184, 188, 461
  - (1) .................................................................. 173, 188
  - (2) .................................................................. 127, 130, 188
  - (3) .................................................................. 160, 190, 196
  - (4) .................................................................. 188
    - (b) .................................................................. 149
  - (5), (6) .................................................................. 189
- s 15 .................................................................. 151, 461
  - (1) .................................................................. 190
  - (2)–(4) .................................................................. 191
  - (5) .................................................................. 149, 191
- s 16 .................................................................. 149, 184, 189, 461
  - (2), (3) .................................................................. 178
- s 17 .................................................................. 111, 150, 184, 190, 461
- s 18 .................................................................. 176, 184, 188, 190, 277
  - (1)–(6) .................................................................. 191
- s 19 (1)–(6) .................................................................. 192
- s 20 .................................................................. 150
  - (1) .................................................................. 192, 277
  - (2) .................................................................. 192, 193
  - (3) .................................................................. 192
- s 21 .................................................................. 181, 182, 184
  - (1) .................................................................. 181, 195, 196
  - (2) .................................................................. 195, 196
  - (3) .................................................................. 195, 196, 206
  - (4), (5) .................................................................. 195, 196
  - (6)–(8) .................................................................. 196
- s 22 .................................................................. 111, 160, 190
- s 23 .................................................................. 143, 180, 184, 332, 338, 342, 397, 497
  - (1)–(6) .................................................................. 195
- s 24 .................................................................. 143, 180, 184, 196, 332
- s 25 .................................................................. 77, 130, 183, 194, 277, 333
  - (1) .................................................................. 193
  - (2) .................................................................. 182, 193
  - (3)–(7) .................................................................. 193
- s 26(1) .................................................................. 194
  - (2) .................................................................. 194
    - (b) .................................................................. 333
  - (3), (4) .................................................................. 194

*Land Drainage Act 1991 (cont.)*
- s 27 .................. 182, 194
- ss 28, 29 .................. 198
- s 30 .................. 198, 199
- s 31 .................. 114, 198
- s 32 .................. 187
- s 33 .................. 111, 185
- s 34(1) .................. 163, 186
  - (2)–(6) .................. 186
- s 35 .................. 187
- s 36, 37 .................. 274
  - (2) .................. 265
- s 37(1) .................. 266
  - (2) .................. 266, 272
  - (3), (4) .................. 272
  - (5) .................. 266, 272
  - (6) .................. 272
- s 38 .................. 111, 121, 140, 166, 268
  - (1), (2) .................. 271
  - (3), (4) .................. 272
  - (5) .................. 273
  - (6) .................. 272, 273
  - (7) .................. 273
- s 39 .................. 121
  - (1)–(3) .................. 272
  - (4)–(7) .................. 273
- s 40 .................. 268
- s 41(1)–(4) .................. 268
  - (5), (6) .................. 269
- ss 42, 43 .................. 269
- s 44 .................. 270
- s 45 .................. 267, 270
- s 46 .................. 253, 271
- s 47 .................. 111, 121, 268, 474
  - (1), (2) .................. 273
  - (3)–(5) .................. 274
- s 48 .................. 267
- s 49 .................. 268
- s 50 .................. 267
- s 51 .................. 267, 271
- s 52(1) .................. 265
  - (2) .................. 266
- s 53 .................. 266
- s 54(1)–(3) .................. 266
  - (4)–(6) .................. 267
- s 55 .................. 111
  - (1) .................. 275
  - (2) .................. 276
  - (3)–(5) .................. 275
- s 57 .................. 121, 151, 260
  - (1), (2) .................. 260
- s 58 .................. 272
  - (1) .................. 121, 260
    - (b) .................. 253

*Land Drainage Act 1991, s 58 (cont.)*
    (2)–(4) ............................................................................................................ 261
    (6) .................................................................................................................. 261
  s 59 ....................................................................................................... 111, 276
    (1), (2) .................................................................................................. 264, 265
    (3) .................................................................................................................. 264
    (4) .................................................................................................................. 265
        (a) ........................................................................................................ 265
    (5) .................................................................................................................. 264
    (6) .......................................................................................................... 150, 265
    (7) .................................................................................................................. 265
  s 60(1), (2) ........................................................................................................... 276
    (3) .................................................................................................................. 275
  s 61(1) ................................................................................................................. 276
  s 61A .......................................................................................... 111, 397, 418, 421
    (1), (2) .......................................................................................................... 419
    (3) .................................................................................................................. 420
    (4)–(6) .......................................................................................................... 419
  s 61B ....................................................................................... 111, 397, 418, 419, 421
  s 61C ................................................................................................................... 421
    (1), (2) .......................................................................................................... 420
    (3), (4) .......................................................................................................... 421
  s 61D ..................................................................................................... 111, 418, 421
  s 61E ...................................................................................................... 111, 416, 418
    (1) .................................................................................................................. 421
    (2) .......................................................................................................... 415, 422
    (3), (4) .......................................................................................................... 421
  s 62 ....................................................................................................... 111, 189
    (2) .......................................................................................................... 189, 461
  s 63(1)–(3) ........................................................................................................... 189
  s 64(1)–(6) ........................................................................................................... 147
  s 65(1) ................................................................................................................. 112
  s 66 ............................................................................................................. 194, 461
    (2)–(5) .......................................................................................................... 145
    (6)–(9) .......................................................................................................... 146
  s 69 ..................................................................................................................... 111
  s 72(1) ............................................. 1, 108, 129, 138–140, 148, 173, 264, 266, 272, 289
    (2) .......................................................................................................... 140, 261
    (3) .................................................................................................................. 261
  s 73(1) ................................................................................................................. 129
  s 110 ................................................................................................................... 276
    (1)–(3) .......................................................................................................... 277
  s 167(1) ........................................................................................................ 173, 174
        (b) ........................................................................................................ 174
  Sch 1 .................................................................................................................. 138
  Sch 2 .................................................................................................................. 139
    paras 4, 5 ...................................................................................................... 139
  Sch 3 ........................................................................................................... 141, 187
  Sch 4 ........................................................................................................... 176, 191
    para 4(1) ....................................................................................................... 184
  Sch 5 .................................................................................................................. 145
Land Drainage Act 1994 ....................................................... 34, 96, 108, 111, 418
Land Drainage (Amendment) Act 1976 ................................................................ 33

Law of Property Act 1925
    s 62(1) .................................................................................................................. 39
        (4) .................................................................................................................. 39
Law Reform (Contributory Negligence) Act 1945 ................................................... 323
Limitation Act 1939 ................................................................................................. 171
Limitation Act 1980
    s 2 ........................................................................................................................... 171
Local Government Act 1929
    s 29 ........................................................................................................................ 297
    s 30(1) .................................................................................................................. 336
Local Government Act 1972 ............................................................................ 205, 460
    ss 122, 123 ........................................................................................................... 225
    ss 126, 127 ........................................................................................................... 225
    s 138 ..................................................................................................................... 463
        (1) ................................................................................................................ 460
        (1A) ............................................................................................................. 461
        (3) ................................................................................................................ 460
        (4), (5) ........................................................................................................ 460
        (6) ................................................................................................................ 461
    s 236 ..................................................................................................................... 145
    s 251(2) ................................................................................................................ 236
Local Government Act 1985 .................................................................................... 334
    s 11(2) .................................................................................................................. 151
Local Government and Housing Act 1989
    s 149(1), (2) ......................................................................................................... 258
    s 155 ..................................................................................................................... 461
        (4) ................................................................................................................ 461
    s 156 ............................................................................................................. 460, 461
Local Government Finance Act 1988 .............................................................. 122, 267
    s 64 ....................................................................................................................... 265
    s 74 ................................................................................................. 252, 257, 258
    s 75 ................................................................................................. 265, 271, 274
    s 143(1), (2) ......................................................................................................... 258
    Sch 11 .................................................................................................................. 270
Local Government Finance Act 1992 .............................................................. 148, 274
    s 1 ................................................................................................. 138, 240, 267
        (2) ................................................................................................................ 138
    Sch 13, para 96 ................................................................................................... 262
        (2) ................................................................................................................ 262
    Sch 14 .................................................................................................................. 262
Local Government (Wales) Act 1994 ............................................................... 148, 334
London County Council (General Powers) Act 1907
    Part VI ................................................................................................................. 151
London County Council (General Powers) Act 1929
    Part IX ................................................................................................................. 151
London County Council (General Powers) Act 1957
    Part VI ................................................................................................................. 151
London County Council (General Powers) Act 1961
    s 66 ....................................................................................................................... 151
London County Council (General Powers) Act 1962
    s 29 ....................................................................................................................... 151
Metropolis Management (Thames River Prevention of Floods) Amendment Act 1879 . 151
Metropolitan Board of Works (Various Powers) Act 1882
    ss 46, 47 .............................................................................................................. 151

Middlesex County Council Act 1898 .................. 30
Mines and Quarries (Tips) Act 1929 .................. 348
Ministers of the Crown Act 1975 .................. 426
Misrepresentation Act 1967 .................. 476
National Parks and Access to the Countryside Act 1949
   s 16 .................. 424, 429, 430
New Roads and Street Works Act 1991 .................. 325
   s 82 .................. 323
Norfolk and Suffolk Broads Act 1988 .................. 413, 420
Nuclear Installations Act 1965
   s 7(1)(a) .................. 4
Occupiers' Liability Act 1957 .................. 472–476
   s 2(1) .................. 472, 473
      (2), (3) .................. 472
      (4)(a) .................. 473
      (5) .................. 473
Occupiers' Liability Act 1984
   s 1(3)–(6) .................. 473
Police Act 1996
   s 3 .................. 461
Protection of Badgers 1992 .................. 422
Public Health Act 1875 .................. 288, 290, 292, 297, 298, 301
   s 4 .................. 283, 286
   s 13 .................. 291
   s 17 .................. 289, 301, 338
   s 21 .................. 304
   s 299 .................. 291, 301
   s 308 .................. 301
Public Health Act 1936 .................. 296, 297
   s 15(1)(I)(b) .................. 285
   s 17 .................. 284, 297
      (3) .................. 287
   s 18 .................. 297
   s 19 .................. 284
   s 20 .................. 296, 297
   s 32 .................. 294, 298
   s 39 .................. 306
   s 259 .................. 333
      (1) .................. 41, 330
         (b) .................. 56, 329
   s 260, 261 .................. 330, 333
   s 262 .................. 333
      (1)–(4) .................. 331
   s 263 .................. 333, 342
      (1) .................. 331
      (2)(3) .................. 332
      (4) .................. 331
   s 264 .................. 333
   s 265 .................. 91, 333
   s 266 .................. 185
      (1) .................. 332
   s 343 .................. 283
      (1) .................. 284

Public Health (Scotland) Act 1897
  s 16(2) ... 329
Public Utilities Street Works Act 1950
  s 18(2) ... 325
Radioactive Substances Act 1960 ... 4
Rating Act 1971 ... 262
Reservoirs Act 1975 ... 347
  s 1(1)–(4) ... 348
  s 2 ... 348
  s 3 ... 349
  s 4(1)–(3) ... 349
    (5) ... 349
  s 6(1)–(3) ... 349
  s 7 ... 349
  s 8(1), (2) ... 350
  s 9(1), (2) ... 350
    (7) ... 350
  s 10(1), (2) ... 351
    (3) ... 351
    (6), (7) ... 351
    (9) ... 350
  s 11(1) ... 351
  s 12 ... 352
  s 13(1)–(3) ... 352
  s 14(1), (2) ... 353
    (4) ... 353
  s 15(1), (2) ... 353, 354
    (5) ... 353
  s 16 ... 354
    (1), (2) ... 353
    (6) ... 353
  s 17(1) ... 354
    (4), (5) ... 354
  s 18(1) ... 354
  s 22(1)–(4) ... 354
  s 28 ... 355
  Sch 2 ... 355
Reservoirs (Safety Provisions) Act 1930 ... 347, 348, 355
River Boards Act 1948 ... 33, 212
Rivers Pollution Prevention Act 1876 ... 288
  s 3 ... 289
Rivers (Prevention of Pollution) Act 1951
  s 2 ... 306
Road Traffic Act 1988
  s 39 ... 472
Salmon and Freshwater Fisheries Act 1975
  s 2(4) ... 167
Scarsbrick Estate Drainage Act 1924 ... 212
Sewers Act 1833 ... 29
Sewers Acts Amendment Act 1849 ... 29
Statutory Water Companies Act 1991 ... 34, 323
Surrey County Council Act 1925 ... 30
Territorial Sea Act 1987
  s 1 ... 232

## Table of Statutes

Thames Barrier and Flood Prevention Act 1972 ............ 152, 154, 203
    s 35 ............ 153
    s 40 ............ 154
    s 56 ............ 154
    s 68 ............ 154
    s 70 ............ 154
Tottenham Urban District Council Act 1900
    s 64 ............ 331
Town and Country Planning Act 1990 ............ 181, 238
    Parts I, II ............ 358
    Part III ............ 424
    Part VII ............ 359
    s 31 ............ 358
        (6)(a) ............ 358
    s 33 ............ 369
    s 36 ............ 358
    s 54A ............ 359, 360
    s 55 ............ 360
        (2)(e) ............ 502
    s 57(1) ............ 359
    s 70(1)(a) ............ 364
        (2) ............ 362
    s 72(1)(a) ............ 364
    ss 77, 78 ............ 358
    s 97 ............ 444, 446
    s 102 ............ 444
    s 106 ............ 246, 363, 367, 444
        (1), (3) ............ 365
    s 107 ............ 444
    s 179 ............ 358
    s 262(1), (3), (6) ............ 426
    s 333 ............ 357
    s 336(1) ............ 323
Unfair Contract Terms Act 1977 ............ 472
    s 2 ............ 295
Victoria (London) Docks Act 1853 (16 & 17 Vict C.cxxxi) ............ 203
Water Act 1973 ............ 33, 296
    s 15 ............ 296
    s 22 ............ 414
    s 24(5) ............ 452
    s 28 ............ 463
    Sch 2 ............ 253
    Sch 3, para 31 ............ 253
    Sch 8, para 33 ............ 297
Water Act 1989 ............ 33, 34, 294
    s 4(1) ............ 151
    s 136(2) ............ 151
    s 140 ............ 137
    Sch 2 ............ 295, 296
        para 1(1), (2) ............ 296
    Sch 14, para 17 ............ 257
Water Consolidation (Consequential Provisions) Act 1991 ............ 34
    Sch 2
        para 1(1), (2) ............ 255, 265

*Water Consolidation (Consequential Provisions) Act 1991, Sch 2 (cont.)*
  para 2(5) .................................................................................... 257, 258, 276
  para 19 ................................................................................................ 140
  para 22(2) ........................................................................................... 461
Water Industry Act 1991 ............................................. 34, 299, 308, 315, 364, 496
  Part III ................................................................................................ 323
  Part IV ........................................................................................ 279, 295
    Ch II ........................................................................................ 293, 296
  s 2 ............................................................................................. 411, 419
  s 3 ...................................................................................... 412, 415, 420
  s 4 ............................................................................................. 415, 431
    (1) ................................................................................................ 431
  s 5 .................................................................................................... 415
  s 18 ................................................... 279, 291, 29, 415, 300, 305, 314, 317
    (8) ................................................................................................ 314
  s 19–21 ............................................................................................. 314
  s 22 .................................................................................................. 314
    (1) ................................................................................................ 301
    (2) ........................................................................................ 301, 317
  ss 23–25 ............................................................................................ 296
  s 37(1) .............................................................................................. 323
  s 94(1) .................................................................................. 279, 299, 301
    (3) ................................................................................................ 279
  ss 95, 96 ........................................................................................... 299
  s 97 ........................................................................................... 279, 307
  s 98 ........................................................................................... 367, 370
    (1), (2) ......................................................................................... 280
  s 99 .................................................................................................. 280
  s 102 ....................................................................................... 280, 284, 296
    (2) ................................................................................................ 287
  s 104 ................................................................................. 280, 284, 293, 367
  s 105 ................................................................................................ 280
  s 106 .................................................................... 89, 314, 364, 370, 495
    (1), (2) ......................................................................................... 282
    (6) ................................................................................................ 282
  s 111 ................................................................................................. 281
  s 115(1) ............................................................................................ 344
    (2)–(5) .......................................................................................... 345
    (6) ................................................................................................ 344
  s 118 ................................................................................................. 281
  s 146(4) ............................................................................................ 345
  s 152 ................................................................................................. 456
  s 155 ................................................................................................. 302
  s 156(7) .................................................................................... 412, 420
  s 158 ........................................................................................... 301, 340
  s 159 ............................................................................ 285, 301, 302, 340
  s 160 ................................................................................................. 301
  s 163 ................................................................................................. 340
  s 165 ................................................................................................. 340
    (1) ................................................................................................ 302
  s 168 ................................................................................................. 340
  s 179 ........................................................................................... 295, 296
    (1), (2) ......................................................................................... 296
    (7) ................................................................................................ 296

*Table of Statutes* xxxvii

*Water Industry Act 1991 (cont.)*
- s 186(3) .................................................................................................. 303
- s 199 ...................................................................................................... 298
  - (1), (2) ............................................................................................... 293
  - (3)–(8) ............................................................................................... 294
- s 200(1)–(3) ........................................................................................... 294
- s 208 ...................................................................................................... 456
- s 209(1) ......................................................................................... 323, 324
  - (4)–(5) ............................................................................................... 323
- s 219(1) .................................................. 281, 283, 284, 295, 297, 431
  - (2) ..................................................................................................... 283
- s 221(1) ..................................................................................................... 1
- Sch 2 .............................................................................................. 295, 296
- Sch 6, para 2 ........................................................................................ 147

Water Resources Act 1991 ............... 34, 96, 113, 151, 199, 277, 436, 450, 461
- Part II, Ch II ...................................................................................... 1, 347
- Part III .................................................................................................. 338
- Part IV ................................................................................. 109, 116, 137
  - Ch II ................................................................................................. 122
- s 2(5) .................................................................................................... 124
- s 3 ......................................................................................................... 135
- s 5 ................................................................................................ 108, 456
- s 6(2) .................................................................................................... 410
- s 7(1), (2) ............................................................................................. 109
- s 9(2)(b) ............................................................................................... 125
- s 85 ............................................................................. 5, 338, 497, 502
  - (1) ................................................................................................. 5, 289
  - (3) ............................................................................................. 289, 306
- s 88(1) .................................................................................................. 497
  - (a) ..................................................................................................... 303
- s 89(1) .................................................................................................. 502
  - (5) ..................................................................................................... 338
- s 100 ..................................................................................................... 338
- s 105(2) ............................................................................... 124, 375, 452
  - (3) .............................................................................................. 124, 167
- s 106 .............................................................................. 120, 124, 304
  - (1) ..................................................................................................... 121
  - (b) ..................................................................................................... 253
  - (2)–(4) ............................................................................................... 122
  - (6) ..................................................................................................... 179
  - (7) ..................................................................................................... 121
- s 107(1) ................................................................................................ 127
  - (2) .......................................................................................... 181, 195, 206
  - (3) .......................................................................................... 182, 194, 333
  - (4) ..................................................................................................... 185
- s 108 .............................................................................. 114, 121, 132, 177
  - (1), (2) ............................................................................................... 263
  - (9) ..................................................................................................... 131
- s 109 ............................................................. 195, 332, 338, 342, 397, 497
  - (1)–(3) ............................................................................................... 179
  - (4) .............................................................................................. 179, 332
  - (5) ..................................................................................................... 179
- s 110 ..................................................................................................... 397
  - (1), (2) ............................................................................................... 179
  - (4)–(5) ............................................................................................... 179

*Water Resources Act 1991 (cont.)*

- s 111 .................... 132, 177
- s 112 .................... 110
- s 113(1) .................... 1, 129, 173
- s 118 .................... 251, 261
  - (1)–(4), (6) .................... 253
- s 133 .................... 252, 257, 276
- s 134 .................... 253, 262
- s 135 .................... 253
  - (1)–(4) .................... 262
- s 137 .................... 129, 253
  - (1) .................... 109, 263
  - (2)–(5) .................... 263
- s 138 .................... 253
  - (1)–(3) .................... 263
- s 139 .................... 121, 260, 272
  - (1) .................... 253, 259
  - (2)–(5) .................... 259
- s 140 .................... 114, 121
  - (1) .................... 109, 260
  - (2), (3) .................... 260
- s 141 .................... 114, 260
  - (3) .................... 109
- s 145 .................... 262
- s 147 .................... 255, 264
  - (1)–(3) .................... 109
- s 148 .................... 109
  - (1)–(4) .................... 255
  - (5) .................... 256, 455
- s 149 .................... 109, 257
  - (1) .................... 176
  - (3) .................... 161
- s 150 .................... 456
- s 154 .................... 110, 256
  - (1), (2) .................... 172
- s 155 .................... 110
  - (1) .................... 172
- s 157 .................... 110
- s 165 .................... 109
  - (1) .................... 127, 161, 163, 188
    - (b), (c) .................... 256
  - (2) .................... 124, 161, 204
  - (3) .................... 124, 161
  - (4) .................... 162, 176, 257
  - (5) .................... 162, 177
  - (6) .................... 161
- s 166(1)–(3) .................... 454
- s 167 .................... 173, 190, 257
  - (1)(b) .................... 172
- s 168 .................... 110
  - (1)–(4) .................... 171
- s 169 .................... 110, 134
  - (1), (3) .................... 134

*Water Resources Act 1991 (cont.)*
>s 172(1), (2) ............................................................................................. 135
>s 177 ........................................................................................ 165, 256, 257
>s 185(2) ................................................................................................. 161
>s 193 ..................................................................................................... 129
>s 194 ................................................................................... 110, 129, 130
>s 207 ..................................................................................................... 463
>>(1)–(3) ............................................................................................ 456
>>(7) .................................................................................................. 456
>
>s 208(1) ................................................................................................ 323
>s 210 ..................................................................................................... 132
>s 211(4) ................................................................................................ 133
>>(5)(b), (c) ...................................................................................... 133
>
>s 221(1) ........................................................................................ 108, 289
>>(7)(b) ............................................................................................. 108
>
>Sch 14 .................................................................................................... 132
>Sch 15 ........................................................................................... 262, 263
>Sch 16 ................................................................................................... 263
>Sch 19 .................................................................................................... 171
>Sch 20, para 6 ...................................................................................... 165
>Sch 21 ........................................................................................... 256, 257
>>para 5 .............................................................................................. 165
>>>(3) ........................................................................................ 166, 172
>
>Sch 25 .................................................................................................... 132
>>para 5(1) ......................................................................................... 133
>>>(2) ................................................................................................ 133
>>>(c) ................................................................................................ 332
>
>Sch 26 ............................................................................................ 132, 133

West Riding of Yorkshire County Council (Drainage) Act 1923 ........................ 30
Wildlife and Countryside Act 1981 ................................... 420, 435, 436, 448
>Part I .................................................................................................... 422
>Part II ........................................................................................... 422, 423
>Part III ................................................................................................. 422
>s 28 ............................................................................................... 369, 439
>>(1)–(6) ............................................................................................ 424
>
>ss 28A–28A ......................................................................................... 424
>s 28E(1)–(3) ......................................................................................... 424
>>(6) .................................................................................................. 424
>
>s 28F ..................................................................................................... 424
>s 28G(1)–(3) ......................................................................................... 426
>28H(1)–(6) ........................................................................................... 427
>s 28I ..................................................................................................... 425
>>(1), (3) ........................................................................................... 427
>>(4)–(6) ............................................................................................ 428
>>(7) .................................................................................................. 427
>
>s 28J ..................................................................................................... 424
>>(1)–(3) ............................................................................................ 429
>>(7)–(8) ............................................................................................ 429
>>(13) ................................................................................................ 429
>
>s 28K .................................................................................................... 424
>>(1)–(4) ............................................................................................ 429
>>(7) .................................................................................................. 430
>
>s 28l ..................................................................................................... 430

*Wildlife and Countryside Act 1981 (cont.)*
    s 28M(1) .................................................................................................. 424
        (2), (3) .............................................................................................. 430
    s 28N(1), (2) ........................................................................................... 430
    s 28P ....................................................................................................... 424
        (1) .......................................................................................... 424, 430
        (2) .......................................................................................... 427, 430
        (3) ................................................................................................... 430
        (4), (5) .................................................................................. 425, 428
        (6) .......................................................................................... 425, 430
        (7) ................................................................................................... 425
        (8) ................................................................................................... 430
        (9) ................................................................................................... 424
        (10) ................................................................................................. 430
    s 31(1) .................................................................................................... 430
    s 37A(1), (2) .......................................................................................... 431
    s 50 ........................................................................................................ 430

# TABLE OF STATUTORY INSTRUMENTS

Agriculture (Maintenance, Repair and Insurance of Fixed Equipment) Regulations 1973 (S.I. 1973 No.1473) .................................................................................. 268
Building Regulations 2000 (S.I. 2000 No.2531) ....................................................... 407
    Sch 1 ............................................................................................................... 407
        Part H ........................................................................................................ 407
Building (Amendment) Regulations 2001 (S.I. 2001 No.3335) ............................... 407
Civil Defence (General Local Authority Functions) Regulations 1993 (S.I. 1993 No.1812) ................................................................................................................ 462
Civil Defence (Grants) Regulations 1993 (S.I. 1993 No.1777) ............................... 462
Coast Protection (Notices) Regulations 1950 (S.I. 1950 No.124) ................... 218, 219
Code of Practice on Environmental Procedures for Flood Defence Operating Authorities (Internal Drainage Boards and Local Authorities) Approval Order 1996 (S.I. 1996 No.3062) ..................................................................................... 422
Conservation (Natural Habitats, etc.) Regulations 1994 (S.I. 1994 No.2716) ... 436, 441, 448
    reg 6 ................................................................................................................ 441
    reg 7 ................................................................................................................ 438
        (1) ............................................................................................................. 437
    reg 8(1) ........................................................................................................... 437
    reg 10 .............................................................................................................. 438
        (1)(c) ................................................................................................. 440, 441
    regs 11–13 ...................................................................................................... 438
    regs 16–21 ...................................................................................................... 439
    regs 22–26 ...................................................................................................... 440
    reg 32 .............................................................................................................. 439
    reg 48 .................................................................................................... 441, 442
        (5) ............................................................................................................. 447
    reg 49 .................................................................................................... 441, 444
    reg 50 ......................................................................................... 443, 444, 446
    reg 51 .................................................................................................... 443, 444
    regs 52, 53 ...................................................................................................... 443
    reg 54–57 ........................................................................................................ 444
    reg 59 .............................................................................................................. 444
    regs 60–62 ...................................................................................................... 445
    regs 65–67 ...................................................................................................... 444
    regs 91, 92 ...................................................................................................... 440
    reg 98 .............................................................................................................. 439
    reg 105 ............................................................................................................ 437
Conservation (Natural Habitats, etc.) Regulations 1997 (S.I. 1997 No.3055) .......... 436
Conservation (Natural Habitats, etc.) Regulations 2000 (S.I. 2000 No.192) .... 436, 438
Contaminated Land (England) Regulations 2000 (S.I. 2000 No.227) ...................... 394
Contaminated Land (Wales) Regulations 2001 (S.I. 2001 No.2197 W.157) ............ 394
Drainage Rates (Appeals) Regulations 1970 (S.I. 1970 No.1152) ................... 270, 271
Drainage Rates (Forms) Regulations 1993 (S.I. 1993 No.223) ........................ 266, 268
Environment Act 1995 (Commencement No.5) Order 1996 (S.I. 1996 No.186) ..... 115
Environmental Impact Assessment (Land Drainage Improvement Works) Regulations 1999 (S.I. 1999 No.1783) ................................................ 396, 402, 404
    Sch 2 ............................................................................................................... 403
    Sch 3 ............................................................................................................... 404

Environmental Impact Assessment (Uncultivated Land and Semi-Natural Areas) (England) Regulations 2001 (S.I. 2001 No.3966) ............................................... 503
Environmental Information Regulations 1992 (S.I. 1992 No.3240) ....................... 450
    reg 2(2) ............................................................................................................ 451
    reg 3 ................................................................................................................. 451
        (1) ............................................................................................................ 451
    reg 4 ................................................................................................................. 451
Environmental Information (Amendment) Regulations 1998 (S.I. 1998 No. 1447) ..................................................................................................................... 450, 451
General Drainage Charges (Anglian Region) Order 1990 (S.I. 1990 No.223) ......... 261
General Drainage Charges (Forms) Regulations 1990 (S.I. 1990 No.564) ............. 263
General Drainage Charges (Relevant Quotient) Regulations 1993 (S.I. 1993 No. 165) ........................................................................................................................ 262
Groundwater Regulations 1998 (S.I. 1998 No.2746) ............................................... 498
Harbour Works (Assessment of Environmental Effects) (No.2) Regulations 1989 (S.I. 1989 No.424) .................................................................................................. 446
Harbour Works (Environmental Impact Assessment) (Amendment) Regulations 2000 (S.I. 2000 No.2391) ........................................................................................ 446
Internal Drainage Boards (Finance) Regulations 1992 (S.I. 1992 No.3079) .... 266, 274
Land Drainage (Election of Drainage Boards) Regulations 1938 (S.R.&O. 1938 No.558) .................................................................................................................... 138
Land Drainage (General) Regulations 1932 (S.R.&O. 1932 No.64)
    reg 2 ................................................................................................................. 192
    reg 7 ................................................................................................................. 141
Land Drainage (Grants) Regulations 1967 (S.I. 1967 No.212) ............................... 255
Land Drainage (River Authorities) Regulations 1965 (S.I. 1965 No.443)
    reg 6 ................................................................................................................. 141
Local Government Act 1985 (Land Drainage Functions) Order 1986 (S.I. 1986 No.208) .................................................................................................................... 150
Local Government Finance (Repeals and Consequential Amendments) Order 1999 (S.I. 1991 No.1730)
    art 2(2) ............................................................................................................. 236
    Sch 2, Part I ..................................................................................................... 236
National Assembly for Wales (Transfer of Functions) Order 1999 (S.I. 1999 No. 672) .................................................................................................................. 406
    Art 2 ......................................................................................................... 113, 120
    Sch 1 ........................................................................................................ 113, 120
National Rivers Authority (Levies) Regulations 1993 (S.I. 1993 No.61) .. 257, 258, 276
    reg 1(2) ............................................................................................................ 257
    reg 3(1) ............................................................................................................ 258
    reg 5(1), (2) ..................................................................................................... 258
    reg 6 ................................................................................................................. 258
    reg 9 ................................................................................................................. 259
Register of Drainage Boards Regulations 1968 (S.I. 1968 No.1672) ....................... 265
Reservoirs Act 1975 (Certificates, Reports and Prescribed Information) Regulations 1986 (S.I. 1986 No.468) ..................................................................... 349
Reservoirs Act 1975 (Registers, Reports and Records) Regulations 1985 (S.I. 1985 No.177) ........................................................................................................... 348, 351
Reservoirs Act 1975 (Registers, Reports and Records) (Amendment) Regulations 1985 (S.I. 1985 No.548) ................................................................................. 348, 351
Reservoirs (Panels of Civil Engineers) (Application and Fees) Regulations 1992 (S.I. 1992 No.1527) ................................................................................................. 349
Reservoirs (Panels of Civil Engineers) (Application and Fees) (Amendment) Regulations 1998 (S.I. 1998 No.2403) ................................................................... 349

Secretaries of State for Transport, Local Government and the Regions and for Environment, Food and Rural Affairs Order 2001 (S.I. 2001 No.2568) .............. 96
Town and Country (Applications) Regulations 1988 (S.I. 1988 No.1812)
    reg 4 ................................................................................................................. 396
Town and Country Planning (Development Plan) Regulations 1991 (S.I. 1991 No.2794) ............................................................................................................. 358
    reg 10 ....................................................................................................... 358, 369
Town and Country Planning (Environmental Impact Assessment) (England and Wales) Regulations 1999 (S.I. 1999 No.293) .............................................. 396, 503
    reg 35(3) .......................................................................................................... 401
    Schs 1–4 .......................................................................................................... 401
Town and Country Planning (General Development Procedure) Order 1995 (S.I. 1995 No.419) ........................................................................................................ 357
    art 3(1) ..................................................................................................... 281, 361
    art 8 .................................................................................................................. 362
    art 10 ........................................................................................... 362, 369, 370
    art 19 ................................................................................................................ 371
    Sch 2 ................................................................................................................. 361
        Part 6, Class A(b) ...................................................................................... 361
        Part 9, Class A ................................................................................... 281, 361
        Part 14, Class A ......................................................................................... 361
        Part 15, Class A(b) .................................................................................... 361
Town and Country Planning (General Permitted Development) Order 1995 (S.I. 1995 No.418) ................................................................................................ 357, 361
    art 3(10), (11) .................................................................................................. 401
    art 4 .......................................................................................................... 361, 386
    Sch 2
        Parts 6, 7 ..................................................................................................... 502
        Part 14A ...................................................................................................... 402
        Part 15A ...................................................................................................... 402
Town and Country Planning (Use Classes) Order 1987 (S.I. 1987 No.764) .... 357, 360
Waste Management Licensing Regulations 1994 (S.I. 1994 No.1056)
    reg 17 ............................................................................................................... 172
    Sch 3
        para 7 .......................................................................................................... 172
        para 9 .......................................................................................................... 173
        para 25 ........................................................................................................ 173
Water Act 1989 (Transfer of Functions) (Appointed Day) Order 1989 (S.I. 1989 No.1530) ............................................................................................................... 296
Water and Sewerage (Conservation, Access and Recreation) (Code of Practice) Order 2000 (S.I. 2000 No.477) ............................................................................ 415
Water Authorities (Precepts to Internal Drainage Boards) Regulations 1974 (S.I. 1974 No.375) ......................................................................................................... 260
Water Supply and Sewerage Services (Customer Service Standards) Regulations 1989 (S.I. 1989 No.1159) ..................................................................................... 299
Water Supply and Sewerage Services (Customer Service Standards) (Amendment) Regulations 1989 (S.I. 1989 No.1383) ................................................................ 299
Water Supply and Sewerage Services (Customer Service Standards) (Amendment) Regulations 1993 (S.I. 1993 No.500) .................................................................. 299
Water Supply and Sewerage Services (Customer Service Standards) (Amendment) Regulations 1996 (S.I. 1996 No.3065) ................................................................ 299
Water Supply and Sewerage Services (Customer Service Standards) (Amendment) Regulations 2000 (S.I. 2000 No.2301) ................................................................ 299

# TABLE OF EUROPEAN SECONDARY LEGISLATION

**Conventions**
European Convention for the Protection of Human Rights and Fundamental Freedoms
  Protocol I
    art 1 .................................................................................. 313, 319, 512, 514
    art 6 .................................................................................................. 357, 514
    art 8 .................................................................................................. 313, 319

**Directives**
Directive on the Assessment of the Effect of Certain Plans and Programmes on
  the Environment (Directive on Strategic Environmental Assessment)
  (2001/42/EC) ............................................................................................ 404–406
Directive on the Assessment of the Effects of Certain Public and Private Projects on
  the Environment (Environmental Impact Assessment Directive – the 'Original'
  Directive) (85/337/EEC) ........................................................... 397–401, 405, 503
    Annex I ............................................................................................... 398, 401
    Annex II .............................................................................................. 398, 399
    Annex III .................................................................................................... 398
Directive on the Assessment of the Effects of Certain Public and Private Projects on
  the Environment (Environmental Assessment Directive – the 'Amending'
  Directive) (97/11/EC) ...................................................... 397, 400, 401, 405, 503
    Annexes I, II ....................................................................................... 400, 401
Environmental Information Directive (90/313/EEC) ................................................ 450
Groundwater Directive (80/68/EEC) ......................................................................... 498
Habitats Directive (92/43/EEC) ......... 102, 403, 431, 432, 434–436, 441, 445, 446, 513
    art 1 ..................................................................................................... 434, 435
    arts 2, 3 ............................................................................................... 435, 436
    art 4 ..................................................................................................... 435, 436
      (2) ..................................................................................................... 437, 438
    art 5(1), (3) ................................................................................... 435, 436, 437
    art 6, 7 ................................................................................. 433, 435, 436
    arts 33–35 .................................................................................................... 436
    Annexes I, II ....................................................................................... 434, 435
    Annex III ..................................................................................................... 437
    Annexes IV, V ............................................................................................. 434
Water Framework Directive (2000/60/EC) ....................................................... 116, 381
Wild Birds Directive (79/409/EEC) ............................... 102, 403, 431–435, 446, 447
    art 2 ..................................................................................................... 432, 433
    art 3 ............................................................................................................. 432
    art 4 ..................................................................................................... 432, 433
      (1), (2) ............................................................................................... 433, 438

**Regulations**
European Community Agri-environmental Regulation (EEC/2078/92) ................... 511

# TABLE OF CASES

A. Prosser and Son Ltd v Levy [1955] 3 All ER 577 ................................................ 326
Aberdeen Magistrates v Menzies (1748) Mor Dict 12 787 ...................................... 53
Abingdon Corp v James [1940] 1 All ER 446 ......................................................... 59
Acton v Blundell (1843) 13 LJ Ex 289 ..................................................................... 68
Acton Local Board v Batten (1885) 28 Ch D 283 .................................................. 292
Adcock and Others v Norfolk Line Ltd and Others, unreported, Court of Appeal
  (Civil Division) 28 May 1993 ............................................................................... 83
AF plc v Tyndale District Council, unreported, Queen's Bench Division, 13 April
  2000 ...................................................................................................................... 75
Airdrie Magistrates v Lanark County Council [1910] AC 286 ............................. 288
Alan Wibberley Building Ltd v Insley [1999] 1 WLR 894 ............................. 65, 345
Alexandrou v Oxford [1993] 4 All ER 987 ............................................................ 465
Alford Drainage Board v Mablethorpe (1985) 227 EC 867 .................................. 266
Allen v Gulf Oil Refining Ltd [1981] AC 1001 ....................................... 87, 90, 312
Andreae v Selfridge and Co Ltd [1938] Ch 1 ....................................................... 227
Andrew v Cod Beck Internal Drainage Board (1982) 261 EG 683 ...................... 168
Anglian Water Services Ltd v Crawshaw Robbins and Co Ltd, unreported, Queen's
  Bench Division, 6 February 2001 ............................................................... 323, 324
Anns v Merton London Borough [1978] AC 728 ................................................. 464
Arkwright v Gell (1839) 5 M&W 203 ............................................................. 42, 43
Armstrong v Turquand (1858) 9 ICLR 32 ............................................................. 485
Attorney-General v Acton Local Board (1882) 22 Ch D 221 ............................... 304
Attorney-General v Copeland [1902] 1 KB 690 ................................................... 335
Attorney-General v Lonsdale (1868) 20 LT 64 ....................................................... 43
Attorney-General v Peacock [1926] 1 Ch 241 ...................................................... 292
Attorney-General v Rowley Brothers and Oxley (1910) 75 JP 81 ................. 40, 331
Attorney-General v St Ives Rural District Council [1961] 2 WLR 111 ............... 336
Attorney-General v Tomline (1879) 12 Ch D 214 ........................................... 28, 54
Attorney-General v Tomline (1880) 14 Ch D 58, CA ........................................... 210
Attorney-General v Waring (1899) 63 JP 789 ....................................................... 338
Attorney-General of Southern Nigeria v John Holt and Co (Liverpool) Ltd [1915]
  AC 620 ............................................................................................................... 211
Austerberry v Oldham Corporation (1885) 29 Ch D 750 ..................................... 499
Baggs v United Kingdom (1985) 9 EHRR 235 .................................................... 313
Baird v Williamson (1863) 15 CBNS 376 ....................................................... 65, 68
Ballard v Leek Urban Council (1917) 87 LJ Ch 146 ........................................... 335
Barret v London Borough of Enfield [1999] 3 All ER 193 .................................... 82
Bartlett v Tottenham [1932] 1 Ch 114 .............................................................. 43, 68
Beal v Thornton Internal Drainage Board [1973] RVR 153 ................................. 168
Beckenham Urban District Council v Wood (1896) 60 JP 490 ............................ 282
Beeston v Weate (1856) 5 E&B 986 ....................................................................... 59
Biard v Deal Corporation (1961) 12 P&CR 398 ................................................... 227
Bickett v Morris (1866) LR 1 Sc&Div 47 ............................................. 40, 48, 51–53
Birch and Birch v Ancholme Drainage Board (1958) 9 P&CR 268 .................... 168
Birse Construction Ltd v Haiste Ltd (Watson and Others, Third Parties) [1996]
  2 All ER 1 .......................................................................................................... 349
Blackdown Properties Ltd v Ministry of Housing and Local Government [1967]
  Ch 115 ................................................................................................................ 284
Bleachers' Association v Chapel-en-le-Frith Rural District Council [1933] Ch 356 ........ 77

Blount v Layard (1888) [1891] 2 Ch 681 ............................................................................... 40
Blue Circle Industries plc v Ministry of Defence [1998] Env LR 22 ........................... 4
Blundell (1843) 13 LJ Ex 289 ................................................................................................ 68
Blundell v Caterrall (1821) 5 B&Ald 268 ......................................................................... 43
Blythe v Birmingham Waterworks Co (1856) 11 Exch 781 ........................................ 83
Borough of Blaenau Gwent v Robinson Jones Design Partnership Ltd and Another
 [1997] 53 Con LR 31 ........................................................................................................ 349
Box v Jubb (1879) 3 Ex D 76 ................................................................................................. 70
Boxes Ltd v British Waterways Board [1971] 2 Lloyd's Rep 183 ....................... 85, 88
Boynton v Ancholme Drainage and Navigation Commissioners [1921] 2 KB 213 .. 212
Bradford Corporation v Pickles [1895] AC 587 ............................................................. 77
Braintree District Council v Gosfield Hall Settlement Trustees, unreported,
 Chelmsford Crown Court, 13 July 1977 .................................................................. 348
Bramlett v Tees Conservancy Commissioners (1885) 49 JP 214 ............................. 201
Bridle v Secretary of State for the Environment, Transport and the Regions (2000)
 97(44) LSG 46 ..................................................................................................................... 363
Bristow v Cormican (1878) 3 AC 641 ............................................................................... 40
Britel Developments (Thatcham) Ltd v Nightfreight Great Britain Ltd [1998] 4 All
 ER 432 ..................................................................................................................................... 59
British Dredging (Services) Ltd v Secretary of State for Wales and Monmouthshire
 [1975] 1 WLR 687; 2 All ER 845 ............................................................ 215, 233, 234
British Gas plc v Stockport Metropolitan Borough Council [2001] Env LR 763 ..... 70, 327
British Railways Board v Tonbridge and Malling District Council (1981) 79 LGR
 565 ........................................................................................................................................... 287
British Waterways Board v Severn Trent Water Ltd [2001] Env LR 780 ......... 88, 302,
 303, 338
Broadbent v Ramsbotham (1856) 11 Exch 602 ............................................................. 62
Broder v Saillard (1876) 2 Ch D 692 ................................................................................. 66
Bromley London Borough Council v Morritt (2000) 79 P&CR 536 ...................... 282
Brown v Dunstable Corporation [1899] 2 Ch 378 ..................................................... 304
Burgess v Northwich Local Board (1880) 50 LJ QB 219 .......................................... 471
Burnside v Emerson [1968] WLR 1490 ......................................................................... 471
Burton v West Suffolk County Council [1960] 2 QB 72 ................................. 341, 471
Butler v River Foss Internal Drainage Board [1966] RVR 282 ................................ 169
Bybrook Barn Garden Centre Ltd v Kent County Council [2001] Env LR
 543 ........................................................................ 56, 74, 75, 82, 88, 89, 330, 331, 341
Cambridge Water Company Ltd v Eastern Counties Leather [1994] 1 All ER
 53 ...................................................................................................... 62, 70, 72, 76, 79, 229
Canterbury City Council v Department of the Environment, unreported, Queen's
 Bench Division, 14 March 1980 ..................................................................... 205, 206
Canvey Island Commissioners v Preedy [1922] 1 Ch 179 ........................................ 211
Caparo Industries plc v Dickman and Others [1990] 1 All ER 568 ........................ 82
Capital and Counties plc v Hampshire County Council [1997] 2 All ER 865 ......... 465
Carter v Boehm (1766) 3 Burr 1905 ................................................................................ 485
Central Electricity Authority v Cumberland River Board [1958] JPL 51 ................. 169
Chamber Colliery Co v Hopwood (1886) 55 LT 449 .................................................. 43
Charing Cross Electricity Supply Co v Hydraulic Power Co [1914] 3 KB 772 ..... 325
Chasemore v Richards (1859) 7 HL Cas 349 ................................................ 39, 44, 62, 77
Chelmer and Blackwater Navigation Ltd v Essex Rivers Catchment Board (1951)
 157 EG 416 ......................................................................................................................... 267
Chippendale v Pontefract Rural District Council (1907) 71 JP 231 .................. 345, 346
Chorley Corporation v Nightingale [1907] 2 KB 637 ................................................ 346
Christchurch Drainage Board v Brown and Others (1987) *The Times* 14
 September .................................................................................................................... 88, 466

## Table of Cases

City of Bradford Metropolitan District Council v Yorkshire Water Services Ltd,
  unreported, Queen's Bench Division, 19 September 2001 .................................. 286
City of Edinburgh v Secretary of State for Scotland (1997) 3 PLR 71 ..................... 360
Clark v Epsom Rural District Council [1928] 1 Ch 287 ............................................ 291
Coe v Wise (1866) LR 1 QB 711 ....................................................................... 201, 212
Collard v River Stour (Kent) Catchment Board [1937] 1 All ER 436 ...................... 267
Collier v Anglian Water (1983) *The Times* 23 March ....................................... 133, 474
Collins v Middle Level Commissioners (1896) LR 4 CP 279 .................................... 201
Commissioners of Sewers for the Parish of Fobbing v R (1886) 11 App Cas 449 .... 50
Computer and Systems Engineering plc v John Lelliot (Ilford) Ltd and Another
  (1990) 54 Build LR 1 ................................................................................................ 482
Cook v Minion (1978) 37 P&CR 58 ............................................................................ 283
Cotton v Derbyshire Dales District Council (1994) *The Times* 20 June .................. 476
Countess of Rothes v Kirkcaldy and Dysart Waterworks Commissioners (1882)
  7 App Cas 694 ........................................................................................................... 202
County Council of Kings County and O'Sullivan v Kennedy [1910] 2 IR 544 ........ 335
Cracknell v Corporation of Thetford (1869) Law Rep 4 CP 629 ........................ 54, 202
Crest Homes (South West) Ltd v Gloucestershire County Council, unreported,
  Court of Appeal, 22 June 1999 ................................................................................. 367
Croft v Rickmansworth Highway Board (1885) 39 Ch D 272 .................................. 335
Crompton v Lea (1874) LR 19 Eq 115 .......................................................................... 69
Crossley v Lightowler (1867) 16 LT 438 ...................................................................... 40
Croysdale v Sudbury-on-Thames Urban District Council [1898] 2 Ch 515 ............ 335
Cullimore v Lyme Regis Corporation [1961] 3 All ER 1008 .................................... 221
Darby v National Trust [2001] EWCA Civ 189 ......................................................... 476
Davey v Harrow Corporation [1958] 1 QB 60 .............................................. 56, 80, 330
Day and Sons v Thames Water Authority [1984] JPL 596 ....................................... 166
Dear v Thames Water (1992) 33 Con LR 43 ................................................. 87, 88, 90
Delaware Mansions Ltd and Others v Lord Mayor and Citizens of the City of
  Westminster [2001] UKHL 55, 25 October 2001 ............................................. 56, 330
Dent v Birmingham Corporation (1897) 66 LJ QB 395 ............................................ 305
Department of Transport v North West Water Authority [1983] 3 All ER 273;
  [1984] AC 336 ................................................................................................... 87, 325
Derry v Peek (1889) 14 App Cas 337 ......................................................................... 485
Dickinson v Grand Junction Canal Co (1852) 16 Jur 200; (1852) 7 Exch 282 .... 44, 52
Doncaster Borough Council v Secretary of State for the Environment (1996)
  74 P&CR 428 .................................................................................................... 281, 361
Donoghue v Stevenson [1932] AC 562 ........................................................................ 82
Dunbar v Edinburgh Corporation 1961 Scots Law Times 45 (Sheriff Court) .. 223, 224
Dunn v Birmingham Canal Co (1872) LR 8 QB 42 .................................................. 325
Durrant v Branksome Urban District Council (1897) 76 LT 739; [1897] 2 Ch
  291 ..................................................................................................................... 301, 338
Dwr Cymru Cyfyngedig v Williams (1991) *The Times* 9 October ......................... 147
Earle and Earle v East Riding of Yorkshire Council [1999] RVR 200 ............. 217, 228
Earl of Norbury v Kitchin (1866) 15 LT 501 ............................................................... 52
East Suffolk Rivers Catchment Board v Kent [1940] 4 All ER 527; [1941]
  AC 74 ............................................................................................... 87, 163, 216, 465
Ellison and Others v Ministry of Defence (1996) 81 Build LR 101 ..................... 62, 70
Embrey v Owen (1851) 6 Ex 353 .................................................................... 39, 41, 52
Enion v Sefton Metropolitan Borough Council, unreported, Court of Appeal,
  9 February 1999 ....................................................................................................... 470
Eton Rural District Council v Thames Conservators [1950] Ch 540 ....................... 186
Falconar v Corporation of South Shields (1895) 11 TLR 223 .......................... 288, 292

## Table of Cases

Farmer Giles Ltd v Wessex Water Authority and Another [1990] 18 EG 102 ......... 169
Farquharson v Farquharson (1714) Mor Dict 12779 ............................................. 47, 53
Fay v Prentice (1845) 1 CB 828 .................................................................................. 326
Fear v Vickers (No.1) (1911) 27 TLR 558 .................................................................. 53
Fellowes v Rother District Council [1983] 1 All ER 513 ................................. 164, 216
Ferrand v Hallas Land and Building Company [1893] 2 QB 135 ............................. 285
Firmstone v Wheeley (1844) 2 Dow & L 203 ............................................................. 68
Fletcher v Smith (1877) 2 App Cas 781 ......................................................... 52, 69, 71
Fobbing Sewers Commissioners v R (1886) 11 App Cas 449 ................................... 210
Fowley Marine (Emsworth) v Gafford [1968] 2 QB 618 ........................................... 51
Freans v O'Brien (1883) 47 JP 472 .............................................................................. 41
Fredin v Sweden (No.1) (1991) ECHR Series A No.192 .......................................... 512
Fyfe Contractors Ltd v Scottish Hydro Electric plc, Scots Court of Session, Outer
  House, 11 June 1996 ............................................................................................. 351
Gann v Whitstable Free Fishers (1865) 11 HL Cas 192 .............................................. 43
Gartner v Kidman (1962) 108 CLR 12 ......................................................................... 64
Gaved v Martyn (1865) 13 LT 74 ................................................................................. 43
Geddis v Proprietors of the Bann Reservoir (1878) 3 App Cas 430 ................... 54, 201
George Legge and Son Ltd v Wenlock Corporation [1938] AC 204 ........................ 288
George Wimpey and Co Ltd v Secretary of State for the Environment and
  Teignbridge District Council [1978] JPL 776 ...................................................... 363
Gerrard v Crowe [1921] 1 AC 395 ............................................................................... 48
Gibbons v Lenfestey (1915) 84 LJPC 158 ................................................................... 64
Gillett v Kent Rivers Catchment Board, etc. [1938] 4 All ER 810 ........................... 162
Gillingham Borough Council v Medway (Chatham) Dock Co Ltd [1993] QB
  343 ................................................................................................................. 61, 356
Gilmore (Valuation Officer) v Baker-Carr [1962] 3 All ER 230 ............................... 262
Glazebrook v Gwynedd River Board [1964] RVR 55 ............................................... 168
Glossop v Heston and Isleworth Local Board (1879) 12 Ch D 102 .... 87, 89, 304, 310, 311
Golden Basket Eggs Ltd v Yorkshire Ouse and Hull River Authority [1971] RVR 21 . 168
Goldman v Hargrave [1967] AC 645 ........................................................................... 82
Good v Epping Forest District Council [1994] JPL 372 ........................................... 365
Goodes v East Sussex County Council [2000] 3 All ER 603 ............ 337, 470, 471, 475
Goodhart v Hyett (1883) 25 Ch D 182 ......................................................................... 59
Grampian Regional Council v City of Aberdeen District Council (1984) 47 P&CR
  633 ................................................................................................... 364, 365, 367
Great Portland Estates plc v Westminster City Council [1984] All ER 744 ............ 362
Greatrex v Hayward (1853) 8 Ex 291 .................................................................... 43, 68
Green v Chelsea Waterworks Co (1894) 70 LT 547 .................................................. 325
Greenock Corporation v Caledonian Railway Co [1917] AC 556 ................. 71, 73, 166
Greenwood Tileries Ltd v Clapson [1937] 1 All ER 765 ............................................ 73
Griffiths v Liverpool Corporation [1967] 1 QB 374 ................................................. 337
Guerra v Italy (1998) 26 EHRR 357 .......................................................................... 313
Halsall v Brizell [1957] Ch 169 .................................................................................. 500
Hammond v Vestry of St Pancras (1874) LR 9 CP 316 ............................................ 325
Hanbury v Jenkins (1901) 2 Ch 401 ............................................................................. 51
Hanley v Edinburgh Corporation [1913] AC 488 ....................................................... 71
Hanscombe v Bedfordshire County Council [1938] Ch 944 ............. 338, 342, 345, 346
Harvey v Walters (1873) LR 8CP 62 ......................................................................... 326
Harvey Nichols and Co Ltd v Thames Water Utilities Ltd, unreported, Technology
  and Construction Court, 16 November 1999 ....................................................... 324
Hatton v United Kingdom (2001) *The Times* 8 October 2001 ................................ 313
Hawkins v Dhawan and Mishiku (1987) 283 EG 1388 ............................................. 326

Hawthorn Corporation v Kannuluik [1906] AC 105 and Hanley v Edinburgh
    Corporation [1913] AC 488) .................................................................................. 469
Haydon v Kent County Council [1978] 1 QB 343 ................................................... 470
Haywood v Brunswick Permanent Benefit Building Society (1881) 8 QBD 403 ...... 50
Hedley v Webb [1901] 2 Ch 126 ............................................................................... 283
Hedley Byrne and Co Ltd v Heller and Partners Ltd [1964] AC 465 ....................... 467
Henderson v Merrett Syndicates Ltd [1994] 3 WLR 761 ......................................... 468
Hesketh v Birmingham Corporation [1924] 1 KB 260 ............................... 87, 304, 310
Hill v Chief Constable of West Yorkshire [1987] WLR 1126 .................................. 464
Hindson v Ashby [1896] 1 Ch 78 .............................................................................. 174
Hobday v Nicol [1944] 1 All ER 302 ........................................................................ 133
Hodgson v York Corporation (1873) 28 LT 836 ........................................................ 54
Holbeck Hall Hotel Ltd v Scarborough Borough Council [2000] 2 All ER
    705 ....................................................................................................... 210, 58, 78, 80
Holborn Trust Co Ltd v Folkestone Corporation (1956) 6 P&CR 86 ...................... 226
Holland v Lazarus (1897) 66 LJ QB 285 .................................................................. 282
Home Brewery plc v William Davis & Co Ltd [1987] 1 All ER 637; [1987] 2
    WLR 117 ............................................................................................. 37, 63, 67, 229
Home Office v Dorset Yacht Co Ltd [1970] 2 All ER 294; [1970] AC 1004 .... 88, 463
Hornsey Local Board v Davis [1893] 1 QB 756 ....................................................... 292
Howard v Ingersoll (1851) 54 US 381 ...................................................................... 174
Hudson v Tabor (1877) 2 QBD 290 ........................................................... 28, 49, 55, 210
Humphrey v Young [1903] 1 KB 44 ......................................................................... 283
Hunter and Others v Canary Wharf and London Docklands Development
    Corporation [1996] 1 All ER 482, affirmed [1997] Env LR 488 .......................... 61
Hunwick v Essex Rivers Catchment Board [1952] 1 All ER 765 ..................... 212, 474
Hurdman v North Eastern Railway Co (1878) 3 CPD 168 ......................................... 66
Hutton v Esher Urban District Council [1974] Ch 167 ............................................ 285
Ingram v Percival [1968] 3 All ER 657; [1969] 1 QB 548 ................................ 43, 161
Irving v Carlisle Rural District Council [1907] JP 212 ............................................ 336
Isle of Ely (1609) 10 Co Rep 141 ............................................................................. 211
John S. Deed and Sons Ltd v British Electricity Authority and Croydon Corporation
    (1950) 114 JP 533 .................................................................................................. 45
Johnson v Essex County Council (1971) 69 LGR 498 ............................................. 339
John White & Sons v White [1906] AC 72 ................................................................ 52
John Young & Co v Bankier Distillery Co [1893] AC 691; (1893) [1891–4] All
    ER 439 ................................................................................................................... 45
Jones v Llanrwst Urban District Council (1910) [1908–10] All ER Rep 922 ............ 39
Jones v Mersey River Board [1957] 3 All ER 375 ................................................... 129
Jones v Mersey River Board (1959) 10 P&CR 305 (Lands Tribunal) ...................... 173
Jordeson v Sutton Southcoates and Drypool Gas Co [1899] 2 Ch 217 ...................... 78
Keaney v Liverpool City Council, unreported, Lands Tribunal, 21 May 1998 ...... 168, 188
Keighley's Case 10 Co Rep 139a ................................................................................ 50
Kerr v Earl of Orkney (1857) 20 D 298 ..................................................................... 71
Kershaw v A. J. Smith and Co Ltd [1913] 2 KB 455 ............................................... 284
Kincaid v Hartlepool Borough Council and Northumbrian Water Ltd, unreported,
    Court of Appeal, 5 December 2000 ..................................................................... 474
Kingsway Furniture (Dartford) Ltd v Hapglow Ltd and Kylefield Ltd (Official
    Referee's Business, 23 March 1990) [1991] *Water Law* 10 ........................ 83, 161
Kitchen Design and Advice Ltd v Lea Valley Water Co [1989] 2 Lloyd's Rep 221 ..... 324
Ladbrokes Ltd v Secretary of State for the Environment [1981] JPL 427 ............... 365
Lakeman v Bournemouth Corporation (1956) 8 P&CR 265 .................................... 225
Lam and Others v Brennan and Another [1997] 3 PLR 22 ...................................... 356

*Table of Cases*

Lambert v Environment Agency, unreported, Lands Tribunal, 22 June 1999 .......... 175
Langbrook Properties Ltd v Surrey County Council [1970] 1 WLR 161 ................... 78
Larner v Solihull Metropolitan Borough Council [2001] RTR 32 ........................... 472
Leakey v National Trust [1980] 1 All ER 17 ........ 49, 56, 62, 67, 76, 80, 210, 306, 311
L. E. Walwin & Partners v West Sussex County Council [1975] 3 All ER 604 ...... 212
Liford's Case (1614) 11 Co Rep 46b ................................................................................ 58
Liggins v Inge (1831) 7 Bing 682 ..................................................................................... 41
London and North West Railway v Fobbing Sewers Commissioners (1896) 75 LT 629 ................................................................................................................................. 210
London Borough of Camden v National Rivers Authority and Wiltshire County Council, unreported, Court of Appeal, 10 October 1996 ...................................... 258
Lopez Ostra v Spain (1994) 20 EHRR 277 .................................................................. 313
Lorrimer v Environment Agency, unreported, Lands Tribunal, 30 March 1999 ...... 169
Lotus Ltd v British Soda Co Ltd [1972] Ch 123 ............................................................ 78
Lucas v South Carolina Coastal Council (1992) 505 US 1003 ................................. 512
Lyme Regis Corporation v Henley (1834) 6 ER 1180 ............................................... 211
Lyon v Fishmongers' Co (1876) 35 LT 569 ................................................................... 43
Mackender v Feldia [1967] 2 QB 590 ........................................................................... 485
Malcolmson v O'Dea (1863) 10 HL Cas 593 ................................................................ 43
Manchester Corporation v Markland [1936] AC 360 ................................................ 325
Marine Industrial Transmissions Ltd v Southern Water Authority [1989] RVR 221 ..... 169
Marriage v East Norfolk Rivers Catchment Board [1949] 2 All ER 1021 ......... 87, 167
Marshall v Ullesswater Steam Navigation Co (1871) LR 7 QB 166 ......................... 39
Mason v Hill (1833) 5 B&Ad 1 ....................................................................... 40, 41, 44
Mason v Shrewsbury and Hereford Railway Co (1871) LR 6 QB 578 ...................... 60
Masters v Hampshire County Council (1915) 84 LJ KB 2194 ................................. 341
Maxey Drainage Board v Great Northern Railway Co (1912) 106 LT 429 ............... 48
Meader v West Cowes Local Board [1892] 3 Ch 18 .................................................. 290
Menzies v Earl of Breadalbane (1828) 3 Bli NS 414 ................ 47, 48, 53, 79, 166, 175
Merlin v British Nuclear Fuels plc [1990] 2 QB 297 ...................................................... 4
Mersey Docks and Harbour Board Trustees v Gibbs (1866) LR 1 HL 93 ............ 86, 90
Metropolitan Borough Council v United Utilities Water Ltd [2001] EWCA Civ 1284 . 287
Micklethwait v Newlay Bridge Co (1886) 51 JP 132 ................................................... 40
Miner v Gilmour (1859) 12 Moo 131 ............................................................................. 39
M'Nab v Robertson [1897] AC 129, HL ....................................................................... 42
Monckton v Severn Trent Water Authority [1988] RVR 247 ....................... 88, 163, 169
Morland v Cook (1868) LR 6 Eq 252 ........................................................ 49, 55, 210, 500
Morris v Thyssen (GB) Ltd, unreported, Queen's Bench Division, 20 May 1983 ... 469
N. Duckitt and Sons v Yorkshire River Authority (1972) 223 EG 492 ..................... 266
Neath Rural District Council v Williams [1951] 1 KB 115 ................................ 56, 329
Newbury District Council v Secretary of State for the Environment [1981] AC 578 .... 364
Newcastle-upon-Tyne Corporation v Houseman (1898) 63 JP 85 ............................ 288
Nicholls v Ely Beet Sugar Factory [1936] Ch 343 ....................................................... 59
Nichols v Marsland (1875) LR 10 Exch 255; (1876) 2 Ex D 1 .............................. 70, 73
Nield v London & North Western Railway (1874) LR 10 Ex 4 ................. 42, 50, 51, 70
Nitro-Phosphate and Odam's Chemical Manure Co v London and St Katherine Docks Co (1878) 9 Ch D 503 ............................................................... 55, 73, 203
Normile v Ruddle (1912) 47 ILT 179 ............................................................................. 54
North Level Commissioners v River Welland Catchment Board [1937] 4 All ER 684 . 128
North Shore Railway Co v Pion (1889) 61 LT 525; (1889) 14 AC 612 ................. 39, 43
Oakes v Mersey River Board (1957) 9 P&CR 145 ..................................... 129, 166, 175
OLL Ltd v Secretary of State for Transport [1997] 3 All ER 987 ............................ 465
Osman v United Kingdom (1998) 5 BHRC 293 ........................................................... 89

## Table of Cases

Pakenham v Ticehurst Rural District Council (1903) 67 JP 448 ..................... 291, 292
Palmer v Bowman [2000] 1 All ER 22 .......................................................... 59, 64, 65
Passley v Wandsworth London Borough Council, unreported, Court of Appeal,
  24 May 1996 ........................................................................................................ 326
Passmore v Oswaldtwistle Urban District Council [1898] AC 387 .......................... 291
Pattinson and Another v Finningley Internal Drainage Board [1970] 2 QB 33 ........ 147
Pattinson and Pattinson v Finningley Internal Drainage Board (1971) 22 P&CR 929 ... 175
Pearce v Croydon Rural District Council (1910) 74 JP 429 .............................. 42, 339
Pemberton v Bright [1960] 1 All ER 792 ................................................................... 74
Pennington v Brinksop Hall Coal Co (1877) 5 Ch D 769 .......................................... 41
Penty v Greater London Council [1983] RVR 86 ..................................................... 169
Peter Marcic v Thames Water Utilities Ltd [2001] Env LR 146; [2002] EWCA 65,
  CA ........................................ 58, 77, 89, 91, 306, 310, 311, 318, 319, 321, 512, 513
Peter Marcic v Thames Water Utilities Ltd (No.2) [2001] 4 All ER 326 ... 306, 319, 321
Peters v Prince of Wales Theatre (Birmingham) Ltd [1943] 1 KB 73 ...................... 326
Pillbrow v Shoreditch Vestry [1895] 1 QB 433 ........................................................ 282
Pinnock v Waterworth (1887) 51 JP 248 ................................................................. 292
Popplewell v Hodkinson (1869) LR 4 Exch 248 ....................................................... 77
Port of London Authority v Essex Rivers Catchment Board [1944] 2 All ER 507 .. 269
Portsmouth Waterworks Co v London Brighton and South Coast Railway Co (1906)
  26 TLR 173 ............................................................................................................ 39
Post Office v Hampshire Country Council [1980] QB 124 ....................................... 295
Potter and Others v Mole Valley District Council and Another (1982) *The Times*
  22 October ............................................................................................................. 75
Powell and Rayner v United Kingdom (1990) 12 EHRR 355 .................................. 316
Pride of Derby and Derbyshire Angling Association v British Celanese Ltd [1953]
  1 Ch 149 ..................................................................................... 88, 305, 310, 469
Pritchard v Clwyd County Council, unreported, Court of Appeal, 16 June 1992 .... 471
Proctor v Avon and Dorset River Catchment Board (1953) 162 EG 161 ................. 167
Provender Millers (Winchester) Ltd v Southampton County Council [1940] 1 Ch
  131 .......................................................................................................... 73, 89, 344
Pyman Bell (Holdings) Ltd v Northmoor District Drainage Board (1995),
  unreported, Lands Tribunal, 20 October 1995 ..................................................... 269
Pyx Granite Co Ltd v Ministry of Housing and Local Government [1958] 1 QB 554 ... 364
R v Baker (1867) LR 2 QB 621 ................................................................................ 210
R v Cambridge Health Authority ex parte B [1995] 1 WLR 898 ............................. 316
R v Cambridgeshire County Council [1936] 3 All ER 352 ...................................... 258
R v Commissioners of Sewers for Essex (1832) 1 B&C 477 ..................................... 50
R v Commissioners of Sewers for Pagham (1828) 8 B&C 355; (1828) 108 ER
  1075 ...................................................................................................... 37, 49, 210, 229
R v Cumberland Justices ex parte Trimble (1877) 41 JP 454 ................................... 329
R v Director of Public Prosecutions ex parte Kebilene [1999] 3 WLR 972 ............. 315
R v Dovermoss Ltd [1995] Env LR 258 ............................................................. 5, 289
R v Environment Secretary ex parte Spath Holme Ltd [2001] 2 WLR 15 ............... 302
R v Falmouth and Truro Port Health Authority ex parte South West Water Ltd
  [1999] Env LR 833; [2000] 3 All ER 306 ............................................... 41, 55, 329
R v Hastings Justices ex parte Pevensey Levels Internal Drainage Board [1962]
  1 All ER 278 ........................................................................................................ 268
R v Leigh (1839) 10 Ad & El 398 ............................................................................ 210
R v Metropolitan Board of Works (1863) 3 B&S 710 ......................................... 44, 62
R v Oxfordshire (Inhabitants) (1830) 1 B&Ad 289 ................................................... 42
R v Secretary of State for the Environment and the Crown Estate Commissioner
  and East Coast Shipping Aggregates Ltd ex parte Bryant, unreported, Queen's
  Bench Division, 30 July 1996 .............................................................................. 233

R v Secretary of State for the Environment ex parte Royal Society for the Protection of Birds (the Lappel Bank case) [1997] Env LR 442 (European Court of Justice) ...... 433
R v Secretary of State for the Environment, Transport and the Regions ex parte First Corporate Shipping Ltd Case C-371/98 [2001] Env LR 34 ............... 434, 437
R v Secretary of State for Wales and A. B. Hutton (Secretary to the Maes Gerddi Residents Association) [1987] JPL 711 ................................................................ 280
R v Spilsby and Skyness Justices ex parte Alford Drainage Board, unreported, Queen's Bench Division, 25 July 1985 ................................................................ 266
R v Wharton (1701) 12 Mod 510 ............................................................................ 56
R (on the application of Holding and Barnes plc) v Secretary of State for the Environment, Transport and the Regions [2001] UKHL 3 ................................. 357
Radstock Co-operative and Industrial Society v Norton-Radstock Urban District Council [1968] Ch 605 ............................................................................................ 76
Rameshur Pershad Narain Singh v Koonj Behari Pattuk (1878) 4 AC 121 ................. 42
Rawstron v Taylor (1855) 156 ER 873 .......................................................................... 42
Ray v Baker (Valuation Officer) (1970) 214 EG 1710, Lands Tribunal ................. 478
Re Coast Protection Act 1949 (1955) 106 L Jo 108, Lands Tribunal ...................... 226
Re Ellenborough Park [1956] Ch 131 ......................................................................... 58
Re Fitzherbert-Brockholes Agreement, River Wyre Catchment Board v Miller [1940] Ch 51 ........................................................................................................ 186
Reece v Miller (1882) 8 QBD 626 ..................................................................... 43, 161
Rhodes v Airedale Drainage Commissioners (1876) 1 CPD 380 ............................... 56
Rhone v Stephens [1994] AC 310 ............................................................................ 499
Rich v Pembrokeshire County Council [2001] EWCA Civ 410 ....................... 471, 475
Rickards v Lothian [1913] AC 263 .................................................................... 70, 326
Rider v Rider [1973] 1 QB 505 ................................................................................ 470
Ridge v Midland Railway Co (1888) 53 JP 55 ........................................................... 47
Rimmer v Crossens Drainage Board (1976) 239 EG 817 ......................................... 175
Rippingale Farms Ltd v Black Sluice Internal Drainage Board [1963] 1 WLR 1347 .... 199
Roberts v Fellowes (1906) 94 LT 279 ......................................................................... 59
Roberts v Gwyrfai District Council [1899] 2 Ch 608 ................................................. 52
Robinson v Cardiff City Council, unreported, 16 October 1987, Cardiff Crown Court . 462
Robinson v Kilvert (1889) 41 Ch D 88 ........................................................................ 61
Robinson v Workington Corporation [1897] 1 QB 619 ................................... 304, 310
Robson v Northumberland and Tyneside River Board (1952) 3 P&CR 150 ............ 170
Rohan Investments Ltd v Cunningham and Others [1999] Lloyd's Rep IR 190 ...... 483
Ross v Fedden (1872) LR 7 QB 661 ........................................................................ 326
Rouse v Gravelworks Ltd [1940] 1 KB 489 ......................................................... 70, 80
Royco Homes Ltd v Eatonwill Construction Ltd, Three Rivers District Council Third Party [1979] Ch 276 .......................................................................... 295, 298
Rugby Joint Water Board v Walters [1966] 3 All ER 497 .......................................... 44
Rydon Construction Ltd v Thames Water Utilities Ltd, unreported, Office of Water Services, 22 April 1998 ....................................................................................... 495
Ryeford Homes Ltd and Another v Sevenoaks District Council and Others [1989] 2 EGLR 281; [1990] JPL 36 ........................................................... 63, 87, 357, 468
Rylands v Fletcher (1866) LR 1 Exch 265, affirmed (1868) Law Rep 3 HL 330 ............................................................................. 64, 69, 70, 311, 318, 355
S v France (1990) 65 D&R 250 ........................................................... 313, 318, 320
St Helen's Smelting Co v Tipping (1865) 11 HLC 642 .............................................. 61
St Margaret's Bay Hotel Ltd v Dover Rural District Council (1960) 12 P&CR 239 ..... 227
Samson v Hoddinott (1857) CBNS 590 ..................................................................... 52
Samuel v Edinburgh and Glasgow Railway Co (1850) 13 D 312 ............................... 72
Saunders v Newman (1818) 1 B&Ald 258 ................................................................. 45

## Table of Cases

Saxby v Manchester, Sheffield and Lincolnshire Railway Co (1869) LR 4 CP 198 .. 75
Scutt and Screeton v Lower Ouse Internal Drainage Board (1953) 4 P&CR 71 ...... 167
Sedleigh-Denfield v O'Callaghan [1940] AC 880 .................................................. 75, 166
Sefton Metropolitan Borough Council v United Utilities Water Ltd [2001] EWCA Civ 1284 .................................................................................................................... 284
Sephton v Lancashire River Board [1962] 1 All ER 183 .......................... 164, 199, 212
Shelfer v City of London Electric Lighting Co [1895] 1 Ch 287 .............................. 320
Shepherd v Croft [1911] 1 Ch 521 ............................................................................. 290
Showan v Yapp, unreported, Court of Appeal (Civil Division), 3 November 1998 ....... 476
Simcox v Yardley Rural District Council (1905) 69 JP 66 ................................ 345, 346
Simpson v Attorney-General [1904] AC 476 ............................................................. 55
Sinclair-Lockhart's Trustees v Central Land Board (1950) 1 P&CR 195 ............... 282
Smeaton v Ilford Corporation [1954] 1 Ch D 450 .......................... 87, 89, 304, 310
Smith v Cawdle Fen, Ely (Cambridge) Commissioners [1938] 4 All ER 64 ... 162, 212
Smith v Kendrick (1849) 7 CB 515 ...................................................................... 37, 67
Smith and Snipes Hall Farm Ltd v River Douglas Catchment Board [1949] 2 KB 500 ................................................................................................ 164, 165, 199, 499
Snook v Grand Junction Waterworks Co (1886) 2 TLR 308 .................................... 325
Southern Water Authority v Nature Conservancy Council [1992] 3 All ER 481 ..... 414
Spring v Guardian Assurance plc [1994] 3 WLR 354 ................................................ 468
Staffordshire Canal Co v Birmingham Canal Co (1866) LR 1 HL 254 ...................... 42
Stapleford v Severn Trent Water Authority [1989] RVR 85 ...................................... 174
Staples v West Dorset District Council (1995) 93 LGR 536 ...................................... 475
Steel Stampings Ltd v Severn Trent Water Authority (1982) 263 EG 359 .............. 169
Stephens v Anglian Water Authority [1987] 1 WLR 1381; [1987] 3 All ER 379 .... 78, 229
Steven Dobson Davison v North West Water Ltd, unreported, Queen's Bench Division, 10 March 1999 .................................................................................................. 324
Stockport Waterworks Co v Potter (1864) 10 LT 748 ......................................... 39, 40
Stollmeyer v Trinidad Lake Petroleum Co [1918] AC 485 ........... ........... 42, 289
Stovin v Wise [1996] 3 All ER 801; [1996] AC 923 ................................ 88, 90, 469
Strange v Andrews [1956] NZLR 948 ..................................................................... 48
Stretton's Derby Brewery Co v Derby Corporation [1894] 1 Ch 431 ..................... 304
Stuckley, Stuckley and Litchfield v North Somerset Drainage Board (1960) 11 P&CR 224 ................................................................................................................... 168
Symes and Jaywick Associated Properties Ltd v Essex Rivers Catchment Board [1937] 1 KB 548; [1936] 3 All ER 908 ...................................................... 211, 212
Tarmac Heavy Building Materials UK Ltd v Secretary of State for the Environment, Transport and the Regions and Buckinghamshire County Council (1999) 79 P&CR 260 ................................................................................................................... 364
Taylor v Bath and North East Somerset District Council, unreported, Queen's Bench Division, 27 January 1999 ....................................................................................... 476
Taylor v St Helens Corporation (1877) 6 Ch D 264 ........................................... 41, 289
Tayside Regional Council v Secretary of State for Scotland, unreported, Scots Court of Session, Outer House, 19 December 1994 ...................................................... 281
Tennent v Earl of Glasgow (1864) 2 M (HL) 22 ......................................................... 72
Tesco Stores Ltd v North Norfolk District Council (1999) 78 P&CR 359 ............... 367
Tesco Stores Ltd v Secretary of State for the Environment and Others [1995] WLR 759 ............................................................................................................................. 366
Thameside Estates Ltd v Greater London Council [1978] RVR 82 ......................... 171
Thamesmead Town Ltd v Allotey (2000) 79 P&CR 557 .......................................... 500
Thames Water Case (2000) 301 ENDS Report ............................................................ 4
Thames Water Utilities Ltd v (1) Skandia Property (UK) Ltd (2) Vala Properties BV, unreported, Court of Appeal, 27 July 1999 ....................................................... 324

Thames Water Utilities Ltd v (1) Videotron Corporation Ltd (2) McNicholas
   Construction Co Ltd, unreported, Court of Appeal, 10 December 1999 ............ 324
Thoburn v Northumberland County Council, unreported, Court of Appeal, 19
   January 1999 .................................................................................................... 469
Thomas v Gower Rural District Council [1922] 2 KB 76 ................................... 88, 339
Tidman v Reading Borough Council [1994] 3 PLR 72 ........................................... 468
Tithe Redemption Commission v Runcorn Urban District Council and Another
   [1954] Ch 383 .................................................................................................... 334
Trafford v R 8 Bing 204 .............................................................................................. 48
Trent River Authority v National Coal Board [1970] 1 All ER 558 ........................ 273
Tulk v Moxhay (1848) 41 ER 1143 ............................................................................. 50
Tutill v West Ham Local Board of Health (1873) LR 8 CP 447 ...................... 341, 345
Umek v London Transport Executive, unreported, Queen's Bench Division, NLJ,
   8 June 1984 ........................................................................................................ 473
Upper District Committee of the County of Renfrew v Woddrop's Trustees 1927
   SLT 69 (Sheriff Court) ...................................................................................... 329
Vestry of St Martin in the Fields v Bird [1895] 1 QB 428 ...................................... 282
Vincent v Thames Conservancy (1953) 4 P&CR 66 ................................................ 171
Vyner v North Eastern Railway Co (1898) 14 TLR 554 ........................................... 55
Vyner v North Eastern Railway Co (1904) 20 TLR 192 ........................................... 55
Walmsley v Featherstone Urban District Council (1909) 73 JP 322 ................ 345, 346
Warner and Another v Kingston Brook Internal Drainage Board [1979] RVR 221 .. 169
Weaver v Family Housing Association (York) Ltd (1975) 74 LGR 255 ................ 282
Webb v Minister of Housing and Local Government [1965] 2 All ER 193 ..... 215, 222
W. E. Black Ltd v Secretary of State for the Environment and London Borough of
   Harrow [1997] Env LR 1 ........................................................................... 364, 496
Weeks and Weeks v Thames Water Authority [1979] JPL 774 ................................ 170
Welsh National Water Authority v Burgess (1974) 28 P&CR 378 .......................... 167
West Leigh Colliery Co Ltd v Tunnicliffe and Hampson Ltd [1908] AC 27 ........... 320
West of Ouse Internal Drainage Board v H. Prins Ltd (1978) 247 EG 295 ............. 267
West Riding of Yorkshire Rivers Board v Tadcaster Rural District Council (1907)
   97 LT 436 ............................................................................................................ 43
Whalley v Lancashire and Yorkshire Railway Co (1884) 13 QBD 131 ..................... 66
Whyte v Redland Aggregates Ltd, unreported, Court of Appeal, 27 November 1997 ... 476
William Leech (Midlands) v Severn-Trent Water Authority (1981) *The Times*
   5 June ................................................................................................................. 281
William Sindall plc v Cambridgeshire County Council [1994] 3 All ER 932 .......... 476
Williams v Morland (1824) 2 B&C 910 ..................................................................... 41
Williamson v Durham Rural District Council [1906] 2 KB 65 ................................ 336
Wilson v Waddell (1876) 2 App Cas 95 ..................................................................... 68
Wincanton Rural District Council v Parsons [1905] 2 KB 34 ................................. 286
Withers v Purchase (1889) 60 LT 819 ........................................................... 51, 53, 59
Wood v Saunders (1875) 10 Ch App 583 ................................................................... 43
Wright v Howard (1823) 1 Si&St 190 ........................................................................ 45
X v Bedfordshire County Council [1995] 2 AC 633 .................................................. 82
Ynys Mon Borough Council v Secretary of State for Wales [1993] JPL 225 .......... 371
Yorkshire Water Services Ltd v Sun Alliance & London Insurance plc and Others
   [1997] 2 Lloyd's Rep 21 ..................................................................................... 83
Young v Sun Alliance and London Insurance Ltd [1977] 1 WLR 104 .................... 481

**European Cases**
Case C-392/96 Commission v Ireland [1999] 3 CMLR 727 ..................................... 399
Case C72/95 Aannemersbedrijf P.K. Kraaijeveld BV and Others v Gedeputeerde
   Staten van ZuidHolland Environnement et Consommateurs [1996] ECR I-5403 .... 398

European Commission v Federal Republic of Germany Case 57/89 [1991] ECR I-883 (the Leybucht Dykes case) .................................................................. 433
European Commission v France Case C-96/98 [2000] 2 CMLR 681 (the Poitevin Marsh case) ............................................................................................... 434
European Commission v French Republic Case C-166/97 [1999] Env LR 781 (the Seine Estuary case) .................................................................................. 433
European Commission v Spain Case 355/90 [1993] ECR 1-4221 (the Marismas de Santona case) ........................................................................................... 433

# Chapter 1

# INTRODUCTION AND BACKGROUND

## 1.1 OBJECTIVES

The purpose of this book is to provide a reasonably comprehensive and accessible account of the law and policy of England and Wales relating to flood defence. Insofar as the general scope of the work is concerned, 'flood defence' is broadly interpreted to encompass the drainage of land, the defence of watercourses and the sea from flooding, the provision of flood warning systems and coast protection activities undertaken to prevent erosion of coastal land. In some contexts, the discussion is more directly focused upon particular kinds of activity and in these contexts the terminology of 'land drainage', 'flood defence' and 'coast protection' is adopted. However, 'flood defence' or, more fully, 'flood and coastal defence' is usefully used as an all-encompassing phrase to cover the full range of activities at issue.

Statutorily, the key terms are defined as the follows:

> 'drainage' includes defence against water, including sea water, irrigation (other than spray irrigation), warping and the carrying on for any purpose of any other practice which involves management of the level of water in a watercourse;[1]

> 'flood defence' means the drainage of land and the provision of flood warning systems;[2] and

---

[1] s.113(1) Water Resources Act 1991 and s.72(1) Land Drainage Act 1991, as amended by s.100 Environment Act 1995. The non-exhaustive formulation of the definition is to be noted: stipulating that 'drainage' *includes* the stated activities, leaves open the possibility that other, unspecified, activities may also be included. On a dictionary definition, 'warping' is the practice of fertilising poor quality land with a deposit of sediment or alluvial material by keeping turbid water standing on that land. For flood defence purposes, 'watercourse' includes all rivers, streams, ditches, drains, cuts, culverts, dykes, sluices, sewers and passages through which water flows, except a 'public sewer' within the meaning of the Water Industry Act 1991 (ss.221(1) and 113(1) Water Resources Act 1991 and s.72(1) Land Drainage Act 1991).

[2] s.113(1) Water Resources Act 1991 and on flood warning systems see 11.3 below. 'Management of the level of a watercourse for any purpose' would seem to encompass a range of practices to ensure a *sufficient* level of flow, as opposed to the alleviation of *excessive* levels of flow. In principle, therefore, this might encompass practices for the irrigation of land or to secure a 'minimum acceptable flow' by means of licensing of abstractions (on abstraction licensing see Part II Chapter II Water Resources Act 1991).

'coast protection' means the protection of the coast against erosion and encroachment by the sea.[3]

In more practical terms, it has been suggested that 'land drainage' means the control of water levels within river or channel systems, often by means of pumped evacuation to enable a developed or agricultural[4] land use to be sustained in areas which could not otherwise support such uses, and the transfer of water to facilitate irrigation and other water uses. By contrast, 'flood defence' has been characterised as those activities for reducing the risk of overland flooding through the management of rivers or channels, control structures, embankments and flood walls, which retain and exclude natural fresh and tidal waters to prevent inundation. Along with these activities 'flood defence' also encompasses the provision of a flood warning service.[5]

Although the concept of 'flood defence' normally encompasses flooding from both watercourses and the sea, a distinction is often drawn between inland or riverine flood defence and 'sea defence' where the defence of estuarial or coastal areas from flooding by tidal waters is involved. 'Coast protection', it should be appreciated, is a significantly different activity in that it is the protection of coastal *land from erosion and encroachment*, rather than from eventual inundation by water, that is involved. That is, it is protection against the loss of land to the sea, rather than the defence of land from flooding, that is primarily sought by coast protection activities, though the contrast between these purposes may sometimes be difficult to disentangle in practice.[6] Another important term is 'coastal defence', which is a composite expression referring to both sea defence and coast protection, that is, any activity relating to the alleviation of tidal flooding or the loss of coastal land.[7]

The practical differences between 'land drainage', 'flood defence' and 'coast protection' are often a matter of degree insofar as individual projects

---

[3] Preamble, Coast Protection Act 1949 and see Ch.5 below on coast protection generally.

[4] For a discussion of the traditional emphasis placed upon land drainage as a means of enhancing agricultural productivity see E. A. G. Johnson, 'Land Drainage in England and Wales' (1954) 3(3) *Proceedings of the Institution of Civil Engineers* 601 and G. Cole, 'Land Drainage in England and Wales' (1976) 30(7) *Journal of the Institution of Water Engineers and Scientists* 345.

[5] House of Commons Agriculture Committee, Sixth Report Session 1997–98, *Flood and Coastal Defence* (1998) HC 707-II, *Memorandum submitted by the Association of Drainage Authorities* p.37

[6] See 5.2 below on the distinction between coastal flood defence and coast protection.

[7] Ministry of Agriculture, Fisheries and Food, and Welsh Office, *Strategy for Flood and Coastal Defence in England and Wales* (1993).

may actually involve two or more of the activities. In some instances it may be a matter of identifying the *main purpose* of a particular project. Nonetheless, the conceptual distinctions between the different kinds of activity are legally important since, to a significant degree, they determine the legislative basis upon which a particular activity or project may be undertaken.

Although this is a book on the law of 'flood and coastal defence', as the expression has now been defined, some unavoidable limitations need to be imposed on the scope of the discussion and it may be useful to make these explicit.

First, it must be emphasised that the account that follows is written from a *legal* perspective, as opposed to that of a hydrological engineer or that of any of the other specialists who are involved in the practice of flood defence. Clearly, securing effective and appropriate flood defence is a multi-disciplinary activity that is not the monopoly of any single discipline. Whilst a range of distinct perspectives will need to be brought to bear upon the practical issues which are encompassed in this work, the legal provisions, policy principles and administrative structures that are considered are a framework within which the different specialist perspectives are accommodated. Suffice to say, the practicalities of flood defence are determined by a range of vitally important political, financial, engineering, social and ecological considerations that fall outside the scope of this work.[8]

Second, the law to be discussed is that of England and Wales, and those aspects of European Community law that have relevance to flood and coastal defence. That is, the law of Scotland and Northern Ireland is not covered, and illustrations from these jurisdictions are only incidentally introduced where they shed light on the law in England and Wales.

Third, it is recognised that there are many situations where the harm caused by flooding is not simply due to an excess of water in an undesired location, but that the *quality* of the intruding water is a key factor. That is, floodwater contaminated by sewage and other kinds of waste, or saline water, may give rise to kinds of harm which would not occur, or would be greatly diminished, if the water was relatively uncontaminated freshwater. Hence, there is a potentially important distinction to be drawn between problems of excess water *quantity* and unsatisfactory water *quality* though this may not always be clearly recognised in practice. Nonetheless, it must be

---

[8] Generally see E. C. Penning-Rowsell, D. J. Parker and D. M. Harding, *Floods and Drainage* (1986).

stressed that this is *not* a book on water quality.[9]

## 1.2 WATER QUANTITY AND WATER QUALITY

Some points arising from the contrast between water quantity and water quality concerns may usefully be elaborated at this early stage by consideration of a couple of examples. In *Blue Circle Industries plc* v *Ministry of Defence*[10] heavy rain caused water from the Aldermaston Atomic Weapons Establishment to flow over neighbouring land owned by the claimant. Because the floodwater was contaminated with radioactive plutonium, which exceeded acceptable levels under the Radioactive Substances Act 1960, a sale of the claimant's property was aborted. Despite decontamination works on the site, which effectively removed the radioactive material, liability[11] was established for an alteration of the physical characteristics of the land. The blighting of the property was recognised to be a foreseeable loss arising from the breach of statutory duty that had occurred.

The point to be emphasised about this situation is that the actual flooding damage was negligible. The overflow of water had passed down a stream through marshland into a lake, apparently without causing damage to any buildings or other structures. It is uncertain whether the circumstances would have given rise to any civil liability[12] if the complaint had been about flooding alone and, even if common law liability had been established, the damage actually done by the floodwater appears to have been of insignificant extent. The *Blue Circle* case graphically demonstrates that a specific incident is capable of giving rise to both water quantity and water quality complaints that may be pursued by markedly different kinds of legal proceedings. Although flooding may be a significant mechanism by which damage by contamination can arise, the situation was one where it was far more sensible for the claimant to pursue proceedings on the basis of contamination harm rather than flood damage.

Another graphic illustration of the contrast is to be seen in criminal proceedings brought by the Environment Agency against *Thames Water*[13] after a sewage pumping station suffered failures of pumping equipment and an emergency pump malfunctioned. The result of this was to pump

---

[9] Generally see W. Howarth and D. McGillivray, *Water Pollution and Water Quality Law* (2001).
[10] [1998] Env LR 22, but contrast *Merlin* v *British Nuclear Fuels plc* [1990] 2 QB 297.
[11] Under s.7(1)(a) Nuclear Installations Act 1965.
[12] Generally see Ch.2 below on civil liability.
[13] See 'Thames Water fined £250,000 for pumping toxic waste into homes' (2000) 301 *ENDS Report* p.50.

surface water drainage and effluent back up the sewers causing it to erupt from street drains and to flood ten residential properties with sewage and pesticide wastes. The residents were immediately evacuated from the properties and underwent medical tests for chemical exposure. The prosecution was brought under environmental legislation relating to water pollution and waste management[14] and the 'complete disregard to persons and the environment' that had been shown by the undertaker resulted in fines totalling £250,000.

Again, the facts *could* be characterised as a 'flood', but to do so would not properly reflect the character of the harm or the seriousness of the incident. Curiously perhaps, no general criminal offence of causing flooding exists.[15] Although it is an offence to cause or knowingly permit the unauthorised entry of polluting matter or effluent into a watercourse, without the need for specific harm to be shown,[16] no offence is committed where an entry of water causes the watercourse to flood and results in damage to downstream properties. Probably, the reasons for this disparity lie in the general lack of control that exists over floodwater, as opposed to situations where polluting matter or effluent is involved and over which persons are assumed to have control and to be responsible for a discharge or escape. Nevertheless, in the circumstances of the *Thames Water* case, a compensatory civil remedy for flooding alone would clearly not have been a proportionate response to the circumstances.

In summary, it is important to note the possibilities for flooding to give rise to civil or criminal proceedings for water contamination and to recognise that there may be a range of situations where this approach is more appropriately pursued. Nonetheless, issues of water quality damage arising from flooding are generally placed outside the scope of this work.

## 1.3 THE MEANING AND CAUSES OF 'FLOODING'

As a natural phenomenon, the periodic inundation of land by water has always occurred and the shape and character of land forms in England and Wales are the result of millions of years of water impacts of this kind. Some of these flows are of a regular kind, as where watercourses have come to follow a fairly consistent channel over time, or patterns of tides have

---

[14] Under s.85(1) Water Resources Act 1991 (in relation to an escape of effluent into an estuary) and under s.33(1)(c) Environmental Protection Act 1990 (in relation to the mismanagement of pesticide waste).

[15] Although, conceivably, some instances of intentional or reckless flooding causing damage to property might be within the Criminal Damage Act 1971.

[16] Under s.85 Water Resources Act 1991 and see *R v Dovermoss Ltd* [1995] Env LR 258.

determined the relatively uniform periodic flow of water over coastal land. In other instances, these flows of water have been more erratic, arising from extreme precipitation or meteorological conditions that do not follow any predictable pattern. Nonetheless, irregular events of this kind have always existed in nature and have had important long-term impacts in determining the shape of the natural environment and the ecosystems that it supports.

By contrast, the concept of 'flooding' is the anthropocentric idea that certain states of water inundation, whether naturally caused or influenced by human activity, are undesirable or unacceptable and should be avoided or counteracted wherever it is feasible to do so. Hence, the idea of 'flooding', as an adversity to be striven against, is antithetical to the natural phenomenon of water inundation as an inevitable and neutral event. 'Flooding' only becomes an issue where land has been developed by human intervention and excess water is likely to be damaging to particular land-uses, built development or human life and property.[17] These concerns do not always arise. For example, some traditional farming practices evolved with periodic water inundation in mind, and the submersion of such land by water may be perceived not only as an inevitable, but also an agriculturally beneficial occurrence.[18] 'Flood defence', therefore, is the cumulative range of operations and activities that are undertaken for the protection of those human interests against which water inundation is recognised to be an adversity. Whilst water inundation may not always be perceived to be problematic, the incompatibility of flooding with most uses of developed land is readily apparent.

Historically, there has been a tendency for the most intensive development of land to have taken place at locations allowing water access either along the coast or alongside navigable watercourses.[19] Whatever the commercial or other advantages of settlement at these locations, many of them are especially vulnerable from a flood risk perspective. Hence, the viability of many intensively developed urban areas has been maintained only by devoting substantial resources and expenditure to sea defences, flood embankments and other flood defence structures. This endeavour has been regarded as justifiable given the importance and value of the developments being protected. Nonetheless, in cost-benefit terms there are always limitations to what protection can be provided by way of flood defence and

---

[17] See Institution of Civil Engineers, *Learning to Live with Rivers* (2001) p.16.
[18] On the traditional practice of flooding 'water meadows' to enhance agricultural productivity see E. A. G. Johnson, 'Land Drainage in England and Wales' (1954) 3(3) *Proceedings of the Institution of Civil Engineers* 601 at p.622.
[19] See Institution of Civil Engineers, *Learning to Live with Rivers* (2001) p.7.

in all contexts it has to be considered whether protection of a particular location is justified on economic and other grounds.[20]

An appreciation of the character of the hazard against which protection is being sought is vitally important.[21] Flooding occurs when the amount of water (from rainfall and other precipitation) arriving or transmitted onto an area of land (by surface flow, watercourse flow or sea inundation) exceeds the capacity of that land to discharge the water (by infiltration, surface flow, watercourse flow or piped drainage). This may arise in any area because of local circumstances such as a torrential downpour or a blocked drain, but is of greatest concern in relation to intensively developed areas of land, in or near to river or coastal flood plains, where the extent of flooding and damage potential is likely to be greatest. Exceedence of the drainage capacity of land is greatly dependent upon the combination of natural drainage characteristics, the inhibition of these through ground being frozen or saturated by previous rainfall, and the effectiveness of artificially constructed drainage structures that serve an area. Inundation by the sea is the result of a combination of the impacts of tides, waves and sea surges and seaward river flow, balanced against the capacity of natural and constructed sea defences to resist these pressures.[22]

In the same way that 'natural inundation' of land by water has been contrasted with 'flooding', a flooding *incident* must be contrasted with its *impact*. The damage caused by a flood is determined not only by the extent of the flooding, but also by the depth of water and the violence of the flow and, perhaps most significantly, the character of land use in the flooded area. On this, land use can be conceived of as varying along a spectrum of intensity, with undeveloped land and agricultural areas at one extreme and intensively developed urban and residential areas at the other. Within the spectrum, financial impacts have been found to be most closely correlated with depth of flooding[23] but other factors such as the duration and the velocity of the floodwater, the presence of contamination, and characteristics of the affected property have also been recognised to be significant factors

---

[20] See 3.2 below on flood defence policy and Ch.12 below on sustainable development.

[21] For general reading on flooding see M. D. Newson, *Flooding and Flood Hazard in the United Kingdom* (1975); R. Ward, *Floods: A Geographical Perspective* (1978); E. C. Penning-Rowsell, D. J. Parker and D. M. Harding, *Floods and Drainage* (1986); L. Mayer and D. Nash, Eds., *Catastrophic Flooding* (1987); E. Zebrowski, *Perils of a Restless Planet* (1997) Ch.5; and E. E. Wohl, Ed., *Inland Flood Hazards: Human, riparian and aquatic communities* (2000).

[22] Generally see Department for Transport, Local Government and the Regions, Planning Policy Guidance Note 25, *Development and Flood Risk* (2001) Appendix A and see 9.8 below.

[23] Association of British Insurers, *Inland Flooding Risk – Issues Facing the Insurance Industry* (2000) p.25.

in determining the extent of structural impacts upon buildings. Not least important, the threat of the loss of life will be greatest where developed areas are vulnerable to rapid inundation, particularly where there is a risk of sea defences or river embankments being overtopped or unable to withstand water pressures. The vulnerability of developed land to rapid inundation is also critical in determining the scope for effective warnings to be given[24] and avoidance measures to be taken to prevent loss of life and property damage.

## 1.4 THE EXTENT OF THE HAZARD

Viewed globally, flooding is the most economically damaging kind of natural disaster. In 1998, some 50,000 lives were lost and damage totalling $93 billion was suffered as a result of natural hazards, though much of this was attributable to Hurricane Mitch in Honduras. Flood events represented 23% of all natural hazard losses by number, 23% of all deaths and 47% of all economic losses, with the greatest economic damage being suffered in Asia. Notwithstanding the tragic losses of human life and enormous economic impacts of flooding, which are suffered worldwide on an annual basis, the underlying trend is for extreme natural events of all kinds to be significantly increasing in number. Hence, a comparison between the numbers of events and their economic implications has shown that impacts have increased nine-fold between the 1960s and the 1990s as a result of population growth, increased urban development, increased wealth and, apparently, an increased willingness to live in riskier locations such as on coasts and in mountain ranges.[25]

In relation to the United Kingdom, annual weather-related insurance claims have typically ranged between £360 million and £2.1 billion between 1989 and 1998, averaging at about £710 million. Flood-related insurance claims have only recently been disaggregated from other weather-related claims but it is estimated that they would typically fall between £50 million and £120 million. However, in 1998, when flooding was particularly serious, floods were estimated to have accounted for claims of about £150 million. Of those claims made for flooding, there seems to be a fairly consistent ratio between claims for damage to commercial and domestic premises with the latter typically constituting between 70% and 75% of all such claims.[26]

---

[24] See 11.3 below on flood warnings.
[25] Association of British Insurers, *Inland Flooding Risk – Issues Facing the Insurance Industry* (2000) p.5.
[26] Association of British Insurers, *Inland Flooding Risk – Issues Facing the Insurance Industry* (2000) p.5.

However, floods are capable of resulting in a wide range of direct and indirect forms of damage, not all of which are likely to be insured, or indeed insurable. 'Direct' damage comprises, loss of life,[27] damage to buildings and contents, damage to vehicles, public and utility infrastructure, communications networks and transport links. 'Indirect' damage encompasses matters such as business disruption, provision of alternative accommodation, costs of emergency operations and less tangible matters such as resulting health and emotional problems.[28] Clearly, however, the wide gulf between the extent of actual damage following a flood, and the extent of that damage which is insurable or actually insured means that insurance data needs to be treated with some caution in assessing the full extent of flooding impacts.[29]

England and Wales seem far better prepared and provided for in respect of flood defence than many other nations. Nonetheless, the impacts of recent flooding events have been substantial. The Easter floods of 1998 resulted in five deaths, about £400 million of damage to property and involved about 11,000 people being evacuated from their homes. The autumn floods of 2000 resulted in about 10,000 properties being flooded and damage that has been initially assessed to be in the order of £1 billion.[30]

Catastrophic though these incidents have been, they represent only the 'tip of the iceberg' insofar as flooding *potential* is concerned. Hence, it is officially estimated that about 10,000 sq km (or 8% of the total land area) of England is at risk from river flooding, including tidal rivers and estuaries and about 2,500 sq km (1.5% of the total land area) is at risk from direct

---

[27] Mercifully, there are relatively few deaths associated with flooding in the United Kingdom in recent years, though about 300 people died as a result of the Easter 1953 Flood (see discussion at 1.9.1 below) and five people died as a result of the flooding in Easter 1998 (see discussion at 1.9.2 below). Generally, over the last few decades, fatalities directly due to flooding have been about one per year which, it has been observed, is far less than any mode of transport: see Institution of Civil Engineers, *Learning to Live with Rivers* (2001) p.20.

[28] See G. Bennett, 'Bristol Floods 1968: Controlled Survey of Effects on Health of Local Community Disaster' *British Medical Journal* 22 August 1970, p.454; P. Bye and M. Horner, *Easter 1998 Floods* (1998) para.1.2, which reported that victims of flooding were experiencing ill health, chronic anxiety and other symptoms of traumatic stress (and see also para.3.4 on human impacts of flooding); E. C. Penning-Rowsell, D. J. Parker and D. M. Harding, *Floods and Drainage* (1986) p.100 for a discussion of medical and other 'intangible' effects of flooding; and A.-M. Ketteridge and M. Fordham, 'Planning for Floods: the UK Emergency Planning Picture' (1995) unpublished paper delivered at the International Emergency Planning Conference, Lancaster, July 1995 (available from Flood Hazard Research Centre, Middlesex University) on evacuation and flooding.

[29] Association of British Insurers, *Inland Flooding Risk – Issues Facing the Insurance Industry* (2000) pp.9 to 10.

[30] See 1.9.3 below on the Autumn 2000 floods.

10   *Introduction and Background*

sea flooding. In effect, about 1.7 million residential properties and 130,000 commercial properties, worth £200 billion, and 1.3 million hectares of agricultural land, worth £7 billion, are at risk from flooding. This amounts to 10% of the population and 12% of the agricultural land being subject to flooding risk.[31]

Alongside these alarming statistics, there is evidence that human activities are at least partially responsible for the increasing frequency and severity of recent flooding. At local and catchment levels, the extent of the problem may have been exacerbated by built development on land that previously served to attenuate flooding by infiltration and natural drainage. Similarly, changes in drainage and other land management practices have reduced the capacity for rainfall to be absorbed without harm to property. At a global level, there is increasing evidence to support the view that climate change is having measurable effects in terms of increasing the frequency and severity of extreme rainfall and causing a gradual but progressive rise in sea levels. Speculation continues as to the precise extent of the flooding impacts that will result from climate change but the substance of the hypothesis is now widely accepted.[32]

## 1.5 RISK

An aspect of flooding that cannot be emphasised too strongly is its inherent uncertainty. Clearly, some areas are more likely to flood than others, but the possibility of flooding at any particular location can never be completely ruled out, no matter what expense is devoted to flood defence measures. Because of the impossibility of securing any absolute guarantee against flooding, the central task of flood defence is conceived of as that of securing protection *against certain levels of flood risk* where the overall costs of achieving this are justifiable. Hence the determination of what degree of risk of flooding is to be regarded as acceptable, and the identification of land which is subject to an unacceptable degree of risk, are critically important.[33]

The inherent uncertainty of flooding, other than when it is immediately imminent, means that the best that can be done is to identify the degree of flood risk associated with a particular area of land. For this purpose, it has been customary to characterise flooding vulnerability in terms of a 'return period' that corresponds to the average duration between flooding events

---

[31] Department for Transport, Local Government and the Regions, Planning Policy Guidance Note 25, *Development and Flood Risk* (2001) para.3.
[32] See 1.7 below on climate change.
[33] Generally see Department of the Environment, *A Guide to Risk Assessment and Risk Management for Environmental Protection* (1995).

of a particular magnitude. Hence, a '1 in 100 years' return period for an area of land will indicate that, on average, that land will be flooded once every 100 years. Similarly, a flood defence structure may be subject to a '1 in 100 years' design specification, meaning that, on average, the structure's flood defence capacity is not likely to be exceeded more than once in 100 years.

However, some care has to be taken in the interpretation of 'return periods' because of their formulation in terms of the *average* frequency of flooding or exceedence of a flood defence design specification. The conclusion that a certain water level is likely to occur only once in 100 years gives no indication as to *when* this will happen, and there is no inconsistency between '1 in 100 year' events taking place in close succession. Certainly, the happening of a '1 in 100 year' event at a particular time is not a rational ground for supposing that the same event could not recur for another 100 years. Because of the possibility of this kind of misconception, it has been suggested that flooding vulnerability is better expressed in terms of percentages rather than return periods. Hence, a corresponding 1% probability of exceedence would express the chance of a flood of a given magnitude occurring *in any one year*. Again, the likelihood of more than one flood of this magnitude happening in close succession would be remote, but the percentage characterisation of the risk involved makes it more explicit that this is statistically capable of occurring.[34]

Whether return periods are expressed as average periods of return between floods of a given magnitude, or as a percentage likelihood of a flood in any particular year, a significant practical difficulty arises for flood defence operating authorities in communicating the inherent uncertainty of flooding to the general public. Hence, a '100-year flood' is commonly understood to be a flood which will occur regularly every 100 years, rather than a flood which will occur *on average* once in 100 years. The contrast between a regular and an uncertain event is difficult to convey without a level of probabilistic thinking that is frequently not appreciated. The difficulties are further compounded by design specifications for flood defences being expressed in terms of return periods. Whereas flood defence engineers appreciate that there must be limits to the effectiveness of any flood defence structure, there is a common public perception amongst those that suffer flooding that defences should provide 'absolute' guarantees against flooding of a kind which are not physically feasible, economically justifiable

---

[34] See Association of British Insurers, *Inland Flooding Risks – Issues Facing the Insurance Industry* (2000) p.6. See also Institution of Civil Engineers, *Learning to Live with Rivers* (2001) p.18, where it is suggested that the expression '100–1 chance flood' might be a better way of communicating a 100-year return period, at least to those members of the public familiar with 'odds' in sports involving gambling.

or environmentally desirable in many instances.[35]

Another aspect of flood return periods that needs to be appreciated is that they relate only to the likelihood or frequency of flooding occurring. They do not indicate the maximum magnitude of the flooding that will occur or the severity of the impacts that will be suffered as a consequence. Clearly, there are major differences between the levels of damage that will be caused by a shallow and slow-flowing body of water and a deep and fast-moving inundation. Also, there are dramatic contrasts between the impacts of flooding on relatively undeveloped agricultural land as opposed to intensively developed urban housing areas. The *risk* of particular flooding, therefore, needs to be considered alongside its potential magnitude and impact, and this involves an assessment of the value and vulnerability of the assets which will be damaged should the risk materialise.[36]

Useful information on the systematic application of risk-based methodology to flood and coastal defence projects is to be found in flood and coastal defence project appraisal guidance. The guidance draws an important distinction between risk *assessment*, involving ascertaining levels of risk inherent in a project, and risk *management*, the related activity of mitigating and monitoring risks. Risk-based methods are seen as a common approach for comparing a wide variety of options and responses in situations of uncertainty. The guidance construes 'risk' in a broad sense to encompass both the probability of an event and the consequences of that event. Hence, the frequency of flooding, expressed in terms of return period or a similar measure, needs to be related to the effects of a flooding incident in a holistic evaluation of risk. Consequences of flooding are recognised to be of an economic, environmental or social kind and some of these are capable of being complex and strongly influenced by human behaviour. It is noted, for example, that the impacts of flooding may be influenced by: the time of day of a flood; the timing and mechanism of any flood warning; the response of the public to the warning; the effectiveness of emergency repair works; and the efforts of emergency services to mitigate impacts. Nonetheless, diverse issues of this kind need to be evaluated in assessing and quantifying risks and determining cost-effective mitigation mechanisms.[37]

Although the identification of land subject to specified levels of flood risk

---

[35] See E. C. Penning-Rowsell, D. J. Parker and D. M. Harding, *Floods and Drainage* (1986) p.154.
[36] See Association of British Insurers, *Inland Flooding Risks – Issues Facing the Insurance Industry* (2000) Ch.3.
[37] Ministry of Agriculture, Fisheries and Food, *Flood and Coastal Defence Project Appraisal Guidance: Approaches to Risk* (FCDPAG4) (2000).

is an essential precursor to effective, risk-based, flood management and planning, caution needs to be exercised in the practical determination of actual boundaries of land falling into particular risk categories. Although factors such as altitude topography, geology, land use, rainfall and drainage patterns may be useful guides, they can never fully determine the circumstances that can, uniquely, combine to cause flooding. Historical information about past flooding events may provide some guidance, if it is available, but determination of risks of extreme flooding events with any degree of confidence will require extrapolation from precise information about past flooding extending over several hundred years. Even then, this information might need to be treated with some circumspection where it is open to differing interpretations.[38] In addition, there is an overriding reservation that future flooding may not follow the pattern of past events. This is especially pertinent if new factors, ranging from changes to local land use to global influences such as the impact of climate change, need to be taken into account. Probably, for this combination of reasons, and others, the widely used flood risk maps produced by the Environment Agency are termed '*indicative*' flood plain maps to avoid any suggestion that they are fully or precisely definitive of those areas where flooding is likely to arise.[39]

## 1.6 CLIMATE CHANGE

Amongst the reasons why assessment of flood risk by extrapolation from past flooding events is methodologically dubious is that it assumes that there is no long-term variability in climatic conditions. That is, it is supposed that past, present and future tendencies for flooding to occur are all roughly the same. This assumption can no longer stand unchallenged alongside the increasing evidence supporting long-term climate change.[40]

The cumulative evidence for global warming is compelling. A rise in global temperatures of about 0.6 degrees centigrade has been recorded, with the 1990s including seven of the ten warmest years on record and 1998 the warmest year in a 140-year record. In England, four of the five warmest years in a 340-year record have been in the 1990s, with 1999 the joint

---

[38] See, for example, Home Office, Scottish Office, Ministry of Housing and Local Government and Ministry of Agriculture and Fisheries, *Report of the Departmental Committee on Coastal Flooding* (1954) Cmd.9165, Appendix C, where archaeological evidence is noted indicating that land levels in south-eastern England have been declining relatively to sea levels at a rate of one foot per century. Also see Philosophical Transactions of the Royal Society of London, *A Discussion on the Problems Associated with the Subsidence of Southeastern England* (1972).
[39] See 11.2.3 below on the Environment Agency's indicative flood plain maps.
[40] Generally see P. Bye and M. Horner, *Easter 1998 Floods* (1998) para.A7.

warmest year ever. Estimates are that, unless action is taken, the world could warm by about 3 degrees centigrade over the next century. Warming is part of a long-term change in overall climatic conditions which includes more extreme and unpredictable global weather patterns involving more intense droughts and flooding in particular areas and sea level rise; and a range of social, economic and environmental impacts are likely to arise as a consequence of these changes.[41]

More specifically, the best predictions are that rainfall could increase by as much as 10% over England and Wales by the 2080s and climate-induced sea level rise could contribute to a 41 cm sea level rise in East Anglia by the 2050s. Moreover, whilst long-term trends may not be reflected in particular years, the overall pattern will be of autumns and winters becoming generally wetter. Springs and summers will become dryer in the south east and wetter in the north west. The predicted consequences of this are that flooding is likely to increase because of the combination of more intense rainfall, rising sea levels and possibly increased storminess, though it is less clear how the frequency of storms and high winds will be affected by climate change. Coastal land could also face a significantly increased risk of flooding and erosion, and land in the flood plains of rivers will, similarly, be placed at a higher risk of flooding which defences may be unable to prevent.[42] Despite these predictions, however, it is not possible to relate any particular flooding event to the general trends that are identified. A research study, commissioned to ascertain the extent to which the Autumn 2000 floods could be attributed to climate change, concluded that, despite the extreme flooding being *consistent with* climate change predictions, it was not possible to say that the floods were *attributable to* climate change, as opposed to natural variability.[43]

The reasons for the climate changes that have been identified, and are being predicted for the future, lie in the emission of 'greenhouse gases', such as carbon dioxide, methane and nitrous oxide, into the atmosphere. These emissions have the effect of disturbing the balance between the radiant energy received from the sun and the energy radiated from the earth. Energy emitted from the earth is trapped and reflected back by greenhouse

---

[41] Department of the Environment, Transport and the Regions, *Climate Change: the UK Programme* (2000) Cm. 4913, p.5. See also Department of the Environment, Transport and the Regions, *Indicators of Climate Change in the UK* (1999) and Department for Transport, Local Government and the Regions, Planning Policy Guidance Note 25, *Development and Flood Risk* (2001) Appendix A.

[42] Department of the Environment, Transport and the Regions, *Climate Change: the UK Programme* (2000) Cm. 4913, pp.31 to 34.

[43] See Department for Environment, Food and Rural Affairs, *To what degree can the October/November 2000 flood events be attributed to climate change?* (2001) and see 1.9.3 below on the Autumn 2000 floods.

gases in the atmosphere and this 'greenhouse effect' has the gradual overall effect of warming the surface of the earth. Although the greenhouse effect occurs naturally, as greenhouse gas concentrations rise above natural levels, as a result of emissions from human activities, the warming effect has the serious climatic consequences that have been outlined.

Clearly, the means of reducing and reversing the climate change trend lies in the reduction of greenhouse gas emissions. However, this involves major changes in energy consumption and the range of human activities that result in greenhouse gas emissions. Moreover, the reductions in emissions must be internationally co-ordinated and adhered to, since it is the *cumulative* effect of emissions from all nations that gives rise to the problem. Recognising this, the United Nations Framework Convention on Climate Change was agreed at the Earth Summit at Rio de Janeiro in 1992, requiring developed countries to return their greenhouse gas emissions to 1990 levels by 2000. The Kyoto Protocol to the Climate Change Convention, agreed in 1997, took the process a stage further in recognising the need for greater reductions in emissions and for specific reduction obligations to be legally binding.

The intricacies of global international agreements on climate change, and the implementation difficulties that they have met with, are beyond the scope of this book,[44] but some broad observations need to be offered on the implications for flooding. The first of these is to note that, although climate change may already be influencing patterns of flooding, it is not possible to be certain whether or not recent flooding events would have occurred regardless of the effect of climate change.[45] The unavoidable fact is that flooding has occurred, for a range of different reasons, throughout history and long before human emissions of greenhouse gases would have had any influence. Hence, there is no reason to conclude that the removal of all greenhouse gases of human origin from the atmosphere would result in the cessation of all flooding.

---

[44] For a general review see D. French, '1997 Kyoto Protocol and the 1992 UN Framework Convention on Climate Change' [1998] *Journal of Environmental Law* 227. For recent developments at European Community level see European Commission, *Decision on the ratification by the EC of the Kyoto Protocol to the United Nations Framework Convention on Climate Change and the joint fulfilment of the commitments thereunder* (COM (2001) 579).

[45] Indeed, there is some evidence that climate change is not the centrally important factor: see House of Commons Agriculture Committee, Sixth Report Session 1997–98, *Flood and Coastal Defence* (1998) HC 707, para.36, where it was observed 'despite the threats posed by a warming global climate, much of the evidence we heard suggested that the most immediate source of increased risk from flood and erosion arose, not from environmental and climatic change, but from a heritage of hard engineered defence structures'.

Second, even if the greenhouse effect is contributing to the worsening of flooding, addressing this problem is, on any estimation, a long-term endeavour. Even making the generous assumption that binding international agreements on greenhouse gas emissions will be reached, fully implemented and will be effective in achieving the desired reductions, the restoration of the atmosphere to its 'natural' state will take many decades. During this period it will be necessary to 'live with' the consequences of global warming, including its flooding consequences. Hence, any suggestion that 'traditional' approaches to flood defence can be lessened, pending the progressive resolution of flooding problems by emission controls, is a rather dangerous kind of misconception. Indeed, in many respects traditional approaches to flood defence will need to be pursued with greater stringency to counteract the possible effects of climate change for as far into the future as can be reasonably foreseen.

The need for immediate measures to accommodate the consequences of climate change in flood defence practice, for at least the next 30 years, has been recognised by the Government. Generally, in respect of flooding, these measures have acknowledged the need to improve flood risk identification, raise awareness of practical steps that can be taken to minimise exposure to flood damage and discourage or restrict development in areas of high flood risk. More specifically, particular measures have been introduced including the requirement to take account of climate change in restricting development of land in flood risk areas, to incorporate allowances for sea level rise in all new and reconstructed coastal defences, and to promote 'high level targets' for flood and coastal defence which are aimed at reducing long-term risk.[46]

The flood and coastal defence implications of climate change are further considered in flood and coastal defence project appraisal guidance, where a range of potential impacts are identified, including sea level rise, ocean circulation changes, precipitation effects, wind effects and surge effects. A broad conclusion is that,

> '[f]or flood and coastal defence, the challenge of dealing with climate change impacts will be a long and sustained process based on building adaptive measures into the maintenance and provision of new defences. A strategic approach to the management of flood and coastal defence will be crucial to this process if appropriate short-term measures and long-term policies are to be identified and implemented successfully.'

---

[46] Department of the Environment, Transport and the Regions, *Climate Change: the UK Programme* (2000) Cm. 4913, pp.139 and 141. On development and flood risk see 9.8 below. On 'high level targets' see 3.2.12 below.

Accordingly, a precautionary approach will be needed, for example, by constructing oversized culverts and bridges, designing defences with provision for future raising and considering overflow routes to minimise risks to life and property. Given that levels of flood risk will almost certainly increase, the need to avoid inappropriate development in high risk areas is re-emphasised. 'No regrets' actions, such as the retention or enhancement of floodplain or wetland areas, should also be considered along with the promotion of managed realignment or relocation of defences as the only long-term solution in some situations.[47]

## 1.7 THE PRECAUTIONARY PRINCIPLE

In most fields of environmental policy and law it is accepted that the 'precautionary principle' should be adhered to. As a principle of international environmental law, this requires that, 'where there are threats of serious or irreversible damage, lack of full scientific certainty should not be used as a reason for postponing cost-effective measures to prevent environmental degradation'.[48] Similarly, it is stipulated that European Community policy on the environment should be based on the 'precautionary principle'.[49] Further guidance on the application of the principle from the European Commission indicates its relevance to contexts where the management of risks which might impinge upon the environment, human, animal or plant health is involved, subject to account being taken of proportionality and the appropriate assessment of costs and benefits.[50]

Insofar as the precautionary principle involves increasing aversity towards risk, its application seems to be reflected in progressively rising standards being applied to flood defence. Public tolerance of urban flooding seems to have declined as standards of living and expectations of the efficiency of public services have increased. Protection against flooding up to a 4%

---

[47] Ministry of Agriculture, Fisheries and Food, *Flood and Coastal Defence Project Appraisal Guidance: Overview* (FCDPAG1) (2001) Ch.6 and particularly p.24. See also Environmental Resources Management, *Potential UK Adaptation Strategies for Climate Change* (2001) published by the Department of the Environment, Transport and the Regions.

[48] Principle 15 of the Rio Declaration and see D. Freestone, The Road from Rio: International Environmental Law after the Earth Summit' [1994] *Journal of Environmental Law* 193; T. O'Riordan and J. Cameron, Eds., *Interpreting the Precautionary Principle* (1994); and E. Fisher, 'Is the Precautionary Principle Justiciable?' [2001] *Journal of Environmental Law* 315. Insofar as flooding is a natural occurrence, however, it may be questioned whether it constitutes 'environmental degradation' within the meaning of the principle.

[49] See Art.174(2) European Community Treaty.

[50] European Commission, *Communication on the Precautionary Principle* COM (2000) 1.

probability (or a 25-year return period) may have been regarded as reasonable a century ago, but is no longer acceptable for modern urban communities.[51] Nowadays, 1% probability (or a 100-year return period) is the normal design standard for defence against river flooding and 0.5% probability (or a 200-year return period) in relation to sea flooding. Increasingly, identification of zones with a 0.1% probability of flooding (or a 1,000-year return period) will become important in identifying those areas that, for planning purposes, are designated as having 'little or no risk of flooding'.[52] As a purely practical matter, flood risk aversity appears to become more precautionary with ever-increasing public expectations.

On first consideration it might be thought that flood risk was an ideal area for a comprehensively precautionary approach to be adopted, given the inherent uncertainties involved and particularly the prospects of increasingly severe flooding as a result of climate change. The implication of applying such an approach might be to require flood defences to be constructed to withstand the greatest possible inundation that could reasonably be predicted by scientific evidence. Notwithstanding first impressions, the need for *proportional* action to be taken in the light of *costs and benefits* greatly reduces the scope for unqualified precaution in relation to flood defence. As has been explained, flooding is best characterised as a *risk* which can be reduced by flood defence measures but never totally eliminated. Moreover, the cost of reducing the risk increases exponentially as progressively improbable flooding events are taken as the standard of protection to be secured against. The potentially unlimited amount that could be spent on flood defence means that the degree of precaution that is allowed for must be balanced against 'cost' measured in economic, environmental and social terms.

Despite the general cost-benefit limitations upon precaution in flood defence, there are some contexts where significant emphasis is placed upon the need for this approach. Historically, the approach towards reservoir safety has always been strongly precautionary in character.[53] More recently, as has been noted, various precautionary measures have been introduced to counteract flooding concerns arising from climate change. Amongst these, the recent planning guidance on development and flood risk demonstrates a consciously precautionary approach. Hence, the guidance stresses the need for proposed new development to be considered against a background of explicit appraisal of the relevant flood risks,

---

[51] See P. Bye and M. Horner, *Easter 1998 Floods* (1998) para.7.1.
[52] See Department for Transport, Local Government and the Regions, Planning Policy Guidance Note 25, *Development and Flood Risk* (2001) discussed at 9.8.3 below.
[53] See 8.4 below on reservoir safety.

## The Precautionary Principle

including allowances for impacts of climate change, and the application of 'sequential approach' of directing development away from zones of greatest flood risk. These precautionary decision-making procedures are balanced against the realisation that 'sustainable development'[54] is not best served by requiring the construction of increasingly more substantial new flood defence structures, which will be excessively burdensome for future generations to maintain, unless the long-term benefits of these are clearly established.[55]

### 1.8 EXTREME FLOODING EVENTS

The characterisation of flooding in terms of 'risk' reflects the fact that there are various of factors that are capable of combining to produce flooding in a widely variable and unpredictable way. Indeed, it is arguable that the more improbable the combination of factors, the less foreseeable the flooding event, the less opportunity there is to make advance provision for it and the more catastrophic the consequent flooding. Nonetheless, the extreme unlikelihood of a flooding event being caused by extraordinary facts can never be totally ruled out and must be weighed into the balance.

Given the background of unpredictability, there is always a danger in taking past flooding events as indicators of future events, but some insights may be provided by a brief examination of the circumstances leading up to the most damaging flooding events of recent times. For this purpose, the East Coast Flood of 1953, the Easter Floods of 1998 and the Autumn Floods of 2000 provide illuminating case studies, not least by demonstrating the wide contrasts between the different kinds of incidents involved and the impacts that the events have had upon flood defence practice.[56]

### 1.8.1 The East Coast Flood 1953

The most dramatic sea flooding incident within living memory occurred on 31 January 1953 when land on the East Coast of Britain suffered extensive flooding after natural and artificial sea defences proved inadequate to withstand exceptional sea conditions. From the Humber estuary to the Straits of Dover, tidal flood defences extending for 1,370 miles suffered some 1,200 breaches with the result that 160,000 acres of land and 24,000 houses were flooded and over 300 people lost their lives. Over 200 major industrial premises were flooded and were out of production for several

---

[54] See Ch.12 below on sustainable development.
[55] Department for Transport, Local Government and the Regions, Planning Policy Guidance Note 25, *Development and Flood Risk* (2001) para.13.
[56] See also Association of British Insurers, *Inland Flooding Risk – Issues Facing the Insurance Industry* (2000) section 4.2, which provides further case studies.

weeks, and farm land was adversely affected by salinity for a considerable period afterwards.[57] Although it was difficult to estimate the extent of the resulting economic loss, one contemporary assessment placed this at about £30 million.[58]

The causes of the incident and the lessons to be learnt from the disaster were investigated in the *'Waverley Report'* which continues to make illuminating, if rather disturbing, reading.[59] The analysis of the circumstances leading up to the flood was that a very high surge of sea water had combined with a fairly high tide and the effect of these had been increased by severe wave action. The 'surge' of water, about nine feet above the normal height of the tide, was produced by pressure of northerly winds of record-breaking strength over the western and central parts of the North Sea. However, the surge was not so great as had previously been recorded, and it did not coincide with the time of high tide or the highest spring tides. Most alarmingly, it was concluded that *had* the surge coincided with the most adverse tidal conditions, and greater seaward flows of fresh water into estuaries, the level of floodwater reached could have been several feet higher than actually occurred. Nevertheless, the height of the waves that were actually produced, and the pressure that was exerted upon sea walls, caused the extensive structural damage to sea defences and the flooding that has been recounted.

The Waverley Committee considering the January 1953 flood had, amongst its terms of reference, the remit to consider what margin of safety for sea defences would be reasonable and practicable having regard to the risks involved and the cost of protective measures. It recognised that the cost of affording protection against the worst possible combination of atmospheric and tidal conditions would have been colossal, and measures designed to secure protection against every conceivable combination of tide and surge

---

[57] See Ministry of Agriculture, Fisheries and Food, *The East Coast Floods 1953* (1962) (discussing the problems for cultivated soils and marshland grazing due to the seawater floods and the measures that were taken to restore flooded land to agricultural use).

[58] Home Office, Scottish Office, Ministry of Housing and Local Government and Ministry of Agriculture and Fisheries, *Report of the Departmental Committee on Coastal Flooding* (1954) Cmd.9165 (the *'Waverley Report'*) para.22. Although, in real terms the cost has been estimated as £5 billion: see House of Commons Agriculture Committee, Sixth Report Session 1997–98, *Flood and Coastal Defence* (1998) HC 707, para.3.

[59] Home Office, Scottish Office, Ministry of Housing and Local Government and Ministry of Agriculture and Fisheries, *Report of the Departmental Committee on Coastal Flooding* (1954) Cmd.9165. An interim report of the Committee, *Flood Warning System* (1953) Cmd.8923, was previously published, though this was incorporated as Appendix A to the final report. See also J. A. Steers, 'The East Coast Floods, January 31 – February 1 1953' (1953) *Geographical Journal* 280.

were ruled out. Even the cost of protecting the *whole* coast against conditions equivalent to those which caused the 1953 flood was thought to be financially prohibitive, though *in some areas* protection against an equivalent event might be taken as the general maximum that could reasonably be afforded. Instead, the view was taken that standards of coast defences must be related to the 'character and amount of the property to be protected'.[60] Hence, the view of the Committee was that,

> 'where flooding would lead to serious damage to property of high value such as valuable industrial premises or compact residential areas or where it would affect any large area of valuable land, the highest measure of protection should be given. . . . in those areas it would be right to aim at a standard of defence which would protect them from a flood like that of January 1953, exceptional though this may be, and in other areas where the value of the property to be protected is not sufficient to warrant so great an expense, at a standard which would reasonably have been thought adequate before the flood of January, 1953. In laying down these standards we do not exclude the possibility of an even higher standard where the property to be protected is of exceptional value though we think that anyone requiring such a higher standard may reasonably be expected to pay for it himself. Similarly, where the value of the area to be protected is conspicuously below the general average, we do not exclude the possibility of a lower standard but in some places where this might have been appropriate, people living under the protection of defences existing before the flood have developed their property with those defences in view and we think that to avoid any breach of public faith those defences should, where practicable, be restored and maintained.'[61]

It is difficult to read this passage without reaching the inference that the Committee had conceded that for many areas of lower priority another flood of the same proportions was, as a matter of financial inevitability, bound to lead to a repetition of the damage and loss of life that had been experienced in 1953, or worse.

On the other hand, the Committee offered some insightful observations as

---

[60] Home Office, Scottish Office, Ministry of Housing and Local Government and Ministry of Agriculture and Fisheries, *Report of the Departmental Committee on Coastal Flooding* (1954) para.4.

[61] Home Office, Scottish Office, Ministry of Housing and Local Government and Ministry of Agriculture and Fisheries, *Report of the Departmental Committee on Coastal Flooding* (1954) para.46. On the 'breach of public faith' issue, contrast the present recognition of the unavailability of public funds to maintain existing defences, and that 'managed retreat' may be an inevitable consequence of the need for sustainable development, discussed at 12.6 below.

to the measures that were needed for areas deserving funding priority, and the particular problem of flooding of London by the Thames was considered in some detail.[62] In January 1953 water levels reached the top of defences along the Victoria and Chelsea Embankments, with defences being overtopped by a few inches at London Bridge and Greenwich, and it was recognised that considerable areas of London lay below the levels that had been reached. Miraculously, because the surge did not correspond with the time of high tide (which would have produced another nine inches of water), extensive flooding of London was narrowly avoided.[63] The exceptionally close proximity of a catastrophe of incalculable[64] proportions for the capital city prompted the Committee to recommend the urgent consideration of a range of major flood defence structures, including various kinds of barriers across the Thames estuary to serve as a defence against future surges and adverse flooding conditions.[65]

A further issue explicitly within the remit of the Committee was the question of what measures should be taken to provide a system of warning to lessen the risk of loss of life and serious damage to property by flooding.[66] On this, it was recommended that a flood warning system operated by the Central Forecasting Office should be provided for the east coast, during those months of the year when the highest tides could be anticipated. Information on water levels would be provided to river boards and to the county police forces, for re-communication to local government authorities. River boards would interpret the information in the light of local conditions and, where necessary, inform the Police that a public flood warning should be issued. The actual communication of flood warnings to members of the public was seen as a matter that was best determined by the Police on a local basis. Remarkably, the use of the BBC to broadcast warnings was advised against since this might cause 'unnecessary alarm' in those areas to which a flood warning did not apply![67]

---

[62] Flooding of London had previously occurred in 1928 and the problem of Thames Flood Prevention had been considered by a Departmental Committee under the chairmanship of Sir William Hart, which reported in 1933. A summary of the main findings of the Committee is provided in Appendix E to the *Waverley Report*.

[63] Home Office, Scottish Office, Ministry of Housing and Local Government and Ministry of Agriculture and Fisheries, *Report of the Departmental Committee on Coastal Flooding* (1954) paras.83 and 84.

[64] Although see the discussion of this as a hypothetical scenario at 11.5.1 below.

[65] Home Office, Scottish Office, Ministry of Housing and Local Government and Ministry of Agriculture and Fisheries, *Report of the Departmental Committee on Coastal Flooding* (1954) para.89 and see 3.7.2 below on the Thames Barrage.

[66] This matter was the subject of an interim report of the Committee, *Flood Warning System* (1953) Cmd.8923, which was later incorporated as Appendix A to the final report.

[67] Contrast the discussion of flood warning systems at 11.3 below.

### 1.8.2 The Easter Floods 1998

The Easter 1998 floods followed a period in which a cool northerly airflow and an area of low pressure which moved south across the United Kingdom resulting in a quantity of rain which caused initial saturation in many catchments. The depression had two associated frontal systems, consisting of cold air over northern areas which moved slowly south and warm air from the south moving slowly north. The merger of these two fronts resulted in a slow-moving and intense frontal zone which resulted in prolonged and heavy rain across central England and Wales. Areas in the central Midlands recorded rainfalls over 75 mm over a 36-hour period, roughly equal to six weeks of average April rainfall falling in a day and a half. In the most seriously affected areas, the combination of already saturated ground and the exceptional rainfall caused rivers to rise at record rates, twice as fast as previously recorded, and the speed and severity of flooding was without precedent in many areas.[68] The impact of this was to cause flooding in some 70 locations across England and Wales in which five people lost their lives, directly or indirectly, as a result of the flooding, and 150 people were treated in hospital for hypothermia and injuries sustained as a result of the flooding; 4,500 residential properties were flooded, particularly in the urban residential areas of Northampton and Leamington, and damage estimated at £400 million was suffered.[69]

In order to assess the performance of the Environment Agency in responding to the Easter 1998 Floods, the Board of the Agency established an independent review. The conclusions of the review, the *'Bye Report'*,[70] were that, despite the exceptional severity of the flooding, the Agency's performance in assessing its extent and severity was generally satisfactory. However, although flood warnings were issued in accordance with current policy in most locations, lack of public awareness, together with nationally inconsistent and inadequate procedures and systems resulted in poor overall performance. The Agency was found to have acted satisfactorily in

---

[68] P. Bye and M. Horner, *Easter 1998 Floods: Report by the Independent Review Team to the Board of the Environment Agency* (1998) (the *'Bye Report'*, available on the Environment Agency website at http://www.environment-agency.gov.uk) para.3.1 and House of Commons Agriculture Committee, Sixth Report Session 1997–98, *Flood and Coastal Defence* (1998) HC 707, para.108.

[69] P. Bye and M. Horner, *Easter 1998 Floods: Report by the Independent Review Team to the Board of the Environment Agency* (1998) para.3.4 and Department for Transport, Local Government and the Regions, Planning Policy Guidance Note 25, *Development and Flood Risk* (2001) para.1.

[70] P. Bye and M. Horner, *Easter 1998 Floods: Report by the Independent Review Team to the Board of the Environment Agency* (1998). See also P. Bye and M. Horner, *Easter 1998 Floods: Preliminary Assessment by the Independent Review Team Report to the Board of the Environment Agency* (1998).

relation to its emergency response responsibilities and had successfully ensured the continuing operation of main river defence systems. Notwithstanding this, and the generally good order of flood defences, flooding at defended locations had resulted from design standards for defences being exceeded, despite such standards having previously been regarded as adequate. In addition, it was thought that the Agency should undertake a review of various organisation, management and investment issues to establish the potential for improving efficiency and effectiveness in the provision, operation and maintenance of flood warning systems and defences.

The implications of the Easter 1998 floods were also considered by the House of Commons Agriculture Committee, alongside a range of associated flood defence issues. Specifically, on the Easter floods the Committee drew attention to the complicated, confusing and regionally variable arrangements which impaired the efficiency and effectiveness of flood warnings. The serious underestimation of the rainfall levels provided by the Meteorological Office was noted and the hope expressed that the Office would always have access to the resources necessary to improve its forecasting techniques in line with best international practice. The limitations of the area for which the Environment Agency provided flood warnings was also seen to be unsatisfactory, with the Agency being encouraged to broaden its flood warning coverage to exposed areas where funding allowed this. Shortcomings were also perceived in the production of flood warning hazard maps by the Agency and these were seen as a high priority in standardising flood warning procedures across the country. Problems were also identified in the functioning of telemetry equipment, operated by the Agency, which failed to record overland flows of water and demonstrated a need for a more strategic, catchment based, approach towards flood prediction. Generally, the Committee found evidence indicating that more needed to be done to raise public awareness, to standardise inter-organisational procedures for flood warnings both regionally and nationally, and for better co-ordination between the Agency, local authorities and emergency services.[71]

The Government responded to the reservations about the performance of the Environment Agency in relation to the Easter 1998 floods, and particularly the critical observations made in the *Bye Report*. In a Parliamentary statement, the Minister expressed the need for there to be 'a seamless and integrated service of flood forecasting, warning and response'. This would necessitate the Agency conducting a thorough review of the

---

[71] House of Commons Agriculture Committee, Sixth Report Session 1997–98, *Flood and Coastal Defence* (1998) HC 707, paras.110 to 114.

whole system to ensure a 'focused delivery' of the service that was needed.[72] In addition, the Minister highlighted a series of specific targets for the Agency, to be achieved by stated deadlines, concerning the checking of flood warning dissemination plans; the development of supervisory responsibilities; the review of management structures; the publication of flood risk maps; the review of dissemination plans for flood warning messages; the assessment of emergency response arrangements; the improvement of telemetered river monitoring equipment; and the completion of a visual survey of flood defences. The Agency's response to these objectives was set out in an *Action Plan* indicating the measures that would be taken to secure their realisation.[73]

### 1.8.3 The Autumn Floods 2000

Autumn 2000 was the wettest in England and Wales since general records began to be kept in 1766, with rainfall amounting to almost twice the average for preceding years. Although some unprecedented bursts of rain were recorded in particular areas, the general picture was of a period of fairly continuous and exceptionally heavy rainfall over a seven-week period between September and November. Hence, unlike the two previous incidents that have been recounted, there was no single or discrete incident that could be identified as a cause of the flooding, but rather a series of events with disastrous cumulative impacts. The continuing rainfall which fell, after catchments in many areas had already become saturated, caused rivers to rise to unprecedentedly high levels, such as the River Ouse at York which exceeded a historic record high level reached in 1625.

The impact of this massive amount of rainfall was to cause extensive and prolonged, and repeated, flooding, with some properties being flooded up to five times. Over 700 locations were affected, in some instances including areas with no previous history of flooding. Ten thousand properties were flooded, 11,000 people were requested to evacuate their homes, and though 280,000 homes were thought to have been protected by flood defences, 37,000 of these properties only narrowly escaped flooding, in some cases by temporarily raising the height of defences with sandbags. There was widespread disruption to transport and power supplies, serious losses to businesses of all kinds, and hundreds of people were left with homes that were uninhabitable, in some instances, for many months afterwards. The costs of the floods have been estimated to be in the order of £1 billion.

---

[72] See Ministry of Agriculture, Fisheries and Food, News Release 409/98, *Morley Acts on Hard Hitting Flood Report*, 20 October 1998.
[73] Environment Agency, *Environment Agency Response to the Independent Report on the Easter 1998 Floods* (1998).

A report on the 2000 floods was commissioned to examine the extent and severity of the flooding, its causes, the effectiveness of flood warning and emergency responses, and the performance of flood defences.[74] *Lessons Learned*, published by the Environment Agency, addressed these issues and concluded that the Agency, local authorities and emergency services had made considerable progress towards delivering the 'seamless and integrated flood warning, response and recovery service' identified by the Minister in the aftermath of the Easter 1998 floods, but the report also identified areas for development and collaboration in the short, medium and long term.

In the Environment Agency's estimation, 28% of flooding was due to overtopping, outflanking or failure of flood defences; 40% because no defences existed; and 32% due to flooding from ordinary watercourses, inadequate local surface water drainage and defences which were the responsibilities of third parties. Of the 10,000 properties that were flooded, 58% were in locations where there were no flood defences.

The Agency's network of monitoring systems performed well and failure rates of monitoring equipment were low, as a result of increased investment following the 1998 floods. Information from the Meteorological Office, predicting heavy rainfall for up to 24 hours ahead, was effectively relied upon by the Agency in deciding when to issue some 1,437 flood warnings, including 190 severe flood warnings. Nonetheless, property occupiers in particular areas, such as North Wales, did not receive a flood warning in advance of their properties being flooded because warning arrangements had not been put in place since the areas were not identified as being of priority need on the basis of previous flooding experience. Otherwise, a general perception was that flood warning systems worked well, communications had been improved and public awareness of the role of the Agency in relation to flooding had improved markedly with dramatic increases in the number of phone calls by members of the public to the Agency's Floodline service.[75]

In respect of the management of particular flooding incidents, a massive collaborative effort had been undertaken between the Agency, local authorities, the police, fire and ambulance services, the armed services, and other public bodies and voluntary sector organisations. A remarkable

---

[74] Environment Agency, *Lessons Learned: Autumn 2000 floods* (2001). See also National Audit Office, *Inland Flood Defence* (2001) HC 299 and Department for Environment, Food and Rural Affairs, *Flood and Coastal Defence: The Autumn 2000 Floods* (2001) on Department for Environment, Food and Rural Affairs website at http://www.defra.gov.uk.

[75] See 11.3 below on flood warnings.

2.5 million sandbags had been put in place to prevent properties from flooding and the logistic demands of evacuating homes and meeting the needs of evacuated persons were self evident. Although emergency plans had generally worked well on a local level, the Agency took the view that more needed to be done to enhance multi-organisational emergency planning structures and to put emergency planning on a sounder statutory and financial footing. Also the problem of public confusion as to responsibilities for flood prevention needed to be addressed to clarify responsibilities in relation to main rivers, ordinary watercourses and drainage and sewerage structures that gave rise to flooding.

Although the general tenor of the Agency's report is that institutional responses were appropriate and flood defences were effective within the scope of their design specifications, the fact remained that a major national disaster had taken place with calamitous implications for individuals, industry and the national economy. Moreover, an important issue for the future is the deteriorating condition of main river flood defences, with visual surveys showing up to 85% of defences, in one region, being categorised as 'fair', 'poor' or 'very poor'. Clearly, the floods had served as a 'timely reminder' that progressive deterioration in flood defences was taking place and an estimated shortfall in capital and maintenance investment, of £100 million per annum, needed to be met if further flooding damage was to be averted. Following the Autumn floods, the Government announced that £51 million would be made available to accelerate river defence works and catchment planning, along with payments by way of 'extraordinary support' in respect of the emergency response costs involved in dealing with the floods. However, this additional funding remains some way below meeting the estimated shortfall. Pertinently, a recent National Audit Office report on inland flood defence in England has noted that existing flood defences reduce the annual cost of flooding by over £2 billion and, requiring an annual investment of £400 million, this 'represents good value for money'.[76]

## 1.9 HISTORICAL DEVELOPMENT OF THE LAW

Insofar as flooding is conceived of as a natural occurrence, it is remarkable that the law should have any bearing upon the matter. Historically, this may have been the legal position, with floods being regarded as consequences of nature or 'acts of God' from which civil liability should not arise.[77] Progressively, the common law has developed from that original position, in regarding flooding increasingly to be caused by (sueable) human beings

---

[76] See also National Audit Office, *Inland Flood Defence* (2001) HC 299, p.3.
[77] See 2.5.3 below on 'acts of God'.

rather than 'nature'. Hence, caselaw principles have defined the rights of riparian owners to allow watercourses to be used for flood defence purposes *to the extent that this does not cause harm to other riparian owners*. The implications of this basic idea have been the subject of extensive litigation, typically concerning the rights of eighteenth century mill owners to an accustomed flow of water, the rights of nineteenth century mine operators to dispose of water removed from lower strata and, over the last century, a series of important cases where culverting of watercourses has given rise to flooding problems.

As will be seen, both in the context of riparian rights and flood defence more generally, the effects of this progression of the civil law have been to impose increasingly extensive obligations upon landowners to take action to avoid flooding nuisances. Hence, the traditional understanding that liability could not arise for flooding of land caused by an omission of a landowner to secure the flow of a watercourse from naturally arising debris or sediment is now extremely doubtful. In its place has been put a 'measured' duty upon landowners to take all reasonable measures to avoid flooding of neighbouring land, taking into account the practicability and cost of such measures. As far as the civil law is concerned, neighbouring land use has significantly displaced 'nature' as the cause of much flooding.[78]

However, the establishment and progressive development of public bodies with powers to undertake flood defence works, to regulate the activities of others and to administer the funding necessary for flood defence works provide the most distinctive elements in the history of flood defence law. Some of the principal landmarks in this legislative progression are as follows.[79]

### 1.9.1 Early Legislation

From the earliest times, the Crown had a duty arising from the royal prerogative to defend the realm against incursion by the sea and the power to order the construction of defences at the expense of those benefited by them.[80] The formalisation of this responsibility, by the establishment of the earliest drainage authority, appears to have been the appointment of a local body established for Romney Marsh by a commission issued by Henry III.

---

[78] Generally see Ch.2 below on the civil law.
[79] For an account of the early history of flood defence law see Royal Commission on Land Drainage in England and Wales, *Land Drainage in England and Wales* (1927) Cmd.2993, pp.8 to 11.
[80] H. Stuart Moore, *Coulson and Forbes on Waters and Land Drainage* (5th ed. 1933) p.42, citing *Hudson* v *Tabor* (1877) 2 QBD 290 (see 2.4.4 below) and *Attorney-General* v *Tomline* (1879) 12 Ch D 214 (see 5.3 below) as authority for this. On the 'beneficiary pays' principle see 6.1.2 below.

## Historical Development of the Law

Following this model, 'commissions of sewers' were more generally provided for in a statute of 1427[81] which ordained that, for a period of ten years, such commissions would be established in all parts of the country where they were needed. Under the Bill of Sewers of 1531, arrangements for the issuing of commissions were made more permanent with subsequent Acts extending the powers of 'commissioners' to inquire as to the defaults of persons causing land to be damaged and to 'tax, distrain and punish' offenders. Further powers allowed commissioners to make statutes and ordinances, to survey and remedy annoyances, to appoint bailiffs to collect money and to punish debtors. However, the rather uncertain powers of commissioners under the Bill of 1531 did not provide powers to execute new flood defence works.

More precise powers were introduced in the Sewers Act 1833 which contained rules with regard to the property qualifications of commissioners, to identify persons who could be ordered to carry out works at their own expense and to define those lands that could be rated to meet the expenses incurred by the commissioners. The 1833 Act also gave commissioners the power to divide their area into districts or 'levels' for the purpose of imposing different rates, subject to the principle that particular land could only be rated in respect of measures which were of benefit to that land. A further permissive power was given to commissioners to construct and maintain new maritime works, or works on navigable rivers, subject to the consent of three-quarters of the owners and occupiers of land to be rated for the works. Further provision for subdivision of areas and differential rating was made by the Sewers Acts Amendment Act 1849.

The Land Drainage Act 1861 established a petition procedure for the appointment of commissioners, requiring the support of one-tenth of the proprietors of relevant land before commissioners were appointed for an area. Upon appointment, commissioners became permanently established in contrast to previous arrangements requiring renewal every ten years. The powers of the commissioners were explicitly defined to allow the cleansing, repairing or maintaining of watercourses and defences; the deepening, widening or straightening or improving of watercourses and the removal of obstructions; and the making of new watercourses, outfalls or defences against water.[82] Obstructions such as mill dams could not be removed without the consent of the owner unless the matter was referred to arbitration and certain matters considered, including the need for payment of compensation. Commissioners were also given powers, for the

---

[81] 6 Hen VI c.5 'Commissions of Sewers Shall be Granted' (1427).
[82] See the present day provisions concerning maintenance, improvement and construction of flood defence works at 4.3.1 and 4.6.1 below.

purpose of defraying costs, to raise a loan on the security of their rates. The Land Drainage Act 1861 also provided for elected drainage boards for 'any bog, moor or other area of land that requires a combined system of drainage, warping or irrigation', having the same powers as commissioners of sewers, but elected by the ratepayers of a district following a petition of proprietors of not less than one-tenth of the area concerned.

The provision for drainage boards for drainage districts was extended by the Land Drainage Act 1918, which enabled the Ministry of Agriculture and Fisheries to constitute such districts either on the petition of proprietors, the petition of the council of any county which lay within the relevant land or on the initiative of the Ministry itself. The 1918 Act also placed the powers of drainage authorities on a firmer basis by authorising authorities to rate land by acreage or annual value and allowing for differential rating or the exemption from rating of a part of a drainage area. Public health and highway authorities were given powers to contribute to the expenses of drainage schemes where they were of benefit to public health or highways. Adjoining drainage authorities were allowed to make arrangements to execute works within each other's area and powers to execute works in neighbouring land for the purpose of securing operation of an outfall were given to drainage authorities. However, default powers were provided allowing the Ministry to take action where persons liable to maintain drainage structures had failed to do so or where a drainage authority had neglected to exercise its powers properly. The Ministry also had powers to initiate drainage schemes for small areas, which did not require a drainage board to be constituted. By the Land Drainage Act 1926 the powers of the Ministry were, with certain restrictions, transferred to county councils and county borough councils who were also given powers to require the cleansing of drains where an obstruction existed.

Alongside the principal national legislation that has been noted, flood defence was also widely provided for in local or special legislation applicable in particular areas and usually providing powers to county councils to undertake specified drainage works within their areas.[83]

### 1.9.2 The Royal Commission

The cumulative result of 500 years of rather piecemeal legislation was a rather confused tangle of authorities exercising a variety of powers and functions with little uniformity and variable effectiveness. The Royal Commission on Land Drainage was established in 1927 to consider the law

---

[83] Examples are the Middlesex County Council Act 1898, Lancashire County Council (Drainage) Act 1921, West Riding of Yorkshire County Council (Drainage) Act 1923 and Surrey County Council Act 1925.

## Historical Development of the Law

and administrative arrangements, and to make recommendations.[84] The conclusion of the Royal Commission was that a satisfactory result could be achieved only by the repeal of all the previous public legislation, and the enactment of single comprehensive statute.

Foremost amongst the defects in the law needing to be addressed was the interpretation of some rather obscure provisions in the Bill of Sewers 1531, which had been narrowly construed to prevent drainage rates being imposed on anyone who did not directly benefit from, or escape danger by, the drainage works in respect of which rates were levied. The interpretation of the principle of drainage rating, 'no benefit, no rate', was differently construed by different bodies but had the general consequence that the funds that could be raised by drainage authorities were inadequate, and a significantly broader basis for funding was needed. Whilst not wishing to totally remove the link between rating and benefit, the Royal Commission sought a wider interpretation of benefit which would ensure that an equitable contribution was made by upper landowners in the whole of a catchment and not collected only from those lower landowners most vulnerable to flooding. Special arrangements would need to be made for the contributions to be made by urban areas but some contribution would be needed from such areas.

Another principal issue considered by the Royal Commission was the problem of fragmentation or lack of co-ordination between activities undertaken by different drainage authorities. On this, the Commission emphasised the need for a 'supreme authority' charged with the supervision of all drainage works within an area comprising the catchment of a river. Hence, in each catchment area, a 'catchment authority' would be responsible for the main river channel and banks, and would work in close collaboration with the drainage authorities concerned with the internal drainage of districts within the catchment area. It was suggested that catchment area authorities should be comprised of representatives of the county councils and county borough councils within the catchment area, together with persons elected by internal drainage authorities or persons directly interested in drainage of lowlands within the catchment.

Inherent in the proposals of the Royal Commission was the need for all the previous legislation and administrative arrangements to be swept away. Hence, it would be necessary for all commissioners of sewers and obsolete or moribund drainage authorities to be abolished and replaced, where appropriate, by new elected drainage boards. Another area of rationalisation

---

[84] Royal Commission on Land Drainage in England and Wales, *Land Drainage in England and Wales* (1927) Cmd.2993.

that was recommended by the Commission related to the need for commutation of liabilities for flood defence. This arose because, apart from contributing to the rates levied by drainage authorities, many landowners were bound, because of their tenure or for other reasons, to maintain watercourses or to repair or contribute towards the repair of sea walls. Quite often, obligations of this kind had been created many years previously and their origins were difficult to trace. Typically, tenure obligations were established at times when landowners held large tracts of land that would benefit from the flood defence works. However, with the fragmentation of large estates into smaller parcels of land, the owners of relatively small areas became increasingly burdened by responsibilities for maintenance work that protected land that was owned by other persons. In addition, maintenance obligations grounded in tenure were found to hamper the work of drainage authorities that were prevented from carrying out works in areas where tenure obligations applied. The solution to the problem recommended by the Commission was that catchment area authorities should be placed under a statutory obligation to require tenure and similar obligations in their areas to be commuted by payment of a capital sum or an annual payment. Thereafter, the commuted obligations would become the responsibilities of the catchment authorities.

### 1.9.3 Modern Legislation

The basis of modern flood defence legislation was the Land Drainage Act 1930. This gave effect to many of the recommendations of the 1927 Royal Commission by creating a new kind of authority, the 'catchment board', which was responsible for the whole area of a river basin. Provision was also made for the conversion of old drainage districts into 'internal' districts, within the area catchment, and within these districts the principle of payment for benefits received was maintained. Hence, catchment boards were empowered to demand a contribution from an internal drainage board for any works carried out by them. Catchment boards were also given powers to charge, or 'precept', the councils of counties and county boroughs throughout the catchment area and the incidence of the precept was not dependent upon the tendency of particular properties, or particular local government districts, to flood. The 1930 Act also recognised the desirability of Exchequer assistance towards the expenditure of catchment boards.[85]

Although the fundamental structure of the 1930 Act has been substantially

---

[85] Home Office, Scottish Office, Ministry of Housing and Local Government and Ministry of Agriculture and Fisheries, *Report of the Departmental Committee on Coastal Flooding* (1954) para.51.

## Historical Development of the Law

maintained, there have been a series of subsequent changes in the law intended, primarily, to give effect to institutional reorganisations. Hence, the River Boards Act 1948 transferred the powers of catchment boards to river boards established under that Act. The 1930 Act was consolidated, with a range of miscellaneous amending legislation,[86] in the Land Drainage Act 1976 which provided for water authorities, established under the Water Act 1973, to exercise the general supervision of all matters relating to land drainage in their areas. Except in relation to certain financial matters, the land drainage functions of water authorities were carried out through regional land drainage committees. Internal drainage districts and internal drainage boards continued to exist under the 1976 Act, though provision was made for a water authority to act as an internal drainage board under certain circumstances. In summary, therefore, the 1976 Act provided for the functions, powers and liabilities of the various drainage authorities, with respect to drainage schemes, drainage works, control of watercourses, flood warning systems and for the financing of water authority activities through precepts on local authorities, and the financing of internal drainage boards through drainage rates.

The Water Act 1989 was primarily enacted for the purpose of privatising the water utility functions of water supply and the provision of sewage services, but transmission of these to water and sewerage undertakers necessitated the establishment of the National Rivers Authority as the public body with primary responsibility for regulation of the aquatic environment. Alongside the regulatory responsibilities of the National Rivers Authority, the functions of the former water authorities in relation to flood defence were transferred to the Authority. Although regional land drainage committees were renamed 'regional flood defence committees', the essential structure of flood defence responsibilities remained as previously provided for. The Environment Act 1995 transferred the functions of the National Rivers Authority to the Environment Agency, which now exercises general supervision over all matters relating to flood defence and exercises essentially the same legal powers and duties as the previous authorities.

As regards the substantive legislation concerning flood defence, the Land Drainage Act 1976 has now been largely repealed and replaced by the Land Drainage Act 1991. The 1991 Act was enacted as part of a consolidation exercise undertaken in relation to water legislation[87] which involved the

---

[86] That is, Land Drainage Act 1961, Land Drainage (Amendment) Act 1976, Drainage Rates Acts of 1958, 1962 and 1963, Part IV Agriculture (Miscellaneous Provisions) Act 1968 and Part V Agriculture Act 1970.

[87] See Law Commission, *Report on the Consolidation of the Legislation in Relation to Water* (1991) Law Com. No.198, Cm. 1483.

substantial repeal of the Water Act 1989 and the re-enactment of its provisions in the Water Resources Act 1991, the Water Industry Act 1991, the Statutory Water Companies Act 1991 and the Water Consolidation (Consequential Provisions) Act 1991. Primarily, the Land Drainage Act 1991 contains provisions which were taken from the Land Drainage Act 1976; however, some provisions from the 1976 Act were consolidated in the Water Resources Act 1991. Broadly, the Water Resources Act 1991 is concerned with the flood defence functions of the Environment Agency, whereas the Land Drainage Act 1991 is concerned with matters relating more specifically to land drainage and particularly the constitutions and functions of internal drainage boards and land drainage functions that may be exercised by local authorities. The Land Drainage Act 1991 has been amended by the Land Drainage Act 1994 in relation to the environmental and recreational duties of internal drainage boards and local authorities. Miscellaneous amendments to the Land Drainage Act 1991 and the Water Resources Act 1991 in respect of flood defence matters were brought about by the Environment Act 1995.

## 1.10 LAYOUT OF THE WORK

The chapters which follow seek to provide a structured exposition and discussion for flood and coastal defence law and policy which should meet the needs of an 'average' reader. Unfortunately such a person does not exist, and particular readers will have markedly different interests in the policies and practices that are covered and, perhaps, what legal requirements apply in the prospect, or aftermath, of a flood. Hopefully, the layout which has been adopted approaches the issues in the most natural progression, but innumerable cross-references have been necessary to indicate the many points where issues are interlinked and represent a 'best effort' to make the successive chapters as reasonably self-contained as possible.

Commentators have suggested that the formidably complex body of law that relates to flood defence may be seen as being based upon four 'key principles'. These may usefully be summarised in the following way. First, primary responsibility for flood defence rests with riparian owners and legislation seeks to maintain the rights of property owners to the greatest possible extent. Second, where legislation is necessary to avoid impossible burdens being imposed upon landowners, it is permissive rather than mandatory and avoids any commitments to public flood defence measures that are unjustifiable for economic or other reasons. Third, notwithstanding general public legislation, the maximum degree of 'subsidiarity' is sought, in that flooding problems are conceived of as predominantly local problems which are best addressed by bodies with local or regional responsibilities.

## Layout of the Work

Finally, those who benefit from flood defence, or create a need for it, are obliged to pay accordingly so that public investment does not result in undue private gain.[88] Although these principles provide a useful 'skeleton' for the subject area, it will be seen that there are many respects in which they are qualified or simply contradicted by the detailed legal measures that are actually provided for. Nonetheless, they may serve as useful 'reference points' in evaluating the detail of what follows.

Both for historical and practical reasons, the most convenient starting point is with private rights and duties in relation to flood and coastal defence (Chapter 2). All too frequently, the responsibilities of private landholders to protect their properties, and to avoid flooding of other properties, are neglected in the hope that 'someone else' will take charge of the problem. Private rights to take flood defence measures are the first, and in many cases the last, resort. Despite action by individuals, many kinds of flood and coastal defence project are beyond the capacity of individuals to address and the next stage is the examination of the public institutional roles of the key bodies (Chapter 3). The Department for Environment, Food and Rural Affairs (in England) and the National Assembly for Wales as the principal policy-making bodies stand at the top of a hierarchy of public bodies with relevant responsibilities. Beneath them are placed the flood defence operating authorities with statutorily defined responsibilities for particular activities: the Environment Agency, internal drainage boards and local authorities. In each case, the constitutional structure of the bodies, their regulatory and operational responsibilities, and their interrelationships are examined (Chapter 4). For reasons of legislative history and difference in function, the roles of coast protection authorities in relation to coastal erosion and encroachment are separately dealt with (Chapter 5). Ultimately, the broad range of statutory powers entrusted to the operating authorities is dependent upon sufficient funds being available to finance the works that they are empowered to undertake (Chapter 6). The somewhat intricate funding arrangements which allow for largely public funds to be collected and used for flood and coastal defence works are therefore considered alongside the tensions which exist between claims upon local and national sources of funds.

Some kinds of flooding have special characteristics which place them into distinct legal categories. Flooding from sewers and flooding from water supply systems fall into specific categories, which necessitates some

---

[88] See E. C. Penning-Rowsell, D. J. Parker and D. M. Harding, *Floods and Drainage* (1986) pp.27 to 29, though the 'principles of British land drainage law' suggested by these authors have been broadly summarised here. See also J. L. Wilkins, 'Land drainage legislation and the engineer – a review and discussion paper' (1980) 107 *Chartered Municipal Engineer* pp.123 (Part I) and 147 (Part II).

investigation of the contrasting degrees of responsibility that are imposed over water industry services and infrastructure (Chapter 7). Local authorities also have some distinct powers which are specially relevant to flooding where public health, highway drainage or reservoir safety are at issue, and these are usefully grouped together to emphasise the diversity and breadth of local authority involvement in flood defence (Chapter 8). However, perhaps most important amongst the flood prevention functions of local authorities is the responsibility for land use planning (Chapter 9). The planning system has recently been recognised to have immense significance in preventing flood-prone development and reducing flooding risks for the future.

Another theme, which has dramatically increased in importance over recent years, is the need to reconcile flood and coastal defence objectives with the need for increasingly high standards of environmental and ecological protection (Chapter 10). The substantial infrastructure of flood defence, much of it located in areas of considerable ecological significance, has to be accommodated in a way that minimises environmental harm and allows for enhancement where possible. This delicate balancing exercise needs to be accomplished with particular sensitivity where sites of designated conservation importance are involved.

Although there is a tendency to emphasise the operational and infrastructural aspects of flood and coastal defence, this should not be allowed to overshadow a vitally important information dimension (Chapter 11). In a range of situations, responsibilities arise to provide information about flooding propensity or to warn of an impending flood. Whilst the provision of flood warnings and other kinds of flood-related information is perceived to be a government policy priority, it raises substantial legal issues, as does the issue of flooding where insurance coverage is concerned.

Finally, but perhaps most fundamentally, the issue of sustainable development in relation to flood and coastal defence must be considered (Chapter 12). Speculation upon matters that extend into the indefinite future may not be a natural ground for legal commentary, but there are a number of critical legal issues that are already emerging as practical concerns. Given the need to enhance the sustainability of flood and coastal defences issues, it must be enquired what changes in practice are involved and what are the cost implications of these.

# Chapter 2

# PRIVATE RIGHTS AND DUTIES

## 2.1 INTRODUCTION

Traditionally, floodwater has been judicially characterised as 'a sort of common enemy . . . against which each man must defend himself'.[1] Defence against flooding was, and in many respects remains, an essentially private matter involving each landowner taking flood defence action to secure his or her property from flooding. As a matter of private law, within broad limits, this has been regarded as a reasonable use of the land which would not give rise to civil liability. The limits are that flood defence, necessarily, has the consequence that water must go elsewhere and in some instances an action which is taken to protect a particular property from flooding amounts to a purposeful direction of water onto adjoining or nearby land. A delicate balance has, therefore, to be drawn between (legitimate) defence of land and (illegitimate) redirection of floodwater onto the land of a neighbour.

A great deal of litigation, particularly in the nineteenth century, was concerned with the delineation of the boundary between legitimate and illegitimate flood defence activities. Broadly, the judicial conclusions were that the principle of good neighbourliness (*sic utere tuo ut alienum non laedas*) applied in a qualified way so far as flood defence was concerned. A degree of selfishness was permitted on the part of a landowner providing that the use that was made of the land was not unreasonable. Nonetheless, the enforcement of private rights between landowners was, until relatively recent times, the principal means by which flood and coastal defence interests of landowners were afforded legal protection. Moreover, outside the scope of modern statutory provisions, private rights remain of considerable importance.

Two main strains are to be discerned in the application of the civil law on flood and coast defence. The first relates to situations where the natural

---

[1] Per Cresswell J in *Smith* v *Kendrick* (1849) 7 CB 515 at p.566, quoting *R* v *Commissioners of Sewers for Pagham Level* (1828) 8 B&C 355, per Lord Tenterden at p.360. Contrast a more modern view that 'water as such is not an enemy of man or beast or land. Indeed, in most circumstances, water can be described as a common friend. Certainly the human race could not survive long without it. Rainwater is generally beneficial and the same can be said of rainwater percolating naturally through the ground', per Piers Ashworth QC in *Home Brewery plc* v *William Davis & Co Ltd* [1987] 1 All ER 637 at p.643.

'riparian' rights of waterside landowners are at issue, normally because flood defence involves an alteration to the natural flow of watercourses that adversely impacts upon upstream or downstream landowners. Second, there are situations where no riparian rights are at issue, because a drainage channel is of artificial construction or because no defined channel exists, for example, where the rights to drain surface or groundwater between neighbouring landowners are at issue. Whilst the first situation primarily involves the application of relatively well-established principles concerning riparian rights to flooding situations, the second situation involves the application of the general law of private nuisance. There may be some significant contrasts between riparian rights and nuisance, particularly in relation to the extent to which the locality is to be taken into account, but the boundaries between the two areas of law are not always clearly defined.

The lack of clear delineation between riparian rights and nuisance is particularly important in relation to relatively recent developments in nuisance which tend to place a greater duty upon landowners to prevent harm to neighbouring land where this is foreseeable and reasonably preventable. Whilst this approach has gained considerable momentum in recent years, it is not always clear to what extent it is similarly applicable to long and substantial lines of authority which point in a different direction so far as riparian rights are concerned. Hence, whether many of the nineteenth century cases on riparian rights and flooding would be decided in the same way today is often a matter of conjecture.

Nonetheless, the approach taken in this chapter is to outline the respective role of riparian rights and nuisance in relation to flood and coastal defence and to indicate the main principles that have been established. The chapter continues by examining some of the situations that have proved to be most contentious in practice, with discussion of mine flooding cases which proved to be the subject of extensive litigation in the nineteenth century, the line of cases on culverting of ditches and watercourses contested in the last century and other problematic issues concerning support and erosion. Finally, general discussion is provided of the special position of public authorities and bodies, acting under statutory duties or powers, in relation to civil liability.

Although placed outside the scope of this chapter, it is necessary to emphasise that many of the issues that arise in private litigation between landowners also need to be examined in a statutory context. Planning permission, for example, will usually be needed to undertake many of the kinds of development which may later become a flood hazard in civil law.[2]

---

[2] See Ch.9 below on town and country planning.

## Introduction

Similarly, powers of flood and coastal defence operating authorities to authorise, or require the removal of, obstructions in watercourses, are likely to be of critical importance in practice.[3] Although these matters are considered elsewhere, it is important to note that many of the issues that previously gave rise to civil litigation are now addressed by statutory mechanisms which, in many instances, may provide a more effective means of addressing a flooding problem.

### 2.2 RIPARIAN RIGHTS

The expression 'riparian rights' refers to those common law powers and duties relating to the use of water associated with the ownership of the bank or bed of a watercourse. The extent of these rights was authoritatively considered in the judgment of Lord Wensleydale in *Chasemore* v *Richards* where it was said,

> '[i]t has been now settled that the right to the enjoyment of a natural stream of water on the surface *ex jure naturae* belongs to the proprietor of the adjoining lands as a natural incident of the soil itself; and that he is entitled to the benefit of it, as he is to all the other advantages belonging to the land of which he is the owner. He has the right to have it come to him in its natural state, in flow, quantity and quality, and to go from him without obstruction, upon the same principle that he is entitled to the support of his neighbour's soil for his own in its natural state. His right in no way depends on prescription or the presumed grant of his neighbour.'[4]

Accordingly, riparian rights depend on the ownership of riparian land,[5] meaning land which is contiguous to the bank or bed of a watercourse or, in the case of tidal waters, land which is in contact with water during ordinary high tides.[6] Riparian rights may be possessed by a freeholder or leaseholder[7] of waterside land and are presumed to be passed by a conveyance of the land.[8] By contrast, land which is separated from a river by a strip of land in separate ownership will not be sufficiently proximate

---

[3] See 4.3 and 4.6 below on flood defence operational powers.
[4] (1859) 7 HL Cas 349 at p.382. See also *Embrey* v *Owen* (1851) 6 Ex 353, per Parke B at p.369; and *Miner* v *Gilmour* (1859) 12 Moo 131, per Lord Kingsdown at p.126.
[5] *Portsmouth Waterworks Co* v *London Brighton and South Coast Railway Co* (1906) 26 TLR 173 at p.175.
[6] *North Shore Railway Co* v *Pion* (1889) 14 AC 612 at p.621; and *Stockport Waterworks Co* v *Potter* (1864) 10 LT 748.
[7] See *Jones* v *Llanrwst Urban District Council* (1910) [1908–10] All ER Rep 922.
[8] See s.62(1) and (4) Law of Property Act 1925, which provides that a conveyance of land will convey all waters and watercourses insofar as a contrary intention is not expressed; and *Marshall* v *Ulleswater Steam Navigction Co* (1871) LR 7 QB 166.

to found a claim based upon riparian rights.[9] Likewise, a contractual right to water use against a riparian owner will not amount to a riparian interest which may be enforced against other riparian owners.[10]

Unless it is expressly provided otherwise, the ownership of both banks of a river carries with it the ownership of the river bed,[11] or, in a situation where a single bank is owned, the river bed up to the centre line (*medium filum*) of the watercourse.[12] This presumption, that the owner of a bank of a river owns the river bed, may be rebutted by sufficient contrary evidence.[13] In every case, however, it is essential that the land that is possessed abuts the water over which rights are claimed.[14] Notwithstanding that a riparian owner has a property right in the bed of river up to the middle line of the stream, this does not allow the river bed to be obstructed in a way that interferes with the flow of the stream.[15]

Subject to statutory provisions, the common law generally provides that,

> 'the possessor of land through which a natural stream runs, has a right to the advantage of that stream flowing in its natural course, and to use it when he pleases for any purpose of his own not inconsistent with the similar rights in the proprietors of the land above and below.'[16]

In particular, riparian ownership may encompass the following matters:

(a) the right to discharge effluent into a watercourse;

(b) the right to abstract water from a watercourse for domestic and agricultural use;

(c) the right to impound or divert the flow of water by placing obstructions in the watercourse;

(d) rights of fishery; and

(e) rights of navigation.

However, alongside these recognised rights, the nature of the uses that can be made of riparian land is to some extent open-ended and may encompass

---

[9] *Attorney-General v Rowley Bros and Oxley* (1910) 75 JP 81.
[10] *Crossley v Lightowler* (1867) 16 LT 438.
[11] *Blount v Layard* (1888) [1891] 2 Ch 681.
[12] *Bickett v Morris* (1866) 30 JP 532; and *Bristow v Cormican* (1878) 3 AC 641 at pp.666 to 667; and on the *medium filum* rule generally, W. Howarth, *Wisdom's Law of Watercourses* (5th ed. 1992) p.17.
[13] *Micklethwait v Newlay Bridge Co* (1886) 51 JP 132.
[14] *Stockport Waterworks Co v Potter* (1864) 10 LT 748.
[15] *Bickett v Morris* (1866) LR 1 Sc&Div 47.
[16] Per Denman CJ in *Mason v Hill* (1853) 5 B&Ad 1 at p.17.

## Riparian Rights

other rights that might qualify as 'riparian' to the extent that they are dependent upon the use of waterside land.[17]

It is notable that, despite the range of uses of water which are permitted to riparian owners, ownership of riparian land does not normally carry with it the *ownership* of flowing water. Water is regarded as being held in public and common ownership in that,

> 'all may reasonably use it who have a right of access to it, and that none can have any property in the water itself, except in the particular portion which he may choose to abstract from the stream and take into his possession, and that during the time of his possession only.'[18]

Because of this, flowing water is not capable of being stolen unless it has been removed from a stream for some purpose.[19] Since riparian owners generally have a limited capacity to take water into their possession for any length of time, it follows that riparian rights are normally concerned with those *activities* that may legitimately be undertaken by the owners of waterside land. They are not normally concerned with the establishment or exercise of anything more than a transient or qualified right of property in the water itself.

### 2.3 WATERCOURSES AND OTHER WATERS

Most fundamentally, riparian rights are dependent upon the ownership of land abutting a '*watercourse*'. Important legal contrasts are drawn between watercourses and other facilities for the containment or transmission of water, and these must be noted.

The rights and duties of riparian owners are defined in terms of the relationship between two or more persons possessing interests in the banks or bed of a 'watercourse', which is defined as a flowing quantity of water which runs in a defined course in such a way as to be capable of diversion.[20] Providing that there exists such a channel, having reasonably defined banks, it need not be shown that water is present continuously. Thus, it will

---

[17] *Pennington v Brinksop Hall Coal Co* (1877) 5 Ch D 769.
[18] Per Parke B in *Embrey v Owen* (1851) 6 Ex 353 at p.369; and see *Williams v Morland* (1824) 2 B&C 910 and *Mason v Hill* (1833) 5 B&Ad 1 at p.24.
[19] See *Freans v O'Brien* (1883) 47 JP 472 and *Liggins v Inge* (1831) 7 Bing 682 at p.693.
[20] *Taylor v St Helens Corporation* (1877) 6 Ch D 264 at p.273. 'Watercourse' may have a different interpretation in statutory contexts. See *R v Falmouth and Truro Port Health Authority ex parte South West Water Ltd* ([1999] Env LR 833 and [2000] 3 All ER 306) where, in interpreting s.259(1) Public Health Act 1936, it was held that rivers and estuaries would not be 'watercourses' within the meaning of this section and see 8.2.1 on statutory nuisance. See also notes to 1.1 above on the statutory definition of 'watercourse'.

not matter that the channel occasionally becomes dry,[21] or even if it ceases to flow during a considerable part of the year.[22]

However, a 'watercourse' does envisage a relatively permanent and defined course for moving water. Thus, the element of permanence was found to be lacking where an artificial marsh of a temporary character, which was present only during the times when it was required by mine owners, was found not to be a watercourse.[23] Similarly, surface water which was intermittently present over an undefined area, without a definite or regular course, was held not to constitute a watercourse,[24] and natural bourne flows of underground water from chalk strata, which at times of flood flowed over the surface of land, have been held not to constitute watercourses.[25] Likewise it has been found that water which percolates through marshy ground did not constitute a 'stream'.[26] The need for moving water to be present has been found lacking in a case concerning abstraction of water from a canal where no flow of water existed.[27]

Although riparian rights arise as a natural incident of the ownership of waterside land, such rights will not normally exist in relation to the artificially constructed channels through which water flows.[28] In circumstances of this kind, riparian rights, if any, will rest upon a different basis to that in respect of natural watercourses.[29] This distinction was emphasised in the observation that,

> '[t]he right to the water of a river flowing in a natural channel through a man's land, and the right to water flowing to it through an artificial watercourse constructed on his neighbour's land, do not rest on the same principle. In the former case each successive riparian owner is *prima facie* entitled to the unimpeded flow of the water in its natural course, and to its reasonable enjoyment as it passes through his land, as a natural incident of his ownership of it. In the latter case any right to the flow of the water must rest on some grant or arrangement, either proved or presumed, from or with the owners of the lands from which the water is artificially brought, or on some other legal origin.'[30]

---

[21] *R v Oxfordshire (Inhabitants)* (1830) 1 B&Ad 289 at p.301.
[22] *Stollmeyer v Trinidad Lake Petroleum Co* [1918] AC 485.
[23] *Arkwright v Gell* (1839) 5 M&W 203.
[24] *Rawstron v Taylor* (1855) 156 ER 873.
[25] *Pearce v Croydon Rural District Council* (1910) 74 JP 429.
[26] *M'Nab v Robertson* [1897] AC 129, HL.
[27] *Staffordshire Canal Co v Birmingham Canal Co* (1866) LR 1 HL 254.
[28] See *Nield v London and North Western Railway Co* (1874) LR 10 Ex 4 and see 2.4.2 below, where flooding from a canal was at issue.
[29] Generally see S. R. Hobday, *Coulson and Forbes on Waters* (1952) p.194.
[30] Per Sir Montague Smith in *Rameshur Pershad Narain Singh v Koonj Behari Pattuk* (1878) 4 AC 121.

The important contrast is that riparian rights arise naturally in a natural watercourse, whereas such rights need to be explicitly created, or presumed to be created, where an artificial watercourse is at issue. Nonetheless, the possibility exists that rights akin to riparian rights may arise in respect of a permanent artificial watercourse where the claimant of such rights is able to establish acquisition either by an express grant,[31] or by means of a prescriptive right[32] acquired through long use of the channel either to receive water or to discharge it,[33] or by statutory authorisation. In each of these situations the extent of the interest acquired will depend upon the scope of the rights originally acquired. Hence, where an artificial channel was intended to be of only a temporary nature it will not give rise to riparian rights, as with a channel used to remove mine waste at the convenience of the mine owners,[34] or an agricultural ditch or drain the operation of which was dependent upon the mode of draining land adopted by the defendant.[35]

As a matter of common law, water that is affected by the regular ebb and flow of the highest tides is termed 'tidal water'.[36] This includes waters where tides have a lateral effect, or a vertical effect due to the arresting of water passing down an estuary into the sea.[37] Normally the foreshore and bed of tidal waters is vested in the Crown,[38] unless its ownership has been alienated prior to Magna Carta. However, in exceptional instances, the ownership of the foreshore may be vested in a private individual,[39] and where this exists the foreshore owner will have similar rights in the sea to those possessed by a riparian owner in respect of an inland watercourse,[40] though there are likely be important exceptions to this in respect of public rights of navigation.[41]

An underground flow of water is capable of giving rise to riparian rights

---

[31] *Wood* v *Saunders* (1875) 10 Ch App 583.
[32] *Gaved* v *Martyn* (1865) 13 LT 74.
[33] A distinction noted by Bowen LJ in *Chamber Colliery Co* v *Hopwood* (1886) 55 LT 449 at p.452.
[34] *Arkwright* v *Gell* (1839) 5 M&W 203.
[35] *Greatrex* v *Hayward* (1853) 8 Ex 291; and *Bartlett* v *Tottenham* [1932] 1 Ch 114.
[36] *Reece* v *Miller* (1882) 8 QBD 626, and generally see G. Newsom and J. G. Sherratt, *Water Pollution* (1972) Appx.II.
[37] *West Riding of Yorkshire Rivers Board* v *Tadcaster Rural District Council* (1907) 97 LT 436; and *Ingram* v *Percival* [1968] 3 All ER 657.
[38] *Malcolmson* v *O'Dea* (1863) 10 HL Cas 593 and *Gann* v *Whitstable Free Fishers* (1865) 11 HL Cas 192.
[39] *Blundell* v *Caterrall* (1821) 5 B&Ald 268, and see W. Howarth, 'Access to the Foreshore' (1992) *Rights of Way Law Review* p.11.
[40] See S. Payne, 'Sewerage Pollution of Beaches – Liability and Clean Up' [1994] *Water Law* 183.
[41] See *Attorney-General* v *Lonsdale* (1868) 20 LT 64; *Lyon* v *Fishmongers' Co* (1876) 35 LT 569; and *North Shore Railway Co* v *Pion* (1889) 61 LT 525.

where it constitutes a stream or watercourse, that is, providing that it has a reasonably well-defined channel and a flow of water. Hence, where a surface watercourse sank below ground, where it continued its course for a distance, and then emerged above ground it was held that it did not cease to be a stream because of the subterranean flow.[42] Different principles will apply, however, where underground water lacks a definite channel of flow and it has been held that the principles relating to underground water in a defined channel are 'inapplicable to the case of subterranean water not flowing in any definite channel . . . but percolating or oozing through the soil, more or less according to the quantity of rain that may chance to fall'.[43] Broadly, therefore, riparian rights may be exercised where a defined underground channel is identified, though establishing this may give rise to some practical difficulties, but riparian rights will not arise where water merely percolates through soil without there being any defined channel.

## 2.4 RIPARIAN DRAINAGE RIGHTS AND DUTIES

Insofar as riparian rights are relevant to flooding, there are three central issues needing to be considered: first, the extent to which a riparian owner is permitted to use a watercourse for the purpose of discharging flood or drainage water; second, the extent to which it is permissible to prevent floodwater from a watercourse from passing onto adjoining riparian land; and, third, the extent to which a riparian owner is bound to maintain the channel of a watercourse in a state which avoids flooding of other land.

### 2.4.1 The Discharge of Floodwater to Watercourses

A basic entitlement of a riparian owner is that of receiving the flow of a watercourse in its natural state in respect of its quality and quantity. Insofar as quantitative issues are concerned, this entitlement is distinctive in giving rise to both rights and duties upon riparian owners. That is, a lower riparian owner will have a *right* to the natural flow of water in the sense that any invasion of this right which causes damage will be actionable unless some justification, such as a statutory right to alter the quantity or quality of the flow, can be shown.[44] However, the qualification to this is that the riparian right to receive the flow of a watercourse is subject to the proviso

---

[42] *Dickinson* v *Grand Junction Canal Co* (1852) 16 Jur 200.
[43] Per Lord Chelmsford LC in *Chasemore* v *Richards* (1859) 7 HL Cas 349 at p.367; *R* v *Metropolitan Board of Works* (1863) 3 B&S 710; and *Rugby Joint Water Board* v *Walters* [1966] 3 All ER 497.
[44] Typically, actions of this kind have arisen where a claimant has been deprived of a natural flow of a watercourse and held to be entitled to that flow by virtue of riparian rights (*Mason* v *Hill* (1833) 5 B&Ad 1); but not where percolating water is not the subject of riparian rights (*Chasemore* v *Richards* (1859) 7 HL Cas 349).

that the water is the *natural* flow, and this will not include water, or effluent, which has been artificially brought on to the upper land and which increases the natural flow, or quality, of the watercourse.[45]

The counterpart of the riparian right to a flow of water is a riparian *duty* to receive the natural flow of the watercourse and to allow that flow to pass down to lower riparian owners, undiminished in quantity or quality. Hence, unless an agreement has been made between riparian owners, or the situation is governed by prescriptive or statutory rights, it is not permissible for a riparian owner to obstruct the flow of a watercourse so as to force water back on upstream proprietors.[46] In early cases at least, this principle was well illustrated by situations where there was a conflict of interests between water mill owners exercising riparian rights. In one instance a downstream mill owner raised the level of the water in a watercourse to the extent that it reduced the flow through an upstream mill. In finding that that the obstruction of flow, to the prejudice of the upstream mill owner, was actionable, the general principle was stated that,

> 'if by any alteration lower down the stream the water be prevented from escaping, as it has usually done, and that be to the prejudice of the owner of the mill, it seems to me to form the ground of an action against the party so obstructing the water.'[47]

Essentially the same principle would be applicable if the result of a downstream obstruction to a watercourse was to cause flooding of upstream land.

By contrast, there are various situations where water, which would not naturally be present in a watercourse, is made to contribute to its flow. In these circumstances, a lower downstream owner will be neither bound nor entitled[48] to receive the non-natural contribution to the flow. In the leading case of *John Young and Co v Bankier Distillery Co*[49] the claimants were owners of a distillery situated on the banks of a stream, the waters of which were used for the purposes of their business. The defendants were owners of a coal mine located on land higher up the stream who, in the course of working the mine, pumped large quantities of water from lower strata into the stream. Because the pumped water was 'hard' in quality, it made the water of the stream less suitable for the claimants' use in distilling. It was

---

[45] *John Young & Co v Bankier Distillery Co* [1893] AC 691.
[46] *Wright v Howard* (1823) 1 Si&St 190.
[47] *Saunders v Newman* (1818) 1 B&Ald 258, per Lord Ellenborough CJ at p.260.
[48] *John S. Deed and Sons Ltd v British Electricity Authority and Croydon Corporation* (1950) 114 JP 533.
[49] (1893) [1891–4] All ER 439.

held that the claimants, as lower riparian owners, were not bound to receive the water pumped from the mine by artificial means which would not have reached the stream otherwise. 'Sensible alteration' to either the quality or the quantity of a watercourse, therefore, is actionable by lower riparian owners. Although the facts were concerned with a deterioration in water *quality*, essentially the same principle would have been applied if there had been a sensible alteration in the *quantity* of water in the stream. Similar reasoning, therefore, has been applied in various situations where operations have brought drainage water to land or watercourses where it would not naturally be present, particularly where the flooding of mines has been at issue.[50]

As a consequence of a riparian owner having a duty to accept the natural flow of a watercourse and a right to contribute water from the riparian land, there will be no liability for erosion or deposition that is caused to adjoining or downstream land. Clearly, there will be situations where downstream riparian owners need to take action to prevent erosion or to remove deposition,[51] but it is for the downstream riparian owners to take necessary measures and to bear the expense of these. Similarly, action may be needed by downstream riparian owners to prevent flooding of their land as a result of the natural flow. In neither case, however, will the need for action by downstream owners give rise to liability on the part of an upstream riparian owner unless that person has in some way interfered with the natural flow. In essence, riparian ownership establishes a sequence of correlative rights and duties allowing water that is naturally present to contribute to the flow of a watercourse and requiring the receipt of that flow by downstream owners. Insofar as these rights and duties are legitimately exercised, no liability for flooding will arise.

### 2.4.2 Alleviating Flooding from Watercourses

The basic principle concerning flood defence in respect of a watercourse is that, providing the flow of a watercourse is not diverted from its normal channel or the course which it customarily takes when in flood (the *alveus* of a river or stream) an owner of waterside land may take reasonable action to prevent floodwater reaching that land. For this purpose, therefore, the riparian owner may construct flood defences even though the amount of water flowing over neighbouring land in times of flood is increased as a result. Although it is possible to state the general principle, with reasonable confidence, the factual complexities that have arisen in applying it to many situations where flood damage has arisen are considerable.

---

[50] See the discussion of the mining cases at 2.5.2 below.
[51] See the discussion of maintenance of a watercourse at 2.4.3 below.

The right of a riparian owner to take action to alleviate flooding was considered by the House of Lords in the early Scots case of *Menzies v Earl of Breadalbane*.[52] Here, the owner of land on the bank of a river commenced the building of a mound which would have had the effect of obstructing a flood channel and directing the flow of the river onto opposite land in times of ordinary flood. It was held that an interdict (injunction) would be granted to prevent further construction of the mound or other work that might have the effect of diverting the flow of the river from its accustomed course in times of flood. It was recognised that it is lawful for an owner of land to build a bulwark to prevent loss of ground by the encroachment of floodwater, but such work must be executed so as not to prejudice the land on the opposite side of the watercourse.

The facts of *Menzies v Earl of Breadalbane* are neatly contrasted with an earlier decision where the opposite conclusion was reached. In *Farquharson v Farquharson*[53] a river was departing from its original course and was encroaching upon ground of the defendant, who constructed a mound, upon existing foundations, to retain the original course. The purpose of the mound was not, therefore, to alter the course of the river, but rather to prevent encroachment and to retain the existing course of the river, and this was held to be lawful. Another fact that may have had some bearing upon the outcome was that the owner of the land on the opposite bank had already embanked his side of the river to prevent flooding and it was recognised to be a local custom that proprietors of opposite sides of rivers embanked against each other.

The principle illustrated by these decisions is apparent: 'you may protect your own property from destruction, but you cannot protect yourself to the prejudice of the opposite proprietor'.[54] However, in many situations a fine factual line must be drawn between (legitimate) protection from encroachment and (illegitimate) diversion of flow of a watercourse. In reality, protecting one bank of a watercourse from flooding will almost invariably increase the risk of flooding to the other bank. Arguably, a strict application of the principle of good neighbourliness would seem to preclude a riparian owner taking *any* action to reduce flooding and would enable neighbouring landowners effectively to dictate what flood defence measures could be taken.[55] Because of this, a delicate balancing of interests has to be undertaken which recognises that *some* increase in the risk of

---

[52] (1828) 3 Bli NS 414.
[53] (1714) Mor Dict 12779 cited in *Menzies v Earl of Breadalbane* (1828) 3 Bli NS 414.
[54] *Menzies v Earl of Breadalbane* (1828) 3 Bli NS 414 paraphrasing the Lord Chancellor at p.419.
[55] See *Ridge v Midland Railway Co* (1888) 53 JP 55 at p.56.

flooding of neighbouring land is permissible as a result of reasonable flood defence measures being carried out.

An illustration of the balancing exercise is to be seen in the Privy Council decision in *Gerrard* v *Crowe*[56] where the parties were owners of land on opposite sides of a river. The respondent's land had been subject to flooding and he had erected an earth embankment about half a mile from the river for the purpose of protecting land behind the embankment. The result of this was that floodwater flowing over the appellant's land was increased and he sought damages and an injunction to compel the removal of the embankment. It was argued, on behalf of the appellant, that the principle of good neighbourliness applied without qualification so that the construction of an embankment was only permissible providing that no more water was made to flow onto neighbouring land.

The Court rejected this view in interpreting *Menzies* v *Earl of Breadalbane*[57] as allowing a landowner to protect land from flooding even where this resulted in water flowing onto neighbouring land. A key feature of that case was that there was an identified flood channel, which was recognised to form part of the *alveus* of the river, and the court would not allow this to be obstructed. Hence, whilst a riparian owner is not allowed to divert or obstruct the channel of a watercourse, this encompasses both the normal channel and any secondary channel which water is accustomed to take in times of flooding. However, in *Gerrard* v *Crowe* the facts were significantly different. The river, in times of flood, did not follow any defined course but merely spread over the respondent's land. No identifiable floodwater drainage channel had been obstructed and, therefore, there could be no liability against the respondent for the construction of the embankment.

Hence, flood defence measures do not need strictly to adhere to the requirements of good neighbourliness and may permissibly increase the flooding of other land providing that there is no diversion or obstruction of a watercourse or an identifiable floodwater channel. However, a landowner taking flood defence measures must use reasonable skill and care and must not do more than is reasonably necessary for that purpose.[58] This principle was illustrated in *Maxey Drainage Board* v *Great Northern Railway Co*[59] where the defendant railway company owned land that was liable to flooding and raised an embankment to prevent this. The effect of the embankment was to divert water which had the result of causing flooding

---

[56] [1921] 1 AC 395, but contrast *Strange* v *Andrews* [1956] NZLR 948.
[57] (1828) 3 Bli NS 414, and also *Trafford* v *R* 8 Bing 204 and *Bickett* v *Morris* (1866) LR 1 HL Sc 47 at p.56 were cited in support of this contention.
[58] *Gerrard* v *Crowe* [1921] 1 AC 395, per Viscount Cave at p.400.
[59] (1912) 106 LT 429.

to the claimant's property. It was found that the defendants were entitled, provided that they used reasonable skill, to do what was necessary to protect their land from flooding and, since they had done this, no liability was established.

Analogous reasoning has been applied in situations where coastal erosion is at issue and in *R v Commissioners of Sewers for Pagham*[60] the issues were characterised as follows:

> 'it is contended that this new groyne has caused the sea to flow with greater violence against the land of [the claimant] and make a greater inroad upon it, than possibly it might otherwise have done; and that as the Commissioners, acting for the benefit of the level, have occasioned this damage, they must make compensation for it. It may be conceived that such is the effect of the groyne, but the sea is a common enemy to all proprietors on that part of the coast, and I cannot see that the Commissioners, acting for the common interest of several landowners, are, as to this question, in a different situation from any individual proprietor. Now, is there any authority for saying that any proprietor of land exposed to the inroads of the sea, may not endeavour to protect himself by erecting a groyne or other reasonable defence, although it may render it necessary for the owner of the adjoining land to do the like? I certainly am not aware of any authority or principle of law which can prevent him from so doing.'

The common law capacity of landowners to undertake flood or coastal defence work for the purpose of protecting their land is traditionally regarded as a *power* rather than a *duty*.[61] Despite numerous instances of statutory responsibilities being imposed in relation to flood and coastal defence works, so far as the common law was concerned, a landowner could not be compelled to undertake works of this kind.[62] The main exception to this was where specific duties arose from the terms on which land was held, particularly where obligations derived from tenure, custom, prescription or other civil law obligations.

In *Morland v Cook*,[63] for example, land which lay below sea level had been partitioned by a deed containing a covenant that required the expense of repairing an existing sea wall to be proportionately borne by the owners of the partitioned land. Part of the land changed hands several times before

---

[60] (1828) 8 B&C 355, per Lord Tenterden at p.360.
[61] See *Hudson v Tabor* (1877) 2 QBD 290, discussed at 2.4.4 below.
[62] However, the present position must take account of the decision in *Leakey v National Trust* [1980] 1 All ER 17, discussed at 2.4.5 below.
[63] (1868) LR 6 Eq 252.

it came into the ownership of the defendant, who claimed no actual knowledge of the covenant imposing liability for maintenance of the sea wall at the time of the purchase. Despite general reservations about burdensome covenants running with land,[64] it was held that the defendant was liable to contribute to the cost of repair of the sea wall. It was emphasised that the fact that the land was below sea level should have caused the defendant to be aware of a responsibility to contribute to the cost of maintaining flood defences and that the covenant was of common benefit to all landowners to whom it applied. Similarly, there have been several cases where common law liabilities for maintaining flood or coastal defences have been recognised to arise through custom or prescription. Normally, the effect of tenure-based obligations of this kind is to require landowners to maintain those parts of defences which are upon their land. However, exceptions have been allowed where an extraordinarily violent storm has destroyed defences, in which case it has been held that the cost of their repair should then fall upon all landowners deriving benefit from the defences, and not merely the owners of the land upon which the defences are situated.[65]

In the past, the obligations upon private landowners to maintain flood defence structures would have been important in relation to particular land to which obligations of this kind attached. However, since the Land Drainage Act 1930 it has been recognised that imposing obligations upon frontagers is capable of operating harshly in situations where particular owners are responsible for an extensive length of frontage but only possess a small proportion of the land that is actually protected by the defences. For this reason successive flood defence authorities have been subject to a statutory duty to commute certain obligations arising from tenure, custom or prescription, so that maintenance obligations may be more equitably distributed.[66] Hence, whatever the common law position may have been in the past, tenure-based flood defence obligations are now likely to be uncommon.

An important contrast needs to be drawn between the situation of a riparian owner and the position of person owning land adjacent to an artificial watercourse. A pertinent illustration of the latter situation is to be seen in *Nield* v *London & North Western Railway*[67] where the defendants were

---

[64] See *Tulk* v *Moxhay* (1848) 41 ER 1143 and *Haywood* v *Brunswick Permanent Benefit Building Society* (1881) 8 QBD 403.

[65] See *Keighley's Case* 10 Co Rep 139a; *R* v *Commissioners of Sewers for Essex* (1832) 1 B&C 477; and *Commissioners of Sewers for the Parish of Fobbing* v *R* (1886) 11 App Cas 449.

[66] See 1.9.2 above and 4.4.9 below on commutation of flood defence obligations.

[67] (1874) LR 10 Ex 4.

owners of a canal that was threatened with inundation by floodwater from a nearby river that had no connection with the canal. Fearing flooding damage to premises located on the banks of the canal, the defendants placed a barricade of planks across the canal to hold back the floodwater. When the water from the river broke into the canal the flow was penned back so that the claimant's premises, which were above the barricade, were flooded. It was held that the defendants were not liable since the floodwater was not brought there by them and there is no duty upon the owners of a canal, analogous to that upon riparian owners of natural watercourses, not to impede the flow of water in it. The claimants had no right to have the floodwater discharge into the canal, so had no grounds for redress when the canal owners impeded the flow of floodwater into the canal for the purpose of protecting their property. On that basis, the question of liability had to be considered as between neighbouring (non-riparian) landowners, and in that respect it was observed,

> 'flood is a common enemy against which every man has a right to defend himself. And it would be most mischievous if the law were otherwise, for a man must then stand by and see his property destroyed out of fear lest some neighbour might say "You have caused me an injury". The law allows what I may term a kind of reasonable selfishness in such matters; it says, "Let every one look out for himself and protect his own interest" and he who puts up a barricade against a flood is entitled to say to his neighbour who complains of it, "Why did not you do the same ?"'[68]

Alongside the construction of flood defence embankments, there may be other activities that a riparian owner may legitimately undertake for the protection of waterside land and its convenient use. Hence, in *Hanbury* v *Jenkins*[69] the placing of stakes and wattles in the bank of a river to prevent erosion by floods and the construction of pens to prevent cattle from straying were actions that were reasonably convenient, or necessary, for the defence or enjoyment of the property of a riparian owner. Similarly, in *Bickett* v *Morris*,[70] though work being undertaken on the bed of a watercourse which interfered with the natural flow of water was generally disapproved of, it was recognised to be subject to exceptions where infinitesimal obstruction was involved such as where stakes were placed in a river.[71]

---

[68] (1874) LR 10 Ex 4, per Bramwell B. at p.6.
[69] (1901) 2 Ch 401.
[70] See *Bickett* v *Morris* (1866) LR 1 Sc&Div 47, per Lord Cranworth at p.59.
[71] Similarly, it has been suggested that it would be legitimate to place stakes in a river bank to prevent erosion even if this would induce a slight alteration of the current (*Withers* v *Purchase* (1889) 60 LT 819 at p.821). See also *Fowley Marine (Emsworth)* v *Gafford* [1968] 2 QB 618 where the laying of moorings was allowed.

### 2.4.3 Maintaining the Channel of a Watercourse

The hydrological efficiency of a watercourse will clearly be reduced where it becomes naturally clogged with silt or vegetation or where flow is restricted by some other kind of natural or artificial obstacle. This is likely to be a cause of concern to upstream or opposite riparian owners if the extent of the obstruction is sufficient to increase the risk of flooding of higher or opposite land or to impair the drainage of such land. Although it is reasonably clear that a riparian owner has the *power* to remove natural and artificial obstructions to the flow of a watercourse, and in some instances may be required to remove artificial obstructions by other riparian owners, it is less certain in what circumstances a *duty* to remove natural obstructions to the flow arises.

As has been noted, there is clear responsibility upon a riparian owner not to place artificial obstacles in the normal or floodwater *alveus* of a watercourse. Hence, a neighbouring riparian owner may require the removal of such an encroachment where this is likely to have a significant effect[72] upon the flow, irrespective of whether any actual damage has been caused.[73] Although most of the decided cases have arisen in situations where lower riparian owners have been deprived of a desired natural flow of water by obstruction or diversion of watercourses,[74] the legal position is essentially the same where the effect of an artificial obstruction is to increase the flow, and the potential for flooding, beyond that which would naturally arise. Certainly, this approach has been taken where the substitution of an artificial channel for a natural watercourse has resulted in a lesser capacity to take floodwaters and caused flooding as a result.[75]

In respect of operations to clear the channel of a watercourse from naturally occurring obstructions, such as where it has become silted with matter carried by the flow, the power to undertake such activities is inherent in the power of a riparian owner to maintain the natural and accustomed flow of

---

[72] See *Embrey v Owen* (1851) 6 Exch 353 concerning 'sensible diminution' of flow.
[73] *Bickett v Morris* (1866) LR 1 Sc&Div 47.
[74] See *Dickinson v Grand Junction Canal Co* (1852) 7 Exch 282 (liability for wrongful abstraction of water to the detriment of downstream mill operators); *Samson v Hoddinott* (1857) CBNS 590 (liability for diversion of stream to the detriment of downstream owner's use for irrigation); *Earl of Norbury v Kitchin* (1866) 15 LT 501 (injunction granted to prevent the damming up or obstruction of the natural flow of a stream); *Roberts v Gwyrfai District Council* [1899] 2 Ch 608 (abstraction of water for drinking water supply purposes to the detriment of downstream mill owner); and *John White & Sons v White* [1906] AC 72 (rights of a mill owner to use the natural flow of a river acquired by prescription).
[75] See *Fletcher v Smith* (1877) 2 App Cas 781 and generally see the discussion of the culverting cases at 2.5.3 below.

a watercourse.[76] A difficulty, however, is that in many watercourses the 'natural' flow changes constantly, and sometimes quite considerably, over time, and there comes a point at which a naturally 'altered' line becomes regarded as the 'customary' course. When this point is reached a riparian owner is no longer allowed to restore the flow to some former line that, historically, it may have followed. Hence, where, after a stream had taken a new course, a riparian owner delayed for a number of years before seeking to erect a bulwark to restore the stream to its former course, it was held that he was not entitled to do so because this would interfere with the rights of others in the new channel.[77] The scouring or dredging of a channel is permitted, therefore, to maintain the line or efficiency of flow of a watercourse, but not significantly to redirect it, even if the aim of such operations is to restore the flow to that which existed at a former time.

The difficulties in distinguishing between 'maintenance' and 'redirection' operations in a watercourse are well illustrated by *Withers* v *Purchase*.[78] Here, the defendants were owners of land and a mill on a river who, for the purpose of allowing water to flow more freely to the mill, undertook dredging and cleansing operations at a point near to where a branch of the river carried water away from the main stream to the claimant's mill. The defendants claimed a right to scour the river of accretions,[79] to preserve it in its natural or accustomed state with regard to volume, velocity and direction and to restore the flow to its former course. However, it was found that the 'accustomed' course should be taken to be that permanent course which the river was actually taking at the time the right to scour was asserted. On the facts, therefore, the large amounts of gravel which were removed and which had accumulated over many years were, at the time the dredging took place, found to have formed a part of the 'permanent' bed of the river. Consequently, the powers of riparian owners had been wrongfully exceeded in removing the material. The inference from this decision must be that the power to undertake operations to remove material which is naturally present in a watercourse needs to be exercised expeditiously and cautiously, or otherwise by agreement with other riparian owners who might be adversely affected.[80] Similar conclusions

---

[76] See *Farquharson* v *Farquharson* (1714) Mor Dict 12779 cited in *Menzies* v *Earl of Breadalbane* (1828) 3 Bli NS 414, discussed at 2.4.2 above.

[77] *Aberdeen Magistrates* v *Menzies* (1748) Mor Dict 12 787 cited in *Bickett* v *Morris* (1866) 1 Sc&Div 47

[78] (1889) 60 LT 819.

[79] On accretion generally, see W. Howarth, 'The Doctrine of Accretion: Qualifications, Ancient and Modern' [1986] *Conveyancer and Property Lawyer* 247.

[80] Similarly see *Fear* v *Vickers (No.1)* (1911) 27 TLR 558 where operations for the removal of debris from the bed of a river had reduced the flow to the claimant's mill and an injunction was granted to require the restoration of the river bed to its state before the wrongful interference.

have been reached in circumstances where removal of established features that constitute a natural barrier to sea encroachment have been at issue.[81]

Although a riparian owner clearly has a *power* to maintain the channel of a watercourse providing that the natural flow is not altered, the more contentious issue is whether, and in what circumstances, a riparian owner is subject to a *duty* to maintain the natural flow of the watercourse. In this respect, the law appears inconsistent with conflicting lines of cases suggesting different principles. Broadly, these may be distinguished as indicating a 'traditional' and a 'modern' approach towards the duty to maintain a watercourse.

### 2.4.4 Maintenance: The Traditional Approach

The traditional view on a riparian owner's duty to maintain the flow of a watercourse is that no such duty exists, in the sense that a riparian owner will not be civilly liable for damage done by water which has overflowed from the watercourse because of the natural silting up of the bed or the accumulation of vegetation. Hence, in *Hodgson* v *York Corporation*[82] the defendants had been authorised under a local Act to abandon a navigation channel providing that satisfactory provision was made to prevent the water from the channel from flowing over adjacent land. Provision was made for escape of water but it was alleged that subsequent flooding had been caused through the resulting watercourse being allowed to become silted up and choked with weeds. It was held that the respondents were not under any common law obligation to remedy any natural and gradual silting up or growth of weeds on the bed of the river for the benefit of adjacent landowners.

The traditional view that maintenance of the channel of a watercourse is permissive without being compulsory is also paralleled by the view taken of obligations in respect of the maintenance of flood defence structures. In

---

[81] See *Attorney-General* v *Tomline* (1879) 12 Ch D 214 where an injunction was granted to prevent removal of gravel from the foreshore where it needed to be retained to prevent the claimant's property from flooding and see 5.3 below.

[82] (1873) 28 LT 836 and similarly see *Normile* v *Ruddle* (1912) 47 ILT 179. Contrast the decision in *Cracknell* v *Thetford Corporation* (1869) LR 4 CP 629, which affirmed the lack of a common law duty to maintain the channel of a watercourse, but noted the possibility of a claimant applying for compensation under the relevant private Act allowing for a river to be made navigable. The imposition of a statutory duty to maintain a channel was established in *Geddis* v *Bann Reservoir (Proprietors)* (1878) 3 App Cas 430 and see 4.9 below.

*Hudson* v *Tabor*[83] the parties were owners of adjoining land that fronted a creek which communicated with the sea. Protection of the land required each owner to maintain a sea wall which ran along the seaward side of both properties; however, the defendant had failed to maintain his length of wall at the same height as that of the plaintiff. Due to an extraordinary high tide, water flowed over the defendant's wall and passed onto the claimant's land causing considerable damage. It was held that, in the absence of a prescriptive or other duty to maintain the wall for the benefit of adjoining landowners, the defendant would not be liable for the damage sustained by the claimant. Most significantly, no common law duty upon owners of flood defence structures to maintain them was recognised.

Similarly, where owners of navigation or boards of conservators are bound to keep a channel in a proper state of repair this has not been construed to impose a duty to cleanse or scour the channel. Hence in *Simpson* v *Attorney-General*[84] the statutory power that was given to maintain and deepen a channel as often as occasion should require was interpreted as a permissive power rather than a duty. Similarly, persons with ownership of locks and other facilities for facilitating the navigation were not bound to keep them in repair if the tolls taken from users of the navigation were not sufficient to defray the cost of maintenance and repair. Likewise, in *Vyner* v *North Eastern Railway Co*[85] it was held that a statutory power to maintain navigation on a river did not impose a duty to maintain certain 'flood banks' which were located beyond the natural banks of the river.

The absence of a general duty upon riparian owners to maintain the flow of a watercourse was also reflected in public health legislation which requires local authorities to serve abatement notices in relation to specified matters which are identified as statutory nuisances.[86] Amongst these, a statutory nuisance will exist where certain watercourses[87] are so choked or silted as to obstruct or impede the proper flow of water. However, no

---

[83] (1877) 2 QBD 290. Contrast *Morland* v *Cook* (1868) LR 6 Eq 252, discussed at 2.4.2 above. Also contrast *Nitro-Phosphate and Odam's Chemical Manure Co* v *London and St Katherine Docks Co* (1878) 9 Ch D 503, discussed at 4.9 below, where it is suggested that a liability to maintain a sea wall at a particular height is capable of arising as a matter of common law, though the basis for this view seems to arise from prescription.

[84] [1904] AC 476.

[85] (1904) 20 TLR 192, though contrast *Vyner* v *North Eastern Railway Co* (1898) 14 TLR 554.

[86] Now provided for under Part III Environmental Protection Act 1990 and see 8.2.1 below on statutory nuisance.

[87] That is, watercourses which are not ordinarily navigated by vessels and see *R* v *Falmouth and Truro Port Health Authority ex parte South West Water Ltd* [2000] 3 All ER 306.

liability will be imposed upon any person unless the nuisance arises or continues due to their default.[88] Interpreting these provisions, it has been suggested that the proviso, requiring default to be shown in allowing the nuisance to arise or continue, was intended to prevent the imposition of any statutory duty upon a riparian owner to maintain the flow of a watercourse and to reflect that there was no common law duty to remove natural obstructions from the stream.[89]

### 2.4.5 Maintenance: The Modern Approach

Despite the longstanding authorities supporting the traditional view that there is no general duty to maintain the flow of a watercourse, this view must now be interpreted alongside more modern authorities to the opposite effect: that, in appropriate circumstances, such a general duty to maintain the flow of a watercourse *does* arise. The modern view has some precursors in early decisions where a duty to maintain the flow of a watercourse by the removal of natural sedimentation and obstructions was at issue.[90] However, the leading modern decision indicating a maintenance duty upon riparian owners to prevent flooding is *Leakey* v *National Trust*,[91] where a landowner was found liable for naturally occurring slides of soil, rocks, tree-roots and other debris from a bank onto a neighbouring property. In deciding the case, the Court stated that there existed a general duty on occupiers in relation to natural hazards occurring on their land, so that where the hazard encroached or threatened to encroach on another's land there was a duty to do all that is reasonable in the circumstances to prevent or minimise the risk of foreseeable damage to the property of others. The breadth of the principle that was expressed and the indication of a greater willingness of courts, generally, to hold landowners liable for the natural state of their

---

[88] s.259(1)(b) Public Health Act 1936 and s.79(1)(h) Environmental Protection Act 1990.

[89] *Neath Rural District Council* v *Williams* [1951] 1 KB 115. However, it has been questioned whether the *Neath* case is reconcilable with the subsequent decision in *Davey* v *Harrow Corporation* [1958] 1 QB 60 where liability in nuisance was established for naturally growing trees: see *Bybrook Barn Garden Centre Ltd* v *Kent County Council* [2001] Env LR 543, per Waller LJ at para.37 and see 2.5.3 below. Most recently, on liability for damage caused by trees, see *Delaware Mansions Ltd and Others* v *Lord Mayor and Citizens of the City of Westminster* [2001] UKHL 55, 25 October 2001.

[90] See *R* v *Wharton* (1701) 12 Mod 510 where it was tersely stated 'if one has a river, and for want of scouring it the neighbouring land is overflown, he is indictable for it' and *Rhodes* v *Airedale Drainage Commissioners* (1876) 1 CPD 380 at 392 to 393 where *Wharton's* case is taken to support the principle that scouring and cleansing of a river bed, so as to keep the stream in its accustomed course and at its accustomed level, is not only permissible but obligatory upon a riparian owner.

[91] [1980] 1 All ER 17.

land seems to indicate a fundamental shift in thinking about the extent of landowners' responsibilities.

Moreover, in one especially pertinent passage from the judgment of Megaw LJ, the application of the principle governing liability for natural states of land to situations where flooding is at issue was analysed as follows.

> 'Take, by way of example, the hypothetical instance [of a] landowner through whose land a stream flows. In rainy weather, it is known, the stream may flood and the flood may spread to the land of neighbours. If the risk is one which can readily be overcome or lessened, for example, by reasonable steps on the part of the landowner to keep the stream free from blockage by flotsam or silt carried down, he will be in breach of duty if he does nothing or does too little. But if the only remedy is substantial and expensive works, then it might well be that the landowner would have discharged his duty by saying to his neighbours, who also know of the risk and have asked him to do something about it, "You have my permission to come onto my land and to do agreed works at your expense", or, it may be, "on the basis of a fair sharing of expense". In deciding whether the landowner has discharged his duty of care...[t]he question of reasonableness of what had been done or offered would fall to be decided on a broad basis, in which, on some occasions, there might be included an element of obvious discrepancy of financial resources.'[92]

It may be significant that these observations were made in the context of an action brought in private nuisance, rather than being specifically concerned with the duties of riparian owners, and it is notable that the leading cases which indicate that a riparian owner is not subject to a duty of this kind were not cited. Nonetheless, it would be remarkable if the law of nuisance imposed a duty that riparian law denied. Certainly, one commentator has expressed the decisive view that there is now a duty upon a riparian owner to cleanse and scour the bed of a watercourse to prevent flooding.[93]

The limitations of the *Leakey* principle, however, also deserve emphasis: liability will only arise where the risk of damage is foreseeable and the landowner has failed do what is reasonable to prevent it. The implications are that an unprecedented flood would probably fall outside the scope of the principle, as would a situation where a landowner would have to bear unreasonable expense to address a foreseeable hazard. The ramifications

---

[92] [1980] 1 All ER 17 at p.37.
[93] J. H. Bates, *Water and Drainage Law* (1990 updated) paras.1.114 and 2.39.

of these matters are discussed in more detail in the later cases on liability for private nuisance in respect of flooding caused by culverts and sewers, in relation to which, the implications of the *Leakey* decision have been most fully considered.[94]

### 2.4.6 Easements concerning Maintenance

A final contingency which needs to be considered, in respect of maintaining the channel of a watercourse, is the circumstances in which a person who is not the owner of the riparian land will be permitted to enter that land for the purpose of undertaking maintenance work, such as the removal of obstructions to the flow to prevent flooding. Whilst it is possible for the non-riparian owner to undertake work of this kind under a contractual agreement or licence with the riparian owner, it may be more appropriate that a continuing arrangement of this kind is constituted as an easement which binds successive owners of the land.

In general terms, an easement is a positive or negative right of one landowner (the dominant owner) over the land (or tenement) of another (the servient owner). Typically, this may consist of a right of way, but in some instances may be associated with rights to take things from the land, such as fish or wood, and properly termed a *profit a prendre*. The essential characteristics for an easement were set out in *Re Ellenborough Park*,[95] where it was established that, first, there must be a dominant and servient tenement; second, the easement must 'accommodate' the dominant tenement (in the sense of benefiting the use or enjoyment of the dominant land); third, the dominant and servient owners must be different people; and, finally, the right which is claimed as an easement must be capable of forming the subject matter of a grant.

It is not necessary to dwell upon the intricacies of easements, but merely to note their potential importance in enabling work to be undertaken for the purpose of preventing flooding.[96] The nature and extent of the right to undertake such works under an easement will depend, in each case, upon the terms of the particular easement that exists. However, in relevant cases it has been found that particular rights have allowed the dominant owner

---

[94] See 2.5.3 below on the culverting cases and see also 2.7 below on *Holbeck Hall Hotel v Scarborough Borough Council* [2000] 2 All ER 705 where the *Leakey* principle was found to be generally applicable to circumstances of coastal erosion. See also the recent application of the *Leakey* principle in the context of sewer flooding in *Peter Marcic* v *Thames Water Utilities Ltd* [2002] EWCA 65, 7 February 2002, discussed at 7.9 below.
[95] [1956] Ch 131.
[96] See *Liford's Case* (1614) 11 Co Rep 46b at 52a.

to enter land at all reasonable times with the equipment needed to take all necessary measures to repair and maintain the banks of a watercourse. Although concerning an artificial water channel, a good example is *Beeston* v *Weate*,[97] where the claimant maintained that the defendant had removed a dam which directed water from a natural stream into a ditch which carried the water onto the claimant's land where it was used to supply water to his cattle. It was established that, for as far back as living memory went, the occupiers of the claimant's land had passed over the defendant's land for the purpose of maintaining the dam and that there had been no objection to this on the part of the defendant or his predecessors. On these facts, it was found that there was ample ground for establishing an easement to pass over the defendant's land to maintain the dam based upon prescription or the explicit grant of an easement at some time in the past.

Similar possibilities exist for easements to arise when a riparian owner acquires the right to go onto the lands of a higher riparian owner to remove vegetation and to repair the banks of a stream which has been raised to make water available to work a mill.[98] However, other rights which have been maintained as easements, such as a right of natural drainage over or under the soil between neighbouring properties, have been rejected by the courts as being natural rights that are incapable of being the subject of an easement.[99]

Notwithstanding a valid easement, the rights of a dominant owner will not exceed the riparian rights of the servient owner and maintenance work that may be undertaken will be subject to the duties to upper or opposite riparian owners not to do anything which will have a significant adverse effect upon the natural flow of the watercourse.[100] Also, it is notable that it may be actionable for either the servient owner or another person to interfere with, or obstruct, the dominant owner in exercising rights under the easement.[101]

A final point on easements, which may be important in some flood defence contexts, is that easements operate for the benefit of dominant owners and not for the benefit of servient owners. The implications of this are that the

---

[97] (1856) 5 E&B 986. For a recent example of litigation concerning easements to conduct drainage works see *Britel Developments (Thatcham) Ltd* v *Nightfreight Great Britain Ltd* [1998] 4 All ER 432.
[98] *Roberts* v *Fellowes* (1906) 94 LT 279.
[99] See the discussion of *Palmer* v *Bowman* [2000] 1 All ER 22 at 2.5.1 below.
[100] See *Withers* v *Purchase* (1889) 60 LT 819, discussed at 2.4.3 above.
[101] See *Nicholls* v *Ely Beet Sugar Factory* [1936] Ch 343. Similarly see *Goodhart* v *Hyett* (1883) 25 Ch D 182 and *Abingdon Corp* v *James* [1940] 1 All ER 446 where building works, obstructing easements of access to water supply pipes for maintenance purpose, were held to be unlawful.

owner of a servient property will not acquire any right to a continuation of a diversion of a stream or whatever other activity has been undertaken in pursuance of an easement. Hence it has been observed that,

> '[an easement] may be discontinued, if it becomes onerous, or ceases to be beneficial to the party entitled. An easement like the present, while it subjects the owner of the servient tenement to disadvantage, by taking from him the use of the water, for . . . beneficial use[s] to which water may be applied, may, on the other hand, no doubt, be attended incidentally with equal or greater advantage to him – as, for instance, by rendering him safe from the danger of inundation. But this will give him no right to insist on the exercise of the easement on the part of the dominant owner, if the latter finds it expedient to abandon his rights.'[102]

The easement at issue in this instance was that of a canal company which was statutorily entitled to take water from a stream which had flowed through the claimant's land. After taking water for the purposes of the canal for many years, the diversion from the stream was discontinued so that the whole flow of the stream was restored. However, during the period when the water had been used for the canal, the channel had become silted up so that when the flow was restored the stream was unable to accommodate the water in times of flood and the claimant's land was flooded as a consequence. Because the canal company was under no duty to continue the diversion, the claimant had no remedy for the flooding caused by its restoration.

## 2.5 RIGHTS BETWEEN LANDOWNERS IN NUISANCE

Riparian rights and duties are only relevant to the legal relationship that subsists between owners of riparian land. Outside that relationship, however, there are many other situations where civil liability for flooding is at issue. Examples arise in situations where a problematic channel has been artificially constructed and so does not give rise to riparian rights, or situations where no particular drainage channel is at issue either where drainage is over the surface, or under the soil, of land between neighbours. Here, the key issues concern the rights of a landowner to drain surface water from his land onto neighbouring land and the circumstances in which liability will arise for such drainage. In situations of this kind, the main civil remedies that are likely to be relevant arise in the law of private nuisance.

---

[102] *Mason* v *Shrewsbury and Hereford Railway Co* (1871) LR 6 QB 578, per Cockburn CJ at p.587.

Broadly stated, private nuisance allows a remedy in a civil action where there has been an unreasonable interference with a landholder's interest in the enjoyment of land.[103] The possible categories of interference with a landowner's enjoyment of land are open-ended, but it is clear that an action in nuisance will be available only where the claimant has a freehold or leasehold interest in the land and will not, therefore, be available to a mere occupier or licensee.[104] The point deserves to be reiterated that flowing water is not normally the subject of ownership,[105] but the lack of such ownership has not prevented nuisance being widely used where enjoyment of ownership of waterside land is impaired due to interference with the quality or quantity of water passing to land.[106] However, nuisance is significantly distinguished from actions based upon fairly specific riparian rights, first, by its open-ended character and, second, because 'reasonable enjoyment' takes account of the actual uses which may be made of land and the behaviour of the parties. Hence, although a nuisance which causes material injury to the value of property will be actionable, lesser nuisances which result in 'sensible personal discomfort' will depend upon the locality in which the nuisance arises and, perhaps, the special sensitivity of a claimant to the nuisance which is complained of.[107] By contrast, these are not matters that need to be considered in circumstances where a riparian owner shows a significant alteration in the quality or quantity of water in a natural watercourse.

The general situation which is likely to ground an action in nuisance is that one landowner has done something on his land which has caused flooding on neighbouring land or interfered with the drainage of that land by transmitting a greater flow of water to pass to it than naturally would occur. Characteristically, situations of this kind arise where a landowner engages in a new land use or undertakes construction work of some kind that allows the transmission of water to neighbouring properties in a way that would not otherwise occur.

However, other aspects of nuisance that must be kept in mind in relation to flooding situations are the need to show causation and reasonable

---

[103] Generally see D. Howarth, *Textbook on Tort* (1995) p.499.
[104] See *Hunter and Others v Canary Wharf Ltd and London Docklands Development Corporation* [1997] Env LR 488.
[105] See 2.2 above on ownership of flowing water.
[106] Generally see W. Howarth and D. McGillivray, *Water Pollution and Water Quality Law* (2001) section 3.8.
[107] *St Helen's Smelting Co v Tipping* (1865) 11 HLC 642. On locality, see *Gillingham Borough Council v Medway (Chatham) Dock Co Ltd* [1993] QB 343, but contrast *Hunter and Others v Canary Wharf Ltd and London Docklands Development Corporation* [1997] Env LR 488. On special sensitivity, see *Robinson v Kilvert* (1889) 41 Ch D 88.

foreseeability of the damage that arises. The fact that the claimant's land has been flooded does not automatically mean that this results from an improper use being made of neighbouring land, and showing causality may often be a serious evidential problem. Even where causality can be established there is a further requirement that the harm that is suffered by the claimant was reasonably foreseeable by the defendant.[108] In *Ellison and Others* v *Ministry of Defence*,[109] for example, the claimant's house was flooded after a heavy storm and it was alleged that the flooding was due to construction works on an adjacent airfield that had allowed water to accumulate and diverted the natural flow. Despite a finding that the water accumulation and diversion of flow had contributed to the flooding, the claimant failed to show that the flooding was a foreseeable result of the defendant's works or that the works were an unreasonable use of the land.

Although the discussion which follows addresses the general relationship between neighbouring landowners in nuisance so far as flooding and drainage is concerned, the later sections examine the caselaw on particular situations which have proved to be especially problematic and have given rise to most litigation: the mining cases, the culverting cases; and issues relating to rights of support and erosion. Although alluded to previously, a continuing theme running through these sections is the extent to which the principle of 'greater neighbourliness', in the sense of creating more extensive liability for naturally occurring states of land, established in *Leakey* v *National Trust*,[110] has had the effect of modifying the traditionally less extensive basis for liability in nuisance.

### 2.5.1 Land Drainage Rights between Landowners

The first situation for consideration is the position of neighbouring landowners where a higher landowner claims the benefit of drainage onto the lower land of a neighbour. This may arise either by allowing water to run over the surface of the land which constitutes the boundary between the properties or by percolation through the soil. It is well established that the lower landowner will have no *right* to receive drainage water which does not follow a defined course[111] but, until relatively recently, it was less clear

---

[108] See *Cambridge Water Company Ltd* v *Eastern Counties Leather* [1994] 1 All ER 53.
[109] [1996] 81 Build LR 101, and on the pleading of this case see the decision of the Court of Appeal, unreported, 18 July 1996. See also R. Kimblin, 'After the Deluge' [2000] *Solicitors Journal* 1092.
[110] [1980] 1 All ER 17 and see the discussion at 2.4.5 above.
[111] *Broadbent* v *Ramsbotham* (1856) 11 Exch 602; *R* v *Metropolitan Board of Works* (1863) 3 B&S 710; and generally see *Chasemore* v *Richards* (1859) 7 HL Cas 349, discussed at 2.2 above.

whether the lower landowner would be subject to a *duty* to receive the water. Put the other way around, the critical question was whether it is possible for a higher landowner to compel his lower neighbour to receive naturally arising drainage water.

The issue was first directly confronted in *Home Brewery plc v Davis and Co*[112] where the drainage of water from the patio and car park areas of the claimants' public house had previously been by natural seepage through the ground to lower adjacent land. The adjoining land originally consisted of disused clay pits and an osier (willow) bed, but the area was to be developed by the defendants as a residential estate. To allow this development to take place, the defendants filled in the clay pits. This had the effect of creating a barrier to the flow of water from the claimants' land, which resulted in flooding of the land and a need for pumps to be used to remove the excess water. The filling of the osier bed had the result of transmitting water onto the claimants' land, resulting in additional flooding. It was maintained that the defendants' actions amounted to nuisance for which the claimant was entitled to damages.

On the fundamental issue of whether an upper landowner has a right to drain land by natural percolation of rainwater into the soil of lower land, it was held that a lower landowner has no right of action arising from the percolation of naturally arising water to lower land. However, the lower landowner is under no duty to receive such water and is entitled to take reasonable steps to prevent the water entering the land even if this has an adverse effect upon the drainage of the higher land. In undertaking operations which obstruct the flow of water from higher land, however, considerable emphasis was placed upon the 'reasonableness' of the lower landowner's use of land.

On the facts, it was found that the defendants had acted reasonably in filling in the clay pits, since this was essential for the development of the land as a residential estate. Accordingly, the claimants had no remedy for the deterioration in drainage of their land attributable to drainage being impeded by the filling of the clay pits. In respect of the additional flooding caused by the infilling of the osier bed, however, it was found that water had been forced onto the claimants' land as a result of this operation.

---

[112] [1987] 1 All ER 637 and see H.W. Wilkinson, 'The Natural Drainage of Land' (1987) *New Law Journal* 867. See also *Ryeford Homes Ltd and Another v Sevenoaks District Council and Others* [1989] 2 EGLR 281 where a landowner erected an embankment to block the natural flow of water percolating from higher land owned by the claimants, resulting in waterlogging and flooding of the higher land, and it was held that the defendants had acted reasonably and could not be liable in nuisance (and see 11.4.1 below).

Because this consequence was reasonably foreseeable on the part of the defendants, it was held that they were liable for the additional costs attributable to pumping and maintenance over the period during which the water from the osier bed was being transmitted to the claimants' land.

Although the *Home Brewery* case was regarded as raising an essentially novel point of law, some guidance was taken from a range of persuasive, if not actually binding, authorities. One line of reasoning which was considered came from *Gibbons* v *Lenfestey*[113] where the right of a higher landowner to transmit water to lower land was characterised as a 'natural servitude' to the extent that natural surface water, even when collected by some means for the purpose of draining the upper property, was bound to be received by the lower owner.[114] However, this was a decision on the law of Guernsey which, as a system based upon Roman law, did not necessarily reflect the position under English common law. A more pertinent authority was *Gartner* v *Kidman*,[115] a decision of the High Court of Australia, which provided an extensive review of cases from different common law jurisdictions and a weighty argument to the effect that the owner of higher land has no right to insist upon a lower neighbour receiving drainage water. This conclusion was also supported by dicta from the House of Lords to the effect that,

> '... if, in what I may term the natural user of that land, there had been any accumulation of water, either on the surface or underground, and if, by the operation of the laws of nature, that accumulation of water had passed off into the close occupied by the [claimant, he] could not have complained that the result had taken place. If he had desired to guard himself against it, it would have lain upon him to have done so, by leaving, or interposing, some barrier between his close and the close of the defendants in order to have prevented that operation of the laws of nature.'[116]

This passage seems to indicate a permissive right of a lower owner to prevent the entry of surface water, that is, that there is no duty to receive such water.

In summary, therefore, the *Home Brewery* case establishes the curious conclusion that natural rights of land drainage are not founded upon

---

[113] (1915) 84 LJPC 158.
[114] On this contrast the approach taken in *Palmer* v *Bowman* [2000] 1 All ER 22 discussed at 2.5.2 below.
[115] (1962) 108 CLR 12.
[116] Per Lord Cairns in *Rylands* v *Fletcher* (1868) LR 3 HL 330 at p.338 and see 2.5.2 below on this case. Notably, however, the issue of rights of drainage between neighbouring landowners was not directly at issue in the case.

reciprocity. The *right* of a higher landowner to drain surface water onto lower land is not matched by a corresponding *duty* upon the lower landowner to receive that water. Notwithstanding this general conclusion, the qualification needs to be emphasised that it is the *natural* drainage of land that is at issue and the same principles will not apply where certain operations have been conducted, for example, where water has been brought onto the higher land artificially.[117]

Most recently, the status of the principle established in the *Home Brewery* case has been considered in *Palmer v Bowman*,[118] where the underlying dispute was between two farmers with the owner of the higher land seeking to secure the maintenance or reinstatement of a boundary ditch which was assumed to be within the defendant's lower land.[119] Although the dispute had proceeded on the basis that the claimant had an easement[120] allowing drainage into the ditch, the abandonment of which was contested, the Court of Appeal took the view that an easement of natural drainage, in the circumstances, was factually and logically misconceived.

The drainage of rainwater from land by percolation or surface flow is a natural process that occurs without the kind of action, on the part of either party, that could give rise to an easement. Because such drainage was considered a natural incident of the ownership of higher land there was no room for argument that the right was previously established by way of an easement. In reaching this conclusion, the Court of Appeal endorsed the principle established in the *Home Brewery* case insofar as it decided that the owner of lower land has no right to complain of natural drainage, since it is nature, not the law, which imposes the burden of receiving such drainage on the lower land. However, no opinion was expressed on whether a lower owner was entitled to obstruct such drainage, as this matter was not at issue.

It is to be emphasised that the previous decisions were concerned with essentially natural drainage rights between neighbouring owners who were seeking to establish what their position would be 'but for' the activities undertaken by their neighbours. That is to be contrasted with the drainage rights that are contested between neighbours where a land use is

---

[117] See *Baird v Williamson* (1863) 15 CBNS 376, discussed at 2.5.2 below.
[118] [2000] 1 All ER 22.
[119] Although, in fact, this was doubtful in view of the subsequent reaffirmation of the 'hedge and ditch' principle by the House of Lords (that ditch is presumed to be owned by the land which it serves to drain in absence of evidence to the contrary) in *Alan Wibberley Building Ltd v Insley* [1999] 1 WLR 894 and generally see 8.3 below on highway drainage.
[120] See 2.4.6 above on easements.

regarded as, inherently, not a natural use of land. An illustration of this is to be found in *Hurdman* v *North Eastern Railway Co*[121] where rubble was placed against a boundary wall to raise the level of the railway land and this caused rainwater to percolate through the wall of a neighbouring house causing damage for which the railway company was found liable.[122] Whilst natural transmission of water might not provide grounds for liability, the direction of water onto neighbouring land by a built structure would not come within this principle.

Another possibility for liability is where water is naturally present on land and action is taken by the landowner to disperse the water in a manner which causes more harm to neighbouring land than would arise if the water level was allowed to subside naturally. This situation is illustrated by *Whalley* v *Lancashire and Yorkshire Railway Co*[123] where, after an unprecedented amount of rainfall, flood water had accumulated against the side of the defendants' railway embankment to such an extent that the embankment was in danger of being washed away. In order to protect the embankment, the defendants cut trenches across it allowing the water to flow onto the land of the claimant and this resulted in damage to his crops. Although it was found that the work was reasonably necessary to protect the embankment and not undertaken negligently, the railway company was held to be liable for damage to the claimant's crops which would not have arisen but for the action that had been taken. Despite the fact that the defendants had not brought the water onto their land, they had no right to protect their property by taking an action that actively and directly transferred the harm to the neighbouring land.

### 2.5.2 The Mining Cases

Historically, many of the situations where a nuisance action has been pursued in relation to flooding have arisen in the context of mining and related operations. Typically, one mine owner has undertaken excavations which have allowed water to be transmitted into the workings of lower mines and the question of liability of the higher mine owner to the lower owner has been at issue. Alternatively, other kinds of land use have resulted in the flooding of mineral workings for which a remedy in nuisance has been sought. Most of the leading cases on issues of this kind date from the nineteenth century, and must be recognised to have been decided in an era when the unrestrained exploitation of coal and other

---

[121] (1878) 3 CPD 168.
[122] Following *Broder* v *Saillard* (1876) 2 Ch D 692.
[123] (1884) 13 QBD 131.

## Rights Between Landowners in Nuisance

minerals was seen as of vital importance for the growth of a range of key industries and the economic prosperity which they brought.

In recent times, however, some of the legal conclusions on land drainage rights that were reached in the context of nineteenth century mining operations have been placed into question insofar as they seemed to allow such operations to take place with relatively little regard for their impact upon neighbouring landowners. It is not easy to reconcile some of the conclusions reached in the earlier cases with the greater emphasis upon good neighbourliness expressed in modern rulings such as the *Leakey*[124] decision. On the other hand, despite the general tendency to seek consistency between the operation of the law of nuisance in different contexts, the view has been expressed that special rules may apply to activities involving mineral extraction.[125] Whether the mining cases have been put in doubt by subsequent decisions and broader policy changes underlying the conception of what constitutes a 'reasonable' use of land, or whether the mining cases accurately reflect the present state of nuisance law as it operates in a specific context, remains to be seen.

A leading decision on flooding of mines is *Smith* v *Kendrick*,[126] where it was anticipated that the removal of a horizontal seam of coal from the defendant's colliery would have the effect of causing a large amount of subterranean water to flow into the adjoining colliery of the claimant which was situated at a lower level. Following the removal of the seam, it was held that the defendant was not liable for the subsequent inundation of the claimant's mine since its removal had taken place for the purpose of obtaining coal and this was a reasonable use of land which was within the defendant's rights as a mining landowner.

The broad principle enunciated was that there was no common law duty upon a mine owner to prevent water flowing into a neighbour's mine. It is for each mine owner to take measures to prevent the entry of water into his mine, if necessary by leaving coal in place as a barrier to water (which had not been done on the facts at issue). Moreover, each mine owner had the right to work his mine in the manner which was most convenient and beneficial, even though, as a consequence, some prejudice might accrue to the owner of an adjoining mine. Significantly, this principle was made subject to the proviso that it is only applicable where harm does not arise from the negligent or malicious conduct of the defendant but, on the facts

---

[124] *Leakey* v *National Trust* [1980] 1 All ER 17 and see 2.4.5 above.
[125] See Piers Ashworth QC in *Home Brewery plc* v *William Davis Ltd* [1987] 1 All ER 637 at pp.642 and 645.
[126] (1849) 7 CB 515.

of the case, there was no evidence that the defendant had done anything other than work the colliery in a customary manner.

Similarly, in *Wilson* v *Waddell*[127] the removal of coal, which had previously formed an impervious barrier, by the lessee of a coal mine enabled rainwater to percolate into the lower workings of another mine operated by the claimant. It was maintained that the defendant's working of the land had interfered with the natural condition of the surface so that water which had previously drained off the surface was now being directed through fissures in the defendant's mine and into the claimant's mine. Nonetheless, in the absence of negligence or malice, it was held that an action for the cost of pumping the water away could not be maintained.

The general approach underlying the mining cases was that one landowner should not, by reasonably altering the condition of his land, deprive the owner of adjoining land of the privilege of using his own land as he might otherwise have done. This principle operates equally where the effect of mining operations is to deprive a landowner of water. Hence, in *Acton* v *Blundell*[128] one landowner who had dug a well on his land could not maintain an action against another landowner who had dug a coal-pit in the neighbourhood which had the effect of drawing water away from the well. Again, the mining operation had been conducted in a proper and reasonable manner for exploiting coal and had not been undertaken negligently, or motivated by malice. Similar conclusions have been reached in situations where the reasonable improvement of agricultural land has resulted in lower owners being deprived of a supply of water, where it has been held that they are not to be entitled to the continuation of the supply in the absence of riparian, prescriptive or other rights to receive it.[129]

By contrast, there are a range of situations where mine owners have been held liable for flooding damage where the effect of their activities is to cause a greater quantity of water to flow into neighbouring mines than would naturally gravitate there. A clear example is *Baird* v *Williamson*[130] where liability was established following the flooding of the claimant's mine after water in the defendant's adjoining mine had been raised by pumping to a level where it could flow from the defendant's mine to the mine of the claimant through a drainage channel. Whilst it was accepted that water which flowed naturally into the claimant's mine would give no grounds for action, the fact that the water was being actively directed into the mine by the defendant placed this situation in a different category.

---

[127] (1876) 2 App Cas 95.
[128] (1843) 13 LJ Ex 289.
[129] *Greatrex* v *Hayward* (1853) 8 Ex 291 and *Bartlett* v *Tottenham* [1932] 1 Ch 114.
[130] (1863) CBNS 376 and see also *Firmstone* v *Wheeley* (1844) 2 Dow & L 203.

A more extreme situation arose in *Crompton v Lea*[131] where the defendants had commenced work on a new seam in a mine which was only a matter of feet below the bed of a watercourse that flowed on the surface. The claimants, who operated a nearby mine, maintained that the effect of the works, if continued, would be that the river would 'inevitably' break into the defendants' mine and flow into the claimants' mine. Notwithstanding the generally wide remit given to mine operators to work their mines in any reasonable and proper manner, it was thought that the operations which were envisaged did not have any reasonable object and an injunction was granted to restrain the continuation of the works.

Perhaps the most celebrated example of a situation where liability for flooding of a mine has been at issue is *Rylands v Fletcher*.[132] Here the defendant owners of a mill contracted with engineers to construct a reservoir but, unknown to anyone, disused mine shafts lay beneath the reservoir so that when the reservoir was filled with water it burst through the shafts and passed into the claimant's mine. Although the contractors should have identified the old mine shafts, the defendant had not been negligent in any respect. Notably, the Court of Exchequer Chamber found for the claimant on the basis of the principle that,

> '[t]he person who, for his own purposes, brings on his land, and collects and keeps there anything likely to do mischief if it escapes, must keep it at his peril, and, if he does not do so, he is *prima facie* answerable for all the damage which is the natural consequence of the escape.'[133]

That principle, and the liability of the defendant, was affirmed in the House of Lords where it was observed,

> '... if the defendants, not stopping at the natural use of their close, had desired to use it for any purpose which I may term a non-natural use, for the purpose of introducing into the close that which in its natural condition was not in or upon it, for the purpose of introducing water either above or below ground in quantities and in a manner not the result of any work or operation on or under the land, so the water came to escape and to pass off into the close of the [claimant], then it appears to me that that which the defendants were doing they were doing at their own peril; and ... the defendants would be liable.'[134]

---

[131] (1874) LR 19 Eq 115. See also *Fletcher v Smith* (1877) 2 App Cas 781 where liability for flooding was established after a natural stream was replaced by an artificial channel which was more likely to overflow.
[132] (1866) LR 1 Exch 265, affirmed (1868) Law Rep 3 HL 330.
[133] Per Blackburn J quoted (1868) Law Rep 3 HL 330 at p.340.
[134] Per Lord Cairns (1868) Law Rep 3 HL 330 at pp.338 to 339.

The so-called 'rule in *Rylands* v *Fletcher*' that was thereby established has been extensively considered in a wide range of contexts in which liability for dangerous activities has been at issue. Generally, it has been thought to illustrate the exceptional operation of strict civil liability in contexts where 'non-natural' use is made of land and escape of hazardous things takes place from the land. Notably though, there have been many other cases where the scope of 'non-natural' use of land has been restrictively construed. For example, liability was not established under the rule for an escape of water from a domestic supply system the installation of which was regarded as a natural use of a residential property.[135] In another case, gravel workings, which caused water to be blown onto the claimant's land causing erosion, did not amount to a non-natural use of the land.[136]

However, the most recent authoritative consideration of the rule in *Rylands* v *Fletcher* has tended to assimilate it to the general law of nuisance. Hence in *Cambridge Water Company Ltd* v *Eastern Counties Leather*[137] it was suggested that the rule should not be regarded as establishing any stricter liability than was otherwise provided for in the law of nuisance. In particular, emphasis was placed upon the need for reasonable foreseeability of harm of the kind that actually arose. Given the reluctance of the courts to apply the rule with the full rigour that it seems to imply, it is debatable whether a defendant would be found liable under the same principle if the facts of *Rylands* v *Fletcher* were to arise today.[138]

In *Ellison and Others* v *Ministry of Defence*,[139] for example, a claim of liability for flooding from nearby land following an exceptional amount of rain was, in part, based upon the rule in *Rylands* v *Fletcher*. It was established that the defendant's use of land involved works that resulted in the accumulation of water and the redirection of the water towards the claimants' properties, and this had largely caused the flood damage. However, the rule was applicable only to things 'collected' on land and involving a 'non-natural' use of the land. On the facts, the water that had accumulated naturally could not be shown to have any special causative

---

[135] *Rickards* v *Lothian* [1913] AC 263. Similarly see *British Gas plc* v *Stockport Metropolitan Borough Council* [2001] Env LR 763 where the passage of water through a service pipe to a block of flats was found to be necessary for the common and ordinary use and occupation of residential properties and not a 'non-natural' use of land and see 7.12 below on liability for flooding from water supply systems.
[136] *Rouse* v *Gravelworks Ltd* [1940] 1 KB 489.
[137] [1994] 1 All ER 53.
[138] Contrast the outcomes in *Nichols* v *Marsland* (1875) LR 10 Exch 255 (see 2.5.3 below); *Nield* v *London & NW Rly Co* (1874) LR 10 Ex 4 (see 2.4.2 above); and *Box* v *Jubb* (1879) 3 Ex D 76.
[139] (1996) 81 Build LR 101 (Queen's Bench Division) and see also unreported, Court of Appeal, 18 July 1996 and see discussion at 2.5 above.

# Rights Between Landowners in Nuisance 71

significance when compared with the overall amount of water generated by the storm. Moreover, the works that had been undertaken by the defendant, involving the construction of a fuel storage area, were categorised as an ordinary use of the land which did not carry any special danger of the kind that was envisaged by the rule. Clearly, the application of strict liability to situations where flooding is involved will be narrowly confined.

## 2.5.3 The Culverting Cases

A large number of the cases that have come before the courts in more recent times have arisen in situations where the culverting of a watercourse has taken place and, for various reasons, it has been alleged that the culvert has caused, or contributed to, flooding. The statutory provisions dealing with culverting and environmental concerns to which culverts give rise are discussed elsewhere,[140] and the present account is limited to the issue of civil liability of the owner of a culvert which gives rise to flooding.

The fundamental principles governing liability for culverts are well established by *Greenock Corporation* v *Caledonian Railway Co*[141] where the defendant municipal authority had undertaken works in a park involving the filling in of the natural channel of a stream and the substitution of a culvert for the channel. Owing to rainfall of extraordinary severity the stream overflowed and water, which would previously have been contained within the banks of the natural stream, poured down a public street to the premises of the claimants causing the demolition of a wall due to the pressure of water which had accumulated behind it. The defendants were found liable for this damage on the basis that it is the duty of anyone who interferes with the course of a stream to ensure that any works which are substituted for the natural channel are adequate to carry off water which is brought down, even where this is the result of extraordinary rainfall. Hence, where flooding results from the lesser capacity of a culvert that is substituted for a natural channel, liability will normally be established.[142]

The strictness of the *Greenock* ruling must be emphasised. Guidance was taken from *Kerr* v *Earl of Orkney*, where liability had been established for flooding following the collapse of a dam, constructed in a natural stream, after heavy rainfall. Here it was observed,

'[the] general principle . . . is – that if a person chooses upon a stream

---

[140] See 4.4.3 below and 8.2.4 below on culverting.
[141] [1917] AC 556 and similarly see *Hanley* v *Edinburgh Corporation* [1913] AC 488.
[142] Essentially the same reasoning has been applied to establish liability for flooding after a natural stream was replaced by an artificial channel (rather than a culvert) which was more likely to overflow: see *Fletcher* v *Smith* (1877) 2 App Cas 781.

to make a great operation for collecting and damming up the water for whatever purpose, he is bound, as the necessary condition of such an operation, to accomplish his object in such a way as to protect all persons lower down the stream from all danger: he must secure them against danger. It is not sufficient that he took all the pains which were thought at the time necessary and sufficient. . . . He creates the danger, and he must secure them against danger, so as to make them as safe notwithstanding his dam as they were before. It is no defence in such a case to allege the dam would have stood against all ordinary rains – –it gave way in an extraordinary and unprecedented fall of rain, which could not be expected. The dam must be made perfect against all extraordinary falls of rain – else the protection is not afforded against the operation which the party must accomplish.'[143]

Similarly, in the circumstances of the Greenock culvert, the extraordinary violence of the rainfall did not provide any defence in circumstances where it was established that the previous course of the natural stream would have been sufficient to have contained the amount of water involved.

Despite the apparently strict and unqualified character of the general principle that was established, the *Greenock* case is also instructive in indicating the extreme rainfall conditions which might allow a party to be absolved from liability. Specifically, the defendants had raised the argument that the amount of rain that had fallen was so exceptional and unprecedented that it constituted a *damnum fatale*, equivalent to what is known as an 'act of God' or *vis major* in English Law. The meaning of this expression had been authoritatively considered in an earlier case where it was summarised as,

> 'one of those things which do not involve any legal liability . . . circumstances which no human foresight can provide against, and of which human prudence is not bound to recognise the possibility, and which when they do occur, therefore, are calamities which do not involve the obligation of paying for the consequences that may result from them'.[144]

The scope for application of this defence had been shown by the decision

---

[143] (1857) 20 D 298 at p.302, per Lord Justice-Clerk Hope. Contrast the emphasis now placed upon *foreseeability* as a basis for liability in nuisance and see *Cambridge Water Company Ltd v Eastern Counties Leather* [1994] 1 All ER 53, discussed at 2.5.2 above.

[144] *Tennent v Earl of Glasgow* (1864) 2 M (HL) 22, per Lord Westbury at pp.26 to 27. The same idea has been expressed as the principle that a person 'is bound to provide against the ordinary operations of nature, but not against her miracles': per Lord Cockburn in *Samuel v Edinburgh and Glasgow Railway Co* (1850) 13 D 312 at p.314.

in *Nichols v Marsland*,[145] where an escape of water from a reservoir was found, as a matter of fact established to the satisfaction of a jury, to have been caused by an act of God which could not reasonably have been anticipated or prevented. Doubts were subsequently expressed as to whether this finding of fact was correct,[146] but the case was decided on the basis that it was correct. The defendant was, therefore, found not to be liable for damage to bridges in a lower watercourse that were destroyed as a consequence of the surge of water resulting from the collapse of the reservoir embankment.

In the circumstances of the *Greenock* case, however, with particular note being taken of the climate of Scotland, it was found that the municipal council had entirely failed to establish any defence on the ground of act of God. Notwithstanding that the rainfall had been of extraordinary severity, floods of this kind must be anticipated to take place from time to time and it was the duty of anyone interfering with the natural channel of a watercourse to substitute a channel that was adequate to cope with extraordinary rainfall. On the facts, therefore, the damage that had occurred was not a *damnum fatale*, or act of God, but rather the direct result of obstruction of the natural watercourse for which the council was wholly responsible.

Another possible defence to the strict obligation to ensure that a culvert is of sufficient capacity to accommodate the natural flow of a watercourse is the possibility that the person installing a culvert is acting under statutory authority to do so and this may prevent liability arising.[147] *Provender Millers (Winchester) Ltd v Southampton County Council*[148] concerned a situation where a highway authority had installed a new culvert in a stream to give additional support to a highway that passed over the stream and to prevent the highway flooding. The result of this was to reduce the flow of the stream which passed to the claimants who were the owners of a downstream water mill. Although the general rights of riparian owners to the natural flow of a watercourse were not in dispute, the central issue was whether the fact that defendants had constructed the culvert in pursuance of their statutory duties provided a defence. On this, it was concluded that, unless it was practically not feasible to perform statutory duties in any

---

[145] (1875) 10 Exch 255 and (1876) 2 Ex D 1. Contrast *Nitro-Phosphate and Odam's Chemical Manure Co v London and St Katherine Docks Co* (1878) 9 Ch D 503 and see 4.9 below on this case. Also contrast *Greenwood Tileries Ltd v Clapson* [1937] 1 All ER 765.

[146] See Lord Parker of Waddington in *Greenock Corporation v Caledonian Railway Co* [1917] AC 556 at p.581.

[147] See 2.9 below on civil liability of statutory bodies.

[148] [1940] Ch 131.

other way, a statutory body undertaking works in a watercourse should not be entitled to invade the riparian rights of others. Moreover, the onus of showing that statutory duties could not be performed in any manner less damaging to riparian owners fell upon the highway authority and, on the facts, the defendants were unable to show that this was the case. Hence, although the possibility of a defence of statutory authority was not completely ruled out, there may be difficulties in showing that there was no way of exercising a statutory responsibility which produced less interference with riparian rights. Although the facts of the case arose from a deficiency, rather than an excess, of water passing to a lower riparian owner, it is thought that the same principle would apply where statutory authority is claimed as a defence to a complaint that works in a watercourse have caused flooding.[149]

The reasoning in the *Greenock* case has been reapplied and extended in several subsequent cases. *Pemberton* v *Bright*[150] illustrates that the obligations upon a person who installs a culvert are not only to ensure that it is designed and constructed to accommodate the flow as effectively as the natural channel, but also to ensure that the culvert is continuously *maintained* to ensure that it operates as effectively as the natural channel. The facts were that the claimants were owners of property by the side of a road, and below the level of the road, alongside which there ran a stream. At a point where the stream passed under a road the county council, as the highway authority, had installed a culvert but had not installed a grid at the upstream end of the culvert to prevent it becoming obstructed by debris. From time to time the entrance to the culvert was cleaned by council employees; however, after extremely heavy rainfall, the culvert became obstructed by branches of trees and other debris. As a consequence, the stream flowed over the road and into the claimants' property causing damage. It was held that the county council were liable in damages because the failure to install a grid amounted to a *potential* nuisance which became an *actual* nuisance when the culvert became obstructed and caused the water to be diverted onto the claimants' land. Damages were apportioned between the council (75%) and the owner of the land on which the upstream end of the culvert was located (25%) on the basis that they were found to have continued the nuisance.

The implications of continuing a nuisance, as opposed to being responsible for its original creation, are most authoritatively illustrated by *Sedleigh-*

---

[149] Hence, the application of the *Provender Millers* ruling was considered in *Bybrook Barn Garden Centre Ltd* v *Kent County Council* [2001] Env LR 543.
[150] [1960] 1 All ER 792.

*Denfield* v *O'Callaghan*[151] where the county council had placed a culvert in a ditch on the defendant's land and covered the top of it with earth. To prevent the possibility of debris obstructing the entrance to the pipe, expert evidence was accepted that proper practice would have been to fix a grid or grating in the ditch a short distance above the entrance to the pipe to intercept debris.[152] The grid that had actually been fixed was placed directly over the opening and this allowed it to become choked with leaves with the result that the flow of water was obstructed and it overflowed onto the claimant's adjoining premises causing damage. A peculiar aspect of the facts was that the pipe had been installed by the county council without the permission or knowledge of the defendant, apparently due to a misunderstanding, so that the original installation amounted to a trespass upon the defendant's land. Nonetheless, for 3 years, the pipe was used to drain the land and the defendant's employees periodically undertook the clearing of accumulated debris from the grid. Hence, the legal issue was whether the defendant could be responsible for a nuisance which he had not created but had known about, or had to be deemed to know about, and where he had 'continued' or 'adopted' the nuisance. Despite some indications that establishing nuisance in these circumstances required it to be shown that there was a positive act causing obstruction of the flow by a defendant,[153] it was held that the defendant was liable because he had 'continued' the nuisance (in the sense of knowing about it, or being presumed to know about it, and failing to take reasonable means to bring it to an end when there was ample time to do so) and had 'adopted' it (in the sense of actually making use of the structure which constituted the nuisance). The broader significance of this ruling is to emphasise that liability for nuisance may arise through the *passive* conduct of the defendant, and that failure to address a potential flooding hazard arising from an unsatisfactory conduit is, potentially, a basis upon which such liability may be established.

The most recent decision in which liability for flooding originating from a culvert has been at issue is *Bybrook Barn Garden Centre Ltd* v *Kent County Council*.[154] Here, the defendant highway authority maintained that

---

[151] [1940] AC 880.

[152] For further discussion of screening requirements see *AF plc* v *Tyndale District Council*, unreported, Queen's Bench Division, 13 April 2000.

[153] See *Saxby* v *Manchester, Sheffield and Lincolnshire Railway Co* (1869) LR 4 CP 198, though adverse comment was made on the clarity of this decision.

[154] [2001] Env LR 543 and see W. Howarth, 'Living with Flooding: nuisance liability and cost allocation' [2001] *Environmental Law Review* 282, and see 2.9 below on other aspects of this case. See also *Potter and Others* v *Mole Valley District Council and Another* (1982) *The Times* 22 October, where it was held that a highway authority was liable for flooding caused by an inadequate culvert. Contrast *AF plc* v *Tyndale District Council*, unreported, Queen's Bench Division, 13 April 2000.

a conduit, which had been put in place some years previously to take the natural flow of water from a ditch passing under a road, had originally been adequate for that purpose. However, because of run off from subsequent road and business park developments in the upper catchment, for which the highway authority was not responsible, the pipe had become inadequate to take the increased flow. A key question, therefore, was the extent to which a culvert could become an actionable nuisance due to contributory factors outside the defendant's control.

Despite previous authorities indicating that liability for nuisance would not arise through factors for which the defendant was not responsible,[155] the Court of Appeal applied the progression of conduit cases previously discussed, to reach the conclusion that the defendant was liable for the nuisance that had arisen. At least from the time when the highway authority became aware, or should have become aware,[156] that the culvert was not adequate to take the amount of water that was now coming down the ditch, it became subject to a duty to abate the nuisance and to prevent flooding. Following *Leakey* v *National Trust*, this was a duty upon the defendant to do what is reasonable having regard, amongst other things, to the expenditure that was needed to address the hazard and the capacity of the defendant to meet that expenditure.[157]

The far-reaching ruling to apply nuisance to situations where the substantial problem lay outside the defendant's control may be regarded as a broad-based policy decision consistent with a trend towards increasing the scope for landowners to be held liable for 'unreasonable' land use which is detrimental to neighbouring land owners. However, there were particular factors about the *Bybrook* case which inclined the Court towards establishing this kind of liability. Specifically, the fact that the culvert was under the control of the defendant gave rise to a 'high obligation' to see that the natural stream continued to flow under the highway and a corresponding duty towards private landowners suffering damage through its inadequacy. Moreover, since the culvert could have been replaced without great difficulty, and without excessive cost to the defendant in relation to the cost of the flooding damage that was likely to be suffered by the claimant, the justification for not taking this action was weak. Additionally, the highway

---

[155] *Radstock Co-operative and Industrial Society* v *Norton-Radstock Urban District Council* [1968] Ch 605 where no liability was established for a sewer which flowed under a watercourse, and contributed to erosion of the claimant's land, where the flow of the watercourse had increased for reasons beyond the control of the defendant.

[156] Following the emphasis placed upon the foreseeability requirement in nuisance emphasised in *Cambridge Water Company Ltd* v *Eastern Counties Leather* [1994] 1 All ER 53 and see 2.5 above.

[157] Per Megaw LJ [1980] 1 All ER 17 at p.37, discussed at 2.4.5 above.

authority would have been placed under a statutory obligation to undertake the necessary work, at its own cost, if an appropriate notice had been served upon it requiring this to be done.[158]

## 2.6 RIGHTS OF SUPPORT

The removal of water from an area of land, either by land drainage or abstraction activities, is capable of having significant effects upon the soil and groundwater characteristics of the area. A number of cases have arisen where the effect of water removal has been to reduce the groundwater support afforded to the foundations of properties, resulting in subsidence. The legal issue arising in situations of this kind is whether damage to property arising from withdrawal of groundwater support is actionable against the person who is responsible for the subsidence due to the removal of the water. Analogous issues might also arise through the converse problem, where an excess of water, generated by land drainage activities, has accumulated around the foundations of a building and has given rise to subsidence. However, there appear to be no decided cases where this aspect of the problem has been specifically at issue.

The general position with regard to surface or groundwater in undefined channels[159] has been outlined previously: in that no riparian rights arise in respect of such water and a landowner may use the water without restriction.[160] Moreover, it has been held that the owner of land under which groundwater percolates has the right to appropriate or divert the water for any use. In so doing, motive is irrelevant and it does not matter that removal of water is motivated by malice.[161] As a consequence of this, an owner of lower land who is disadvantaged through removal of a supply of groundwater will have no remedy against the person who is responsible for the removal.[162]

The position with regard to the removal of groundwater that supports buildings is, therefore, legally curious. It is clear that adjacent landowners owe each other a general right of support, so that liability will arise if one

---

[158] Under s.25 Land Drainage Act 1991, and see 4.7.1 below on this. See also the discussion of *Peter Marcic* v *Thames Water Utilities Ltd* [2002] EWCA 65, 7 February 2002, at 7.9 below, where the *Leakey* principle was applied to a nuisance arising from a sewer flooding.

[159] See *Bleachers' Association* v *Chapel-en-le-Frith Rural District Council* [1933] Ch 356 on the evidential difficulties in establishing that underground water flows in a defined channel.

[160] *Chasemore* v *Richards* (1859) 7 HL Cas 349 and see 2.2 above.

[161] *Bradford Corporation* v *Pickles* [1895] AC 587.

[162] *Popplewell* v *Hodkinson* (1869) LR 4 Exch 248.

landowner removes soil causing the collapse of a neighbour's property.[163] Hence, liability arose in one instance where subjacent support was removed by causing rock salt to liquefy and then removing it[164] and in another case where a bed of wet sand or running silt was removed.[165] However, support by water is placed in a different legal category from support by soil and other minerals. The effect of the legal characterisation of water which percolates through soil, or otherwise flows in an undefined channel, is such that no claim to a right to support from such water has been legally recognised.

The 'artificial and illogical'[166] distinction that has been drawn between groundwater and other substances which provide support to properties has been contested, without success, on various grounds. In *Langbrook Properties Ltd v Surrey County Council*[167] the claimants were property developers who were engaged in developing a site. Nearby, the local highway authority was engaged in road construction works that necessitated the diversion of an aqueduct and the repositioning of water mains. The excavations for these works, which went below the water table, were kept dry by pumping water away. The effect of the removal of the water was to cause settlement of the neighbouring land and subsidence of the claimants' buildings, for which they claimed damages in both nuisance and negligence. Following previous authorities, it was held that no liability of this kind could arise in nuisance. In respect of negligence, it was held that the position was the same, since, if it was not actionable to cause damage by the abstraction of underground water maliciously (in nuisance) it would be illogical if an action was possible where the abstraction was merely done carelessly (in negligence).

A later attempt to impose liability for property damage due to subsidence resulting from the removal of groundwater arose in *Stephens v Anglian Water Authority*.[168] Here the defendant water authority abstracted percolating water under land close to the claimant's house in such volume that the land subsided causing damage to the house. It was alleged that the defendants had been negligent in undertaking the water abstraction despite warnings of the likely effect of this upon neighbouring properties. Notably, the action was framed in negligence, rather than nuisance, since it was claimed that the defendants owed a duty of care to the claimant and had failed to

---

[163] See 2.7 below on the *Holbeck Hall Hotel v Scarborough Borough Council* [2000] 2 All ER 705 and rights of support.
[164] *Lotus Ltd v British Soda Co Ltd* [1972] Ch 123.
[165] *Jordeson v Sutton Southcoates and Drypool Gas Co* [1899] 2 Ch 217.
[166] Per Slade LJ in *Stephens v Anglian Water Authority* [1987] 3 All ER 379 at p.383.
[167] [1970] 1 WLR 161.
[168] [1987] 3 All ER 379.

adhere to that duty. It was reaffirmed that a landowner is entitled to abstract subterranean water flowing in undefined channels, regardless of the consequences to neighbouring land and irrespective of motive in so doing. Hence, the position in negligence was no different to that in nuisance, in that no duty to neighbouring landowners for consequent damage arose as a consequence of the allegedly negligent abstraction activities.

The absence of common law rights in subterranean water is remarkable in allowing conduct that is directly contradictory to the general principle of good neighbourliness insofar as, in an extreme case, a landowner may purposefully and maliciously deprive a neighbour of a water supply. Beyond that, the possibility of uncompensatable damage being caused to property, due to water removal and consequent loss of groundwater support, seems difficult to reconcile with the general principles that apply in finding liability in nuisance or negligence. Whether the decided cases need to be reviewed in the light of subsequent emphasis upon the foreseeability of damage, as a general basis for liability in nuisance,[169] remains to be seen.

On the other hand, the conclusions which have been reached on the absence of liability for the removal of groundwater are consistent with the conception of groundwater being unowned public property which is available for use by any person with the capacity to exploit it. From the point of view of a person who is seeking to abstract groundwater, or to conduct drainage activities that may involve the diversion of groundwater from neighbouring land, the absence of this kind of liability may be seen as advantageous. Whether the exercise of private rights to improve the 'efficiency' of land drainage is conducive to sustainable development in drainage is a different matter, and the broader implications of particular drainage activities of this kind are considered later in this work.[170]

## 2.7 LAND EROSION

One potential effect of flooding is the erosion of land, particularly where water is periodically forced over land by pressure of gravity, winds or tidal movements. Indeed, in many of the cases on riparian rights previously considered, the prospect of damage to land by erosion is likely to have been a significant consideration.[171] However, outside the sphere of riparian rights, there are some situations where erosion has been the central aspect of civil litigation.

---

[169] See *Cambridge Water Company* v *Eastern Counties Leather* [1994] 1 All ER 53 and see discussion at 2.5 above.
[170] See Ch.12 below on sustainability.
[171] See *Menzies* v *Earl of Breadalbane* (1828) 3 Bli NS 414, discussed at 2.4.2 above.

A good example of the problem of erosion is to be seen in *Rouse* v *Gravelworks Ltd*[172] where the defendants conducted gravel excavation operations with the result that the area from which the gravel had been removed eventually filled with water. The neighbouring claimant's field lost support as a result of the excavations and his land was further eroded as a result of the action of water and wind so that he was prevented from making profitable use of part of the field. It was held that extraction of gravel was a reasonable use of the defendants' land and the effects upon the claimant's field were not caused by the action of the defendants, but by the natural action of water and wind, over which the defendants had no control.

Although the facts of this case provide a useful illustration of the problem of erosion, it is rather doubtful whether the same legal outcome would be reached today. Indeed, the validity of the decision has been expressly doubted in the *Leakey* case,[173] where it was established that liability in nuisance could arise in situations where naturally arising states of land were the subject of complaint.[174] Clearly the supposition that there is no liability for damage to land arising by natural agency had been greatly diminished by the *Leakey* principle, though important issues remain as to the extent of the 'measured' duty of care upon a landowner to address potential natural hazards and the reasonable foreseeability of harm from such hazards.

These matters have recently been considered in the context of coastal erosion in the decision in *Holbeck Hall Hotel* v *Scarborough Borough Council*.[175] The dramatic circumstances of the case were that the land on which the claimant's hotel had been located suffered a massive landslip resulting in the collapse of the soil under the seaward wing of the building and requiring its eventual demolition. The defendant was the owner of land that had previously been between the hotel grounds and the sea and it was contended, following the *Leakey* principle, that it was subject to a duty to maintain the seaward land and to provide support for the claimant's land.

Although it was accepted that the *Leakey* principle was generally applicable

---

[172] [1940] 1 KB 489.
[173] Per Megaw LJ in *Leakey* v *National Trust* [1980] 1 All ER 17 at p.33 and see discussion at 2.4.5 above.
[174] Specifically, the *Rouse* case was thought to be irreconcilable with *Davey* v *Harrow Corporation* [1958] 1 QB 60 where liability was established for the encroachment onto neighbouring land of roots and branches of trees, causing damage, and it was affirmed that no distinction should be drawn between trees that were self-sown and trees that had been deliberately planted.
[175] [2000] 2 All ER 705 and see J. Wightman, 'Liability for Landslips: Should Landowners be Responsible for the Consequences of Erosion?' [2000] *Environmental Law Review* 285.

to the circumstances where rights of support were at issue, the Court declined to find the defendant liable for the damage that had arisen. In particular, the 'measured' duty of care that the principle envisaged would only arise where the hazard to the claimant's land was known, or should have been known, or was reasonably foreseeable by the defendant. The difficulty, on the facts, was that, although the defendant appreciated the possibility of a minor land slip occurring, it could not have anticipated a catastrophic event of the magnitude that actually occurred. It would not have been possible to have identified the full gravity of the hazard without extensive geological investigations which went beyond an initial study that had been undertaken on behalf of the defendant. Moreover, as it transpired, the latent geological fault that gave rise to the slip had actually extended beyond the defendant's land to the land of the claimant, though the claimant had no more knowledge of this than the defendant. In all the circumstances, it was concluded that it would not be reasonable to impose liability for damage which was greater in extent than any eventuality that was reasonably foreseeable, or foreseeable only after extensive geological investigations, especially where the danger existed as much on the claimant's land as that of the defendant.

Although the facts of the *Holbeck Hall* case are far from typical, in that coastal erosion is usually of a more gradual character, it does clearly establish that the general responsibilities for preventing erosion of neighbouring land are much more extensive than indicated by the previous state of the law. Coastal erosion, in particular, is a significant problem in many vulnerable areas and difficult legal issues need to be confronted. A problem, in both private and public law, is likely to be the difficulty of reconciling costs and benefits with regard to the issue of reasonableness. Specifically, in what circumstances will potentially massive expenditure by coastal and waterside landowners be required to prevent erosion and encroachment for the sake of preserving neighbouring land? Alternatively, it might be asked, in what circumstances is it more environmentally rational to accept the 'managed retreat' of the coastline or alongside watercourses in those locations where land can only be preserved at disproportionate expense?[176]

## 2.8 NUISANCE AND NEGLIGENCE

As it has recently been observed, 'the situations in which liability for nuisance has been established vary enormously. and it is not always easy to reconcile the reasoning as to why liability has been found to exist in one situation but not in another'. Moreover, 'the tort of nuisance, uncertain in

---

[176] See the discussion of 'managed retreat' of the coastline at 12.6 below.

its boundary, may comprise a wide variety of situations, in some of which negligence plays no part, in others of which it is decisive'.[177] However, the common feature of nuisance is that of an interference with the claimant's land arising from something emanating from the defendant's land.

In most of the situations where liability for flooding is at issue, the key characteristic of nuisance, that it concerns rights and duties between landowners, is unproblematic. Insofar as the claimant seeks to establish that wrongful land use by a neighbour is the cause of flooding, nuisance is clearly appropriate. However, there are situations where nuisance is not readily available because the flooding is alleged to arise because of some action undertaken on land by a person other than its owner. Characteristically, works undertaken by flood and coast defence operating authorities on land which is not within their ownership may fall within that category. More broadly, any action taken by a person who is not a landowner which causes flooding of land of another would be more appropriately considered in an action in negligence than in nuisance. Similarly, where personal injury arising from a failure to maintain or warn of the danger of a flood or coastal defence structure is at issue, an action in negligence would be more appropriate.[178]

In the most general terms, negligence arises where there has been a breach of the duty to 'take reasonable care to avoid acts or omissions which you can reasonably foresee would be likely to injure your neighbour'.[179] The potential extent of this form of liability is of considerable breadth and generality so that, as it has been put, 'the categories of negligence are never closed'.[180] Nonetheless, courts have tended to determine liability for negligence in accordance with three elements: first, a requirement upon the defendant to exercise care where it is reasonably foreseeable that failure to do so will cause consequent damage to the claimant; second, a need for sufficient proximity between the parties; and, third, the situation must be one in which the court considers it 'fair, just and reasonable' that a duty should be imposed and there is no ground of public policy[181] for excluding

---

[177] *Bybrook Barn Garden Centre* v *Kent County Council* [2001] Env LR 543, per Waller LJ at p.550 in part quoting Lord Wilberforce in *Goldman* v *Hargrave* [1967] AC 645 at p.657.
[178] See 11.4.3 below on occupiers' liability.
[179] *Donoghue* v *Stevenson* [1932] AC 562, per Lord Atkin at p.580.
[180] *Donoghue* v *Stevenson* [1932] AC 562, per Lord Macmillan at p.619. However, courts will be guided by previous cases in which liability has been established, and the reasonableness or otherwise of imposing a duty between the parties: see *Caparo Industries plc* v *Dickman and Others* [1990] 1 All ER 568.
[181] On public policy generally see *Barret* v *London Borough of Enfield* [1999] 3 All ER 193 and contrast the more restrictive approach in *X* v *Bedfordshire County Council* [1995] 2 AC 633.

## Nuisance and Negligence

such a duty.[182] Hence, in relation to flooding, liability in negligence generally depends upon the claimant showing that the proximity between the parties is such that the defendant owes a duty of care to avoid this, that the harm which has been suffered is a reasonably foreseeable consequence of the defendant's act. Alternatively, negligence is commonly characterised as a failure to adhere to the standard of conduct of a 'reasonable person'.[183]

Because many of the situations involving flooding which might otherwise be categorised as negligence fall within statutory compensation provisions, at least so far as the activities of flood and coastal defence operating authorities are concerned, there are relatively few cases on flooding where negligence has been argued.[184] However, there are some situations where private bodies or individuals are placed under a duty to take positive actions to prevent damage from a known flooding hazard of which they are not the owner. In situations of this kind, the contested issue is whether sufficient steps have been taken to *prevent* flooding,[185] rather than the question of whether the defendant's use of land has *caused* flooding, and these are appropriately considered under negligence.

A good example of the scope of liability in negligence for inadequate measures to prevent flooding is to be seen in *Adcock and Others* v *Norfolk Line Ltd and Others*,[186] which concerned liability for serious flooding damage following an exceptionally high tide which resulted in the inundation of a substantial area of low-lying land occupied by some 74 houses and 20 business premises, and with resulting damage amounting to about £1 million. The flooding was found to be due to the breaching of a temporary sandbag wall that had been placed on a wharf to maintain sea defences until permanent works were completed. Liability for damage caused through the collapse of the sandbag wall was established against the lessees of the wharf, the main contractor undertaking the work, sub-contractors of the

---

[182] Generally see M. Brazier and J. Murphy, *Street on Torts* (17th ed. 1999) pp.97 to 98 and Ch.5 generally.
[183] Per Alderson B in *Blythe* v *Birmingham Waterworks Co* (1856) 11 Exch 781 at p.784.
[184] Contrast the application of negligence to situations where flooding originates from water supply pipes, discussed at 7.12 below and see 4.3.2 below on statutory compensation for flood defence operations.
[185] On the issue of whether a public liability insurance policy requires an indemnity to be paid where preventative operations have been undertaken, as opposed to the payment of an indemnity where flood damage has actually occurred, see *Yorkshire Water Services Ltd* v *Sun Alliance & London Insurance plc and Others* [1997] 2 Lloyd's Rep 21.
[186] Unreported, Court of Appeal (Civil Division) 28 May 1993. Similarly see *Kingsway Furniture (Dartford) Ltd* v *Harpglow Ltd and Kylefield Ltd* (1990) unreported but noted [1991] *Water Law* 10, where liability in negligence was established after the defendants removed a flood defence wall without providing an alternative means of protection.

main contractor and the regional water authority (which admitted liability in relation to the exercise of its statutory powers). However, an appeal by the subcontractors contested the apportionment of liability which had been determined between the four defendants.[187]

The assessment of the relative responsibilities of the different defendants for the inadequate sandbag wall involved an intricate analysis of the reasons for its failure. These had been identified as fivefold:

(1) the failure to specify an adequate height;

(2) the failure to build to the (inadequate) height which had been specified;

(3) the use of inappropriate and over-filled sandbags;

(4) the failure to bond or compact the bags and the generally haphazard construction of the wall; and

(5) the failure to correct the previous failings by direction, inspection or maintenance.

In respect of the design, it was found that the water authority and the main contractor were responsible for the negligent design, first, by a failure to require sandbags of a suitable size to be used and, second, through a failure to specify an adequate height for the wall. The authority had specified that the wall should be the same height as that of adjacent flood defences (2.74 m above the mean sea level or 'ordnance datum'). However, the authority had not made clear to the subcontractors that the effective height of a sandbag wall was the height of the dips between the top bags and not their crests, and a 'freeboard' allowance of 0.3 m on top of the wall had not been required. Had the wall been properly constructed, to an effective height of 2.74 m above ordnance datum, it was found that it would 'very likely' have withstood the tide.

Despite the inadequate height which had been specified by the water authority, the subcontractors had actually built a wall to an effective height of only 2.5 m above ordnance datum, with the result that there had been a displacement of the top layer of bags followed by the lower bags. On the kind of sandbags used, it was found that the subcontractors had used plastic builders' bags which the senior technician for the water authority had rejected in advising that hessian bags should be used, preferably of a standard size (and these could be supplied by the authority). The subcontractors disregarded this advice and used bags that were eight times

---

[187] Under ss.1(1) and 2(1) Civil Liability (Contribution) Act 1978.

larger than standard bags. It was found that the weight of the larger bags made them difficult to manoeuvre into position, and left interstices where they were over-filled or inadequately compacted, and their use was negligent. Similarly, inadequate construction of the wall resulted from the bags being unevenly or 'haphazardly' laid and bonded together.

In respect of failure to observe or correct faults, it was found that all four defendants were to some degree responsible. The lessees of the wharf failed to check the adequacy and integrity of the wall and whether it was of sufficient height. The failings of the wall also reflected a failure on the part of the main contractors to check the work of their subcontractors. The water authority was also in breach of an inspection duty when it 'passed' the wall during construction and on two subsequent inspections.

Taking account of all these factors, the Court of Appeal confirmed the ruling of the lower court that the liability should be apportioned in the following proportions: the lessees, 5%; the water authority, 35%; the main contractors, 25%; and the subcontractors, 35%.

Although the facts of the *Adcock* case illustrate preventative action needing to be taken some time in advance of the actual flooding danger arising, the possibility of negligence being established against private concerns and a public body are potentially far reaching. The circumstances, however, should be contrasted with those in which a flooding event is imminent where, presumably, the standard of what is 'reasonable' in relation to flood prevention would be lowered by the urgency of the situation. Hence, where a sandbag wall needs to be built as an emergency operation,[188] in the face of an impending flood, the standards required would not be so exacting as those where the parties had ample time to design and construct the wall.

Another example of a situation where negligence, in failing to take preventative action, formed the principal basis of an action for flood-related damage was *Boxes Ltd* v *British Waterways Board*.[189] Here the claimant's factory abutted the bank of a canal which the defendant canal authority had statutory powers to regulate and maintain. Due to congestion of the canal, barges moored against a stone wharf, which was owned by the claimants, and struck it with such force that a lower part of the wall collapsed and water seeped through into the claimant's premises. The claimant sought damages for the cost of engineering works that were necessary to repair the wall to prevent penetration by the canal water. The

---

[188] See 11.3.4 below on emergency response obligations.
[189] [1971] 2 Lloyd's Rep 183.

defendant authority argued that it was only under a duty to maintain the canal in a navigable state and that byelaws prohibited the mooring of barges alongside the wall. Although it was clear that the damage had actually been caused by the operators of barges wrongfully mooring against the wall, the defendant owed a duty of care, as controller of the canal, because it carried out operations which could be a danger to others if reasonable care was not exercised. The duty to regulate and supervise the canal traffic effectively encompassed a duty to prevent damage to the wall, and the defendant was under a duty to take action as soon as it was known that water was escaping. Although the proceedings had originally been formulated in negligence or nuisance, it was agreed that the case was really one of negligence, since if there had been no negligence there would have been no nuisance.

## 2.9 CIVIL LIABILITY OF PUBLIC BODIES

The previous discussion of private rights and duties in respect of flood defence, at least so far as nuisance is concerned, has tended to suppose that one private landholder will be seeking to establish liability on the part of another private landholder. Although the assumed status of the parties as private individuals is a convenient supposition for the purpose of providing an exposition of basic principles concerning riparian rights and private nuisance, the reality may often be different. In a range of situations, the victim of flooding is actually seeking to recover compensation against a public or statutory body, rather than a private individual. Hence, discussion in later chapters is provided of a range situations where civil liability is alleged against flood or coastal defence operating authorities in exercising their operational functions; local highway authorities exercising functions in relation to drainage of highways; and sewerage and water undertakers involved in water utility service activities. It is clearly established that, in the absence of statutory authority, a public body is capable of being civilly liable in the same way as a private person.[190] However, in all these contexts, a common issue is raised as to whether the statutory provisions under which the authority or body is acting will serve as a defence to civil liability that would otherwise arise.

At the broadest level of generality, it is fair to state that statutory bodies have extensive immunity from civil liability of a kind which is not possessed by private persons and this immunity is available in proceedings brought in private nuisance or in negligence. However, the legal basis and extent of this immunity is a matter of some complexity and far from being

---

[190] *Mersey Docks and Harbour Board Trustees* v *Gibbs* (1866) LR 1 HL 93.

fully resolved.[191] As will be seen, cases that have arisen in different contexts, and have been decided at different times, seem to rest upon markedly different principles and justifications without any definitive test applicable to all situations. Hence, the best that can be done for the present is to provide an initial indication of the factors that have been found persuasive in relevant cases where civil liability of statutory bodies has been in contention.

Statutory bodies are *less likely* to be civilly liable for flood-related damage where:

(a) liability is excluded by the statute under which the body exercises functions;[192]

(b) the relevant statute provides an alternative enforcement mechanism or provision for payment of compensation which precludes civil litigation;[193]

(c) the body is bound to exercise a statutory *duty*, rather than a permissive statutory *power*;[194]

(d) the duty upon the body is owed to the public at large, rather than a particular claimant;[195]

(e) the body possessing a statutory power is guilty of a failure to act (nonfeasance) as opposed to a wrongful act (misfeasance);[196]

(f) the exercise of the statutory power resulted in no additional damage beyond that which would have occurred had no action been taken;[197]

(g) the body possesses insufficient control over the activity which is alleged to give rise to liability;[198]

---

[191] See B. Markesinis, J.-B. Auby, D. Coester-Waltjen and S. Deakin, *Tortious Liability of Statutory Bodies: A Comparative and Economic Analysis of Five English Cases* (1999) and P. Craig and D. Fairgrieve, 'Barratt, Negligence and Discretionary Powers [1999] *Public Law* 626.

[192] *Allen* v *Gulf Oil Refining Ltd* [1981] AC 1001.

[193] See *Marriage* v *East Norfolk Rivers Catchment Board* [1949] 2 All ER 1021, discussed at 4.3.2 below.

[194] See *Department of Transport* v *North West Water Authority* [1983] 3 All ER 273, discussed at 7.11 below.

[195] *Dear* v *Thames Water* (1992) 33 Con LR 43 and *Ryeford Homes Ltd and Another* v *Sevenoaks District Council and Others* [1989] 2 EGLR 281, discussed at 11.4.1 below.

[196] *Hesketh* v *Birmingham Corporation* [1924] 1 KB 260, discussed at 7.8 and 7.9 below.

[197] See *East Suffolk Catchment Board* v *Kent* [1940] 4 All ER 527, discussed at 4.3.1 below.

[198] *Glossop* v *Heston and Isleworth Local Board* (1879) 12 Ch D 102; *Smeaton* v *Ilford Corporation* [1954] Ch 450 and see 7.8 and 7.9 below; and *Dear* v *Thames Water* (1992) 33 Con LR 43.

(h) the imposition of liability upon the body would have adverse economic consequences in diverting resources away from more pressing public needs;[199]

(i) the imposition of liability would inhibit the proper exercise of discretion by the body;[200] or

(j) finding liability would involve a court substituting its own judgment on a discretionary or policy matter for that of the statutory body (particularly where the weighting of competing public interests is involved).[201]

Statutory bodies are *more likely* to be civilly liable where:

(a) a body has acted outside its statutory powers;[202]

(b) the relevant statute provides no alternative remedy;[203]

(c) the duty of the body is owed to an individual rather than the public at large;[204]

(d) the body exercising a power is guilty of a wrongful act (misfeasance) as opposed to a failure to act (non-feasance);[205]

(e) the exercise of the statutory power resulted in additional damage beyond that which would have occurred had no action been taken;[206]

(f) the body possesses sufficient control over the activity which is alleged to give rise to liability;[207]

(g) the cost of taking preventative measures is not excessive by comparison to the harm that will arise if no such measures are taken;[208]

(h) the exercise of a statutory power is undertaken in a manner which

---

[199] *Stovin* v *Wise* [1996] 3 All ER 801.

[200] *Dear* v *Thames Water* (1992) 33 Con LR 43.

[201] *Home Office* v *Dorset Yacht Co Ltd* [1970] 2 All ER 294, per Lord Diplock at pp.331 to 332.

[202] *Pride of Derby and Derbyshire Angling Association* v *British Celanese Ltd* [1953] Ch 149, discussed at 7.8 below; *Thomas* v *Gower Rural District Council* [1922] 2 KB 76; and see 8.3.3 below.

[203] *British Waterways Board* v *Severn Trent Water Ltd* [2001] Env LR 780, discussed at 7.7.2 below.

[204] See *Christchurch Drainage Board* v *Brown and Others* (1987) *The Times* 14 September, discussed at 11.4.1 below and *Boxes Ltd* v *British Waterways Board* [1971] 2 Lloyd's Rep 183, discussed at 2.8 above.

[205] *Thomas* v *Gower Rural District Council* [1922] 2 KB 76, discussed at 8.3.3 below.

[206] See *Monckton* v *Severn Trent Water Authority* [1988] RVR 247.

[207] See the discussion of water suppliers' liabilities at 7.11 below.

[208] See *Bybrook Barn Garden Centre* v *Kent County Council* [2001] Env LR 543, discussed at 2.5.3 above.

*Civil Liability of Public Bodies* 89

results in more harm to the claimant than is necessary;[209] or

(i) the alleged harm involves an infringement of human rights, particularly where this precludes comprehensive exclusion of a duty of care.[210]

Although it is difficult to identify any single factor as definitive of whether civil liability will, or will not, be imposed upon a statutory authority or body, to varying degrees, the range of factors which have been listed have been influential upon courts addressing the issue in different flood-related contexts considered later in this work. For the present, it is useful to take a couple of examples to illustrate the way in which the issue of civil liability of a public authority has been addressed.

In *Bybrook Barn Garden Centre Ltd v Kent County Council*,[211] it may be recalled, a local highway authority was found to be liable to a private landowner for the failure to provide a culvert of sufficient capacity to accommodate the water flow and consequent flooding damage. A factor that received consideration in this case was the significance of the status of the defendant as a public body. In relation to this, it was recognised that there was a line of cases where courts had expressed a reluctance to allow private law remedies to be used, in effect, to compel a public body to exercise a statutory power which was intended to be exercised on a discretionary basis and with regard to the policy priorities which arise in expending limited public resources. Hence when local authorities had responsibility for sewage treatment works they were held not to be liable for effluent discharges which had become unsatisfactory due to subsequent development of the area served by a treatment works and the connection of properties to the sewerage system which they were powerless to prevent.[212]

Underlying the reluctance to impose liability on public bodies was a concern that imposition of liability would have an undesirable constraining effect upon the allocation of public resources. Hence, it has been observed,

> 'the creation of a duty of care upon a highway authority . . . would inevitably expose the authority's budgetary decisions to judicial

---

[209] See *Provender Millers (Winchester) Ltd v Southampton County Council* [1940] 1 Ch 131, discussed at 2.5.3 above and 8.3.6 below.

[210] See *Osman v United Kingdom* (1998) 5 BHRC 293 and *Peter Marcic v Thames Water Utilities Ltd* [2001] Env LR 146 and [2002] EWCA 65, 7 February 2002, discussed at 7.9 below.

[211] [2001] Env LR 543 and see 2.5.3 above.

[212] *Smeaton v Ilford Corporation* [1954] Ch 450 and now see s.106 Water Industry Act 1991, discussed at 7.2 below, on the right of connection to sewers. See *Glossop v Heston and Isleworth Local Board* (1879) 12 Ch D 102 and discussion in 7.8 and 7.9.3 below.

inquiry. This would distort the priorities of local authorities, which would be bound to try to play safe by increasing their spending on road improvements rather than risk enormous liabilities.... They will spend less on education or social services. . . . [I]t is important, before considering a duty of care owed by public authorities, to consider the cost to the community of the defensive measures which they are likely to take to avoid liability . . .'[213]

On the other hand, it is well established that public bodies do not enjoy any special immunity so far as liability for nuisance is concerned unless this is explicitly provided for by statute.[214] Essentially, a public body will be liable for nuisance in the same circumstances as a private person would be. Whilst statutory powers may be taken into account in determining the extent of this liability, the allocation of statutory powers alone does not give rise to nuisance liability. If the situation were otherwise, the statutory allocation of a *power* to a public body could be translated into a *duty* to act by private individuals using nuisance actions, effectively, to compel public bodies to undertake major programmes, sometimes at great expense and with adverse consequences to services provided to the public at large.

In the circumstances of the *Bybrook* case, the defendant highway authority was under a statutory duty to maintain the highway subject to an exemption from liability where reasonable care had been taken to secure that it was not dangerous to traffic.[215] However, it was not established that the exemption from liability, allowed where the highway was made reasonably safe for traffic, applied where the exercise of the highway authority's power to undertake drainage work was at issue.[216] More broadly, it was found that the highway authority did not have any statutory immunity from actions in nuisance where flooding damage was at issue. Because of this, the authority was subject to the strict liability that generally applies to those with responsibility for culverts,[217] and the authority was found liable for the damage which had arisen.

A contrasting outcome is to be seen in *Dear* v *Thames Water*.[218] Here, the claimant's house was subject to periodic flooding from a culverted watercourse which, over some years, had become inadequate to take the

---

[213] Per Lord Hoffmann in *Stovin* v *Wise* [1996] AC 923 at p.958.
[214] *Mersey Docks and Harbour Board Trustees* v *Gibbs* (1866) LR 1 HL 93, though contrast *Allen* v *Gulf Oil Refining Ltd* [1981] AC 1001 where statutory immunity was provided for activities that would otherwise have constituted an actionable nuisance.
[215] Under ss.41 and 58(1) Highways Act 1980, discussed at 8.3.3 and 11.4.2 below.
[216] On the general drainage powers of highway authorities see 8.3 below.
[217] See 2.5.3 above on liability for flooding caused by culverts.
[218] (1992) 33 Con LR 43, and discussed at (1993) *Water Law* 116.

increased flow generated by development of the catchment area. An action in negligence and nuisance was brought against both the sewerage undertaker and the local authority, which carried out the periodic cleaning of the culvert. However, the action in negligence failed because it was found that the defendants owed a statutory duty only to the public generally,[219] rather than to particular individuals such as the claimant. Clearly, the court was concerned that a public power to act should not be translated into a duty to act by means of private litigation. The action in nuisance also failed since it was found that liability for the culvert remained with the riparian property owners, which included the claimant. The periodic cleansing of the culvert which was undertaken at the initiative of the local authority, but without any legal obligation to so, had not given it sufficient practical control to establish liability. Although it was accepted that the sewerage undertaker had statutory powers to abate the nuisance,[220] this was not sufficient to establish that it had a duty to do so or had sufficient control over the watercourse to be liable in nuisance.

Although it was evident that there were many other householders in the area who were experiencing similar flooding to that suffered by the claimant, it was stressed in the *Dear* case that the proceedings were not to determine, generally, how flooding in the area was to be alleviated. The matters at issue were merely concerned with the extent of the claimant's individual common law rights.[221] Hence, the Court was concerned that any outcome should not constrain broad-based and discretionary policy decisions as to how best to allocate resources to combat flooding in the area. Matters of this kind might, possibly, be addressed through statutory enforcement procedures or be the subject of challenge through judicial review,[222] but should not be dictated by the enforcement of individual private rights alone.

---

[219] See 7.2 below on sewerage undertakers' responsibilities under the Water Industry Act 1991.
[220] Under s.265 Public Health Act 1936 and see 8.2.1 below on statutory nuisance.
[221] Contrast *Peter Marcic v Thames Water Utilities Ltd* [2001] Env LR 146 and [2002] EWCA 65, 7 February 2002, discussed at 7.9 below, where an infringement of human rights was alleged to arise as a result of sewerage flooding.
[222] See 7.2 below on enforcement mechanisms under the Water Industry Act 1991.

# Chapter 3

# INSTITUTIONAL RESPONSIBILITIES

## 3.1 INTRODUCTION

Although the civil law has traditionally emphasised the rights of individuals to protect their land from flooding and erosion, the practical scope for an individual landowner to take effective action of this kind is normally quite limited. For technical or economic reasons the protection of individual properties from flooding is not feasible unless substantial areas of land are under the control of a single landowner. Within limits, the common law has recognised various kinds of tenure-based obligations and contractual agreements as being mutually enforceable between neighbouring landowners as a means of securing flood defence, and the funding needed to provide or maintain defences. However, this approach has its limitations beyond essentially local flood defence initiatives. Recognising that security against flooding hazards to life and property are public concerns, and that flood defence can only be undertaken efficiently and effectively where a collective, rather than an individual, approach is adopted, the case for public regulation has long been recognised.[1] Nonetheless, profound and controversial issues remain as to the institutional structures which are most appropriate to flood and coastal defence, the powers and duties which should be allocated to relevant public bodies, and the mechanisms by which they should be funded. This chapter, and the three which follow, seek to address these issues.

The allocation of public responsibilities for flood and coastal defence in England and Wales is somewhat complex, but may be regarded as a tiered structure of powers and duties assigned to interrelated bodies with varying degrees of executive and operational responsibilities. Whilst overall administrative control is retained by central government, operational powers are progressively devolved to regional and local bodies, subject to supervisory controls exercised by bodies placed at a higher level in the 'pyramid' of administrative, regulatory and operational functions. Not least important is the relationship between the public bodies involved in flood defence and the responsibilities of private landowners who may desire, or be required, to undertake a range of activities for the purpose of protecting their land from flooding. A broad outline of the allocation of

---

[1] E. C. Penning-Rowsell, D. J. Parker and D. M. Harding, *Floods and Drainage* (1986) pp.4 to 5.

# Introduction

## Flood Defence Responsibilities in England and Wales

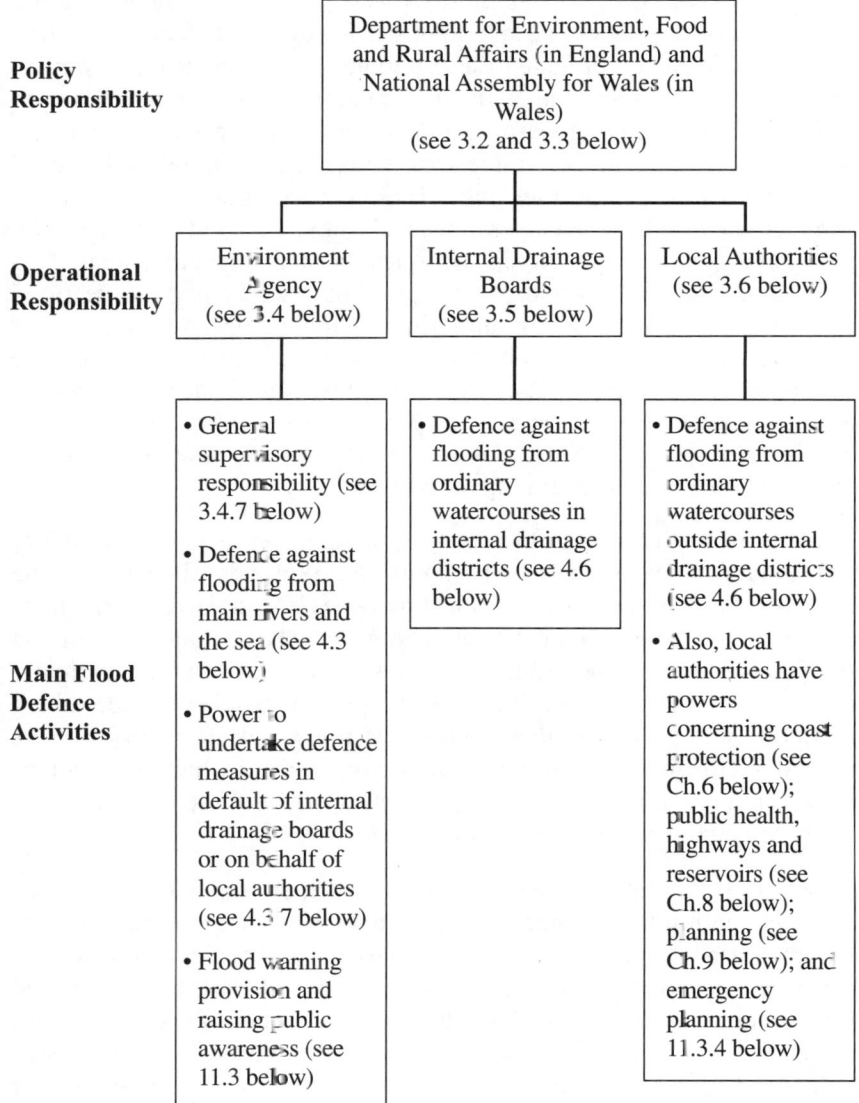

*This table is adapted from information kindly provided by the Flood Management Division, Department for Environment, Food and Rural Affairs.*

flood defence responsibilities is given in the following paragraphs, before examining more detailed matters later in the chapter.

At the apex of the pyramid of responsibilities, the main ministerial responsibilities for policy and the administration of flood defence legislation lie with the Secretary of State for Environment, Food and Rural Affairs in respect of England and the National Assembly for Wales in relation to Wales.[2] The respective government departments undertake research and provide an administrative framework within which flood and coastal defence 'operating authorities' provide flood warning services, undertake and regulate flood defence operations and, subject to guidance, generally plan and implement operational strategies for their respective areas. To a large extent, control over the exercise of the largely permissive flood defence powers of operating authorities is maintained by the need for capital expenditure to be supported by government funding. Hence, the conditional allocation of funding, to require compliance with central guidance, means that executive responsibility is effectively retained, despite the rather open-ended statutory powers to undertake flood defence work that are given to operating authorities.

At a level beneath central government, a general supervisory responsibility for flood defence matters in England and Wales is allocated to the Environment Agency, which for most purposes is bound to act through its regional flood defence committees. The Agency has a major operational role in undertaking flood defence activities, though its powers are normally restricted to works in main rivers and the sea. Alongside the undertaking of flood defence works, the Agency has important regulatory powers allowing it to withhold consent for various operations which other bodies or private individuals may seek to undertake where these operations are likely to have an adverse effect upon flood defence.

Along with the Environment Agency, as the principal flood defence operating authority, the other operating authorities are internal drainage boards and local authorities, with maritime local authorities acting as coast protection operating authorities. Internal drainage boards are established for certain low-lying areas where drainage is a matter of special concern and operations in respect of land drainage on ordinary watercourses need to be conducted on a continuing basis. Local authorities are possessed of similar permissive powers, to undertake drainage work on ordinary watercourses within their areas where no internal drainage board exists.

---

[2]  Notably, however, land use planning falls within the remit of the Department for Transport, Local Government and the Regions in England though in Wales this is a responsibility of the National Assembly in relation to Wales. Generally see 9.2 below on planning administration.

# Introduction

Maritime local authorities also have special powers in relation to coastal erosion and sea encroachment. However, these powers to undertake flood and coastal defence work may only be exercised within the jurisdiction of the respective boards and authorities, and will be subject to the supervision of the Agency and, perhaps most significantly, subject to funding constraints and guidance requirements imposed by the Department for Environment, Food and Rural Affairs and the National Assembly for Wales.

Finally, at the lowest level on the pyramid of flood defence responsibilities, are the significant obligations that fall to private landowners where defence facilities on private land have not been adopted by operating authorities. Although, historically, private landowners may not generally have been subject to a duty to undertake flood defence work, unless this arose by virtue of tenure or similar land-related obligations, it is evident that the duty upon landowners to prevent flooding has been subject to progressive expansion.[3] Moreover, where a private landowner seeks to undertake work for the protection of land from flooding, the operations that are proposed will normally be subject to control by public bodies. Usually, this will involve consent or authorisation by the Environment Agency or another operating authority, but important control mechanisms are also provided through the land use planning system[4] and other systems of regulation administered by local authorities.

Within this broad outline, the main purpose of this chapter is to examine the respective functions of the public bodies involved in flood and coastal defence. In doing so, emphasis will be placed on compositions, constitutions and the broad institutional roles and policies of the different bodies. Other matters, such as the application of particular operational and regulatory powers, and the more detailed implications of funding constraints, will be set aside for consideration in later chapters.

## 3.2 DEPARTMENT FOR ENVIRONMENT, FOOD AND RURAL AFFAIRS

### 3.2.1 Administrative Background

Until June 2001 the Government department with principal responsibility for flood defence in England was the Ministry of Agriculture, Fisheries and Food. However, following a reorganisation of departmental responsibilities, this Ministry was abolished and all its functions passed to the new Department for Environment, Food and Rural Affairs. Another significant aspect of the reorganisation was the abolition of the former Department of

---

[3] See Ch.2 above on duties upon landowners.
[4] See Ch.9 below on the planning system.

the Environment, Transport and the Regions, which had previously been responsible for environmental protection and wildlife conservation matters including land use planning. As a consequence of the reorganisation, responsibility for environmental protection and wildlife conservation passed to the Department for Environment, Food and Rural Affairs, whilst planning became a responsibility of the new Department for Transport, Local Government and the Regions.[5] These changes concerned government responsibilities in relation to England and did not affect matters within the jurisdiction of the National Assembly for Wales.[6]

However, it must be appreciated that the full implications of the fairly recent Government departmental reorganisation are likely to take time to become apparent. The closer link between flood defence and environmental matters, which has been facilitated by bringing these matters together within the same department, may have important longer-term implications upon the policy and practice of flood defence. Conversely, the separation of land use planning from other areas of environmental responsibility is an innovation that will require careful co-ordination to ensure that the planning system gives sufficient prominence to environmental protection issues. At the time of writing, it is too early to gauge the implications of the administrative changes. Indeed, many of the key flood defence policy statements, which continue to apply until new guidance is promulgated, remain publications of the former Ministry of Agriculture, Fisheries and Food and the Welsh Office.

As the principal government department with responsibility for flood defence, land drainage and coastal defence policy in England, the Department for Environment, Food and Rural Affairs has key executive responsibilities for funding, policy guidance and research. More specific, and in some respects project-related, guidance is given in relation to legislation that is administered by the Department. Primarily, this involves administration of provisions from the Water Resources Act 1991 and the Land Drainage Acts 1991 and 1994, in respect of flood defence from rivers and the sea, and the Coast Protection Act 1949, in relation to schemes for protection against coastal erosion and sea erosion. Although these Acts empower operating authorities to undertake flood defence, land drainage and coast protection works it must be stressed that they do not require any specific works to be undertaken or provide criteria as to the circumstances in which the various powers are to be exercised. Largely, the actual use that is to be made of the various powers is a matter of policy which must be adhered to if government funding is to be made available for the support

---

[5] See Secretaries of State for Transport, Local Government and the Regions and for Environment, Food and Rural Affairs Order 2001, S.I. 2001 No.2568.
[6] See 3.3 below on the National Assembly for Wales.

of a particular project. Hence, for example, it will be increasingly necessary for flood defence powers to be exercised in accordance with conservation and other duties imposed on the various bodies involved. Likewise, environmental and social considerations will need to be weighed into the balance in determining which projects will be allocated funding priority.

### 3.2.2 Overall Policy Objectives

The most comprehensive statement of Government policy objectives and priorities on flood and coastal defence is presently to be found in the *Strategy for Flood and Coastal Defence* which was published by the Ministry of Agriculture, Fisheries and Food and the Welsh Office in 1993. Although some modifications of this policy are apparent from subsequent ministerial statements,[7] it remains the central statement of government policy on flood and coastal defence.

The overall policy objective for flood and coastal defence is:

> 'to reduce the risk to people and the developed and natural environment from flooding and coastal erosion by encouraging the provision of technically, environmentally and economically sound and sustainable defence measures.'

Within the overall objective, a number of more specific objectives are envisaged and these are described under the following subheadings.

### 3.2.3 Flood Warning Systems

Due to the potential for reducing risks to life and property through advance preparations by individuals, operating authorities and the emergency services, the encouragement of adequate and cost-effective flood warning systems is regarded as having a priority claim upon grant aid. The Environment Agency has the lead operational role in relation to issuing flood warnings and grant aid has been provided towards the cost of equipment allowing improvements in Agency practice. Similarly, funds have been provided for the Storm Tide Warning Service, operated by the Meteorological Office, which provides advance warnings of high sea levels drawing upon a network of tide gauges, along with funding research to provide improved mathematical models of storm surges.[8]

---

[7] In some respects the information in the 1993 strategy document has been developed and updated in the *Memorandum submitted by the Ministry of Agriculture, Fisheries and Food*, submitted to the House of Commons Agriculture Committee, Sixth Report Session 1997–98, *Flood and Coastal Defence* (1998) HC 707-II *Minutes of Evidence and Appendices* p.194, which has also been drawn upon in the following account.

[8] Generally see 11.3 below on flood warnings.

### 3.2.4 Encouraging Sound and Sustainable Measures

Government encouragement of adequate, technically and environmentally sound and sustainable flood and coastal defence measures is sought through a number of strategic mechanisms. These involve initiatives such as the establishment of coastal defence groups, comprising local authorities, the Environment Agency and other bodies with responsibilities for particular stretches of the coast. Coastal defence groups are now in existence for the entire English coastline and a national Coastal Defence Forum has been established to provide a lead for these groups. Further mechanisms in pursuance of a strategic approach to flood and coastal defence policy involve encouragement of local Environment Agency plans[9] and shoreline management plans.[10] The aim of these plans is to ensure that individual schemes are undertaken in accordance with a strategic framework which recognises broader issues such as natural processes, planning pressures, current and future land use and defence needs, and environmental considerations within a catchment area of a watercourse or sediment cell of the coastline. A sea defence wall can result in coastal erosion elsewhere and a new development can result in increased flood risk at other locations. Accordingly, the Agency is producing plans for all main catchment areas, and coastal defence groups are developing shoreline management plans. Grant funding is being made available for associated studies, so that strategic objectives may be set for flood defence and coastal management in conformity with these plans.

The Government also pursues its overall policy objectives for flood and coastal defence by encouraging operating authorities to prepare water level management plans[11] for appropriate areas. Particularly in relation to important wildlife habitats, operating authorities are urged to promote a balanced and integrated approach towards flood defence, conservation and agriculture by means of active planning for water level requirements for the various activities involved. Hence, guidance has been issued on the preparation of water level management plans and grant aid is made available for works and associated studies, with particular emphasis upon sites of special scientific interest. An enhanced grant rate is offered to internal drainage boards for works on conservation sites of international

---

[9] See Environment Agency, *Local Environment Agency Plans* (1999).
[10] See Ministry of Agriculture, Fisheries and Food, *Shoreline Management Plans: A guide for coastal defence authorities* (1995) and see 5.5 below on shoreline management plans.
[11] See Ministry of Agriculture, Fisheries and Food, Welsh Office, Association of Drainage Authorities, English Nature and National Rivers Authority *Water Level Management Plans: A procedural guide for operating authorities* (1994) and Ministry of Agriculture, Fisheries and Food, *Water Level Management Plans: Additional Guidance Notes for Operating Authorities* (1999) and see discussion at 10.7 below.

## Department for Environment, Food and Rural Affairs

importance. Close co-ordination between the Department for Environment, Food and Rural Affairs, the operating authorities and English Nature is being maintained to ensure that plans are completed for all relevant sites of special scientific interest.[12]

### 3.2.5 Technical and Indicative Standards

Another key role of the Department for Environment, Food and Rural Affairs is that of providing guidance to operating authorities on technical standards, environmental factors, project appraisal and post project evaluation techniques. In respect of this, the Department aims to ensure that flood defence and coastal defence schemes are properly assessed in accordance with technical criteria. This is done through written guidance concerning environmental matters and project appraisal,[13] summary reports of post project evaluation, the provision of advice on technical and environmental issues and dissemination of results from the Department's research and development programme. In relation to a specific project proposal, operating authorities will be required to consider a range of options for defence works, including a 'do nothing' option and a 'do the minimum' option, with a view to adopting the option which is technically and environmentally sound and offers the best value for money. The range of options needing to be considered will depend upon the scale of the investment that is envisaged and the possibilities for alternative approaches. Hence, there may be shoreline management situations in which the preferred option is that of allowing natural processes to take their course and an appropriate decision in such cases might be to allow 'managed realignment' of the coastline.[14]

Various measures are adopted to assess the efficiency and effectiveness of flood and coastal defence projects. Amongst these, reports are published by the Department of post project evaluations in respect of grant-aided defences.[15] Although these have generally reflected that projects operate soundly, where shortcomings have been identified these are indicated in guidance to operating authorities. General flood and coastal defence

---

[12] See 10.4 below on sites of special scientific interest.
[13] Ministry of Agriculture, Fisheries and Food, *Flood and Coastal Defence Project Appraisal Guidance Notes*: this is a series of publications including *Overview (including general guidance)* (FCDPAG1) (2001); *Strategic Planning and Appraisal* (FCDPAG2) (2001); *Economic Appraisal* (FCDPAG3) (1999); *Approaches to Risk* (FCDPAG4) (2000); *Environmental Appraisal* (FCDPAG5) (2000); and *Post Project Evaluation* (FCDPAG5) (forthcoming).
[14] See Ch.12 below on sustainability.
[15] See Ministry of Agriculture, Fisheries and Food, *Flood and Coastal Defence – Post Project Evaluation Summary Report 1995/96* (1997) Publication PB 3040.

performance indicators, concerning schemes approved, administrative costs, aggregate cost-benefit ratios and ongoing schemes, are published in annual reports. Surveys of coast protection works have also been commissioned to ascertain the condition of works and to allow the review of local authority plans for coastal defence works in respect of those works showing the most significant deterioration.

The Department also provides indicative standards to assess the need for flood defence measures, which may also be used as a guide for surveys of existing defences. In this respect, project appraisal guidance notes provide an indication of the need for, and adequacy of, defences, though it is recognised that they are not intended as a prescriptive standard for all future defence works and their status is subsumed to the greater need for technical, environmental and economic soundness. Essentially, the final choice for a flood defence project is that option which offers the best cost-benefit outcome. In some circumstances, however, it is recognised that the preferred option may fall short of the indicative standard of protection suggested by a project appraisal guidance note if the additional cost of achieving that standard of protection is not justified.

### 3.2.6 Guidance on Priorities for Grant Funding

Guidance on priorities for grant funding are established by the Department for Environment, Food and Rural Affairs and communicated to the operating authorities and the public generally. On an annual basis, the Environment Agency and local authorities assess their medium-term local or regional needs and submit expenditure plans, and these are evaluated by the Department to establish a priority programme for expenditure which is justified on the basis of urgency and priority. This evaluation of funding priorities is used as a baseline against which a medium-term level of Government support is determined.

In assessing grant funding priorities, emphasis is placed upon the need for protection of life, and this has the implication that funding will be directed towards those areas where greatest numbers of people live and work. In consequence, a broad hierarchy of priorities (in descending order of importance) has been formulated:

(1) flood warning systems;

(2) urban coastal and tidal defences;

(3) urban flood defence and environmental assets of international importance;

(4) rural coastal and tidal defences, existing rural flood defences and drainage works, and environmental assets of national significance; and

(5) new rural flood defence works and environmental assets of local significance.

Alongside need and urgency, this hierarchy is intended to guide operating authorities in their strategic planning and to indicate the relative importance that will be attached to flood defence measures in relation to expenditure programmes. Hence, the categories featuring in the hierarchy form the basis of a 'priority scoring system' which involves each proposal being given a rating accordingly. In the light of demand and available funds, an indicative minimum score is set so that applications rated below this level will not be likely to be approved for funding.

The need for flood defence measures to take account of the interrelationship between processes and measures elsewhere within a catchment or coastal cell is addressed by the Department in influencing the technical, environmental and economic aspects of each proposed scheme. In this respect, for example, making use of natural defence capacity of a soft defence feature such as a beach, as opposed to the construction of a concrete sea defence wall, has been encouraged by extending grant eligibility for monitoring and replenishment of soft defence features and the removal of perceived differences of treatment between soft and hard defence features. Although general maintenance of defence structures is not grant aided, future maintenance is a factor for consideration in determining which projects will be grant aided. In essence, a bid for a capital grant needs to be supported by evidence of a planned and costed maintenance programme, which will ensure that satisfactory maintenance is provided for and conducted in accordance with environmental and other relevant guidance.

### 3.2.7 Guidance on Environmental Matters

Alongside previous matters directed towards the provision of environmentally sound and sustainable flood defence, a *Code of Practice on Environmental Procedures for Flood Defence Operating Authorities*[16] emphasises that:

'[f]lood and coastal defence works should be environmentally acceptable as well as technically sound and economically viable. They should also be sustainable and based on an understanding of river and coastal processes. By working with these processes as far as possible

---

[16] Ministry of Agriculture, Fisheries and Food and Welsh Office (1996).

and avoiding their disruption, except where important man-made or natural assets are at risk, the possibility of committing future generations to inflexible and expensive options for defence should be minimised. This can only be achieved, however, if a strategic approach is adopted which covers all relevant issues at an appropriate scale in both space and time.'

The implications of this policy statement on the longer-term environmental planning for sustainable development are considerable.[17] The opportunities for protection and enhancement of important wildlife habitats are stressed and grant aid may be available for enhancement works where these are integral to a flood defence scheme. Other aspects of the emphasis placed upon environmental and ecological features of flood defence are the need to adhere to environmental assessment requirements[18] and to consult with English Nature and other conservation bodies before submitting a scheme for grant approval. Biodiversity action plans for coastal and wetland habitats may also be relevant to particular projects and it is envisaged that flood defence works, including water level management plans, should make a contribution to biodiversity action plans. Not least significant are the requirements of the European Community Wild Birds and Habitats Directives[19] in establishing stringent conditions to guard against adverse effects upon special protection areas and special areas of conservation designated under the Directives.

### 3.2.8 Guidance on Climate Change

Another respect in which Departmental guidance is likely to have a major effect on future flood and coastal defence activities is the prospect of increasing influence of climate change upon sea levels and the frequency, intensity and duration of rainfall.[20] Since 1989, operating authorities have been encouraged to take account of relative sea level rise in designing coastal defence schemes. The basis of the allowances which must be made to take account of climate change impacts have been reports of the Intergovernmental Panel on Climate change, which have provided estimates of the future rise in global sea levels. However, the precise implications of these impacts upon sea levels, and weather conditions in particular areas, are subject to considerable uncertainty and research is being undertaken to provide more precise and specific assessments of the implications of climate change in particular localities.

---

[17] See Ch.12 below on sustainable development.
[18] See 9.14 below on environmental impact assessment.
[19] See 10.5 below on the Wild Birds and Habitats Directives.
[20] See 1.6 above on climate change.

### 3.2.9 Discouragement of Inappropriate Development

In respect of inappropriate development, the Department's stated objective is to discourage development which increases flood risk or which interferes with the activities of flood and coastal protection authorities and, generally, to minimise development in areas which are subject to flood risk. In relation to this, the Department for Transport, Local Government and the Regions has recently adopted town and country planning guidance which significantly strengthens the controls upon inappropriate development and requires account to be taken of matters such as climate change and rising sea levels.[21] In addition, strategic flood and coastal defence plans for river catchment and coastal management units should be used to assist planning authorities in identifying areas where future land use might have a significant impact upon flood and coastal defences.

### 3.2.10 Research and Development

In respect of research and development, the Department aims to fund a programme that gives value for money through reducing uncertainty in the prediction of forces that cause flooding and coastal erosion and improving the technical means of responding to these uncertainties. Close liaison is advocated with other research and development funding bodies, such as the Environment Agency, to ensure complementary work is undertaken and to encourage the effective dissemination of results. Dissemination of the results of research and development projects is provided to operating authorities and others through annual reports, newsletters and conferences.[22]

### 3.2.11 Sponsorship of the Environment Agency

The Department for Environment, Food and Rural Affairs has policy responsibility for all Environment Agency functions and, alongside the National Assembly for Wales, has responsibility for sponsoring the Agency. Previous ministerial arrangements involved members of the Board of the Agency being appointed by the Department of the Environment, Transport and for the Regions and the Ministry of Agriculture, Fisheries and Food in relation to England. However, a result of the changes in Government departmental arrangements is that the Department for Environment, Food and Rural Affairs now appoints all the corresponding members of the Board including those especially concerned with flood and

---

[21] See the discussion of Department of the Environment, Transport and the Regions, Planning Policy Guidance Note 25, *Development and Flood Risk* (2001) at 9.8 below.

[22] Generally see Ministry of Agriculture, Fisheries and Food, *Report of the Advisory Committee on Flood and Coastal Defence Research and Development* (1999) and *Research and Development Annual Reports* on Department for Environment, Food and Rural Affairs website: http://www.defra.gov.uk/environ/fcd/default.

coastal defence matters, alongside those members appointed by the National Assembly for Wales. The power of appointment of members of the Agency's Board has to be seen alongside the important ministerial power to give directions of various kinds to the Agency as to the exercise of its functions, discussed below.[23]

### 3.2.12 High Level Targets

Although the *Strategy for Flood and Coastal Defence*, originally published in 1993, remains the principal policy statement, it must be read subject to subsequent developments which have had important impacts upon flood and coastal defence practice. Not least significant amongst these are actions that have been taken in response to the 1998 report of the House of Commons Agriculture Committee on *Flood and Coastal Defence*.[24] The Government response to the Report led to the publication of an *Elaboration of the Environment Agency's Flood Defence Supervisory Duty*[25] and the establishment of 'high level targets' for flood and coastal defence in England and similar targets for Wales.[26]

The high level targets for the flood and coastal defence operating authorities in England were published in 1999, following the publication of interim targets, as a means of securing more certain delivery of the national policy and strategy for flood and coastal defence. Generally, the targets relate to improving arrangements for the collection and provision of information, particularly in relation to inspection of the status of flood defence structures, and the establishment of a national flood and coastal defence database. The underlying aim is to build upon best practice in the delivery of flood and coastal defence policy 'on the ground' by securing greater consistency in flood defence activities undertaken by all operating authorities. Accordingly, the targets which have been established, from 1 April 2000, will be periodically reviewed and progress towards their realisation monitored.

Generally, the targets require flood and coastal defence operating authorities to provide policy statements as to how they intend to contribute to the

---

[23] See 3.2.14 below on directions to the Environment Agency.
[24] House of Commons Agriculture Committee, Sixth Report Session 1997–98, *Flood and Coastal Defence* (1998) HC 707 and see also House of Commons Agriculture Committee, Fifth Special Report Session 1997–98, *Replies by the Government and the Environment Agency to the Sixth Report from the Agriculture Committee Session 1997–98 'Flood and Coastal Defence' (HC 707)* (1998) HC 1117.
[25] See 3.4.7 below on the *Elaboration* of the Environment Agency's flood defence supervisory duty.
[26] See also National Assembly for Wales, *High Level Targets for Flood and Coastal Defence and Elaboration of the Environment Agency's Flood Defence Supervisory Duty* (2001) which makes corresponding provision in relation to Wales.

delivery of national policy on flood and coastal defence. Statements will be provided in relation to the area covered by each operating authority, in a fairly standard form, including information about the flood and erosion risks in the area, plans for mitigation of that risk, and plans for the management and inspection of flood defence works, including any new works, where appropriate. In each instance, deadlines are specified by which the relevant target must be met. Within this overall structure the specific targets, and the bodies to whom they are addressed, may be summarised as follows.[27]

*Target 1: Policy statements*
Produce, and copy to Environment Agency and the Department, a publicly available policy statement setting out plans for delivering the Government's policy aims and objectives, and the Agency report to the Department on completion of the policy statements and information collated from them. (Addressed to all operating authorities.)

*Target 2: Provision of flood warnings*
In conjunction with local authorities, emergency services and other partners to develop a method for categorising flood risk to an area for flood warning purposes; determine where a flood warning service can be provided and the appropriate dissemination arrangements using the method developed; determine and publish flood warning service standards for each area at risk of flooding; and report to the Department on achievement of service standards. (Addressed to the Environment Agency.)

*Target 3: Emergency exercises and plans*
Arrange, in conjunction with local authorities, emergency services and other partners, a programme of flood emergency exercises at national, regional and local levels, periodically conduct exercises and report to the Department. (Addressed to the Environment Agency.)

*Target 4: National Flood and Coastal Defence Database*
Develop a national flood and coastal defence database and maintain it thereafter, including information from operating authorities and on assets that provide a flood and coastal defence service that are in private or other ownership. (Addressed to the Environment Agency, though requiring collaboration by operating authorities.)[28]

---

[27] The full text can be found on the Department for Environment, Food and Rural Affairs website: http://www.defra.gov.uk/environ/fcd/default.
[28] See also National Audit Office, *Inland Flood Defence* (2001) HC 299 Ch.4 on the condition of flood defences in England.

## Institutional Responsibilities

*Target 5: Flood defence inspection and assessment of flood risk*
Ensure that a programme is in place for the regular inspection of all the defence assets included in the database and main rivers and critical ordinary watercourses[29] and report annually to the Department assessing the risk of flooding and the action taken or proposed. (Addressed to the Environment Agency.)

*Target 6: Coast protection inspections and assessment of coastal erosion risk*
Ensure that a programme is in place for the regular annual inspection of all coast protection assets included in the database, including those which are in private or other ownership and report to the Department on the assessment of risk of coastal erosion. (Addressed to coast protection authorities through Coast Defence Group.)

*Target 7: Expenditure programmes*
Provide to the Department a prioritised forward programme of capital and maintenance work for the assets on the database, covering the current and following 3-year period and including, where appropriate, proposed expenditure on any assets in third party or other ownership. (Addressed to all operating authorities.)

*Target 8: Shoreline Management Plans*
Following from Target 1, have in place and provide to the Department a programme for completing strategy plans necessary to implement shoreline management plans and updating plans in accordance with guidance.[30] (Addressed to relevant operating authorities.)

*Target 9: Biodiversity*
In addition to statutory obligations, when carrying out flood and coastal defence works, aim to avoid damage to environmental interest, ensure no net loss of habitats covered by Biodiversity Action Plans, seek opportunities for environmental enhancement and report annually on these matters. (Addressed to all operating authorities, with reporting by the Environment Agency.)

*Target 10: Water Level Management Plans*
In partnership with English Nature, complete water level management

---

[29] 'Critical ordinary watercourses' are defined as watercourses which are not classified as 'main rivers' but which the Environment Agency and other operating authorities agree are critical because they have the potential to put large numbers of people and property at risk from flooding. See 3.4.8 below on main rivers.
[30] See 5.5 below on shoreline management plans.

plans[31] in European sites and other sites of special scientific interest,[32] have a programme for implementing and reviewing plans and report annually to the Department on progress. (Addressed to relevant operating authorities, with reporting by the Environment Agency.)

*Target 11: Coastal Habitat Management Plans*
Identify sites where a coastal habitat management plan[33] is needed and produce a programme for completion and report annually to the Department. (Addressed to English Nature in collaboration with Environment Agency and other operating authorities.)

*Target 12: Development in areas of flooding*
Report annually to the Department on local authority development plans identifying flood risk statements or policies and report on planning applications identifying cases where sustained objections on flood risk grounds have been made and final decisions.[34] (Addressed to Environment Agency in collaboration with local planning authorities.)

*Target 13: Development in areas at risk of coastal erosion*
Report to the Department on local authority development plans identifying coastal erosion statements which reflect the assessed risk, and planning applications where coastal erosion was a material consideration and any conflict with assessed risks of coastal erosion. (Addressed to coast protection authorities through Coastal Defence Group.)

*Target 14: Internal Drainage Board administration and membership*
Produce and distribute to internal drainage boards guidance on the means by which efficiency can be improved through amalgamations and consortia, and ensuring that relevant interests are reflected in membership of boards, and report annually to the Department. (Addressed to the Association of Drainage Authorities in collaboration with the Department and Environment Agency, with reporting by Association of Drainage Authorities.)

### 3.2.13 Statutory Functions

A range of statutory powers and duties concerning flood and coastal defence are allocated to the Secretary of State for Environment, Food and Rural Affairs in relation to England, though in relation to Wales these

---

[31] See 4.9 below on water level management plans.
[32] See Ch.10 below on European sites and sites of special scientific interest.
[33] See English Nature, *Coastal Habitat Management Plans: An Interim Guide to Content and Structure* (2000).
[34] Generally see 9.8 below on planning and flood risk.

responsibilities are exercised by the National Assembly for Wales.[35] Most of these arise under the Environment Act 1995, the Water Resources Act 1991, the Land Drainage Acts 1991 and 1994, and the Coast Protection Act 1949, and are briefly summarised in the following paragraphs. However, it should be noted that, as originally enacted under the Water Resources Act 1991 and the Land Drainage Act 1991, many flood defence responsibilities, were entrusted to 'the Secretary of State and the Minister of Agriculture, Fisheries and Food'[36] or whichever of these was appropriate in particular contexts. As has been noted, in relation to England at least, the reorganisation of government departments now means that the Secretary of State for Environment, Food and Rural Affairs has responsibility for exercising powers and duties which were previously allocated to the different Ministers who respectively exercised environmental and agriculture responsibilities.

### 3.2.14 Environment Act 1995

Under the Environment Act 1995, which provides for the establishment of the Environment Agency, the Board of the Agency is appointed by the Secretary of State, who is bound to appoint persons who have experience of, or have shown capacity in, some matter relevant to the functions of the Agency.[37] The Secretary of State also has the power to appoint the chairmen and a number of other members of the Agency's regional flood defence committees.[38]

The Secretary of State must give the Agency guidance with respect to the objectives that are considered appropriate for the Agency to pursue in discharging its functions. This guidance must encompass guidance as to the contribution that the Agency is to make towards attaining the objective of sustainable development.[39] The Secretary of State may also give the Agency directions of a general or specific character, with which it is bound to comply, with respect to the carrying out of any of its functions and, specifically, this may encompass directions necessary for the implementation of European Community or international obligations.[40]

---

[35] See 3.3 below on the National Assembly for Wales.
[36] See s.221(1) Water Resources Act 1991, s.72(1) Land Drainage Act 1991 and s.56(1) Environment Act 1995.
[37] s.1(2)(a) Environment Act 1995. See 3.4 below on the Environment Agency.
[38] s.15(1)(a) Environment Act 1995. See 3.4.5 below on regional flood defence advisory committees.
[39] s.4(2) and (3) Environment Act 1995 and see 3.4.2 below.
[40] s.40(1), (2) and (8) Environment Act 1995. For example, see the direction on flood warnings discussed at 11.3.2 below (though this was actually issued to the National Rivers Authority under previous powers under ss.5 and 221(7)(b) Water Resources Act 1991).

## Department for Environment, Food and Rural Affairs

The Secretary of State is placed under the same duty as the Environment Agency as regards environmental and recreational matters. This requires that, when any proposals relating to the flood defence functions of the Agency are being considered, ministerial powers are exercised so as to further conservation and enhancement of natural beauty and the conservation of flora, fauna and geological or physiographical features of special interest. Further general duties require the Secretary of State to have regard to freedom of public access to certain areas and the desirability of facilities for public access to buildings and sites of archaeological, architectural, engineering or historic interest.[41]

### 3.2.15 Water Resources Act 1991

The Water Resources Act 1991, Part IV of which provides for the flood defence function of the Environment Agency, incorporates a range of supervisory and appeal provisions allowing scrutiny or confirmation of actions of the Agency by the Secretary of State. Hence, for example, the Agency is bound to submit to the Secretary of State, for confirmation, any scheme for special drainage charges in the interests of agriculture.[42] Appeals against determinations of contributions to the Agency from internal drainage boards and local authorities are considered by the Secretary of State.[43] The Secretary of State may direct the Agency as to the form of statements concerning recovery of precepts or contributions from internal drainage boards.[44]

Perhaps of greatest practical importance, however, are the ministerial powers under the Water Resources Act 1991 concerning grants for flood defence works. In respect of this, the Secretary of State may make grants to the Agency towards improvements in flood defence works or the construction of new works, subject to the approval of the Treasury, and subject to further requirements that the work will be properly undertaken.[45] Similarly, grants can be made by the Secretary of State towards the cost of flood warning systems,[46] and in respect of various other purposes connected with drainage. These include payments arising from the compulsory acquisition of land[47] and payments arising from the Agency exercising its general flood defence and drainage works powers.[48]

---

[41] s.7(1) and (2) and see 10.2 below on general environmental duties.
[42] s.137(1) Water Resources Act 1991 and see 6.3.10 below on special drainage charges.
[43] s.140(1) Water Resources Act 1991.
[44] s.141(3) Water Resources Act 1991.
[45] s.147(1) to (3) Water Resources Act 1991 and generally see Ch.6 below on funding.
[46] s.148 Water Resources Act 1991.
[47] See 4.3.3 below on the compulsory acquisition of land.
[48] s.149 Water Resources Act 1991 and see s.165 and 4.3.1 below on general flood defence works powers.

A range of land acquisition and works powers of the Agency are subject to ministerial approval. Hence, compulsory purchase of land by the Agency for the purpose of carrying out its functions is subject to approval by the Secretary of State[49] and, similarly, the acquisition of rights by the Agency in relation to land resulting from accretion due to drainage works.[50] Likewise the disposal of land that has been compulsorily acquired by the Agency is subject to approval by the Secretary of State.[51] Compulsory works powers, allowing building or engineering operations to be undertaken by the Agency, are exercisable only after a compulsory works order has been granted by the Secretary of State.[52] The Secretary of State may also designate a person for the purpose of exercising powers of entry for enforcement purposes.[53]

An operationally important, ministerial power under the 1991 Act is that of amending definitive maps of main rivers, which serve to define the extent of the Agency's functions in relation to watercourses. Hence, at any time, the Secretary of State may send the Agency one or more new maps to be substituted for the main river maps which must be kept by the Agency.[54] A final point to note is that the Secretary of State is empowered to make regulations for the purpose of carrying into effect the provisions of the Water Resources Act 1991 concerning flood defence and other flood defence provisions of the Act.[55]

### 3.2.16 Land Drainage Act 1991

Significant ministerial control is retained over internal drainage boards, provided for under the Land Drainage Act 1991, through appointment of members of boards,[56] involvement in the procedures for review of boundaries of districts,[57] and the powers to confirm the reorganisation of internal drainage districts which vest in the Secretary of State.[58] In certain instances the Secretary of State may transfer the functions of an internal drainage board to the Agency and, when appropriate, transfer those functions back to the board.[59] The Secretary of State is also responsible for giving consent

---

[49] s.154 Water Resources Act 1991.
[50] s.155 Water Resources Act 1991.
[51] s.157 Water Resources Act 1991.
[52] s.168 Water Resources Act 1991.
[53] s.169 Water Resources Act 1991 and see 3.4.11 below on powers of entry.
[54] s.194 Water Resources Act 1991 and see 3.4.8 below on main rivers.
[55] s.112 Water Resources Act 1991.
[56] s.1(4) Land Drainage Act 1991 and see 3.5.2 on the composition of internal drainage boards.
[57] s.2 Land Drainage Act 1991 and see 3.5.3 on the boundaries of internal drainage boards.
[58] s.3 Land Drainage Act 1991.
[59] ss.4 and 5 Land Drainage Act 1991.

for the Agency to exercise powers of a board in circumstances of default,[60] and may also determine that powers of the Agency are to be exercised by local authorities in circumstances of default.[61]

Supervision of local authority activities in exercising general drainage powers under the Land Drainage Act 1991 is initially the responsibility of the Agency. However, the reasonableness or otherwise of the Agency declining a local authority request to exercise its general flood defence works powers is subject to determination by the Secretary of State.[62] Under the Land Drainage Act 1994, the Environment Agency, internal drainage boards, local authorities and the Secretary of State are placed under similar environmental and recreational duties in respect of land drainage functions as those provided for under the Environment Act 1995.[63] In relation to the environmental and recreational duties, the Secretary of State is empowered to issue directions to internal drainage boards and to approve codes of practice.[64]

A wide variety of powers are provided for under the Land Drainage Act 1991 in relation to the supervision of a range of operational and funding matters, and these are exercisable by the Secretary of State. For example, the Secretary of State may: authorise landowners to carry out drainage works;[65] determine proposals to commute land drainage obligations;[66] confirm subdivision of a flood defence district for raising expenses;[67] consider appeals in relation to certain claims of exemption from rating;[68] consent to borrowing by internal drainage boards and local authorities;[69] make grants towards expenditure of internal drainage boards and other drainage bodies;[70] authorise internal drainage boards to acquire land compulsorily;[71] and hold inquiries for flood defence purposes.[72] Although some of these powers may be only infrequently exercised, special practical

---

[60] s.9 Land Drainage Act 1991 and see 3.5.5 on the supervisory role of the Environment Agency.
[61] s.10 Land Drainage Act 1991.
[62] s.17 Land Drainage Act 1991.
[63] ss.61A and 61B Land Drainage Act 1991, inserted by Land Drainage Act 1994, and see 10.3.1 below.
[64] ss.61D and 61E Land Drainage Act 1991, inserted by Land Drainage Act 1994, and see 10.3.2 below.
[65] s.22 Land Drainage Act 1991 and see 4.8.1 below on authorisation of works by landowners.
[66] s.33 Land Drainage Act 1991 and see 4.4.9 below on commutation of obligations.
[67] s.38 Land Drainage Act 1991 and see 6.4.7 below on differential drainage rates.
[68] s.47 Land Drainage Act 1991 and see 6.4.8 below on exemption from drainage rates.
[69] s.55 Land Drainage Act 1991 and see 6.4.10 below on borrowing powers.
[70] s.59 Land Drainage Act 1991 and see 6.4.2 below on grants.
[71] s.62 Land Drainage Act 1991 and see 4.6.1 below on compulsory acquisition.
[72] s.69 Land Drainage Act 1991.

significance must be attached to those concerning funding. The power to award grants to flood defence bodies is of fundamental practical importance, and the funding implications are considered in detail later in this work.[73] Finally, it may be noted that the Secretary of State is empowered to make regulations for the purpose of prescribing anything which may be prescribed under the Land Drainage Act 1991 or generally for the purpose of carrying the Act into effect.[74]

### 3.2.17 Coast Protection Act 1949

Part I of the Coast Protection Act 1949[75] is concerned with coast protection from erosion and encroachment by the sea and, under the new departmental arrangements, the responsibility for administration of this Part of the Act will rest with the Secretary of State for Environment, Food and Rural Affairs in England and the National Assembly for Wales in Wales. Ministerial powers under the Act allow for orders providing for the constitution of 'coast protection authorities' comprising representatives of maritime local authorities;[76] to cause local enquiries to be held where there is an objection to coast protection work;[77] to confirm works schemes;[78] to acquire land compulsorily;[79] to exercise default powers;[80] to confirm orders concerning the excavation of materials from the seashore;[81] and, perhaps most practically important, ministerial powers are provided for to make contributions towards the expenses of coast protection authorities subject to Treasury approval.[82]

## 3.3 THE NATIONAL ASSEMBLY FOR WALES

Although the allocation of flood defence powers and duties to the 'Secretary of State' means, in relation to England, the Secretary of State for Environment, Food and Rural Affairs, this must be contrasted with the allocation of responsibilities for these matters in relation to Wales. Although

---

[73] Generally see Ch.6 below on funding.
[74] s.65(1) Land Drainage Act 1991.
[75] Generally see Ch.5 below on coast protection.
[76] s.2 Coast Protection Act 1949 and see 5.4.1 below on coast protection authorities.
[77] s.5(4) Coast Protection Act 1949 and see s.17(4) and (5) in relation to works carried out by authorities other than coast protection authorities.
[78] ss.6(3) and 8(4) Coast Protection Act 1949, and see 5.4.4 below on works schemes, and to consider appeals in relation to works schemes providing for coast protection charges under s.7(6) Coast Protection Act 1949.
[79] s.14 Coast Protection Act 1949, and see 5.4.7 below on the compulsory acquisition of land, and see s.28 on the power of a Minister to facilitate coast protection work.
[80] s.15(4) Coast Protection Act 1949 and see 5.4.13 below on ministerial default powers.
[81] s.18(4) Coast Protection Act 1949 and see 5.4.11 below on prohibition of excavations.
[82] ss.20 and 21 Coast Protection Act 1949 and see 6.6 below on funding.

previously the responsibilities of the 'Secretary of State' had been exercised by the Secretary of State for Wales in relation to Wales,[83] these powers are now exercised by the National Assembly for Wales as provided for under the Government of Wales Act 1998.[84]

The Government of Wales Act 1998 established the National Assembly for Wales as a body corporate exercising various functions on behalf of the Crown.[85] Amongst the areas in which legislative functions are transferred to or conferred upon the Assembly is that of 'water and flood defence'[86] in relation to which, as a result of the devolution of power which is provided for, secondary legislation will in future be enacted by the Assembly. Primary legislation will remain the responsibility of the United Kingdom Parliament, though it is the duty of the Assembly to enact secondary legislation to transpose European Community Directives into national law.[87] The overall effect of these provisions is a major transfer of responsibilities from the Secretary of State for Wales to the Assembly as a secondary regulatory body and a new sponsor of the Environment Agency.[88] Hence, insofar as 'ministerial' powers are under consideration, in relation to flood defence, this is to be understood as shorthand for the allocation of powers to the Assembly that has been outlined.

More detailed provision for the transfer of powers to the National Assembly for Wales is made under the National Assembly for Wales (Transfer of Functions) Order 1999.[89] This Order provides for the exercise by the Assembly of statutory functions that were previously vested in Ministers of the Crown, and Schedule 1 provides a list of specific enactments in relation to which the transfer of functions is brought about. Within Schedule 1, all the key Acts concerning flood and coastal defence are listed, though with some qualifications to the extent of the transfer of functions. Hence, in relation to the Coast Protection Act 1947 functions are

---

[83] A specific example of a matter reserved exclusively for the Secretary of State for Wales was the duty upon him to maintain a committee of his appointees to advise him on the work of the Environment Agency in Wales (under s.11 Environment Act 1995).
[84] Generally see R. Lee. 'Devolution and the Environment: Wales' in N. Faris and S. Turner, Eds., *Public Law and the Environment: New Directions?* (1999).
[85] See Part I Government of Wales Act 1998.
[86] ss.21 and 22 and Schedule 2 Government of Wales Act 1998 and see Art.2 and Schedule 1 National Assembly for Wales (Transfer of Functions) Order 1999 (S.I. 1999 No.672) which transfers functions under the Water Resources Act 1991 with certain exceptions.
[87] ss.29 and 106 Government of Wales Act 1998.
[88] s.147 Government of Wales Act 1998 allows the Environment Agency to report to the Assembly on the exercise of its Welsh functions and to be subject to the financial scrutiny of the Auditor General for Wales (provided for under ss.90 to 96).
[89] S.I. 1999 No.672.

transferred subject to the retention of certain powers allocated other than to 'the Minister' or 'the Minister of Agriculture, Fisheries and Food' in the Act.[90] Functions under the Water Resources Act 1991 are transferred to the Assembly with certain qualifications[91] along with functions under the Land Drainage Act 1991.[92] In addition, but again with qualifications, functions under the Town and Country Planning Act 1990 pass to the Assembly.[93]

The implications of this transfer of jurisdiction in respect of ministerial powers for flood and coastal defence are, at the time of writing, difficult fully to assess. The National Assembly for Wales has only been operative since 1999, and relatively little opportunity has been provided for secondary legislation to be enacted for Wales which differs from that operative in England. Previously, the Welsh Office and the government departments responsible for flood and coastal defence in England have liaised closely and have tended to produce joint publications on key policy matters. However, there are differences to be seen in relation to guidance that has been promulgated by the Assembly in relation to planning matters[94] and substantial differences of approach to flood and coastal defence may become increasingly apparent in future years.

## 3.4 THE ENVIRONMENT AGENCY

### 3.4.1 Introduction

The following subsections provide an account of the statutory status and organisational structure of the Environment Agency followed by some general discussion of the Agency's overall flood defence function. A more detailed account of flood defence operations and regulation undertaken by the Agency, funding issues, information, flood warning services and

---

[90] Specifically, this arises in relation to ss.2, 5(4), 8(4), 17, 18(2) and the Treasury function under s.32(5) of the Coast Protection Act 1949, and see Ch.5 below on the 1949 Act.

[91] In relation to flood defence, the transfer excludes certain ministerial powers in relation to schemes for the transfer to the Agency of functions in relation to main rivers (under s.108 Water Resources Act 1991) and certain matters relating to revenue from internal drainage boards (under ss.140 and 141 Water Resources Act 1991).

[92] The exceptions to this arise in relation to s.31 Land Drainage Act 1991 (concerning the composition and incidental powers of the Agricultural Land Tribunal) and a range of matters where functions of the former Minister of Agriculture, Fisheries and Food are excluded from the transfer.

[93] See J. Bosworth and T. Shellens, 'How the Welsh Assembly will Affect Planning' [1999] *Journal of Planning and Environment Law* 219 and generally see Ch.9 below on planning.

[94] See 9.7 below on planning guidance for Wales.

## The Environment Agency

general environmental duties of the Agency is provided in later chapters.

The Environment Agency, with responsibility for England and Wales,[95] acquired its functions under the Environment Act 1995.[96] The 1995 Act brought about a consolidation of the pollution control functions previously administered by different authorities including the responsibilities for the aquatic environment previously possessed by the former National Rivers Authority. A main purpose of the consolidation was to achieve greater harmonisation and co-ordination of pollution control in relation to the environment *as a whole*. However, the comprehensive transfer of responsibilities from the Authority has the consequence that flood defence is now within the functions of the Environment Agency.

The Environment Agency is a non-departmental public body and, as such, its Board and management is given a broad freedom to exercise its responsibilities within an explicit statutory framework.[97] However, a fairly extensive range of powers and duties relating to the Agency have been allocated to the Secretary of State for Environment, Food and Rural Affairs and the National Assembly for Wales. These powers and duties are legislative in some instances, allowing or requiring secondary regulations to be made, administrative, in providing for the appropriate Minister to determine appeals of various kinds, and executive in allowing the Minister to give general or specific directions or guidance of various kinds to the Agency.

Outside the scope of the 1995 Act, the Agency is a statutory consultee in respect of the formulation of development plans and in relation to various categories of planning application.[98] These roles are of particular practical importance in anticipating and opposing development plans and particular developments that are capable of being problematic with regard to flood defence. Another notable feature, not directly addressed by the 1995 Act, is the status of the Agency as a competent authority for the purposes of certain European Community Directives concerned, for the most part, with

---

[95] In relation to Scotland, Part I of the Environment Act 1995 provides for establishment of the Scottish Environment Protection Agency. In this work, the 'Environment Agency' or the 'Agency' is used to refer to the Environment Agency *for England and Wales*.

[96] On the transfer date, 1 April 1996, see Environment Act 1995 (Commencement No.5) Order 1996 (S.I. 1996 No.186) and see s.2(1) Environment Act 1995 on the functions of the Environment Agency.

[97] The Agency is not to be regarded as the servant or agent of the Crown, or as enjoying any status, immunity or privilege of the Crown; or by virtue of any connection with the Crown, as exempt from any tax, duty, rate, levy or other charge, whether general or local; and the Agency's property is not to be regarded as property of or property held on behalf of the Crown (s.1(5) Environment Act 1995).

[98] See Ch.9 below on planning.

water quality.[99]

Insofar as flood defence is concerned, the impacts of the 1995 Act were less significant than in other areas, in that the Agency acquired essentially the same powers and duties as were previously administered by the National Rivers Authority. Hence, most of the substantive law under which the Agency operates remains as it was provided for under previous legislation. In particular, the regulation of flood defence, under Part IV of the Water Resources Act 1991, the Land Drainage Act 1991, as amended, and the Coast Protection Act 1949, remains substantially unchanged by the administrative reorganisation brought about by the 1995 Act.[100] Nonetheless, the transmission of flood defence functions to the Agency has involved some significant changes of approach resulting from the broader remit of the Agency as compared with its predecessor bodies[101] and as a result of fundamental new obligations to which it is subject.

Perhaps most significantly amongst the regulatory innovations, the Agency is given an explicit duty with regard to sustainable development,[102] is subject to a statutory duty to have regard to costs and benefits,[103] and made subject to reformulated general environmental duties.[104] These general duties are capable of arising in relation to any function of the Agency, including flood defence. In theory, their disregard would expose the Agency to judicial review proceedings; however, in practice, the effect of the duties may be limited by their generality.

### 3.4.2 The Principal Aim and Objectives

The Environment Agency is to be guided by a 'principal aim' in respect of the contribution that it is to make towards achieving 'sustainable

---

[99] Although the European Community Water Framework Directive (2000/60/EC) requiring River Basin Management Plans, and 'appropriate authorities' to administer these, with the implication that water management will have an increasingly quantitative dimension under the regimes that are envisaged. Generally see W. Howarth and D. McGillivray, *Water Pollution and Water Quality Law* (2001) sections 5.7 to 5.10.

[100] Although some minor changes were introduced under the 1995 Act, for example, on the definition of 'drainage' and in respect of grants for drainage work (under ss.100 and 101 Environment Act 1995).

[101] Generally, see House of Commons Environment Committee, *The Government's Proposals for an Environment Agency* (1992) HC 55 and House of Commons Environment Committee, *Environment Bill: Hearings of the Draft Environment Agencies Bill* (1994) HC 40.

[102] s.4(1) and (2) Environment Act 1995, and see 3.4.1 below on the principal aim of the Environment Agency.

[103] s.39 Environment Act 1995 and see discussion at 3.4.3 below on the costs and benefits duty.

[104] s.7(1) Environment Act 1995 and see the discussion of environmental duties at 10.2 below.

development'.[105] The most commonly cited definition of 'sustainable development' is 'development that meets the needs of the present without compromising the ability of future generations to meet their own needs'.[106] The general idea was elevated into an imperative of international environmental law by the Rio Declaration[107] in 1992 which required, amongst other things, that the right to development must be fulfilled equitably so as to meet developmental and environmental needs of present and future generations, and maintained that environmental protection must constitute an integral part of the developmental process which cannot be considered in isolation from it.[108]

However, the major task for governments that have endorsed the need for sustainable development is that of interpreting and applying the broadly formulated principle in national contexts and requiring public bodies, such as the Environment Agency, to be responsive to its implications. The formula which has been adopted in the 1995 Act is that, in discharging its functions in accordance with its statutory responsibilities, and taking into account any likely costs and benefits, the Agency is to make the contribution towards attaining the objective of achieving sustainable development indicated in ministerial guidance. For that purpose the Ministers[109] must, from time to time, give guidance with respect to objectives that they consider it appropriate for the Agency to pursue in discharging its functions and in attaining sustainable development. The Agency is bound to have regard to this guidance.[110]

The actual guidance on sustainable development that has been given to the Agency is contained in a memorandum issued by the relevant Departments, *The Environment Agency and Sustainable Development*.[111] This states that

---

[105] For further discussion of sustainable development, see Ch.12 below.

[106] Report of the World Commission on the Environment and Development, *Our Common Future* (1987) (the 'Bruntland Report').

[107] The 'Rio Declaration' was one of the outcomes of the United Nations Conference on Environment and Development, the 'Earth Summit', held in Rio de Janeiro, Brazil in June 1992. Generally, see S. Johnson, *The Earth Summit: The United Nations Conference on Environment and Development* (1993).

[108] See Principles 3 and 4 of the *Declaration* and see Ch.12 below on sustainable flood defence.

[109] The 'Ministers' now means the Secretary of State for Environment, Food and Rural Affairs and the National Assembly for Wales (s.56(1) Environment Act 1995, as amended) and see 3.2 and 3.3 above.

[110] s.4(1) to (4) Environment Act 1995.

[111] Department of the Environment, Ministry of Agriculture, Fisheries and Food and Welsh Office (1996). This should be read alongside Department of the Environment, Ministry of Agriculture, Fisheries and Food and Welsh Office, *The Environment Agency Management Statement* (1996) and more generally, on sustainable development, HM Government, *A Better Quality of Life: A Strategy for Sustainable Development for the UK* (1996).

the Ministers consider it appropriate for the Agency to act in accordance with general principles that require it to take a holistic approach to the protection and enhancement of the environment, whilst taking proper account of likely costs and benefits. Hence, where practicable and permissible, the Agency should seek to exercise its functions in combination so as to take a long-term perspective with regard to the contribution that can be made to sustainable development, the enhancement of biodiversity and the protection of the natural heritage.

In relation to flood and coastal defence, the guidance to the Agency on sustainable development reaffirms that the aim of government policy is to reduce risks to people, and the developed and natural environment, from flooding and coastal erosion. However, appropriate opportunities should be taken to enhance the environment and effects on wildlife habitats are regarded as a key consideration. Moreover, flood defence measures should be part of a strategic plan for the coastal area or river catchment concerned and must be shown to be in the national economic and environmental interest in respect of costs and benefits. Hence, 'sustainable' flood and coastal defence schemes are regarded as those which take account of natural processes and other defences and developments within a river catchment or coastal sediment cell and which avoid, as far as possible, committing future generations to inappropriate options for defence.[112]

The Ministers are also bound to give guidance to the Agency with respect to objectives that they consider it generally appropriate for the Agency to pursue in discharging its functions.[113] In relation to this, separate Ministerial guidance has been provided in *The Environment Agency Management Statement*.[114] This requires the Agency to adopt, across all its functions, an integrated approach to environmental protection and enhancement; develop approaches which deliver environmental requirements and goals without imposing excessive costs on regulated organisations or society as a whole; operate to high professional standards, based on sound science, information and analysis of the environment and processes which affect it; and organise its activities in ways which reflect good environmental and management practice and provide value for money for those who pay its charges and taxpayers as a whole.

---

[112] Department of the Environment, Ministry of Agriculture, Fisheries and Food and Welsh Office, *The Environment Agency and Sustainable Development* (1996) *Part II Explanatory Document accompanying the Statutory Guidance* Ch.6 'Guidance material on particular functions', paras.6.29, 6.30 and 6.45. See Ch.12 below on sustainable flood defence.

[113] Under s.4(2) Environment Act 1995.

[114] Department of the Environment, Ministry of Agriculture, Fisheries and Food and Welsh Office, *The Environment Agency Management Statement* (1996).

### 3.4.3 The Costs and Benefits Duty

Another important general responsibility imposed upon the Environment Agency is the explicit duty to have regard to costs and benefits in exercising its powers. This requires the Agency, in considering whether or how to exercise any power conferred upon it, to take reasonable account of the likely costs and benefits of the exercise or non-exercise of the power.[115] For these purposes, 'costs' is stated to include costs to any person and costs to the environment.[116] However, the cost-benefit responsibility imposed upon the Agency does not affect its obligation to discharge any *duties*, comply with any requirements, or pursue any objectives, imposed upon or given to it otherwise than under this provision.[117] Significantly, therefore, the obligation to have regard to costs and benefits applies to the *powers* but not to the *duties* of the Agency. This is particularly significant in the context of flood defence where powers, rather than duties, to act predominate in relation to undertaking works of various kinds.

The ministerial guidance that has been given to the Agency in relation to its principal aim and objectives[118] emphasises the link between the cost-benefit duty and the recognition that sustainable development involves reconciling the need for economic development with that of protecting and enhancing the environment without compromising the ability of future generations to meet their needs. Accordingly, decisions of the Agency should not only ensure that financial and other considerations are taken into account, but that environmental considerations are given a central role unless this is unreasonable to do so.[119]

Practical reinterpretation of the duty with regard to costs and benefits has been provided by the Agency in *Sustainable Development: Taking Account of Costs and Benefits*.[120] This recognises that the duty does not prescribe any particular technique and that the cost of applying the duty should be proportionate to the benefit to be gained. Hence, in relation to small-scale licence or consent applications a detailed survey of all related costs and benefits might be more expensive, in terms of diverted Agency resources, than any eventual benefit secured. Similarly, there may be situations where it is not reasonable fully to apply the duty on a case-by-case basis, such as

---

[115] s.39(1) Environment Act 1995.
[116] s.56(1) Environment Act 1995.
[117] s.39(2) Environment Act 1995.
[118] Under s.4 Environment Act 1995 and see 3.4.2 above on the principal aim and objectives of the Agency.
[119] Department of the Environment, Ministry of Agriculture, Fisheries and Food and Welsh Office, *The Environment Agency Management Statement, The Environment Agency and Sustainable Development* (1996) Ch.5 'Costs and Benefits' para.5.2.
[120] Environment Agency (1999).

where action needs to be taken urgently in an emergency, or in relation to taking legal action. Nonetheless, where the duty is applicable, it is suggested that the Agency's activities should be assessed by the use of techniques which may be used to identify and assess costs, benefits and relevant risks.

In the context of flood defence, the duty to undertake cost-benefit assessment in determining whether powers of the Agency should be exercised, or how they should be exercised, is underscored by the fact that projects which cannot be justified as cost effective will be unlikely to secure government funding.[121] Hence, in many contexts, cost-benefit assessment is already provided for as a part of the funding determination procedure. Outside contexts where government funding is being sought, however, there are other determinations where costs and benefits need to be considered by the Agency. For example, where an application for a flood defence consent,[122] allowing an activity to be undertaken by another person or body, needs to be determined by the Agency, it would be necessary for the Agency to take account of costs and benefits in making its determination.

### 3.4.4 Organisation and Staffing

Although it is commonplace to associate the 'Agency' with the employees that constitute its workforce, in legal terms its identity is more narrowly defined as being the members of its Board.[123] Hence, the Agency is statutorily defined as a corporate legal body consisting of not less than eight nor more than fifteen members appointed by the relevant Ministers.[124] Formally, the Board of the Agency has responsibility for approving the Agency's Corporate Plan, budget and Annual Report and Accounts. The Board also advises in respect of Government consultations, responses to Parliamentary Select Committee investigations and provides general advice to the Government in relation to proposed European Community

---

[121] See Ch.6 below on funding generally.

[122] See 4.4 below on regulatory powers of the Environment Agency.

[123] Although, things required to be done by the Agency may be done by any employee of the Agency who has been authorised by the purpose: Schedule 1 para.6 Environment Act 1995 (subject to the obligation to carry out flood defence functions through regional flood defence committees under s.106 Water Resources Act 1991).

[124] That is, the Secretary of State for Environment, Food and Rural Affairs and the National Assembly for Wales. Under Art.2 and Schedule 1 National Assembly for Wales (Transfer of Functions) Order 1999 (S.I. 1999 No.672), with specified exceptions, all functions of a Minister of the Crown under Environment Act 1995 are, so far as exercisable in relation to Wales, transferred to the Assembly. However, this only encompasses s.1(2)(b) Environment Act 1995, concerning appointments to the Agency previously made by the Secretary of State for Wales, where his function is transferred to the Assembly to the extent that it may make such appointments as will ensure that there is at all times one member of the Agency appointed by the Assembly.

## The Environment Agency 121

and national legislation impacting upon the Agency's functions.

The Agency staff in 1999–2000 consisted of 10,151 persons, though it is anticipated that, due to the significant additions to its workload, the total would increase to over 10,600 over the two following years. Of the total, 5,782 are devoted to water management generally and flood defence occupies the greater proportion of these, with 3,736 persons being primarily involved in this sector of activity.[125]

A range of Agency advisory committees are provided for under Part I of the Environment Act 1995. These include an Advisory Committee for Wales and Regional Environment Protection Advisory Committees.[126] Alongside the statutory advisory committees, the Board of the Agency has established six non-statutory advisory committees to assist it in policy and strategic deliberations relating to different functions and sectors of activity, including water and flood defence.[127] However, for flood defence purposes, the principal responsibilities are discharged through Regional Flood Defence Committees.

### 3.4.5 Regional Flood Defence Committees

The Agency is generally required to discharge its flood defence function through regional flood defence committees, ten of which are presently established.[128] These committees are to discharge the flood defence functions of the Agency for their respective areas and, where the area of more than one regional flood defence committee is involved, flood defence activities may be conducted jointly by committees or in accordance with arrangements made by the Agency.[129]

The Agency may give a regional flood defence committee directions of a general or specific character as to the carrying out of its flood defence functions, other than internal drainage functions,[130] if the carrying out of a function is likely materially to affect the Agency's management of water

---

[125] Environment Agency, *Corporate Plan 2001/02* (2000) p.72.
[126] Under ss.11 and 12 Environment Act 1995.
[127] Environment Agency, *Annual Report and Accounts 1998/99* (1999) p.12.
[128] House of Commons Agriculture Committee, Sixth Report Session 1997–98, *Flood and Coastal Defence* (1998) HC 707-II, *Memorandum Submitted by the Environment Agency* p.3.
[129] s.106(1) Water Resources Act 1991.
[130] 'Internal drainage functions' means the functions of the Authority under ss.108, 139 and 140 of the Water Resources Act 1991, and ss.2 to 9 (concerned with transfer to and supervision by the Agency of internal drainage boards), 38, 39 and 47 (concerned with differential drainage rates and exemptions from such rates), and 57 and 58(1) (concerned with provisions with respect to contributions by the Agency to the expenses of internal drainage boards and the expenses of the Agency as such a board) Land Drainage Act 1991 (s.106(7) Water Resources Act 1991).

for a purpose other than flood defence. Regional flood defence committees may, in turn, delegate duties to subcommittees or local flood defence committees for districts within their region.[131] However, the Agency is not to make arrangements any other body or committee to carry out any of its functions with respect to the issuing of levies or the making of drainage charges,[132] and the Agency may not authorise any other body or committee to borrow money for purposes connected with the Agency's flood defence function.[133] Essentially, this insulation of the flood defence function from other functions of the Agency is intended to 'ring fence' income and expenditure from other Agency financial resources. Hence regional flood defence committees have a high degree of autonomy in the exercise of their powers, whilst being bound by duties imposed upon the Agency generally and subject to a degree of overall supervision particularly where flood defence interacts with other functions of the Agency.

Provision for regional flood defence committees is now made under the Environment Act 1995 in relation to flood defence functions under the Water Resources Act 1991. Accordingly, each area will have a regional flood defence committee which will undertake flood defence responsibilities for that area, though works may be undertaken beyond the seaward boundaries of the area of the adjacent committee. The Agency is bound to maintain a principal office for the area of each regional flood defence committee.[134] The boundaries of regional flood defence committees are provided for under Schedule 4 to the Environment Act 1995, which allows the relevant Minister to make orders altering the boundaries of committees or to amalgamate them, subject to publicity, consultation and other procedural requirements.

In respect of composition of regional flood defence committees, and subject to transitional arrangements, the chairman and other members are to be appointed by the relevant Minister,[135] two members are appointed by the Agency and a number of members appointed by or on behalf of the constituent councils[136] of the region. In relation to the appointment of a

---

[131] Schedule 5 para.12 Environment Act 1995.
[132] Levies are provided for under the Local Government Finance Act 1988, and the making of charges is provided for under Chapter II of Part VI Water Resources Act 1991.
[133] s.106(2) to (4) Water Resources Act 1991.
[134] s.14 Environment Act 1995.
[135] That is, either the Secretary of State for Environment, Food and Rural Affairs or the National Assembly for Wales.
[136] The 'constituent councils' for this purpose include every county, county borough, metropolitan district or London borough council any part of which is in the area of the regional flood defence committee, including the Common Council of the City of London for the committee comprising any part of the City (s.15(6) Environment Act 1995).

person as a chairman or member of a committee by the Minister, or as a member appointed on behalf of the constituent councils, the appointment is to have regard to the desirability of appointing a person who has experience of, and has shown capacity in, some matter relevant to the functions of the committee.[137] The Agency is empowered to make determinations varying the total number of members of a committee, but the total number of members must not be less than 11 and may not be more than 17 members unless a ministerial order to that effect has been made. In any case, however, the total number of members appointed by the Minister and the Agency must be one less than the number appointed by the constituent councils.[138] Detailed matters concerning the membership and procedure of regional flood defence committees are provided for under Schedule 5 to the Environment Act 1995, which specifies matters such as the terms of appointment, payments, delegation of functions and rules of procedure.

### 3.4.6 Local Flood Defence Committees

Powers are provided to allow local flood defence schemes to be established by the Environment Agency, within the area of a regional flood defence committee, and for the constitution, membership, functions and procedures of a local flood defence committee for that district. Twenty local flood defence committees are presently in existence.[139] The mechanism for creation of local flood defence schemes involves a regional flood defence committee submitting a proposed local scheme to the Agency for an area in which there is no scheme in force or for variation and replacement of an existing scheme. Before submission of the scheme, the regional flood defence committee must consult every local authority whose area falls within the area and organisations representing persons interested in flood defence or agriculture. The Agency must send the proposed scheme to the appropriate Minister, who may approve it, with or without modifications, and fix a date for it to come into force.[140]

A local flood defence committee is normally to consist of not less than 11 and not more than 15 members. However, on recommendation by a regional flood defence committee, ministerial approval may be given for a local committee to comprise more than 15 members. A local committee is to consist of a chairman and members appointed from the regional flood

---

[137] s.15(1) and (5) Environment Act 1995.
[138] s.16 Environment Act 1995.
[139] House of Commons Agriculture Committee, Sixth Report Session 1997–98, *Flood and Coastal Defence* (1998) HC 707-II, *Memorandum Submitted by the Environment Agency* p.3.
[140] s.17 Environment Act 1995.

defence committee and members appointed on behalf of constituent councils. The number of members appointed by the constituent councils is to be one more than the number of members appointed by the regional flood defence committee.[141] Detailed matters relating to the membership and procedure of local flood defence committees are provided for under Schedule 5 to the Environment Act 1995.

### 3.4.7 The Flood Defence Function

Of fundamental importance is the concise statement in the Environment Act 1995 that 'the Agency shall in relation to England and Wales exercise a general supervision over all matters relating to flood defence'.[142] This allocation of overall supervisory responsibility is made subject to the obligation upon the Agency to carry out its flood defence functions through regional flood defence committees.[143] Nonetheless, it is remarkable in constituting one of the few mandatory *duties*, as opposed to powers, that are imposed on public bodies under flood defence legislation. Another exceptional example of a flood defence *duty* arises in relation to the surveying responsibility of the Agency. In respect of this, the Agency must, from time to time, carry out surveys of the areas in relation to which its flood defence function is carried out.[144] This duty is of considerable importance in relation to the need to advise local planning authorities of those areas that are subject to flood risk and to provide information to the public generally in relation to flood defence matters.[145]

Despite its fundamental importance, no further details of the overall supervisory duty of the Agency or the manner in which it is to be exercised are provided for in legislation, other than in relation to the extent of the Agency's flood defence jurisdiction. On this, it is provided that the flood defence function of the Agency extends to the territorial sea adjacent to England and Wales so far as the area of any regional flood defence committee includes any area of the territorial sea or provision is made for the exercise of any power in relation to the territorial sea.[146] Where the flood defence function is to be carried out at a place beyond the seaward

---

[141] s.18 Environment Act 1995.
[142] s.6(4) Environment Act 1995.
[143] s.106 Water Resources Act 1991 and see 3.4.5 below on regional flood defence committees.
[144] s.105(2) Water Resources Act 1991 and see 11.2.3 below on the surveying duty. Another *duty* in relation to flood defence requires the Agency to have due regard to the interests of fisheries including sea fisheries when exercising its flood defence powers (s.105(3)).
[145] See Ch.9 below on planning and Ch.11 below on information.
[146] s.2(5) Water Resources Act 1991. Provision for the exercise of flood defence functions in relation to the territorial sea is made under s.165(2) and (3).

boundaries of a regional flood defence committee, that place is assumed to be within the area of the adjacent committee.[147]

However, the Government responded to the 1998 House of Commons Agriculture Committee report with a commitment that the Agency would develop its supervisory responsibilities for all flood defence matters including the adequacy of defences owned by others.[148] A result of this was the publication of the *Elaboration of the Environment Agency's Flood Defence Supervisory Duty*[149] which, in some respects, provides a counterpart to the high level targets[150] for flood and coastal defence which were also established in response to the Select Committee report. The main purpose of the *Elaboration* is to provide more detail on the practical implications of the statutory supervisory duty in relation to flood defence and, particularly, to respond to concerns raised by the Select Committee.

The *Elaboration* affirms the responsibility of the Agency for inspecting, and assessing the condition of, flood defences on main rivers[151] and the compilation and maintenance of a national database, comprising additional information provided by internal drainage boards and local authorities in respect of defences for ordinary watercourses (including 'critical' ordinary watercourses[152]) for which it is responsible. The Agency will also be responsible for inspecting sea and coastal defences except where maritime local authorities are responsible for coast protection works solely for protection against erosion or encroachment of defences that are in the ownership of the maritime authorities. Again, the Agency will be supplied with information on the state of coastal defences that, along with other information, will be stored on the National Flood and Coastal Defence Asset Database which will be used to supply Ministers and the public with information.

The Agency is responsible for assessment of the risk associated with sea and main river flood defences and, in partnership with other operating authorities, must agree methods of risk assessment and standards of defence. These methods will be used by all operating authorities to assess

---

[147] s.9(2)(b) Water Resources Act 1991.
[148] See House of Commons Agriculture Committee, Sixth Report Session 1997–98, *Flood and Coastal Defence* (1998) HC 707 and House of Commons, Agriculture Committee, Fifth Special Report for Session 1997–98, *Replies by the Government and the Environment Agency to the Sixth Report from the Agriculture Committee Session 1997–98 'Flood and Coastal Defence'* (HC 707) (1998) HC 1117.
[149] (1999) available on the Department for the Environment, Food and Rural Affairs website: http://www.defra.gov.uk/environ/fcd/default.
[150] See 3.2.12 above on the high level targets.
[151] See 3.4.8 below on 'main rivers'.
[152] See 3.4.8 below on 'critical ordinary watercourses'.

risk associated with all defences on main rivers, critical ordinary watercourses and coastal defences. Where cause for concern is found, the operating authority will draw this to the attention of the owner of a defence and seek remedial action. In conjunction with other operating authorities, the Agency will provide the Ministers with annual reports on the achievement of high level targets.

The Agency, in conjunction with the other operating authorities, must endeavour to provide efficient and effective flood warnings[153] and to ensure that appropriate emergency planning, operational and emergency responses, incident management and aftercare are provided. This will involve the carrying out of flood emergency exercises, alongside operating authorities, emergency services and others, at national regional and local levels.[154] The Agency will also agree and implement methods for raising public awareness of flood risk, along with other operating authorities.

The *Elaboration* also reaffirms the role of the Agency in respect of providing guidance to local planning authorities regarding development of areas at risk of flooding, or developments that give rise to a risk of flooding elsewhere, and the obligation to report to Ministers concerning adverse policies in development plans and instances where planning permission has been given contrary to Agency advice.[155] The Agency will produce annual statistics of applications for consent to carry out works on main rivers and ordinary watercourses on the basis of information provided by all operating authorities. The Agency will also prepare water level management plans where needed, and give advice to other operating authorities to assist in the preparation of plans for their areas, with reports being provided to the Ministers on the preparation of such plans and on the impact of flood and coastal defence operations on habitats covered by biodiversity action plans.

Most recently the Agency has provided further detail on its flood defence function in *Reducing Flood Risk*.[156] This reaffirms the Agency's overall long-term objective with respect to flooding:

> '[f]lood warning and sustainable defences will continue to prevent deaths from flooding. Property damage and distress will be minimised. The role of wetlands in reducing flood risks will be recognised and all the environmental benefits from natural floods will be maximised.'

---

[153] Generally see 11.3 below on flood warnings.
[154] See 11.3.4 below on emergency responses.
[155] See 9.8 below on development and flood risk.
[156] Environment Agency, *A Framework for Change: Reducing Flood Risk* (2001).

## The Environment Agency

In addition, a range of goals and actions for the Agency and others, and their respective outcomes, are set out:

(1) flood warnings will be given in good time, acted upon and damage minimised;

(2) people will accept the need to avoid flood risks, take warnings seriously;

(3) nationally consistent standards of flood defences will be put in place to meet the challenges of climate change;

(4) flood defences will be designed and constructed to deliver optimum environmental benefits;

(5) flood risks arising from land use and climate change will be recognised, understood and fully taken into account in planning decisions;

(6) properties at risk will be designed or modified to cope with the likely consequences of being flooded;

(7) flood defences that may be required because of new development will be fully funded by developers as part of that development, and should not lead to additional flood risk;

(8) innovative uses of technology will improve the ability to predict and cope with floods; and

(9) benefits for water resources and wildlife will be achieved from natural flood events.

In some respects, the role of the Agency is central in meeting these outcomes; in other respects it is a substantial partner in achieving the outcome or has an involvement in building greater understanding. Further objectives for flood defence and target dates by which they are to be met are set out in the Agency's *Corporate Plan*.[157]

### 3.4.8 Main River Functions

Primarily, the powers conferred on flood defence operating authorities, under the Water Resources Act 1991 and the Land Drainage Act 1991, are exercisable only by the Environment Agency in relation to 'main rivers'.[158] The principle of catchment boards having primary responsibility for main

---

[157] See, most recently, Environment Agency, *Corporate Plan 2001/02* (2000) p.49.
[158] s.107(1) and 165(1) Water Resources Act 1991 and s.14(2) Land Drainage Act 1991.

rivers was first established by the Land Drainage Act 1930[159] and essentially the same responsibilities now rest with the Agency. Following the commencement of the 1930 Act, disputes arose between catchment boards and internal drainage boards as to the precise limits of their respective jurisdictions in respect of main rivers. Resolution of these disputes served to determine the operational significance of a watercourse being designated as a 'main river'.

A key determination was *North Level Commissioners v River Welland Catchment Board*[160] where the claimant internal drainage board sought a declaration that the defendants had been made responsible for the maintenance of a flood defence structure, on the ground that it was a 'bank' of a main river under the 1930 Act which was, therefore, the responsibility of the Catchment Board. The particular structure, Barrier Bank, was situated at some distance from the main river channel and had a long history of statutory maintenance obligations, but it was established that it was the responsibility of the claimants before the 1930 Act came into effect. The statutory scheme for the transfer of responsibilities to the Catchment Board had indicated that all 'rights, powers, duties, obligations and liabilities' over or in connection with the main river were to be transmitted to the Board. Curiously, earlier statutes had referred to the Barrier Bank as a 'bank' of the main river and, therefore, the internal drainage board argued that responsibility for it had been transferred to the Catchment Board under the 1930 Act.

Against this, it was noted that the area of the Catchment Board was designated on a map of the catchment area determined by the Ministry of Agriculture. The definitive map revealed that the catchment area boundary ran along the middle of the Barrier Bank, with half of it being placed in the catchment area of another main river. However, the area of the main river within the catchment area, indicated in red in the definitive map, did not include the Barrier Bank. Moreover, the definition of 'bank' used in the 1930 Act referred to structures 'adjoining or confining' the main river channel. On the facts, the Barrier Bank was located, at some points, a distance of three-quarters of a mile from the main river channel. Hence, it did not serve to 'confine' the flow within the ordinary channel of the main river, but was intended to protect land that was remote from the main river, from flooding. In addition, the court was concerned that the interpretation sought by the claimants would have indirectly resulted in maintenance *obligations* being transferred to the Catchment Board by the 1930 Act,

---

[159] See 1.9.3 above on the Land Drainage Act 1930.
[160] [1937] 4 All ER 684.

whereas the Act generally sought only to provide *powers* to maintain main river flood defence works. For a range of reasons, therefore, the conclusion was that the obligation to maintain the Barrier Bank had not been transferred to the Catchment Board and remained a responsibility of the internal drainage board.

Under present provisions, main rivers[161] are conclusively defined by 'main river maps' relating to areas of regional flood defence committees, showing in a distinctive colour the extent to which any watercourse in an area is to be treated as a main river, and indicating which watercourses are designated under special drainage schemes.[162] Watercourses which are not designated as main rivers are termed 'ordinary watercourses'.[163] In practice, about 36,600 km of watercourses are designated as main rivers.[164]

The Agency is bound to keep the main river map for the area of a regional flood defence committee at the principal office of the Agency for that area and to provide reasonable facilities for inspecting the map and taking copies of extracts from it. Main river maps are subject to amendment by the Ministers by the substitution of the whole or part of an existing map and a specification of the date on which the substitution takes effect. Alternatively, the Agency may apply to a Minister for a variation of a main river map following the consideration of any objections.[165]

No statutory criteria are provided to determine the circumstances in which a watercourse should be designated as a main river. Clearly, however, designation is of considerable importance in allowing the Agency to exercise its flood defence powers and undertake operations in relation to key watercourses. Likewise, designation will allow the Agency to exercise control over operations in a watercourse through the exercise of its

---

[161] 'Main river' includes any structure or appliance for controlling or regulating the flow of water into, in or out of the channel which is situated in the channel or in any part of the banks of the channel and is not vested in or controlled by an internal drainage board. 'Banks' means banks, walls or embankments adjoining or confining, or constructed for the purposes of or in connection with, any channel or sea front, and includes all land and water between the bank and low-watermark (s.113(1) Water Resources Act 1991). On the meaning of 'banks' under previous legislation, see *Jones* v *Mersey River Board* [1957] 3 All ER 375, discussed at 4.3.4 below and *Oakes* v *Mersey River Board* (1957) 9 P&CR 145, discussed at 4.3.2 below.
[162] However, if any question arises whether any work, or proposed work, is drainage work in connection with a main river, the question is to be referred to one of the Ministers for decision or, if either of the parties so requires, to arbitration (s.73(1) Land Drainage Act 1991). See 6.3.10 below on special drainage schemes under s.137 Water Resources Act 1991.
[163] s.72(1) Land Drainage Act 1991.
[164] Environment Agency, *A Framework for Change: Reducing Flood Risk* (2001) p.17.
[165] ss.193 and 194 Water Resources Act 1991.

consenting powers, requiring works to be undertaken[166] and the enforcement of Agency flood defence byelaws.[167] In addition, the responsibilities of the Agency in relation to the provision of flood warning services will normally arise only in relation to those main rivers that constitute a flooding hazard. Conversely, where a watercourse is *not* designated as a main river it will generally be dealt with under the flood defence powers of internal drainage boards and local authorities which are provided in respect of ordinary watercourses.[168]

Given the operational significance of a watercourse being designated as a main river, it might be thought that the criteria to be applied would be transparent and fully appreciated by all with an interest in the matter. However, this is not the case, since there is considerable ignorance on the part of the public, and some local authorities, and the need for greater clarity and rationality in the allocation of responsibilities has been recognised.[169] The more fundamental point has been made that where the quality of life of people is at risk, the status of the watercourse giving rise to that risk should not be the factor determining whether action is taken. Moreover, although statutory provision is made for ordinary watercourses to be reclassified as main rivers by a process of 'en-maining',[170] in practice, this involves each regional flood defence committee taking the initiative of applying to the relevant Minister for a river or section of river to be en-mained.

Over the years significant differences have arisen between regions of the Environment Agency with regard to which rivers are classified as main rivers and ordinary watercourses. In the North West region, for example, many small watercourses are classified as main rivers simply because in the late 1970s internal drainage boards for that region opted for their own abolition and all the watercourses were en-mained. As a consequence, the region has the second highest length of main river, though it is one of the smaller Agency regions both in size and in terms of the number of properties at risk. More generally, there is a tendency for main rivers to be historically determined, with only minor changes being made from time to

---

[166] That is, under powers provided under s.25 Land Drainage Act 1991, discussed at 4.7.1 below.
[167] See 4.4.1 below on consenting powers and 3.4.10 below on byelaws.
[168] See s.14(2) and Land Drainage Act 1991, in respect of the general drainage powers of internal drainage boards and local authorities, and see 4.6 and 4.7 below.
[169] See P. Bye and M. Horner, *Easter 1998 Floods* (1998) para.1.6(12) which reported that members of the public do not understand why some watercourses are described as *main river*, or the significance of this term in determining whether the Agency is able to provide flood defence.
[170] Under s.194 Water Resources Act 1991.

time, usually by agreement with local authorities. An explanation for this is the unwillingness of flood defence committees to acquire responsibilities for additional lengths of watercourse with consequent future maintenance costs. Hence the criticism has been made, in a recent National Audit Office report, that the present system of en-maining is bureaucratic and complicated, and leads to inconsistencies in the standard of flood defences and warning services between regions. Accordingly, it should be considered whether clearer principles for classifying watercourses are needed to provide a more balanced approach to service provision nationally.[171]

The statutory provisions envisage a fairly decisive distribution of responsibilities between the Agency and other operating authorities, according to whether a watercourse is a main river or an ordinary watercourse. However, this division of responsibility has recently been blurred in relation to 'critical ordinary watercourses', which comprise ordinary watercourses that are recognised to have the potential to put large numbers of people and property at risk of flooding, usually in intensively developed urban areas. In relation to critical ordinary watercourses, the Agency has undertaken to act in partnership with other operating authorities to agree methods of identifying those ordinary watercourses that have critical flooding potential. On the basis of the agreed methodology, internal drainage boards and local authorities will identify and assess the condition of critical ordinary watercourses. In conjunction with the Agency, operating authorities will assess the flood risk associated with defences on critical watercourses and, where these give cause for concern, identify potential solutions.[172] Hence, the Agency has acquired some responsibilities in relation to non-main river watercourses for the purposes of realising high level targets for flood and coastal defence.[173]

### 3.4.9 Transfer of Functions and Arrangements with Other Authorities

The Environment Agency may at any time prepare, and submit to either of the Ministers for confirmation, a scheme making provision for the transfer from any drainage body[174] to the Agency of all rights, powers, duties,

---

[171] See National Audit Office, *Inland Flood Defence* (2001) HC 299 paras.2.27 to 2.35. Generally see E. C. Penning-Rowsell, D. J. Parker and D. M. Harding, *Floods and Drainage* (1986) p.161 on the difficulties involved in en-maining watercourses.

[172] See Ministry of Agriculture, Fisheries and Food, *Elaboration of the Environment Agency's Flood Defence Supervisory Duty* (1999) and discussion at 3.4.7 above.

[173] See 3.2.12 above on the high level targets and note Target 5 in particular.

[174] 'Drainage body' means an internal drainage board or other body having power to make or maintain works for the drainage of land (s.108(9) Water Resources Act 1991).

obligations and liabilities, including liabilities incurred in connection with works, over or in connection with a main river, and any property held by the drainage body in connection with the functions transferred. The Minister to whom a scheme is submitted may confirm the scheme in accordance with the procedure set out in Schedule 14 to the Water Resources Act 1991. Where liabilities are incurred in connection with a scheme of this kind by the transfer of liabilities from a local authority to the Agency, the Agency may require the local authority to contribute towards the discharge of those liabilities.[175]

For the purpose of improving the drainage of any land, the Agency may enter into an arrangement with a navigation or conservancy authority for a range of purposes where the Ministers approve the agreement. This may allow the transfer to the Agency of the whole or part of the undertaking of the navigation or conservancy authority or any of the rights, powers, duties, liabilities and obligations of that authority or any property vested in the authority. Alternatively, the agreement may allow the Agency to alter or improve any of the works of the navigation or conservancy authority, or the making of payments by the Agency to the navigation or conservancy authority, or vice versa, in respect of any matter for which provision is made by the arrangement.[176]

### 3.4.10 Flood Defence Byelaws

The Agency is empowered to make byelaws for the purpose of carrying out its function in relation to flood defence and land drainage, primarily in relation to main rivers.[177] Hence, Schedule 25 to the Water Resources Act 1991 allows the Agency to make byelaws in relation to any particular locality or localities as necessary for securing the efficient working of any drainage system including the proper defence of land against sea or tidal water. In particular, byelaws may be made for the purposes of:

(a) regulating the use, and preventing the improper use, of any watercourses, banks or works vested in the Agency or under its control or for preserving them from destruction;

(b) regulating the opening of sluices and flood gates in connection with any works under (a);

(c) preventing the obstruction of any watercourse vested in the Agency or

---

[175] s.108 Water Resources Act 1991.
[176] s.111 Water Resources Act 1991.
[177] s.210 and Schedules 25 (powers) and 26 (procedures) Water Resources Act 1991 (Schedule 25 as amended by Schedule 22 para.190 Environment Act 1995 to make reference to s.2(1)(a)(iii) of that Act concerning flood defence).

under its control by the discharge into it of any liquid or solid matter or by reason of such matter being allowed to flow or fall into it; and

(d) compelling persons having control of any watercourse vested in the Agency or under its control, or of any watercourse flowing into it, to cut the plant growth in or on the bank of the watercourse and, when cut, to remove them.

Restrictions on these powers are imposed insofar as regulation of the use of watercourses must not prevent reasonable facilities being afforded for watercourses to be used for the purpose of watering stock. Also, byelaws are not to conflict or interfere with the operation of any byelaw made by a navigation, harbour or conservancy authority.[178] Under Schedule 26 to the 1991 Act, the procedural provisions relating to Agency byelaws require these to be confirmed by the relevant Minister, who may, with or without a local inquiry, refuse or confirm any proposed byelaw or confirm it with modification.

Contravention of an Agency byelaw is an offence.[179] Without prejudice to criminal proceedings, the Agency, in enforcing a byelaw, may take such action as is necessary to remedy the effect of the contravention and may recover the expenses reasonably incurred from the person in default.[180]

Present Agency byelaws have been enacted on a regional basis, and often made by different predecessor bodies of the Agency; hence some variations can be seen between byelaws applying in different regions. Nonetheless, the Southern Water Authority Land Drainage and Sea Defence Byelaws 1981 provide an example of the kinds of main river activity that may be subject to byelaw control.[181] These Byelaws regulate the use, maintenance

---

[178] Schedule 25 para.5(1) and (2) Water Resources Act 1991.

[179] The maximum penalty for the offence, on summary conviction, is a fine not exceeding level 5 on the standard scale, presently £5,000, and a further fine not exceeding £40 for each day on which the contravention continues after conviction (s.211(4) Water Resources Act 1991). For an illustration of byelaw regulation see *Hobday v Nicol* [1944] 1 All ER 302, where a byelaw of the Lee Conservancy Board prohibited the construction of any 'structure' on the bank of a main river and it was held that a number of tanks, filled with earth and placed along the bank, constituted 'structures' for the purposes of the byelaw. For further discussion of the implications of byelaw regulation see *Collier v Anglian Water* (1983) *The Times* 23 March, discussed at 11.4.3 below.

[180] s.211(5)(b) and (c) Water Resources Act 1991. On internal drainage board and local authority flood defence byelaws see 3.5.7 below.

[181] See also the Anglian Water Authority Land Drainage and Sea Defence Byelaws 1987, which are similar in most respects though incorporating a contrasting provision for the control of construction and deposition on 'washlands', which are defined as areas of land adjoining a main river which have been confined by a bank or other structure designed for the storage of water.

## Institutional Responsibilities

and discontinuance of various kinds of 'river control works', comprising diverse structures for the control, measurement and regulation of water flow, and prohibit the interference with such works. Further prohibitions are imposed upon activities involving diversions or obstructions of flow. Provision is made to require occupiers of banks to control infestation by burrowing vermin which may damage banks, to require the removal of vegetation which may obstruct flows and to carry out repairs on buildings or structures which may cause an obstruction. Various provisions are made to prevent damage to banks by vehicles, grazing animals, excavations and other activities, the planting of trees, dredging, and the deposition of various materials on banks. Prohibitions are imposed on the mooring of vessels so as to obstruct flow and provision is made for the removal of vessels that have been abandoned. Powers are also given to allow the Agency to impose speed limits upon vessels to prevent damage to banks or drainage works. Largely similar powers and prohibitions are also provided for in relation to the protection of sea defences.

### 3.4.11 Powers of Entry

Although general powers of entry by staff of the Environment Agency are provided for in relation to pollution control functions,[182] separate powers are provided for in relation to entry for land drainage purposes. Hence, any person designated in writing for the purpose by the Ministers or the Agency may enter any premises for specified enforcement purposes. Entry may be for the purpose of ascertaining whether specified provisions are being or have been contravened. In addition, entry may be for the purpose of carrying out inspections, measurements and tests on any premises entered or any articles found on such premises and the authorised person may take away such samples of water, land or articles as the Minister or the Agency considers appropriate for the purpose and has authorised the person to carry out or to take away.[183] These powers of entry apply to any enactment under, or for the purposes of which, the Agency carries out functions,[184] including flood defence activities under the Water Resources Act 1991, the Land Drainage Act 1991, subordinate legislation and Agency byelaws.[185]

Powers of entry for other purposes authorised by Ministers or the Agency are also provided for. These allow any designated person to enter premises

---

[182] s.108 Environment Act 1995.
[183] s.169(1) Water Resources Act 1991.
[184] However, Schedule 22 para.165 Environment Act 1995 amends s.169 Water Resources Act 1991 by a stipulation that the powers of entry described may not be used for the Agency's pollution control functions.
[185] s.169(3) Water Resources Act 1991.

for the purpose of determining whether, and in what manner, any power or duty conferred on either of the Ministers or the Agency should be exercised or performed or exercising or performing any such power or duty. Persons designated in writing for these purposes may carry out such inspections, measurements and test on any premises or vessel entered by that person under the powers, or of any articles found on the premises that are appropriate for the purpose and the person has been authorised to carry out or take away.[186]

### 3.4.12 Incidental Functions

Although the functions of Agency are exhaustively defined by statute, subject to guidance, some flexibility is allowed in their interpretation. Quite widely formulated incidental general powers are provided clarifying, and in some respects broadening, the activities in which the Agency may engage. Accordingly, for relevant purposes,[187] the Agency may do anything which, in its opinion, is calculated to facilitate, or is conducive or incidental to, the carrying out of its functions. Without prejudice to the extreme generality of this power, it may, for the purposes of, or in connection with, the carrying out of its functions, acquire and dispose of land and other property and carry out such engineering or building operations, as it considers appropriate.[188]

Also of significant general importance is the capacity of the Agency to institute criminal proceedings in England and Wales.[189] No explicit general power is given to the Agency to instigate or participate in civil proceedings, such as those involving the seeking of an injunction to prevent the continuation of an activity that is contrary to flood defence law. However, it may be arguable that the use of the civil law in this way is permissible despite the absence of a general power of the Agency to seek injunctions.[190]

---

[186] s.172(1) and (2) Water Resources Act 1991.

[187] 'The relevant purposes' is a reference to the purposes of s.37(1) Environment Act 1995 (concerning incidental general functions of the Agency) as it applies in relation to the Agency and the construction of any other enactment which confers any power on or in relation to the Agency (s.10(1) Environment Act 1995).

[188] s.10(2) Environment Act 1995. In relation to the former National Rivers Authority similar incidental functions were provided for under s.3 Water Resources Act 1991.

[189] s.37(1) Environment Act 1995. In England and Wales, a person who is authorised by the Agency to prosecute on its behalf in proceedings before a magistrates' court is entitled to prosecute in any such proceedings although not a barrister or a solicitor (s.54 Environment Act 1995).

[190] See S. Tromans, *The Environment Acts 1990–1995* (1996) p.533.

## 3.5 INTERNAL DRAINAGE BOARDS

### 3.5.1 Introduction

Internal drainage boards are established for particularly low-lying areas of England and Wales where flood defence and land drainage measures are necessary, on a continuing basis, to sustain primarily agricultural, but some developed land uses.[191] The essentially local functions of boards may be traced back many years, though the present provisions governing their operating may be seen to have been largely defined by the Land Drainage Act 1930. The continuing justification for these relatively autonomous and primarily self-funding bodies for areas of special drainage need was reaffirmed in 1985 when a Government Green Paper noted the justification for bodies to give detailed attention to local issues and to avoid the costs of drainage operations, intended to benefit particular landowners, falling to bodies with catchment-level responsibilities or being placed upon the public purse more generally. Although the principle of local funding being reflected in local control was broadly accepted, emphasis was placed upon the need for boundaries to be drawn with sufficient breadth to allow boards to operate efficiently and upon the accountability of boards to owners of land and constituent local authorities which provide their funds.[192]

The present practical position with regard to internal drainage boards is usefully summarised in a memorandum by the Association of Drainage Authorities submitted to the House of Commons Agriculture Committee in 1998.[193] This memorandum reports that, though the numbers of internal drainage boards in England and Wales have been significantly reduced over the last 20 years, presently 247 boards exist,[194] covering 1.2 million hectares, and with responsibility for 18,000 km of drainage channels, 273 km of culverts and over 600 pumping stations alongside responsibilities regulating the activities of others to prevent obstructions to watercourses.

The areas for which internal drainage boards are established, based upon watercourse catchments, tend to be flat lowland areas subject to high flood

---

[191] Generally see P. Bye and M. Horner, *Easter 1998 Floods* (1998) para.A.5.

[192] See Ministry of Agriculture, Fisheries and Food, *Financing and Administration of Land Drainage, Flood Prevention and Coast Protection in England and Wales* (1985) Ch.4.

[193] Association of Drainage Authorities, *Memorandum submitted by the Association of Drainage Authorities*, submitted to the House of Commons Agriculture Committee, Sixth Report for Session 1997–98, *Flood and Coastal Defence* (1998) HC 707-II.

[194] Although 247 internal drainage boards are in existence, these are served by 68 management units and, in 2001, 15 of the boards were in the process of amalgamating down to 4 (House of Commons Agriculture Committee, Third Report Session 2000–01, *Flood and Coastal Defence Follow Up* (2001) HC 172, *Memorandum Submitted by the Environment Agency* para.2.6).

risk, predominantly in Cambridgeshire, Lincolnshire, Yorkshire, Norfolk, Kent, Somerset and the valleys of the Rivers Severn and Trent. Much of this area, particularly in eastern England, is reclaimed land which is below sea level, with 615,000 hectares being dependent upon pumping to sustain the full range of land uses. Many of the areas for which boards are established tend to be traditionally associated with agricultural land use and boards continue to serve areas that are recognised to have some of the best farmland in Europe. However, the present tendency is for an increasing number of industrial and energy-related land uses to be based within internal drainage districts and to be dependent upon flood defences provided by boards.

The legal functions of internal drainage boards are kept largely separate from those of the Environment Agency, with the functions of the former being specified in Part II of the Land Drainage Act 1991 and those of the latter being set out in Part IV of the Water Resources Act 1991. Nonetheless, internal drainage boards share some common features with the Agency in respect of powers that they possess to undertake and maintain drainage works. Close similarities are also to be seen between the flood defence powers of internal drainage boards and local authorities, which are also provided for under the Land Drainage Act 1991. As indicated below, a number of the powers given to internal drainage boards are also given to local authorities and are considered in common in the following discussion.

However, perhaps the central distinction between the flood defence functions of internal drainage boards and local authorities, and the flood defence function of the Environment Agency, relates to the watercourses over which powers may be exercised. Whilst the Agency is primarily responsible for main rivers,[195] internal drainage boards and local authorities have responsibilities for non-main rivers, termed 'ordinary' watercourses, and surrounding land which will derive benefit or avoid danger as a result of flood defence and land drainage operations.

For the purpose of establishing internal drainage boards, internal drainage districts are identified within the areas of regional flood defence committees, and internal drainage boards established for each internal drainage district.[196] An internal drainage board is to exercise a general supervision over all matters relating to the drainage of land within its district and to have those powers and duties which are provided for under the Land Drainage Act 1991. Whilst the following subsections outline the general legal status of internal drainage boards, their functions in relation to flood defence

---

[195] See 3.4.8 above on main rivers.
[196] See s.6 Land Drainage Act 1976 and s.140 Water Act 1989 on the previous provisions

operations and regulation, their funding position, their general environmental duties and their role in the land use planning process are considered in later chapters.

### 3.5.2 Composition and Constitution

An internal drainage board is a body corporate consisting of members elected and holding office in accordance with Schedule 1 to the Land Drainage Act 1991 along with a bare majority of members appointed by those local authorities which are 'billing authorities' for council tax purposes.[197]

The *elected* members holding office under Schedule 1 are owners or occupiers of certain land within the internal drainage district who are elected by the agricultural ratepayers for a 3-year term in accordance with regulations made by the Minister. The members are elected under a voting system which allows up to 10 votes per person and may be cast according to the value of the agricultural land and buildings occupied, thereby giving more votes to those occupiers who contribute higher drainage rates.[198]

Local billing authorities which are subject to special levies[199] issued by an internal drainage board are entitled to *appoint* (rather than 'elect') members of that board. Broadly, the numbers of local authority appointees must not exceed the number of elected members of the board by more than one, and comprise a number of members which is in proportion to the amount of a board's total income that the authorities contribute. In making appointments, the local authorities are to have regard to the desirability of appointing persons who have knowledge or experience, or who have shown capacity, in matters relating to the functions of the board.[200]

The expenses and proceedings of internal drainage boards are governed by

---

[197] s.1(3) Land Drainage Act 1991, as amended by s.1 Local Government Finance Act 1992 (s.72(1) Land Drainage Act 1991 originally provided for 'charging authorities'); s.1(2) of the 1992 Act defines 'billing authority' to include, in relation to England, a district council or London borough council, the Common Council of the City of London and, in relation to Wales, a county council or county borough council; s.1(4) Land Drainage Act 1991 provides for 'first members' of internal drainage boards to be appointed by the Minister together with persons appointed by billing authorities.

[198] Part I Schedule 1 Land Drainage Act 1991 and see Land Drainage (Election of Drainage Boards) Regulations 1938, S.R.&O. 1938 No.558, as amended. However, for internal drainage boards in existence before the Land Drainage Act 1930 came into effect, certain provisions from Schedule 1 to Water Resources Act 1991 apply only so far as they are provided for under a scheme for the reorganisation of an internal drainage district (under s.3 of the 1991 Act or s.7(4) Land Drainage Act 1976, the corresponding provision).

[199] See 6.4.9 below on special levies.

[200] Part II Schedule 1 Land Drainage Act 1991.

Schedule 2 to the Land Drainage Act 1991.[201] This covers matters such as the payment of expenses to members and officers of boards; the making of rules governing procedure, election of chairmen and delegation of matters to committees; and requirements to submit an annual report and to provide annual accounts. Hence, the annual report and accounts of an internal drainage board must be sent to the appropriate Minister,[202] and copies must also be sent to the Environment Agency and the appropriate county council or unitary authority.[203]

### 3.5.3 Boundaries and Reorganisation

The Land Drainage Act 1991 provides for the continuation of internal drainage boards existing under previous legislation. Otherwise, the bare statement is provided that internal drainage boards are to be the boards for internal drainage districts, which comprise areas within the jurisdiction of regional flood defence committees that 'derive benefit, or avoid danger' as a result of drainage operations.[204] Interpretation of this phrase involves an appreciation that catchment areas and internal drainage districts were previously defined by mechanisms under the Land Drainage Act 1930. The 1930 Act required catchment boards to submit, for ministerial confirmation, schemes for reorganisation of internal drainage boards which served to define the boundaries of districts of such boards.[205] Although provision is made for the alteration of boundaries, the implementation of the 1930 Act in this respect largely served to define the boundaries of internal drainage boards in a way that continued to apply under successive legislation.

The difficulties inherent in the issue of what land 'derives benefit or avoids danger' as a result of drainage operations was practically, if somewhat arbitrarily, resolved by the 'Medway Letter' of 1933.[206] This document set

---

[201] s.1(5) Land Drainage Act 1991.
[202] 'The Minister' for the purposes of the Land Drainage Act 1991 means the Secretary of State for Environment, Food and Rural Affairs or the National Assembly for Wales depending upon the location of an internal drainage board (see 3.2 and 3.3 above). 'The relevant Minister' in relation to internal drainage districts which are partly in Wales or to the boards for such districts means both the Secretary of State for Environment, Food and Rural Affairs and the National Assembly for Wales (see s.72(1) Land Drainage Act 1991).
[203] Schedule 2 paras.4 and 5 Land Drainage Act 1991.
[204] s.1(1) Land Drainage Act 1991.
[205] s.4(1)(b) Land Drainage Act 1930.
[206] That is, the letter sent by the Minister of Agriculture and Fisheries to the Clerk of the River Medway Catchment Board on 28 June 1933 as a response to a public inquiry into schemes prepared by the Board for the Upper Medway and Lower Medway Drainage Districts under s.4(1)(b) Land Drainage Act 1930. The text of the letter appears as an appendix to A. S. Wisdom, *Land Drainage* (1966).

out the general principles that were to be applied by catchment boards in defining the boundaries of internal drainage districts. In relation to non-tidal areas, the view was taken that agricultural land up to 8 ft above the highest known flood may properly be brought within a drainage district, though the general limit for developed land was identified as flood level. The higher level in relation to agricultural land was intended to reflect the adverse effects of shallow water saturation upon agricultural productivity, whereas saturation of this kind was not generally thought to have an adverse effect upon developed areas. In relation to tidal areas, the view was taken that the boundary line should include agricultural land to a limit of 5 ft above ordinary spring tides, where land adjacent to a sea embankment is below the level of ordinary spring tides, and in urban areas only to tidal levels. Exceptions to this general guidance were allowed for in certain situations, for example, where higher land derived benefit from drainage operations through not being cut off in times of flood. Nonetheless, the principles established by the Medway Letter served to define internal drainage districts in a way that has continued to apply to many present boundaries.

Where a petition for the alteration of the boundaries of an internal drainage district is made to the Environment Agency by a sufficient number of 'qualified persons' or by a 'qualified authority',[207] and the boundaries of the district have not been reviewed in the previous 10 years, the Agency is bound to review those boundaries. The process of review involves the Minister being informed, and the publication of a notice concerning the review and a statement that representations may be made to the Agency within 30 days. The Agency is then bound to consider any representations made and to consult the internal drainage board concerned. The Minister must then be informed whether the Agency proposes to submit a scheme for the reorganisation of the internal drainage district. Where the Agency does not propose to submit a scheme for reorganisation, but considers that an order subdividing a district for the purposes of raising expenses should be made by the drainage board,[208] the Agency may direct that board to make

---

[207] Subject to Schedule 2 para.19 of the Water Consolidation (Consequential Provisions) Act 1991, which makes provision with respect to qualification by reference to drainage rates levied on land in respect of years beginning before 1993. 'Qualified persons' are persons who are the owners and occupiers of any land in the district in respect of which a drainage rate is levied. 'A sufficient number of qualified persons' means not less than forty, or not less than one-fifth of the number of persons who are qualified or persons for whom the assessable value of their land, for the purposes of the last drainage rate levied in the district, is not less than one-fifth of the assessable value of all the land in respect of which that rate was levied (s.72(2) Land Drainage Act 1991). 'Qualified authority' in relation to an internal drainage district, means a billing authority for an area wholly or partly included in that district (s.72(1)).

[208] An order subdividing a district may be made under s.38 Land Drainage Act 1991.

an order on specified terms. However, a direction of this kind will not come into effect unless confirmed by the Minister if the internal drainage board objects to the direction.[209]

Schemes for the reorganisation of internal drainage districts are further provided for whereby the Agency may, and must if directed by the Minister, submit to him for confirmation a scheme for the constitution of new internal drainage districts and boards and other matters. Other matters within such schemes may include:

(1) the alteration of boundaries of any internal drainage board;

(2) the amalgamation of the whole or any part of an internal drainage district with another district;

(3) the abolition of Commissioners of Sewers;

(4) the abolition or reconstruction of any internal drainage district and drainage board;

(5) the constitution of new internal drainage districts;

(6) the constitution of internal drainage boards for all or any of the separate internal drainage districts constituted by the scheme;

(7) the amendment of the method of constituting an internal drainage board; and

(8) the making of alterations in, or additions to, local Acts and awards; and

any supplemental or consequential matters.

Provision is made for a reorganisation scheme to be submitted to the relevant Minister and a copy to every internal drainage board, local authority, navigation, harbour and conservancy authority affected by it, and for publication in newspapers allowing for representations to be made within 1 month of publication. The Minister may confirm the scheme, with or without modification, in accordance with the detailed provisions set out in Schedule 3 to the Land Drainage Act 1991.[210]

On a petition by the Agency presented to the Minister, he may transfer to

---

[209] s.2 Land Drainage Act 1991. These provisions do not require the Agency to carry out a review or publish any notice on a petition which, in the opinion of the Minister, is frivolous (s.2(7)).
[210] s.3 Land Drainage Act 1991. See also reg.7 Land Drainage (General) Regulations 1932, S.R.&O. 1932 No.64, and reg.6 Land Drainage (River Authorities) General Regulations 1965, S.I. 1965 No.443.

the Agency the powers, duties, liabilities, obligations and property, including maps, deeds and other documents, of the drainage board of any internal drainage district. Where this is done, the Agency becomes the drainage board for that district.[211] The converse provision is that where, by virtue of a scheme for the reorganisation of internal drainage districts, or an order for the transfer of functions to the Agency, the Agency is the drainage board of an internal drainage district, the Minister may constitute an internal drainage board for that district and transfer to it the property and liabilities of the Agency as the drainage board for that district. An order of this kind requires a petition for constituting an internal drainage board for that district to be made to the Agency by a sufficient number of qualified persons, or by a qualified authority. The Agency must send a copy of the petition to the Minister, who is bound to consider the views of the Agency before making an order of this kind.[212]

### 3.5.4 Supervisory Role of Internal Drainage Boards

Internal drainage boards have a duty to exercise general supervision over all matters relating to the drainage of land within their districts.[213] Largely, the supervisory duty is exercised through determining consent applications for flood defence works undertaken, or proposed to be undertaken, by others, or by taking enforcement action in relation to certain obstructions in ordinary watercourses.[214]

### 3.5.5 Supervisory Role of the Environment Agency

A consequence of the general supervisory role of the Environment Agency in relation to flood defence matters is that it exercises supervision over the activities of internal drainage boards. Hence, for securing the efficient working and maintenance of existing drainage works and the construction of new drainage works, the Agency may give general or specific directions for the guidance of internal drainage boards with respect to their powers and duties. The consent of the Agency is required, but may not be unreasonably withheld, for an internal drainage board to construct drainage works, or alter existing drainage works, if they will affect the working of any drainage works belonging to another internal drainage board. An internal drainage board may not, except where maintenance of an existing

---

[211] s.4 Land Drainage Act 1991.
[212] s.5 Land Drainage Act 1991.
[213] s.1(2)(a) Land Drainage Act 1991, though contrast the general supervisory role of the Environment Agency, discussed at 3.4.7 above, and note the supervision of internal drainage boards by the Agency, discussed at 3.5.5 above.
[214] See 4.5 below on the operational and regulatory powers of internal drainage boards.

work is involved, construct or alter any structure, appliance or channel for the discharge of water from their district into a main river except by agreement with the Agency or, in default, by determination of the Minister.[215]

In the event of an internal drainage board acting in contravention of these provisions, the Agency may execute any works and do anything necessary to prevent or remedy any damage resulting from the action of the internal drainage board. The Agency may also recover from the board the expenses reasonably incurred in exercising that power. Questions as to whether the consent of the Agency is unreasonably withheld, or whether a conditional consent is unreasonable, must be referred to the Minister.[216] The Agency has powers in relation to the prohibition of obstructions in watercourses[217] which are exercisable concurrently with the powers of an internal drainage board.[218]

Further supervision of the activities of internal drainage boards arises through the Agency being empowered to exercise the powers of a board where it has failed to take satisfactory action in relation to flood defence measures. Hence, default powers will arise if the Agency is of the opinion that land is injured or likely to be injured by flooding or inadequate drainage which might be remedied wholly or partially by an internal drainage board exercising its powers. This will arise where powers of a board are either not being exercised at all or are not being exercised to the necessary extent, and in either instance the Agency may exercise all or any of the powers. Before exercising default powers in this manner, however, the Agency is required to give 30 days' notice of its intention to do so. If the drainage board objects, the Agency must obtain the consent of the Minister before exercising the powers. The Minister may hold a public local inquiry with respect to the objection.[219]

In exercising the powers of an internal drainage board in circumstances of default, the Agency is entitled to inspect and take copies of any deeds, maps, books and other documents in the possession of the internal drainage board relating to land drainage in the district of the board. Any person who intentionally obstructs or impedes any person authorised for this purpose will commit an offence.[220]

---

[215] s.7(1) to (3) Land Drainage Act 1991.
[216] s.7(4) and (5) Land Drainage Act 1991.
[217] Under ss.23 and 24 Land Drainage Act 1991 and see 4.4.2 below.
[218] s.8 Land Drainage Act 1991.
[219] s.9(1) to (4) Land Drainage Act 1991.
[220] s.9(5) and (6) Land Drainage Act 1991. The penalty for the offence, on summary conviction, is a fine not exceeding level 4 on the standard scale, presently £2,500.

An alternative to the default powers being exercised by the Agency is that they may be exercised by certain local authorities. Hence, the Agency may, on application of the council of any county, metropolitan district or London borough, direct that the power to act in default of an internal drainage board is to be exercised by that council instead of the Agency. If the Agency refuses such an application, the council may appeal to the Minister, who may require the Agency to comply with the application.[221]

### 3.5.6 Relationships with Other Operating Authorities

Although internal drainage boards are subject to overall supervision by the Environment Agency, provision is made for undertakings of various kinds to be entered into between boards and the Agency. Hence, the Agency may enter into an agreement with any internal drainage board for the carrying out by the board of any work in connection with a main river which the Agency is authorised to carry out. Conversely, with the consent of an internal drainage board, the Agency may carry out and maintain works which the board is authorised to carry out or maintain them on such terms as are agreed, or the Agency may agree to contribute to the expense of carrying out maintenance of any works by an internal drainage board. Between two internal drainage boards agreements may be made for one board to carry out or maintain works in the district of another board on such terms as may be agreed, or for one board to agree to contribute towards the expense of works by the board for another district.[222]

As between an internal drainage board and a local authority, the flood defence powers of a local authority may normally only be exercised where an internal drainage board does not exist, or with the consent of an internal drainage board. In local authority areas where no internal drainage board exists the potential problem of overlapping flood defence powers does not arise. In practice, it appears that local authorities tend to be more concerned in providing flood defence for urban areas and rarely become involved in the projects for the purpose of draining agricultural land of the kind that are characteristically undertaken by internal drainage boards.

Minor watercourses generally remain the primary responsibility of riparian owners but, as will be seen, internal drainage boards have powers to give consent for private drainage works or to require the removal of certain obstructions which interfere with flood defence.[223]

---

[221] s.10 Land Drainage Act 1991.
[222] s.11 Land Drainage Act 1991.
[223] See 4.7 below on regulatory powers of internal drainage boards.

### 3.5.7 Byelaws

Quite extensive provision is made for internal drainage boards and certain local authorities to make flood defence byelaws. Given the similarities, it is convenient to consider the byelaw-making powers of internal drainage boards and local authorities together.[224]

An internal drainage board or a local authority, other than a county council, may make such byelaws as are necessary for securing the efficient working of the drainage system in its district or area. Without prejudice to the generality of this, particular byelaws may be made for purposes encompassing:

(1) the regulation of proper use of watercourses or works vested in the internal drainage board or authority;

(2) the opening of sluices and flood gates;

(3) the prevention of obstruction of watercourses vested in the board or authority; and

(4) compelling persons having control of watercourses vested in the board or authority to cut and remove vegetable growths.[225]

However, the powers to make byelaws may not be exercised by an internal drainage board in connection with a main river or its banks, or any drainage works in connection with a main river. Insofar as local authorities are concerned, the byelaw-making powers may be exercised only so far as necessary for the purpose of preventing flooding or remedying or mitigating damage caused by flooding.[226]

Procedural requirements stipulate that byelaws will not be valid unless confirmed by the relevant Minister.[227] Further provision concerning the making of byelaws is made in Schedule 5 to the Land Drainage Act 1991 which deals with matters such as publicity of application for confirmation, confirmation, commencement, publicity of a confirmed byelaw and revocation.[228]

---

[224] See 3.4.10 above on the byelaw-making powers of the Environment Agency.
[225] s.66(2) Land Drainage Act 1991. However, in relation to (1), no byelaw will be valid if it prevents reasonable facilities being afforded to enable a watercourse to be used by stock for drinking purposes (s.66(4)).
[226] s.66(3) Land Drainage Act 1991.
[227] s.66(5) Land Drainage Act 1991.
[228] The procedure for making byelaws is subject to s.236 Local Government Act 1972.

Contravention of, or failure to comply with, a byelaw is an offence.[229] Where contravention of, or failure to comply with, a byelaw occurs an internal drainage board or a local authority may take such action as is necessary to remedy the effect of the contravention or failure, providing that the consent of the Environment Agency has been obtained for such works. Following work being undertaken by the board or authority, it may recover the expenses reasonably incurred from the person in default. Although it is envisaged that local authority byelaws will normally be made by district or unitary authorities, subject to a power of appeal, default powers are provided to allow byelaws to be made by a county council where notice is given to the district council. Byelaws may not authorise the carrying out of any works in connection with a main river and byelaws must not conflict with the operation of any byelaws made by a navigation authority, harbour authority or conservancy authority.[230]

Byelaws of particular internal drainage boards or local authorities will differ in each case, but an example is provided by the River Stour (Kent) Internal Drainage Board Byelaws 1991. These Byelaws allow the Board to control activities increasing the flow of waters in the district, the use and maintenance of sluices and other drainage structures, and the diversion of obstruction of water flows. Various measures prohibit or allow control of activities which may damage banks or other structures by detrimental substances or the lighting of fires. Provision is made to require persons to remove vegetation in or alongside watercourses, prohibiting obstructions or requiring the repair of buildings or other structures that may impede the flow of a watercourse. Various mechanisms are provided to prevent damage to banks through infestation by burrowing animals, by grazing animals and by vehicles. Storage of materials on banks is prohibited, as are dredging operations and various kinds of excavations unless the consent of the Board is obtained. Prohibitions are imposed upon activities obstructing tidal outfalls, interference with sluices, damage to banks or other property of the Board and obstruction of officers of the Board exercising functions under the Byelaws.

### 3.5.8 Powers of Entry

In relation to flood defence, the powers of entry given to staff of internal drainage boards and relevant local authority personnel are the same. Notably however, the land drainage powers of entry of persons authorised

---

[229] The penalty for the offence, on summary conviction, is a fine not exceeding level 5 on the standard scale, presently £5,000, and continuing contravention after conviction is subject to a further daily fine of £40 for every day on which the contravention continues (s.66(6) Land Drainage Act 1991).

[230] s.66(7) to (9) Land Drainage Act 1991.

by internal drainage boards are analogous but separately provided for from those of Environment Agency staff.[231] Hence, any person authorised by an internal drainage board, or a local authority, after producing, if so required, a duly authenticated document showing authority, may at all reasonable times:

(1) enter any land for the purpose of exercising any function of the board, or any function of the local authority under the Land Drainage Act 1991;

(2) without prejudice to (1), enter and survey any land and take levels of the land and inspect the condition of any drainage work on it; and

(3) inspect and take copies of any Acts of Parliament, awards or other documents in the possession of any internal drainage board, local authority or navigation authority which relate to drainage of the land and confer any powers or impose any duties on that board or authority.[232]

A person who is authorised to enter land may take with him such other persons and such equipment as may be necessary and if the land is unoccupied he must, on leaving, leave it as effectually secured against trespassers as he found it. Except in an emergency, admission to land may not be demanded unless written notice of the intended entry has been given to the occupier and, if the land is used for residential purposes or the demand is for admission with heavy equipment, notice of this must be given not less than 7 days before the demand for entry is made. Where injury is sustained by any person by reason of the exercise of any of the powers of internal drainage boards or local authorities, the board or authority is liable to make full compensation to the injured person. In a case of dispute, the amount of compensation payable is determined by the Lands Tribunal. Any person intentionally obstructing or impeding any person exercising a power of entry conferred on an internal drainage board or local authority will commit an offence.[233]

---

[231] See 3.4.11 above on powers of entry relating to Environment Agency staff.
[232] s.64(1) Land Drainage Act 1991. See *Pattinson and Another* v *Finningley Internal Drainage Board* [1970] 2 QB 33 where it was unsuccessfully argued that the powers of entry were only for maintenance of existing works. See also *Dwr Cymru Cyfyngedig* v *Williams* (1991) *The Times* 9 October, where the powers of entry of a water undertaker under warrant (now see Schedule 6 para.2 Water Industry Act 1991) allowed the undertaker to enter land for the purpose of gaining entry to *adjoining* land.
[233] s.64(2) to (6) Land Drainage Act 1991. The penalty for the offence, on summary conviction, is a fine not exceeding level 4 on the standard scale, presently £2,500.

## 3.6 LOCAL AUTHORITIES

### 3.6.1 Introduction

Alongside the Environment Agency and internal drainage boards, the other principal flood and coastal defence operating authorities are the 400 local authorities. In maritime areas, it may be noted that 88 local authorities comprise 'coast protection authorities' under the Coast Protection Act 1949, though the special role of these authorities is considered elsewhere in this work.[234] Also notable is the fact that local authorities have a range of other responsibilities that may impact upon flood defence and land drainage, particularly in respect of public health, highways, reservoirs and land use planning, and these are considered elsewhere in this work. The discussion that follows, therefore, concentrates primarily on the general flood defence functions of local authorities as these are provided for under Part II of the Land Drainage Act 1991, which makes diverse provision for securing the drainage of land, and other miscellaneous and supplemental matters which arise under Part V of the Act.

Local authorities are implicitly placed alongside the Environment Agency and internal drainage boards as operating authorities by the opaque statutory formula 'any other body having the power to make or maintain works for the drainage of land'.[235] 'Local authorities', for these purposes, includes county councils, county borough councils (in Wales), borough councils (in England), metropolitan and non-metropolitan district councils, London boroughs and the Common Council of the City of London.[236] However, there are significant differences in the flood defence and land drainage powers allocated to different levels and categories of local authority.

Local government in most areas follows a two-tier structure involving county and district authorities, with administrative functions distributed correspondingly. However, in consequence of the reorganisation of local government in both England and Wales,[237] unitary authorities now exist in some areas and possess the powers of both county and district councils. In Wales, all authorities are now unitary authorities, but in England unitary authorities exist in metropolitan districts and London boroughs and further areas where unitary authorities have been recently established. Where a two-tier system of local government is in place, contrasts exist between the drainage powers that are allocated at district level and at county level.

---

[234] See Ch.5 below on coast protection.
[235] See s.72(1) Land Drainage Act 1991 which uses the term 'drainage bodies'.
[236] s.72(1) Land Drainage Act 1991, as amended by Local Government (Wales) Act 1994.
[237] See Local Government Act 1992 and Local Government (Wales) Act 1994.

## Local Authorities

Where a unitary local authority exists it may exercise any drainage power. The London unitary authorities are separately provided for in some respects.[238]

Perhaps most notably, the general flood defence works powers allocated to local authorities[239] are not generally available to county councils.[240] The effect of this is that, normally, works of this kind should be undertaken only by district or unitary authorities. However, this is subject to default provisions that allow works to be undertaken by county councils or the Environment Agency where a district council fails to act. Hence, where a non-metropolitan district authority fails to exercise the works powers, they may be exercised by a county council, either at the request of the district council or where 6 weeks' notice has been given by the county council. Where the works powers have not been exercised by a metropolitan district council or a London borough council or the Common Council of the City of London they may be exercised by the Agency, either at the request of the council or following 6 weeks' notice. In either instance, the district council receiving notice that either a county council or the Agency is intending to exercise the works powers may appeal to the Secretary of State, and the powers may not be exercised unless confirmed on appeal.[241]

### 3.6.2 Supervision by the Agency

The Environment Agency retains a supervisory role over land drainage work undertaken by local authorities through a consent system. Hence, before work is carried out by a local authority under the general drainage works powers, or the powers to dispose of spoil, consent is required from the Agency and work must be conducted in accordance with any reasonable conditions imposed by the Agency in giving its consent. Before giving consent in respect of drainage works in connection with a watercourse under the control of an internal drainage board, the Agency is bound to consult with the board. In respect of consents required for local authority works, it is stipulated that consent must not be unreasonably withheld and is deemed to have been given if not determined within 2 months of the application being made. Questions as to whether a consent is 'unreasonably withheld' or whether a condition is 'reasonable' are to be determined by the Minister. These requirements will not apply in respect of work carried

---

[238] See 3.7 below on administration in London.
[239] See 4.6.1 below on the general flood defence works powers of local authorities.
[240] s.14(4)(b) Land Drainage Act 1991. See also s.15(5) on the powers given only to district or unitary authorities in respect of the disposal of spoil and see 4.6.2 below on the disposal of spoil.
[241] s.16 Land Drainage Act 1991.

out in an emergency, but the local authority must inform the Agency of the circumstances and the work carried out as soon as practicable.[242]

### 3.6.3 Arrangements with Other Persons

Any local authority, other than a council of a non-metropolitan district, may, by agreement with any person and at that person's expense, carry out and maintain drainage works which that person is entitled to carry out and maintain. Hence, county or unitary authorities may undertake drainage work on behalf of owners or occupiers of land providing that this work is reimbursed, and such work may be conducted either within or outside the area of the authority. However, the obligation of the person on behalf of whom the work is undertaken to meet the expense may be reduced where the appropriate Minister has made a grant to the local authority in respect of the work that is carried out.[243]

### 3.6.4 Powers of Entry and Byelaws

The powers of entry of local authority personnel and the powers of a local authority to make byelaws are essentially the same as those of internal drainage boards and have been considered above.[244]

## 3.7 LONDON

### 3.7.1 Administrative Arrangements

Under previous legislation,[245] flood defence functions in respect of a 'London excluded area' were conferred upon London borough councils and the Common Council of the City of London. These councils were empowered to exercise functions concurrently with the former Greater London Council in relation to certain metropolitan watercourses, though the Greater London Council had exclusive powers in relation to 'main' metropolitan watercourses. However, with the abolition of the Greater London Council, its flood defence functions passed to the Thames Water Authority, and were subsequently transferred to the National Rivers

---

[242] s.17 Land Drainage Act 1991.

[243] s.20 Land Drainage Act 1991, and see s.59(6) on grants to drainage bodies and 6.4.2 below.

[244] See 3.5.8 above on powers of entry and 3.5.7 above on byelaws.

[245] That is, the Land Drainage Act 1976, s.116(1) of which defined the 'London excluded area' though this was subsequently amended by the Local Government Act 1985 (Land Drainage Functions) Order 1986, S.I. 1986 No.208. The 1986 Order also subsequently identified the metropolitan watercourses in relation to which the concurrent powers of the Greater London Council applied and the main metropolitan watercourses.

Authority, and now rest with the Environment Agency.[246]

Hence, the present position is that flood defence functions under the Water Resources Act 1991 and the Land Drainage Act 1991 now apply to watercourses in the former London excluded area as they apply in other areas. The Environment Agency will exercise its functions primarily in respect of main rivers in the London area, whilst local authorities will exercise functions in relation to ordinary watercourses.[247] Hence, the general position is that London borough councils, as unitary authorities, will have the same powers as those possessed by district and county councils in other parts of the country. More specifically, this means that London borough councils will be able to exercise permissive powers under the Land Drainage Act 1991 in relation to ordinary watercourses. With some exceptions,[248] the powers under the Act may also be exercised by the Common Council of the City of London.

However, alongside the powers provided for under the principal national enactments, flood defence works are also provided for in the London area under local enactments which continue in force. The Thames River (Prevention of Floods) Acts 1879 to 1962[249] apply to the whole of the tidal Thames and generally allow the Environment Agency to require the execution of flood defence works, and give powers to approve works conducted by others, for the protection of land from flooding by the Thames. For these purposes, the Agency must prepare a plan of flood defence works that are required under the Acts and must serve notice on owners of premises who are required to undertake works. Owners of premises are placed under a duty to execute required works on their premises and, in cases of default, the Agency may carry out the works at the owner's expense. Similar powers allow the Agency to require owners of premises to undertake works of maintenance where banks are identified as being insufficient for effectual flood protection. The Acts also allow the Agency to exercise a general supervision over all banks of the Thames and flood works conducted upon those banks.

---

[246] See s.11(2) Local Government Act 1985, ss.4(1) and 136(2) Water Act 1989.
[247] See 3.4.8 above on main rivers.
[248] Exceptions arise under ss.10, 15 and 57 Land Drainage Act 1991.
[249] The Thames River (Prevention of Floods) Acts 1879 to 1962 comprise the following enactments: Metropolis Management (Thames River Prevention of Floods) Amendment Act 1879; ss.46 and 47 Metropolitan Board of Works (Various Powers) Act 1882, as amended; Part VI London County Council (General Powers) Act 1907, as amended; Part IX London County Council (General Powers) Act 1929, as amended; Part VI London County Council (General Powers) Act 1957, as amended; s.66 London County Council (General Powers) Act 1961; and s.29 London County Council (General Powers) Act 1962. Generally see *Halsbury's Laws of England*, Fourth Edition Reissue, Vol.49(2) *Water* (1997) para.753.

### 3.7.2 The Thames Barrier

Perhaps the most distinguishing feature of flood defence in relation to the London area is the Thames Barrier which serves to protect the City from flooding. As has been seen,[250] the 1953 floods graphically demonstrated the vulnerability of large parts of the London area to flooding from the tidal Thames and the *Waverley Report* stressed the urgent need for a major infrastructure project to safeguard the area from sea surges and other conditions which might give rise to a flooding hazard. Although several schemes were proposed for structures for this purpose, it was not until 1965 that government approval was eventually given for a structure comprising a line of movable flood gates. Although constructed by the former Greater London Council and completed in 1984, the Thames Barrier is now operated by the Environment Agency.

The Thames Barrier is the world's largest movable flood barrier, spanning 520 m across the River Thames at Woolwich Reach. The Barrier comprises four main gates, each over 60 m wide, which can be lowered into the bed of the river to minimise interference with the natural flow of the river and avoid imposing any headroom restriction for shipping. When raised, the gates provide a barrier that is designed to protect the capital from flooding until at least the year 2030. Normally, the Barrier is closed two or three times a year to protect London from flooding; however, between November 2000 and March 2001 the Barrier was closed a remarkable 23 times. The Environment Agency's explanation for this lies in a varying combination of high spring tides, depressions in the North Sea, wind effects up the English Channel and high river flows which were experienced over the period. Nonetheless, there has also been a significant general upward trend in the use of the Barrier over the last decade, though the Agency is unable to say whether this trend is related to global climate changes.[251]

The legal basis for the construction of the Thames Barrier, and its future operation, is a local Act of Parliament, the Thames Barrier and Flood Prevention Act 1972. The preamble to this Act notes the sinking of land in the south-east of England relative to sea levels, the risk of tidal surges and the increasing danger of serious flooding of areas adjoining the tidal Thames, and the consequent justification for the works and measures that are provided for in the Act. Accordingly, powers are provided for the acquisition of lands, properties and easements, and the extinction of certain easements, with compensation being payable in certain cases. A range of

---

[250] See 1.8.1 above on the 1953 Floods.
[251] See Environment Agency website http://www.environment-agency.gov.uk and Environment Agency, 'Sharp rise in Thames Barrier closures', *Environment Action*, Issue 29, July 2001. On climate change see 1.6 above.

works powers enabled the Barrier to be constructed, amongst other things, by allowing dredging and the disposal of spoil to be undertaken and the closure of the river to navigation where this was needed to allow works to proceed.

As regards the continuing operation of the Thames Barrier, specific powers are conferred upon the Environment Agency to close the Barrier's flood gates at such periods as are considered necessary or desirable, but only for specified purposes. Hence the gates may be closed,

(1) at any time when there is reason to believe that, unless this is done, floods may be caused by the overflow of the river upstream of the barrier, or in any other case of emergency;

(2) for the purpose of enabling experiments to be carried out in connection with the development of the most effective use of the Barrier for flood defence;

(3) for the purpose of testing the Barrier;

(4) for the purpose of exercising and instructing staff in the operation and control of the Barrier; and

(5) for the purpose of maintaining, extending, enlarging, altering, replacing, repairing or renewing the Barrier, or any part of it, where this is reasonably necessary.

Providing that the gates are closed for the specified purposes, no liability will arise against the Agency in relation to any vessel that it obstructed, delayed or interfered with. However, in determining whether to open or close the gates, the Agency is to have regard to the need to minimise risk of danger to life and property arising from downstream flooding, to use its best endeavours to secure minimum obstruction of navigation and other river users and comply with a Ministerial direction.[252] Further limitations are imposed so that closure of the gates for purposes (2) to (5) may only be exercised in accordance with a scheme made by the Agency and approved by the relevant Ministers.[253] The power to close the gates for purposes (4) or (5) may not be exercised so as to close the river to navigation completely.[254]

---

[252] That is, a direction from the Secretary of State for Environment, Food and Rural Affairs.

[253] That is, the Secretary of State for Environment, Food and Rural Affairs and the Secretary of State for Transport, Local Government and the Regions.

[254] Generally see s.35 Thames Barrier and Flood Prevention Act 1972 and see Thames Barrier Byelaws 1983.

Other powers provided for under the Thames Barrier and Flood Prevention Act 1972 allow the Environment Agency to require the occupier of any land to close any flood dam, within the former 'London excluded area' and upstream or downstream of the Barrier, to prevent flooding. The failure of an owner to close a flood dam will entitle a person authorised by the Agency to enter land to close the dam and the owner will be guilty of an offence, subject to a due diligence defence.[255] Powers are also provided under the Act in relation to a wide range of proposed sea defence works, in respect of which the Agency may apply to the relevant Minister for an order.[256] In relation to such an application an order may be made conferring upon the Agency such compulsory powers for the works as are considered necessary or expedient, including providing for the extinguishment of rights of navigation, the diversion of watercourses and the obstruction of highways or rights of way.[257]

A range of criminal offences are provided for under the 1972 Act. Hence, any person who, without lawful authority or excuse, closes or opens any of the flood defence gates of the Barrier, or in any other way interferes with the Barrier or its operation, or attempts to do so, is guilty of an offence.[258] More generally, any person who wilfully obstructs or impedes any person acting in the execution of the 1972 Act, or of any order or byelaw made under it, or in compliance with any notice or direction given under it, is guilty of an offence.[259]

## 3.8 ASSESSMENT OF FLOOD DEFENCE ADMINISTRATION

Despite constitutional changes in the responsible bodies, the general structure of flood defence administration remains broadly along the lines suggested by the Royal Commission of 1927 and as originally implemented in the Land Drainage Act 1930.[260] Broadly, as has been seen, the Environment

---

[255] s.68 Thames Barrier and Flood Prevention Act 1972, as amended.
[256] That is, the application must be made to the Secretary of State for Environment, Food and Rural Affairs and the Secretary of State for Transport, Local Government and the Regions if the proposed works include works in, on, under or over tidal waters or tidal lands, or the Secretary of State for Environment, Food and Rural Affairs in any other case.
[257] Generally see s.56 Thames Barrier and Flood Prevention Act 1972.
[258] s.40 Thames Barrier and Flood Prevention Act 1972, as amended. On summary conviction, this offence carries a penalty of imprisonment for a term not exceeding 6 months or a fine not exceeding the prescribed sum, presently £5,000, or to both, or on conviction on indictment to imprisonment for a term not exceeding 14 years or a fine, or to both.
[259] s.70 Thames Barrier and Flood Prevention Act 1972, as amended. Where no other penalty is provided for, a person committing this offence will be liable, on summary conviction, to a fine not exceeding level 3 on the standard scale, presently £1,000.
[260] See 1.9.3 above on the Land Drainage Act 1930.

## Assessment of Flood Defence Administration

Agency exercises overall supervision for flood defence and conducts operations on main rivers and sea defences, though exercising functions through its regional flood defence committees. The composition of these committees, with a majority of members being appointed by local authorities, reflects the fact that funding is largely provided by precepts upon the authorities and seeks to relate funding to representation. Internal drainage boards have been established, primarily, for the purposes of agricultural land improvement and, again, composition of these boards reflects their funding position, with income from landowners who benefit from drainage improvements being related to representation on boards. Outside internal drainage districts, local authorities act as flood and coastal defence operating authorities in relation to ordinary watercourses and in respect of certain sea defences, and have corresponding powers to undertake flood and coastal defence works.

The overall issue is whether this rather intricate distribution of responsibilities between the different operating authorities, subject to overall ministerial supervision, is the most effective and efficient means of securing flood defence policy objectives. Over the years, the question has been raised many times as to whether more integration of flood defence administrative responsibilities would be generally beneficial.[261] Recently, the arguments have been considered by the House of Commons Agriculture Committee,[262] which noted the 'complicated mosaic' of different organisation duties allocated in relation to the administration, financing and delivery of flood defence, arising from the separation of national policy from its delivery at regional and local levels, and the further separation between flood defence and coastal protection. 'Considerable problems' and 'significant gaps' were identified in attempting to co-ordinate or integrate the activities of operating authorities and individuals to achieve a more holistic approach to the implementation of national policy for flood and coastal defence.

---

[261] For example, in 1982 the Monopolies and Mergers Commission suggested that flood defence administrative arrangements were too complex and recommended that a review should be undertaken (see Ministry of Agriculture, Fisheries and Food, *Financing and Administration of Land Drainage, Flood Prevention and Coast Protection in England and Wales* (1985) Preface). Similar administrative arrangements under previous legislation were described as 'a chaos of authorities with an absence of authority': see J. L. Wilkins, 'Land drainage legislation and the engineer – a review and discussion paper' (1980) 107 *Chartered Municipal Engineer* 123 (Part I) at p.126. Generally see E. Penning-Rowsell and J. W. Handmer, 'Flood Hazard Management in Britain: A Changing Scene' (1988) 154(2) *The Geographical Journal* 209.

[262] House of Commons Agriculture Committee, Sixth Report Session 1997–98, *Flood and Coastal Defence* (1998) HC 707, and see also Agriculture Committee, Third Report Session 2000–01, *Flood and Coastal Defence Follow Up* (2001) HC 172. See also Institution of Civil Engineers, *Learning to Live with Rivers* (2001) p.71.

According to the Agriculture Committee, the fragmentation of policy responsibility which it identified was the product of relatively self-contained legislation that had been formulated at a time when socio-economic and political needs were different and when scientific understanding of water cycles and erosion were far more rudimentary than today. The results of the different legislation, and the 'arbitrary' administrative consequences to which it gave rise, was a source of bewilderment amongst the public over organisational responsibilities and, potentially, a serious negative impact on the delivery of vital flood defence and warning services. Alongside this, concerns were expressed that much local-level decision-making was being excessively driven by short-term economic circumstances and localised priorities.

The appropriate remedy for the unsatisfactory division of responsibilities identified by the Agriculture Committee was a radically more integrated or unified approach to flood defence administration. Hence, the Committee's recommendation was that,

> 'the Government should rationalise the legislative base of flood and coastal defence policy in England and Wales as soon as possible, with, among other aims, the ending of the artificial distinction between sea defence and coast protection responsibilities. . . . coastal groups [should] take responsibility for coastal flooding and erosion. Similarly, the logical basis for dividing responsibilities for main river and non-main river flood defence between the Environment Agency and local authorities should be re-evaluated by the Ministry. . . . the regional flood defence committees [should] take on responsibilities for flood defences activities on non-main rivers currently undertaken by local authorities and riparian owners.'[263]

An important implication of this proposal was the future role envisaged for local flood defence committees and internal drainage boards. On this, the Committee was firmly convinced that the functions of local committees and boards would be more appropriately discharged by regional flood defence committees which should become responsible for delivery of all inland flood defence policy under the supervision of the Environment Agency.[264] However, this did not necessarily imply the abolition of internal drainage boards. Boards would be retained to fulfil a consultative role, and an element of local level funding would be retained for projects agreed by

---

[263] House of Commons Agriculture Committee, Sixth Report Session 1997–98, *Flood and Coastal Defence* (1998) HC 707, para.67, recommendation k.
[264] House of Commons Agriculture Committee, Sixth Report Session 1997–98, *Flood and Coastal Defence* (1998) HC 707, para.76, recommendation o.

## Assessment of Flood Defence Administration

regional flood defence committees which would have to ensure democratic accountability and full reflection of stakeholder interests.

Although the Agriculture Committee raised the possibility of a single national agency being responsible for flood defence, on balance it thought it inappropriate to recommend this. The potential benefits of a national agency in improving the efficiency and effectiveness in delivering national policy had to be weighed against any reduction in democratic accountability, particularly at the local level. Hence, a preference remained for a more strongly regional level of administration, and accountability, provided by regional flood defence committees.[265]

In response,[266] the Government was critical of the Agriculture Committee's proposals for rationalisation of responsibilities insofar as they would involve replacing one artificial distinction (between flood defence and coastal protection) with another artificial distinction (between coastal defence and inland defence). Instead, the Government preferred to rely upon the Environment Agency, in fulfilling its supervisory role, to ensure consistency in the actions of all operating authorities, whether on the coastline or in river systems. The suggestion that flood defence responsibilities of riparian owners should be transferred to regional flood defence advisory committees was strongly resisted, because a transfer of such responsibilities to the public sector was seen to be excessively costly and difficult to justify.

In relation to the Agriculture Committee's proposals for transfer of functions from local flood defence committees and internal drainage boards to regional flood defence committees, the Government was not in favour of making fundamental changes to the existing institutional arrangements though it recognised that guidance should be prepared on the continuing need for local committees. In respect of internal drainage boards, the Government thought that the boards were good examples of bodies with local responsibilities which remained pertinent to the needs of particular areas and the expenditure of income from local beneficiaries, though it was recognised that greater standardisation in arrangements might be beneficial.

Most recently, the issue of fundamental reform of flood and coastal defence administrative arrangements has been revisited by the Agriculture

---

[265] House of Commons Agriculture Committee, Sixth Report Session 1997–98, *Flood and Coastal Defence* (1998) HC 707, para.79, recommendation p.

[266] See House of Commons Agriculture Committee, Fifth Special Report Session 1997–98, *Replies by the Government and the Environment Agency to the Sixth Report from the Agriculture Committee Session 1997–98 'Flood and Coastal Defence' (HC 707)* (1998) HC 1117.

Committee which reaffirmed its desire to see 'Byzantine arrangements' streamlined in relation to the formulation, implementation and financing of Government policy.[267] No change in Government policy was indicated in response to this restatement of the Committee's recommendation, though it was recognised that a future funding review might make recommendations with institutional implications.[268]

---

[267] House of Commons Agriculture Committee, Third Report Session 2000–01, *Flood and Coastal Defence Follow Up* (2001) HC 172.

[268] House of Commons Agriculture Committee, Eighth Special Report Session 1999–2000, *Reply by the Government to the Third Report of the Agriculture Committee, Session 2000–01 'Flood and Coastal Defence Follow Up'* (2001) HC 437. See the discussion of the Flood Defence Funding Review at 6.1.3 below.

# Chapter 4

# OPERATIONAL AND REGULATORY POWERS

## 4.1 INTRODUCTION

This chapter provides an account of the powers of flood and coastal defence operating authorities to undertake works and to supervise or regulate works carried out by other persons or bodies. Broadly, the discussion is arranged to parallel the institutional discussion of the flood defence bodies in the previous chapter but, again, the special arrangements concerning coast protection are considered separately.[1] Another topic treated separately is the role of the Environment Agency in providing a flood warning service[2] which, though arguably the exercise of an 'operational' power by the Agency, has features and implications which set it apart from other kinds of construction and maintenance activities which are considered in this chapter.

## 4.2 THE MINISTERS

In taking an institutionally orientated approach, the operational and regulatory powers of the Secretary of State for Environment, Food and Rural Affairs and the National Assembly for Wales can be dealt with fairly briefly. As regards the carrying out of flood and coastal defence operations, the involvement of the Ministers is minimal since it is envisaged that most operations will be undertaken by the operating authorities or by private individuals. Clearly, ministerial guidance and funding decisions will have fundamental implications in determining which flood defence operations are undertaken, and how they are conducted, but the Ministers are not directly involved in the actual operations which are normally undertaken by operating authorities.

In respect of ministerial regulatory powers, as has been seen, the Ministers have extensive powers to determine flood and coastal defence policy and to implement policy through directions and guidance to operating authorities. Clearly, executive responsibility for flood and coastal defence, and the appropriate contribution to be made to policy implementation by operating authorities, is retained by the Ministers and may be exercised through a

---

[1] See Ch.5 below on coast protection.
[2] See 11.3 below on flood warnings.

range of mechanisms that are considered elsewhere.[3]

Most of the regulatory powers possessed by the Ministers are exercisable in relation to the activities of operating authorities, and only exceptionally do ministerial powers apply in relation to private persons and bodies. However, an exceptional example of this is to be found in the power of the Ministers to authorise a person with an interest in land to carry out drainage works where those works cannot be carried out because of the objection or legal disability of another person whose land would need to be entered upon for the purpose of conducting the works. In such circumstances, the landholder who seeks to undertake the works may apply to the appropriate Minister for an order authorising works to be executed with a view to improvement of land. The procedural requirements require the application to be made in a prescribed form, and to contain particulars of the proposed works, the persons by whom they are to be carried out and any further specified particulars. Further provisions concern publicity and the facility for objections to be made to a proposed order, and allow for public inquiries to be held. However, the appropriate Minister has the final discretion to allow the proposed works and to authorise persons to undertake them and to maintain them thereafter, though compensation may be payable to persons who suffer injury as a result of an order.[4]

The power of the Ministers to authorise drainage works by particular landowners is rather exceptional, though it may be noted that the same procedure is also available to authorise internal drainage boards and local authorities to undertake works on land outside their district or area.[5] In most respects, regulatory powers in relation to flood defence works are exercised by operating authorities, either by way of the Environment Agency supervising the activities of other operating authorities, or by an operating authority regulating the activities of a private person or body in relation to flood defence.

## 4.3 THE ENVIRONMENT AGENCY: OPERATIONAL POWERS

### 4.3.1 General Flood Defence Works Powers

The Environment Agency has a range of statutory powers to carry out flood defence works in connection with main rivers[6] which allow it to undertake the following activities:

---

[3] See 3.2 and 3.3 above on ministerial policy and see 6.2 below on central government funding.
[4] s.22 Land Drainage Act 1991.
[5] See s.14(3) Land Drainage Act 1991.
[6] See 3.4.9 above on main rivers.

(1) to cleanse, repair or otherwise maintain existing watercourses or drainage works in an efficient state;

(2) to improve existing works by deepening, widening or otherwise improving any existing watercourse or removing or altering mill dams, weirs or other obstructions to watercourses, or raising, widening or otherwise improving any existing drainage work; and

(3) to construct new works by making any new watercourse or drainage work or erecting any machinery or doing any other act required for the drainage of land.[7]

Also, irrespective of whether the works are in connection with a main river, the Agency has the power to maintain, improve, or construct drainage works for the purpose of defence against sea water or tidal water,[8] and that power may be exercised above and below the low-water mark.[9] The Agency may also undertake works in the sea or any estuary that are necessary to secure an adequate outfall for a main river. However, none of these provisions will authorise any entry on the land of any person except for the purpose of maintaining existing works.[10]

A range of additional powers to undertake flood and coastal defence works arise where the Agency has entered into agreements with various persons and bodies. Hence, by agreement with any person, the Agency may carry out, improve or maintain any drainage works which that person is entitled to conduct, though such works are to be undertaken at that person's expense, subject to a ministerial grant being paid in relation to the expense involved.[11] With the consent of an internal drainage board, and notwithstanding the general restriction of Agency powers to main rivers,

---

[7] s.165(1) Water Resources Act 1991. Notably, powers of the Agency to undertake flood defence work are not limited by the fact that some other person is under an obligation to undertake work by reason of tenure, custom, prescription or otherwise (s.185(2)).

[8] On 'tidal waters' see *Kingsway Furniture (Dartford) Ltd v Hapglow Ltd and Kylefield Ltd* (Official Referee's Business, 23 March 1990 [1991] *Water Law* 10) where a civil action was brought for the removal of a sea defence contrary to flood defence byelaws and the outcome depended on whether the relevant waters were 'tidal' or not. Following previous authorities it was stated that waters were tidal 'where there is a real and perceptible ebb and flow of the tide, whether lateral or vertical', that is, salinity was not relevant. See also *Ingram v Percival* [1969] 1 QB 548 and *Reece v Miller* (1882) 8 QBD 626.

[9] However, the powers of the Agency to carry out flood defence works on coastal and estuarine land do not extend to coastal protection against erosion which is separately provided for under the Coast Protection Act 1949 and discussed at Ch.5 below.

[10] s.165(2), (3) and (6) Water Resources Act 1991 and see 3.4.11 above on powers of entry and 4.3.3 below on compulsory powers.

[11] Grants may be paid under s.149(3) Water Resources Act 1991.

the Agency may carry out and maintain any works in the district of the board which the board is entitled to carry out or maintain, on such terms as to payment or otherwise as are agreed between the board and the Agency.[12] The Agency may enter into an agreement with any local authority or navigation authority for the carrying out by that authority of any work in connection with a main river which the Agency is authorised to carry out.[13]

In respect of the practical application of the general flood defence works powers of the Agency, and the exercise of these powers by predecessor bodies, some guidance as to the legal implications may be gained from a brief survey of the relevant caselaw.

The overriding principle, which is repeatedly emphasised by the caselaw, is that the general flood defence works powers are *powers* and not *duties* of the Agency. A facility exists for a Minister to give a direction to the Agency that it must exercise the flood defence powers in particular circumstances or in a particular manner,[14] thereby imposing a duty upon the Agency to act accordingly. However, in the absence of a ministerial direction of this kind, the exercise or non-exercise of the powers is a matter for the discretion of the Agency.

Early cases served to establish the permissive rather than mandatory character of the general flood defence powers. In *Smith* v *Cawdle Fen, Ely (Cambridge) Commissioners*[15] it was unsuccessfully argued that flooding of the claimant's land was due to the failure of the defendant Drainage Commissioners to provide a bank of sufficient height to withstand flooding. This claim was dismissed on the basis that the Commissioners were under no statutory duty to execute the works which, it was alleged, they had failed to execute. Similarly, in *Gillett* v *Kent Rivers Catchment Board, etc.*[16] the claimants' lands were flooded by the allegedly negligent failure of a Catchment Board to maintain a drain free from weeds. Although it was found that the Board had actually taken reasonable steps to clear the drain, the court found that no duty was owed to the claimants, under the Land Drainage Act 1930, requiring the work to be undertaken.

---

[12] s.11(2)(a) Land Drainage Act 1991 and see 3.5.6 on the relationships between operating authorities.
[13] s.165(4) and (5) Water Resources Act 1991.
[14] s.40 Environment Act 1995 and see 3.2.14 above. Note also the speculative discussion in 7.8.9 on the possibility that a failure to exercise a power to alleviate flooding might be capable of constituting a contravention of a human right. In such situations, a ministerial direction requiring a flood defence operational power to be exercised might be especially appropriate.
[15] [1938] 4 All ER 64.
[16] [1938] 4 All ER 810.

However, given that the Environment Agency is not under a duty to exercise its general flood defence works powers in any particular case, there is a separate issue of whether, in circumstances where it actually opts to exercise those powers, it may become civilly liable for negligence because of a failure to act appropriately. This issue is illustrated by the leading case of *East Suffolk Rivers Catchment Board* v *Kent*[17] where the claimant was the occupier of farmland adjacent to a tidal river which had become flooded after a high tide and exceptional gale caused the breach of a protection wall. Staff of the defendant Catchment Board, in exercise of their statutory powers to repair drainage works,[18] undertook work to close the breach in the wall but carried out the work so inefficiently that the land continued to be flooded for 178 days whereas, had the work been properly conducted, it was found that the wall might have been repaired in 14 days. The claimant alleged negligence upon the part of the Board and claimed losses attributable to the land continuing to be flooded for the longer period because of its delay in undertaking the repairs.

The House of Lords decided in favour of the Catchment Board. Reaffirming that there was no statutory duty requiring the Board to intervene, and that it would not have been liable if it had done nothing to repair the wall, the Court considered what duty was owed where the Board had chosen positively to exercise its statutory powers. Insofar as the Board owed any duty, it was a duty only to avoid causing further damage to the claimant's property and not a duty to undertake works with reasonable efficiency and speed. Hence, if the Board had chosen to abandon its attempt to repair the wall, there would have been no liability on its part, providing that it had done nothing to exacerbate the damage to the claimant's property. In the circumstances, the actions of the Board did not cause the claimant's loss, which was caused by the operations of nature for which the Board was not responsible.

The key principle arising from the *Kent* case is, therefore, that the discretion given to a body with statutory flood defence powers allows that body a discretion both in deciding *whether* to exercise those powers and in deciding *how* to exercise those powers; that is, providing that nothing is done to make a situation worse than it would have been if no action whatever had been taken.[19] In reaching this conclusion, the special position

---

[17] [1941] AC 74. See 1.9.3 above on the status of 'catchment boards' as predecessors of the Agency under the Land Drainage Act 1930.

[18] Under s.34(1) Land Drainage Act 1930, corresponding to s.165(1) Water Resources Act 1991 discussed above.

[19] Contrast *Moncktor* v *Severn Trent Water Authority* [1988] RVR 247, where the defendant's regrading works on a watercourse were found to have increased the speed of flow and caused reasonably foreseeable erosion damage to the claimant's bridge, and the defendant was found liable for compensation in negligence or nuisance.

of a statutory body, as contrasted with a private contractor who might be engaged to undertake flood defence work, was noted. The exceptional circumstances which had given rise to the breach of the wall adjacent to the claimant's property had also caused no less than 22 breaches of sea walls on the same tidal river, and about 30 within the area of the Catchment Board. The Board was obliged to exercise its responsibilities for the benefit of its area as a whole and to do so within limits that were imposed upon its funding. In the circumstances, it was recognised that the Board may have had to deploy its most skilled staff in other locations and that the outlay involved in repairing particular damage to flood defence structures might have been greater than its limited finances would permit.

The *Kent* case contrasts markedly with the decision in *Smith and Snipes Hall Farm Ltd* v *River Douglas Catchment Board*[20] where the construction of new flood defence works was undertaken under an agreement with owners of land alongside a watercourse that was prone to flooding. The terms of the agreement were that the defendant Catchment Board would widen, deepen and make good the banks of the watercourse and take over responsibility for the future maintenance of the work.[21] In return, the landowners covenanted to contribute towards the cost of the work. However, the work was badly carried out by the Board since, for reasons of economy, the bank was constructed of soil from the bed of the watercourse and lacked a clay core which would have ensured its stability. As a result of the inadequate construction, the watercourse burst through the bank and flooded land of the claimants, who were successors in title to the original landowner convenantees.

The contrast between these facts and those in the *Kent* case was that the agreement that had been made between the Catchment Board and the landowners was regarded as a basis for a contractual, rather than a tortious, remedy. That is, despite the rather general language in which the agreement was expressed, there was an implied obligation that the work should be undertaken with reasonable skill and care so as to make the bank reasonably fit to prevent flooding. On the basis of expert evidence, to the effect that

---

[20] [1949] 2 KB 500 and see *Sephton* v *Lancashire River Board* [1962] 1 All ER 183. Also contrast the analysis provided by Robert Goff J in *Fellowes* v *Rother District Council* [1983] 1 All ER 513 (discussed at 5.4.2 below) where it is suggested that 'there is no rule that . . . liability [for an action under a statutory power] is contingent on the defendant causing the [claimant] fresh or additional damage'. Hence, a statutory body 'may be responsible for the consequence of a negligent act done in a purported exercise of the power (but not in fact within the limits of a discretion bona fide exercised) even though no fresh or additional damage is caused' (at p.522).

[21] This involved the Catchment Board making an application to the Minister to have the watercourse designated as a 'main river' to enable the Board to exercise its functions in relation to the watercourse. See 3.4.8 above on main rivers.

the unsatisfactory construction of the bank made it 'doomed to failure', the Court concluded that there had been a breach of contract which gave rise to liability on the part of the Catchment Board.

Significantly, the principles concerning statutory liability of flood defence bodies for negligence established by the *Kent* case were not relevant to the issue of contractual liability. In reflecting upon this contrast it was observed,

> '[the *Kent* case] does show, however, that, in considering whether the board broke its duty in tort, it is material to inquire into the expense of the works which it is said they ought to have constructed. An adjacent landowner must not be too critical if the board prefers thrift to efficiency, I suppose on the principle that he should not look a gift horse in the mouth and must be prepared to take it with some faults. But the duty in contract is a very different thing. There is no question of a gift horse there. The landowner paid his contribution in return for the board's promise, and they are in duty bound to fulfil it.'[22]

On that basis, there would seem to be a substantial difference between the permissive statutory powers of the Environment Agency to undertake flood defence works, and the undertaking of works by the Agency in accordance with the various kinds of agreement which it is empowered to enter into. Insofar as the Agency does enter into agreements to undertake flood defence works, it may become subject to contractual duties to ensure that the works are properly conducted, in accordance with the terms of the agreement, and be liable for failings in this respect.[23]

### 4.3.2 Compensation

Although the general flood defence works powers allow the Environment Agency to undertake various kinds of maintenance, improvement and construction works, they do not allow such works to be undertaken without compensation being paid to those who suffer damage or whose rights are otherwise interfered with as a result. Hence, where injury is sustained by any person through the exercise of general flood defence works powers by the Agency, it will be liable to make full compensation to that person and, in the case of dispute as to the amount of compensation, the matter will be determined by the Lands Tribunal.[24] Compensation is also payable where injury is sustained by reason of the exercise of a power of entry by the Agency.[25]

---

[22] Per Denning LJ *Smith and Snipes Hall Farm Ltd v River Douglas Catchment Board* [1949] 2 KB 500 at p.518.
[23] See also the discussion of duties under local and private legislation at 4.9 below.
[24] s.177 and Schedule 21 para.5 Water Resources Act 1991.
[25] Schedule 20 para.6 Water Resources Act 1991 and see 3.4.11 above on powers of entry.

A starting point in a claim for compensation for damage arising from flood defence works is the need for a claimant to show that, regardless of the statutory provisions allowing for compensation, there is a valid claim for compensation as a matter of common law. That is, the claimant must show that the actions complained of would provide grounds for an action in nuisance or negligence had they been done by a private defendant. Essentially, this involves reconsideration of the principles upon which civil liability for flooding is based,[26] but it is fairly clear that most kinds of flood defence works would give rise to this kind of liability. For example, in *Day and Sons* v *Thames Water Authority*[27] the court recognised that the installation of a flood gate in an artificial flood-relief channel gave rise to a foreseeable risk that the structure might fail to operate satisfactorily and cause flooding of neighbouring land as a result. The essential ingredients of the tort of nuisance having been shown, it was clear that a private action on the same facts would have been well founded, and statutory compensation would, therefore, be payable.[28]

A contrasting example is *Oakes* v *Mersey River Board*[29] where damage to a wall supporting the bank of an island arose after flood defence work was undertaken on the opposite bank of the river. The work involved the deposit of dredged material on the opposite bank, in accordance with statutory powers of the River Board,[30] and this was claimed to have diverted the flow and caused the damage to the wall. However, it was found that these facts would not have given rise to a common law action by the claimant. No obstruction of the channel had taken place and measures to maintain the flow of a watercourse within its accustomed course are not normally actionable as a matter of common law.[31] The key point remains that action by a flood defence operating authority will only justify compensation where, in principle, the same facts would give rise to common law liability.

Where statutory liability to pay compensation arises for damage sustained as a result of flood defence operations, compensation is payable both for damage which results inevitably from *authorised* operations and also for damage which results from operations being *negligently* performed. An illustration of the latter is to be seen in *Scutt and Screeton* v *Lower Ouse*

---

[26] See Ch.2 above on civil liability for flooding.
[27] [1984] JPL 596.
[28] See the discussion of *Greenock Corporation* v *Caledonian Railway Company* [1917] AC 556 and *Sedleigh-Denfield* v *O'Callaghan* [1940] AC 880 at 2.5.3 above.
[29] (1957) 9 P&CR 145.
[30] Under s.38 Land Drainage Act 1930, now see Schedule 21 para.5(3) Water Resources Act 1991, and see 4.3.4 below on the disposal of spoil.
[31] See *Menzies* v *Earl of Breadalbane* (1828) 3 Bli NS 414, discussed at 2.4.2 above.

*Internal Drainage Board*[32] where contractors for the Board had been engaged to clear reeds and other vegetation from a watercourse. Although it had been made clear to the contractors that vegetation that had been cut had to be cleared from the watercourse, they had failed to do this. As a result, a screen at the entrance to a culvert had become obstructed causing flooding of the claimants' farmland. The negligent undertaking of the maintenance work was sufficient to establish a claim for compensation for consequent damage to the claimants' crops.

An important aspect of compensation for damage resulting from flood defence works being provided for under statute is that statutory compensation is the only available remedy available. For example, in *Marriage v East Norfolk Rivers Catchment Board*[33] the Catchment Board deposited river dredgings on the south bank of a river. The result of this was to prevent the escape of water by a route that it had previously taken and to cause the water to pass to the north of the river and to sweep away a bridge, for which the owner claimed damages in private nuisance. It was held that where a statute that authorised the works to be undertaken provided a statutory right to compensation, there was no further right of common law action in nuisance. In relation to works that were authorised by the statute, the claimant's only remedy was to apply for compensation under the statute. Similarly, in *Proctor v Avon and Dorset River Catchment Board*[34] an action for an injunction to restrain a River Board from dredging a river which, it was alleged, would have had an adverse effect upon rights of fishery in the river was dismissed. Notably, this decision was reached despite a statutory duty upon the Board to have due regard to fishery interests.[35]

However, insofar as an injury resulting from a flood defence operation can be compensated for by a money payment, a wide range of injuries have been found to justify compensation claims. In *Welsh National Water Authority v Burgess*[36] compensation was found to be payable to the owner of fishing rights on one bank of a river after works had been carried out on the banks and bed of the river. Compensation was assessed by the Lands Tribunal as the difference in value of the fishery before, and after, the works had been undertaken. On appeal by the Water Authority, it was found that the compensation award should not be reduced because the

---

[32] (1953) 4 P&CR 71.
[33] [1949] 2 All ER 1021.
[34] (1953) 162 EG 161.
[35] s.62(2) Land Drainage Act 1930 and now see s.105(3) Water Resources Act 1991. See also s.2(4) Salmon and Freshwater Fisheries Act 1975 which provides for an offence relating to the disturbance of fisheries.
[36] (1974) 28 P&CR 373.

claimant owned only the bed of the river up to a middle line. Likewise, compensation would not be reduced because of allegations that the work undertaken by the Authority was carried out negligently and, therefore, outside the statutory powers of the Authority.

However, a point to be kept in mind in assessing compensation for flood defence works is that financial losses incurred by particular landowners are capable of being offset against the benefits to the land of the work that is undertaken. Where greater 'betterment' is shown, no 'injury' will have been suffered and no compensation will be payable.[37] In *Glazebrook* v *Gwynedd River Board*[38] works had been undertaken for the widening and deepening of a stream to improve the drainage of agricultural land. The effect of this scheme, according to the claimant, was to drain an area of bog which had previously provided a productive area for wildfowl shooting, and had made it necessary for him to provide an alternative water supply for his cattle. Whilst these detriments were recognised and quantified, they proved to be slightly less than the value of the increased agricultural productivity of the land as a result of the drainage scheme. In effect, the claimant had suffered no overall loss and his entitlement to compensation was assessed as nil.[39]

Broadly, the kinds of situations in which statutory compensation has been found to be payable in the past may be subdivided into, first, those where the damage arises during the period when the work is undertaken and, second, those where the damage becomes apparent as a later consequence of the work having been undertaken. A good illustration of 'initial' damage is to be seen in *Golden Basket Eggs Ltd* v *Yorkshire Ouse and Hull River Authority*[40] where a flood alleviation scheme involved the use of a pneumatic hammer to drive steel piles into the bed of a river, causing considerable noise and vibration. The claimants occupied a poultry rearing house near to the river and suffered a disastrous decline in egg production and a deterioration in the condition of the poultry. These effects were found to be a result of the disturbance due to the flood defence works and compensation was payable for the loss.

---

[37] See *Keaney* v *Liverpool City Council*, unreported, Lands Tribunal, 21 May 1998, where no compensation was awarded because of the failure to show loss and the apparent increase in the value of the claimant's property as a result of the work that had been undertaken.

[38] [1964] RVR 55.

[39] For further decisions on compensation for agricultural damage see *Beal* v *Thornton Internal Drainage Board* [1973] RVR 153; *Birch and Birch* v *Ancholme Drainage Board* (1958) 9 P&CR 268; *Stuckley, Stuckley and Litchfield* v *North Somerset Drainage Board* (1960) 11 P&CR 224; and *Andrew* v *Cod Beck Internal Drainage Board* (1982) 261 EG 683.

[40] [1971] RVR 21.

A relatively small amount of compensation for temporary disturbance due to flood defence works was also found to be payable in *Penty v Greater London Council*,[41] but more substantial sums were found to be payable because of the continuing diminution in the value of a listed residential property due to extensive flood defence works carried out alongside it. The effect of the works was to raise the level of an adjoining road by 2 ft above the level of the front entrance to the property, making access awkward, diminishing the privacy of the ground floor rooms and generally detracting from the attractiveness of the front elevation of the building. These were held to be matters that could properly be included in the claim for statutory compensation.

Other examples of damage occurring during flood defence works have involved damage arising during works where earth movements have had the effect of removing support for structures of various kinds. Hence, liability to pay compensation was established in one instance where works resulted in the collapse of a river bank[42] and in another instance after the collapse of a wall.[43]

Not all the adverse effects of flood defence works will be immediately apparent, and several reported cases have concerned damage to bridges and other structures being undermined or subsiding some time after the completion of works.[44] Although the duration between the completion of the works and the appearance of the damage unavoidably generates disputes as to cause and effect, it is clear that compensation will be payable where a link between the works and the subsequent damage can be established.

The potential evidential problems are well illustrated by *Butler v River Foss Internal Drainage Board*[45] where a house developed cracks 2 months after drainage work had been conducted on an adjacent watercourse. The cracks became progressively worse and required walls to be shored up, the

---

[41] [1983] RVR 86.
[42] *Steel Stampings Ltd v Severn Trent Water Authority* (1982) 263 EG 359.
[43] *Farmer Giles Ltd v Wessex Water Authority and Another* [1990] 18 EG 102. Contrast *Central Electricity Authority v Cumberland River Board* [1958] JPL 51 where no evidence could be provided to link the collapse of a river wall with flood defence work.
[44] See *Monckton v Severn Trent Water Authority* [1988] RVR 247 (liability for damage to a bridge); *Warner and Another v Kingston Brook Internal Drainage Board* [1979] RVR 221 (liability for damage to a bridge); *Marine Industrial Transmissions Ltd v Southern Water Authority* [1989] RVR 221 (liability for damage to a quay).
[45] [1966] RVR 282. Contrast *Lorrimer v Environment Agency*, unreported, Lands Tribunal, 30 March 1999, where damage to the foundations of a wall was alleged to have resulted from river dredging works, but the evidence showed no causal link between the damage and the works.

watercourse culverted and underpinning work carried out on the foundations of the house. A claim to compensation by the owner of the house necessitated a detailed investigation of circumstances, revealing that the house was built upon relatively shallow foundations, erosion of waterside land had taken place over some time and a length of bankside wall had collapsed some years previously. Despite the factors indicating a long-term natural action by the watercourse, it was found that an excavator used in the drainage works had weakened the soil support given to the house and the effect of the drainage had been to cause a swifter flow of water against the bank alongside the house. On the balance of the evidence, therefore, it was found that the claimant was entitled to compensation for the trespass and withdrawal of support, and the compensation awarded was calculated to allow redress of the damage to the property that had been caused.

Another example, involving a contrasting kind of injury, is *Robson* v *Northumberland and Tyneside River Board*[46] where a farmer had installed a weir in a watercourse to direct water to water turbines used for generating electricity for use on the farm. The effect of works, conducted under a flood relief scheme, had been to carry a large amount of silt down the watercourse which had rendered the turbines unworkable. Although it was recognised that 'sooner or later' the farmer would have had to resort to the public electricity supply, this had to be done earlier than would have otherwise have been necessary. As a consequence, the farmer was awarded compensation for the additional expense and inconvenience caused along with a contribution towards the cost of making connection to the public electricity supply.

Although the general basis for the assessment of compensation is the difference between the value of a property before works are undertaken and its value afterwards, application of the 'before and after' test may generate some complexities in practice. In *Weeks and Weeks* v *Thames Water Authority*[47] the claimant was the owner of a cottage adjoining a stream in a 'setting of exceptional charm'. However, the property underwent an adverse change of character as a result of flood defence improvement works involving the grubbing up of trees and shrubs and the loss of land along the waterside. Although the claimant accepted an initial sum from the Water Authority as compensation for permanent damage which had been caused, he brought further claims for losses incurred as a result of a delay in selling the house, at a lower price than anticipated, and interest which had been paid on a bridging loan over the period when the house was unsold. Whilst the Lands Tribunal reaffirmed that the assessment of

---

[46] (1952) 3 P&CR 150.
[47] [1979] JPL 774.

compensation should be the difference in value in the property before and after the execution of the works, the assessment had to be made at the date of the execution of the works. Applying that date for assessment, account had to be taken of a fall in property prices since the claimant had originally placed the cottage on the market. Moreover, the Tribunal declined to award the claimant any interest on the sum awarded or to allow the claimant to recover interest paid on the bridging loan that he had taken out due to the delay in selling the property.[48] Hence, damages were restricted to 'injurious affectation' to the property and did not encompass the further economic consequences arising from the alleged 'blight' due to the works.

A final point to note about statutory compensation for injury sustained as a result of flood defence works is that it is the duty of the Lands Tribunal to assess the amount of compensation which is payable 'once and for all'. That is, it must seek to take account of future damage that may arise after a determination has been made, as well as the damage that has already arisen at the time of the determination. Hence, it is for a claimant to make a claim for compensation within the statutory limitation period of 6 years and failure to do so within that period will render the claim time barred under the Limitation Act 1980.[49]

### 4.3.3 Compulsory Works Orders

Where the Agency is proposing to carry out engineering or building operations, or to discharge water into any inland waters or underground strata, it may apply to either of the Ministers for a compulsory works order. An application of this kind allows the Minister to grant the compulsory powers or authority which are necessary to enable operations to be undertaken in connection with the flood defence function of the Agency. Detailed procedural matters concerning compulsory works orders are provided for under Schedule 19 to the Water Resources Act 1991, which covers matters such as applications, publicity concerning orders, consideration of objections, notice of an order, compulsory acquisition provisions, and compensation. Subject to the requirements of Schedule 19, a compulsory works order may confer the power to acquire land compulsorily, apply relevant land and works powers of the Agency, impose conditions, amend or repeal local statutory provisions and contain supplemental, consequential or transitional provisions.[50]

---

[48] See *Thameside Estates Ltd* v *Greater London Council* [1978] RVR 82 where, with regret, the Lands Tribunal felt itself unable to award interest upon compensation to reflect the duration between an injury being suffered and the date when compensation was assessed.

[49] See *Vincent* v *Thames Conservancy* (1953) 4 P&CR 66, concerning the Limitation Act 1939; now see s.2 Limitation Act 1980.

[50] s.168(1) to (4) Water Resources Act 1991.

The provisions in a compulsory works order apply without prejudice to general powers allowing the Agency to acquire land, subject to ministerial authorisation, in connection with the carrying out of any of its functions. Hence, the Agency may be authorised by a Minister to purchase land compulsorily where it is required for the purpose of its functions. The power to authorise acquisition includes the power to authorise the acquisition of interests of rights over land, either by the creation of new interests or by the acquisition of existing interests or rights.[51] A further power is provided for allowing the Agency, subject to ministerial authorisation, to acquire accretions of land resulting from drainage works. This power allows the acquisition of land by agreement or compulsorily, and arises in connection with the tidal waters of a main river or where drainage works have been transferred from another operating authority to the Agency, and there has been or is likely to be an accretion of land.[52]

### 4.3.4 Power to Dispose of Spoil

An important contrast needs to be drawn between flood defence work undertaken by the Environment Agency, under the general works powers, for which statutory compensation may be payable to landowners who suffer damage as a result, and the disposal of spoil arising from certain dredging operations, for which no compensation may be payable.[53] Hence, the Agency is empowered, without having to make payment, to appropriate and dispose of any matter removed in the course of carrying out work for the widening, deepening or dredging of any watercourse. Along with this, the Agency may deposit any matter removed on the banks of the watercourse or a width of land adjoining the watercourse which is sufficient to enable the matter to be removed and deposited by mechanical means in one operation. However, this power does not authorise the deposit of any matter in such a manner as to constitute a 'statutory nuisance'.[54] The

---

[51] s.154(1) and (2) Water Resources Act 1991 and see also s.37(1) Environment Act 1995.
[52] s.155(1) Water Resources Act 1991.
[53] However, see Schedule 21 para.5(3) Water Resources Act 1991, which provides that where injury is sustained by reason of spoil being deposited on the banks of a watercourse in specified circumstances (under s.167(1)(b)) the Agency *may* pay such compensation as it may determine and if the injury could have been avoided if powers to deposit spoil were exercised with reasonable care full compensation will be payable.
[54] That is, a statutory nuisance under Part III Environmental Protection Act 1990, discussed at 8.2.1 below. Notably also, material removed in dredging, particularly where it is contaminated, may come within the waste licensing requirements under Part II Environmental Protection Act 1990, but see Waste Management Licensing Regulations 1994, S.I. 1994 No.1056 as amended, particularly reg.17 and exemptions from licensing provided by Schedule 3 para.7 (relating to spreading of dredgings from

Agency may enter into an agreement with the council of any district or London borough in England, or any county or county borough council in Wales, for the disposal by the council of any matter removed in connection with flood defence works and for the payment by the Agency to the council of a specified sum in respect of the disposal of the matter by the council.[55]

The interpretation of previous powers to dispose of spoil from dredging operations was fully considered in *Jones* v *Mersey River Board*[56] where the River Board had exercised its general flood defence works powers to widen a river and had, allegedly, deposited spoil over an area of adjoining agricultural land which was beyond the 'banks' of the watercourse. The claimant, who farmed the land, sought compensation from the Board, and the Court of Appeal had to decide upon the extent to which the power to dispose of the spoil excluded a right to compensation and whether the land on which the deposit was made fell within the meaning of the 'banks' of the river.

On the first point, it was found that the power of the Board to deposit spoil was limited to deposits which were undertaken for the purpose of maintaining or improving those banks, so that compensation would be excluded where deposits were made for that purpose. However, where an operation extended beyond the maintenance or improvement of banks, as had happened in relation to spoil being placed on the claimant's adjoining land, then compensation would be payable.

On the second point, it was held that the word 'banks', as it featured in the statute,[57] meant so much of the land adjoining or near to a watercourse as performed, or contributed to the performance of, the function of containing

---

inland waters on agricultural land), para.9 (relating to spreading of dredgings from inland waters on land in connection with reclamation or improvement) and para.25 (relating to the spreading of dredgings on the banks or towpaths of waters). See also the system of licensing deposits of waste at sea under Part II Food and Environment Protection Act 1985. Generally see J. Brook, H. Paipai, S. E. Magenis, S. L. Challinor, M. van Zijderveld, J. Gibson and L. Moore, *Guidance on the disposal of dredged material to land* (1995) Construction Industry Research and Information Association Report 157.

[55] s.167 Water Resources Act 1991.
[56] [1957] 3 All ER 375, Court of Appeal, concerning the interpretation of s.38(1) Land Drainage Act 1930, broadly corresponding to s.167(1) Land Drainage Act 1991. See also *Jones* v *Mersey River Board* (1959) 10 P&CR 305 (Lands Tribunal, concerning the amount of compensation payable) and (1960) 175 EG 49 (Court of Appeal, concerning an alleged failure to mitigate the loss).
[57] s.81 Land Drainage Act 1930, corresponding to s.113(1) Water Resources Act 1991, which defines 'banks' to mean 'banks, walls or embankments adjoining or confining, or constructed for the purposes of or in connection with, any channel or sea front, and includes all land and water between the bank and low-watermark' (and similarly see s.72(1) Land Drainage Act 1991).

the watercourse.[58] That is, the banks of a watercourse are not limited to the slope or vertical face meeting the channel but include further land adjoining the watercourse where that land serves the purpose of containing the water in the channel. Although the issue was primarily to be determined on the facts of each case, it was apparent that the power to deposit spoil did not arise in relation to the deposit of material on surrounding fields.

It is important to note that the wording of the present power is slightly different from the statutory provision which was at issue in the *Jones* case. It no longer needs to be shown that the deposit of spoil is for the purpose of maintenance or improvement of banks. Also, although the present wording allows for the deposit of spoil on the 'banks' of a watercourse, it qualifies this by allowing the deposit to be made on such width of land adjoining a watercourse as is sufficient to enable the spoil to be removed and deposited by mechanical means in *one operation*.[59] The purpose behind this wording is, presumably, an attempt to instil more precision into determining the area alongside a watercourse over which spoil may be spread though, arguably, the matter is now dependent upon the capacity of the machine which is being used for a dredging operation.

The issue of the area over which dredged spoil may be spread, amongst other salient points, was considered in *Stapleford v Severn Trent Water Authority*[60] where the Water Authority had undertaken deepening and widening work on a watercourse which flowed alongside the claimant's land. The claimant requested that dredged material should be spread over a depression in his land, rather than at the side of the watercourse. This was agreed to and done by contractors engaged by the Authority, but the infilling of the depression with clay and only a small amount of topsoil cover meant that the land did not drain. The claimant rectified this by installing drains in the waterlogged area and importing topsoil to spread over the area, and claimed compensation from the Authority for the remedial work.

A key issue arising from these facts was whether the infilling of the depression had been undertaken by the Authority in exercising powers under land drainage legislation and, specifically, its power to dispose of spoil.[61] This issue depended upon whether the spoil had been deposited on the depressed area in 'one operation'. On the facts, the spoil had been removed from the channel of the watercourse by an excavator and then

---

[58] Following *Howard v Ingersoll* (1851) 54 US 381 and *Hindson v Ashby* [1896] 1 Ch 78.
[59] s.167(1)(b) Water Resources Act 1991.
[60] [1989] RVR 85.
[61] Under s.33 Land Drainage Act 1976, now s.167(1) Land Drainage Act 1991.

transported to the depressed area by a dumper truck, and the question arose as to whether or not this constituted a single operation. It was found that the statutory provision had to be interpreted narrowly so that, in effect, the area in which deposit was allowed was determined by the length of the jib on the excavator in making a 180-degree turn from the watercourse.

A consequence of the finding that the deposit of spoil was conducted outside the statutory powers of the Authority was that the dispute had to be regarded as a private contractual matter and not within those circumstances for which statutory compensation could be awarded. Nonetheless, the Lands Tribunal made an assessment of the damage suffered by the claimant as a result of the inadequate work, and deducted from that an amount which represented betterment, in improving the claimant's land, to reach a figure of £2,000. Presumably, had the matter been pursued in contractual litigation, the same amount of compensation would have been awardable.

The essential difficulty arising in the *Stapleford* case, and several others, is that of defining a practical boundary between the uncompensatable bankside disposal of spoil and those flood defence operations for which statutory compensation is payable. In principle, this issue parallels the question of whether the action complained of would give rise to civil liability if a private person had conducted it. A private person would not normally be liable at common law for maintaining a watercourse by depositing spoil on its banks,[62] and the statutory provisions echo this by excluding liability for similar deposits of spoil.[63]

The problematic situations arise where damage is suffered to some further interest that is alleged to beyond the 'banks' of the watercourse in some sense. Hence in *Rimmer* v *Crossens Drainage Board*[64] the complaint was about the deposit of spoil in a manner that made a roadway alongside the watercourse unusable. On the facts, it was found that the use of the track had actually been abandoned and no compensation was payable since the claimant had not suffered any loss. Nonetheless, in principle, it is apparent that a spoil depositing operation could cause some claimants exceptional inconvenience for reasons of this kind. Another exceptional example is *Pattinson and Pattinson* v *Finningley Internal Drainage Board*[65] where the Board's power to remove and deposit spoil without compensation being payable was recognised. It was found that the 'matter' which could

---

[62] See *Menzies* v *Earl of Breadalbane* (1828) 3 Bli NS 414, discussed at 2.4.2 above.
[63] See *Oakes* v *Mersey River Board* (1957) 9 P&CR 145, discussed at 4.3.2 above.
[64] (1976) 239 EG 817. Also see *Lambert* v *Environment Agency*, unreported, Lands Tribunal, 22 June 1999, on the measures necessary to restore the surface of a roadway.
[65] (1971) 22 P&CR 929.

be removed did not encompass trees and a hedge, and compensation was payable in respect of these. In addition, the drainage works involved the widening of the watercourse and, though no compensation was payable for the removal and deposit of spoil, the effect of the widening was to prevent the claimant using a strip of waterside land and compensation was also payable for this loss. Although it could not be said that the land was 'matter removed', it was clear that it was an injury to the claimant's interests for which compensation was payable. Clearly, there may be difficulties in the categorisation of situations where the deposit of spoil actually involves an injury of a compensatable kind.

### 4.3.5 Powers concerning Schemes for Small Areas

Where land is capable of improvement by drainage works but the establishment of an internal drainage board would be impracticable, the Agency (or a local authority other than a district council) may enter land and carry out a scheme for the drainage of a small area of land. Detailed requirements concerning such schemes are set out in Schedule 4 to the Land Drainage Act 1991, but essentially a scheme of this kind must identify the works to be conducted, the area to be improved, the estimated expense, the maximum amount recoverable by the Agency and the manner in which the expenses are to be apportioned between the lands which are to be improved. The powers to undertake drainage of a small area are subject to limitations on the maximum costs that are recoverable from the owners of the improved lands. The present maximum rate is £50 per hectare, but this may be varied by ministerial order.[66]

### 4.3.6 Powers under Agreements

Further operational powers of the Environment Agency arise from its capacity to enter into certain agreements concerning flood defence works. The power of the Agency to enter agreements is relatively open-ended in that it may by agreement with any person carry out, improve or maintain, at that person's expense, any drainage works that that person is entitled to undertake. The qualification to this is that the expense should be borne by the other person subject to the possibility that the work may be the subject of a ministerial grant.[67] The apparently unqualified nature of the power to enter agreements with 'any person' implies that works on ordinary watercourses might be allowed under this provision, though it is not clear under what circumstances the Agency would find it appropriate to be

---

[66] s.18 Land Drainage Act 1991.
[67] s.165(4) Water Resources Act 1991. Ministerial grants may be payable under s.149(1) and see 6.3.4 below.

undertaking work of a kind that would ordinarily be undertaken by a private waterside landowner.

Other powers of the Agency to undertake flood defence work by agreement arise in relation to the powers of other operating authorities. Hence the Agency may, with the consent of an internal drainage board, carry out and maintain works which that board might undertake in its district on agreed terms. The converse of this is that the Agency may enter into an agreement with an internal drainage board allowing the board to carry out, on agreed terms, any work in connection with a main river that the Agency is entitled to undertake.[68] Alternatively, the Agency may agree to contribute to the expense of carrying out or maintaining works which a drainage board undertakes.[69]

### 4.3.7 Powers arising from Default

A further possibility is that flood defence operations may be undertaken by the Environment Agency in circumstances where other operating authorities have failed to exercise their powers or have failed to exercise those powers appropriately. This situation must be distinguished from circumstances where main river functions are transferred to the Agency from another operating authority.[70]

Exercise by the Agency of powers of an internal drainage board is stated to be without prejudice to the power of the Agency to exercise certain regulatory powers concurrently with a board.[71] The power of the Agency to act in default of an internal drainage board arises in specific circumstances where land is damaged, or likely to be damaged, by flooding or inadequate drainage. The Agency may then exercise the powers of the drainage board where the relevant powers are not being exercised by the drainage board or are not being exercised to the necessary extent. Where this occurs the Agency may exercise all the powers of the board, including any power for the purpose of defraying expenses incurred or for incidental purposes.[72] That is, the Agency may meet relevant expenditure from income that would have otherwise passed to the board.

---

[68] Similar provisions allow the Agency to enter into an agreement with any local authority or navigation authority for the carrying out, by that authority, on such terms as to payment or otherwise as may be agreed, of any work in connection with a main river which the Agency is authorised to carry out (s.165(5) Water Resources Act 1991).

[69] s.11(1) and (2) Land Drainage Act 1991. On transfer arrangements with navigation and conservancy authorities see s.111 Water Resources Act 1991.

[70] Under s.108 Water Resources Act 1991 and see 3.4.9 above.

[71] Under s.8 Land Drainage Act 1991, and see 4.4.7 below.

[72] s.9(1) Land Drainage Act 1991.

Before exercising the powers of an internal drainage board in default, the Agency is bound to give the board 30 days' notice of an intention to do so. If, before the expiry of this notice, the drainage board raises an objection, the Agency may not exercise the powers except with the consent of the relevant Minister. The Minister may cause a public local inquiry to be held with respect to any objection to the Agency exercising the powers.[73]

Where the Agency actually exercises the powers of an internal drainage board in accordance with these provisions, any person authorised by the Agency may, to the extent reasonably necessary, inspect and take copies of any deeds, maps, books, papers or other documents which are in the possession of the board and relate to the drainage of land or the provision of flood warning systems in that district. Obstruction of a person exercising powers authorised by the Agency for this purpose is made an offence.[74]

The Agency also has default powers allowing it to exercise the land drainage powers of local authorities in certain circumstances. Hence where the general drainage works powers[75] conferred upon a metropolitan district council, a London borough council or the Common Council of the City of London are not exercised by that council they may be exercised by the Agency and the expenses incurred will be recoverable by the Agency from the council. However, the facility for the Agency to exercise these powers in default of a local authority doing so is provided for only where this is done at the request of the relevant council or where 6 weeks' notice has been given by the Agency. Provision is made for a council to object to the powers being exercised by the Agency by appeal to the Secretary of State; and where this is done and the Agency is informed of the appeal, the powers may not be exercised unless the Minister confirms their exercise.[76]

## 4.4 THE ENVIRONMENT AGENCY: REGULATORY POWERS

### 4.4.1 Controls over Structures in Main Rivers

The powers of the Environment Agency to undertake flood defence operations must be contrasted with those situations where the Agency has power to regulate activities undertaken by others. Perhaps the most significant of the regulatory powers arises from a general prohibition that is imposed upon the erection of any structure in, over or under a watercourse

---

[73] s.9(2) to (4) Land Drainage Act 1991.
[74] s.9(5) and (6) Land Drainage Act 1991. On summary conviction, the offence is punishable by a maximum fine not exceeding level 4 on the standard scale, presently £2,500.
[75] Under s.14(1) Land Drainage Act 1991 and see 4.6.1 below on these powers.
[76] s.16(2) and (3) Land Drainage Act 1991.

which is part of a main river except with the consent of the Agency and in accordance with plans and sections approved by the Agency. Similarly, without the consent of the Agency, to carry out any work of alteration or repair on any structure in, over or under a watercourse which is part of a main river is prohibited if the work is likely to affect the flow of the watercourse or to impede drainage work. The erection or alteration of any structure designed to contain or divert floodwaters of any part of a main river is also prohibited without the Agency's consent, and must be in accordance with plans and sections approved by the Agency.[77]

Work carried out in contravention of the prohibition upon erection of structures in watercourses and other prohibitions may be removed, altered or pulled down by the Agency, and it may recover from the person in default the expenses incurred in so doing. However, the prohibitions upon erection and alteration of structures are not to apply to work carried out in an emergency providing the person carrying out the work informs the Agency that it has been carried out, and the circumstances in which it was carried out, as soon as practicable.[78]

In relation to a consent for the lawful erection or alteration of a structure in, over or under a main river and the erection of a structure to contain or divert floodwaters, the Agency may require the payment of an application fee by a person who applies for consent. The amount of the fee is to be £50 or a sum specified by statutory instrument.[79] In determining an application of this kind, the consent of the Agency is not to be unreasonably withheld, and is deemed to have been given if it is not determined within a 2-month period following the date of the application, or 2 months after payment of an application fee, whichever of these is the later. The consent may be given subject to any reasonable condition as to the time and manner in which the work is to be carried out. If any question arises as to whether consent is unreasonably withheld, or whether a condition is unreasonable, the matter must, if the parties agree to arbitration, be referred to a single arbitrator appointed by agreement between the parties or, in default of agreement, by the President of the Institution of Civil Engineers. If the parties do not agree to arbitration, the matter is referred to and determined by the relevant Minister.[80]

---

[77] s.109(1) to (3) Water Resources Act 1991.
[78] s.109(4) and (5) Water Resources Act 1991.
[79] s.110(1) and (5) Water Resources Act 1991, as amended by Schedule 22 para.147 Environment Act 1995 which states that 'prescribed' means specified in accordance with an order made by the Ministers (s.106(6) Water Resources Act 1991, as added).
[80] s.110(2) and (4) Water Resources Act 1991, as amended.

### 4.4.2 Obstructions in Ordinary Watercourses

The Land Drainage Act 1991 also imposes prohibitions upon the erection of certain kinds of obstruction in ordinary watercourses unless the relevant internal drainage board has given consent. Where, however, a watercourse is outside the district of an internal drainage board the powers concerning obstructions are exercisable by the Agency. Hence, outside an internal drainage district, no person may erect, raise or alter any mill dam, weir or other like obstruction, or erect any culvert that would be likely to affect the flow of an ordinary watercourse without the consent of the Agency.[81]

Provision is made for obstructions which are erected, raised or altered in contravention of the above provisions to be deemed a nuisance. In relation to such nuisances, the Agency may act, in relation to areas outside internal drainage districts, by serving notices to require abatement. Hence, where a person is served with a notice requiring an obstruction to be removed, it will be an offence to act in contravention of the notice. Without prejudice to criminal proceedings, the Agency may take such action as is necessary to remedy the effect of the contravention and may recover the expenses reasonably incurred from the person in default.[82]

### 4.4.3 Culverting Policy

Alongside the two previous sections, concerning structures in main rivers and obstructions in ordinary watercourses, it is pertinent to note the policy of the Environment Agency concerning the installation of culverts in watercourses since this is likely to be one of the most common operations for which consent is required. In short, the Agency is strongly opposed to the culverting of watercourses and considers that it is beneficial for watercourses to remain open whenever possible for both flood defence and environmental reasons. The Agency's *Policy Statement Regarding Culverts*[83] emphasises a series of detrimental consequences of culverting including: loss of and adverse effects on environmental features and wildlife habitats; increased likelihood of flooding due to blockage; increased impact of flooding; loss of floodwater storage; increased difficulties in providing for drainage connections; difficulties in the repair, maintenance and replacement of culverts; increased health and safety hazards; reduced groundwater recharge; and increased difficulty in detecting the origins of

---

[81] s.23 Land Drainage Act 1991.
[82] s.24 Land Drainage Act 1991. A person convicted of the offence will be liable on summary conviction to a fine not exceeding level 5 on the standard scale, presently £5,000, and a further fine of £40 for each day on which the contravention continues.
[83] Environment Agency, *Policy Regarding Culverts: Policy Statement* (1999) and see also *Policy Regarding Culverts: Explanation of Policy* and *Policy Regarding Culverts: Technical Guidance on Culverting Proposals* (1999).

pollution and in monitoring water quality. Given this combination of adverse features the circumstances in which the Agency is likely to give consent to a culverting application are likely to be very limited and the general preference is to have existing culverts restored to open channels.

On the other hand, the Agency is bound to treat each application for consent on its merits and it recognises that there may be situations where culverting is unavoidable. For example, it is difficult to avoid culverting of short lengths of watercourses for access purposes or where highways cross watercourses. However, even in exceptional cases, alternatives, such as open span bridges or the diversion of watercourses, should be considered and the length of culvert should be restricted to the minimum that is necessary to meet the applicant's objectives. Where appropriate, measures to mitigate the adverse effects of culverting and to secure environmental enhancement should be incorporated into a culverting proposal.

The implication of the Agency's policy statement is that the legal powers that have been described,[84] allowing for consent to be given for culverting, will be narrowly construed by the Agency. Although, as has been seen, consent for structures in main rivers or obstructions in ordinary watercourses may not be 'unreasonably' withheld by the Agency, the broad opposition to culverting expressed in the policy is justified by the general need for the Agency to have regard to nature conservation in exercising its functions.[85]

### 4.4.4 Powers concerning Repairs to Watercourses

Within the functions of the Agency concerning main rivers is a stipulation that it will have the same powers as internal drainage boards in respect of securing certain drainage obligations. Specifically, this concerns the powers of internal drainage boards to enforce obligations to repair any watercourse, bridge or drainage against any person who by reason of tenure, custom, prescription or otherwise was bound to do the work.[86] Hence, the powers of the Agency in relation to main rivers encompass powers to compel certain repair work to be done by others.[87]

---

[84] Note also the need for highway authorities to obtain the consent of the Agency before conducting works affecting a watercourse, under s.339 Highways Act 1980, and the power of the Agency to oppose the granting of planning permission under the Town and Country Planning Act 1990 where adverse impacts on watercourses may arise (see Ch.9 below on planning).
[85] See 10.2 below on the general environmental duties upon the Agency.
[86] s.21 Land Drainage Act 1991 provides for the power of internal drainage boards to enforce repair obligations. Notably, the repair obligation must have been in existence before the commencement of the Land Drainage Act 1991 and does not apply to obligations enacted or re-enacted by the Land Drainage Act 1991 or the Water Resources Act 1991 (s.21(1) Land Drainage Act 1991).
[87] s.107(2) Water Resources Act 1991.

The effect of this extension of internal drainage board powers to the Agency is that it may serve a notice upon any person who is liable to do any work in relation to a watercourse, bridge or drainage work, by reason of tenure, custom, prescription or otherwise, and who has failed to do that work. A notice of this kind will require the recipient to undertake the necessary work with 'all reasonable and proper dispatch'. If the recipient fails, within 7 days, to comply with the notice, the Agency may do whatever is necessary for the purpose. Expenses that are reasonably incurred by the Agency may be recovered from the person who is liable to make the repair.[88]

### 4.4.5 Powers to Maintain the Flow of a Watercourse

Another respect in which the powers available to internal drainage boards are extended to the Agency concerns the power to require works for maintaining the flow of a watercourse. This power is extended to the Agency in relation to ordinary watercourses that do not fall within an internal drainage district.[89] However, the power to require the maintenance of flow of a watercourse is also made available to the Agency in relation to main rivers. In effect, the Agency has the same powers to secure the maintenance of flow of a main river, or an ordinary watercourse outside an internal drainage district, as are exercisable by internal drainage boards in respect of ordinary watercourses within their districts.[90]

The consequence of empowering the Agency to secure the flow of main rivers is that enforcement action may be taken where the flow of a watercourse is impeded, other than where the impediment is due to mining operations. This allows the Agency to serve a notice requiring the condition of the watercourse to be remedied on any person having control of the relevant part of the watercourse, owning or occupying adjoining land or whose act or default has caused the impediment to the flow. Works on land which is not owned by the recipient of the works notice will require the consent of the owner of the land unless that person cannot be ascertained after reasonable inquiry. The notice that is served must indicate the nature of the works to be conducted and the period within which they must be carried out and the right of appeal against the service of the notice.[91] Subject to a successful appeal, the failure to undertake the works in accordance with the notice will be an offence. Without prejudice to criminal proceedings, the Agency may itself carry out the required works and recover the

---

[88] s.21 Land Drainage Act 1991.
[89] s.25(2) Land Drainage Act 1991.
[90] s.107(3) Water Resources Act 1991.
[91] A right of appeal is provided for under s.27 Land Drainage Act 1991.

expenses reasonably incurred from the person upon whom the notice was served.[92]

### 4.4.6 Supervision of Internal Drainage Boards

For the purpose of securing the efficient working and maintenance of existing drainage works and the construction of such new works as may be necessary, the Agency is empowered to give general or special directions to internal drainage boards with respect to the exercise and performance by those boards of their powers and duties. Moreover, an internal drainage board may not construct any drainage works or alter any existing drainage works if the construction or alteration will in any way affect the interests of, or the working of, any drainage works belonging to any other drainage board. In addition, an internal drainage board may not, otherwise than for maintaining an existing work, construct or alter any structure, appliance or channel for the discharge of water from its district into a main river except on such terms as are agreed by the Agency and the board, or in default of agreement determined by the relevant Minister. For the purpose of giving consent to the construction or alteration of drainage works by an internal drainage board, the consent of the Agency is not to be unreasonably withheld and may be given subject to reasonable conditions.[93]

If an internal drainage board acts in contravention of the requirements for Agency consent or agreement, the Agency itself has the power to carry out and maintain any works or to do anything which is necessary to prevent or remedy any damage which may result or has resulted from the contravention. The Agency is also entitled to recover from the drainage board any expenses that have been reasonably incurred in the exercise of the power to undertake or maintain works in accordance with this power. Any question as to whether the consent of the Agency is unreasonably withheld, whether a condition of a consent is reasonable or whether expenses have reasonably been incurred by the Agency, must be referred to the relevant Minister for determination and the Minister must lay before Parliament a report giving particulars of his decision.[94]

### 4.4.7 Concurrent Powers

The powers of an internal drainage board in relation to the enforcement of repairing obligations concerning ordinary watercourses, bridges and

---

[92] s.25 Land Drainage Act 1991. The maximum penalty for the offence, on summary conviction, is a fine not exceeding level 4 on the standard scale, presently £2,500.
[93] s.7(1) to (3) Land Drainage Act 1991.
[94] s.7(4) to (6) Land Drainage Act 1991.

drainage works,[95] and powers to prohibit obstructions in ordinary watercourses,[96] are exercisable by the Agency concurrently with the drainage board.[97]

### 4.4.8 Supervision of Local Authorities

The supervision of local authority land drainage activities by the Agency is retained through a requirement that the Agency must give consent for various works. Hence, a local authority may not undertake work in accordance with its general drainage works powers,[98] or a county council undertake work on behalf of a district council,[99] except with the consent of the Agency and in accordance with any conditions imposed in a consent. Before giving consent for these purposes, the Agency is bound to consult any internal drainage board in respect of works concerning a watercourse under the control of the board. The Agency's consent must not be unreasonably withheld and may be deemed to have been given if neither given nor refused within 2 months of the application being made. Questions as to whether consent is unreasonably withheld or whether conditions are reasonable are to be referred to and determined by the Ministers. These requirements do not apply to works carried out in an emergency, but in such circumstances the local authority carrying out the work must inform the Agency, as soon as practicable, as to the work and the circumstances in which it was carried out.[100]

A lesser supervisory power appears to be provided to the Agency in relation to schemes for drainage of small areas undertaken by a local authority. Either the Agency or a local authority other than a district council is empowered to establish a scheme of this kind and undertake the required works subject to certain ministerial controls.[101] However, where a local authority formulates the scheme, the requirement is that the local authority must *consult* the Agency, rather than gaining the consent of the Agency.[102]

---

[95] Under s.21 Land Drainage Act 1991 and see 4.7.2 below on the enforcement of repair obligations.

[96] s.23 Land Drainage Act 1991 and also the power to serve abatement notices for offending obstructions under s.24. See 4.7.3 below on the prohibition of obstructions in watercourses.

[97] s.8 Land Drainage Act 1991.

[98] Under s.14 Land Drainage Act 1991, and the disposal of spoil under s.15, and see 4.6.1 and 4.6.2 below.

[99] Under s.16 Land Drainage Act 1991 and see 3.6.1 below on default powers of county councils.

[100] s.17 Land Drainage Act 1991.

[101] See 4.3.5 above on the Environment Agency undertaking schemes for the drainage of small areas.

[102] s.18 and Schedule 4 para.1(1) Land Drainage Act 1991.

Notably also, other powers of the Agency allow it to exercise varying degrees of supervision over the land drainage activities of local authorities where authorities act under other legislation. Thus, for example, a highway authority is required to obtain consent from the Agency before certain works are undertaken in any watercourse or drainage channel.[103] Under public health legislation a duty is placed upon a local authority to consult the Agency or an internal drainage board in relation to certain proposals for the culverting of watercourses.[104]

### 4.4.9 Commutation of Obligations

As has been previously discussed, the historic system of providing for flood defence through tenure obligations imposed upon private landholders has been recognised for some time to be inefficient and inappropriate.[105] The policy of the Land Drainage Act 1930, and subsequent legislation, has been to require tenure obligations concerning flood defence to be transferred to public bodies with flood defence responsibilities at catchment level.

Present provision for the commutation of tenure-based land drainage obligations requires or allows these obligations to be assumed by the Agency or an internal drainage board. In relation to main rivers, where any person is under an obligation imposed by tenure, custom, prescription, or otherwise to undertake land drainage work, such as repairing banks or walls or maintaining watercourses, the Agency will be under a *duty* to take steps to commute the obligation.[106] In relation to ordinary watercourses, where any person is under the same obligations relating to tenure and the other matters the Agency, or an internal drainage board, *may* commute the obligation with the consent of a Minister. Where commutation of obligations in respect of an ordinary watercourse is proposed, the Agency must give the Minister notice of the proposal and its terms, and the period within which objections may be made. If within 1 month of this notice, the person on whom the obligation is imposed raises an objection to the Agency, the decision as to whether the obligation should be commuted must be referred to the Minister, whose decision will be final.[107]

It is evident that the kinds of obligation that are open to commutation are only those which attach to the ownership of land. Hence, in *Eton Rural*

---

[103] s.339 Highways Act 1980 and see 8.3 below on highway drainage.
[104] Under s.266 Public Health Act 1936 and see 8.2.4 below.
[105] See the discussion of tenure obligations at 1.9.2 above.
[106] s.107(4) Water Resources Act 1991.
[107] s.33 Land Drainage Act 1991.

*District Council* v *Thames Conservators*[108] it was contended that a contractual undertaking to keep a ditch which formed a part of a main river 'clean, open and free from obstructions' was subject to commutation, so that the catchment board was bound to take steps for the commutation of the obligation. However, the phrase 'tenure, custom, prescription or *otherwise*' was narrowly construed to extend only to interests relating to land and, therefore, excluded the purely contractual obligation to maintain the ditch.

The financial consequences of commutation of land drainage obligations are that any person who would be entitled to any exemption from drainage charges, but for the commutation, will be entitled absolutely to a like exemption. The sum to be paid by the owner in respect of the commutation must be determined by the Agency as a sum paid by way of a capital sum or a terminal annuity for a period not exceeding 30 years at the option of the owner. The determination of this sum is to be made by ascertaining the amount which fairly represents the probable average cost of carrying out and maintaining the works which are needed in relation to the commuted obligation. However, no account is to be taken of costs attributable to improvements in drainage, of alterations in cultivation, of land drained by a main river, that have taken place since 1 January 1900 if these have caused an increase in the volume of water being discharged into that river. A person aggrieved by a determination of the sum to be paid on commutation of a drainage obligation may, within 3 months of the Agency's determination, require the matter to be referred to an agreed arbitrator or, in default of agreement, to the President of the Institution of Civil Engineers.[109]

### 4.4.10 Powers to Vary Awards

Provision is made for variation of any award made under a public or local Act that contains any provision affecting or relating to the drainage of land, including provisions concerning the powers and duties of any drainage body or other person relating to the drainage of land. This allows the Agency to submit to a Minister for confirmation a scheme for revoking, varying or amending the relevant statutory provision. In particular, such a scheme may provide for commuting of the obligation of any person to repair or maintain drainage works and may contain necessary incidental, consequential or supplemental provisions. On the application of any

---

[108] [1950] Ch 540. Similarly, see *Re Fitzherbert-Brockholes Agreement, River Wyre Catchment Board* v *Miller* [1940] Ch 51 where no obligation to commute was established where payment was made voluntarily under a covenant which was not binding.
[109] s.34(1) to (6) Land Drainage Act 1991.

person who is under an obligation of this kind, or an internal drainage board, the appropriate Minister may direct the Agency to submit a scheme for variation of the award.[110] The detailed procedural provisions concerning orders for variations of awards are set out in Schedule 3 to the Land Drainage Act 1991.[111]

### 4.4.11 Powers to Vary Navigation Rights

Powers are provided to vary or extinguish certain navigation rights for flood defence purposes. These allow an application to be made to the Minister for this purpose by the Agency, in relation to any watercourse, or by an internal drainage board, in relation to ordinary watercourses within their districts. On receipt of an application of this kind, the Minister must be satisfied that a navigation authority is not exercising, or not properly exercising, the powers vested in it and that it is desirable that they should be exercised to secure the better drainage of any land. If satisfied of these matters, the Minister may revoke or amend the provisions of any local act relating to navigation over any canal, river or navigable waters and the corresponding powers and duties of the responsible navigation authority. However, the ministerial powers to make an order of this kind may not be exercised in relation to any waters within the ebb and flow of the tide at ordinary spring tides except with the consent of the Secretary of State for Transport, Local Government and the Regions. Orders of this kind are subject to procedural requirements detailed in Schedule 3 to the Land Drainage Act 1991.[112]

## 4.5 OPERATIONAL AND REGULATORY POWERS: INTERNAL DRAINAGE BOARDS AND LOCAL AUTHORITIES

The operational and regulatory powers of internal drainage boards and local authorities are, primarily, provided for under the Land Drainage Act 1991. These may be considered relatively briefly since, in many respects, they are the same or similar to the powers of the Environment Agency, which have previously been discussed. Also, within their respective districts and areas, the powers of internal drainage boards and local authorities are the same and, therefore, may be considered together in the subsections that follow. However, there are some differences between the powers of boards and local authorities and these must be noted.

---

[110] s.32 Land Drainage Act 1991.
[111] See the discussion of duties arising under local and private legislation at 4.9 below.
[112] s.35 Land Drainage Act 1991.

## 4.6 OPERATIONAL POWERS: INTERNAL DRAINAGE BOARDS AND LOCAL AUTHORITIES

### 4.6.1 General Flood Defence Works Powers

The general flood defence works powers of the Environment Agency have been previously discussed[113] and essentially the same powers are available to internal drainage boards and local authorities. However, in the case of an internal drainage board, these powers may only be exercised within its district, and in the case of a local authority, the powers may only be exercised for the purpose of a scheme for drainage for a small area[114] or for the purpose of preventing flooding, or mitigating damage caused by flooding, in its area.[115] Also, in the case of local authorities, the powers are not available to a county council unless it is acting in default of a non-metropolitan district council.[116]

Otherwise than in connection with a main river, the general flood defence works powers of internal drainage boards or local authorities allow operations to be carried out for the following purposes:

(a) to cleanse, repair or otherwise maintain existing watercourses or drainage works in an efficient state;

(b) to improve existing works by deepening, widening or otherwise improving any existing watercourse or removing or altering mill dams, weirs or other obstructions to watercourses, or raising, widening or otherwise improving any existing drainage work; and

(c) to construct new works by making any new watercourse or drainage work or erecting any machinery or doing any other act required for the drainage of land.[117]

As with the allocation of these general powers to the Environment Agency the permissive rather than mandatory character of the powers must be reaffirmed. Hence, liability will not generally arise where an internal drainage board or local authority fails to exercise the powers, though this must be read subject to the same qualifications that were raised in relation

---

[113] On the corresponding powers of the Environment Agency, see s.165(1) Water Resources Act 1991, and see 4.3.1 above.
[114] Under s.18 Land Drainage Act 1991, and see 4.6.3 below.
[115] s.14(1) Land Drainage Act 1991.
[116] s.14(4) Land Drainage Act 1991, and see s.17 on the default powers of county councils, discussed at 3.6.1 above.
[117] s.14(2) Land Drainage Act 1991. See *Keaney* v *Liverpool City Council*, unreported, Lands Tribunal, 21 May 1998, where it was held that work undertaken under an 'estate action environmental scheme' did not constitute works within s.14 Land Drainage Act 1991.

to the circumstances in which the liability against the Agency might arise.[118]

Where the powers are exercised by an internal drainage board or local authority and this results in injury being sustained by any person, then compensation will be payable to the injured person. In a case of dispute as to the amount of compensation payable, the amount will be determined by the Lands Tribunal.[119] Again, this parallels the liability of the Agency to compensate those injured as a result of flood defence operations.

Notably, the general flood defence works powers given to internal drainage boards and local authorities do not authorise any person to enter on land except for the purpose of maintaining existing works.[120] As has been seen, powers of entry of boards and authorities are otherwise provided for.[121]

Separate provision is also made for internal drainage boards and local authorities to acquire land in connection with the performance of their functions, including the exercise of the general flood defence works powers. Hence, boards and authorities may acquire land within or outside their districts or areas by agreement or may acquire such land compulsorily if authorised by the relevant Minister. Internal drainage boards may exercise the power to acquire land so as to acquire an interest in, or rights over, land by way of creating new rights in land as well as acquiring existing interests in the land, subject to legislation concerning compulsory purchase.[122] The disposal of land by internal drainage boards is subject to the restriction that, except with the consent of the relevant Minister, land must not be disposed of otherwise than by way of a short tenancy, for a consideration which is less than the best that can reasonably be obtained. Also, except with Ministerial consent, a drainage board may not dispose of land which has been acquired compulsorily or, at a time when the board was authorised to acquire it compulsorily, by agreement.[123]

---

[118] See 4.3.1 above on the potential liability of the Environment Agency. See also the discussion of possible human rights implications at 7.9.8 below.
[119] s.14(5) Land Drainage Act 1991.
[120] s.14(6) Land Drainage Act 1991.
[121] See 3.5.8 and 3.6.4 above on powers of entry of internal drainage boards and local authorities.
[122] s.62 Land Drainage Act 1991. Generally see Acquisition of Land Act 1981. The exercise of the general flood defence works powers is included in the purposes for which the council of any district of London borough or the Common Council of the City of London may be authorised to purchase land compulsorily. Similar compulsory purchase powers are afforded to county authorities where they act in default of a district authority in exercising general drainage powers (under s.16 Land Drainage Act 1991 and see 3.6.1 above) again, subject to ministerial authorisation (s.62(2)).
[123] s.63(1) to (3) Land Drainage Act 1991.

Although internal drainage boards and local authorities normally undertake works in accordance with their general flood defence works powers within their own district or area, there may be situations where works need to be undertaken outside the district or area which is intended to be benefited. Hence, subject to any arrangements between the Agency and an internal drainage board[124] and supervisory powers of the Agency over works carried out by local authorities,[125] internal drainage boards and local authorities may conduct work, for the benefit of their district or area, on ordinary watercourses where these are outside their district or area. However, such works are limited to works under powers which are conferred upon persons with an interest in the relevant land and who desire the drainage works for that purpose.[126]

### 4.6.2 Power to Dispose of Spoil

As with the Environment Agency, special powers are given to internal drainage boards and local authorities in relation to the disposal of spoil arising from flood defence operations. Hence, without having to make payment, an internal drainage board or local authority may appropriate and dispose of any matter removed in the course of carrying out work for the widening, deepening or dredging of an ordinary watercourse. Matter which is removed may be deposited on the banks of the watercourse, on such width of land adjoining the watercourse as is sufficient to enable the matter to be removed and deposited by mechanical means in a single operation.[127]

However, the power to dispose of spoil by a local authority may not be exercised except for the purpose of works in pursuance of a scheme for drainage of a small area[128] or so far as may be necessary for the purpose of mitigating any damage caused by flooding in its area. In no case will the power to dispose of spoil be exercised so as to constitute a statutory nuisance.[129]

Where injury is sustained by any person by an exercise of the power to dispose of spoil, the internal drainage board or local authority may pay the

---

[124] Under s.11 Land Drainage Act 1991, and see 4.6.4 below.
[125] Under s.17 Land Drainage Act 1991.
[126] s.14(3) Land Drainage Act 1991. See also 4.8.1 below on the power of Ministers to authorise landowners to carry out drainage works (under s.22).
[127] s.15(1) Land Drainage Act 1991. On the corresponding power of the Environment Agency to dispose of spoil under s.167 Water Resources Act 1991, see 4.3.4 above.
[128] Under s.18 Land Drainage Act 1991, and see 4.6.3 below.
[129] Under Part III Environmental Protection Act 1990, and see 8.2.1 on statutory nuisance.

## Operational Powers: Internal Drainage Boards and LAs

person such compensation as they think fit and where the injury could have been avoided if the power had been exercised with reasonable care a dispute as to the amount of compensation must be referred to the Lands Tribunal. Alternatively, where disposal of spoil cannot be undertaken within the power given to an internal drainage board or local authority, the board or authority may enter into an agreement for the disposal of spoil on payment to the council of any district or London borough or any Welsh country or county borough council.[130]

### 4.6.3 Drainage of Small Areas (by Local Authorities)

As for the Environment Agency,[131] certain local authorities, but not internal drainage boards, are empowered to exercise powers in relation to schemes for the drainage of small areas. Hence, local authorities other than English non-metropolitan district councils are empowered to make schemes for drainage of small areas, for which the creation of an internal drainage board would not be justified, and to enter land for the purpose of carrying out such drainage works as are desirable in accordance with the provisions of a scheme. The detailed provisions concerning such schemes are set out in Schedule 4 to the Land Drainage Act 1991.[132]

Local authorities are required to consult the Agency on the making of a scheme for drainage of a small area; to give notice to owners and occupiers of land affected; to allow objections to be made; and for matters to be determined by one of the Ministers, if necessary, after a local inquiry.[133] Other requirements for a scheme are that it must state the works to be carried out; the area to be improved; the estimated expenses; the maximum amount recoverable by the local authority in respect of the expenses; and the manner in which the expenses of the work and its maintenance are to be apportioned between the land to be improved. Ordinarily, the expense of the work should not exceed £50 for each hectare of land improved, but this limit may be varied by ministerial order and a ministerial power allows the limit to be dispensed with if the proposed works are urgently required in the public interest. In accordance with the apportionment provisions set out in a particular scheme, the expenses of carrying out the works and maintaining them will be recoverable by a local authority from the owners of land to which the scheme relates.[134]

---

[130] s.15(2) to (5) Land Drainage Act 1991.
[131] See 4.3.5 above on the powers of the Environment Agency in relation to schemes for small areas.
[132] s.18(1) and (2) Land Drainage Act 1991.
[133] Schedule 4 Land Drainage Act 1991.
[134] s.18(3) to (6) Land Drainage Act 1991.

### 4.6.4 Works by Arrangement

Flood defence works powers of internal drainage boards and local authorities are also capable of arising where they are the subject of particular kinds of arrangement. Two kinds of arrangement are statutorily provided for in this respect: arrangements between internal drainage boards and navigation or conservancy authorities; and arrangements between internal drainage boards or local authorities and other persons who are entitled to carry out flood defence works.

In relation to arrangements between internal drainage boards and navigation or conservancy authorities, agreements of this kind may be entered into for the improvement of drainage of any land situated in the board's district. The effect of the arrangement may allow the transfer to the board of any undertaking of the navigation or conservancy authority or any rights, powers, duties, liabilities or obligations or property of the authority. Alternatively, the arrangement may provide for the alteration or improvement by the board of any of the works of the authority or the making of payments by the board to the authority in relation to matters which are the subject of the arrangement.[135]

Arrangements between internal drainage boards and navigation or conservancy authorities are limited by the stipulation that they may not relate to main rivers or drainage works in connection with a main river. Also, arrangements require the approval of the relevant Minister. Procedural requirements also apply requiring notice of a proposed arrangement to be published as required by the Minister, and for the final arrangement to be published in a prescribed form.[136]

The second kind of arrangement that is provided for allows either internal drainage boards or local authorities to enter an arrangement with a person who is entitled to carry on or maintain flood defence works. In relation to internal drainage boards this allows the board to enter into an agreement to undertake works at the expense of the person who is entitled to carry out the work, either within or outside the district of the board. However, these powers are not exercisable by the board in relation to a main river or any flood defence works in connection with a main river.[137]

In relation to local authorities, an arrangement with another person entitled to undertake flood defence works allows an authority, other than an

---

[135] s.19(1) Land Drainage Act 1991.
[136] s.19(2) to (6) Land Drainage Act 1991 and see reg.2 Land Drainage (General) Regulations 1932, S.R.&O. 1932 No.64.
[137] s.20(1) and (3) Land Drainage Act 1991.

English non-metropolitan district council, to undertake work at that person's expense within the area of the authority.[138]

## 4.7 REGULATORY POWERS: INTERNAL DRAINAGE BOARDS AND LOCAL AUTHORITIES

In relation to regulatory powers of internal drainage boards and local authorities, comparison may again be drawn with the Environment Agency, which has extensive powers to regulate activities of other bodies and persons which are likely to impact upon flood defence.[139] In respect of internal drainage boards and local authorities, regulatory powers are of narrower compass, but nonetheless important in relation to ordinary watercourses.

### 4.7.1 Works to Maintain Watercourses

Where an ordinary watercourse is in such a condition that the proper flow of water is impeded, an internal drainage board[140] or local authority is empowered to require works to be undertaken for the purpose of maintaining the flow of the watercourse. Unless the unsatisfactory condition of the watercourse is attributable to mining operations, the board or authority is entitled to serve notice on the person responsible requiring the condition to be remedied. A notice of this kind may be served on any person having control of the watercourse where the impediment occurs, owning or occupying adjoining land or due to whose act or default the impediment occurs. The notice must indicate the nature of the works to be carried out, and the period within which they must be undertaken, and must indicate the existence of a right of appeal against the notice.[141]

Failure to carry out the works required by a works notice within the required period will allow the internal drainage board or local authority to exercise default powers which allow it to undertake the works and recover the expense reasonably incurred from the person on whom the notice was served. Without prejudice to this, the person failing to undertake works in accordance with the notice will be guilty of an offence. In prosecution proceedings of this kind, it will not be open to the defendant to raise any issue that could not have been raised in an appeal against the service of the works notice.[142]

---

[138] s.20(2) Land Drainage Act 1991.
[139] See 4.4 above on the regulatory powers of the Environment Agency.
[140] Alternatively, in relation to ordinary watercourses which are not in an internal drainage district, the same powers are given to the Environment Agency (s.25(2) Land Drainage Act 1991).
[141] s.25(1) to (5) Land Drainage Act 1991.
[142] s.25(6) and (7) Land Drainage Act 1991. On summary conviction, the offence is punishable by a fine not exceeding level 4 on the standard scale, presently £2,500.

Before a local authority exercises its powers in respect of requiring works to maintain the flow of an ordinary watercourse, it must notify the internal drainage board if the watercourse is part of an internal drainage district or, if not, it must notify the Environment Agency. Where a local authority has other powers for securing the appropriate flow of water in any watercourse under its jurisdiction the power to serve a notice requiring works to be undertaken to maintain the flow[143] must not be exercised by a local drainage board except by agreement with the local authority or where, after reasonable notice, the local authority has failed to exercise other powers.[144]

Notably in this respect, local authorities have other powers[145] to secure the proper flow of watercourses and it seems to be envisaged that these should be used as a matter of first resort. Also, where a watercourse is under the jurisdiction of a navigation authority, harbour authority, conservancy authority or board of conservators which are exercising their powers, the power to require works to maintain the flow of a watercourse must not be exercised except with the consent of the relevant authority or board. In addition, the power to require works to maintain the flow of a watercourse will not apply in relation to main rivers in respect of which separate powers are provided.[146] An appeal against the service of a notice requiring works to maintain the flow of an ordinary watercourse may be allowed in specified circumstances such as where the alternative works have been unreasonably declined or where the period allowed for the works is not reasonably sufficient.[147]

### 4.7.2 Enforcement of Repair Obligations (by Internal Drainage Boards)

Internal drainage boards are given specific powers to compel others to undertake various kinds of repair work in relation to ordinary watercourses. Hence, enforcement action may be pursued if any person fails to fulfil an obligation, predating the commencement of the Land Drainage Act 1991, by reason of tenure, custom, prescription or otherwise, which gives rise to a liability to repair, maintain or do other work in relation to a watercourse, bridge or drainage work. In such circumstances, the board may serve a notice requiring the person to do the necessary work with 'all reasonable

---

[143] Under s.25 Land Drainage Act 1991.
[144] s.26(1) and (2) Land Drainage Act 1991.
[145] Obstructions may also be dealt with by local authorities under public health powers, or by byelaws made under s.66 Land Drainage Act 1991.
[146] s.26(3) and (4) Land Drainage Act 1991, and see s.107(3) Water Resources Act 1991, concerning main river functions of the Environment Agency, discussed at 3.4.8 above.
[147] s.27 Land Drainage Act 1991.

and proper dispatch'. If a person fails, within 7 days, to comply with a notice of this kind the board may undertake such works as are necessary under the notice. Following the exercise of default powers by a board, it may recover all expenses that are reasonably incurred from a person who was liable to undertake the repairs.[148]

### 4.7.3 Prohibition of Obstructions in Watercourses (by Internal Drainage Boards)

Specific prohibitions are imposed upon the placing of various obstructions in ordinary watercourses and powers of consenting and enforcement in relation to these are given to internal drainage boards. Hence, no person may erect any mill dam, weir or other similar obstruction to the flow of a watercourse, or raise or otherwise alter any such obstruction, or erect a culvert that would be likely to affect the flow of a watercourse, or alter a culvert in a way that would be likely to affect the flow. However, this prohibition applies only where the obstruction has not been consented to by the relevant internal drainage board and exceptions are provided for in relation to works under the control of a navigation, harbour or conservancy authority, and for works which are carried out or maintained under statutory powers.[149]

In determining a consent for an obstruction in an ordinary watercourse, the internal drainage board is not to withhold its consent unreasonably, and if the applicant is not notified of the determination within 2 months from the application and payment of the fee, the board is deemed to have consented. Any question as to whether consent has been unreasonably withheld is to be referred to a single arbitrator agreed between the parties or, in the absence of agreement, the President of the Institution of Civil Engineers on the application of either party. For the determination of an application for consent, the board may require a fee of £50 or such other sum as may be prescribed.[150]

If an obstruction or culvert is erected or altered in contravention of the prohibition and without consent, the internal drainage board will be empowered to serve a notice requiring the nuisance to be abated within a specified period. This notice must be served upon a person with the power

---

[148] s.21(1) to (5) Land Drainage Act 1991. See s.107(2) Water Resources Act 1991 on the corresponding powers of the Environment Agency to compel works to be conducted by third parties, discussed at 4.4.4 above.

[149] s.23(1) and (6) Land Drainage Act 1991.

[150] s.23(2) to (5) Land Drainage Act 1991, as amended by Schedule 22 para.192 Environment Act 1995. On the power of the Environment Agency to give consent for structures in main rivers see s.109 Water Resources Act 1991, discussed at 4.4.1 above.

to remove the obstruction and a failure to comply will constitute an offence. Where a person acts in contravention of a notice of this kind, or fails to comply with it, the internal drainage board may take such action as is necessary to remedy the effect of the contravention or failure and may recover the expenses reasonably incurred from the person in default. The exercise of default powers by the board is without prejudice to it taking criminal proceedings against a person who has failed to comply with a notice.[151]

## 4.8 POWERS OF LANDHOLDERS

The powers and duties of landholders in relation to flood defence have been largely considered in Chapter 2 as a matter of civil law. Notwithstanding the general *power* of a landowner to undertake flood defence work, as has been seen, there are various contexts where a *duty* will arise for a landowner to take action to prevent flooding and be liable in private nuisance where there is a failure to do so which results in harm to neighbouring landowners. Hence, there is a significant contrast between the *powers* possessed by public flood defence bodies and the statutory *duties* that may be imposed upon private landholders in relation to flood defence matters. It is out of place to talk of 'regulatory' powers of landholders over others, but the statutory provisions may allow landowners certain procedural rights to compel work to be undertaken or to require other landholders to fulfil flood defence obligations.

### 4.8.1 Authorisation of Landowners to Carry Out Works

In a situation where landholder 'A' is suffering from flooding because works need to be undertaken on land held by 'B', it might be most appropriate for the two to enter into a private agreement whereby A is allowed to enter B's land for the purpose of conducting whatever work is needed. However, there may be situations where B is not agreeable to a private arrangement of this kind. For example, the operation which is envisaged may be damaging to B and A is not prepared to offer recompense or there may be legal reasons, such as the terms of a lease, which prevent B from entering into the agreement which is being offered.

To address these kinds of issue, statutory provision is made to allow the relevant Minister to authorise landowners to carry out certain drainage works on the same basis as internal drainage boards and local authorities

---

[151] s.24 Land Drainage Act 1991. On summary conviction, the offence may be punished by a fine not exceeding level 5 on the standard scale, presently £5,000, and a further fine, not exceeding £40 for each day on which the failure continues.

may be authorised to undertake work.[152] Specifically, the ministerial powers arise where any person is interested in land and of the opinion that it is capable of improvement by drainage works, but the works cannot be carried out because of the objection of a legal disability upon a person whose land would be entered upon or interfered with for the purpose of the work. In those circumstances, the person seeking to undertake the work may make an application to the Minister for an order allowing drainage works to be undertaken insofar as they are expedient for the improvement of land.[153]

An application for authorisation for drainage works must be in a prescribed form and must contain particulars of the proposed works, the persons by whom they are to be carried out, any further particulars that are prescribed and the applicants must give security for expenses involved. The application is to be publicised, and a period allowed for objections, so that notice is given to persons whose land is to be entered or interfered with, the Environment Agency and the internal drainage board for the district, if any. Provision is made for public inquiries to be held where certain objections are made and sustained. Following such an inquiry, if necessary, the Minister may either refuse the application or allow it with or without alteration.[154] However, the Minister is not entitled to make any order which authorises any work whereby streams, reservoirs or feeders supplying 'ornamental waters' will be cut through, diverted or interfered with except with the agreement of the owner of the ornamental waters.[155]

The effect of an order of this kind is to authorise persons to carry out the relevant works and to maintain them thereafter. However, persons who are interested in land affected by the order, unless they are amongst those authorised to carry out the works, will be entitled to compensation for any injury suffered as a result of the works. Compensation which is payable in respect of such injury will be determinable by the Lands Tribunal.[156]

### 4.8.2 Orders Requiring Cleansing of Ditches

Where a ditch is in such a condition as to cause damage to land or to prevent the improvement in the drainage of *any* land, the owner of the land may

---

[152] Under s.14(3) Land Drainage Act 1991 an internal drainage board or local authority is deemed to have the same powers as 'persons interested in land' which is capable of being drained or improved and desiring to carry out drainage works for that purpose.
[153] s.22(1) Land Drainage Act 1991.
[154] s.22(2) to (5) Land Drainage Act 1991.
[155] s.22(8) Land Drainage Act 1991. No definition of 'ornamental waters' is provided.
[156] s.22(6) and (7) Land Drainage Act 1991.

make an application to the Agricultural Land Tribunal.[157] Following such an application, the Tribunal may make an order requiring a person named in the order to carry out such remedial work as is specified in the order. Accordingly, an order of the Tribunal may name any person who is an owner or occupier of land through which the ditch passes or which abuts the ditch and any person who has the right to carry out the work specified or any part of it. Orders of this kind may specify that more than one person is required to carry out the work and may specify the respective work to be undertaken, or may indicate that persons have joint liability, if necessary, specifying the contributions that are to be made to the cost of the work. For these purposes, 'ditch' includes a culverted or piped ditch but excludes a watercourse vested in, or under the control of, a drainage body. 'Remedial work' means work for the cleansing of the ditch, removing from it any matter which impedes the flow of water or otherwise for putting it in proper order and for protecting it.[158]

An order made by the Agricultural Land Tribunal is sufficient authority for a person named under the order to undertake the work specified in the order and, so far as is necessary, to enter specified land for that purpose. In the event of work specified in an order not having been carried out after 3 months, the appropriate Minister or any authorised drainage body may enter land, where this is necessary and after 7 days' notice, and carry out the work. The expenses reasonably incurred in carrying out the work may then be recovered from the person who ought to have undertaken the work under the order. 'Expenses' for these purposes may include compensation which is payable to any person who sustains injury as a result of the work being undertaken unless the person sustaining injury is the person who failed to undertake the work under the order. Disputes as to the amount of compensation are to be determined by the Lands Tribunal.[159]

The Agricultural Land Tribunal has powers to make orders authorising works to be undertaken in connection with ditches where this is required for the drainage of land. Orders of this kind may be made on the application of an owner or occupier of land where the work needs to be undertaken on other land. The power to make such orders arises where the drainage of any land requires the carrying out of any work in connection with a ditch

---

[157] The constitution and procedure of the Agricultural Land Tribunal is provided for under the Agriculture Act 1947. Special provision is also made for the composition and incidental powers of the Agricultural Land Tribunal for the purpose of hearing applications under ss.28 and 30 Land Drainage Act 1991, concerned with orders requiring the cleansing of ditches and authorisation of drainage works in connection with a ditch (under s.31 Land Drainage Act 1991).
[158] s.28 Land Drainage Act 1991.
[159] s.29 Land Drainage Act 1991.

passing through other land; the replacement or construction of such a ditch; or the alteration or removal of any drainage work in connection with such a ditch. An order of this kind will authorise the applicant to carry out the specified works and, so far as may be necessary, to enter land for that purpose. Provision is also made for compensation to be payable to persons suffering injury as a result of the work being conducted and for disputes as to the amount of compensation to be determined by the Lands Tribunal.[160]

## 4.9 PRIVATE AND LOCAL LEGISLATION

Although the body of this chapter has been largely concerned with flood defence operations and regulation arising under the Water Resources Act 1991 and the Land Drainage Act 1991, it must be noted that there are many instances where flood defence obligations are otherwise provided for. The significance of obligations of this kind has already been alluded to in the discussion of *Smith and Snipes Hall Farm Ltd* v *River Douglas Catchment Board*,[161] where it was seen that the responsibilities of the Catchment Board, arising from an agreement to maintain a flood bank, were regarded as contractual rather than tortious in character. Three broader implications follow from this. First, it is apparent that operational flood defence obligations are capable of arising outside the provisions of the 1991 Acts. Second, where a flood defence operating authority, or other statutory body, has acquired rights and duties under previous agreements, or under private or local legislation, it may continue to be bound by these. Third, whilst the general strategy of the 1991 Acts is to provide only permissive powers in relation to flood defence, this approach is not always followed under agreements and earlier legislation, and many examples are to be found of mandatory duties applying in particular localities, of a kind which do not exist under the 1991 Acts.

Generalisation about the effects of private and local legislation is impossible, since the provisions of each Act will be differently formulated. Nonetheless, some examples may usefully illustrate the operation of such legislation and its potential for continuing application to the activities of internal drainage boards or the Environment Agency.

In *Rippingale Farms Ltd* v *Black Sluice Internal Drainage Board*[162] a local Act dating from 1765 had required Commissioners to 'keep in repair' a particular dyke out of money raised under the Act. By an order of 1935, under the Land Drainage Act 1930, responsibilities of the Commissioners

---

[160] s.30 Land Drainage Act 1991.
[161] [1949] 2 KB 500, discussed at 4.3.1 above.
[162] [1963] 1 WLR 1347. See also *Sephton* v *Lancashire River Board* [1962] 1 All ER 183, discussed at 5.3 below.

had been transferred to the defendant Internal Drainage Board. The claimant occupied farmland adjoining the dyke and suffered damage when it overflowed. An action was brought for breach of statutory duty in respect of the failure of the defendant to use reasonable care to keep the bank of the dyke in repair, as required under the 1765 Act.

The circumstances raised two key issues: the extent of the duty under the 1765 Act and whether that duty was transferred to the defendants. On the first point it was clear that a positive duty was imposed, requiring that certain 'marsh and fen land shall and may be drained and improved' and kept in repair at all times thereafter. The Act provided a detailed specification of the particular works that were to be undertaken and enabled the Commissioners to levy rates on the lands which were benefited. Although this may not have been an 'absolute' duty to keep the dyke in repair, it was construed to be a duty to use reasonable care in securing the maintenance of the dyke. Conceivably, failure to fulfil the duty may have been excused due to lack of funding but, since the defendant was able to raise the relevant expenses by means of a drainage rate under the 1930 Act, this argument was not relevant.

The second issue was whether this duty had been transferred to the defendant. The argument of the Internal Drainage Board on this point was that the responsibility did not devolve because the *positive duty* under the 1765 Act had been entirely replaced by the *permissive powers* given to internal drainage boards under the 1930 Act. The validity of the argument depended upon the effect of the 1930 Act and orders made under it to reconstitute the former Commissioners as the subsequent Internal Drainage Board. In the first place, it was found that nothing under the 1930 Act relieved the Commissioners of duties under the 1765 Act. Beyond that, a ministerial Order made in 1935 reconstituting the Drainage Board had provided that 'the existing rights, powers, duties, obligations and liabilities' of the Commissioners were to be transferred to the Board except insofar as they were 'inconsistent with or contrary or repugnant to' the provisions of the 1930 Act. On this, it was found that there was nothing inconsistent between the Board having powers under the later Act alongside duties in the earlier Act. Hence, the 1930 Act had contemplated that earlier local Acts should continue to apply to relevant internal drainage boards.

The direct consequence of this ruling was that the defendant was liable to the claimant for the flooding damage arising from the breach of statutory duty, under the 1765 Act, in failing to exercise reasonable care in maintaining the state of the dyke. The broader implication was that there were likely to be many internal drainage boards and catchment boards, and now the Environment Agency, who were similarly bound to fulfil duties under earlier private and local enactments. Despite the general approach of flood defence legislation, from 1930 onwards, seeking to avoid allocating *duties* to flood defence operating authorities, the survival of many earlier enactments has the consequence that substantial flood defence duties may continue to apply in particular localities.

The practical consequences of the survival of earlier legislation depend, in each instance, upon the wording used in each relevant private or local Act. However, there are several examples of early legislation imposing relatively strict duties upon those with responsibilities for flood defence structures. Hence, in *Collins* v *Middle Level Commissioners*[163] a local drainage Act required the Commissioners to construct a cut, with proper walls, gates, and sluices, to keep out the waters of a tidal river. Liability was established after sluices had allowed water to flow into the cut causing it to burst its banks and flood adjoining lands. Despite the fact that the force of tidal waters had broken the sluices, it was admitted, for the purpose of the proceedings, that this constituted negligence on the part of the Commissioners. In *Bramlett* v *Tees Conservancy Commissioners*[164] the Commissioners were placed under a duty to maintain walls and works alongside a river, and this was construed as a duty to protect all lands that could be harmed by the overflow of tidal waters. Hence, liability on the part of the Commissioners was established on the basis of their failure to fulfil a statutory duty to provide a reasonably sufficient sea wall or embankment to protect lands from being flooded. The strictness of these duties, by comparison with the powers available under present flood defence legislation, will be readily apparent.

However, the most remarkable examples of duties to prevent flooding are to be found in private or local legislation enabling various kinds of water undertaking to be conducted. In *Geddis* v *Proprietors of the Bann Reservoir*[165] a local Act incorporated certain persons for the purpose of supplying water to mill owners on the banks of a river. For this purpose, the defendants were authorised by the Act to construct a reservoir to ensure an adequate supply of water to the river at all times of the year. In addition, they were empowered to 'maintain, repair, widen, deepen, scour, cleanse, and keep proper and sufficient conduits, aqueducts, channels and watercourses' etc. However, after a time, the defendants neglected to cleanse the channel of a particular watercourse which had become silted, with the result that it overflowed its banks and caused damage to the

---

[163] (1896) LR 4 CP 279. See also *Coe* v *Wise* (1866) LR 1 QB 711 where drainage commissioners were found liable for a negligent failure to maintain a cut and sluice.
[164] (1885) 49 JP 214.
[165] (1878) 3 App Cas 430.

adjoining land of the claimant. Despite the apparently permissive form of the power to cleanse the watercourse, it was held that it should be exercised in such a way as to prevent avoidable harm being caused to others. The local Act did not authorise neighbouring land to be flooded unless it was impossible to avoid or prevent this by any reasonable use of the statutory powers. Hence, the defendants were under an effective *duty* to exercise the 'power' to cleanse the watercourse and to prevent it flooding the claimant's land.[166]

Perhaps the most extreme example of a statutory duty to prevent flooding is to be seen in *Countess of Rothes* v *Kirkcaldy and Dysart Waterworks Commissioners*[167] where a local and personal Act provided that the Commissioners, with responsibilities for reservoirs and other water supply works,

> 'should be bound to make good to the Countess of Rothes and her heirs ... all damages which may be occasioned to her or them, by reason of or in consequence of any bursting, or flow, or escape of water from any reservoir, or aqueduct, or pipe, or other work connected therewith.'

During a period of extraordinary rainfall a great quantity of water was continuously discharged from a reservoir into a watercourse from which it overflowed onto the claimant's land and caused damage for which compensation was sought. Although the defendants argued that it would be unreasonable to interpret the clause so widely that they would be liable for a flood which would have happened irrespective of their activities, a majority of the House of Lords held that the words should be construed in a broad way. The clause constituted an 'obligation of absolute protection' against flooding and it was no defence for the defendants to show that the circumstances at issue had arisen without any negligence on their part. Although it appears extraordinary that statutory wording should be interpreted to impose a duty which it may be beyond the powers of a party to fulfil, the decision has to be seen against a background of a local Act which was effectively drafted by the promoters of the Act. They sought the legislative powers to carry out their activities and should have taken care to define with precision and accuracy the limits of their liability. As such the wording of the Act had to be construed *contra proferentem* (against he who proffers) and given the interpretation which was most favourable to the claimant.

---

[166] Contrast *Cracknell* v *Corporation of Thetford* (1869) Law Rep 4 CP 629 where accumulations of weed and silt caused a river to overflow its banks but, under a private Act, the defendant had no powers allowing it to clear the weed and silt, unless this was required for the purposes of navigation, and was found not to be liable for the flooding.

[167] (1882) 7 App Cas 694.

Finally, it is notable that provisions under private and local statutes did not only apply to flood defence and other statutory bodies, and there are examples of situations where obligations were statutorily imposed upon private persons in relation to flood defence structures on their land. As has been seen, a relatively modern example of this kind of obligation is to be found in Thames Barrier and Flood Prevention Act 1972 which imposes a duty upon certain private landowners to ensure the closure of certain flood dams when required to do so.[168]

An earlier example of the operation of a special Act imposing a flood defence duty upon landowners is to be seen in *Nitro-Phosphate and Odam's Chemical Manure Co* v *London and St Katherine Docks Co.*[169] Here, a dock company has been authorised by special Act to make and maintain a retaining bank at a height of about 4 feet above the level of the Trinity high-water mark to protect surrounding land which was below that level. However, the company allowed the bank to be retained several inches below the specified level at one point, with the consequence that the bank was overtopped by an exceptionally high tide and the property of a neighbouring landowner was damaged as a result. Despite the possibility that some of the damage arose because of an 'act of God',[170] it was held that the defendants were liable for the failure to adhere to the statutory duty to keep the bank at the required height.

---

[168] See 3.7.2 above on the Thames Barrier and Flood Prevention Act 1972.
[169] (1878) 9 Ch D 503 (concerning the Victoria (London) Docks Act 1853 (16 & 17 Vict. C.cxxxi) and other special Acts).
[170] See 2.5.3 above on 'acts of God'.

# Chapter 5

# COAST PROTECTION

## 5.1 INTRODUCTION

Although distinguished from flooding, the protection of land, and particularly coastal land, from erosion is a major problem in many areas. The natural forces which cause the removal of soil from some coastal land and its deposition elsewhere have shaped the coastline of England and Wales over many centuries without, or despite, human intervention. Nonetheless, the need to challenge the natural processes underlying coastal erosion has been recognised in some locations and legal machinery provided for this. Clearly, the application of coast protection measures can only be used selectively, since the problems in many areas seem insurmountable by the application of any realistic deployment of resources.

> 'The depredations of coastal erosion are particularly obvious on the vulnerable eastern English coast, which is mostly composed of softer rocks and clay. Archival and cartographic evidence indicates that the East Riding of Yorkshire has suffered continual loss of land to the sea since records began; a loss that at present amounts on average to 12 hectares of land a year. Similarly, county archives show that Norfolk has lost 21 coastal towns and villages since the eleventh century.'[1]

For various reasons, the law of coast protection needs to be considered separately from other areas of flood and coastal defence law. Initially, it may be recalled, the flood defence works powers of the Environment Agency allow it to undertake work in estuarial and coastal locations for securing defence against sea or tidal water and the power to undertake such works may be exercised above or below the low-water mark.[2] In practice, this means that most of the coastal defences in England and Wales are the responsibility of the Agency. Also, as has been noted, the Agency performs an important role in surveying coastal defences and, with the provision of information from other operating authorities and individuals, compiling a national coastal defence database.[3]

---

[1] House of Commons Agriculture Committee, Sixth Report Session 1997–98, *Flood and Coastal Defence* (1998) HC 707, para.4.
[2] s.165(2) Water Resources Act 1991 and see 4.3.1 above.
[3] See 3.2.12 above on high level target 4 concerning the national coastal defence database. Generally see House of Commons Committee of Public Accounts, Thirteenth Report Session 1992–93, *Coastal Defences in England* (1992) HC 85.

## Introduction 205

However, alongside the responsibilities of the Agency for coastal *flood defence*, separate legal provision is made for *coast protection* under the Coast Protection Act 1949. Although not precisely or authoritatively defined, the essential distinction is that 'coast protection' involves the protection of coastal land against erosion and encroachment, whilst coastal flood defence is concerned with the protection of land from flooding by the sea. Some further guidance is provided by the definition of 'coast protection work' which is stated to mean any work of construction, alteration, improvement, repair, maintenance, demolition or removal for the purpose of the protection of land, and includes the sowing or planting of vegetation for that purpose.[4] However, the distinction between flood defence and coast protection is not an easy one to draw, and it has been recognised that the two functions may overlap where a particular project has the dual purpose of preventing erosion and preventing flooding so that, in the past, litigation has been required to determine whether particular projects were primarily for coast protection or coastal flood defence purposes.[5]

The legal problems are neatly illustrated by *Canterbury City Council* v *Department of the Environment*,[6] where an action was brought by the local authority for a declaration that a proposed works scheme to protect Whitstable comprised 'coast protection works' within the Coast Protection Act 1949. Whitstable had been built upon former marshland, lying about 8 ft above ordinance datum, and had suffered several incidents of sea flooding. Previous schemes had been accepted as coast protection works and had allowed a sea wall to be built up to a height of 19 ft above ordinance datum, but flooding was not prevented by this. It was then proposed that a new sea wall should be constructed at 22 ft above ordinance datum, but the relevant government department disputed that this would constitute 'coast protection works' since its main purpose was to prevent flooding, rather than erosion or encroachment.

Underlying this dispute was an issue of funding. At the time, coast protection works were administered by the Department of the Environment and were supported by 80% public funding. Alternatively, flood defence works were administered by the regional water authority and the Minister

---

[4] s.49(1) Coast Protection Act 1949. Generally note that the 1949 Act has been extensively amended, particularly by Local Government Act 1972 and Government of Wales Act 1994, though details of the amendments are omitted in the following references to sections of the 1949 Act.

[5] See House of Commons Environment Committee, Second Report Session 1991–92, *Coastal Zone Protection and Planning* (1992) HC 17-II, Appendix 11, *Memorandum by the Flood Hazard Research Centre, Middlesex Polytechnic* p.316.

[6] Unreported, Queen's Bench Division, 14 March 1980. Generally see E. C. Penning-Rowsell, D. J. Parker and D. M. Harding, *Floods and Drainage* (1986) p.167 on the controversies surrounding Whitstable's flood and coastal defences.

of Agriculture, Fisheries and Food and attracted only 65% public funding. It was, therefore, of considerable financial importance to the claimant that the project fell into the former rather than the latter category.[7]

Nonetheless, to resolve the dispute it was necessary to decide whether the works should be classified as 'coast protection' or 'flood defence'. On this, the wording of the Coast Protection Act 1949, defining 'protection' as 'protection against erosion or encroachment by the sea'[8] was found to be sufficient to encompass the works that were envisaged and it did not matter that the corresponding provisions under land drainage legislation might also have been applicable.[9] Moreover, previous works had been undertaken under the 1949 Act, without any objection being raised by the defendant, and a greater height of sea wall should not change the essential character of the work to be undertaken which, it was held, was coast protection work. Nevertheless, the judgment is revealing in rejecting a clear dichotomy between the two kinds of project and accepting that there may be an overlap. As the point was put,

> '[i]f erosion remains unchecked it seems to me encroachment by the sea is likely to follow and so, in all probability, does flooding. The interaction of the three are often inseparable and, if erosion can be prevented, so often can consequential encroachment and flooding.'[10]

## 5.2 IMPLICATIONS OF COAST PROTECTION–FLOOD DEFENCE DISTINCTION

Despite the difficulties in distinguishing coast protection from coastal flood defence, the contrast is of considerable legal and administrative importance because of the division of responsibilities to which it gives rise. Whilst the Environment Agency has responsibility for coastal flood defence, some 88 maritime local authorities, as 'coast protection authorities, are made operationally responsible for coast protection and have regulatory powers under the Coast Protection Act 1949.

Whether the distinction between coast protection and coastal flood defence is a rational or practically useful one is another matter. The House of Commons Agriculture Committee has observed that the distinction has

---

[7] Clearly, given the present ministerial and funding arrangements this issue would no longer arise.
[8] s.49(1) Coast Protection Act 1949.
[9] s.17(1) Land Drainage Act 1976, and now see s.107(2) Water Resources Act 1991 and s.21(3) Land Drainage Act 1991, and the discussion of the general works powers of the Environment Agency at 4.3.1 above.
[10] *Canterbury City Council* v *Department of the Environment*, unreported, Queen's Bench Division, 14 March 1980, per Willis J at p.7 transcript.

## Implications of Coast Protection–Flood Defence Distinction 207

arisen from relatively self-contained legislation formulated at a time when socio-economic and political needs were different from those of the present. Moreover, this legislation had been enacted at a time when scientific understanding of the interrelationships between natural cycles of erosion and deposition, both in river catchments and at the coast, were far more rudimentary than today. In a present-day context, the Committee thought that the distinction gave rise to concerns about a lack of public clarity over organisational responsibilities and a potentially serious negative impact upon delivery of vital services.[11]

Notwithstanding that coast protection and coastal flood defence are processes that are 'inextricably bound together', difficult decisions have to be made between the exercise of mainly permissive powers by maritime local authorities in respect of coast protection and similar powers of the Environment Agency in respect of flood defence. The result is a considerable overlapping of responsibilities for coast defences. Of the 1,019 km of defences around the English coast, 693 km are maintained by the Environment Agency, 169 km by maritime local authorities and 157 km are in private ownership. The effects of this 'seemingly arbitrary' division of coast defence responsibilities were graphically demonstrated to members of the Agriculture Committee in a visit to the Norfolk coast. Here, along a 14 km sea frontage, the Agency had constructed a broken line of offshore reefs, consisting of massive blocks of stone, supplemented by nourishment of the supporting beaches. However, following this length of coastline, responsibility was assumed by the local district council, as the coast protection authority, which had deemed that coastal defences were not capable of repair, following their failure in 1992. Over this length of coastline, cliff faces were rapidly eroding with average losses of 7.5 m a year, and low property values had prevented proposed coast protection schemes qualifying for a ministerial grant.[12] Clearly, 'flood defence' and 'coast protection' approaches to similar kinds of problem can lead to significantly different kinds of action, or inaction, in practice.

The view of the Agriculture Committee was that there should be a rationalisation of the legislative base of flood and coastal defence policy in England and Wales, with the objective of ending the artificial distinction between sea defence and coast protection responsibilities. The counterparts of this recommendation were that 'coastal groups' of local authorities should be given statutory status to exercise their responsibilities for coastal

---

[11] House of Commons Agriculture Committee, Sixth Report Session 1997–98, *Flood and Coastal Defence* (1998) HC 707, paras.62 to 63.
[12] House of Commons Agriculture Committee, Sixth Report Session 1997–98, *Flood and Coastal Defence* (1998) HC 707, paras.64 to 66.

flooding and sea defence through a more strategic approach, though membership of existing groups should be vetted to ensure they represent the full spectrum of stakeholder interests. In addition the Committee thought that Shoreline Management Plans should be given a statutory status.[13]

In response, the Government were unreceptive in suggesting that the Agriculture Committee's main proposal would replace one artificial distinction (between flood defence and coast protection) with another (between coastal defence and inland defence). The Government preferred to rely upon the Environment Agency, in fulfilling its supervisory responsibility, to provide an appropriate level of oversight, guidance and monitoring to ensure consistency of action by all operating authorities, both on the coastline and on river systems.[14]

Equally, it may be noted that the allocation of ministerial responsibilities for coast protection and flood defence ought to facilitate a high degree of co-ordination. Although, before 1985, the Coast Protection Act 1949 was administered by the Secretary of State for the Environment in England and the Secretary of State for Wales, one consequence of the Government Green Paper on financing of flood defence was to transfer responsibility from the Secretary of State for the Environment to the Minister of Agriculture, Fisheries and Food.[15] That is, central government responsibilities for coast protection and flood defence in England were placed within the same Ministry. However, this adjustment of ministerial responsibilities was felt, by the Agriculture Committee, to fall short of the radical reorganisation of institutional and administrative responsibilities that was needed.[16]

As a result of recent ministerial reorganisations,[17] responsibility for coast protection now rests with the Department for Environment, Food and Rural Affairs in relation to England and the National Assembly for Wales

---

[13] House of Commons Agriculture Committee, Sixth Report Session 1997–98, *Flood and Coastal Defence* (1998) HC 707, paras.67, 77, 82 and 85. See 5.5 below on shoreline management plans.

[14] House of Commons Agriculture Committee, Fifth Special Report Session 1997–98, *Replies by the Government and the Environment Agency to the Sixth Report from the Agriculture Committee Session 1997–98 'Flood and Coastal Defence'* (1998) HC 1117 p.viii.

[15] See HM Government, *Financing the Administration of Land Drainage, Flood Prevention and Coast Protection in England and Wales* (1985) Ch.6.

[16] House of Commons Agriculture Committee, Sixth Report Session 1997–98, *Flood and Coastal Defence* (1998) HC 707, para.75.

[17] See 3.2 and 3.3 above on ministerial responsibilities and the National Assembly for Wales.

in relation to Wales. The fact that the same Ministers are now responsible for flood defence and coast protection in each jurisdiction, and exercise control over funding and may give guidance to the Environment Agency, should allow flood defence and coast protection to be more effectively co-ordinated at ministerial level.

On the other hand, the legal and administrative complexity of the coastline is a significant factor to be taken into account. A House of Commons Environment Committee report on *Coastal Zone Protection and Planning* in 1992, noted that there were over 80 Acts of Parliament dealing with the regulation of activities taking place in the coastal zone and it was estimated that there were as many as 240 Government departments, local authorities and public agencies at national and local level that had responsibilities for the coastal zone. The result of this was that control and responsibility for the coastal zone was seen to be fragmented and confused. The confusion was exacerbated by there being different jurisdictions for different bodies for specific purposes and a perceived lack of communication and consultation between bodies. Understandably, a recommendation of the Environment Committee was that there should be a review of the organisations with an interest in the coastal zone in order to reduce unnecessary duplication of responsibilities and to improve co-ordination.[18] Largely, however, the position remains that coast protection and coastal flood defence activities need to be conducted with regard to a range of interests that are potentially more complex than those which are likely to be encountered in relation to inland flood defence.[19]

## 5.3 COMMON LAW AND COAST PROTECTION

It is instructive to draw out some points of contrast between the provisions of the Coast Protection Act 1949 and common law responsibilities for coast protection. Although the 1949 Act was enacted, amongst other things, for the protection of the coast against erosion and encroachment by the sea, to some extent these matters were already provided for prior to the Act and previous provisions may continue to apply alongside the Act.[20]

---

[18] House of Commons Environment Committee, Second Report Session 1991–92, *Coastal Zone Protection and Planning* (1992) HC 17-I paras.19 and 32.

[19] See European Commission, *Communication from the Commission to the Council and the European Parliament on Integrated Coastal Zone Management: A Strategy for Europe* COM (2000) 547 final and European Commission, *Proposal for a European Parliament and Council Recommendation concerning the implementation of Integrated Coastal Zone Management in Europe* COM (2000) 545 final. See also Department of the Environment, *Policy Guidelines for the Coast* (1995).

[20] Generally see A. Wharam, 'The Prevention of Floods' [1974] *Journal of Planning and Environment Law* 333.

It may be recalled[21] that there is a longstanding common law right for a coastal landholder to erect groynes or other defences to protect land from erosion or encroachment, even if the effect of this is to make it necessary for a neighbour to do the same, on the basis that 'every landowner exposed to the inroads of the sea has the right to protect himself, and is justified in making and erecting such works as are necessary for that purpose'.[22] However, the traditional *right* of a private landholder to take coast protection measures falls short of a general *duty* to do so. Hence, no liability will arise where a person fails to maintain a coastal flood or protection facility, to the detriment of neighbouring land, if there is no obligation upon others to do so.[23] As a matter of common law, duties upon coastal landowners to prevent erosion and encroachment may arise by tenure,[24] custom,[25] prescription[26] or under contract.[27] To the traditional categories may also be added the modern qualification that a 'measured' duty may arise, under certain circumstances, to take reasonable steps to protect neighbouring land threatened by flooding or erosion, but the scope of this may be limited in practice.[28] Notably, the 1949 Act expressly recognises pre-existing obligations to undertake coast protection work arising by reason of 'tenure, custom, prescription or otherwise', so that common law obligations of this kind continue to apply.[29]

In addition, there are many illustrations of civil liability arising where persons have been responsible for active interference with natural features or built structures which serve a coast protection purpose. In *Attorney-General* v *Tomline*,[30] for example, the defendant was the owner of the foreshore and claimed a right to remove shingle from the beach, which he then sold for ballast. The claimant was the owner of adjacent land which was protected from inundation by the sea by the natural bank which the defendant was progressively reducing by extracting the shingle. An

---

[21] Generally see Ch.2 above on the civil law.
[22] *R* v *Commissioners of Sewers for Pagham* (1828) 108 ER 1075, per Bayley J at p.1077 and see 2.4.2 above.
[23] See *Hudson* v *Tabor* (1877) 2 QBD 290 and see 2.4.4 above.
[24] See *Fobbing Sewers Commissioners* v *R* (1886) 11 App Cas 449 and *R* v *Baker* (1867) LR 2 QB 621.
[25] See *London and North West Railway* v *Fobbing Sewers Commissioners* (1896) 75 LT 629.
[26] See *R* v *Leigh* (1839) 10 Ad & El 398; *Fobbing Sewers Commissioners* v *R* (1886) 11 App Cas 449; and *Hudson* v *Tabor* (1877) 2 QBD 290, discussed at 2.4.4 above.
[27] *Morland* v *Cook* (1868) LR 6 Eq 252, discussed at 2.4.2 above.
[28] See discussion of *Leakey* v *National Trust* [1980] 1 All ER 17 at 2.4.5 above and *Holbeck Hall Hotel Ltd* v *Scarborough Borough Council* [2000] 2 All ER 705 at 2.7 above.
[29] See s.15 Coast Protection Act 1949, discussed at 5.4.9 below. Contrast the discussion of commutation of tenure-based flood defence obligations, discussed at 4.4.9 above.
[30] (1880) 14 Ch D 58.

injunction was sought to restrain the activity and it was held that it should be granted.

The basis for this decision lay in the right of a landowner whose land was defended by the natural barrier to have that barrier protected from damage by anyone, its owner included. This right derived from the duty of the Crown to protect the realm from incursions by the sea through constructing appropriate defences and by leaving natural defences unimpaired.[31] The public duty upon the Crown to maintain sea defences, however, is characterised as a duty of 'imperfect obligation', in the sense that courts have no jurisdiction to compel the Crown to perform the duty. However, where land is granted to a person who is subject to the jurisdiction of a court, the public duty not to damage sea defences may be enforced by a neighbour who is likely to suffer injury as a result of the contravention. In effect, therefore, the removal of the bank constituted a nuisance against which the neighbouring landowner had a right of action.

Analogous reasoning has been applied in situations where the duty of the Crown in relation to sea defence has been passed to statutory bodies, so that bodies with coast protection responsibilities will be entitled to restrain private persons from interference with sea defences.[32] Notably, the power to prevent harm to coastal defences, as a result of excavating materials from the seashore, is also provided for under the Coast Protection Act 1949.[33]

However, the counterpart of sea defence being a duty of imperfect obligation upon the Crown is that, where the duty of the Crown has been explicitly devolved to a statutory body, that body will become subject to a *duty* to maintain sea defences. An example of this is to be seen in *Lyme Regis Corporation v Henley*[34] where a claimant brought an action against the Corporation after his property had been flooded due to the failure of the Corporation to maintain sea walls. It was found that the Crown's duty to repair the sea walls had been passed to the Corporation by a royal charter which was explicit in making the transmission of responsibility subject to a duty to maintain the walls as consideration for the grant. Despite arguments that the charter could only be enforced by the Crown, it was held that the claimant was entitled to damages.

Most characteristically, an obligation to maintain a coast protection

---

[31] Citing *Isle of Ely* (1609) 10 Co Rep 141 where it was said 'the King ought of right to save and defend his realm as well against the sea, as against the enemies, that it should not be drowned or wasted'. See also *Attorney-General of Southern Nigeria v John Holt and Co (Liverpool) Ltd* [1915] AC 620.
[32] See *Canvey Island Commissioners v Preedy* [1922] 1 Ch 179 and *Symes and Jaywick Associated Properties Ltd v Essex Rivers Catchment Board* [1937] 1 KB 548.
[33] See s.18 Coast Protection Act 1949, discussed at 5.4.11 below.
[34] (1834) 6 ER 1180.

structure has arisen in the past where commissioners, a statutory body or, perhaps, a private individual have become subject to a statutory duty to maintain the structure.[35] An illustration of this is to be seen in *Sephton v Lancashire River Board*[36] where the River Board had acquired functions under a local Act[37] requiring commissioners to take all reasonable steps to maintain sea embankments and had empowered the levying of drainage rates for these purposes. As a result of the failure of the Board to maintain the embankment, and to make good losses of clay suffered through erosion, the bank became unstable and burst, causing the flooding of the claimant's land. It was found that the defendant was under a statutory duty to maintain the bank, and had failed to do so, and that the claimant was entitled to damages for the flooding suffered as a consequence. In essence, therefore, the local Act had created a *duty* to maintain a sea defence and this duty had been transmitted to the defendant.

A contrasting decision is *Hunwick v Essex Rivers Catchment Board*[38] where the claimant, who had been walking on a footpath along the top of a sea wall, suffered injury after part of the wall collapsed and sued the Catchment Board for negligence. It was accepted that the Board was responsible for the repair of the wall, as it had acquired statutory duties as successor to the commissioners of sewers, but the extent of the duty was contested. It was accepted that the Board was under a duty to maintain the wall to restrain incursion from the sea, but found that it was not empowered to dedicate, construct or maintain a highway on the wall.[39] Consequently, since there was no duty to maintain the highway, no duty could be owed to the claimant. Although this decision must now be read subject to subsequent statutory provision for occupier's liability,[40] it usefully illustrates that statutory duties to maintain defence coast defence structures should not be extended to encompass other kinds of duty.

In summary, therefore, the largely permissive coast protection powers

---

[35] See 4.9 above on duties under local and private legislation.

[36] [1962] 1 All ER 183, following *Coe v Wise* (1866) LR 1 QB 711. See also *Boynton v Ancholme Drainage and Navigation Commissioners* [1921] 2 KB 213, but contrast *Smith v Cawdle Fen, Ely (Cambridge) Commissioners* [1938] 4 All ER 64.

[37] The Scarsbrick Estate Drainage Act 1924. Under the Land Drainage Act 1930 and the River Boards Act 1948, and instruments under these Acts, functions and liabilities were transferred successively to a catchment board and to the defendant River Board.

[38] [1952] 1 All ER 765. The status of the same sea wall was considered in *Symes and Jaywick Associated Properties Ltd v Essex Rivers Catchment Board* [1936] 3 All ER 908.

[39] Contrast the decision in *L. E. Walwin & Partners v West Sussex County Council* [1975] 3 All ER 604 where it was found that nothing under the Coast Protection Act 1949 expressly or implicitly authorised a coast protection authority to obstruct or stop up a highway and that there was nothing that could be done under the royal prerogative relating to sea defences that could not be done under the 1949 Act.

[40] See 11.4.3 below on occupier's liability.

under the Coast Protection Act 1949 have to be considered alongside a range of pre-existing, and continuing, common law and local statutory duties which may impose a private or public responsibility to maintain sea defence structures. Although provision is made for the Minister to repeal or amend any provision in a local Act which is inconsistent with the 1949 Act or is no longer required,[41] the effect of the Environment Agency or a coast protection authority having acquired statutory duties imposed upon previous flood defence authorities is that there may be many local situations where permissive powers are actually overridden by statutory duties.

## 5.4 THE COAST PROTECTION ACT 1949

Broadly, the Coast Protection Act 1949 provides for coast protection authorities with general powers to execute coast protection work and provides authorities with powers to authorise others to undertake such work. Other than where maintenance is involved, coast protection works schemes may be established, subject to ministerial confirmation, and statutory provision is made for charges to be levied on land which is benefited by such schemes. Coast protection authorities are empowered to require coastal works to be undertaken by others and to recover their own costs where these are not provided for under a charging scheme. Requirements are imposed that consent must be given by authorities for work to be undertaken by others and powers are provided allowing authorities to take action in relation to activities which may be harmful to coast defence. Further provisions are concerned with funding for coast defence, compensation and ministerial powers. The detail of these matters is considered in the following sections.[42]

### 5.4.1 Coast Protection Authorities and Boards

The council of each 'maritime district'[43] in England, or maritime county or

---

[41] s.31(1) Coast Protection Act 1949.
[42] Generally see Ministry of Health, *Coast Protection Act 1949* (1950) Circular 9/50; R. J. Roddis, *The Law of Coast Protection* (1950); and K. T. Salt, 'Problems Arising under the Coast Protection Act, 1949' [1956] *Journal of Planning Law* pp.170 to 177, 247 to 253 and 338 to 340.
[43] 'Maritime district' means a district, or Welsh county or county borough, any part of which adjoins the 'sea' (s.49(1) Coast Protection Act 1949). However, for the purposes of Part I of the 1949 Act, the expression 'sea' excludes any of the waters specified in Schedule 4 to the Act and the expression 'seashore' does not include the bed or shore of any of those waters (s.49(2)). The effect of this is that the jurisdiction of coast protection authorities is excluded in relation to certain lands which are above high-water limits, though these areas will be the responsibility of the Environment Agency insofar as flood defence is concerned. Specifically, the areas are listed under Schedule 4, as amended, which defines points at various river estuaries that serve as jurisdictional limits upon the powers of coast protection authorities.

county borough in Wales, is identified as the cost protection authority for its area and has powers and duties in connection with the protection of coastal land in its area conferred under the 1949 Act.[44] However, the Minister is empowered to make an order,[45] where this is expedient for the protection of land in any area, providing for the constitution of a 'coast protection board', which will then be the coast protection authority for that area.[46]

A coast protection board consists of representatives of the council of every maritime district within the area, but an order constituting a board may require other bodies and persons to be represented on the board. These include representatives of any county council within the area; the Environment Agency; sea defence commissioners; internal drainage boards; harbour authorities; local fisheries committees; conservancy or navigation authorities; the authorities or bodies responsible for the maintenance of any highway, railway, canal or inland navigation (which might be injuriously affected by the action of the sea); and any other body or person having powers or duties relating to the protection of land in the area under any enactment.[47]

The contents of an order providing for a coast protection board may make various provisions concerning the representation of constituent authorities on the board; the tenure and remuneration of members; allowing the board to hold land; authorising the board to contribute to expenses of coast protection work; making provision for the raising or borrowing of money, the apportionment of expenses between constituent authorities and the issuing of precepts; and various incidental and consequential matters which are expedient for the purposes of the order.[48]

### 5.4.2 Powers of Coast Protection Authorities

A coast protection authority has the power to carry out such coast protection work, within or outside its area, as is necessary or expedient for the protection of any land within its area from erosion or encroachment by the sea. For this purpose, it may enter into an agreement with any other person for the carrying out of the work, which the authority is empowered

---

[44] s. 1(1) and (2) Coast Protection Act 1949.
[45] The procedure governing the making of orders is provided for in Schedule 1 to the Coast Protection Act 1949, which deals with matters such as: the publication of draft orders; the service of notice upon local authorities and persons and bodies exercising jurisdiction in the area; the consideration of objections; and provision for application to the High Court by persons aggrieved by the order.
[46] s.2(1) Coast Protection Act 1949.
[47] s.2(2) Coast Protection Act 1949.
[48] s.2(5) Coast Protection Act 1949.

to carry out under the 1949 Act. An authority may also purchase or lease any land which is required for the carrying out of coast protection work or land which is to be protected by *new* coast protection work, that is, work not involving maintenance or repair. However, the powers to undertake work and acquire land are solely for the purpose of removing any constitutional limitation upon the capacity of an authority.[49] In effect, though authorities have generally formulated coast protection works powers, these will not serve as a defence in respect of other kinds of civil liability to which they may be subject.

Although the powers of coast protection authorities are generally formulated, to allow work to be undertaken involving construction, alteration, improvement, repair, maintenance, demolition or removal,[50] these operations must be for the purpose of protecting land from erosion and encroachment. The implication of this is that works which are undertaken for other purposes will be outside the powers of authorities. An illustration of this constraint is to be seen in *Webb* v *Minister of Housing and Local Government*[51] where a coast protection authority had secured ministerial approval for a coast protection works scheme and a compulsory purchase order to allow various works to be undertaken alongside a shoreline.[52] Although it was accepted that a sea wall needed to be constructed to prevent the land from erosion, the compulsory purchase order encompassed a strip of land, about 12 ft wide, running alongside the wall which was intended to be used as a paved way, or promenade, to facilitate public access along a right of way. The disputed issue was whether compulsory purchase of the strip of land needed for this purpose was within the powers of the authority, and whether the Minister had the power to approve the purchase.

On the facts, it was found that the strip of land for the promenade was not necessary for maintenance of the wall and that there was no justification for compulsory purchase, since the owners of the land would have been willing to enter into voluntary access agreements with the authority. The ruling, therefore, was that the compulsory purchase order should be quashed: landowners are entitled to have their land taken from them only for purposes lawfully authorised and not for ulterior or political reasons. The same point may be generally made in relation to all the powers of coast protection authorities, that exercise of these powers other than for the

---

[49] s.4 Coast Protection Act 1949.
[50] s.49(1) Coast Protection Act 1949.
[51] [1965] 2 All ER 193. See also B*ritish Dredging (Services) Ltd* v *Secretary of State for Wales and Monmouthshire* [1975] 2 All ER 845, discussed at 5.4.11 below.
[52] See 5.4.4 below on works schemes and 5.4.7 below on compulsory purchase.

purpose of preventing erosion and encroachment will be *ultra vires*. Technically, the use of coast protection powers for a flood defence purpose would be similarly invalid but, because of the difficulties of distinguishing the two concepts, explained above, the scope for raising an argument of this kind may be limited.

Another point deserving to be emphasised is the status of the powers of coast protection authorities, as *powers* rather than *duties*. Although the 1949 Act provides for directions to be given by the Minister, requiring an authority to exercise its powers in a particular manner,[53] outside of this exception an authority will have a wide discretion as to when and how it chooses to execute coast protection works. The similarities with the position of operating authorities in relation to the exercise of flood defence powers is readily apparent.[54] In either case, the discretion of the authorities is confined only by the need to ensure that powers are not exercised either for an *ultra vires* purpose or exercised negligently.

The basic principle that there will be no liability for the failure of a coast protection authority to exercise a power is centrally important. Thereafter, the inadequate exercise of a power should follow the same principles as apply in relation to flood defence operating authorities, to the effect that actual exercise of a power should not give rise to liability in negligence unless it creates a new harm or exacerbates a problem that would arise regardless of whether the power was exercised or not. Hence, the principle established in *East Suffolk Rivers Catchment Board* v *Kent*,[55] indicating limited scope for liability in negligence, is equally pertinent to the position of coast protection authorities.

However, this is not to say that the possibility of successful proceedings in negligence, against a coast protection authority, is totally excluded. A relevant, if somewhat inconclusive, illustration is to be seen in *Fellowes* v *Rother District Council*[56] where part of the claimant's garden had been washed away by the sea. Although the factual issues were not finally determined, he alleged that the coast protection authority was liable in negligence because, in the course of repairing groynes on the beach adjoining the property, it had lowered the height of a particular groyne and this had created a scouring effect which had caused the land to be eroded.

Preliminary proceedings on the legal issues determined that a claimant bringing an action against a public body purporting to act in pursuance of

---

[53] Under s.29 Coast Protection Act 1949 and see 5.4.13 below.
[54] See 4.3 and 4.6 above on the powers of flood defence operating authorities.
[55] [1940] 4 All ER 527, discussed at 4.3.1 above.
[56] [1983] 1 All ER 513.

a statutory power could only succeed if the following factors could be established:

(a) that the act complained of was not within the limits of discretion, exercised in good faith, under the relevant power;

(b) that, having regard to the circumstances and the legislation, there was sufficient proximity between the claimant and the authority to give rise to a duty of care to prevent the damage complained of;

(c) that there was no ground for negativing, reducing or limiting the duty of care; and

(d) that it was reasonably foreseeable that the act of the defendant was likely to cause damage of the type in fact suffered.

On the *assumption* that it could be shown that the lowering of the groyne was outside the discretionary powers conferred under the 1949 Act, it was found that there was a sufficient relationship of proximity to create a duty of care to avoid damage of the kind that was at issue and there were no grounds for negativing or limiting the duty of care. Significantly, the fact that the Act provided for statutory compensation[57] did not affect the duty of care because the statutory remedy applied only in relation to the legitimate exercise of powers of the authority. Nonetheless, to succeed the claimant would still have to establish that the damage was reasonably foreseeable by the authority, that the lowering of the groyne was likely to cause the erosion damage to occur and that the claimant's land had, in fact, been eroded as a result of the lowering of the goyne.

The ruling in the *Fellowes* case is very difficult to interpret, perhaps because of the unsatisfactory way in which the 'disembodied' issues of law had been formulated. Without examination of the factual background, the 'assumption' that the lowering of the groyne was outside the discretionary powers of the coast protection authority seems dubious. Similarly, the need for the claimant to establish that the damage was reasonably foreseeable, and that the damage actually occurred because of the actions of the authority, are matters which it would be difficult to substantiate.[58] Perhaps the most that can be confidently concluded is that the *Fellowes* decision retains the possibility of actions in negligence against coast protection authorities, but indicates that the factual situations in which liability will arise are very narrow in scope.

---

[57] See 5.4.8 below on compensation.
[58] See the discussion of *Earle and Earle* v *East Riding of Yorkshire Council* [1999] RVR 200 at 5.4.8 below.

### 5.4.3 General Coast Protection Work

Otherwise than in relation to works schemes,[59] the carrying out of coast protection work by a coast protection authority requires it to publicise details of the proposed work, and its estimated cost, and to give notice, in local newspapers or in a manner directed by the Minister, that objections may be registered.[60] Similar notice must be served on the Environment Agency, any internal drainage board in whose district the work is to be carried out, and other prescribed bodies and authorities or persons as directed by the Minister. Objections to the proposed works may be served upon the Minister stating the ground of the objection. Where an objection involves an allegation that the work will be detrimental to the protection of any land, or will interfere with the exercise of statutory functions, a local inquiry must be held or an opportunity given for the objector to be heard by a person appointed by the Minister. The Minister must then either approve the proposal, with or without modifications, or direct the authority not to carry out the proposed work. However, these general requirements will not prevent an authority carrying out coast protection work which is urgently necessary for the protection of any land in their area. Where such work is undertaken, notice must be given, as soon as possible, to the Environment Agency and any internal drainage board where they are not represented on the authority.[61]

A coast protection authority is empowered to sell any materials which have been severed from any land in carrying out coast protection work. 'Materials' is defined to include minerals and turf, but not seaweed, and 'minerals' includes coal and stone and any metallic or other mineral substance.[62] However, this power arises only where, after 14 days from the severance from the land, the materials are not claimed by the person to whom they belong. Moreover, where an authority sells any materials under this power it will be bound to pay the proceeds to the person to whom the materials belonged.[63]

### 5.4.4 Works Schemes

The general provisions relating to coast protection work by a coast protection authority do not apply in relation to works undertaken in accordance with a works scheme.[64] Hence, where a coast protection

---

[59] Under s.9(4) Coast Protection Act 1949 and see 5.4.4 below on works schemes.
[60] See the Coast Protection (Notices) Regulations 1950, S.I. 1950 No.124.
[61] s.5 Coast Protection Act 1949.
[62] s.49(1) Coast Protection Act 1949.
[63] s.23 Coast Protection Act 1949. Compare the provisions for disposal of spoil in relation to flood defence activities, discussed at 4.3.4 above.
[64] s.9(4) Coast Protection Act 1949.

authority proposes to undertake new coast protection work, that is, excluding maintenance or repair work, and this cannot be carried out except by the exercise of compulsory purchase powers, the authority is bound to prepare a works scheme for the carrying out of the work. A scheme of this kind must indicate the nature of the proposed work, specify what work will be carried out on land not vested in the authority, or which it is proposed to acquire, and state the estimated cost of the work.[65] Provision is also made for a works scheme to indicate land that will be benefited by the scheme (termed 'contributory land') in respect of which coast protection charges are to be payable.[66]

A works scheme will not take effect unless confirmed by the Minister.[67] The procedures leading up to confirmation require the coast protection authority to publish details of the proposed scheme in local newspapers circulating in the area or as directed by the Minister,[68] naming a place where a copy of the notice can be inspected and indicating that objections should be served on the Minister within a prescribed period. Notice of the proposed scheme must also be served on the owners or occupiers of any land on which work is to be carried out; the Environment Agency and any internal drainage board for the district in which the work is to be carried out; other prescribed bodies; and authorities or persons which the Minister may direct.[69]

Following the publication of notice of a proposed works scheme, any person may serve on the Minister and the coast protection authority their notice of objection to the scheme. Where an objection to a proposed works scheme is sustained on certain grounds the Minister must cause a local inquiry to be held or to give the objector an opportunity of being heard by a person appointed by the Minister. Relevant grounds of objection are that work under the scheme is unnecessary, would cause hardship to the objector or that the work will be detrimental to the protection of specified land. Following the inquiry, the Minister must either confirm the scheme, with or without modifications, or quash it.[70]

Following confirmation of a works scheme by the Minister, the coast protection authority has power to take all steps necessary for carrying out the work provided for under the scheme. However, where a scheme

---

[65] s.6(1) and (2) Coast Protection Act 1949.
[66] s.7(1) Coast Protection Act 1949, and see ss.10 and 11, discussed at 5.4.5 below on coast protection charges.
[67] s.6(3) Coast Protection Act 1949.
[68] See the Coast Protection (Notices) Regulations 1950, S.I. 1950 No.124.
[69] s.8(1) Coast Protection Act 1949.
[70] s.8(5) and (6) Coast Protection Act 1949.

specifies work which is to be undertaken on land which is not vested in, or proposed to be acquired, by the authority, the owner of that land may serve a notice stating that he proposes to carry out the work. Where the owner serves notice to this effect within a specified period the authority may not carry out the work. The exception to this is that where the owner fails to carry out the work in accordance with the scheme, the authority may give notice that unless the work is carried out within a specified period the authority will itself carry out the work.[71]

Where a works scheme is approved and carried into effect by a coast protection authority, the question arises as to who is responsible for future maintenance of those works. Remarkably, the 1949 Act contains no express provision requiring a coast protection authority to maintain works undertaken under a works scheme,[72] though the method of calculating coast protection charges seems to presuppose that an authority will have future responsibility for the works.[73] Default powers of the Minister which may be exercised where an authority neglects to carry out works may be used to compel the authority to carry out continuing maintenance.[74] However, it is more likely that continuing maintenance will be provided for as a condition of any ministerial grant which is made for the works to be undertaken. The potential legal difficulty is whether a condition in a grant agreement, between an authority and the Minister, would be enforceable by a property owner, or whether the owner would only be able to enforce the condition by requesting the Minister to exercise his default powers to compel the authority to undertake the maintenance work.[75]

### 5.4.5 Coast Protection Charges

The 1949 Act provides that a works scheme may indicate 'contributory land', which is benefited by the carrying out of the work, and in respect of which 'coast protection charges' are to be payable and levied by reference to interests in the land. In particular, a charge is not to exceed the amount by which the value of an interest immediately after the completion of works is greater than the value of that interest had the works not been

---

[71] s.9(1) to (3) Coast Protection Act 1949.
[72] However, Ministry of Health, *Coast Protection Act 1949* (1950) Circular 9/50 *Explanatory Memorandum* para.10 indicates that coast protection charges are based on the *assumption* that works carried out under works schemes will thereafter be maintained by the coast protection authority.
[73] See s.7(3) Coast Protection Act 1949 on the calculation of coast protection charges, discussed at 5.4.5 below.
[74] Default powers of the Minister are provided under s.29 Coast Protection Act 1949 and discussed at 5.4.13 below.
[75] See K. T. Salt, 'Problems Arising under the Coast Protection Act, 1949' [1956] *Journal of Planning Law* at p.248.

undertaken. This before-and-after calculation of the increased value to contributory land due to the works is made on the assumption that the works will be maintained without expense to the person having the interest in the land. However, if any of the work undertaken under a works scheme is carried out at the expense of a person having an interest in the land, the maximum protection charge must be reduced by the reasonable cost of carrying out that work.[76]

Where the levying of coast protection charges is provided for under a works scheme, the scheme must specify the persons and amounts of charges, and the interest in land by reference to which the charge is levied. Alternatively, a works scheme may state that the coast protection authority will, within a specified period,[77] determine the interests in land and the amount of the charge leviable. Provision is made for appeals to the Minister, after which he may confirm, reduce or cancel the charge levied. Disputes as to the calculation of increased value to contributory land due to the works, and whether the maximum charge is exceeded, are to be determined by arbitration.[78] Payments of coast protection charges become due on the completion of the work or when a person is served with a notice specifying the amount of the charge, or following an appeal.[79] Provision is made to allow coast protection charges to be made payable in instalments over a specified period not exceeding 30 years, along with a reasonable rate of interest.[80]

Despite the continuing existence of statutory provisions concerning coast protection charges, the practical reality is markedly different. A departmental circular, issued by the Ministry of Housing and Local Government in 1962,[81] announced the outcome of a review in which all local authority associations had indicated that they were in favour of abandoning charges. The Minister accepted this recommendation and advised that no more works schemes should be made for the purpose of recovering compulsory contributions from private interests. Consequently, it was decided that the works scheme procedure should be allowed to fall into abeyance except insofar as it was necessary to obtain compulsory powers to carry out operations on land which was not in local authority ownership. For works

---

[76] s.7(1) to (3) Coast Protection Act 1949.
[77] The failure to determine charges within the specified period may have the effect of invalidating the determination, see *Cullimore v Lyme Regis Corporation* [1961] 3 All ER 1008.
[78] s.7(4) to (7) Coast Protection Act 1949.
[79] s.10(1) Coast Protection Act 1949.
[80] s.10(2), (3) and (5) Coast Protection Act 1949.
[81] Ministry of Housing and Local Government, *Coast Protection Act, 1949* (1962) Circular 41/62.

schemes which had not yet been completed charges should be waived, but where charges had already been paid recovery of the outstanding charges would continue. Nonetheless, the Minister reminded local coast protection authorities of their powers to obtain contributions to coast works by agreement and expressed the view that where the sole interest involved was a private or commercial body authorities should consider whether it would be more appropriate for them to make a contribution towards works carried out by that body.

The 1962 ministerial announcement reflected that, in practice, it had been found that coast protection charges brought in only a small contribution to the cost of the work involved and generated more administrative difficulties than they were worth.[82] The effect of the change in policy was most significant in relation to those works schemes which had been planned with coast protection charges in mind.[83] However, because provision is made for coast protection charges to be paid over a period of up to 30 years,[84] in some cases charges may have continued to be paid for some time after the announcement. Despite the practical abandonment of coast protection charges, the administrative mechanism by which this was done did not involve any change to the statutory provisions which, theoretically, continue to allow for charges to be levied. Notwithstanding the change in policy on charges, works schemes remain of importance as a means of securing compulsory acquisition powers where these are needed to undertake the works that are envisaged.[85]

### 5.4.6 Maintenance and Repair of Works

Within the 1949 Act a general division is made between the approach taken to new works, provided for under works schemes, and the measures which apply to maintenance and repair of existing works. In respect of the latter, where it appears to a coast protection authority that works in its area are in need of maintenance or repair, it may serve on the owner and occupier of the land a notice specifying the works which are necessary and indicate a period after the expiry of which the authority will carry out the work if it has not been previously completed. Following the expiry of the period indicated in the notice, the authority may take all necessary steps for

---

[82] See, for example, on the difficulty of identifying 'contributory land', K. T. Salt, 'Problems Arising under the Coast Protection Act, 1949' [1956] *Journal of Planning Law* at p. 174.

[83] See *Webb* v *Minister of Housing and Local Government* [1965] 2 All ER 193, for example.

[84] Under s.10(2) Coast Protection Act 1949.

[85] See also s.14 Coast Protection Act 1949 on compulsory acquisition of land, discussed at 5.4.7 below.

carrying out the works. However, where work is urgently necessary for the protection of land in the area of a coast protection authority, it may take all steps necessary for repairing the works without having served any notice or before the period stated in a notice has expired.[86]

Where maintenance or repair work is undertaken by a coast protection authority which is not the subject of a works scheme, and in respect of which no scheme for maintenance and repair is in operation, the authority may recover the reasonable cost of carrying out the work from the owner or occupier of the land on which the works are situated. Recovery of such costs requires the owner or occupier of the land to be served with a notice in respect of the work, stating that the works are works to which the cost-recovery power applies, that the authority proposes to exercise that power and indicating the effect of this. Provision is made for the owner or occupier to make an objection to a magistrates' court on specified grounds. If a ground of complaint is accepted by the court, it may grant an order directing that the cost of the work should be recovered against an owner or occupier other than the complainant; that the authority should be prevented from recovering the cost or a specified part of it; that the work specified is not maintenance or repair; or that the authority should be allowed to make a scheme for maintenance and repair. Where the authority is empowered to make a scheme for maintenance and repair, statutory provisions relating to preparation and confirmation of the scheme apply to such a scheme similarly as they apply to a works scheme.[87]

Underlying the powers in relation to maintenance and repair works, and the recovery of costs, is the potential difficulty of distinguishing between *new* works and the maintenance of *existing* works. This issue arose in *Dunbar v Edinburgh Corporation*[88] where a coast protection authority had served a notice upon the claimant requiring the 'repair' of a sea wall on her property. It appeared that the works which were required involved replacing a vertical wall at the foot of a slope by a sloping bulwark and a completely new wall erected at the top of the slope. The question whether this work involved 'maintenance' involved a detailed examination of what works, if any, were presently in existence, and the condition of those works, and an assessment of the contrast between the existing works and those that were being required by the notice. As the point was made,

---

[86] s.12 Coast Protection Act 1949, though land which is maintained by railway or canal authorities is excluded from this provision; s.28(1) provides for ministerial orders to allow persons subject to repair notices to enter land for the purpose of carrying out the required work and for related purposes.
[87] s.13(1) to (6) Coast Protection Act 1949 and on works schemes see 5.4.4 above.
[88] 1961 *Scots Law Times* 45 (Sheriff Court).

'[i]s what is proposed to be done a work of new construction, or reconstruction or of maintenance and repair? For new construction the [claimant] is clearly not liable under the present notice. For maintenance and repair she clearly might be liable. For reconstruction, in my opinion, she might in certain circumstances be liable provided that the works being reconstructed are substantially the same as those which previously existed and provided that a substantial amount of the original stone was being built into the reconstructed works. . . . But it seems to me that if they are made to a totally different design and a substantial amount of new material is involved, then the work becomes a work of new construction rather than of reconstruction or repair.'[89]

On the facts, the proposed works were found to be new works, or at least works of reconstruction involving new materials, and could not be classified as works of maintenance or repair.

### 5.4.7 Compulsory Acquisition of Land

A coast protection authority may acquire land compulsorily subject to ministerial authorisation in accordance with the Acquisition of Land Act 1981. This power applies to the purchase, lease or exchange of any land, either within or outside its area, which an authority requires for the carrying out of coast protection work thereon, or land for the protection of which it proposes to carry out work other than work of maintenance or repair.[90] However, where land is to be protected but works are to be undertaken on other land, the power of compulsory acquisition will only be exercisable if the value of the protected land after the completion of the work is greater than it would have been had the work not been carried out. In estimating the value of the land on completion of the work, it will be assumed that the works which are undertaken will be maintained without expense to any person interested in the land. Disputes as to any enhanced value of the land consequent upon works being undertaken will be referred to arbitration.[91]

Associated with the power to acquire land compulsorily is a power of a coast protection authority to acquire information about the ownership of land. This allows an authority to require the occupier of any land, and any person who receives rent in respect of the land, to state the nature of his interest in land and to provide the name and address of any other person known to have an interest in the land either as freeholder, mortgagee,

---

[89] 1961 *Scots Law Times* 45, per Sheriff W. Ross McLean at p.49.
[90] Acquisition of land is provided for, under s.4(3) Coast Protection Act 1949, although acquisition of Crown land is excluded (under s.32(2)).
[91] s.14 Coast Protection Act 1949.

owner, lessee or otherwise. Failure to provide information when required, or knowingly misstating information, is an offence.[92]

Provision is also made for a coast protection authority to acquire convenient access to land on which coast protection work has been, or is proposed to be, carried out. This allows the authority to obtain a right of passage over land by agreement or compulsorily, subject to statutory requirements and regulations concerning acquisition, and to secure the right perpetually or for some fixed or determinable term. 'Right of passage', for these purposes, applies to persons, vehicles, plant and materials and encompasses a right to carry out work for facilitating passage.[93]

Where land is acquired by a coast protection authority for protection by coast defence work, by agreement or compulsorily, it may be disposed of or appropriated in accordance with relevant local government legislation.[94] The powers of a district council in England, or a county or county borough council in Wales, to provide various facilities for public recreation or convenience are exercisable in respect of land which is acquired for the purpose of coast protection work. However, the land must not be used in a manner which interferes with the coast protection work, or the maintenance or repair of such work.[95]

### 5.4.8 Compensation

A claim for compensation may be made to a coast protection authority if the value of any person's interest in land has depreciated,[96] or a person has suffered damage by being disturbed in the enjoyment of land, in consequence of work being carried out by the authority. A claim for compensation of this kind is, however, subject to the proviso that compensation for the act or omission causing the depreciation or disturbance will only be payable if the complaint would have been actionable if the act or omission had been done otherwise than under the statutory powers of the authority. Alternatively, compensation may be payable where the value of an interest in land has depreciated after a coast protection authority has refused consent for coast protection work to be carried out, or made such consent subject to conditions. A claim for compensation must be made to the coast protection authority within 1 year of the completion of the work giving rise

---

[92] s.26 Coast Protection Act 1949. On summary conviction, the offence carries a maximum fine not exceeding level 1 on the standard scale, presently £200.
[93] s.27 Coast Protection Act 1949.
[94] See ss.122, 123, 126 and 127 Local Government Act 1972.
[95] s.22 Coast Protection Act 1949.
[96] See *Lakeman* v *Bournemouth Corporation* (1956) 8 P&CR 265 where interest in land was held to include a tenancy agreement for 3 years for a beach kiosk.

to it and provision is made for arbitration of disputes about compensation.[97]

Significantly, the provision for payment of compensation is made subject to the proviso that the work would be actionable if it had been done otherwise than under the statutory powers of the authority. Though somewhat obscurely worded, the import of this is that the claimant must have suffered harm of a kind which would be compensatable under the general civil law if it had been inflicted by a private individual.[98] This begs the question as to what kinds of harm to interests in land would be generally compensatable. It has been recognised that, in an action arising from disturbance caused by coast protection operations, no liability will arise for activities that are reasonably carried out and where reasonable and proper steps are taken to ensure that no undue inconvenience is caused to neighbours.[99] More generally, it may be observed that private nuisance will take account of all the circumstances in determining whether there has been a compensatable interference with the 'enjoyment of land' and the public utility of acts that are alleged to constitute a nuisance would normally be a factor to be weighed into the balance. In the context of coast protection it might also be relevant that acts complained of as causing a 'depreciation' in the value of land would commonly have the opposite effect in protecting or enhancing the value of that land. Hence, it would be a misconception to suppose that matters such as inconvenience and disturbance, which will unavoidably arise in relation to any major coast defence works, will automatically give rise to a claim for statutory compensation under the 1949 Act.

Nonetheless, the compensation provisions under the 1949 Act have been tested on numerous occasions. In early decisions, it was established that determinations of coast protection charges were ascertained by the difference in value of contributory land resulting from the execution of a works scheme. The market valuations used for this purpose took account of matters including injurious affectation of properties and so would not be altered by the hypothetical vendor of a property being entitled to compensation. Consequently, only where the depreciation of an interest was so great that the value of the property after a scheme had been carried out fell below its previous value would any entitlement to compensation arise, and then only to the extent of the difference between the pre-scheme and post-scheme values.[100]

---

[97] s.19(1) to (3) Coast Protection Act 1949. On arbitration, see s.24(1) which requires matters in dispute to be referred to the Lands Tribunal.
[98] On civil liability generally, see Ch.2 above.
[99] See *Holborn Trust Co Ltd* v *Folkestone Corporation* (1956) 6 P&CR 86.
[100] See *Re Coast Protection Act 1949* (1955) 106 L Jo 108, Lands Tribunal.

## The Coast Protection Act 1949

In *St Margaret's Bay Hotel Ltd* v *Dover Rural District Council*[10] the payability of compensation was dealt with alongside the issue of the appropriate level of coast protection charges. Here the Lands Tribunal accepted a nominal valuation of a sea wall, on the basis that there would be no market for a structure which required costly works, and low valuations of properties were accepted on the basis that vehicular access would have been impossible after a relatively short period because of the progress of erosion. A claim that coast protection charges should be reduced to compensate owners of the land for greater public use of the area as a result of increased accessibility because of the works which had been carried out was rejected, since it was not shown that any new public right of access had been created.

Because coast protection charges under works schemes have fallen into abeyance since 1962,[102] compensation will now need to be assessed separately from the pre-scheme and post-scheme valuations of properties that were previously used to assess coast protection charges. This approach is illustrated by *Biard* v *Deal Corporation*[103] where four references to the Lands Tribunal were heard together since they all concerned compensation for damage and depreciation to land arising from the construction of a sea wall under a coast protection scheme. As a general principle, the Tribunal regarded itself as being bound by the decision in *Andreae* v *Selfridge and Co Ltd*[104] which decided that no compensation would be payable for inconvenience arising from building operations which were conducted reasonably and with proper steps being taken to avoid undue disturbance of neighbours. Accepting that a certain amount of noise, dust and personal inconvenience was unavoidable during construction activities, the Tribunal, however, did not accept that the approach was appropriate where physical damage to property was at issue.

On the facts of the *Biard* case, various complaints had arisen from works concerned with a new sea wall, which had involved clouds of cement dust being emitted from an uncovered cement silo which, it was found, amounted to a failure to take proper precautions to reduce the nuisance to a minimum and gave rise to liability on the part of the coast protection authority. In respect of complaints about noise, however, it was not found that there was sufficient evidence to establish that the authority had failed to exercise proper skill and care in executing the works. Also, in respect of cracks in the walls of one claimant's house, there was insufficient evidence

---

[101] (1960) 12 P&CR 239.
[102] See the discussion of coast protection charges at 5.4.5 above.
[103] (1961) 12 P&CR 398.
[104] [1938] Ch 1.

to establish that these had been caused by the operation of pile-driving hammers used in the works. Nonetheless, compensation was awarded for physical damage to the claimants' houses due to the cement dust and for consequent redecorating and cleaning costs arising from this.

In contrast to those situations where the complaint arises from disturbance during the construction of coast protection works, other types of claim arise because of the long-term effects of works. A particular problem is where the effect of undertaking coast protection at one point in the coastline is alleged to increase the problem of erosion at another point. Disputes of this kind give rise to two kinds of difficulty: the factual issue of whether works at one point have, on the balance of probabilities, actually caused erosion at another location; and the legal issue of whether a coast protection authority would be civilly liable for any loss of land at the other location even if the causal connection is shown.

The factual and legal issues are extensively considered in *Earle and Earle v East Riding of Yorkshire Council*[105] where the claimants were owners of farmland which had suffered considerable erosion, of some 4.6 m annually, which they alleged had been accelerated because of works which had been conducted by the defendant coast protection authority. The works comprised two rock groynes and a rock revertment wall linking the heads of the groynes along the base of a cliff which, it was claimed, had caused sediment to be taken away from the coast alongside the claimants' land. The difficulty in establishing this contention was that data for the coastline demonstrated that it had been eroding for many centuries. Although some increase in the rate of erosion was evident over recent years, this did not constitute proof that the works had been the reason for the increased erosion of the claimants' land or that the rate of erosion would have been any less if an alternative scheme of works had been undertaken or if no works had been undertaken.

Having failed to establish the factual issue, that the works had caused erosion to be accelerated, the claimants' case failed. However, because other similar claims had been referred to the Lands Tribunal for consideration, it went on to address the issues of law which would be of general application to the outstanding claims. The key legal issue was whether the actions of the coast protection authority would have given rise to civil liability had they been done otherwise than under the exercise of the statutory powers. Notably, although there was no allegation that the works had been undertaken negligently, it was claimed that had an alternative system of works been adopted the removal of sediment from the

---

[105] [1999] RVR 200.

claimants' land would have been reduced, and the failure to adopt the alternative system would be sufficient to establish an action in nuisance.

The legal difficulty for the claimants was the authority of *R* v *Commissioners of Sewers for Pagham*[106] which had established that a person who protects his land from the 'common enemy' of the sea will not be liable in nuisance to another person who is adversely affected as a result. Hence, there is no absolute requirement of nuisance that a landowner must refrain from any activity which injures a neighbour's enjoyment of land.[107] Nonetheless, the *Pagham* case needed to be read subject to later authorities on nuisance emphasising that liability would not arise in relation to reasonable use of land.[108] In the circumstances, and despite arguments that the alternative coast protection scheme would have been less damaging to the claimants' land, the Tribunal accepted that the scheme which had been adopted was, on the face of things, a reasonable use of the land. Given that the Tribunal did not accept that the existing scheme had caused the erosion which was complained of it would, of course, have been impossible to have shown that the alternative would have been any less damaging.

### 5.4.9 Subsisting Obligations

Although the preceding subsections have been primarily concerned with the operational powers of coast protection authorities, the 1949 Act also provides authorities with important powers that are of an essentially regulatory character. These powers enable authorities to exercise enforcement control over other persons or bodies who neglect to carry out activities relating to coast protection, and to authorise particular works and activities to be undertaken where no interference with coast protection is involved.

Where a person is subject to an obligation to maintain or repair coast protection works, which arises independently of the 1949 Act, by reason of tenure, custom, prescription or otherwise, then this obligation will not extend to works constructed under the Act.[109] Hence, a person who is subject to a subsisting obligation of this kind will not become liable to maintain or repair any works constructed, altered or improved under a coast protection works scheme[110] or a scheme for recovering the cost of

---

[106] (1828) 8 B&C 355 and see the discussion at 2.4.2 above.
[107] Similarly, see *Home Brewery plc* v *William Davies & Co Ltd* [1987] 2 WLR 117, discussed at 2.5.1 above, and *Stephens* v *Anglian Water Authority* [1987] 1 WLR 1381, discussed at 2.6 above.
[108] Citing *Cambridge Water Company Co* v *Eastern Counties Leather plc* [1994] 2 AC 264.
[109] See 5.3 above on common law obligations relating to coast protection.
[110] See s.6 Coast Protection Act 1949 on works schemes, discussed at 5.4.4 above.

maintenance or repair works.[111]

On the other hand, nothing in the 1949 Act operates to release any person from any subsisting obligation in relation to coast protection work.[112] Moreover, the Act provides a mechanism for the enforcement of such obligations by a coast protection authority. This allows an authority to serve a notice upon a person who is liable to carry out 'necessary or expedient' coast protection work, and who fails to carry out such work, requiring the work to be carried out within a specified period. If the person upon whom the notice is served fails to comply with the notice, the authority may carry out the work and recover the expense reasonably incurred from that person.[113]

Where coast protection work that has been neglected is the responsibility of 'sea defence commissioners' the 1949 Act provides for a mechanism to address this.[114] This allows a coast protection authority to represent to the Minister that any sea defence commissioners have failed to carry out any work that the commissioners are authorised or required to carry out under a local Act for the protection of land in the area of the authority. If, after giving the commissioners an opportunity to respond, the Minister is satisfied of the failure to carry out necessary or expedient work by the commissioners, he may make an order authorising the coast protection authority to carry out the work and to recover the reasonably incurred expenses from the commissioners.[115]

### 5.4.10 Consents and Notification concerning Works

A general prohibition is imposed upon the carrying out of any coast protection work, other than work of maintenance or repair, without the consent of the coast protection authority for the area. Similarly, a prohibition is imposed in relation to activities that involve a contravention of any condition of a consent that is granted for coast protection work.[116] The coast protection authority is empowered to institute proceedings for this offence.[117]

---

[111] s.15 (1) and (2) Coast Protection Act 1949. See s.13 on recovery of cost of maintenance of works constructed under works schemes and see 5.4.6 above.

[112] Note that the powers and duties to commute tenure-based *flood defence* obligations possessed by flood defence operating authorities (see 1.9.2 and 4.4.9 above) are not given to coast protection authorities.

[113] s.15(3) and (4) Coast Protection Act 1949.

[114] 'Sea defence commissioners' means a body established by or under a local Act wholly or mainly for the purpose of carrying out coast protection work (s.49(1) Coast Protection Act 1949).

[115] s.15(5) Coast Protection Act 1949.

[116] s.16(1) Coast Protection Act 1949.

[117] s.16(5) Coast Protection Act 1949. The maximum penalty for the offence is, on summary conviction, a fine not exceeding level 3 on the standard scale, presently £1,000, under s.43 Coast Protection Act 1949, as amended.

Without prejudice to criminal proceedings for coast protection works conducted without, or in contravention of, a consent, provision is made for the removal of unlawfully constructed works. Hence, a coast protection authority may serve a notice on any person who has constructed, altered or improved such works without authority requiring the works to be removed within a specified period of not less than 30 days. If, within the specified period, the person on whom the notice has been served fails to comply, the authority may remove or alter the works in the manner specified in the notice. The authority will then be entitled to recover the expenses incurred from the person on whom the notice was served.[118]

The procedure for determination of an application for consent for coast protection works by a coast protection authority requires that, before determination of the application, the authority must given notice to certain bodies. In particular, the authority to which the application is made is to give notice of the application to any other coast protection authority which adjoins its area; the Environment Agency; and any internal drainage board whose district is within the area of the authority determining the application. The authority is bound to consider representations of any of the consultees in making its determination.[119]

Significant exceptions are provided for in relation to the offence concerning coast works constructed without, or in contravention of, a consent. Hence, the offence will not arise in relation to works undertaken by a coast protection authority; a body or person acting under statutory powers; an authority for the protection of a highway or railway; or a harbour authority.[120] However, where works are conducted by these authorities, or under statutory powers, notification requirements apply. Failure to observe the notification requirements will be an offence for which a coast protection authority may instigate proceedings against the relevant 'undertaker'.[121]

The notification requirements, applicable where undertakers are exempt from consenting requirements, require the undertaker to give at least 28 days' notice of the intended work to the coast protection authority for the area in which the work is to be carried out, coast protection authorities in adjoining areas, the Environment Agency and any internal drainage board whose district is in the area. The work must not be carried out before the

---

[118] s.16(2) and (3) Coast Protection Act 1949.
[119] s.16(4) Coast Protection Act 1949. Alongside consent from the coast protection authority, it is likely that planning permission will also be required from the local planning authority (see Ch.9 above on planning law generally).
[120] s.17(1) Coast Protection Act 1949.
[121] Under s.17(2) and (6) Coast Protection Act 1949. The maximum penalty for the offence is, on summary conviction, a fine not exceeding level 3 on the standard scale, presently £1,000, under s.43 Coast Protection Act 1949, as amended.

expiry of the notice and if any objection has been served on the Minister by any of the consultees the work must not be carried out except under ministerial direction.[122]

The procedure to be followed where an objection is raised normally requires the Minister, and any other Minister concerned with the relevant undertaker, to allow the objector an opportunity of being heard by a person appointed for this purpose. Following this, the appropriate Minister must either direct that the undertaker may carry out the work originally indicated, or subject to modifications or conditions, or that the undertakers may not carry out the work.[123]

Despite the requirement of notification of a coast protection authority being generally imposed upon undertakers, this will not prevent coast protection work being carried out by an undertaker where this is urgently necessary for the protection of any land. Where the power to undertake urgent work without notification is exercised, however, the undertaker must, as soon as possible after the commencement of the work, give the authority notice of the nature of the work.[124]

### 5.4.11 Prohibition of Excavations

A restriction is imposed upon the excavation or removal of any materials, on or forming part of the seashore, other than minerals more than 50 ft below the surface, where the excavation is the subject of an order made by a coast protection authority. Authorities are empowered to make orders applying the restriction to any part of the seashore within their areas, up to 3 nautical miles seaward from the baselines from which the breadth of the territorial sea is measured. Exceptions are provided for to allow excavations to be undertaken by, or on behalf of, the Secretary of State for Transport in the exercise of powers relating to the safety of navigation under Part II of the Coast Protection Act 1949.[125]

The general effect of an order of this kind is to make it unlawful to excavate or remove materials from the seashore, subject to any exceptions or

---

[122] s.17(3) Coast Protection Act 1949.
[123] s.17(4), (5) and (8) Coast Protection Act 1949.
[124] s.17(7) Coast Protection Act 1949.
[125] s.18(1) to (3) Coast Protection Act 1949 and see s.1 Territorial Sea Act 1987 on the baselines for measuring the breadth of the territorial sea. The procedure for making an order is contained in Schedule 2 to the 1949 Act and Part II of that Schedule allows for the making of interim orders where, because of an emergency, it is urgently necessary that excavation of removal of material should be restricted. The expression 'sea' does not include waters which are specified in Schedule 4 to the Act and the expression 'seashore' will not include the bed or shore of those waters (s.49(2) Coast Protection Act 1949).

conditions contained in the order. The authority is placed under a duty to enforce this offence.[126] However, provision is also made for the authority to grant licences for operations that would otherwise be in contravention of an order and, providing an operation is conducted under a licence and without contravention of any licence condition, no offence will be committed.[127]

In *British Dredging (Services) Ltd* v *Secretary of State for Wales and Monmouthshire*[128] a coast protection order had been made in relation to commercial sand extraction operations along a length of seashore. The coast protection authority formed the view that the effect of the operations was gradually to erode the clay sub-stratum of the beach. The effect of the order was to make it unlawful to remove sand except under licence, so that the licensing procedure allowed the authority to control the rate of sand removal. The order was contested by companies involved in sand extraction and was considered at a public inquiry. The inspector reported to the Minister that whilst changes were occurring to the foreshore, the reasons for these were not properly understood. They could be due wholly or in part to the sand extraction operations, to storms, or to alterations in local tidal conditions brought about by the construction of a harbour. In the view of the inspector a detailed study of the foreshore and seabed was needed, there was a serious danger of over-exploitation and it was important, for providing a bulwark against the sea, that the quantity of sand should not exceed the natural replenishment of the beach. The inspector recommended the confirmation of the order and the use of a licensing system, conducted on a scientifically conceived and properly monitored basis, and that the coast protection authority, in administering the system, should have due regard to the interests of the extracting companies as well as the needs of coast protection.

Following the confirmation of the order by the Minister, the extracting companies brought an application to have the order quashed on the basis that it was *ultra vires* because there was no evidence that the protection of the coast against erosion or encroachment would be served by the order. It was held that the order was not *ultra vires* since the authority had powers to make an order, not only where it was conclusively shown that extraction

---

[126] Under s.43 Coast Protection Act 1949, as amended, the maximum penalty for the offence, on summary conviction, is a fine not exceeding level 3 on the standard scale, presently £1,000.

[127] s.18(5), (7) and (8) Coast Protection Act 1949, though an authority may be required to consult with any drainage authority before granting a licence relating to land with which the drainage authority is concerned (s.18(6)).

[128] [1975] 1 WLR 687. See also *R* v *Secretary of State for the Environment and the Crown Estate Commissioner and East Coast Shipping Aggregates Ltd ex parte Bryant*, unreported, Queen's Bench Division, 30 July 1996, noted [1997] *Water Law* 93.

of materials was causing erosion or encroachment, but also where there was reasonable apprehension of erosion or encroachment by any cause. Accordingly, it appeared to the authority necessary or expedient to make the order to discharge its statutory duty. Hence, the Minister had not exceeded his powers under the 1949 Act, or come to a conclusion which, on the evidence before him, he could not reasonably have reached, or taken into account any matters which he ought not to have considered or vice versa.

Notably, in relation to the *British Dredging* decision, a basis for the confirmation of the order was that conclusive proof that erosion or encroachment due to the extraction activities did not need to be shown. It was sufficient that there was a 'reasonable apprehension' on the part of the coast protection authority that an order was necessary or expedient. As the point was put in the judgment,

> '[t]here is nothing in the [1949] Act which restrains the coast protection authority from acting until catastrophe occurs before making their order. They do not have to stand by while a seashore becomes more and more denuded of sand until a point is reached when the protection afforded by the sand, for example, to a sea wall, has vanished, so that during the next winter's gales the sea wall is breached, and the land behind is flooded, or the foundations of the buildings on the cliff above are weakened. It must always be difficult to foresee the effect of sea and wind and tide on a seashore.'[129]

Given the dynamic state of the shoreline, the capacity of a coast protection authority to take a preventative or precautionary approach is valuable in view of the difficulties in showing a clear causal relationship between a coastal activity and erosion or encroachment. In the circumstances of the case, it was also recognised that the order would also allow a more controlled scientific investigation to be undertaken of the impact of the extraction upon erosion.

### 5.4.12 Powers of Entry

A person authorised by a coast protection authority, on producing an authenticated document showing authority if required, has the right to enter any land on which the authority is empowered to carry out work at all reasonable hours. The right of entry also extends to any land that it is reasonably necessary to enter in order to gain access to the land on which work is undertaken. Entry is also permitted for the purpose of inspecting or surveying land for the purpose of determining how the functions of an authority are to be exercised or to determine whether any notice, order,

---

[129] [1975] 1 WLR 687, per Park J at p.692.

direction or byelaw served, given or made is being or has been complied with. In addition, entry is allowed for the purpose of estimating any amount of compensation that may be payable or the value of any interest in land.[130]

The power of entry allows the person entering to take with him such other persons as may be necessary, but unoccupied land that has been entered must be left as effectually secured as when entered. Likewise, the power of entry includes the power to authorise the entry or passage of such vehicles, plant and material as may be necessary and to authorise the carrying out of work for facilitating their passage. However, admission to land that is used for residential purposes may not be demanded unless 24 hours' notice of the intended entry has been given to the occupier. In the event of depreciation and disturbance caused by entry onto land for works purposes provisions relating to compensation will apply.[131]

Where admission has been refused, or refusal is apprehended, or where land is unoccupied or the owner is absent, or in a case of urgency, provision is made for entry under warrant issued by a magistrate. However, this requires it to be shown that there is a reasonable ground for entry onto the land in one of the foregoing circumstances. Where a warrant is granted, entry may be by force and the warrant will continue to operate until the purpose for which entry is necessary has been satisfied.[132]

Any person who wilfully obstructs a person exercising a power of entry will be guilty of an offence.[133] Restrictions are also imposed upon the disclosure of information with regard to any manufacturing process or trade secret by any person authorised to enter any factory or workplace.[134]

### 5.4.13 Default Powers of the Minister

If a complaint is made to the Minister that a coast protection authority has failed to take sufficient measures for the protection of any land in its area, or he is of the opinion that an investigation should be made into the need

---

[130] s.25(1) Coast Protection Act 1949, though entry upon Crown land is excluded (s.32(2)).
[131] s.25(2),(3), (5) and (6) Coast Protection Act 1949 and on compensation see s.19, discussed at 5.4.8 above. Contrast the powers of entry for flood defence purposes, discussed at 3.4.11 and 3.5.8 above.
[132] s.26(4) and (7) Coast Protection Act 1949. Assistance may also be provided to a coast protection authority by allowing it to enter land under a ministerial order where this is necessary because of a covenant or restriction affecting the use of the land (s.28(2)).
[133] s.26(8) Coast Protection Act 1949. The maximum penalty is, on summary conviction, a fine not exceeding level 3 on the standard scale, presently £1,000. The penalty is provided for under s.43 Coast Protection Act 1949, as amended.
[134] s.25(9) Coast Protection Act 1949. This offence is punishable, on summary conviction, by a fine not exceeding level 3 on the standard scale, presently £1,000, or to imprisonment not exceeding 3 months.

for such measures or the sufficiency of any measures which have been taken, he may cause a local inquiry to be held into the matter. Following a local inquiry, if the Minister is satisfied that there has been a failure on the part of a coast protection authority he may make an order declaring it to be in default and directing it to exercise any of its powers under the 1949 Act in a manner, and within a time, specified in the order.[135] The Minister is also empowered to cause a local inquiry to be held in connection with any matter arising under the 1949 Act.[136]

### 5.4.14 Grants and Contributions towards Expenses

Because of the progressive integration of approaches to funding between coast protection and flood defence, the general issues relating to funding are considered together later in this work.[137] However, there are some specific provisions relating to funding under the Coast Protection Act 1949 that may usefully be noted here.

Subject to such conditions as the Treasury may determine, the Minister may make grants towards any expenditure incurred under the 1949 Act by a coast protection authority or incurred by a council of a county or a county borough in carrying out coast protection work under enactments relating to highways.[138]

Where the Minister makes a grant towards expenditure incurred by a maritime district council under the 1949 Act, the council for the relevant county must pay the district council an agreed contribution towards the expenditure or, in default of agreement, an amount determined by the Minister. The requirements concerning county council contributions determined by the Minister prevent him imposing any contribution requirement that exceeds the amount of the ministerial grant that has been, or will be, provided. In addition, the amount that a county council may be obliged to contribute was originally limited to an amount corresponding to a one penny in the pound levied over the whole county. However, since the replacement of domestic rating by the community charge, and subsequently the council tax, the maximum amount is determined by a formula which relates the amount that could have been raised at the time when domestic rating ceased with any increase or decrease related to retail prices indices.[139]

---

[135] s.29(1) and (2) Coast Protection Act 1949.
[136] s.46(1) Coast Protection Act 1949.
[137] See Ch.6 below on funding.
[138] s.21 Coast Protection Act 1949.
[139] s.20(1) and (2) Coast Protection Act 1949, and see s.251(2) Local Government Act 1972 and Art.2(2) and Schedule 2 Part I Local Government Finance (Repeals and Consequential Amendments) Order 1991, S.I. 1991 No.1730. Domestic rating ceased on 31 March 1990.

Other provisions allow coast protection expenses to be met by county councils by enabling a council to make payment towards any person, other than a district council, in respect of work for the protection of land in the county. A district council in England, or a county borough council in Wales, where these are not coast protection authorities or constituent authorities of a coast protection board, may also contribute to the cost of carrying out any coast protection work which is necessary or expedient for protection of land within their area. Also, a coast protection authority may contribute towards the cost of coast protection work, either within or outside their area, which is necessary or expedient for the protection of any land within its area.[140] In addition, it has been noted that private and commercial interests will, in many cases, benefit from works that coast protection authorities carry out under the Act, and it is suggested that 'appropriate contributions' should be obtained in these cases.[141]

## 5.5 POLICY AND SHORELINE MANAGEMENT PLANS

The provisions of the Coast Defence Act 1949 operate in a policy context which has much in common with that appertaining to flood defence as discussed previously. Hence the principal policy statement, the *Strategy for Flood and Coastal Defence*,[142] tends to emphasise common principles, such as the need for adequate, technically, environmentally and economically sound and sustainable flood *and coastal defence* measures. Similarly, as will be seen, there is a high degree of integration of the public funding mechanisms that apply to flood and coastal defence with the Department for the Environment, Food and Regional Affairs and the National Assembly for Wales applying common principles to grant applications for either purpose.

However, a distinctive feature of coast protection is the emphasis that is increasingly being placed upon the need for more co-ordinated guidance of the activity through establishment of shoreline management plans. Hence, the Ministers have encouraged the formulation of coast protection defence groups comprising operating authorities and other bodies with coastal responsibilities, providing a forum for discussion and co-operation. The object is to promote a strategic approach to coastal defence through the exchange of information and understanding between relevant bodies and to disseminate good practice in the planning and implementation of policy at an appropriate level.

---

[140] s.20(4) to (6) Coast Protection Act 1949.
[141] Ministry of Health, *Coast Protection Act 1949* (1950) Circular 9/50 *Explanatory Memorandum* para.15 (commenting on sections 4, 7 to 11 and 14 of the Act).
[142] Ministry of Agriculture, Fisheries and Food and Welsh Office (1993), discussed at 3.2 above.

For the purpose of establishing shoreline management plans, the coastline of England and Wales has been divided into 11 major 'sediment cells', comprising lengths of coastline which are relatively self-contained insofar as the movement of sand and shingle are concerned. The sediment cells form discrete units for plans that should cover an entire cell, though sub-cells are also identified as more practical units for initial production of plans. Nonetheless, the exercise of planning on the basis of hydrological or geological features allows effective consideration to be given to various issues that extend beyond the jurisdiction or powers of particular coast protection authorities. Hence, coastal groups are encouraged to consider natural coastal processes, coastal defence needs, environmental considerations, planning issues, and current and future land use in formulating shoreline management plans.[143]

Officially, coastal groups have only a 'voluntary' status, and shoreline management plans lack the statutory status afforded to development plans established under the Town and Country Planning Act 1990. Nevertheless, there is a recognition that shoreline management plans have a valuable role to play, insofar as planning authorities are advised to take 'due account' of these plans insofar as they are concerned with coastal land use.[144] Also, where a shoreline management plan is in place, the Ministers have indicated that they will expect any coast protection scheme that is submitted for grant aid to be consistent with the plan. Therefore, despite plans not being approved by the Minister they will fulfil an important role in determining the acceptability of a particular coast protection proposal.[145] Notwithstanding the importance of plans in funding and land-use planning determinations, however, there have been calls for coastal groups to be given more formal powers and for shoreline management plans to be afforded statutory status.[146]

---

[143] Generally see Ministry of Agriculture, Fisheries and Food, Welsh Office, Association of District Councils, English Nature and National Rivers Authority, *Shoreline Management Plans: A Guide for Coastal Defence Authorities* (1995).
[144] See 9.8 below on planning and flood risk and Ch.9 on planning generally.
[145] Ministry of Agriculture, Fisheries and Food, Welsh Office, Association of District Councils, English Nature and National Rivers Authority, *Shoreline Management Plans: A Guide for Coastal Defence Authorities* (1995) para.4.3.
[146] House of Commons Agriculture Committee, Sixth Report Session 1997–98, *Flood and Coastal Defence* (1998) HC 707, paras.82 and 85. Although see House of Commons Agriculture Committee, Fifth Special Report Session 1997–98, *Replies by the Government and the Environment Agency to the Sixth Report from the Agriculture Committee Session 1997–98 'Flood and Coastal Defence'* (1998) HC 1117 response to recommendations (q) and (s).

# Chapter 6

# FUNDING

## 6.1 INTRODUCTION

Previous chapters have described the operating authorities with public responsibilities for flood and coastal defence, and discussed the range of operations that may be undertaken for these purposes. However, the point has been repeatedly made that the powers to undertake works and activities of various kinds are almost invariably of a permissive kind, so that it is only in exceptional circumstances that an authority will be legally obliged to carry out any particular works or activity at any particular time. The practical reality is, therefore, that flood and coastal defence works are only undertaken in circumstances where funding is available to allow an authority to do so. Hence, the purpose of this chapter is to examine the legal provisions and administrative practices that determine when funding will become available.

Initially, the chapter is concerned with the policies and practices of central government in providing flood and coastal defence funding. Alongside this, the statutory provisions allowing for funding need to be considered and the diverse mechanisms by which operating authorities may recover their costs from other bodies and individuals. The point is fairly made that this is a discussion of the mechanisms for funding *public* bodies with relevant functions, and it should not be overlooked that private responsibilities for flood and coastal defence remain to be discharged, normally, at the expense of individual landholders.

After some introductory observations, the plan of the chapter broadly follows the pattern previously adopted in considering the public bodies concerned with flood and coastal defence, from the Ministers down through the successive operating authorities. In each case, the objective is to identify the mechanisms by which a body provides or receives funds for relevant work or activities. In all respects, these mechanisms need to be facilitated by enabling legislation though, as will be seen, the actual use of legislative powers in relation to funding is profoundly affected by policy considerations and administrative practices.

### 6.1.1 An Outline of Funding Arrangements

The central principles concerning funding for flood and coastal defence operating authorities are concisely set out in a ministerial memorandum

240  Funding

submitted to the House of Commons Agriculture Committee in 1998[1] and are usefully restated as follows.

(1) The Environment Agency's non-grant aided flood defence expenditure is funded primarily from levies on local authorities and also from internal drainage board contributions.[2]

(2) Internal drainage boards are funded, primarily, by the combination of special levies on local authorities and drainage rates payable on agricultural land and buildings.[3]

(3) Where local authority flood and coastal defence schemes are grant aided,[4] the Ministry issues supplementary credit approvals to enable local authorities to borrow to cover the residual cost of a scheme.

(4) Local authority costs are funded in accordance with general funding arrangements for local authorities; hence, flood and coastal defence revenue expenditure, including Environment Agency levies and internal drainage board special levies, is reflected in the standard spending assessments for local authorities and revenue support grants made available to them.[5]

(5) Revenue support grants are distributed to each receiving authority so that if it were to spend at the level of its standard spending assessment then, subject to certain qualifications, all billing authorities[6] could set broadly the same council tax for dwellings in the same valuation band in any area.

(6) There are two parts to the standard spending assessment which relate to flood and coastal defence, the first concerning the day-to-day costs

---

[1] House of Commons Agriculture Committee, Sixth Report Session 1997–98, *Flood and Coastal Defence* (1998) HC 707-II, *Memorandum Submitted by the Ministry of Agriculture, Fisheries and Food*, Annex C, p.204.

[2] Although an exception to this is the funding of the Anglian Region of the Agency by 'general drainage charges' payable by agricultural landholders in certain areas. See 6.3.9 below on general drainage charges. See 6.3.5 below on Environment Agency levies on local authorities and 6.3.8 below on internal drainage board contributions.

[3] See 6.4.9 below on special levies on local authorities and 6.4.4 below on drainage rates payable on agricultural land.

[4] See 6.3.2 and 6.4.2 below on the provision of ministerial grants for flood and coastal defence schemes.

[5] Although flood and coastal defence expenditure appear as two separate sub-elements in the standard spending assessments of local authorities.

[6] On local 'billing' authorities see s.1 Local Government Finance Act 1992 which identifies billing authorities as those authorities required to levy and collect council tax in relation to dwellings in their areas. These authorities comprise district and London borough councils, and the Common Council of the City of London, in relation to England, and county and county borough councils in Wales.

# Introduction 241

associated with these services, and the second relating to the cost of servicing borrowing undertaken on the strength of supplementary credit approvals.

(7) An authority's share of the national total of standard spending assessments for day-to-day expenditure on flood and coastal defence is its share of the budgeted expenditure in the previous year. The national totals reflect an estimate by the Ministry of expenditure on Environment Agency levies and internal drainage board special levies, together with the authority's own spending.

(8) The element of standard spending assessment relating to the cost of servicing borrowing is based on a notional debt for each authority, reflecting the supplementary credit approvals that have been issued to the authority.

(9) The overall effect of these arrangements is that nearly all of the day-to-day costs of flood and coastal defence which would otherwise fall upon local authorities and their council tax payers are met by central government through the revenue support grant, as are the majority of debt charges.

At the time of the Agriculture Committee's report, the actual sources and levels of funding provided for flood and coastal defence in England were indicated as follows.

*Revenue Support Grant:* £225.4 million
(paid to local authorities to fund levies to the Environment Agency and internal drainage boards, and flood and coastal defence spending by local authorities).

*Ministerial Grants:* £69.4 million
(for expenditure by operating authorities on flood warning systems and capital works).

*Ministerial Supplementary Credit Approvals:* £12.0 million
(used to support the balance of capital works undertaken by local authorities).

*Drainage Rates:* £11.0 million
(paid by agricultural landholders and used to fund expenditure by internal drainage boards).

*General Drainage Charges payable by agricultural landholders:* £2.8 million
(used to fund Environment Agency expenditure in the Anglian Region only).

*Contributions from Beneficiaries:* £3.0 million (estimated) (used to fund expenditure by operating authorities).

Hence, for 1997–98, the overall cost of publicly undertaken flood and coastal defence works amounted to approximately £323.6 million, including borrowing approvals, though £16.8 million of this was contributed by farmers and landholders benefited by particular works. Despite the considerable amounts of expenditure involved, the Agriculture Committee concluded that there was a significant shortfall in annual expenditure. Specifically, it suggested that additional expenditure of between £30 and £40 million was needed to ensure Environment Agency inland and sea defences were maintained and restored to minimum standards. That figure did not include estimated expenditure required for the upgrading of defence works in private or local authority ownership, and the total national shortfall would be proportionately higher.[7]

Following the Agriculture Committee's Report, further studies were undertaken by the Ministry of Agriculture, Fisheries and Food as part of the 1998 Comprehensive Spending Review. These studies concluded that the annual shortfall in capital works and maintenance investment was approximately £100 million to maintain existing standards of defence works, without making any allowances for the impact of climate change. Since then, additional funding of £23 million has been made available as a result of the 1998 Review. Further announcements of £30 million over 3 years were made as a result of the spending review of 2000; an additional £51 million over 4 years to accelerate flood defence works, catchment area assessment studies and flood warning system improvements; and an £11.6 million package of measures was provided to meet the cost of emergency responses provided in the aftermath of the Autumn 2000 floods. The National Assembly for Wales also announced, in January 2001, that £25 million of expenditure was planned over the following 3 years.[8]

Notwithstanding the recent investment announcements, the Agriculture Committee remained of the view that these will not be sufficient to clear the backlog of flood defence works in England and that the Government should reassess the provision of funding as a matter of urgency. In response, the Government has pointed out that aggregate annual investment in flood and coastal defence is currently about £400 million. Funding for capital works is set to increase by 50% from £76 million in 2000–01 to £114 million in 2003–04. In addition, some £268 million is provided to

---

[7] House of Commons Agriculture Committee, Sixth Report Session 1997–98, *Flood and Coastal Defence* (1998) HC 707, para.45 and see Institution of Civil Engineers, *Learning to Live with Rivers* (2001) pp.44 to 46.

[8] Environment Agency, *Lessons Learned: Autumn 2000 Floods* (2001) pp.39 to 40.

support local authority expenditure on flood and coastal defence through revenue support grant arrangements. Presently, the Government is of the opinion that this reflects a 'realistic' view of what operating authorities can achieve in building up their defence programmes, but it has instigated further research to identify long-term investment needs, taking account of climate change and future technical options for flood defence.[9]

Although the sums of money involved in flood and coastal defence are very large, the critical issue is whether they represent good value for money. On this, it has been estimated that, if there were no form of defence, the annual average value of damage from flooding and coastal erosion in England and Wales would be in the order of £2.1 billion.[10] Hence a recent report by the National Audit Office, concerning inland flood defence in England, concluded that an annual investment by operating authorities of some £400 million represents good value for money.[11]

### 6.1.2 Allocation of Costs

Although achieving a satisfactory level of protection against flooding and coastal erosion is, unavoidably, a costly exercise, there are difficult policy issues to be addressed in the allocation of costs. Potentially, costs could be met from national, regional or local public funding or from private funding, and the challenge is to allocate costs at the appropriate level. At each level, an assessment has to be made of the respective public and private benefit that a project involves and to allocate costs appropriately through legal and administrative mechanisms.

A useful insight into cost-allocation issues is provided by a Government Green Paper published in 1985, *Financing and Administration of Land Drainage, Flood Prevention and Coast Protection in England and Wales*.[12] The Green Paper highlighted a range of institutional and funding issues, many of which remain topical despite the passage of time. In the light of a general need to control public expenditure, the question was posed as to whether the arrangements struck the right balance in the financing of flood defence work. It was recognised that, insofar as the object of such work is to protect property from flooding, the immediate beneficiaries are the

---

[9] House of Commons Agriculture Committee, Eighth Special Report of Session 1999–2000, *Reply by the Government to the Third Report of the Agriculture Committee, Session 2000–01 'Flood and Coastal Defence Follow Up'* (2001) HC 437, para.18.
[10] House of Commons Agriculture Committee, Sixth Report Session 1997–98, *Flood and Coastal Defence* (1998) HC 707, para.6.
[11] National Audit Office, *Inland Flood Defence* (2001) HC 299, p.3. See also Association of British Insurers, *Flooding: A Partnership to Protecting People* (2001) p.3 which estimates the return on annual investments at 675%.
[12] HM Government (1985) Cmnd.9449.

owners of the property which is protected and it was justifiable, therefore, that beneficiaries should contribute all, or a substantial part, of the cost of schemes which protect their properties.

However, there were (and remain) considerable practical difficulties in securing adherence to the 'beneficiary pays' principle, in requiring contributions to works in proportion to the benefit received by individual landowners. There are several examples of statutory mechanisms, designed to secure funding contributions from landowners, which have proved unworkable in practice. For example, the facility for drainage work undertaken for the benefit of agricultural land to be funded by 'general drainage charges'[13] upon such land at a flat rate charge per hectare had proved to be an extremely complicated method of calculating the charge to occupiers. Charges of this kind have only been applied by the Anglian Region of the Environment Agency. Even then, the amount raised is only a small proportion of the total precept and the administrative burden involved in maintaining detailed records of agricultural holdings has meant that the costs of collection of the general rates constituted a relatively high proportion of the overall amount collected. A further statutory facility for levying 'special drainage charges'[14] upon landowners in respect of schemes for the benefit of agricultural land in a particular area had never actually been used in practice. In part, this may have been because most of the areas of special drainage need were already covered by internal drainage boards, but the low limit of the special drainage charge which could be imposed was also a contributory factor. Another example, from coast protection funding, is the provision for 'coast protection charges'[15] in relation to land which is the subject of a coast works scheme where, again, the administrative difficulties in ascertaining and collecting such charges, and the relatively low amounts actually collected, caused the practice of imposing the charges to fall into abeyance.

Hence, the theoretical attractiveness of the beneficiary pays principle has to be balanced against the practical difficulties involved in identifying who benefits from flood defence work, by how much they benefit and what legal and administrative mechanisms can be efficiently used to recover an appropriate proportion of the benefit. Despite the 1985 Green Paper prompting an anticipation that significant changes in law and administrative practice for flood and coastal defence funding were in prospect, this did not happen.[16] Essentially, the problematic issues identified in 1985 remain.

---

[13] See 6.3.9 below on general drainage charges.
[14] See 6.3.10 below on special drainage charges.
[15] See 5.4.5 above on coast protection charges.
[16] See A. Longworth, 'Land Drainage Law' [1991] *Water Law* 188.

# Introduction

The difficulties in identifying and quantifying private benefits, and devising efficient mechanisms for recouping them, have the consequence that the cost of many kinds of flood and coastal defence work is placed upon the public purse. The 'corpses' of various kinds of cost recovery schemes remain in the legislation, but do not reflect the actual practice of funding flood and coastal defence works which is greatly more dependent upon public funding than the 'beneficiary pays' principle would suggest.

## 6.1.3 The Flood Defence Funding Review

At the time of writing, the Department for Environment, Food and Rural Affairs and the National Assembly for Wales is undertaking a major review of flood and coastal defence funding. During the Government Spending Review in 2000 it was recognised that there was scope to make funding mechanisms and institutional arrangements for flood and coastal defence more effective, fair and efficient, and a review of these matters was instigated. The terms of reference of the review required consideration of current funding mechanisms for flood and coastal defence in England and Wales; examination of the scope for reform to ensure a rational and fair distribution of the burden of financing flood defences; consideration of whether expenditure is properly directed towards sustainable and coherent priorities; and consideration of whether administrative arrangements correspond with funding mechanisms.

A Flood and Coastal Defence Funding Review Steering Group was established comprising representatives from the Ministry of Agriculture, Fisheries and Food (and later the Department for Environment, Food and Rural Affairs); the Treasury; the Department of the Environment, Transport and the Regions (and later the Department for Transport, Local Government and the Regions); the National Assembly for Wales; and the Environment Agency. The Steering Group commissioned research from independent consultants which identified three potential drawbacks in existing funding mechanisms:

(1) the time-lag involved in local authorities recovering flood defence spending from central government with consequent shortfalls in funding in years in which there is increased expenditure;

(2) a distortion between expenditure on capital projects and on operational expenditure to reduce flood risk, causing capital solutions to be preferred where other solutions might have been cheaper; and

(3) the overall level of funding is not directly linked to minimising the total costs of flooding, so that there is little incentive for private provision of defences and as a result economically efficient defences are not built.

There was recognised to be a public interest in increasing funding available for flood defences, since this investment would secure protection from risks which outweighed its costs. Consequently, it was suggested that those who benefit from flood defences should contribute a greater part of their costs. The consultants' report suggested that such contributions might be met by charges on the development of new property in the flood plain by way of a capital contribution by developers,[17] with this charge being used to support defences for poorly defended areas. In addition, charges reflecting local programmes of flood defences could be charged to all householders and businesses in protected flood plains and collected through the Council Tax or National Non-Domestic Rates.[18]

Although recognising the continuing need for Government investment, the Review Steering Group shared the view that the upward trend in expenditure on flood defence heightened the need to explore new sources of funding. Accordingly, the Group supported some aspects of the new mechanisms for funding which had been proposed. In particular, it was thought that, although a 'development charge' might be premature given new arrangements for controlling development in the flood plain,[19] a 'connection charge' might be more appropriate. A connection charge would be a one-off payment made by all developers in the flood plain to recover general flood defence costs not attributable to any particular development. Also, in view of technical advances enabling flood plains to be defined with greater accuracy, an investigation of the viability of a 'flood plain levy', charged upon those occupying flood plains and enabling a direct contribution to be made to the cost of flood defences, might be advantageous.[20]

Following the Report of the Review Steering Group, and other influential commentaries on the issues by the Institution of Civil Engineers and the Environment Agency,[21] the funding of flood and coastal defence is presently

---

[17] It was envisaged that this payment might be payable by way of a planning obligation (under s.106 Town and Country Planning Act 1990). See 9.5 and 9.8.10 below on planning obligations and developer contributions.

[18] Oxford Economic Research Associates, *The Flood and Coastal Defence Funding Review: A Discussion of Funding Options* (2001) (a Report submitted to the Flood and Coastal Defence Funding Review Steering Group).

[19] See Department for Transport, Local Government and the Regions, Planning Policy Guidance Note 25, *Development and Flood Risk* (2001) discussed at 9.8 below.

[20] Department for Environment, Food and Rural Affairs, HM Treasury, Department for Transport, Local Government and the Regions, National Assembly for Wales and Environment Agency, *The Flood and Coastal Defence Funding Review: Report to Ministers by the Review Steering Group* (2001).

[21] See Institution of Civil Engineers, *Learning to Live with Rivers* (2001) and Environmental Agency, *Review of the Appraisal Framework* (2001).

the subject of a consultation exercise.[22] The consultation paper recognises that funding for flood defence will continue to be primarily provided by central government, but endorses the view that there may be a strong case for new funding sources which derive from the affected areas. The consultation focuses upon the option of the development connection charge whilst leaving open the possibility of other kinds of local charge, providing that these can meet requirements of 'practicability and fairness' and tests for good taxation requiring 'equity and collectability'.

The consultation also recognises that funding and institutional arrangements are inextricably linked and possible changes to institutional arrangements would need to be informed by any decisions on funding mechanisms. Hence, following the proposals of the Steering Group, associated consultation is being undertaken on a 'broad-based regional model' for institutional arrangements. Most significantly, the proposals to secure a more integrated, strategic and streamlined approach to flood defence involve the establishment of 'Regional Customer Bodies', to be responsible for flood and coastal defence in areas defined by river catchments. These Bodies would comprise representatives from local authorities and relevant regional bodies, and would contract with operating authorities for the flood defence services that are required. The Bodies would have the option of raising funds locally to support an enhanced flood defence service, though the means to allow this would depend upon the outcome of the consultation on the funding options.

Although it is premature to comment on the outcome of the funding review consultation, it is evident that the 'beneficiary pays principle' seems to be undergoing a significant revival. Whether the new mechanisms being proposed for supporting flood defence funding by charges upon individual beneficiaries will fare any better than past attempts to achieve similar objectives, remains to be seen. However, insofar as past attempts to secure funding from beneficiaries have foundered on the difficulties of identifying precisely who benefits from a particular flood defence project, and by how much, the technical advances that have taken place in identifying flood plains may allow some of the past obstacles to practicability to be surmounted.[23]

---

[22] See Department for Environment, Food and Rural Affairs and National Assembly for Wales, *The Flood and Coastal Defence Funding Review: Consultation Document* (2002).

[23] See, for example, the difficulties of identifying 'contributory land' for the purpose of coast protection charges, under s.7 Coast Protection Act 1949, discussed at 5.4.5 above.

## 6.2 CENTRAL GOVERNMENT FUNDING

The Department for the Environment, Food and Rural Affairs and the National Assembly for Wales provide funding for the Environment Agency and internal drainage boards, and grant-in-aid to local authorities for the construction of new flood and coastal defence works. The national policy objectives which ultimately determine when ministerial funding will be provided have been previously discussed[24] and the legal basis upon which funding will be provided to particular operating authorities is considered later in this chapter in relation to the respective operating authorities. However, an issue that needs to be dealt with at this juncture is the question of relative priority between competing bids for Government funding.[25]

On priority, it must be appreciated that there is never likely to be sufficient funds available to meet the cost of every proposal for new flood and coastal defence work that is put forward. Unavoidably, some projects will need to be ranked above others because they represent a better use of limited public resources, perhaps because they represent better value for money or because of the nature of the risks that are secured against. Clearly, a number of factors will need to be carefully weighed into the balance in determining which projects represent a priority claim upon the limited funds that are available. It might seem consistent to seek a common standard of defence in all flood alleviation measures; however, such an approach would mean that all defences would have to be built to the same standard without regard to the value of the assets to be protected. Alternatively, funding could be allocated to flood defence projects upon a strict cost-benefit analysis so that the most valuable protection would be given the highest priority. This would have the consequence that less valuable properties would be protected to a lower standard than more valuable properties. Present guidance generally aims to secure a consistency of approach, in terms of cost-benefit, rather than a consistency of standard, in the sense of applying the same return period specification to all projects. However, this has been criticised in that levels of protection may be dependent, for example, upon higher property values in different parts of the country, and neglect to take proper account of the human impacts of flooding within the cost-benefit analysis.[26]

Financial support for flood and coastal defence projects is based upon project submissions from operating authorities to the relevant Ministry

---

[24] See 3.2.2 above on national policy.
[25] Generally see National Audit Office, *Inland Flood Defence* (2001) HC 299 paras.3.11 to 3.16.
[26] Institution of Civil Engineers, *Learning to Live with Rivers* (2001) p.20.

which, to be successful, have to meet national policy objectives for works. Initial eligibility for funding is dependent upon compliance with project appraisal guidance notes,[27] but this initial screening still leaves a far greater number of projects that are eligible for funding than can actually be funded in any single year.

In 1998 the Ministry of Agriculture, Fisheries and Food introduced a 'priority scoring system' under which every project proposal that is eligible for funding is assessed against national criteria to determine an order of funding priority. The priority scoring system has three stages requiring: first, that projects must comply with 'threshold requirements'; second, that proposals must score above a certain number of points on the basis of specific characteristics; and, third, that projects must be approved by a ministerial panel of coastal engineers. The priority scoring system ranks schemes according to component scores based on 'urgency', 'priority' and 'economics'.[28]

After 3 years of operation of the priority scoring system, an analysis of its operation was undertaken. This indicated, overall, that urban coastal or tidal flood or coast protection schemes tended to achieve the highest scores and schemes in rural areas and non-tidal schemes scored lowest. The 'urgency' component generally carried the greatest weight, though it was recognised that there was often a misleading degree of subjectivity or vagueness in the urgency justifications that were offered. Nonetheless, the analysis of the priority scoring system concluded that national policy priorities were generally reflected in the system. However, concerns were raised as to whether the system directed funding to the areas of greatest need, whether small-scale projects were placed at a disadvantage in securing funding and other issues were identified needing further consideration.[29]

Most recently, consultation has been initiated on a revised version of the prioritisation system for funding that will provide the basis for grant allocations for 2003–04 onwards. In the new system, it is proposed that there will be three basic elements to be considered, economic, social and environmental, and these matters will be quantified to comprise the overall

---

[27] See 3.2.5 above on project appraisal guidance notes.
[28] House of Commons Agriculture Committee, Sixth Report Session 1997–98, *Flood and Coastal Defence* (1998) HC 707, para.28. It appears that the priority scoring system does not apply in Wales, where each proposed scheme is considered on its individual merits: see Ministry of Agriculture, Fisheries and Food, *Water Level Management Plans: Additional Guidance Notes for Operating Authorities* (1999) para.8.2.
[29] Ministry of Agriculture, Fisheries and Food, *Consultation on Flood and Coastal Defence Funding Scheme Prioritisation System* (2001).

score for a project. It is recognised that each of the three elements gives rise to a wide range of issues but some trade-off had to be made between the practicability of the system and its comprehensiveness.[30]

Broadly, the proposals envisage that the 'economic' element will comprise a cost-benefit ratio for each project. The 'social' element will be based upon the number of houses that have their risk of flooding or erosion significantly reduced by the proposal, which is adjusted to reflect the level of risk to safety involved and the vulnerability of the population that is protected. The 'environment' element is based upon the area of designated habitat[31] that is protected or created by the project, with an adjustment being made for the designation status and further account being taken of protected heritage sites. Clearly, different projects will score differently depending upon whether they are intended to protect urban areas or designated habitat sites, and it is recognised that some habitats may be placed outside the prioritisation system because of mandatory obligations to undertake ecological protection work. On the other hand, a proposed flood warning scheme will typically score highly on the 'social' index if it enhances the safety of a significant number of households, though it would be unlikely to secure any credit under the 'environmental' index. Although there are still issues to be decided in relation to securing fairness between large-scale and small-scale projects, the intention is that the emphasis upon quantification under the new scheme should reduce the discretionary or subjective aspects of the existing system and generally enhance transparency.

At the time of writing, the Department for Environment, Food and Rural Affairs is undertaking consultation on guidance to resolve any uncertainties as to how flood and coastal defence operating authorities should identify legitimate spending for nature conservation purposes.[32] The consultation document stresses that all the relevant bodies are subject to conservation duties[33] and that the impact of flood and coastal defence schemes upon biodiversity should be taken into account when allocating grant aid. To some extent, the high level targets[34] that have been established for operating authorities indicate that conservation work may be legitimately undertaken using flood and coastal defence funding. In particular, the targets require the avoidance of environmental damage, no loss of habitats covered by

---

[30] Department for Environment, Food and Rural Affairs, *Review of Scheme Prioritisation System for DEFRA Grant Aid: Second Consultation* (2001).
[31] See Ch.10 below on habitat designations.
[32] Department for Environment, Food and Rural Affairs, *Consultation on the role of flood and coastal defence in nature conservation in England* (2001).
[33] See 10.2 and 10.3 below on general environmental duties.
[34] See 3.2.12 above on high level targets.

biodiversity action plans and that opportunities should be sought for environmental enhancement.[35] Accordingly, new schemes, for which funding is sought, should ensure that there is no overall environmental damage or loss of important habitats as a minimum, and the corresponding costs are legitimately included within a funding application. Moreover, operating authorities are encouraged to consider enhancement measures as an essential part of all schemes and should provide statements of the scope for such measures and the corresponding costs. As a broad guide, it is suggested that enhancement measures will be within the share of funds available for this purpose if they are proportionate in scale to the works which are proposed; they are linked, spatially and temporally; the costs and benefits of enhancement works are taken into account; and opportunities are sought for partnerships when providing extensive facilities which have little bearing upon the works.

## 6.3 THE ENVIRONMENT AGENCY

### 6.3.1 General Funding Position

In general terms, the Environment Agency's flood defence function is funded by grants from the Department for Environment Food and Rural Affairs and the National Assembly for Wales and the exercise of borrowing powers in relation to capital projects. In addition, it may raise the funding that is needed for flood defence work through levies on local authorities, by contributions from internal drainage boards and through general or special drainage charges upon the occupiers of land outside an internal drainage district.

The statutory provisions relating to funding of the Environment Agency allow the appropriate Ministers, after consultation with the Agency and with approval of the Treasury, to determine the financial duties of the Agency.[36] Hence, the appropriate Minister may, with Treasury approval, provide the Agency with grants of such amounts, and on such terms, as thought fit.[37] In addition, the Agency will be entitled to borrow in accordance with its borrowing powers.[38] The Agency is bound to keep proper accounts and records and to prepare an annual statement of accounts giving a true and fair view of the income and expenditure of the Agency. The statements

---

[35] See high level target 9A and see also target 10 (concerned with Water Level Management Plans) and target 11 (concerned with Coastal Habitat Management Plans).
[36] Subject to special duties with respect to flood defence revenue, as provided for under s.118 Water Resources Act 1991.
[37] s.47 Environment Act 1995.
[38] ss.48 to 50 Environment Act 1995.

of accounts must comply with any requirement imposed by the Ministers, with the consent of the Treasury.[39] The accounts of the Agency are to be audited and the Comptroller and Auditor General is entitled to inspect the contents of all accounts and accounting records of the Agency and may report to the House of Commons on the results of any inspection carried out.[40]

The most recent statement of the Agency's financial position is to be found in the Agency's *Annual Report and Accounts 2000/01* covering the financial year to 31 March 2001. In summary, this indicates that the Agency had an operating budget of about £642 million, with 43% of this spent on flood defence compared with 33% spent on environmental protection and 22% spent on the Agency's other water management functions.[41] The total expenditure on flood defence of £311.5 million consisted of £90.1 million on main river inland waters; £13.6 million on main river tidal waters; £6.9 million on sea defence; £9.4 million on flood warning; £47.8 million on items listed as 'other works'; £141.0 million on depreciation and expenditure on capital works; and £2.7 million spent on internal drainage boards. The total income relating to flood defence of £292.2 million consisted of £227.3 million from local authority levies; £3.0 million from general drainage charges; £7.5 million from internal drainage boards; £0.7 million in contributions from beneficiaries; £13.2 million listed as 'other income'; £35.0 million in capital grants and contributions; and £5.5 million as interest receivable.[42] With regard to capital expenditure, a total of £114.9 million was met in part by grants of £26.4 million from the Ministry of Agriculture, Fisheries and Food and by grants of £0.7 million from the National Assembly for Wales.

For most purposes, Agency funding in respect of flood defence is kept financially separate from funding provided for its other functions and constraints are imposed upon the use of this funding to ensure that it is expended in the locality in which it was raised. Specifically, this applies where funding is raised, or held, by the Agency in relation to a particular local flood defence district under the following powers:

(a) under local government regulations allowing levies to be raised;[43]

---

[39] See, Environment Agency, *Annual Report and Accounts 1998/99* (1999) *Direction on the annual accounts* at p.140.
[40] s.46(1), (3) and (4) Environment Act 1995.
[41] Environment Agency, *Annual Report and Accounts 2000/01* (2001) p.59.
[42] Environment Agency, *Annual Report and Accounts 1999–2000* (2000) p.106. A deficit between the expenditure and income for the year of £30.8 million was largely met by a transfer from the Agency's capital reserves.
[43] s.74 Local Government Finance Act 1988, concerning the power to issue levies, and see s.133 Water Resources Act and 6.3.5 below.

(b) by general drainage charges;[44]

(c) by special drainage charges;[45]

(d) by contributions from internal drainage boards;[46]

(e) by a resolution allocating revenue in lieu of contributions for a local flood defence district;[47]

(f) in consequence of transfer of property, rights or liabilities from a former water authority where a sum is required to be spent upon the discharge of land drainage functions in or for the benefit of a particular local land drainage district;[48] and

(g) in respect of any sums raised by the Agency in a flood defence district by a precept under previous flood defence legislation.[49]

Where revenue raised by the Agency falls into any of these categories it may only be spent on the carrying out of the Agency's functions in, or on behalf of, the local flood defence district in which it was raised. However, where no local flood defence scheme is in force, the corresponding area of a regional flood defence committee is treated as a single local flood defence district. In effect, therefore, income from the stated categories must be spent within the district for which it was raised or, at least, within the area of the relevant regional flood defence committee.[50]

The two exceptions to the general requirement that locally raised money should be locally expended are, first, that this does not apply to amounts paid towards research-related activities or towards meeting the Agency's administrative expenses. Second, an exception is made for amounts to be paid towards expenses incurred by the Agency, or any regional flood defence committee, under arrangements made by the Agency concerning matters involving the area of more than one regional flood defence committee.[51]

---

[44] Under s.134 and 135 Water Resources Act 1991, and see 6.3.9 below.
[45] Under s.137 and 138 Water Resources Act 1991, and see 6.3.10 below.
[46] Under s.139(1) Water Resources Act 1991, and see 6.3.6 below.
[47] Under s.58(1)(b) Land Drainage Act 1991, and see 6.3.8 below.
[48] Under a transfer scheme made under Schedule 2 to the Water Act 1989, insofar as the water authority was required to spend the sums for the benefit in or for the benefit of a particular local land drainage district under Schedule 3 para.31 Water Act 1973.
[49] That is, under s.46 Land Drainage Act 1976.
[50] s.118(1), (2), (4) and (6) Water Resources Act 1991. Notably also, income falling within the specified categories is to be disregarded from any amount which may become payable to the Secretary of State in the event of the Environment Agency having a surplus on its capital or revenue accounts (under s.44(4) Environment Act 1995).
[51] s.118(3) Water Resources Act 1991, and on arrangements concerning matters involving more than one regional flood defence committee see s.106(1)(b).

A significant proportion of the overall income of the Agency is raised through charges imposed upon the recipients of the services that it provides. General provision for incidental charges to be levied by the Agency is made, through a power allowing it to fix and recover charges for services and facilities provided in the course of carrying out its functions.[52] This is stated to be without prejudice to other powers of the Agency to recover charges including drainage charges. General provision is also made for charging schemes to be established in relation to environmental licences and licences for abstraction and impounding.[53] Before implementation, charging schemes of this kind require consultation and ministerial approval and regard must be had to the desirability of ensuring that the amounts recovered by the Agency are amounts that are appropriate to meet costs and expenses incurred in carrying out its functions.[54] More specific flood and coastal defence charging mechanisms are considered later in this chapter.

### 6.3.2 Grants to the Environment Agency

The Ministers may make grants towards expenditure incurred by the Environment Agency in the improvement of existing drainage works or the construction of new works. Grants are to be of such amounts as are sanctioned by the Treasury and will be subject to conditions prescribed in regulations approved by the relevant Minister and the Treasury. In particular, no grant may be made towards improvement or construction of works unless the plans and sections for the work have been approved by the Minister and he is satisfied that the work is being, or has been, properly carried out. With Treasury approval, the Minister may also make grants to the Agency in respect of the following matters:

(a) expenditure properly incurred by the Agency with a view to carrying out drainage works, where this is expenditure for which a grant would have been payable had the work been properly carried out;

(b) enabling the Agency to determine whether drainage works, or drainage works of a particular description, should be carried out;

(c) obtaining or organising information, including information about natural processes affecting the coastline, to enable the Agency to

---

[52] s.43 Environment Act 1995.
[53] s.41(5) to (7) Environment Act 1995.
[54] Final approval of a proposed charging scheme by the Secretary of State requires the consent of the Treasury. Following approval, it is the duty of the Agency to take appropriate steps to bring the attention of persons likely to be affected to the provisions of the charging scheme (s.42(7) and (8) Environment Act 1995).

formulate or develop its plans with respect to the defence of any part of the coastline against sea water; and

(d) obtaining information, at any time after carrying out drainage works, with respect to the quality or effectiveness, or the effect on the environment, of those works or any matter of a financial nature relating to those works.[55]

Where the Agency is about to incur expenditure for which a grant would be payable, or expenditure which has been incurred for work which has been properly carried out, the Minister may make advances to the Agency on account of the expenditure.[56]

The detailed provisions concerning grant applications by the Agency are provided for in the Land Drainage (Grants) Regulations 1967[57] which require applications to be made in the form required by the Minister. Applications are to be supplemented by information as to the finances of the Agency and plans and sections of the proposed works. Estimates also need to be provided of costs of the proposed works and these may need to be supported by technical reports to ascertain the effectiveness of the works. Provision is also made for grants to be a fixed sum or a percentage of the total cost and requiring proper accounts to be kept, inspection of the work to be allowed and for modification of proposals with Ministerial consent.

### 6.3.3 Grants for Flood Warning Systems

The relevant Minister may make grants of amounts, sanctioned by the Treasury, towards expenditure incurred by the Agency in providing or installing apparatus, or carrying out other engineering or building operations, for the purposes of a flood warning system.[58] However, this is subject to the proviso that the work is approved and that the Minister is satisfied that it is being, or has been, properly carried out in accordance with conditions imposed by the Minister and approved by the Treasury. Where expenditure is about to be incurred by the Agency in respect of work for which a flood warning system grant may be payable, the Minister, with the approval of the Treasury, may make advances to the Agency on account of the expenditure.[59]

---

[55] (b) to (d) were added by s.101 Environment Act 1995 with the proviso that they are without prejudice to other powers to make grants or otherwise to impose conditions.
[56] s.147 Water Resources Act 1991.
[57] S.I. 1967 No.212, as amended. These Regulations continue to apply by virtue of Schedule 2 para.1(1) and (2) Water Consolidation (Consequential Provisions) Act 1991.
[58] See 11.3 below on flood warning systems.
[59] s.148(1) to (4) Water Resources Act 1991.

256  *Funding*

For the purposes of making grants, 'flood warning system' is defined as any system whereby, for the purpose of providing warning of any danger of flooding, specified information is obtained and transmitted, whether automatically or otherwise, with or without provision for carrying out calculations and for transmitting the results of those calculations. The specified information concerns:

(a) rainfall, as measured at a particular place within a particular period;

(b) the level of flow of any inland water, or part of an inland water, at a particular time; or

(c) any other matters appearing to the Agency to be relevant for that purpose.[60]

### 6.3.4 Other Grants for Flood Defence Purposes

With Treasury approval, Ministerial grants and advances may be made in respect of expenditure incurred, or to be incurred, to the Agency under its general flood defence works powers.[61] Specifically, grants and advances of this kind may be made in relation to:

(a) payments arising from the exercise of any power of the Agency to acquire land by agreement or compulsorily;[62]

(b) payments for providing housing accommodation for persons employed, or to be employed, by the Agency in controlling works of a kind, or so located, that those persons will be required to reside in the vicinity of the works;

(c) payments for, or in respect of, injury sustained by any person by the exercise by the Agency of its general flood defence works powers;[63] and

---

[60] 'Inland water' means (a) any river, stream or other watercourse, whether natural or artificial and whether tidal or not; (b) any lake or pond, whether natural or artificial, and any reservoir or dock; and (c) any channel, creek, bay, estuary or arm of the sea. 'Rainfall' includes any fall of snow, hail or sleet (s.148(5) Water Resources Act 1991).

[61] That is, functions of the Agency under s.165(1)(b) and (c) Water Resources Act 1991 (concerning improvement of existing works and construction of new works) and see 4.3.1 above on the general flood defence works powers.

[62] Under s.154 Water Resources Act 1991 and see 4.3.3 above on acquisition of land.

[63] That is, payments under s.177 and Schedule 21 Water Resources Act 1991 concerned with compensation in respect of the exercise of the general flood defence works powers and see 4.3.2 above on this.

## The Environment Agency

(d) payments of compensation in respect of injury sustained by the exercise of the Agency's power to dispose of spoil in relation to flood defence works.[64]

In addition the Minister may, with Treasury approval, make grants or advances to the Agency in respect of expenditure incurred, or to be incurred, in the carrying out of works for the rebuilding or repair of any bridge maintained by the Agency other than works of a routine kind. Also, grants may be made towards the cost of any works executed by the Agency that would otherwise be at another person's expense.[65]

### 6.3.5 Levies on Local Authorities

For the purpose of its flood defence function, the Environment Agency is a 'levying body' under local government legislation with a power to make regulations authorising the issue of a levy upon local authorities.[66] Hence, in order to meet its 'qualifying expenses' in respect of a local flood defence district, the Agency may issue a levy to local councils[67] for each financial year subject to a prescribed maximum amount.[68]

The detailed matters concerning the power of the Environment Agency to raise revenue by issuing levies to local authorities in respect of expenses of flood defence districts are provided for in the National Rivers Authority

---

[64] That is, payments under s.177 and Schedule 21 Water Resources Act 1991 in relation to the power to dispose of spoil in connection with flood defence works under s.167 Water Resources Act 1991 and see 4.3.4 above on the disposal of spoil.

[65] s.149 Water Resources Act 1991. On work carried out by the Agency at another person's expense see s.165(4) Water Resources Act 1991 and 4.3.6 above.

[66] s.133 Water Resources Act 1991, that is, a levying body for the purposes of s.74 Local Government Finance Act 1988.

[67] 'Local council' means, in relation to a flood defence district, the council of any county, county borough, metropolitan district or London borough any part of whose area is comprised in that district and the Common Council of the City of London if any part of the City of London is within the district (reg.1(2) National Rivers Authority (Levies) Regulations 1993 (S.I. 1993 No.61).

[68] s.45(2) and (3) Land Drainage Act 1976, as amended by Schedule 14 para.17 Water Act 1989. Despite the repeal of the 1976 Act, the Agency's power to issue levies upon local authorities is retained by Schedule 2 para.2(5) Water Consolidation (Consequential Provisions) Act 1991 and must be exercised in accordance with the National Rivers Authority (Levies) Regulations 1993 (S.I. 1993 No.61). The annual 'qualifying expenses' for a district are ascertained by deducting from the 'relevant expenditure' any amount defrayed out of any reserve, replacement or sinking fund and any income not derived from the levies issued to local authorities and adding any amount required as new working capital. The 'relevant expenditure' for a district means expenditure by the Agency in respect of flood defence functions in, or for the benefit of, the district and includes an appropriate proportion of the Agency's administrative expenses and expenses in relation to research-related activities.

(Levies) Regulations 1993.[69] These Regulations include provision for the power to issue levies; the maximum amount of levies; the apportionment of expenses that are met by levies where a district comprises more than one local authority; the duty of a certain authority to notify the Agency of the council tax base[70] for its area; the power of the Agency to issue a levy in substitution of a previous levy; the method of payment of levies; and the anticipation by a local authority of a levy which may be issued to it.[71]

The 1993 Regulations determine that the maximum amount of the Agency's levy is to be based upon the estimated penny rate product that would be raised for an area in a financial year.[72] However, this formula need not apply where special consent is given by the majority of local authority members of a local flood defence committee or, where no local committee exists, by a majority of the local authority members of a regional flood defence committee who were appointed by councils with areas within the local flood defence district.[73]

The Agency is under a duty to prepare a statement of the purposes to which the amount demanded by any levy is intended to be applied, and the basis on which it is calculated, and a local authority is not liable to pay the amount demanded until it has received such a statement.[74] Otherwise, a

---

[69] S.I. 1993 No.61, hereafter the '1993 Regulations', made under ss.74, 143(1) and (2) Local Government Finance Act 1988 and s.149(1) and (2) Local Government and Housing Act 1989. The 1993 Regulations continue to operate under Schedule 2 para.2(5) Water Consolidation (Consequential Provisions) Act 1991.

[70] The Agency must secure that its expenses in relation to a district are met by levies which are borne *proportionately* by local authorities, if there are more than one in a district, under a formula by which appropriate proportions are determined. This requires an annual determination of the 'council tax base' for the area, or the part of the area, of each local council which falls within the district in accordance with reg.6 of the 1993 Regulations.

[71] See also *London Borough of Camden v National Rivers Authority and Wiltshire County Council*, unreported, Court of Appeal, 10 October 1996, concerning the power of the Environment Agency to impose levies upon local authorities generally where a particular local authority has mistakenly provided incorrect information as to the product of a penny rate for its area.

[72] For any particular year, this is to be based upon the figure for 1992, but made subject to an increase or decrease, in line with the retail prices index, applying the index for September 1992 as the reference point (reg.5(2) 1993 Regulations). The maximum amount that may be levied in an area in any financial year is normally 1.7 times the estimated penny rate product (s.46(5) Land Drainage Act 1976, repealed but continuing in effect for the purpose of reg.5(1) 1993 Regulations). See *R v Cambridgeshire County Council* [1936] 3 All ER 352 on the basis on which an estimation may be made.

[73] s.46(7) Land Drainage Act 1976, repealed but continuing in effect for the purpose of reg.5(1) 1993 Regulations.

[74] s.46(8) Land Drainage Act 1976, repealed but continuing in effect for the purpose of reg.3(1) 1993 Regulations.

local council to which a levy is issued in respect of a financial year must pay the Agency the amount of the levy in that financial year at such time and in such instalments, if any, as are agreed between the Agency and the council or, in default of agreement, at prescribed times.[75]

### 6.3.6 Contributions from Internal Drainage Boards

The Environment Agency must, by resolution, require every internal drainage board to make such contributions towards the expenses of the Agency as it considers to be 'fair'. By contrast with the provisions for the calculation of levies upon local authorities, there is no statutory formula for ascertaining the precise amounts of contributions by internal drainage boards. However, some constraints upon what is a 'fair' contribution are imposed. Hence, where a 'main' internal drainage district contains two or more 'minor' districts the Agency must not require the main board to make contributions in relation to the minor districts. Despite this, the Agency may require the drainage board for the main district to pay the Agency an amount equal to the aggregate of the contributions of the boards for the minor districts. Following a requisition of this kind, the board of the main district must raise the amount paid to the Agency by means of drainage rates[76] levied by that board within, or special levies[77] issued in respect of, the main district or such part of it as is situated within a minor district.[78]

Where the Agency makes a resolution as to what is a fair contribution, this may be acted upon immediately notwithstanding any appeals that may be brought in relation to the resolution.[79] Despite the immediate effect of a resolution, provision is made for appeals by any internal drainage board that is aggrieved by the resolution. Likewise, appeals may be made by any county, county borough or London borough that is aggrieved because the amount of the contribution required of an internal drainage board is considered to be inadequate. Appeals are to be made to the relevant Minister within a 6-week period after the notice of the resolution from the Agency is communicated to the internal drainage board. The Minister may, after considering the objections made to him, and holding a public inquiry if he thinks fit, may make such an order as he thinks 'just'. If the Agency has already acted upon a resolution that is the subject of an appeal, the Minister must require whatever adjustment to the sums recovered or paid

---

[75] reg.9 1993 Regulations.
[76] On drainage rates see 6.4.4 below.
[77] On special levies see 6.4.9 below.
[78] s.139(1) to (4) Water Resources Act 1991.
[79] s.139(5) Water Resources Act 1991.

under the resolution as is necessary to give effect to his decision.[80]

The Agency may issue a precept to any internal drainage board requiring payment of any amount that must be contributed to the Agency. The internal drainage board is then bound to pay the amount demanded in the precept. The Agency is bound to prepare, in such a form as the relevant Minister may direct,[81] a statement of the purposes to which the amount demanded by any precept is intended to be applied and the basis on which it is calculated. The internal drainage board is not liable to pay the amount demanded by the Agency until it has received a statement of this kind.[82]

### 6.3.7 Contributions to Internal Drainage Boards

Under certain circumstances an internal drainage board may apply to the Agency for a contribution towards its expenses. This arises where the district of a board receives a quantity of water from lands at a higher level or because of the period that will elapse before the district obtains any relief from the operations of the Agency on a main river. Where these circumstances are established, the board may be entitled to a 'fair' contribution towards its expenses and the Agency may resolve to make the board such a contribution, if any, as is specified by the resolution.[83]

### 6.3.8 Contributions where the Agency is the Internal Drainage Board

Where the Agency acts as the drainage board for an internal drainage district by virtue of a scheme for the reorganisation of districts or an order for the transfer of functions,[84] the Agency may, by resolution, specify the amount of any contribution that it would, otherwise, make or require to be made from the board.[85] Where a contribution from or to a drainage board would otherwise be required, expenses incurred by the Agency in acting as the drainage board must be defrayed out of sums received by the Agency in acting as the board. The Agency is bound to publish resolutions of this

---

[80] s.140(1) to (3) Water Resources Act 1991.
[81] The prescribed form is provided for in the Water Authorities (Precepts to Internal Drainage Boards) Regulations 1974, S.I. 1974 No.375.
[82] s.141 Water Resources Act 1991.
[83] s.57(1) and (2) Land Drainage Act 1991.
[84] On schemes for the reorganisation of districts see s.3 Land Drainage Act 1991, discussed at 3.5.3 above. On orders for the transfer of functions see s.4 Land Drainage Act 1991, discussed at 3.5.3 above.
[85] s.58(1) Land Drainage Act 1991, that is, any contributions to an internal drainage board under s.57 Land Drainage Act 1991 or contributions from a board under s.139 Water Resources Act 1991.

kind and provision is made for a 'sufficient number of qualified persons',[86] or the council of any county, county borough or London borough, aggrieved by the resolution, or the failure to pass a resolution, to appeal to the relevant Minister. The Minister, after considering any objections made to him, may make such an order as he thinks just.[87]

### 6.3.9 General Drainage Charges

Although used only in the Anglian Region of the Environment Agency,[88] provision is made for general drainage charges to be imposed upon agricultural landholders in each local flood defence district that is outside an internal drainage district. General drainage charges may be raised in respect of the Agency's flood defence expenditure in the district, whereas 'special drainage charges'[89] require agricultural landholders to contribute to the cost of a particular drainage scheme that involves improvement or maintenance works in relation to particular watercourses in their area. As has been noted, revenue that is raised from general charges should be expended only on flood defence activities in or for the benefit of the areas in which the charges were raised.[90]

Generally, the Agency is empowered to raise general drainage charges from occupiers of land at an amount per hectare of 'chargeable land' in a local flood defence district in accordance with provisions relating to the assessment of charges and determination of the 'relevant quotient'. 'Chargeable land' means agricultural land and buildings in so much of the area of a regional flood defence committee as does not fall within an internal drainage district, excluding rough grazing land and woodlands

---

[86] Where reference is made to the making of any petition by 'a sufficient number of qualified persons': (a) the qualified persons are the occupiers of any land in the district on which a drainage rate is levied; and (b) their number will be sufficient if (i) they are not less than 40; or (ii) they are not less than one-fifth of the number of persons who are qualified to make the petition; or (iii) the assessable value of the land in respect of which they are qualified persons, under the last drainage rate, is not less than one-fifth of the total assessable value of the land in respect of which that rate was levied. Where a district is subdivided, the occupiers of land qualified to make a petition for subdivision will also be sufficient where they are not less than one-fifth of the number of persons who are qualified to make the petition within the sub-district, or the assessable value of the land in respect of which they are qualified persons is not less than one-fifth of the assessable value of the land in respect of which the rate was levied in the sub-district (s.72(2) and (3) Land Drainage Act 1991).
[87] s.58(2), (3), (4) and (6) Land Drainage Act 1991.
[88] See 6.1.2 above on the allocation of costs. See General Drainage Charges (Anglian Region) Order 1990, S.I. 1990 No.223.
[89] See 6.3.10 below on special drainage charges.
[90] s.118 Water Resources Act 1991 and see 6.3.1 above.

other than commercial woodlands.[91] However, the Agency may not levy a general drainage charge in respect of a district unless the regional flood defence committee for the relevant area have recommended that such a charge should be raised. For the purposes of such a recommendation, the area of a regional flood defence committee in relation to which no local flood defence scheme is in force is to be treated as a single local flood defence district, and any part of the area of the committee in which no scheme is in force is to be treated as a single local flood defence district.[92]

A general drainage charge raised by the Agency for a local flood defence district for any year is to be at a uniform amount per hectare of chargeable land in the district. The uniform amount is to be ascertained by multiplying the 'relevant quotient' by one penny and by numbers specified by either Minister in an order for that purpose. Apart from any adjustment to take account of grazing land, the numbers specified in an order must be such as will secure, so far as reasonably practicable, that the aggregate amount produced will be equal to an amount which would have been produced by a rate for the financial year beginning in 1989 levied at one penny in the pound multiplied by the 'relevant quotient'.[93] For the purposes of this calculation, an order may be made to apply to all general drainage charges or charges to be raised in particular flood defence districts specified in the order.[94]

The detailed provisions concerning the amount and assessment of general drainage charges are set out in Schedule 15 to the Water Resources Act 1991. This Schedule contains various supplemental provisions with respect to drainage charges concerning matters such as publication; liability of occupiers; assessment of chargeable land; appeals against demands; and proceedings for the recovery of charges. Notable also is the requirement

---

[91] s.145 Water Resources Act 1991. 'Agricultural land' means (a) land used as arable, meadow or pasture ground only; (b) land used for a plantation or a wood or for the growth of saleable underwood; and (c) land exceeding one-tenth of a hectare used for the purpose of poultry farming, market gardens, nursery grounds, orchards or allotments (including allotment gardens within the meaning of the Allotments Act 1922) but does not include land occupied together with a house or park, gardens (other than aforesaid) or pleasure grounds, land kept or preserved mainly or exclusively for purposes of sport or recreation or land used as a racecourse. 'Agricultural buildings' has the meaning provided by s.26(4) General Rate Act 1967 (as amended by the Rating Act 1971) and see *Gilmore (Valuation Officer)* v *Baker-Carr* [1962] 3 All ER 230 (where a broiler house was held not to be agricultural land or an agricultural building).

[92] s.134 Water Resources Act 1991.

[93] The relevant quotient is determined by calculations made in accordance with: General Drainage Charges (Relevant Quotient) Regulations 1993, S.I. 1993 No.165, and see Local Government Finance Act 1992 Schedule 13 para.96.

[94] s.135(1) to (4) Water Resources Act 1991, amended by Schedule 13 para.96(2) and Schedule 14 Local Government Finance Act 1992.

that demands for drainage charges must be made in a prescribed form.[95]

### 6.3.10 Special Drainage Charges

Although never used in practice, apparently for reasons of impracticability,[96] statutory provision is made for special drainage charges to be imposed by the Environment Agency upon agricultural landholders, requiring contributions to the cost of local drainage schemes that involve improvement or maintenance works in relation to particular local watercourses. Hence, where the interests of agriculture[97] require the carrying out, improvement or maintenance of drainage works in connection with particular watercourses in the area of a regional flood defence committee, the Agency may submit to either of the Ministers for confirmation a scheme for special drainage charges with respect to those watercourses. A scheme of this kind must designate the relevant watercourses and make provision for raising charges and designate agricultural land that will benefit from the works. Upon confirmation of the scheme, the designated watercourses will be treated as part of a main river.[98] A special drainage charges scheme may make provision for certain rights, powers, duties, obligations and liabilities to be transferred to the Agency[99] and may provide for revocation or amendment of previous schemes.[100]

The procedural provisions relating to the establishment of schemes for imposing special drainage charges are provided for in Schedule 16 to the Water Resources Act 1991. Amongst other things, this Schedule provides for requirements relating to consultation before the submission of a proposed scheme to either of the Ministers; confirmation of the scheme by the Minister; the giving of notice of an order confirming a scheme; and challenges to unconfirmed orders by persons aggrieved. Where a scheme has been put in place, a special drainage charge must be levied by the Agency at a uniform rate in respect of chargeable land in the designated area. The amount of the uniform rate is to be determined by the regional flood defence committee but is not to exceed the maximum amount specified in the ministerial order and may not, without parliamentary approval, exceed 25p per hectare.[101]

---

[95] See General Drainage Charges (Forms) Regulations 1990, S.I. 1990 No.564.
[96] See 6.1.2 above on the 'beneficiary pays' principle
[97] On the definition of 'agriculture' see notes to 6.3.9 above.
[98] See 3.4.8 above on main rivers.
[99] As provided for under s.108(1) and (2) relating to schemes for transfer to the Agency of functions in relation to a main river, and see 3.4.9 above.
[100] s.137(1) to (5) Water Resources Act 1991.
[101] s.138(1) to (3) Water Resources Act 1991. See also Schedule 15 Water Resources Act 1991 which governs the assessment, incidence, payment and enforcement of special drainage charges, discussed at 6.3.9 above.

## 6.4 INTERNAL DRAINAGE BOARDS

### 6.4.1 General Funding Position

In general terms, the expenses of internal drainage boards are met by the receipt of ministerial grant aid towards the costs incurred in carrying out drainage schemes, contributions from the Environment Agency, drainage rates imposed on agricultural hereditaments and levies on local billing authorities. Contributions from the Agency to internal drainage boards have been previously discussed, as have contributions to the Agency from internal drainage boards and the provisions that apply where the Agency acts as the internal drainage board.[102]

### 6.4.2 Grants to Drainage Bodies

The appropriate Minister, subject to Treasury approval, and subject to conditions, may make grants to drainage bodies,[103] including internal drainage boards,[104] for expenditure incurred in carrying out drainage schemes. Similarly, advances may be made for this purpose, in relation to future expenditure, where it appears that the work will be properly carried out.[105]

Specifically, the Minister, with Treasury approval, may make grants to internal drainage boards in respect of expenditure properly incurred in relation to:

(a) drainage works where, if the works are properly carried out, a grant would be payable;

(b) enabling internal drainage boards to determine whether drainage works, or drainage works of a particular description, should be carried out;

(c) obtaining or organising information, including information about natural processes affecting the coastline, to enable boards to formulate or develop plans with respect to the defence against sea water of any part of the coastline; or

---

[102] See 3.4.9 and 3.5.5 above on the Environment Agency acting as an internal drainage board.

[103] 'Drainage body' means the Environment Agency, an internal drainage board or any other body having the power to make or maintain works for the drainage of land (s.72(1) Land Drainage Act 1991).

[104] But excluding the Environment Agency, in respect of which powers to make grants in connection with drainage works are otherwise provided for (see s.147 Water Resources Act 1991 and discussion at 6.3.2 above).

[105] s.59(1) to (3) and (5) Land Drainage Act 1991.

(d) obtaining, at any time after the carrying out of drainage works, information with respect to the quality or effectiveness, or the effect on the environment of those works, or any matter of a financial nature relating to those works.[106]

In addition, the appropriate Minister, with Treasury approval, may make a grant to a board in respect of works undertaken on behalf of other persons[107] and reimbursement of costs from the person on behalf of whom the work has been undertaken will exclude any payment made by way of a grant. Grants may also be payable to a board in respect of expenditure incurred in carrying out works for the rebuilding or repair of any bridge maintained by the board unless these are maintenance works of a routine kind.[108]

### 6.4.3 Raising the Expenses of Internal Drainage Boards

With the exception of those expenses of an internal drainage board that are met by ministerial grants and contributions from the Environment Agency, expenses of boards are to be met by drainage rates on agricultural land and special levies issued to local billing authorities.[109] The expenses of a board that are raised by drainage rates are to be defrayed out of such rates without regard to the purposes for which expenses were incurred.[110]

Each internal drainage board must prepare a register containing prescribed information concerning drainage hereditaments in its district and a map showing particulars of hereditaments.[111] The register is to be maintained by the drainage board and is open to public inspection at the office of the board

---

[106] s.59(4) Land Drainage Act 1991, as amended by s.101(2) Environment Act 1995. The powers to make grants in relation to (b) to (d) are stated to be without prejudice to other powers to make grants or to impose conditions upon grants (under s.59(1), (2) and (4)(a) Land Drainage Act 1991).

[107] Under s.20 Land Drainage Act 1991 and see 4.6.4 above.

[108] s.59(6) and (7) Land Drainage Act 1991.

[109] s.36(1) Land Drainage Act 1991. That is, drainage rates raised in accordance with Chapter II of Part IV Land Drainage Act 1991 and previous provisions and special levies issued in accordance with regulations under s.75 Local Government Finance Act 1988 (see 6.4.9 below).

[110] s.36(2) Land Drainage Act 1991.

[111] s.52(1) Land Drainage Act 1991 and see Register of Drainage Boards Regulations 1968 (S.I. 1968 No.1672) which prescribe the form of the register, specify the information to be provided and the details to be shown on the map. The Regulations continue to have effect under Schedule 2 para.1(1) and (2) Water Consolidation (Consequential Provisions) Act 1991. On the meaning of 'hereditament' see s.64 Local Government Finance Act 1988, indicating that a 'hereditament' is a right to use land for certain purposes including the leasing of the land.

at reasonable times.[112] For the purpose of compiling the register, a board may serve on the owner of any hereditament a notice requiring the recipient to state his name and address and that of any other person who is an occupier of the hereditament. Failure, without reasonable excuse, to comply with a notice, or making a statement which is known to be false or recklessly making a statement which is false is an offence. Unless a reasonable excuse is shown, a person may be guilty of a further offence where the failure to comply with a notice continues after a conviction.[113]

The proportion of expenses of an internal drainage board to be raised through drainage rates must be equal to the 'agricultural proportion' of land values.[114] The proportion of the expenses of a board which is to be raised from special levies is the balance of the expenses which remains after the deduction of the proceeds of drainage rates. For these purposes, a drainage board must determine the aggregate value of the chargeable (agricultural)[115] properties in the district and the aggregate value of other land in the district. The 'agricultural proportion' is then determined by dividing the value of chargeable properties by the value of the other land in the district.[116]

In respect of non-agricultural properties drainage expenses are provided for by special levies issued to local billing authorities. In relation to the value of 'other' (non-agricultural) land a series of options are provided for in relation to properties shown in local non-domestic rating lists, domestic properties, other properties which are contained in the registers maintained by drainage boards, land which did not comprise agricultural land at 31 March 1990 (to which a nil value is given) and further properties where the value is calculated as an average of the previous categories.[117]

Drainage rates are to be made in a prescribed form[118] and to be treated as made on the date when a resolution is passed by the board authorising the rate.[119]

---

[112] s.52(2) Land Drainage Act 1991.
[113] s.53 Land Drainage Act 1991. The offence is punishable, on summary conviction, by a fine not exceeding level 4 on the standard scale, presently £1,000.
[114] See *Alford Drainage Board* v *Mablethorpe* (1985) 227 EC 867 and *N. Duckitt and Sons* v *Yorkshire River Authority* (1972) 223 EG 492, concerning the determination of annual value of agricultural land by an internal drainage board.
[115] A 'chargeable property' means a hereditament comprising agricultural land or buildings in respect of which drainage rates may be assessed: s.72(1) Land Drainage Act 1991.
[116] s.37(1) and (2) Land Drainage Act 1991.
[117] s.37(5) Land Drainage Act 1991, as modified by Internal Drainage Boards (Finance) Regulations 1992, S.I. 1992 No.3079.
[118] Under the Drainage Rates (Forms) Regulations 1993, S.I. 1993 No.223.
[119] See *R* v *Spilsby and Skyness Justices ex parte Alford Drainage Board*, unreported, Queen's Bench Division, 25 July 1985, concerning the duty to pay drainage rates notwithstanding that an appeal had been lodged with the Lands Tribunal.

## Internal Drainage Boards

A drainage rate will not be valid unless a notice of it stating the amount of the rate, the respective amounts of the board's expenses to be raised by means of drainage rates and special levies and the date is given within 10 days of it being made. Publicity requirements are provided for.[120] A drainage rate may be amended to conform with the statutory requirements where an error arises. Provision is also made for the service of notice of amendments and repayment of overpaid amounts or recovery of underpaid amounts.[121]

Arrears of drainage rates may be recovered by an internal drainage board in the same way as arrears for non-domestic rates may be recovered by a billing authority.[122] In proceedings for the recovery of drainage rates the defendant is not entitled to raise any matter which might have been raised in an appeal to the appropriate valuation tribunal or in an appeal to the Crown Court.[123] The powers to recover arrears are in addition to any powers conferred upon a drainage board by a local Act, but no distress for arrears may be levied on goods or chattels other than a person from who the arrears are entitled to be recovered. No proceedings may be brought for the enforcement of any charge on land created by a local Act for securing payment of arrears of any rate. A drainage board is not required to enforce payment of any drainage rate where the amount payable is insufficient to justify the expense of collection.[124]

### 6.4.4 Levying and Assessment of Drainage Rates

Internal drainage boards are entitled to make a drainage rate in respect of agricultural land and buildings in its district.[125] Subject to powers to make amendments, a drainage rate is to be made before 15 February in respect of the following financial year, but it is not invalidated because it is made on or after that date. Although drainage rates are levied upon the occupiers

---

[120] s.48 Land Drainage Act 1991.
[121] s.50 Land Drainage Act 1991.
[122] s.54(1) Land Drainage Act 1991, as amended by s.1 Local Government Finance Act 1992. That is, recovery is under Local Government Finance Act 1988 though the drainage board may by resolution authorise a member of the board to institute or defend proceedings (s.54(2) Land Drainage Act 1991).
[123] s.54(3) Land Drainage Act 1991, that is defences which might be raised in an appeal under s.45 (concerning appeals against determinations of annual value) or s.51 (concerning appeals against other drainage rates). See *Chelmer and Blackwater Navigation Ltd* v *Essex Rivers Catchment Board* (1951) 157 EG 416.
[124] s.54(4) to (6) Land Drainage Act 1991.
[125] See *Collard* v *River Stour (Kent) Catchment Board* [1937] 1 All ER 436 where it was found that tidal land was not exempt from drainage rates. See *West of Ouse Internal Drainage Board* v *H. Prins Ltd* (1978) 247 EG 295 on the assessment of agricultural value of agricultural buildings.

of hereditaments in the district, the owner of a hereditament is deemed to be its occupier during any period during which it is unoccupied.[126]

Drainage rates are to be assessed on the person who, at the date of making the rate, is the occupier of the relevant hereditament. Hence, the full rate for the financial year will be recoverable from the occupier, but persons who are in occupation for only part of the year will be liable to pay only a proportionate part. Accordingly, where occupation changes during the year, the previous occupier may recover proportionate amounts of the rate from subsequent occupiers, subject to any agreement to the contrary. Where the name of the occupier is not known, that person may be assessed as 'the occupier' of the relevant premises, but a demand for a drainage rate must be in the prescribed form.[127]

Subject to certain exceptions,[128] a drainage rate made by an internal drainage board must be assessed at a uniform rate per pound on agricultural land and buildings throughout the district. The annual value of any chargeable property must, subject to provision for adjustments, be an amount which is equal to the yearly rent at which the holding might reasonably be expected to have been let by a prudent and willing landlord to a prudent and willing tenant on a tenancy from year to year commencing 1 April 1988 on relevant terms.[129]

In determining the yearly rent for which a property might reasonably be expected to be let, the liability to pay drainage rents is to be disregarded, but account may be taken of all other relevant factors. Such factors include the character and situation of the holding, the productive capacity of the holding and its related earning capacity, and the level of rents for comparable lettings. In determining the level of rents for comparable lettings, certain matters are to be disregarded including elements in the rent due to

---

[126] s.40 Land Drainage Act 1991.
[127] s.49 Land Drainage Act 1991, and see Drainage Rates (Forms) Regulations 1993, S.I. 1993 No.223.
[128] See 6.4.7 below on subdivision of districts for rating purposes (under s.38 Land Drainage Act 1991) and 6.4.8 below on exemptions from rating (under s.47).
[129] s.41(1) to (4) Land Drainage Act 1991 and see the Agriculture (Maintenance, Repair and Insurance of Fixed Equipment) Regulations 1973, S.I. 1973 No.1473, as amended. 'Relevant terms' means a letting of the property incorporating terms concerning liability for destruction of crops in accordance with good husbandry requirements; a covenant requiring insurance against specified fire damage; a power of the landlord to re-enter in default of the tenant performing obligations under the agreement; a covenant by the tenant not to assign or sub-let without the landlord's consent; and a requirement that the property is let on specified terms relating to maintenance repair and insurance of fixed equipment. See *R v Hastings Justices ex parte Pevensey Levels Internal Drainage Board* [1962] 1 All ER 278 on the need for fairness in the assessment of annual values.

*Internal Drainage Boards* 269

appreciable scarcity of comparable holdings, elements in rents attributable to the occupation of other land in the vicinity and the effect on rents of allowances or reductions made in consideration of the charging of premiums.[130]

Applying the agricultural valuation principles, internal drainage boards were bound to determine the annual value for each chargeable property in their district by 31 December 1992.[131] After that date, where any property in a district becomes chargeable property or any agricultural property becomes part of a district, the board is bound to determine its annual value as soon as practicable. This determination will have effect from the date of valuation. Where a determination is made, either initially or at a subsequent valuation date, the board is to serve a notice of the determination on the relevant occupier, along with a statement of right of appeal against the determination. To allow boards to comply with these obligations, occupiers of chargeable property are bound to afford reasonable facilities for inspecting the property.[132]

### 6.4.5 Adjustment of Annual Values

Provision is made for the adjustment of annual values to secure a fair distribution of the rating burden. Hence, if the amount of the annual value for any chargeable property in a district is increased or reduced, the internal drainage board may make a determination accordingly. The occupier of a chargeable property who is of the opinion that the annual value of the property should be altered may also request the board to make a determination. The board must either comply with the request or, if it is considered that no alteration of value is required, refuse the request. The basis for adjustment of annual value in these circumstances is that there have been changes to relevant circumstances and to other alterations of annual values which have been made or proposed by the board. That is, there has been a change to the circumstances by reference to which the annual value of the property in question, or any other chargeable property in the district, was fixed.[133]

Where a determination has been made in accordance with the provisions for adjustment of annual values, the internal drainage board is bound to

---

[130] s.41(5) and (6) Land Drainage Act 1991. See *Pyman Bell (Holdings) Ltd v Northmoor District Drainage Board* (1995) unreported, Lands Tribunal, 20 October 1995, on the assessment of annual value of agricultural land.
[131] See *Port of London Authority v Essex Rivers Catchment Board* [1944] 2 All ER 507 illustrating the absence of any duty upon internal drainage boards to make a determination of annual values on an annual basis.
[132] s.42 Land Drainage Act 1991.
[133] s.43 Land Drainage Act 1991.

serve notice of the determination, together with a statement of the rights of appeal, on the occupier of the chargeable property. Following an adjustment of annual value at the initiative of the board, the annual value of the property must, for the purpose of any subsequent drainage rate, be the value specified in the determination. Where the determination is made as a consequence of a request by an occupier, the annual value of the property is to be that specified in the determination for any drainage rate within the financial year in which the request for the determination was made, and subsequently. Consequently, provision is made for the repayment of any sum overpaid and the recovery of any sum underpaid.[134]

### 6.4.6 Appeals against Determinations of Annual Value and Drainage Rates

In relation to either an initial or subsequent determination of annual value by an internal drainage board, an occupier may appeal. An occupier wishing to appeal must serve notice of objection upon the board, stating the grounds of the objection, within a 28-day period from the service of the determination or such longer period as the board may allow. Where a notice of objection is served upon the board, it may cancel the determination and may make a fresh determination. However, where the board does not cancel the determination, it is bound to transmit the notice and a notice of the determination to the clerk of the 'appropriate tribunal'. This transmission of the notice constitutes a lodging of an appeal against the determination by the person who served the notice to a valuation tribunal established for the area.[135]

The President of the valuation tribunal must arrange for the appeal to be heard and determined. This involves a tribunal being constituted to determine appeals concerning determinations of annual value in accordance with the General Rate Act 1967,[136] which allows the objector, any other person who is an occupier of the land and the drainage board to appear and to call and examine witnesses in a public hearing. An appeal lies from the valuation tribunal to the Lands Tribunal. The outcome of the appeal will be a decision to quash the determination, to alter it or to dismiss the appeal. Where a determination of annual value is quashed or altered on appeal,

---

[134] s.44 Land Drainage Act 1991.
[135] s.45 Land Drainage Act 1991, as amended. The 'appropriate tribunal' for the area is established under regulations under Schedule 11 Local Government Finance Act 1988, as amended, and where the land falls into the areas of different tribunals the appropriate tribunal is determined by the Drainage Rates (Appeals) Regulations 1970, S.I. 1970 No.1152, as amended.
[136] See s.88(5) General Rate Act 1967, as amended and repealed with savings.

the amount of annual value must be recalculated, and any sum overpaid must be repaid and any sum underpaid recovered as arrears of drainage rates.[137]

On matters other than determinations of annual value, appeals may be made to the Crown Court by any person who is an occupier in a drainage district and who is aggrieved by a drainage rate. Notice of the appeal must be given to the Crown Court, the internal drainage board and the occupier of the hereditament if the appellant is not in occupation. The notice must specify the grounds of the appeal and must be given within 28 days of the date on which the rate is made or the notice of amendment served on the appellant. It is open to the Crown Court to confirm the rate, to annul it or to modify it. However, the appellant and the respondent to an appeal may agree in writing to refer the dispute to arbitration by a person agreed between them or, in default of agreement, to a person appointed by the relevant Minister.[138]

### 6.4.7 Differential Drainage Rates

After consultation with the Environment Agency, an internal drainage board may divide its district into sub-districts for the purpose of levying differential drainage rates or issuing differential special levies. Hence, if it is regarded as 'just' to do so, the board may exercise its powers concerning drainage rates to make and levy differential drainage rates or differential special levies.[139] An order which is made for these purposes may determine the proportions of the expenses of the board which are to be raised in the respective sub-districts within the district.[140]

Where an order subdividing an internal drainage district does not determine the proportions of the expenses of an internal drainage board which are to be raised in the respective sub-districts, a general formula is applied. This requires that expenses incurred in connection with new works or the maintenance or improvement of existing works in a sub-district are to be raised in that sub-district. In addition, in each sub-district there must be raised a proportionate part of the charges incurred by the board in respect of contributions to the Environment Agency, or amounts corresponding to

---

[137] s.46 Land Drainage Act 1991, as amended, and further on jurisdiction and procedure see Drainage Rates (Appeals) Regulations 1970, S.I. 1970 No.1152, as amended.
[138] s.51 Land Drainage Act 1991.
[139] s.38(1) Land Drainage Act 1991. That is, the board may exercise its powers under Chapter II of Part IV of the Land Drainage Act 1991 (concerning drainage rates) and powers under any regulations made under s.75 Local Government Finance Act 1988, as amended (concerning special levies).
[140] s.38(1) and (2) Land Drainage Act 1991.

such contributions,[141] and other expenses and charges not directly attributable to the maintenance of particular works.[142]

Where an order subdividing a district is in force, the proportions of the expenses of the board raised in a sub-district, must, in each financial year, bear the same proportions to each other as the aggregate values of chargeable properties and the values of other land in the sub-district. Hence, provisions concerning the apportionment of drainage expenses of boards in a district are to be applied to determine aggregate amounts for sub-districts.[143]

The procedure relating to the making of an order for subdivision of a drainage district requires the internal drainage board to submit the proposed order to the relevant Minister and publish a notice stating that the order has been submitted to the Minister. The notice must also state that a copy of the order is open to inspection at a specified place and that representations may be made to the Minister within 1 month after the publication of the notice. The order will not take effect unless and until confirmed by the Minister.[144]

A power is given to a 'sufficient number of qualified persons'[145] or a 'qualified authority'[146] to petition for the making, revocation or varying of sub-districts of an internal drainage district. Hence, where a petition for the making, variation or revocation of an order subdividing a district is made to an internal drainage board, the board is bound to consider the petition. If directed, it must make, vary or revoke the order, either in accordance with the petition or in accordance with the petition as modified by the direction. For these purposes, a direction may be given by either of the Ministers if the Environment Agency is the board and, where the Agency is not the board, a direction may be given by the Agency. Where the board objects to a direction which is given by the Agency, it will not take effect until it is confirmed, with or without modifications, by the relevant Minister.[147]

---

[141] That is, contributions to the Agency under s.139 Water Resources Act 1991 (see 6.3.6 above on this) and amounts specified under s.58 Land Drainage Act 1991 as corresponding to such contributions (see 6.3.8 above on this).
[142] s.38(3) Land Drainage Act 1991.
[143] s.38(4) Land Drainage Act 1991. That is s.37(2) to (6) are to be used for determining aggregate amounts for sub-districts and see 6.4.7 above on the apportionment of drainage expenses.
[144] s.38(5) and (6) Land Drainage Act 1991.
[145] On 'sufficient number of qualified persons' see notes to 6.3.8 above.
[146] 'Qualified authority', in relation to an internal drainage district, means a billing authority for an area wholly or partly included in that district (s.72(1) Land Drainage Act 1991, as amended).
[147] s.39(1) to (3) Land Drainage Act 1991.

## Internal Drainage Boards

The procedures relating to petitions for the subdivision of internal drainage districts require the internal drainage board to inform the Environment Agency or, if the Agency is the board, one of the Ministers. The board must also publish a notice stating that the petition has been received for the making, variation or revocation of an order subdividing the district and that representations may be made to the board within a stated period of not less than 30 days. After considering a petition, and not later than 6 months after it is received, the drainage board must inform the Agency, or one of the Ministers if the Agency is the drainage board, whether it proposes to make, vary or revoke an order subdividing a district and the terms of any order or variation which is proposed.[148]

### 6.4.8 Exemption from Drainage Rates

After consultation with the Environment Agency, an internal drainage board may determine that no drainage rates will be levied on the occupiers of hereditaments in any portion of the district.[149] Specifically, a determination allowing exemption from drainage rates may be made because of the height above sea level of the land which is the subject of the exemption or 'for any other reason'.[150]

The procedures involved in allowing exemption from drainage rates follow those relating to orders for the subdivision of a drainage district. Hence the internal drainage board will be required to submit the proposed order to the relevant Minister and publicise the order by a notice indicating where the proposal may be inspected and inviting representations to be made.[151] Where the occupier of any hereditament in a district requests the board to make or amend an order for exemption so as to exempt that portion of the district, the board must consider the request and, if directed, must comply with it. If the request is refused by the drainage board, the person making the request may appeal to the Environment Agency or, if the board is the Agency, to the relevant Minister. As the case may be, the Agency or the Minister may direct the board to make or amend the order as requested. The failure of a board to refuse or to comply with a request within 3 months

---

[148] s.39(4) to (7) Land Drainage Act 1991, though provision is made for petitions not to be considered where they are made within 10 years of a previous petition or subdivision of a district, or where, in the opinion of the Agency or Minister, a petition is frivolous (s.39(6)).

[149] See *Trent River Authority v National Coal Board* [1970] 1 All ER 558 where it was found that a 'portion' of a district means a portion of the surface area and there is no power to exempt underground workings from drainage rates despite the fact that they derived no benefit from drainage operations.

[150] s.47(1) Land Drainage Act 1991.

[151] s.47(2) Land Drainage Act 1991, applying s.38(5) to (7) to exemption orders and see 6.4.7 above on this.

### 6.4.9 Special Levies

As has been noted, the expenses of an internal drainage board, insofar as they are not met by contributions from the Environment Agency, are met by a combination of drainage rates upon agricultural land occupiers and special levies upon local authorities to raise the balance of the expenses of the board which are outstanding after deduction of the amount raised through drainage rates.[153] Accordingly, provision is made for a board to meet an appropriate part of its expenses by the issue of a special levy upon a local billing authority in respect of any financial year in accordance with regulations made under the local government legislation.[154]

The Internal Drainage Boards (Finance) Regulations 1992[155] modify the power of internal drainage boards to issue special levies upon local billing authorities. These Regulations require a special levy to be issued before the 15 February in the preceding financial year, though the levy is not invalidated where it is issued after that date. Where more than one billing authority is located within a district, the internal drainage board must secure that its expenses which are to be met by special levies are met by billing authorities proportionately. This must be done by reference to the aggregate annual value of the land, other than agricultural land or buildings, within each billing authority's area or that part of the land which lies within the district.

An internal drainage board which has issued a special levy in respect of a financial year may issue a new special levy in substitution. This may arise because of a failure to secure that its expenses are proportionately met by local billing authorities or if it appears necessary for the board to do so in order to make the levy conform with the provisions of the relevant regulations. For example, this may be done to correct clerical or arithmetical errors or to make corrections which are necessary because of boundary changes in the district or the district of a billing authority.

A special levy must be issued within 10 days of being made. The levy must

---

[152] s.47(3) to (5) Land Drainage Act 1991.
[153] See s.36 Land Drainage Act 1991 (on raising of expenses of internal drainage boards), discussed at 6.4.3 above, and s.37 (on the apportionment of drainage expenses), discussed at 6.4.7 above.
[154] That is, regulations under s.75 Local Government Finance Act 1988, as amended.
[155] S.I. 1992 No.3079. These Regulations were needed to take account of the system of local government finance introduced by the Local Government Finance Act 1992 for the financial year 1993–94 onwards.

state the amount, the billing authority to which it is issued and the date of issue and must be issued to every billing authority for any area wholly or partly included in the district. A board must maintain a record of any special levy issued showing the amount of the levy, the dates on which it was made and issued, the billing authority to which it was issued and the proportion of expenses raised in each financial year from the proceeds of drainage rates and special levies. The record must be made available for public inspection by members of the public at all reasonable times at the board's principal office.

A billing authority to which an internal drainage board has issued a special levy must pay the amount of the levy in that year at a time and in such instalments, if any, as agreed between the authority and the board. In default of agreement, the levy is payable by two equal instalments on 1 May and 1 November in the relevant financial year. Where, at a time when a billing authority makes a calculation of its budget requirements, a board with power to issue a levy to that authority has not issued a levy in respect of that financial year, the authority may take into account, in estimating its expenditure, its estimate of the amount of any special levy that it expects to be issued by the board.

### 6.4.10 Borrowing Powers

An internal drainage board may borrow, on the security of its property or income, for the purpose of defraying any costs, charges or expenses incurred in the execution of the Land Drainage Act 1991 or for the purpose of discharging any loan contracted under the Act. However, the consent of the relevant Minister is required for borrowing by a board other than for the purpose of discharging any loan previously contracted. Money may be borrowed by a board for a period, not exceeding 50 years, as the relevant Minister may determine. Where a board borrows sums for which only a part of the district will be liable, the money which has been borrowed must be repayable only out of rates levied on, or special levies issued or contributions received in respect of that part of the district.[156]

### 6.4.11 Local Authority Contributions to Drainage Expenses

A local authority[157] may contribute, or undertake to contribute, to the expenses of carrying out or maintaining any drainage works by a drainage body such an amount as is considered proper, having regard to the public benefit derived therefrom. Hence, contributions may be made by a local

---

[156] s.55(1) and (3) to (5) Land Drainage Act 1991.
[157] 'Local authority' for this purpose includes the Sub-Treasurer of the Inner Temple and the Under Treasurer of the Middle Temple (s.60(3) Land Drainage Act 1991).

authority to drainage works undertaken by an internal drainage board, or drainage works undertaken by another local authority. Making contributions of this kind is stated to be a purpose for which local authorities may borrow.[158]

## 6.5 LOCAL AUTHORITIES AND LAND DRAINAGE FINANCE

Many of the financial provisions concerning local authority land drainage expenses are similar to, or intimately connected with, the financial position of internal drainage boards and have been implicitly covered in the previous discussion. They may, however, be summarised at this juncture.

A local authority may receive a ministerial grant in the same way as an internal drainage board.[159] Local authorities may contribute, or undertake to contribute, an appropriate amount to the expenses of the carrying out or maintenance of any drainage works by a drainage body and have the power to borrow for this purpose.[160] More general powers are provided to allow the council of a county or London borough and the Common Council of the City of London may borrow for the purposes of the Land Drainage Act 1991.[161]

Generally, the expenses of the council of a metropolitan district or London borough under the Land Drainage Act 1991, or the flood defence provisions under the Water Resources Act 1991, must be defrayed as general expenses or, if thought fit, must be defrayed as special expenses charged to such parts of the metropolitan district or borough as thought fit.[162] However, a major expense of local authorities in relation to flood defence is likely to arise in respect of levies which are payable to the Environment Agency[163] and in respect of these more specific provisions apply.[164] These require that amounts due to the Agency from a county council in respect of levies must be defrayed, as the council thinks just and equitable, having regard to the benefit, if any, derived by various areas, in any of the following ways:

---

[158] s.60(1) and (2) Land Drainage Act 1991.
[159] Under s.59 Land Drainage Act 1991, as amended.
[160] s.60(1) and (2) Land Drainage Act 1991. For these purposes a 'drainage body' would include the Environment Agency, an internal drainage board or another local authority.
[161] s.55(2) Land Drainage Act 1991.
[162] s.61(1) Land Drainage Act 1991.
[163] Under s.133 Water Resources Act 1991.
[164] Under s.110 Land Drainage Act 1976. Although s.110 has been repealed, it is saved by Schedule 2 para.2(5) Water Consolidation (Consequential Provisions) Act 1991 for the purposes of the National Rivers Authority (Levies) Regulations 1993, S.I. 1993 No.61, as amended, and see 6.3.5 above on these Regulations.

(a) as general expenses;

(b) as special expenses chargeable on parts of the county within the area of the appropriate regional flood defence committee; or

(c) by apportioning the expenses between, and charging them on, such parts of the county, in such proportions as the council thinks fit, and by the issue of precepts to billing authorities.

Similarly, any amounts which are due from a London borough council or metropolitan district council by way of levies to the Agency are defrayed as either general expenses or special expenses. The expenses of a county, metropolitan district or London borough council incurred under the Land Drainage Act 1991 or the flood defence provisions of the Water Resources Act 1991 may be defrayed as general expenses or as special expenses charged on such parts of the county, district or borough as the council thinks fit, unless an expense is statutorily required to be otherwise defrayed.[165] Examples of expenses which are otherwise defrayed arise in relation to certain works undertaken by agreement,[166] the recovery of expenses from a person in default,[167] and expenses from the owner or occupier of land under a scheme for drainage of a small area.[168]

## 6.6 FUNDING OF COAST PROTECTION WORKS

The funding of coast protection works has previously been considered[169] and it has been noted that ministerial grants are payable towards expenditure by coast protection authorities.[170] Since 1985, when responsibility for flood protection and coast protection were consolidated within the same ministries, the administration of funding for these activities has been harmonised. Hence, as has been seen,[171] the criteria which are applied for funding coast protection projects are the same as those applicable to projects for flood defence purposes.

---

[165] s.110(1) to (3) Land Drainage Act 1976, repealed with savings
[166] Under s.20(1) Land Drainage Act 1991 and see 4.6.4 above.
[167] Under s.25 Land Drainage Act 1991 and see 4.4.5 above.
[168] Under s.18 Land Drainage Act 1991 and see 4.6.3 above.
[169] See 5.4.14 above on coast protection funding.
[170] s.21 Coast Protection Act 1949.
[171] See 6.2 above on central government funding.

# Chapter 7

# SEWERAGE AND WATER SUPPLY

## 7.1 INTRODUCTION

Although the preceding discussion has focused upon the legal implications of flooding from watercourses and the sea, another important cause of flooding is the overloading of sewerage systems, particularly where they receive surface water run-off. Here, the immediate problem is frequently of an infrastructural kind, with sewers becoming increasingly inadequate to accommodate increasing amounts of waste water from catchments which have been subject to building development and have placed increased demands upon the sewerage system.[1] Understandably, sewerage undertakers are commonly perceived as the culprits of the situation for not enlarging sewer capacity sufficiently to accommodate the increase in flow. However, this perception fails to take account of the legally curious position in which undertakers are placed by having no effective power to prevent connections to sewers. This general lack of legal control over the quantities of effluent passed into sewers has the counterpart that undertakers, traditionally at least, have not normally been found liable for sewer flooding which is a consequence of overloading.

Another water utility issue, which is conveniently considered alongside sewer flooding, is that of escapes of water from water supply pipes of various kinds. In circumstances where a water main has fractured and flooded surrounding properties, again, there is a natural inclination to look to water undertakers, as the owners of the main, as the targets for liability. Here, however, the legislation follows the intuition and, within quite broad limits, water suppliers are strictly liable for flooding caused by escapes of water from their pipes. The contrast is evident: whilst sewerage undertakers have no overall control of what enters their sewers, water suppliers do have control over the content of water supply pipes, and legal responsibility reflects this control.

Although the broad principles and contrasts are usefully sketched out at this juncture, the issues of detail arising from sewerage and water supply responsibilities are of some complexity, and most of these can only be

---

[1] For a general background see R. W. P. May, P. Martin and N. J. Price, *Low-cost Options for Prevention of Flooding from Sewers* (1998) Construction Industry Research and Information Association Report C506.

outlined in the discussion which follows.[2] Two matters, however, which are of some gravity and justify more detailed comment are the knotty problem of determining whether or not a drainage channel is a 'public sewer', for the purpose of establishing the responsibilities of sewerage undertakers, and the recently raised issue of whether sewage flooding constitutes a breach of human rights legislation which justifies a reassessment of sewerage undertakers' traditional liabilities. These matters, and other issues brought within this chapter, are all to be viewed against the background of a privatised system of water utility services which has existed in England and Wales since 1989. The contrasts between the obligations imposed upon essentially private commercial organisations to provide water services and the allocation of obligations upon public bodies in respect of general flood and coastal defence, described in earlier chapters, will be readily apparent.

## 7.2 SEWERAGE RESPONSIBILITIES

The regulatory framework for sewerage undertakers is provided for in Part IV Water Industry Act 1991 which imposes a general duty upon undertakers to provide, improve and extend a system of public sewers and to cleanse and maintain sewers so as to ensure that an undertaker's area is effectually drained. In addition, an undertaker must make provision for emptying sewers and for effectually dealing with their contents, by means of sewage disposal works or otherwise.[3] However, a sewerage undertaker may enter into an 'agency agreement' with a local authority in respect of sewerage services, with the exception of functions relating to sewage disposal and the discharge of trade effluent into sewers, and such agreements will allow the authority to provide sewerage services on behalf of the undertaker. Agency agreements do not affect any remedy that is available against an undertaker in respect of a failure to comply with its statutory sewerage duties.[4]

The general duties of a sewerage undertaker may be enforced by the Secretary of State or, with his authorisation, by the Director General of Water Services[5] and provision is made for enforcement orders and proceedings where conditions of an undertaker's appointment or statutory or other requirements are contravened.[6]

---

[2] Generally see J. H. Bates. *Water and Drainage Law* (1990 updated) Ch.9; J. F. Garner and S. H. Bailey, *The Law of Sewers and Drains* (8th ed. 1995); J. D. Leeson, *Environmental Law* (1995) Ch.8; and W. Howarth and D. McGillivray, *Water Pollution and Water Quality Law* (2001) Chs.7, 11 and 17.
[3] s.94(1) Water Industry Act 1991.
[4] s.97 Water Industry Act 1991.
[5] s.94(3) Water Industry Act 1991.
[6] s.18 Water Industry Act 1991.

More specifically, a sewerage undertaker is under a duty to provide a public sewer to drain domestic premises in its area where specified persons make a requisition. Hence a sewer may be requisitioned by owners or occupiers of premises in the locality or a local authority within whose area the locality is situated.[7] The premises must be those on which there are buildings, or on which building work is proposed, where specified financial conditions are satisfied.[8]

Alternatively, a sewerage undertaker may, either of its own volition or in response to an application from the owner, make a declaration vesting a sewer or any sewage disposal works in itself. In making a declaration, the undertaker must have regard to all the circumstances but, in particular, it must consider certain matters: whether the sewer is adapted to any general system provided, or to be provided; whether the sewer is constructed under a highway; the number of buildings to be served, or likely to be served; the method of construction and state of repair of the sewer; and whether the declaration would be detrimental to an owner who objects.[9] Any person who immediately before the declaration was entitled to use the sewer will continue to be entitled to use it to the same extent as if the declaration had not been made.[10]

A person constructing or proposing to construct a sewer may apply to a sewerage undertaker requesting it to declare that the sewer will be vested in it, providing that it is constructed in accordance with an agreement between the undertaker and the person making the application.[11] An 'adoption' agreement of this kind will provide that, on satisfactory completion of the work and at some future date, the undertaker will make a vesting declaration. A declaration made in accordance with this procedure will be enforceable against the undertaker by future owners or occupiers of the premises that are served by the sewer.[12] However, provision is made for an owner of sewer who is aggrieved by the refusal of an undertaker to make a vesting declaration, or by an offer to make an agreement on objectionable terms, to appeal to the Secretary of State.[13]

---

[7] s.98(1) and (2) Water Industry Act 1991.
[8] s.99 Water Industry Act 1991, which also provides for the costs to be paid to the sewerage undertaker.
[9] See *R* v *Secretary of State for Wales and A. B. Hutton (Secretary to the Maes Gerddi Residents Association)* [1987] JPL 711.
[10] s.102 Water Industry Act 1991.
[11] In practice, agreements of this kind are likely to follow the guidelines provided for construction of sewers established by the water industry: see Water UK and WRc, *Sewers for Adoption* (5th ed. 2001).
[12] s.104 Water Industry Act 1991.
[13] s.105 Water Industry Act 1991.

The owner or occupier of premises or the owner of any private drain or sewer draining premises is normally entitled to have the drain or sewer communicate with the public sewers of an undertaker and to discharge foul water and surface water from the premises.[14] The 'right of connection' is subject to restrictions concerning discharges from manufacturing processes and prohibited substances, and connection may be declined where the mode of construction or condition of the drain or sewer is such that the connection would be prejudicial to the undertaker's sewerage system. Where separate sewers are provided by the undertaker for foul water and surface water, the right of connection only allows discharges to be made to the appropriate sewer and there is no right of direct connection in relation to a storm-water overflow sewer.[15] Notably also, restrictions are imposed upon the substances which may be allowed to enter public sewers[16] and the consent of the undertaker is required for the discharge of trade effluent.[17]

## 7.3 THE DEFINITIONS OF 'SEWER' AND 'DRAIN'

Important, but practically problematic, issues arise in applying the terminology in which statutory responsibilities for sewerage is couched, and particularly the distinction between a 'sewer' and a 'drain'. Although the terms 'sewer' and 'drain' have no precise meaning as a matter of common law,[18] they are explicitly defined under the Water Industry Act 1991 as follows.

> 'Drain' is defined as meaning a drain used for the drainage of one building or yards appurtenant to buildings within the same 'curtilage'.

> 'Sewer' is defined as including all sewers and drains (not being drains within the meaning given above) which are used for the drainage of buildings and yards appurtenant to buildings.[19]

---

[14] See *William Leech (Midlands)* v *Severn-Trent Water Authority* (1981) *The Times*, 5 June, on the duty of a sewerage undertaker to make a connection to a sewer.
[15] s.106(1), (2) and (6) Water Industry Act 1991. See *Tayside Regional Council* v *Secretary of State for Scotland*, unreported, Scots Court of Session, Outer House, 19 December 1994, where, under Scots legislation, it was held that a local authority was not entitled to refuse to allow connection to a sewer even in circumstances where the sewer was already overloaded.
[16] s.111 Water Industry Act 1991.
[17] s.118 Water Industry Act 1991.
[18] Note also that in other contexts the word 'sewer' may be more generally interpreted. Hence in *Doncaster Borough Council* v *Secretary of State for the Environment* (1996) 74 P&CR 428 it was held that a drainage ditch came within the meaning of 'sewer' so that explicit planning permission was not required to undertake operations for the removal of silt and vegetation (under Art.3(1) and Schedule 2 Part 9 Class A Town and Country Planning (General Development Procedure) Order 1995, S.I. 1995 No.419).
[19] s.219(1) Water Industry Act 1991.

## Sewerage and Water Supply

The statutory definitions of 'drain' and 'sewer' seem rather uninformative, but their mutual exclusivity serves to emphasise a key point of contrast. This is that 'drain' is the name given to a drainage channel that serves one or more buildings or areas within a single curtilage, whereas a 'sewer' is a drainage channel that serves different buildings or areas that are not within the same curtilage. Hence, the 'general rule' has been stated that where a pipe receives the waste water from two or more houses it is a sewer but where it receives the waste water of one house only it remains a drain. However, it is recognised that the general rule may be subject to exceptions where a sewer takes the sewage of one house only or of no houses at all. An example of this could arise where a main sewer is laid down in a new street where no houses are yet built, but where it is intended that houses will be built. Subsequently, the buildings may be commenced at the lower end of the street and when the drain of one house is connected with the main sewer the connecting pipe will be a drain and not a sewer, but the sewer itself will no less continue to be a sewer, though it receives the waste water from only a single property.[20]

The underlying difficulty in the distinction between sewers and drains is that everything is dependent upon how the boundaries between properties are drawn and their respective 'curtilages'. 'Curtilage' has been defined as being surrounding land which is used for the comfortable enjoyment of a house and as an integral part of that enjoyment, even though this land is not marked off or enclosed. Hence, land has been found to be part of the curtilage if it serves the purposes of the house in some reasonably useful way.[21]

Nonetheless, the practical difficulties in determining the extent of a 'curtilage' in relation to adjoining buildings is well illustrated by *Weaver v Family Housing Association (York) Ltd*.[22] Here the cellar of the claimant's property had become flooded with sewage due to blockages in underground pipes. The question as to who was responsible for maintaining the pipes, or improving the drainage system, depended upon whether the pipes constituted a 'drain' or a 'sewer'. This depended upon whether the houses

---

[20] *Beckenham Urban District Council* v *Wood* (1896) 60 JP 490 and see *Holland* v *Lazarus* (1897) 66 LJ QB 285. See also *Bromley London Borough Council* v *Morritt* (2000) 79 P&CR 536 where it was held that a pipe laid across the defendant's land was a sewer because it had been constructed as such and despite the fact that it only served a single property; and see the discussion of functionality at 7.4 below.

[21] See *Sinclair-Lockhart's Trustees* v *Central Land Board* (1950) 1 P&CR 195, though other dicta have emphasised the need for 'enclosure' or 'land within an enclosure': see *Weaver* v *Family Housing Association (York) Ltd* (1975) 74 LGR 255, per Lord Simon at p.262.

[22] (1975) 74 LGR 255. See also *Vestry of St Martin in the Fields* v *Bird* [1895] 1 QB 428 and *Pillbrow* v *Shoreditch Vestry* [1895] 1 QB 433.

were 'within the same curtilage' or whether the terrace constituted 'one building'.[23] The claimant's property was part of a terrace of eight houses, built under a continuous slate roof and originally in common ownership, but other properties in the terrace were now owned by the defendants. On the facts, it was held that the terrace constituted more than one building and the houses within the terrace were not within the same curtilage, with the consequence that the drainage system was established to be a 'sewer' which it was the local authority's responsibility to maintain. Nevertheless, the essentially factual nature of this determination was emphasised.[24] Conflicting criteria had to be weighed against one another. Structural unity, original unity of ownership and a shared drainage system tended to indicate a single curtilage, whereas separate occupation, the absence of intercommunication and separate lavatories and outside storage facilities tended to indicate multiple curtilages.[25]

The statutory definitions of 'drain' and 'sewer' are made subject to a proviso that references to a 'pipe', 'sewer' or 'drain' are to include references to a tunnel or conduit and any accessories for the pipe, sewer or drain. Accordingly, references to the laying of a pipe will include references to the construction of a tunnel or conduit, to the construction or installation of any accessories and the making of a connection between one pipe and another. Perhaps most importantly, a *'public* sewer' means a sewer that is vested in a sewerage undertaker in its capacity as such and 'private sewer' is to be construed accordingly.[26] Hence, the allocation of responsibility for a particular drainage channel to an undertaker involves two determinations being made: first, that the channel is a sewer, rather than a drain; and, second, that the channel is a public sewer, rather than a private sewer.

The rather terse statutory definitions that are provided of the terms 'sewer' and 'drain' have given rise to a substantial body of litigation revolving around the issue of whether a particular facility falls within one or other of the definitions. Most commonly these cases have been brought to ascertain the maintenance responsibilities of sewerage undertakers, or previous bodies with sewerage responsibilities. However, analogous concerns arise where the issue of responsibility for flooding is in contention where, again, it needs to be asked whether a particular water channel is a *'sewer'* and, if so, whether it is a *'public'* sewer.

---

[23] Under s.4 Public Health Act 1875; now see s.219(1) Water Industry Act 1991.
[24] Remarkably, courts have refused to establish a rule as to whether semi-detached houses constitute a 'single building' or not: see *Humphrey* v *Young* [1903] 1 KB 44 and contrast *Hedley* v *Webb* [1901] 2 Ch 126.
[25] See also *Cook* v *Minion* (1978) 37 P&CR 58.
[26] s.219(1) and (2) Water Industry Act 1991 and, similarly, see s.343 Public Health Act 1936. On the vesting of sewers in sewerage undertakers see 7.6 below.

## 7.4 THE FUNCTIONAL DEFINITION OF 'PUBLIC SEWER'

Despite the potential complexity involved in establishing whether a particular drainage channel is a 'public sewer',[27] as a broad generality, most of the issues come down to a test of functionality: the question of whether a particular drainage facility is either initially constructed or, in some instances, actually used for the drainage of buildings and yards. The application of the basic functionality test, however, is sometimes obscured by circumstances where changes of use are evident or where older cases, which seem to have added a 'proper outfall' requirement to the statutory definition of 'sewer', need to be interpreted in context.

### 7.4.1 Purpose of Construction

A useful illustration of the functional approach to determining whether a particular water channel is a sewer is to be found in *Blackdown Properties Ltd* v *Ministry of Housing and Local Government*.[28] Here the claimants were the owners of land where houses had been built and, in accordance with the requirements of the defendant local authority,[29] a foul sewer had been constructed. Following the construction of this sewer, and again with local authority consent, the claimants decided to alter the sewerage system by constructing another sewer that communicated with the original sewer part way along its length. Although the upper part of the original sewer had been used for a few months, it became redundant and was sealed-off by the claimants. Following this, the authority gave notice[30] that the whole of the original sewer, including the part which had been sealed-off, should become vested in the authority since it appeared that the authority envisaged that it might subsequently be used to serve other properties. The Minister allowed the adoption of the sealed-off length of sewer and the claimants contested this ruling as being wrong in law.

The claimants' argument was that the sealed-off length of pipe was not a 'sewer' within its statutory meaning,[31] because it was not being used as a sewer at the time when the notice was given by the local authority. Whilst it was accepted that a sewer could cease to be a sewer as a result of alteration of a system of drainage,[32] no alteration had taken place in the

---

[27] Generally see J. F. Garner and S. H. Bailey, *The Law of Sewers and Drains* (8th ed. 1995) Ch.1.
[28] [1967] Ch 115. See also *Sefton Metropolitan Borough Council* v *United Utilities Water Ltd* [2001] EWCA Civ 1284.
[29] Under s.19 Public Health Act 1936 and now see s.104 Water Industry Act 1991.
[30] Under s.17 Public Health Act 1936 and now see s.102 Water Industry Act 1991.
[31] Under s.343(1) Public Health Act 1936 and now see s.219(1) Water Industry Act 1991.
[32] See *Kershaw* v *A. J. Smith and Co Ltd* [1913] 2 KB 455.

## The Functional Definition of 'Public Sewer' 285

circumstances at issue; the pipe had merely been sealed-off. It was concluded that the defining characteristic of a sewer, that it was 'used for the drainage of buildings and yards', was descriptive of a sewer's original function and not its actual use at any later time. Hence, the critical question concerned the function for which the pipe was constructed and, on the facts, the pipe at issue was constructed as a sewer and its subsequent abandonment did not alter its status as such.

Determination of the status of a water channel as a sewer is not especially problematic where its initial purpose is to convey sewage from buildings and yards. Importantly in this respect, 'sewage' is broadly construed to encompass both foul water originating from premises and also rain or surface water that is conveyed from roofs and yards. It has been emphasised that foul water drainage is not a defining characteristic of a sewer, and pipes conveying 'clean' surface water are equally capable of constituting sewers.[33] However, potential difficulties arise where a channel or conduit is used for a range of purposes including the conveyance of sewage.

In *Hutton* v *Esher Urban District Council*[34] the defendant council had formulated a scheme whereby a large pipe would take flood water from a river in times of flood and transmit the water to an outfall on another river. In addition, the pipe would take surface water from 5 miles of road and effluent from some 750 existing houses, from shops and offices and from future houses to be built in the area. The implementation of the project involved the outfall being constructed on land on which the claimant's bungalow stood and this would necessarily involve its demolition. Accordingly, the district council gave the claimant notice of its intention to undertake the work, which was claimed to involve the construction of a 'public sewer'. Amongst other things,[35] the claimant contested whether the project was properly characterised as the construction of a 'public sewer' insofar as the pipe was primarily intended as a flood alleviation and highway drainage measure rather than a means of draining surface water from buildings and curtilages. Notwithstanding that two out of the three purposes for which the pipe was being constructed would not have justified it being classified as a 'public sewer', the court found that the fact that it was also being constructed to drain premises was sufficient for it to be classified as a public sewer.

---

[33] *Ferrand* v *Hallas Land and Building Company* [1893] 2 QB 135, per A. L. Smith LJ at p.144.
[34] [1974] Ch 167.
[35] The claimant also, unsuccessfully, contested whether the power, under s.15(1)(I)(b) Public Health Act 1936 (now see s.159 Water Industry Act 1991) was exercisable in relation to 'land' which included buildings.

The *Hutton* case illustrates that a drainage channel may constitute a public sewer despite the fact that it serves purposes other than conveying sewage effluent. Whilst the multifunctionality of a drainage channel need not disqualify it from being a sewer, it should be noted that this purpose was evident at the time the pipe was constructed. The case may be contrasted, therefore, with other situations where the status of a channel is alleged to have been changed by subsequent use.

Most recently, the purposive approach has been applied in *City of Bradford Metropolitan District Council* v *Yorkshire Water Services Ltd*,[36] where an abatement notice had been served against the sewerage undertaker in relation to a statutory nuisance which had arisen following a discharge of sewage from a pipe, the responsibility for which was disputed.[37] The pipe ran from a gully in an unadopted road to a public sewer and served to drain water from the road as well as receiving water from a farmhouse. The public sewer record[38] was uninformative as to the ownership of the pipe and it became necessary to ascertain the purpose for which it was constructed in accordance with the public health legislation operative at that time.[39] Centrally, the issue was whether the highway and the farmhouse constituted separate 'premises'.

On this point, the situation in *Wincanton Rural District Council* v *Parsons*[40] was found to be analogous. Here, a drain had been constructed which ran from a house under a road to a point where it was joined by a drain from another house. Over part of the length under the road, the drain received surface water from the road, which had not been adopted by the local authority. A statutory nuisance arose at a point along the drain where it was receiving sewage from only one house and surface water run-off from the road. It was found that the drain was constructed for private purposes and did not become a sewer until the point where the connection from the second house was made. Following this, in the *Bradford* case, it was found that the main purpose of the pipe was to receive effluent from a single property, the farmhouse, and the fact that surface water from the road was also received by the drain did not convert it into a public sewer. The implication of this was that the abatement notice had been wrongly served upon the sewerage undertaker and responsibility for the pipe and the statutory nuisance lay with its private owner.

---

[36] Unreported, Queen's Bench Division, 19 September 2001.
[37] On statutory nuisance see 8.2.1 below.
[38] See 7.5 below on sewer maps.
[39] That is, s.4 Public Health Act 1875 and see 7.6 below on the vesting of sewers in sewerage undertakers.
[40] [1905] 2 KB 34.

## 7.4.2 Changes in Use

The functional definition of public sewer has proved problematic in relation to watercourses which have changed their use over time and increasingly come to receive water which is drained from developed areas. In many instances, it is the preference of local authorities, or other bodies with maintenance responsibilities, to transfer these responsibilities to sewerage undertakers, but this may only be done where the status of the relevant channel can be established to meet the criteria required for a public sewer.

An example of a progressive change in the use of drainage channel is to be seen in *British Railways Board* v *Tonbridge and Malling District Council*[41] where the responsibility for a culvert which ran under a railway line was at issue. The culvert had originally been constructed under a private Act of Parliament, which required the railway company to make and maintain culverts of sufficient dimensions to convey water from lands near the railway without obstructing or impounding the water to the prejudice of neighbouring land. This involved the construction of a culvert which was sufficient to take the flow of three natural watercourses that drained into the catchment area which, at the time of construction, was almost entirely agricultural land. However, due to subsequent residential and street development in the catchment, the position had been reached where buildings and curtilages constituted about 18% of the catchment area and the surface water flow originating from these constituted 30% of the flow in normal periods and 47% during times of peak flow. At this stage the British Railways Board, as the successor to the original railway company, requested a declaration[42] that the conduit should be vested in the district council as the local authority responsible for sewers.[43] The effect of a declaration of this kind would have been to transfer the responsibility for upkeep of the conduit to the local authority.

The local authority declined the request for a vesting declaration on the basis that the culvert was not a sewer and, therefore, the power of vesting did not apply. In considering this issue, the Court of Appeal found that the relevant question is whether the circumstances were such that the culvert had substantially lost its original character and taken on the character of a sewer. On the facts, it was evident that there had been no change in the function of the culvert in receiving the flow from the three watercourses. The fact that the surface drainage from built-up areas had been channelled

---

[41] (1981) 79 LGR 565. See also *Sefton Metropolitan Borough Council* v *United Utilities Water Ltd* [2001] EWCA Civ 1284.
[42] Under s.17(3) Public Health Act 1936; now see s.102(2) Water Industry Act 1991.
[43] That is, the predecessor of the present sewerage undertaker.

into the watercourses did not convert them into sewers or drains. Consequently, the conduit continued to function to receive the watercourses and had not become a sewer, with the consequence that it could not become vested in the local authority.

Although most of the cases on the meaning of 'sewer' involve pipes and conduits of various kinds, it is significant that a sewer need not be of artificial construction and, in the past, it has been possible for a natural watercourse to have become a sewer through becoming used, substantially, for the purpose of conveying sewage from premises.

The conversion of a natural watercourse into a sewer is illustrated by *Falconar* v *Corporation of South Shields*[44] where the claimant sought an order to restrain the sanitary authority for the district from diverting foul water from houses into a stream which, she claimed, formed the boundary of her property, and causing the stream to become a nuisance. The sanitary authority contested this in maintaining that the stream had become a sewer many years previously and that, as a consequence, it was vested in the authority and not the claimant. Again, stressing the factual nature of the issue to be decided, it was held that the ditch had actually been used to receive surface and foul water drainage for many years. As a consequence, the sanitary authority was bound to carry out operations necessary for the preservation of public health in relation to the channel that had changed character completely and had become a sewer.

The *Falconar* decision needs to be read with some caution, however, since it is relatively unusual for open natural watercourses to be categorised as sewers. Moreover, the circumstances in which the watercourse became a sewer in *Falconar* would no longer be lawful. The question whether it is legally possible for the status of a natural stream to be changed into that of a sewer was directly considered in *George Legge and Son Ltd* v *Wenlock Corporation*.[45] Here, it was argued that a culverted water channel which ran through the claimants' land had become a sewer, through the discharge of sewage into it from houses which had taken place over the previous 25 years, and the defendant sanitary authority was, therefore, bound to maintain the culvert. Significantly, the Public Health Act 1875 had generally made it an offence to use any sewer for conveying sewage into a natural watercourse unless rendered innocuous to the quality of the receiving watercourse. In addition, the Rivers Pollution Prevention Act 1876 had created a statutory offence for any person to cause any sewage

---

[44] (1895) 11 TLR 223. Similarly see *Newcastle-upon-Tyne Corporation* v *Houseman* (1898) 63 JP 85.
[45] [1938] AC 204. Similarly see *Airdrie Magistrates* v *Lanark County Council* [1910] AC 286.

matter to flow into any stream.[46] The consequence of these provisions was that any conversion of a watercourse into a sewer of the kind that was alleged was necessarily unlawful and the question whether a natural watercourse could become a sewer as a result of receiving discharges of sewage, at least since 1876, had to be answered in the negative. Notwithstanding this, the possibility remains that, as in the *Falconar* case, there are some watercourses that became sewers before this mechanism was made unlawful.

### 7.4.3 The Significance of Culverting

Despite the historical possibility of an open natural watercourse having become a sewer, through a change in its purpose before this was made unlawful, the normal practice is for sewers to be constructed from pipes or culverts.[47] In such instances, the issue is whether the emplacement of a culvert is, by itself, sufficient to convert a natural watercourse into a sewer.

For statutory purposes, a 'watercourse' is defined to include all rivers and streams and all ditches, drains, cuts, culverts, dykes, sluices, sewers (other than public sewers) and passages through which water flows.[48] In *R v Dovermoss Ltd*[49] a distinction was drawn between a 'watercourse', comprising the channel in which water flows, and the flowing water which may, or may not, be present in that channel at any particular time. The implication of this interpretation is that a river channel will remain a 'watercourse', despite the water departing from the channel in times of flood or the temporary absence of water during times of drought.[50]

---

[46] See s.17 Public Health Act 1875 and s.3 Rivers Pollution Prevention Act 1876; and now see s.85(3) Water Resources Act 1991 (preventing the discharge of sewage effluent into watercourses).
[47] On culverting of watercourses generally see 2.5.3 above.
[48] s.72(1) Land Drainage Act 1991 and see s.221(1) Water Resources Act 1991 which incorporates a similar definition with the explicit exclusion of mains and other pipes which belong to the Environment Agency or a water undertaker, or are only used for the purposes of providing a supply of water to any premises.
[49] [1995] Env LR 258. The potential for flooding to give rise to criminal liability for water pollution is also well illustrated by this case: polluting matter entered waters *of* a watercourse notwithstanding that those waters had, during a period flooding, departed from their normal course and run over an adjoining field where they were contaminated by the entry of polluting matter contrary to s.85(1) Water Resources Act 1991. Contrast *Taylor v St Helens Corporation* (1877) 6 Ch D 264 where a watercourse was more broadly defined, for purposes of civil law, as meaning either (a) an easement or right to the flow of water; (b) the channel itself; or (c) the land over which the water flows.
[50] See *Stollmeyer v Trinidad Lake Petroleum Co* [1918] AC 485 where it was held that a stream which ceased to flow for a considerable time each year did not cease to be river.

Critically, the responsibilities relating to watercourses rest, primarily, with their riparian owners, though, as has been seen, there are extensive powers given to flood defence operating authorities to undertake works of various kinds in privately owned watercourses.[51] Nonetheless, responsibilities for watercourses that fall outside the meaning of 'public sewers' will not fall to sewerage undertakers to maintain and undertakers have no general powers to undertake works for the purpose of maintaining watercourses.

The general principle is that a watercourse does not become a sewer merely because it has been culverted or piped. This is illustrated by *Shepherd* v *Croft*[52] where a contract for the sale of a property was disputed by the purchasers because a piped water channel which ran underground was alleged to be a public sewer. It was contended that this constituted a latent defect in the property, which made it less suitable for building development, and a ground upon which the contract should be rescinded. It was found that the underground culvert contained the waters of a natural watercourse that flowed through the property along with water from various roads and streets within the district. However, it was not connected with the sewage system apart from one place where the local authority had made connection of a storm overflow with a road gully that emptied into the watercourse. The finding, therefore, was that the natural watercourse did not become a sewer merely by being culverted; hence, it was not vested in the local authority, which was, therefore, not responsible for the repair of the pipes.

*Shepherd* v *Croft* may usefully be compared with the *British Railways Board* case and the *Hutton* case, discussed previously. In each instance, the initial purpose of constructing a conduit was found to be determinative of the status of the channel. Culverting, by itself, is subsumed to the overriding question of the purpose for which it is undertaken and the function that the culvert is intended to perform.

### 7.4.4 The 'Proper Outfall' Requirement

The early cases on the meaning of 'sewer', as it featured in the Public Health Act 1875, are sometimes taken to have established a requirement that for a water channel to be a sewer it had to have a 'proper outfall'.[53] Hence, in a leading case, *Meader* v *West Cowes Local Board*,[54] it was held

---

[51] See 4.3 and 4.6 above on flood defence operations.
[52] [1911] 1 Ch 521.
[53] See also the discussion of the 'proper outfall' requirement in relation to highway drains at 8.3.2 below.
[54] [1892] 3 Ch 18. For a discussion see W. Howarth and A. Brierley, *Infiltration Drainage – legal aspects* (1995) p.30 (Construction Industry Research and Information Association, Project 448 Report 25).

that a pipe that terminated in a pit or cesspit would not qualify as a sewer even though it drained water from a building. This ruling arose from circumstances where a property was drained by a system of pipes that ran into a cesspool that communicated with the foreshore of a tidal river. When the owner of the foreshore built upon it and stopped the drain, the cesspool overflowed and caused a nuisance. The claimant brought the action to restrain the local authority from permitting the nuisance to continue and alleged that the pipes were a 'sewer' and the cesspool a 'thing belonging thereto',[55] with the consequence that the authority was bound to keep the system in order.

It was held that the claimant had no right to make the continuation through the foreshore and the unlawful outfall that had been constructed had to be discounted. The remaining system of pipes, terminating in a pit on the claimant's property, did not serve to carry the sewage away and, therefore, could not be considered to be a sewer. In effect, the lack of a 'proper outfall' disqualified the essentially private drainage system from being classified as a 'sewer' and prevented it being vested in the authority under the 1875 Act. As the principle was later expressed,

> '[a] sewer within [the 1875 Act] must be in some form of line of flow by which sewage or water of some kind, such as would be conveyed through a sewer, should be taken from a point to a point and then discharged. It must have a terminus *a quo* and a terminus *ad quem*. There must be a line of flow from one to the other ... if you have a thing which conveys sewage, but has no outflow at all, but simply terminates in a pit on the land of the person who lays the pipe, that is not a sewer.'[56]

The requirement of a proper outfall, established by the *Meader* decision, was considered in *Clark* v *Epsom Rural District Council*[57] where a sewage disposal works originally passed effluent into a ditch leading to a river, but where subsequently the outfall was stopped and the effluent flowed over adjoining land. The claimant claimed entitlement to a declaration that the

---

[55] See s.13 Public Health Act 1875 which had the effect of vesting 'all existing and future sewers' in local authorities together with 'all building works material and things belonging thereto' with certain exceptions.

[56] Per Buckley J in *Pakenham* v *Ticehurst Rural District Council* (1903) 67 JP 448 at p.449.

[57] [1928] 1 Ch 287. Despite the finding that the drainage system at issue fell within the meaning of a 'sewer', the claimant failed in this action because the proper remedy was an appeal to the Ministry of Health under s.299 Public Health Act 1875 (allowing for complaints to be made to the Ministry in cases of local authority default and for orders to be made requiring authorities to perform their duties); now see s.18 Water Industry Act 1991. See also *Passmore* v *Oswaldtwistle Urban District Council* [1898] AC 387 on the inappropriateness of judicial review in circumstances where a statute provides for a specific method of enforcement.

system had become vested in the local authority under the Public Health Act 1875 and that the authority was bound to maintain it. Whilst the principle established in *Meader* was not disputed, the view was taken that the system at issue did actually have a proper outfall, albeit one that was not operating effectively at the time of the litigation. Moreover, the wording of the 1875 Act should be broadly construed to vest in local authorities sewers of 'good, bad and indifferent' degrees of efficiency.[58] *Meader*, therefore, was distinguished on the basis that the 1875 Act had never intended to bring about the vesting of essentially private sewerage systems in local authorities.[59]

Following this line of reasoning, it may be seen that it is the private character of a drainage system that prevents it being adopted as a public sewer, rather than the presence or absence of any particular kind of 'proper outfall'. This approach is evident in the decision in *Attorney-General* v *Peacock*[60] where the drainage for a residential estate, consisting originally of 48 houses, incorporated an elaborate system of channelling discharges from the houses along lines of pipes into settling tanks and then raising the waste water to the surface by means of pumping before finally disposing of it through sub-soil pipes radiating from a distribution chamber. The system had been considered and approved by the local authority before construction, but became unsatisfactory after the pipes became blocked and the pumping was abandoned. At this stage, sewage flooded some of the houses and a notice was served upon the defendant, who owned the unsold part of the estate, requiring him to abate the nuisance. After attempts to do

---

[58] Similarly see *Acton Local Board* v *Batten* (1885) 28 Ch D 283 where it was suggested that the word 'sewer' under the Public Health Act 1875 should receive the broadest possible interpretation and a drain should be held to be a 'sewer' where more than one house connected with it.

[59] See also *Pakenham* v *Ticehurst Rural District Council* (1903) 67 JP 448 which illustrates both possibilities: first, a number of pipes which conveyed sewage to an open ditch, from properties *on the same estate*, was held not to be a sewer because there was no proper outfall; second, a system of drainage established by agreement *between two neighbouring landowners* converted what had originally been a cesspool into a catchpit from which the sewage flowed onto the neighbouring land and eventually into a ditch constituting a small watercourse and this was held to be a sewer. Notably, the fact that sewage flowed through an open ditch for part of the course did not prevent this being a sewer (similarly see *Falconar* v *South Shields Corporation* (1895) 11 TLR 223, discussed at 7.4.2 above, on an open channel serving as a sewer).

[60] [1926] 1 Ch 241. See also *Pinnock* v *Waterworth* (1887) 51 JP 248 where a pipeline which received sewage from several houses and conveyed these to a cesspool was held to be a sewer which was vested in the local authority. See also *Hornsey Local Board* v *Davis* [1893] 1 QB 756 where it was held that a conventional sewer could be adopted by a local authority, despite the absence of a proper outfall, though the *Meader* case was not considered.

so proved ineffectual, an injunction was granted requiring him to restrain from continuing the nuisance.[61] Against this, the defendant contended that the drainage system constituted a 'sewer' which was vested in the local authority and that the nuisance was due to the failure of the authority to fulfil its statutory obligations.

In finding for the defendant, the argument from *Meader*, that a line of pipes that does not terminate in an outfall is incapable of constituting a 'sewer', was discounted. Despite the practical ineffectiveness of the drainage system at issue, and the fact that it ultimately involved dispersal of waste water to the sub-soil, it was found that the system constituted a 'sewer' vested in the local authority. Moreover, the nuisance which had arisen was attributed to the persistent disregard of statutory sewerage duties by the authority. With hindsight therefore, the 'proper outfall' requirement for a drainage system to constitute a sewer may actually be better characterised as a means of excluding essentially private systems of drainage rather than a stipulative requirement as to the manner in which effluent must ultimately be discharged from a drainage system.

## 7.5 SEWER MAPS

If it has been determined, in accordance with the previous considerations, that a particular water channel is a 'sewer', the next question is whether it is a *public* sewer which is the responsibility of the sewerage undertaker for the area in which it is located. As a practical matter, this may be most readily ascertained by consulting sewer maps which undertakers are bound to maintain. Hence, every sewerage undertaker is bound to keep records of the location and other relevant particulars:

(a) of every public sewer or disposal main which is vested in the undertaker;

(b) of every sewer in relation to which a declaration of vesting has been made by the undertaker but has not taken effect; and

(c) of every drain or sewer which is the subject of any agreement to make a declaration which has been entered into by the undertaker.

The 'relevant particulars' for these purposes comprise information as to the description of effluent for which the drain, sewer or disposal main is to be used, whether it is vested in the undertaker, whether it is subject to a vesting declaration, or whether it is subject to an agreement to make a declaration.[62]

---

[61] See the discussion of statutory nuisance at 8.2.1 above.
[62] s.199(1) and (2) Water Industry Act 1991. A 'declaration of vesting' is provided for under Chapter II of Part IV Water Industry Act 1991. Agreements to make declarations are provided for under s.104 Water Industry Act 1991 and see 7.2 above.

The records maintained by a sewerage undertaker are to be kept separately in relation to the area of each local authority. The undertaker must secure that the contents of the records are available, at all reasonable times, for inspection by the public free of charge at an office of the undertaker. Any information that is required to be made available to the public must be made available in the form of a map. There is a duty upon the undertaker to modify records as soon as reasonably practicable after the completion of relevant works. Where records are modified, the date of modification and the completion of the relevant works must be incorporated in the records.[63]

However, there are a number of reasons why sewer maps may not accurately record the location and existence of all public sewers. When sewerage undertakers were first established, by the Water Act 1989, the obligation to record sewers on maps did not apply to any drain, sewer or disposal main which was laid before 1 September 1989. This dispensation did not apply except where the undertaker did not know of, or have reasonable grounds for suspecting, the existence of a sewer, or it was not reasonably practicable for the undertaker to discover its existence and it had not done so. However, since 1 September 1999, the dispensation in relation to the exclusion from sewer maps of old drains, sewers or disposal mains will only apply where specified conditions are satisfied. Amongst the conditions is a requirement that after 1 September 1999 maps should contain any particulars that were shown, on 31 August 1989, on a sewer map kept by a local authority.[64] In effect therefore, undertakers were given a 10-year period to transfer information from local authority sewer maps to the sewer maps now maintained by undertakers.

Sewerage undertakers must provide local authorities, free of charge, with copies of records kept in sewer maps, and modifications of those records, and to ensure that every local authority is informed of the contents of records relating to its area. In turn, a local authority is bound to ensure that information provided to it by a sewerage undertaker in the form of a map is made available for inspection by the public, at all reasonable times, free of charge.[65]

Although sewer maps may provide important information to members of the public and local authorities, the legal status of this information is not specified. It is not clear, for example, whether a person who acted in

---

[63] s.199(3) to (6) Water Industry Act 1991.
[64] s.199(7) and (8) Water Industry Act 1991. The reference to a 'map kept by a local authority' refers to sewer maps kept by local authorities under s.32 Public Health Act 1936.
[65] s.200(1) to (3) Water Industry Act 1991.

reliance upon information in an inaccurate sewer map would have any claim for consequent loss against the sewerage undertaker who is bound to maintain the map.[66] Notably also, the sewer maps are dependent upon the completeness and accuracy of information which has been previously supplied to local authorities under their duties to keep sewer maps under previous legislation. The absence of any requirement that sewer maps should contain information about old sewers, except insofar as this has been confirmed by 'reasonably practicable' investigation, means that sewer maps are capable of being significantly incomplete and misleading without there necessarily being any breach of statutory duty on the part of an undertaker. In cases of uncertainty, therefore, it may be necessary to investigate the historical basis upon which a sewer may have become vested in an undertaker.

## 7.6 THE VESTING OF SEWERS IN SEWERAGE UNDERTAKERS

Recognising the practical value of sewer maps for most purposes, the legally definitive issue is whether a sewer is actually a 'public sewer' that is vested in the undertaker. In respect of this, there are three possible mechanisms by which a sewer may become vested in an undertaker:

(a) under a scheme under Schedule 2 to the Water Act 1989 (concerning schemes for the initial transfers of property, rights and liabilities from water authorities to sewerage undertakers);

(b) under Schedule 2 to the Water Industry Act 1991 (concerned with transitional provisions on termination of appointments of sewerage undertakers); or

(c) under section 179 Water Industry Act 1991 (concerned with the vesting of works in an undertaker).[67]

The circumstances envisaged under (c) are fairly explicit in that section 179 provides for vesting of works, undertaken since the commencement of the 1991 Act, in an undertaker. This states that every 'relevant pipe', including any sewer or disposal main, which has been laid in exercise of any power conferred by Part VI of the 1991 Act (concerned with undertakers'

---

[66] See *Post Office* v *Hampshire Country Council* [1980] QB 124 (where negligently given information about the location of a telephone cable constituted a basis for a claim in negligence) though possibilities may exist for liability for incorrect information to be disclaimed: see s.2 Unfair Contract Terms Act 1977. See also the discussion of *Royco Homes Ltd* v *Eatonwill Construction Ltd, Three Rivers District Council Third Party* [1979] Ch 276 at 7.6 below.

[67] As required by s.219(1) Water Industry Act 1991.

powers and works) or otherwise by an undertaker must vest in the undertaker. That is, sewerage works constructed by the undertaker itself will vest in the undertaker.[68] In addition, every sewer or sewage disposal works with respect to which a declaration of vesting by the undertaker has taken effect are stated to vest in an undertaker.[69] Also vested in the undertaker are every sewer which is laid in the area of the undertaker under highways legislation[70] and which is not a sewer belonging to a road maintained by a highway authority.[71]

The circumstances envisaged under (b) are also relatively straightforward, if somewhat unlikely in practice, in that the Secretary of State is empowered to apply to the High Court for a special administrative order directing that an administrator should take over the running of an undertaker's business in certain extreme circumstances.[72] The effect of an order of this kind, amongst other things, would be to vest the undertaker's sewers in the administrator.

However, some complexity surrounds (a), whereby a sewer may become vested in an undertaker under a scheme under Schedule 2 to the Water Act 1989. Schedule 2 to the 1989 Act required the former water authorities to make schemes for the division of their property, rights and liabilities to their successor companies. These schemes took effect following approval by the Secretary of State[73] and, amongst other things, had the effect of transferring rights over public sewers from water authorities to sewerage undertakers. The inherent difficulty in this lies in ascertaining precisely what rights over sewers were transferred by this mechanism.

Alongside sewers constructed by water authorities, otherwise vested in them under the Water Act 1973[74] or highways legislation, the transfer encompassed sewers that were the subject of previous vesting. Accordingly, earlier provisions under the Public Health Act 1936, governing the original vesting of sewers in local authorities, continue to determine whether a particular sewer has been transferred to a present-day sewerage undertaker. On the vesting of sewers, section 20 of the 1936 Act originally provided

---

[68] s.179(1) and (7) Water Industry Act 1991.
[69] That is, under Chapter II of Part IV Water Industry Act 1991 (concerned with the provision of sewerage services) and see, in particular, s.102 allowing for the adoption of sewers subject to specified circumstances and procedures, discussed at 7.2 above.
[70] Under Part XI Highways Act 1980, concerned with the making up of private streets.
[71] s.179(2) Water Industry Act 1991. On highway drains generally see 8.3.2 above.
[72] See ss.23 to 25 and Schedule 2 Water Industry Act 1991.
[73] Schedule 2 para.1(1) and (2) Water Act 1989 and see Water Act 1989 (Transfer of Functions) (Appointed Day) Order 1989, S.I. 1989 No.1530, which brought about the transfer from 1 September 1989.
[74] See s.15 Water Act 1973, a forerunner of s.179 Water Industry Act 1991.

for this in the following way.

'All sewers within the meaning of the Public Health Act 1875, and sewage disposal works which by virtue of the provisions of that Act were immediately before the commencement of [the Public Health Act 1936] vested in a local authority, shall continue to be vested in them, and there shall also vest in them –

(a) all combined drains[75] constructed before the commencement of [the Public Health Act 1936] which, by virtue of the Public Health Act 1875, would immediately before the commencement of [the Public Health Act 1936] have been vested in the local authority as sewers but for the provisions of some enactment or statutory scheme relating to the construction of combined drains, or of an order made under such an enactment or scheme;

(b) all sewers and sewage disposal works constructed by them at their expense, or acquired by them;

(c) all sewers constructed under any enactment relating to the sewering of private streets to the satisfaction of the council carrying that enactment into execution, except any such sewer which by virtue of section 29 of the Local Government Act 1929[76] will vest in the county council; and

(d) all sewers and sewage disposal works with respect to which a declaration of vesting under the foregoing provisions of [the Public Health Act 1936] has taken effect.'[77]

Amongst the various effects of this section of the Public Health Act 1936 is the possibility that the responsibility of a present-day sewerage undertaker for a particular sewer is capable of depending on whether it constituted a

---

[75] Although the expression 'combined drains' was not defined under the 1875 or 1936 Acts, it has been suggested that it refers to the practice of draining buildings in combination where a common line of pipes takes effluent from internal drains of several buildings through private land to a cesspool, cesspit or 'other receptacle for drainage' or into a sewer. However, every combined drain having a proper outfall would be a 'sewer' under the 1875 Act and vested in the local authority, so separate provision for combined drains was not strictly necessary (see J. F. Garner and S. H. Bailey, *The Law of Sewers and Drains* (8th ed. 1995) p.50).

[76] Amongst other things, s.29 Local Government Act 1929 had the effect of making county councils highway authorities and vesting highway drains in them; now see s.100(9) Highways Act 1980 and discussion at 8.3.2 above.

[77] s.20 Public Health Act 1936, subsequently replaced by Schedule 8 para.33 Water Act 1973; and now see s.219(1) Water Industry Act 1991. On vesting under the 1936 Act see ss.17 and 18 of that Act.

'public sewer' within the meaning of the 1875 Act; hence, the early cases on this point may remain of relevance in some exceptional instances.

There are also other problematic issues in tracing historic responsibilities for sewers where the mechanism by which responsibility for them has been acquired by a public body has not been formally recorded. A good illustration is to be found in *Royco Homes Ltd v Eatonwill Construction Ltd, Three Rivers District Council Third Party*,[78] which concerned the question of whether a local authority had 'acquired' a sewer within the meaning of the 1936 Act. The claimants were builders who proposed to develop land for housing. Before doing this, they enquired with the local authority as to the location of the nearest public sewer to the site and were informed, on the basis of information from the statutory sewer map,[79] that a public sewer was located in a highway within 100 feet of the site. In reliance upon this, the claimants purchased the site, proceeded to build houses upon it and, with local authority approval, made a connection to the sewer. At this stage, the defendants, another firm of building contractors, informed the claimants that, contrary to the previous information, the sewer had never been formally vested in the local authority and remained in their ownership. Consequently, the defendants claimed to be entitled to seal-off the connection that the claimants had made to the sewer until satisfactory terms or compensation for the making of the connection with the, allegedly, private sewer were agreed between the parties.

It transpired that, although the defendants' sewer had been constructed in accordance with the local authority's adoption criteria, and it had been the intention of the local authority to adopt the sewer, no resolution had ever actually been made formally to vest the sewer in the council. The issue for the court, therefore, was whether there was any other basis upon which adoption of the sewer could have taken place. On this, it was held that the provision for sewers which were 'acquired' by a local authority was to be widely construed to embrace all forms of acquisition. On the facts, the maxim of *quicquid plantatur solo, solo cedit* (whatever is affixed to the soil belongs to the soil) applied. The effect of this was that a permanent sewer that had become attached to land owned by the local authority had become a part of that land, with the effect that the sewer passed into the ownership of the local authority. As a consequence, the sewer became a public sewer, over which the defendants had relinquished rights of ownership, so that they had no right to object to the connection made by the claimants.

---

[78] [1979] Ch 276.
[79] Under s.32 Public Health Act 1936; now see s.199 Water Industry Act 1991, and see 7.5 above.

## The Vesting of Sewers in Sewerage Undertakers

The final outcome in this case had the effect of rectifying the 'oversight' of the local authority in omitting formally to adopt the sewer as had been originally contemplated, and avoided the possibility of the local authority becoming liable for negligently providing incorrect information to the claimants. Nonetheless, the facts clearly illustrate the potential problems that may arise in identifying public sewers where, historically, these have been created or adopted by informal mechanisms that have not been officially recorded.

### 7.7 STATUTORY PROVISIONS ON SEWERS AND FLOODING

#### 7.7.1 Customer Service Standards

If it has been determined that, by any of the mechanisms that have been described, a sewer is a public sewer and vested in the relevant sewerage undertaker, then the natural counterpart of this is that the undertaker should be responsible for the satisfactory functioning of that sewer. More specifically, this responsibility should encompass a duty upon the undertaker to ensure that the sewer does not cause flooding of other properties.

To some extent, responsibility to prevent flooding from sewers is provided for by the Water Industry Act 1991. This provides for a general duty upon sewerage undertakers to cleanse and maintain sewers and to ensure that their areas are properly drained, and for enforcement of this duty by the Secretary of State.[80] A more detailed indication of what the general duty entails is provided by a mechanism for 'performance standards' for the provision of sewerage services to be specified by the Secretary of State, or the Director General of Water Services with the approval of the Secretary of State. This mechanism allows standards to be prescribed for sewerage services, which should be achieved in individual cases, and to require under-takers to pay persons specified sums of money where they are affected by the failure to meet those standards. Hence regulations may be enacted for this purpose to require sewerage undertakers to inform persons of their rights, to provide for disputes to be referred to the Director, and to make provision for procedures that must be followed and to provide for exemptions.[81]

In accordance with the powers to specify performance standards for sewerage services, the Water Supply and Sewerage Services (Customer Service Standards) Regulations 1989[82] have been made. These Regulations

---

[80] See s.94(1) Water Industry Act 1991 on the general duty concerning provision of a sewerage system and s.18 on enforcement orders.
[81] s.95 Water Industry Act 1991 and see s.96, as amended, on the procedure that must be followed for making regulations of this kind.
[82] S.I. 1989 No.1159 and see the Amendment Regulations S.I. 1989 No.1383, S.I. 1993 No.500, S.I. 1996 No.3065 and S.I. 2000 No.2301.

require undertakers to make payments to customers in relation to any failure to meet standards involving flooding from sewers. Hence, where effluent from an undertaker's sewer enters a customer's building, including a space beneath a suspended floor of a building, in relation to each incident, the undertaker must remit sewerage charges for the year or pay the customer £1,000, whichever is the lesser. This payment must normally be made automatically by the undertaker, whether or not the customer makes a claim. A failure to make the payment within 20 working days will require the undertaker to pay a further 'penalty sum' of £20 for domestic premises or £50 for other premises. However, this obligation does not apply in specified circumstances: where a payment has previously been made within the same financial year; the entry of effluent is caused by exceptional weather conditions; industrial action by the undertaker's employees; actions of the customer; any defect, inadequacy or blockage in the customer's drains or sewers; or, in the case of a customer whom it is impractical for the undertaker to identify as being affected, where the claim is not made within 3 months. Notably, the making of a payment under the Regulations does not constitute an admission of liability on the part of the undertaker and the acceptance by a customer of a payment or credit is without prejudice to any other legal liabilities of either the undertaker or the customer.

The limitations of the system of customer services standards and the payments that are provided for under the present scheme are fairly self-evident. Where a customer suffers damage resulting from sewer flooding, even where the exceptions do not apply, the amount of the payment which is provided for will, in many cases, fail to cover the cost of the damage which has been suffered. Moreover, the more pressing objective of many customers who suffer flooding from sewers will be to secure an improvement in the state of the sewer which is the cause of the problem, particularly where flooding by sewage is a recurring event.

Perhaps most notably, in respect of statutory liability, the Water Industry Act 1991 does not incorporate any express provision making sewerage undertakers generally liable for loss or damage in the event of flooding from sewers. The only exception to this arises where the Secretary of State or the Director General makes an enforcement order against a sewerage undertaker, requiring it to take specified actions in relation to the contravention of a statutory or other requirement.[83] Where this occurs, the obligation to comply with an enforcement order is a 'duty owed to any person who may be affected by a contravention of the order' so that any breach of the enforcement order which causes loss or damage will be

---

[83] See s.18 Water Industry Act 1991 on enforcement orders.

actionable by that person.[84] Other than within this relatively narrow exception, however, civil liability will arise only through application of the general principles of civil law relating to negligence and private nuisance and the normal requirements for liability in such actions will need to be established before a remedy will be given.

### 7.7.2 Discharges from Sewers

Despite the general duty of sewerage undertakers to drain their areas,[85] and various works powers that allow sewers to be constructed and maintained by undertakers,[86] the statutory authority of undertakers to make discharges from sewers into watercourses has, until recently, been rather obscure. The traditional view had been that duty to drain areas, and to construct sewers for that purpose, implied a power to discharge from those sewers into the nearest convenient watercourse. Hence, in *Durrant v Branksome Urban District Council*[87] a local authority was found to have the right to discharge water from its drains into a natural watercourse providing that it was free from foul or noxious matter that might impair the purity of the stream. Notably, the drainage implications of this power were recognised, in that a discharge of this kind can cause an increase and acceleration of the flow of the receiving watercourse. Nevertheless, it was found to be lawful for the local authority to drain land into a watercourse, even if, in times of flood, the effect of this was to swell the flow of the watercourse to a greater extent than would have happened but for that drainage.

The relevance of the *Durrant* case to modern circumstances, however, is placed in doubt by several features of the case. First, it was primarily a dispute about water quality, revolving around the question of whether the effect of the drainage was to carry sand and silt into the stream that would not naturally have been present. Second, it was concerned with the interpretation of the Public Health Act 1875 which explicitly authorised certain discharges into watercourses, except where the discharge impaired the purity of the stream.[88] Third, the 1875 Act explicitly provided for compensation to be paid, or an injunction to be granted, in circumstances where a claimant could show harm arising from a misuse of the powers of the local authority.[89] Finally, the 1875 Act was premised upon sewerage functions being exercised by *public* authorities and, since privatisation of

---

[84] s.22(1) and (2) Water Industry Act 1991.
[85] Under s.94(1) Water Industry Act 1991, and see 7.2 above.
[86] See particularly ss.158 to 160 Water Industry Act 1991, providing powers to lay pipes in streets, in other land and to carry out works for sewerage purposes.
[87] (1897) 76 LT 739.
[88] See s.17 Public Health Act 1875.
[89] See ss.308 and 299 Public Health Act 1875.

the water industry, this is no longer the case.[90]

By further contrast, there are significant differences in the provisions now made under the Water Industry Act 1991 that, as a consolidation Act, must be interpreted accordingly. Hence, unless there was an ambiguity, the 1991 Act should be construed by looking at its provisions alone, and not by interpreting those provisions by reference to earlier statutes that have now been repealed.[91] Consequently, the decision in the *Durrant* case is no longer directly relevant to the interpretation of the present legislation.

The interpretation of the relevant parts of the 1991 Act was recently considered in *British Waterways Board* v *Severn Trent Water Ltd*[92] where, for some years previously, a sewerage undertaker had made a discharge of surface water into a canal under a licence granted by a canal authority. The canal authority sought to terminate the licence and require the removal of the sewer by the undertaker, in accordance with the terms of the licence. Although it was clear that the undertaker had statutory powers to lay sewers,[93] it contended that these powers implied a statutory power authorising the continued use of the sewer for making the discharge into the canal, without the need for the consent of the canal authority.

Most significantly, it was found that the 1991 Act provided no *explicit* power allowing sewerage undertakers to make discharges to watercourses.[94] The argument that such a power should be *implied* foundered on the doubtful assumption that Parliament had intended to allow the interests of individual landowners to be impaired without compensation being payable. Consequently, it was found that if a sewerage undertaker needed to acquire the right to discharge into a watercourse of another, in order to carry out its statutory drainage duty, it could do so only by acquiring that right compulsorily,[95] with the authority of the Secretary of State. Where compulsory purchase powers were exercised, an obligation to pay compensation would arise, thereby ensuring that harm to landowners was fully reimbursed. Therefore, as between the canal authority and the

---

[90] See 7.2 above on sewerage undertakers.
[91] See *R* v *Environment Secretary ex parte Spath Holme Ltd* [2001] 2 WLR 15.
[92] [2001] Env LR 780 and see D. Wilkinson 'Discharge of Water by Statutory Sewerage Undertaker into Watercourse into Watercourse Owned by Another' [2001] *Water Law* 107.
[93] Under s.159 Water Industry Act 1991.
[94] Contrast the explicit power given to *water* undertakers to make discharges into watercourses under s.165(1) Water Industry Act 1991 and the power of highway authorities to discharge drainage water into any inland or tidal waters under s.100(2) Highways Act 1980, and see 8.3.3 below.
[95] Powers of sewerage undertakers to acquire land and rights compulsorily are provided for under s.155 Water Industry Act 1991 subject to the Compulsory Purchase Act 1965, as amended by the Compulsory Purchase Act 1991.

sewerage undertaker, the narrow point that was decided was that there was no implied right of the undertaker to dis-charge from the sewer into the canal without an obligation to pay compensation.

The broader implications of this decision, however, are of potential relevance to situations where a discharge from a sewer into a watercourse causes a watercourse to flood or exacerbates flooding problems. On this, the 1991 Act states that a sewerage undertaker will not be authorised injuriously to affect the 'supply, quality or fall of water contained in ... any reservoir, canal, watercourse, river or stream'. This prohibition is made subject to the consent of any person who, apart from the 1991 Act, would have been entitled to prevent, or to be relieved against, the injurious affection.[96] In the *British Waterways Board* case it was observed that the purpose of this provision was to ensure that those who may be adversely affected by a discharge, either through its quality or quantity, are protected from damage. Into this category would come those downstream of the discharge who are riparian owners and who may be at risk from flooding or other harm. Hence, the effect of the statutory provision is to make clear that common law remedies, particularly in nuisance, are not affected by the exercise of the undertaker's statutory powers to lay pipes.[97] In effect, the position is, not only that an undertaker has no statutory power to make a discharge to a watercourse unless a discharge consent is obtained,[98] but that the further need for the consent of the owners of a watercourse ensures that consequent damage, including flooding damage, is properly taken into account.

The practical implications of this are difficult to assess. On the one hand, the statutory provisions suggest that unconsented sewer discharges that cause or exacerbate flooding should give rise to liability on the part of the sewerage undertaker. Presumably, the liability would be capable of extending to all persons adversely affected, perhaps encompassing landowners with property alongside a watercourse for a considerable distance downstream from the point of discharge. On the other hand, the difficulties which were apparent in the *Durrant* case seem to present a formidable obstacle to liability being established in practice. That is, it must be shown that the discharge from the sewer actually *causes* a significant difference to the quality or quantity of the receiving watercourse by comparison with its former state, before the sewer was installed. Although, it is generally accepted that drainage has the effect of accelerating the rate of surface water run-off, attempting to establish that flooding would not have occurred if a particular sewer had not been in place is likely to raise considerable evidential difficulties.

---

[96] s. 186(3) Water Industry Act 1991.
[97] See *British Waterways Board* v *Severn Trent Water Ltd* [2001] Env LR 780, per Keene LJ at para.84.
[98] That is, a consent granted under s.88(1)(a) Water Resources Act 1991.

## 7.8 CIVIL LIABILITY OF SEWERAGE UNDERTAKERS: THE TRADITIONAL APPROACH

The general bases of civil liability for flooding have been previously considered,[99] but it is pertinent here to survey those rulings concerning the liability of sewerage undertakers, and previous public bodies with corresponding responsibilities, to illustrate the distinctive principles that apply and to take account of recent developments. Although many of the decided cases concerning sewerage undertakers have concerned contamination of waters by inadequate treatment of sewage effluent, many of the general principles governing pollution liability are similarly applicable to flooding damage. Hence, the traditional position has been that where an action in negligence or private nuisance is pursued on the basis that the nuisance arises from the overloading of a sewer, and this is attributable to connections to the sewerage system that an undertaker is powerless to prevent,[100] the undertaker will not be liable despite any sewage flooding that has arisen.[101] Similarly, where householders have rights of drainage from their premises an injunction will not be granted to restrain the exercise of those rights if this would involve the closure of a sewer which is causing flooding, or would prevent further connections to a sewer which the undertaker is statutorily bound to permit.[102]

The traditional position is illustrated by *Hesketh* v *Birmingham Corporation*[103] where the defendant local authority was the owner of a sewer that ran alongside a natural watercourse. The authority had constructed a number of storm-water outlets in the sewer to relieve the pressure upon it in times of heavy rain by discharging the excess water into the watercourse. Although the stream was initially of sufficient capacity to accommodate the surplus water, the development of neighbouring land caused the stream to become inadequate. Following a heavy storm, a discharge of surplus water caused the adjoining land and the claimant's house to be flooded. It

---

[99] See Ch.2 above on civil liability.
[100] That is, because of the right of connection of householders' drains to the sewerage system under s.106 Water Industry Act 1991, and see 7.2 above.
[101] *Smeaton* v *Ilford Corporation* [1954] Ch 450 (concerning sewage flooding from a manhole in the street and overflowing into the claimant's premises).
[102] *Brown* v *Dunstable Corporation* [1899] 2 Ch 378 (where an 'absolute' right of householders to connect drains to sewers (under s.21 Public Health Act 1875; now see s.106 Water Industry Act 1991) prevented an injunction being granted to prevent further connections being made). See also *Attorney-General* v *Acton Local Board* (1882) 22 Ch D 221 (concerning the rights of a sanitary authority to direct sewage effluent into sewers vested in the sanitary authority of an adjoining district).
[103] [1924] 1 KB 260. Similarly see *Glossop* v *Heston and Isleworth Local Board* (1879) 12 Ch D 102; *Stretton's Derby Brewery Co* v *Derby Corporation* [1894] 1 Ch 431; and *Robinson* v *Workington Corporation* [1897] 1 QB 619.

was held that the defendant had statutory authority to discharge the surplus water from the sewer into the watercourse and it was not liable for the nuisance. In addition, the defendant's neglect to enlarge the capacity of the stream did not constitute negligence for which an action could be sustained. Fundamentally, the court stressed a distinction between instances of *non-feasance* (where a body had failed to act) and *misfeasance* (where a wrongful action was taken). In cases of non-feasance, and in the absence of negligence, the civil law provided no remedy against a body acting within the scope of its statutory powers. The appropriate remedy, in a case of non-feasance, therefore, is an enforcement order, made in accordance with the statutory provisions, by the Secretary of State or the Director General of Water Services.[104]

By contrast, there have been instances where misfeasance has been found against bodies exercising the functions of present-day sewerage undertakers. In *Dent v Birmingham Corporation*,[105] for example, the diversion of sewage from one drain into another that was already surcharged with sewage, with resulting damage to an adjoining property, was found to be an act of misfeasance for which the liability of the authority was established. Generally, however, the scope for showing either misfeasance or negligence is limited due to the lack of any duty, under the Water Industry Act 1991, upon sewerage undertakers to undertake any particular works.

An alternative statement of the general position now applicable to sewerage undertakers' liabilities in respect of inadequate sewage treatment works is to be found in *Pride of Derby and Derbyshire Angling Association* v *British Celanese Ltd*.[106] Here, a distinction was drawn between actions based upon nuisance and actions based upon negligence. In respect of negligence, it was recognised that non-feasance, in the sense of failing to perform a statutory responsibility, did not give rise to a cause of action against a local authority in respect of the unsatisfactory operation of its sewerage system. However, in respect of nuisance, the central question was whether the thing complained of as a nuisance was expressly or impliedly authorised by the statute in accordance with which the works were constructed. In addressing that issue, the question of whether the nuisance arose through non-feasance or misfeasance was not relevant to the overriding question as to whether the body had a statutory defence to the nuisance. On the facts of the *Pride of Derby* case, the local statute under which the defendant's sewage treatment works operated gave no authority for the defendant to cause a nuisance by pouring noxious and polluting

---

[104] Under s.18 Water Industry Act 1991; see 7.2 above.
[105] (1897) 66 LJ QB 395.
[106] [1953] Ch 149.

effluent into a river,[107] and it was found liable to the claimants for consequent damage to a fishery in the river.

Nevertheless, whether interpreted as an exclusion of liability for nonfeasance by sewerage undertakers or the exclusion of liability as a matter of statutory construction, the traditional position was that few instances of flooding from sewers were found to give rise to liability of sewerage undertakers or previous bodies with corresponding responsibilities. The policy rationale for this probably lay in a reluctance of Parliament to allow a private individual to compel an undertaker to exercise a power owed to the public generally. That is, civil proceedings should not be used as a means of forcing an undertaker to exercise its powers for the benefit of an individual claimant where this may be to the detriment of other, potentially more deserving, members of the public.[108]

Although the traditional approach of declining to impose civil liability upon sewerage undertakers for sewer flooding, except in instances of misfeasance, has been reaffirmed on numerous occasions over the last century, it has recently been denied whether this still represents the state of the law. Specifically, the recent Court of Appeal decision in *Peter Marcic* v *Thames Water Utilities Ltd*[109] has suggested that the old authorities concerning sewer flooding can no longer stand alongside the decision in *Leakey* v *National Trust*.[110] The *Leakey* case established the principle that an occupier of land on which a natural or man-made hazard arises owes a general duty to neighbouring occupiers to take reasonable steps to deal with the hazard. Critically, the *Marcic* case affirms that this principle applies to sewer flooding. The implications of this momentous change of approach to civil liability for sewer flooding are fully considered in the following sections, alongside the human rights issues raised by the *Marcic* case.

## 7.9 SEWAGE FLOODING AND HUMAN RIGHTS

The litigation in *Peter Marcic* v *Thames Water Utilities Ltd*[111] concerned the civil liability of a sewerage undertaker for damage caused by the

---

[107] Under ss.109 and 113 Derby Corporation Act 1901, s.39 Public Health Act 1936 and s.2 Rivers (Prevention of Pollution) Act 1951; now see s.85(3) Water Resources Act 1991.
[108] Generally see 2.9 above on civil liability of statutory bodies.
[109] [2002] EWCA 65, 7 February 2002.
[110] [1980] 1 All ER 17 and see 2.4.5 above.
[111] [2001] Env LR 146 (High Court) and [2002] EWCA 65, 7 February 2002 (Court of Appeal). See also *Peter Marcic* v *Thames Water Utilities Ltd (No.2)* [2001] 4 All ER 326, concerning the preliminary assessment of the proper measure of damages, discussed at 7.9.7 below. See also W. Howarth, 'Sewage Flooding and Human Rights' [2001] *Water Law* 169 (on the High Court decision) and D. Wilkinson, 'Old Laws Fail to Contain Liability for Sewage Flooding: A Floodgate for Human Rights Claims?' [2002] *Journal of Water Law* 45 (on the Court of Appeal decision).

flooding of a sewer to the property of the claimant. In the Court of Appeal, the undertaker was found to be liable for this damage. This decision has raised profound doubts about the continuing applicability of many of the longstanding common law authorities on civil liability for sewer flooding. Beyond that, the decision is perhaps most remarkable in illustrating the application of the European Convention on Human Rights and Fundamental Freedoms, implemented nationally by the Human Rights Act 1998, to the predicament of a person suffering from sewage flooding. Although, at the time of writing, it is understood that the decision in the *Marcic* case may be subject to an appeal to the House of Lords, the case is of such fundamental importance that it requires fairly detailed consideration.

### 7.9.1 The Facts of the *Marcic* Case

The claimant, Mr Marcic, was the occupant of a residential property in the area of the defendant sewerage undertaker which, at the time of the proceedings, in 2001, had suffered at least 16 flooding incidents since 1992. The flood water originated from a combined foul and surface water sewer which ran under the road alongside the claimant's property. At times of heavy rain, water from the overcharged sewer flowed over the garden in front of the claimant's house and rose to a level of three-quarters of an inch below the threshold of the front door. When the water subsided, deposits of sludge and debris were left on the garden and it was alleged that the house had suffered from dampness, cracking of walls and subsidence as a result of the flooding. The effect of this, it was alleged, was to make the property unsaleable. The claimant, at his own expense, undertook various flood alleviation works in the grounds of the property at a cost of £16,000. Although these may have prevented water entering the house, they did not prevent the recurrence of flooding of the garden.

The claimant notified his local authority, which at the time was the area sewerage management contractor for the sewerage undertaker,[112] and cleaning of the claimant's drains was undertaken, though this did not have any significant effect upon the recurrence of the flooding. Similarly unsuccessful cleansing of the public sewer by the defendants was undertaken. Correspondence with the Secretary of State prompted the advice that the complaint should be referred to the appropriate Customer Services Committee of the Office of Water Services as a precursor to investigation of the complaint, though no approach was actually made to the Office of Water Services by the claimant.

It was recognised by both parties that any significant alleviation of the

---

[112] See s.97 Water Industry Act 1991 on agency agreements and see 7.2 above.

flooding problem would involve major construction works and engineering experts agreed on a range of schemes that would alleviate the problem ranging, in cost, up to at least £200,000. In some respects, however, these schemes were dependent upon the Environment Agency granting consents to allow discharges to be made to downstream watercourses. In respect of this, difficulties were evident because of concerns that the effect of works would be to transfer the flooding problem downstream. Nonetheless, it was concluded that flood alleviation works were necessary to prevent the flooding and works would only be undertaken provided that the necessary funding could be made available by the sewerage undertaker.

In effect, it was the unwillingness of the sewerage undertaker to make available the funding to implement a suitable programme of flood alleviation works that prompted the claimant to pursue an action in nuisance. Although it was not suggested that the sewers were not built in accordance with the standards that prevailed at the time of their construction, or that they had not been properly maintained, it was clear that they were presently inadequate to prevent flooding of the claimant's property. Accordingly, it was alleged that the undertakers were liable for the flooding as a matter of common law and also under the Human Rights Act 1998.

### 7.9.2 Determining Priorities for Sewerage Improvements

The situation in the *Marcic* case, concerning sewage flooding in the area of Thames Water Utilities Ltd, and the mechanisms by which it was addressed, provides a valuable insight into the practical operation of the sewerage services provisions of the Water Industry Act 1991. The defendant was the statutory sewerage undertaker for some 80,000 kilometres of public sewers, 361 treatment works and over 2,000 pumping stations, serving 5.4 million properties and a population of about 12 million people. The undertaker's revenue came from water and sewerage charges which were periodically limited by the Director General of Water Services who made allowances for work to be undertaken to remove properties from a list of those which have been shown to be at risk from internal flooding. The process of setting charges by the Director General took account of the expenditure required to achieve a reasonable level of flood alleviation by removing an appropriate number of properties from the list of those susceptible to internal flooding. Accordingly, the undertaker was to endeavour to achieve performance targets for flooding alleviation on the basis of the expenditure allowed by the Director General.

To determine targets for flood alleviation, the Director General operated a flood risk categorisation system which determined the maximum amount of expenditure which would be allowed for this purpose. The three categories of risk were identified as follows:

> *Category A* comprised properties that are statistically categorised as being at risk of internal flooding twice or more in ten years.
>
> *Category B* comprised properties that are statistically at risk of internal flooding once or more, but less than twice, in ten years.
>
> *Category X* applied to all other properties with a history of flooding, including properties subject only to external flooding.[113]

Accordingly, the Director General had determined that the undertaker should remove 1,500 category A or category B properties from the risk of flooding over the period between 2000 and 2005 and £46 million was allowed as the expenditure needed to achieve this.

The determination of which particular properties would actually benefit from flood alleviation works was made by the undertaker on the basis of a points system which sought to assess the impact upon customers of particular flooding incidents. Hence, points were allocated depending upon whether the flooding was of foul or surface water; whether the flooding was internal or external; whether the property was a school, hospital or nursing home; and whether the customer had been forced to vacate the property temporarily. Additional points were added to take account of the frequency with which incidents occurred, though on a different basis depending on whether the flooding was external or internal. The points total was then compared with the estimated cost of the works needing to be undertaken and a 'threshold of viability' applied, whereby 100 points needed to be reached for each £1 million of required expenditure. However, there was a facility for instances which fell below this threshold to be referred to the undertaker's 'review group', which could take account of additional factors such as special vulnerability of the customer, due to age, sickness or disability, and whether the matter had received press coverage or a Member of Parliament or a local councillor had become involved.

---

[113] For this purpose, sewerage undertakers are required to keep records of incidents that result in internal flooding of properties (referred to as 'DG5' incidents). The Office of Water Services publishes information on the number of properties flooded each year, as well as the number of properties considered to be at risk of flooding once in ten years and twice in ten years. In 2000-01, 5,644 properties were estimated to be at risk of flooding twice in ten years and 20,368 once in ten years. See Office of Water Services, *Levels of Service for the Water Industry in England and Wales* (2001) p.29 (available on http://www.ofwat.gov.uk/pdffiles/los2001.pdf). See also Institution of Civil Engineers, *Learning to Live with Rivers* (2001) p.32 where concern is expressed about the low level of investment to overcome the risk of sewer flooding.

## 310 Sewerage and Water Supply

The result of applying the points system to Mr Marcic's property was that there was no realistic prospect of the necessary flood alleviation works being carried out in the foreseeable future. This was because of the number of other properties for which flood alleviation works, according to the points system and respective costs, constituted a higher priority. It is notable that, during the 1999-2000 financial year, 851 properties were affected by internal flooding incidents due to overloaded sewers and 911 properties affected by internal flooding incidents from other causes. The total number of properties thought to be in Category A, at risk of internal flooding twice or more in ten years, was 3,600 and the number of properties in Category B, at risk of being flooded once of more but less than twice in ten years, was 14,655. Hence, on the basis of the risk categories, there were over 18,000 properties that would be given funding priority over Mr Marcic's property. Consequently, it was argued that expending funds to address the flooding problems at that property would involve an improper diversion of funds from other properties that were assessed to have greater flooding risk.

Looking at the issues from a financial perspective, it was found that the average cost of alleviating flooding problems amounted to roughly £30,000 per property, though this unit cost reflected that it was less expensive to undertake schemes that benefited groups of properties, as opposed to individual properties in isolation. Although the information was imprecise, it was estimated that it would cost the undertakers in the order of £1,000 million to alleviate the flooding problems of all customers who were in a similar position to Mr Marcic or worse.

### 7.9.3 The Common Law Claim

The first basis on which Mr Marcic contended that he was entitled to a remedy for the sewer flooding was as a matter of common law liability for nuisance. In proceedings before the High Court,[114] it was accepted that the traditional approach towards finding civil liability of sewerage undertakers prevailed. Hence, following the body of caselaw previously considered,[115] in cases of non-feasance, a sewerage undertaker would not be liable for a nuisance caused by an escape or discharge of sewage by reason of increases in flow in the sewerage system. This outcome was the same whether the action was based upon nuisance, the principle in *Rylands* v

---

[114] [2001] Env LR 146.
[115] In particular, *Glossop* v *Heston and Isleworth Local Board* [1897] 12 ChD 102; *Robinson* v *Workington Corporation* [1897] 1 QB 619; *Hesketh* v *Birmingham Corporation* [1924] 1 KB 260; *Pride of Derby and Derbyshire Angling Association* v *British Celanese Ltd* [1953] 1 Ch 149; *Smeaton* v *Ilford Corporation* [1954] 1 Ch D 450; and see the discussion at 7.8 above.

*Fletcher*[116] or breach of statutory duty, and the same outcome would be reached in situations where negligent non-feasance was alleged.

Significantly, the High Court declined to follow the decision in *Leakey* v *National Trust*,[117] to the effect that the sewerage undertaker should have been subject to a measured duty to take reasonable steps to abate the nuisance. The explanation for declining to apply this authority was that there was no suggestion that the principle required or authorised work to be done on neighbouring land. Moreover, the principle depended upon the existence of negligence and the only negligence in the circumstances was that of an undertaker to fulfil its general statutory duty with regard to drainage. Hence, 'negligence' of this kind would not be actionable because of the pre-existing law on non-feasance.

In the proceedings in the Court of Appeal, however, a radically different view was taken of the common law claim. The view of the High Court, that it was bound by previous decisions[118] to find that no liability would arise from non-feasance on the part of the sewerage undertaker, was mistaken. In the first place, the Court of Appeal thought that the circumstances in the *Marcic* case could be distinguished from the facts of previous instances where the claimant was seeking to use a civil law remedy to enforce a statutory duty. By contrast, the court found that Mr Marcic was not seeking to enforce a statutory duty, but rather to secure a remedy for a private nuisance which arose independently of any statutory powers of the undertaker. As the point was made, the claimant 'is not complaining of failure on the part of Thames to drain his property. He is complaining of the fact that their drainage of the property of others is resulting in discharge from Thames' system which is damaging to his property'.[119] The distinction between enforcing a statutory duty and securing a remedy for a nuisance seems a fine one, which appears difficult to reconcile with the previous cases. Nevertheless, the court thought that the two kinds of situation could be distinguished and that this provided a ground for not following past decisions where liability had been denied.

More fundamentally, the Court of Appeal found that the previous common law authorities could not survive the development of the law which had taken place in *Leakey* v *National Trust*.[120] The previous distinction between misfeasance and non-feasance could not stand alongside the finding that a person who owns and controls land cannot remain passive in the face of

---

[116] See 2.5.2 above on *Rylands* v *Fletcher*.
[117] [1980] 1 QB 485 and see the discussion at 2.4.5 above.
[118] Particularly *Glossop* v *Heston and Isleworth Local Board* [1879] 12 Ch 102.
[119] [2002] EWCA 65 para.100, per Phillips LJ.
[120] [1980] 1 All ER 17 and see 2.4.5 above.

a hazard arising on the land, even if the landholder is not responsible for the creation of the nuisance. Hence, once Mr Marcic had shown that the nuisance originated from land in the possession or control of the undertaker, the onus shifted to the undertaker to show that it had taken all reasonable steps to prevent the nuisance. On this, the court was not willing to accept that a body with the financial resources of the defendant was in a position to justify its inaction. In addition, it was not open to the undertaker to claim that the sewer flooding was justified by its statutory powers, since the nuisance that had been caused was not an inevitable consequence of the statutory powers that were being exercised.[121] Hence, the undertaker was placed in a similar position to a private landowner on whose property a hazard accumulates. On the basis that the sewerage undertaker had knowledge of the flooding hazard and failed to demonstrate that it was not reasonably practicable for it to take action, it was found liable notwithstanding the statutory provisions under which it operated.

### 7.9.4 The Human Rights Issues

The unique feature of the *Marcic* case was the claimant's assertion that the failure to prevent sewage flooding, on the part of the undertaker, constituted an infringement of human rights which were protected under the European Convention on Human Rights.[122] Specifically, the Human Rights Act 1998 provides that it is unlawful for a public authority, or a body whose functions are functions of a public nature, to act in a way which is incompatible with a 'Convention right' provided for under the 1998 Act, unless, as a result of primary legislation, the authority could not have acted differently.[123] More particularly, the Convention rights that had been infringed were those concerning respect for private and family life and the protection of property. On these, the Convention provides, under Article 8 that,

(1) everyone has the right to respect for his private and family life, his home and his correspondence;

---

[121] Following *Allen* v *Gulf Oil Refining Ltd* [1981] AC 1001 where it was held that immunity from action in nuisance would only be allowed where the nuisance was an 'inevitable' result of the exercise of statutory powers and the burden of proving this rested upon the defendant.

[122] Generally see W. Upton, 'The European Convention on Human Rights and Environmental Law' [1998] *Journal of Planning and Environmental Law* 315; J. Thornton and S. Tromans, 'Incorporating the European Convention on Human Rights: Some Thoughts on the Consequences for UK Environmental Law' (1999) *Journal of Environmental Law* 35; and B. Pontin, 'Beyond nuisance? Enforcing the right to a healthy environment within the framework of the Human Rights Act 1998' [2001] *Environmental Law and Management* 305.

[123] s.6(1) and (3) Human Rights Act 1998.

(2) there shall be no interference by a public authority with the exercise of this right except as in accordance with the law and is necessary in a democratic society in the interests of national security, public safety or the economic well-being of the country, for the prevention of disorder or crime, for the protection of health or morals, or the protection of the rights and freedoms of others.

Article 1 of the First Protocol to the Convention, concerned with protection of property, provides as follows:

Every natural or legal person is entitled to the peaceful enjoyment of his possessions. No one shall be deprived of his possessions except in the public interest and subject to the conditions provided for by law and by the general principles of international law.

The preceding provisions shall not, however, in any way impair the right of a State to enforce such laws as it deems necessary to control the use of property in accordance with the general interest or to secure the payment of taxes or other contributions or penalties.

Although the connection between the Convention rights and the predicament of the claimant was not immediately obvious to the High Court, the caselaw concerning human rights was supportive. Hence, the nuisance of noise from an airport had been found to constitute an admissible complaint under both of the Articles[124] and the effect of noise and emissions from a nuclear power station had also been found to be actionable in another case, though the payment of compensation was found to justify the interference as not going beyond what was necessary in a democratic society.[125] Other cases have established that toxic emissions from a factory polluting an applicant's home[126] and interference with an applicant's home by fumes and smells emanating from a waste treatment plant[127] are within the scope of Article 8 insofar as they infringe the right to respect for private and family life and a person's home.

The application of this body of case law to the situation of Mr Marcic allowed the inference that he constituted a 'victim' and, therefore, a proper

---

[124] *Baggs* v *United Kingdom* (1985) 9 EHRR 235. See, subsequently, *Hatton* v *United Kingdom* (2001) *The Times* 8 October 2001 where it was held that the United Kingdom Government had failed to protect the right to respect for private and family life, under Art.8 of the Convention, by neglecting to conduct independent research into the implications of night flights on sleep patterns of those living near Heathrow Airport.
[125] *S* v *France* (1990) 65 D&R 250.
[126] *Guerra* v *Italy* (1998) 26 EHRR 357.
[127] *Lopez Ostra* v *Spain* (1994) 20 EHRR 277.

claimant against the sewerage undertaker as a 'public authority'. The sewerage undertaker was guilty of an 'act' incompatible with a Convention right, since the 1998 Act provides that an 'act' includes 'a failure to act'[128] and this was construed to encompass a failure to put an end to an infringement where the defendant could reasonably have done so.

The argument was raised as to whether the sewerage undertaker was the appropriate defendant. The undertaker contended that the relevant omission was that of the Secretary of State and the Director General of Water Services who had failed to take enforcement action, which would have had the effect of remedying the contravention and/or allowing the claimant a civil remedy.[129] However, it was found that the possibility of their being other defendants did not serve as a defence to the action which had been brought against the particular undertaker. Similarly unsuccessful was the argument that the claimant had failed to exhaust his remedies by not following up the suggestion that he should register the complaint with the Director General through the appropriate Customer Services Committee.

Another unsuccessful argument put forward by the sewerage undertaker was to the effect that it could not be guilty of infringement of a Convention right in circumstances in which it could not have acted any differently.[130] That is, that the undertaker was legally bound to accept connections to the sewer and so could not prevent the consequent flooding.[131] This argument was not accepted on the basis that the exception for situations where the defendant could not have acted differently would only apply where the defendant's inactivity was a *necessary* consequence of the legislation. Clearly, the defendant could, legally, have acted differently in the sense of actually undertaking the works required to prevent the sewer flooding.

### 7.9.5 The High Court's Approach to Human Rights

On the issue of contravention of human rights, the initial conclusion of the High Court was that the defendant's failure to carry out the works necessary to bring an end to the sewer flooding, in principle, constituted an interference with the claimant's Convention right to respect for his home. Likewise, it was found that there had been an infringement of the claimant's Convention right to the peaceful enjoyment of his possessions insofar as diminution in the value of his property should be regarded as partial expropriation without compensation. The claims for infringement of Convention rights could not be sustained in relation to circumstances

---

[128] s.6(1) and (6) Human Rights Act 1998.
[129] See ss.18 to 22 Water Industry Act 1991 and particularly s.18(8).
[130] Under s.6(2)(a) and (6) Human Rights Act 1998.
[131] Under s.106 Water Industry Act 1991 and see 7.2 above.

arising before 2 October 2000, the date at which the Human Rights Act 1998 came into force. Nonetheless, as a matter of principle, the continuation of the flooding after that date was actionable under the 1998 Act.

Despite these fundamentally important findings, the High Court took the view that Convention rights were subject to qualifications that needed to be considered in order to strike a 'proportional' balance between the interests of the community as a whole and the protection of individual rights.[132] On this, it was pertinent that the right to respect for a person's home was qualified by wording that allowed actions that were 'necessary in a democratic society in the interest of the economic well-being of the country or for the protection of the rights and freedoms of others'. Similarly, the right to peaceful enjoyment of possessions was subject to the competing consideration of the 'general interest'. In each instance, the burden rested upon the defendant to show that these exceptions constituted a justification for the infringement of the claimant's rights that had arisen.

The difficulties involved in determining whether a sewerage undertaker had surmounted the 'justification burden' were recognised. Prior to the Human Rights Act 1998, the Water Industry Act 1991 had allocated responsibility to the Secretary of State and the Director General of Water Services to determine whether enforcement proceedings should be brought. Determinations of this kind involved the exercise of discretion, with appropriate weight being given to factors such as the amount of funds made available to an undertaker and the priority to be given to a particular complainant as compared with others suffering a comparable predicament. The underlying political issue was whether undertakers should be under a duty to provide a faultless sewerage system for everyone, regardless of the cost involved, or whether undertakers should be under some lesser duty and, if so, what the extent of this duty should be.

Previously, the mechanism for resolving political and economic issues of this kind had been through control, exercised by the Director General of Water Services, over the charges which undertakers were allowed to impose upon their customers. In turn, these controls determined the amount that undertakers were able to spend upon improvements to their sewerage systems. Essentially, social and economic factors needed to be balanced to prioritise and facilitate improvements within a budget dictated by the amounts that customers could reasonably be expected to pay. The task of determining a proportionate balance, between the interests of a

---

[132] On the need for a 'proportional' interpretation of rights under the European Convention on Human Rights see *R v Director of Public Prosecutions ex parte Kebilene* [1999] 3 WLR 972.

particular claimant and those of the community as a whole, was recognised to be beyond the expertise of the court.

Nonetheless, on the basis that the sewerage undertaker was the defendant in the proceedings at issue, there was precedent for the High Court to consider the merits of a claim that an appropriate balance had not been struck.[133] Hence, allowing the undertaker a 'wide margin of discretion', it was justifiable for the court to consider the merits of the mechanisms used by the undertaker to determine priorities in improvement of the sewerage system.

In taking stock of the economic information and the system for determining the sewerage undertaker's flood alleviation priorities, the question of law needing to be addressed was whether the disadvantage at which the claimant was placed was within the scope of the qualifications provided to his Convention rights. That is, was the interference that had been suffered, in apparent contravention of Convention rights, justified in the interests of the economic well-being of the country or the public interest? Bearing in mind that the burden of showing justification lay upon the defendant, and recognising that the undertaker must be allowed a margin of discretion in determining its flooding alleviation priorities, it was concluded that justification had not been established.

In particular, there were a number of respects in which the points system operated by the undertaker was regarded as questionable by the High Court. In working out priorities, account was taken of the time which had elapsed since a flooding incident in relation to internal flooding but not in relation to external flooding and consideration should have been attached to the relatively recent flooding experienced by the claimant. Similarly, the points system failed adequately to reflect the frequency of flooding events and to give sufficient weighting to the high frequency of flooding that the claimant had suffered. No account was taken of the period of nine years during which the claimant had been waiting to have something done about the flooding problem, or the value of the property flooded, the diminution in value or the cost of repairs where damage had been suffered. Likewise, the points system failed to take account of the fact that a customer may have spent money in trying to address the flooding problem. On the other hand, the points system took account of matters which, it was thought, should not be relevant, such as whether or not a complaint had received press coverage.

---

[133] See *Powell and Rayner* v *United Kingdom* (1990) 12 EHRR 355 (concerning the appropriateness of measures to control, abate and compensate for aircraft noise) and *R* v *Cambridge Health Authority ex parte B* [1995] 1 WLR 898 (where consideration was given to the reasonableness of a decision of a health authority not to allocate funding for medical treatment).

Despite these 'apparent faults' in the fairness of the points system, it was conceded that the sewerage undertaker's case might turn out to be fair, or at least within the margin of discretion allowed, but more evidence of the numbers involved in each class under the points system, and the respective costs involved in undertaking remedial measures, was needed to establish its fairness. The failure of the defendant to provide the necessary justification had the consequence that the High Court had to rule in favour of the claimant. Given the continuing refusal of the undertaker to carry out the necessary works, the claimant had a good cause of action for infringement of his Convention rights as from the commencement of the operation of the Human Rights Act 1998, on 2 October 2000.

### 7.9.6 The Court of Appeal's Approach to Human Rights

The approach of the High Court towards the contravention of human rights contrasts strikingly with the approach taken by the Court of Appeal. On appeal, the sewerage undertaker reaffirmed its view that the statutory scheme struck a fair balance between the rights of individuals and the general interests of the community and incorporated mechanisms to ensure this, within the margin of discretion allowed to Parliament. The proper remedy, therefore, was to register a complaint through the Office of Water Services, since this mechanism allowed an enforcement order to be made requiring the undertaker to perform its statutory duty.[134] Where an enforcement order is made, it is open to the claimant to seek compensation for any infringement of that order.[135] In the event of no order being made, it would be possible for the claimant to challenge the decision through judicial review proceedings.

However, the Court of Appeal took the view that the statutory enforcement mechanism was not adequate to address situations where a breach of human rights was at issue. The exclusion of any right to compensation, except where an infringement of an enforcement order was involved, may have raised conflicts with human rights law where a breach of statutory duty was involved, but Mr Marcic's claim was not only for breach of statutory duty. He was also claiming compensation for interference with his human rights, and the statutory scheme did not cater for this eventuality and specifically excluded any right to compensation for contraventions arising before any enforcement order was made. The statutory procedure for issuing enforcement notices might provide a satisfactory means of striking the necessary balance for claimants who are being denied the benefits that the undertaker is required to provide, but it did not address a

---

[134] Under s.18 Water Industry Act 1991.
[135] Under s.22(2) Water Industry Act 1991.

situation where the actions of an undertaker constituted a breach of human rights.[136]

Beyond these findings, the Court of Appeal identified a number of 'unanswered questions' arising from the proceedings, to some extent interlinking common law with human rights issues. Amongst these, it was observed that, where a nuisance results from an existing sewerage system becoming overcharged, liability should not depend upon whether or not there are steps which the undertaker should reasonably have taken to abate the nuisance. Isolated and infrequent flooding may not justify the expenditure necessary to remove the risk, and the need for disproportionate expenditure might be a ground for declining to grant an injunction. Nevertheless, it does not follow that a householder who suffers flooding in these circumstances should receive no compensation. As the point was made,

> '[i]t seems to us at least arguable that to strike a fair balance between the individual and the general community, those who pay to make use of a sewerage system should be charged sufficient to cover the cost of paying compensation to the minority who suffer damage as a consequence of the operation of the system.'[137]

This result could be achieved if the principle in *Rylands* v *Fletcher*[138] was applied to liability for sewage flooding, though it was recognised to be questionable whether this could be achieved without 'a degree of modification of legal principle'. Nonetheless, it was indicated that such modification of the common law may be necessary if the common law is to 'march in step' with the requirements of the Human Rights Convention.[139]

In addition, the Court of Appeal seemed to indicate a significantly more negative view of whether a fair balance might have been struck by the system of priorities for sewer improvements adopted by the sewerage undertaker. The High Court had been 'prepared to contemplate' that the funding priorities of the undertaker might have been 'entirely fair' in the final outcome, notwithstanding that nothing was done to remedy the claimant's flooding problem in the foreseeable future. The Court of Appeal doubted this.

On this matter, reference was made to the European Commission of Human Rights decision in *S* v *France*[140] where nuisances generated by a nuclear power station near the claimant's home had been found to

---

[136] [2002] EWCA 65 para.110.
[137] [2002] EWCA 65 para.114, per Phillips LJ.
[138] See 2.5.2 above on *Rylands* v *Fletcher*.
[139] [2002] EWCA 65 para.115, per Phillips LJ.
[140] (1990) 65 D&R 250.

constitute an infringement of human rights under Article 8 and Article 1 of the First Protocol of the Human Rights Convention. However, payment of compensation had the result that the interference with the claimant's rights did not go beyond what was necessary in a democratic society. Hence, determinations of whether an interference is 'necessary in a democratic society', and whether a fair balance had been struck, should be determined by a 'principle of proportionality', which meant that particular individuals should not be obliged to bear an unreasonable burden. The implication of this was that, where an authority carries on an undertaking in the general interests of the community, it may have to pay compensation to individuals whose rights are infringed in order to achieve a fair balance between the interests of the individuals and the community. As Phillips LJ expressed the point,

> '[w]e have referred to these matters, which have not been explored in the present action, lest sewerage undertakers assume from our judgment that their liability to pay compensation for damage done by discharge from an overcharged sewer is dependent upon whether or not there are measures which they should reasonably have taken to prevent the discharge. That does not necessarily follow from our judgment.'[141]

It is difficult to read this passage without taking it to mean that compensation will be payable for sewage flooding regardless of whether there is anything that an undertaker could reasonably have been expected to do to prevent it. Insofar as human rights infringements arise in respect of sewer flooding, a form of absolute liability seems to be being advocated which is capable of overriding previous principles governing civil liability.

### 7.9.7 Compensation for Human Rights Contraventions

Following the High Court determination of liability for contravention of human rights, subsequent High Court proceedings, in *Peter Marcic v Thames Water Utilities Ltd (No.2)*,[142] were pursued to determine, as a preliminary matter, the remedy available to the claimant. In the initial proceedings, it had been held that a mandatory injunction requiring work to be carried out to address the sewer flooding would not be granted. It was clarified that the reasons for not granting the injunction were that it would have to specify the works precisely and that specification was a matter of engineering expertise that was not before the court. Moreover, performance of the injunction would require the co-operation of third parties, although the defendant had powers allowing the compulsory purchase of land.[143]

---

[141] [2002] EWCA 65 para.119, per Phillips LJ.
[142] [2001] 4 All ER 326.
[143] [2001] 4 All ER 326, at para.7.

The alternative remedy of an award of damages was the subject of a dispute as to the basis upon which compensation should be assessed. The claimant contended that the appropriate measure of damages should be the difference between the value of the property as it was, with the propensity to flood, and the value of the property as it would be if works to prevent flooding had been properly undertaken. The defendant contested this on the basis that it contravened the general principle that damages in substitution for an injunction should only be allowed where 'small' and easily estimated payments of money are involved.[144] However, the court found, in favour of the claimant, that the 'difference in value' measure would be appropriate where it was the claimant, rather than the defendant, that was seeking compensation in lieu of an injunction.

Another aspect of the dispute was whether an award of difference in value compensation was 'premature', in the sense of compensating the claimant for future losses which might, or might not, actually be suffered, depending upon whether or when the work was undertaken. In essence, the claimant would be securing an unjustified gain in respect of 'future wrongs' if he were to be compensated for a continuing loss which, at some point in the future, was actually rectified. On this point, the High Court found that compensation for future wrongs was not inconsistent with human rights law requiring 'just satisfaction' to be provided.[145]

Accordingly, in relation to the infringement of Convention rights, the High Court concluded that, to meet the requirements of the 1998 Act, on 2 October 2000 the defendants should have put in place measures to bring the nuisance to an end. These measures should have ensured that the nuisance would have ended by a reasonable 'completion date' for the necessary works. As from the completion date, the claimant's damages would be assessed as the diminution in value of the property below its value with the works completed and without the prospect of future flooding. Depending upon the ascertainment of the completion date, therefore, Mr Marcic would be entitled to the difference between the value of the property with the propensity to flood and its value without that propensity. Although, in principle, damages for inconvenience, distress and vexation arising out of the flooding might be awarded in relation to events after the completion

---

[144] See *Shelfer* v *City of London Electric Lighting Co* [1895] 1 Ch 287.
[145] See s.8(4) Human Rights Act 1998, requiring a court to take account of the principles applied by the European Court of Human Rights in determining the amount of an award, and *S* v *France* (1990) 65 D&R 250 where compensation was found to have been justifiably awarded in relation to *future* noise constituting an interference with Convention rights. Contrast *West Leigh Colliery Co Ltd* v *Tunnicliffe and Hampson Ltd* [1908] AC 27 where it was held that depreciation in the value of property brought about by the apprehension of future damage could not be compensated for.

date, it was thought that these heads of claim would be adequately reflected in the diminution in value of the house.[146]

This resolution of the claim to a remedy for contravention of the claimant's human rights as a result of the sewer flooding is informative as to the general manner in which such issues should be approached. However, the subsequent finding of the Court of Appeal that the defendant was liable *as a matter of common law* has had the consequence that the defendant's liability for nuisance extended to the period before the 1998 Act came into operation. Nonetheless, the Court of Appeal was prepared to assume that the common law damages that the claimant would be entitled to should afford him 'just satisfaction' in a similar manner to that in which damages would be assessed for a human rights violation.[147]

### 7.9.8 Implications of the Marcic Decision

As previously noted, the Court of Appeal decision in the *Marcic* case is presently the subject of an application for leave of appeal to the House of Lords and the final outcome, therefore, remains to be seen. Insofar as the Court of Appeal decision is concerned, however, the decision represents a radical departure from the previous understanding of the common law regarding sewerage undertakers' liabilities. In addition, it might be argued that the alleged violation of human rights at issue extends some way beyond the existing jurisprudence of the European Court of Human Rights.

The practical implications of the new requirement to alleviate sewer flooding, or to compensate victims of flooding, are momentous. The estimated cost of £1,000 million, to prevent sewer flooding in the Thames Water region alone, is indicative of the enormous financial implications nationally. Whilst the cost of compensating those suffering the consequences of sewer flooding would probably be significantly less than the cost of rectifying the problems, it will be considerable nonetheless. The Court of Appeal judgment recognised the implications of this: that those paying sewerage service charges will have to meet the significant costs of protecting the minority who presently suffer sewer flooding. Similarly, the limits upon sewerage services charges, imposed by the Office of Water Services, will need to take account of this.[148]

Although flooding from sewers is undeniably a serious problem, a broader issue is whether reasoning analogous to that applied in the *Marcic* case may be applied to situations where non-sewer flooding is at issue.

---

[146] [2001] 4 All ER 326, at para.18.
[147] [2002] EWCA 65, 7 February 2002, para.104.
[148] See Office of Water Services, *Flooding from Sewers: a way forward* (2002).

Essentially, the question is whether the general body of flood defence law can be distinguished from the law relating to sewer flooding. In effect, the issue is whether flood and coastal defence operating authorities are legally bound to exercise their statutory powers to undertake defence works where a failure to do so would involve a contravention of human rights by allowing flooding to take place. This conclusion would be remarkable since, as has been seen,[149] statutory responsibilities have been purposefully formulated as *powers* to recognise the potentially unlimited amount which is capable of being expended upon flood and coastal defence, and that the need for operations must be reconciled with the practical limits upon availability of funding. A finding that a flood defence operating authority was bound to undertake work, or compensate a flooding victim for the failure to do so, because infringements of human rights are involved, would have the surprising effect of turning a substantial body of permissive *powers* into mandatory *duties*, without any apparent mechanism to ensure availability of commensurate funding.

Another potentially remarkable aspect of applying the reasoning from the *Marcic* case to other sectors of flood defence activity is the difficulty, or impossibility, of providing any absolute guarantee of protection of human rights, insofar as non-sewer flooding is properly regarded as a human right. As has been seen,[150] the *absolute* protection of any area from flooding is not possible. The best that can be done is to secure the protection of land within the design specification of an appropriate flood defence structure, which usually means protection against a 1 in 100 year event for river flooding or a 1 in 200 year event for sea flooding. The critical question is whether the human right to protection against flooding is a right to a *reasonable* level of protection, as indicated by the relevant return period, or whether it is a right to protection of an unqualified kind. If it is the latter, then no amount of expenditure on flood defence will even provide an absolute guarantee that human rights will never be infringed.

## 7.10 WATER SUPPLY

The other kind of flooding problem which may arise in relation to water utility activities is that of flooding from water supply pipes of various kinds. The following sections consider the two main possibilities: flooding from water supply pipes vested in a water undertaker, subject to statutory and common law liabilities, and flooding arising from water supply pipes within premises and outside the responsibilities of a water undertaker.

---

[149] See 4.3.1 and 4.6.1 above on flood defence operational powers.
[150] See 1.5 above on risk.

## 7.11 STATUTORY LIABILITY FOR ESCAPE OF WATER

The general responsibility for water supply in England and Wales falls upon water undertakers, comprising undertakers appointed for the purposes of Part III of the Water Industry Act 1991 and including statutory water companies which are responsible for the supply of water for domestic and other purposes in many areas under the Statutory Water Companies Act 1991. In each instance the water undertaker will be subject to a general duty to develop and maintain a water supply system to ensure the provision of water supplies to premises in its area and for maintaining, improving and extending water mains and other pipes as is necessary for meeting obligations under Part III of the Water Industry Act 1991.[151] The detail of water supply obligations upon undertakers is outside the scope of this work,[152] but the issue of liability for escapes of water from supply pipes is relevant.

The notable contrast with sewage flooding is that, under statute, water undertakers will normally be strictly liable for escapes of water from their water supply pipes. Hence, where an escape of water, however caused, occurs from a pipe vested in a water undertaker and this causes loss or damage,[153] the undertaker will be civilly liable for that loss or damage, subject only to stated exceptions.[154] An exception arises where the loss or damage is wholly due to the fault of the person who suffers the loss or any employee, agent or contractor of that person. Also, no liability will arise in respect of loss or damage for which the undertaker would not otherwise be liable and which is sustained by the Environment Agency or by certain relevant undertakers or other bodies or persons. However, liability may be reduced where contributory negligence is found or where a contribution may be recovered from a third party where the liability was due to the fault of that party.[155]

---

[151] s.37(1) Water Industry Act 1991.
[152] See W. Howarth and D. McGillivray, *Water Pollution and Water Quality Law* (2001) Chs.7 and 17.
[153] See *Anglian Water Services Ltd* v *Crawshaw Robbins and Co Ltd*, unreported, Queen's Bench Division, 6 February 2001, para.149, where 'loss or damage' was found to mean loss of property or damage to property, so that non-physical damage could not be recovered.
[154] s.209(1) Water Industry Act 1991 and, for similar liability in relation to the Environment Agency, see s.208(1) Water Resources Act 1991.
[155] s.209(2) to (5) Water Industry Act 1991. The 'relevant undertakers' include statutory undertakers (within the meaning of s.336(1) Town and Country Planning Act 1990), gas and electricity suppliers, highway authorities and persons to whom a right to compensation is conferred by s.82 New Roads and Street Works Act 1991. On contributory negligence see the Law Reform (Contributory Negligence) Act 1945 and on contributions from third parties see the Civil Liability (Contribution) Act 1978. The application of the Civil Liability (Contribution) Act 1978 to this context

Subject to the exceptions, the liability of a water undertaker will be strict and will arise in relation to escapes of water 'however caused'. From a claimant's point of view, this should be unproblematic where there has been a sudden and catastrophic bursting of a water main and where the link between the escape of water and the damage is readily apparent. However, there may be other situations where a person suffering water damage has greater difficulty in establishing a causal link between the escape and the damage.

A good illustration of this problem is to be seen in *Harvey Nichols and Co Ltd v Thames Water Utilities Ltd*[156] where the basement of a department store in central London was subject to severe water ingress which had the effect of delaying structural work that was being undertaken and causing the claimant expense in rectifying the problem.[157] The central matter at issue was the source of the water entering the basement, that is, whether it was water originating from a leak in a pipe vested in the defendant or whether it was groundwater that was naturally present. Ascertaining the source of the water involved evidence being presented by an array of experts who presented geological and hydrological information of various kinds. Ultimately, it was concluded that the surrounding water table was below the level of the water ingress in the basement, and the variability of the water flow and unseasonable fluctuations suggested a non-natural source. Accordingly, on the balance of probabilities, the source of the water was found to be a leakage from the water main for which the undertaker was found to be liable. Nonetheless, establishing this primarily factual point raised no small number of extremely technical evidential difficulties.

---

was considered in *Thames Water Utilities Ltd v (1) Videotron Corporation Ltd (2) McNicholas Construction Co Ltd* (unreported, Court of Appeal, 10 December 1999) where the defendants had fractured a water main whilst digging a trench and the claimants were bound to provide compensation to occupiers that had been flooded as a result under s.209(1) Water Industry Act 1991. It was found that, though the defendants were responsible for the initial flooding, the claimants had responded with insufficient speed in isolating the main, and liability should be apportioned, 92% to the defendants and 8% to the claimants. Also see *Anglian Water Services Ltd v Crawshaw Robbins and Co Ltd*, unreported, Queen's Bench Division, 6 February 2001.

[156] Unreported, Technology and Construction Court, 16 November 1999. Also on the need for a claimant to show causality, see *Steven Dobson Davison v North West Water Ltd*, unreported, Queen's Bench Division, 10 March 1999, where a leaking water main was found not to have contributed to a road traffic accident. On the insurance implications of claims for damage from a burst water main see *Kitchen Design and Advice Ltd v Lea Valley Water Co* [1989] 2 Lloyd's Rep 221.

[157] Also, on the restoration works which may be undertaken in the aftermath of flooding from a burst water main, see *(1) Skandia Property (UK) Ltd (2) Vala Properties BV v Thames Water Utilities Ltd*, unreported, Court of Appeal, 27 July 1999.

Outside the sphere of statutory strict liability for water escapes from supply pipes, and special provisions governing reservoirs,[158] the fact that an injury involving the escape of water is the result of an action taken under statutory authority will not afford a defence where negligence or some lack of proper precaution is shown.[159] Hence, water undertakers and others who are entitled to accumulate water artificially will normally be liable for acts undertaken in accordance with their powers, though not *duties*, and will be liable where powers are negligently exercised. Pertinently, undertakers will be negligent if they fail to take reasonable precautions in laying or maintaining water mains or in detecting or remedying leaks that occur.[160]

In the absence of negligence, as a general principle, a statutory body is not liable for a nuisance that is attributable to the performance by it of a *duty* imposed upon it by statute.[161] However, a statutory body will be liable for nuisance in the exercise of a *power* conferred by statute, even without negligence, if it is expressly made liable for nuisance by statute or not exempted from such liability.[162] Hence in *Department of Transport* v *North West Water Authority*[163] a water main running under a street burst and caused damage to a street, but this was not found to be attributable to any negligence on the part of the water undertaker. The undertaker's liability in nuisance in respect of damage to the street was disputed but, in accordance with the relevant legislation,[164] it was found that a statutory body would not be liable in nuisance for an act that was undertaken in accordance with a statutory *duty* even in the absence of any statutory exemption from such liability.

## 7.12 CIVIL LIABILITY FOR WATER SUPPLY SYSTEMS

The statutory liability of water undertakers for escapes of water from their supply pipes may be contrasted with the position under common law where

---

[158] See 8.4 below on reservoir safety.
[159] See, for example, *Dunn* v *Birmingham Canal Co* (1872) LR 8 QB 42.
[160] *Manchester Corporation* v *Markland* [1936] AC 360, though contrast *Green* v *Chelsea Waterworks Co* (1894) 70 LT 547 and *Snook* v *Grand Junction Waterworks Co* (1886) 2 TLR 308.
[161] Per Lord Fraser of Tullybelton in *Department of Transport* v *North West Water Authority* [1984] AC 336 at p.359, citing *Hammond* v *Vestry of St Pancras* (1874) LR 9 CP 316.
[162] Per Lord Fraser of Tullybelton in *Department of Transport* v *North West Water Authority* [1984] AC 336 at p.359, citing *Charing Cross Electricity Supply Co* v *Hydraulic Power Co* [1914] 3 KB 772.
[163] [1984] AC 336.
[164] s.18(2) Public Utilities Street Works Act 1950 (now see New Roads and Street Works Act 1991) provided that if any nuisance was caused by the discharge of water from supply works, nothing in the Act would exonerate the undertakers from any action in proceedings by street undertakers.

an escape of water takes place from an internal water supply system that is the responsibility of the owner of the property. Typically, this might arise where frost damage, vandalism or lack of maintenance causes a water supply pipe or structure to burst or overflow and results in damage to an adjoining property. In such circumstances, liability for water damage is entirely dependent upon whether negligence can be shown.

The general situation is well illustrated by *Ross* v *Fedden*[165] where the claimant occupied an upper floor and the defendant a lower floor of business premises. After their respective premises had closed for the weekend, water escaped from a water closet on the defendant's premises and percolated through the floor into the claimant's premises where damage was caused to the claimant's stock. The escape of water arose because of a defect in a valve in the pipe supplying water to the water closet and an obstruction of the waste pipe, neither of which were known to the defendant or could have been detected without examination. It was held that, in the absence of negligence, there was no liability for the water damage that had occurred in the defendant's premises. Another illustration is provided by *Peters* v *Prince of Wales Theatre (Birmingham) Ltd*[166] where the damage arose because an exceptionally severe frost had caused pipes in a fire sprinkler system to burst and this had resulted in water percolating into lower shop premises. Again, it was held that, in the absence of any negligence on the part of the defendants, no liability would arise.

Most authoritatively, the possibilities for liability for water damage of this kind were considered in *Rickards* v *Lothian*[167] where an escape of water into lower premises was found to have been caused by a malicious act of a third person who had turned on a tap in a washbasin and blocked the overflow. The basic principle was reaffirmed, that negligence against the owner of the upper premises needs to be shown before liability would arise

---

[165] (1872) LR 7 QB 661. Contrast *A. Prosser and Son Ltd* v *Levy* [1955] 3 All ER 577 where negligence was established in circumstances where water piping was found to have been in an unsatisfactory condition and the defendant had failed to show that the escape of water was due to vandalism. Contrast also situations where an actionable nuisance has been found to arise where water is *purposefully* allowed to fall from eaves and gutters onto neighbouring land (*Fay* v *Prentice* (1845) 1 CB 828) though the right of 'eavesdropping' may be the subject of an easement (*Harvey* v *Walters* (1873) LR 8CP 62).

[166] [1943] 1 KB 73. Contrast *Passley* v *Wandsworth London Borough Council*, unreported, Court of Appeal, 24 May 1996, where the bursting of pipes on the roof of a block of flats was found to be foreseeable in the British climate, and the landlord was held liable for failing to keep the pipes in repair.

[167] [1913] AC 263 (Privy Council). See also *Hawkins* v *Dhawan and Mishiku* (1987) 283 EG 1388.

and the defendant, who had neither instigated nor foreseen the vandalism and could not reasonably have prevented it, was not liable. In addition, an argument that accumulation of water in a property was a 'non natural' use of that property, for which strict liability under the principle of *Ryland* v *Fletcher*[168] should arise in the event of an escape, was rejected. Having a supply of water for reasonably incidental use in a property did not give rise to strict liability and, in the absence of any lack of proper and reasonable care, the defendant was not liable for the escape that had occurred.

More recently, similar reasoning has been applied in *British Gas Plc* v *Stockport Metropolitan Borough Council*[169] where water escaped from a crack in a large diameter service pipe, which was vested in a local authority, and caused the partial collapse of a disused railway embankment. Here, it was found that the principle of strict liability would not apply where water was being supplied for common and ordinary use. Specifically, the supply of water in a large diameter pipe to a block of flats, in the circumstances at issue, did not bring the situation within the *Rylands* v *Fletcher* principle.

---

[168] See 2.5.2 above on *Rylands* v *Fletcher*.
[169] [2001] Env LR 763.

# Chapter 8

# PUBLIC HEALTH, HIGHWAYS AND RESERVOIRS

## 8.1 INTRODUCTION

Although the powers of local authorities that are specifically concerned with flood defence and coast protection have already been discussed, local authorities also possess various other responsibilities with important flood defence implications. This chapter considers three relevant areas that are primarily local authority responsibilities: public health legislation insofar as it addresses water quantity concerns; the drainage of highways; and the statutory regime for reservoir safety. Further local authority responsibilities arise in relation to the operation of the town and country planning system, and the role of land-use planning in relation to the avoidance of flooding is examined in Chapter 9.

## 8.2 PUBLIC HEALTH

### 8.2.1 Statutory Nuisances

Part III of the Environmental Protection Act 1990 provides for a range of powers of local authorities[1] in relation to statutory nuisances. 'Statutory nuisances' are defined to encompass a range of matters, including premises, smoke, fumes, dust and noise which are, in each case, 'prejudicial to health or a nuisance'. In relation to local environmental problems of these kinds, it is the duty of the local authority to inspect its area to detect such nuisances, or to take reasonably practicable steps to investigate complaints and, where satisfied that a statutory nuisance exists, to serve abatement notices upon those responsible.[2] If a person on whom an abatement notice is served, without reasonable excuse, contravenes or fails to comply with any requirement or prohibition imposed by the notice, that person will be guilty of an offence.[3]

---

[1] 'Local authority', for this purpose, means, in Greater London, a London borough council, the Common Council of the City of London and, as respects the Temples, the Sub-Treasurer of the Inner Temple and the Under-Treasurer of the Middle Temple respectively. In England, outside Greater London, 'local authority' means a district council and in Wales a county council or county borough council (s.79(7)(a) Environmental Protection Act 1990, as amended).

[2] ss.79(1) and 80(1) Environmental Protection Act 1990.

[3] s.80(4) Environmental Protection Act 1990. This offence is generally punishable, on summary conviction, by a fine not exceeding level 5 on the standard scale, presently

Although most of the matters which are identified as statutory nuisances are unlikely to have any connection with flood defence, a residual category which is provided for is 'any matter declared by any enactment to be a statutory nuisance'.[4] This encompasses certain nuisances in relation to watercourses[5] that were identified as statutory nuisances in earlier public health legislation. In particular, a statutory nuisance may arise in relation to any part of a non-navigated watercourse that is so choked or silted up as to obstruct or impede the proper flow of water and thereby to cause a nuisance. This is subject to the proviso that this category of statutory nuisance will not serve to impose liability on anyone other than the person by whose act or default the nuisance arises or continues.[6]

The issue of liability for statutory nuisance was considered in *Neath Rural District Council* v *Williams*,[7] where a natural watercourse on the defendant's land became silted up. The silting was found to be due to natural causes for which the defendant was not responsible, but the effect was to cause a nuisance by contributing to flooding. It was held that the defendant's failure to comply with an abatement notice requiring the removal of the obstruction was not unlawful. This outcome was reached on the basis that the proviso, requiring default to be shown in allowing the nuisance to arise or continue, was intended to prevent the imposition of any statutory duty upon a riparian owner to maintain the flow of a watercourse and to reflect that, at that time, there was thought to be no common law duty to remove naturally occurring obstructions from the stream.

As has been noted,[8] the assumption that there is no common law duty to remove natural obstructions from a watercourse to prevent flooding is now doubtful. Moreover, the *Neath* case is difficult to reconcile with subsequent common law decisions where liability has been recognised in respect of

---

£5,000, together with a further fine of one-tenth of that amount for each day on which the offence continues after conviction (s.80(5)). In relation to industrial, trade or business premises the maximum fine is £20,000 (s.80(6)).

[4] s.79(1)(h) Environmental Protection Act 1990.

[5] See *R* v *Falmouth and Truro Port Health Authority ex parte South West Water Ltd* [2000] 3 All ER 306 where it was held that an estuary did not constitute a 'watercourse' within the meaning of these provisions.

[6] s.259(1)(b) Public Health Act 1936.

[7] [1951] 1 KB 115. For a contrasting example, see *Upper District Committee of the County of Renfrew* v *Woddrop's Trustees* 1927 SLT 69 (Sheriff Court) where a statutory nuisance arose through the defendant's ditch having become so silted up and overgrown that water flowed onto neighbouring land where it stagnated and became a breeding ground for mosquitoes which affected nearby residential properties (under s.16(2) Public Health (Scotland) Act 1897). See also *R* v *Cumberland Justices ex parte Trimble* (1877) 41 JP 454.

[8] Generally see 2.4.3 above on the common law obligation to maintain watercourses.

naturally arising nuisances.[9] The more likely interpretation of the law is that statutory nuisance provisions are capable of applying to watercourses which have become silted, whether naturally or otherwise, and an abatement notice will be appropriately served upon the person responsible where a flooding nuisance is established as a result of such obstructions.

### 8.2.2 Powers concerning Ponds and Ditches

A number of other powers of local authorities, which may have implications for land drainage, are also provided for under the Public Health Act 1936. Closely related to statutory nuisance is a power of a parish or community council or local authority to 'deal with' any pond, pool, ditch, gutter or place containing, or used for the collection of, any drainage, filth, stagnant water or matter which is likely to be prejudicial to health. Where water in this state is identified, action may be taken by draining, cleansing or covering it, or otherwise preventing it from being prejudicial to health, providing that this does not interfere with any private right, or with any public drainage, sewerage or sewage disposal works. Similarly, works may be executed for the purpose of maintenance or improvement, which are incidental to the power to deal with water-related nuisances. In addition, a parish council or local authority may contribute towards the expenses incurred by any other person in taking the actions referred to.[10] Although the circumstances at issue would tend to be linked to water quality concerns, or perhaps nuisances arising through infestation by insects or vermin, it is notable that a mechanism for addressing these concerns is through improvements in land drainage.

Provision is also made for the 'cleansing' of offensive watercourses or ditches which lie near to, or form, the boundary between local authorities. Hence where such a ditch is so foul and offensive as injuriously to affect the district of a local authority, it may register a complaint against a neighbouring local authority. A magistrates' court, having jurisdiction in the place where the watercourse or ditch is situated, may make such an order as it considers reasonable with respect to its cleansing and the execution of any work appearing to be necessary, and persons by whom, and the proportions in which, the costs are to be paid.[11]

---

[9]  See *Davey* v *Harrow Corporation* [1958] 1 QB 60 where liability in nuisance was established for naturally growing trees, and see also *Bybrook Barn Garden Centre Ltd* v *Kent County Council* [2001] Env LR 543, per Waller LJ at para.37 and see 2.5.3 and 2.9 above. Most recently, on liability for damage caused by trees, see *Delaware Mansions Ltd and Others* v *Lord Mayor and Citizens of Westminster* [2001] UKHL 55, 25 October 2001.

[10] s.260 Public Health Act 1936. See also s.259(1) which states that a statutory nuisance will arise where any pond, ditch, gutter or watercourse is so foul or in such a state as to be prejudicial to health or a nuisance.

[11] s.261 Public Health Act 1936.

### 8.2.3 Culverting of Watercourses

If a local authority considers that any watercourse or ditch which is situated on land laid out for building, or on which building land abuts,[12] should be wholly or partially filled up or covered over, the authority may require the owner of the land to do so before the building work commences. Alternatively, the authority may require the owner to substitute a pipe, drain or culvert with all the necessary gullies and other means of conveying surface water into and through it.[13]

In relation to the power of the authority to require infilling or culverting of watercourses and ditches, any question as to the reasonableness of the works that are required may, on the application of either party, be determined by a magistrates' court. Any person, who on land to which a notice of this kind applies, begins or proceeds with any building operations before executing the works required by the notice will commit an offence. However, the power to require infilling or culverting works will not authorise the authority to require works to be executed by any person other than the owner of land which is laid out for building without the consent of that person, or prejudicially to affect the rights of any person who is not the owner of the land concerned.[14]

It is an offence to culvert or cover any stream or watercourse except in accordance with plans and sections approved by the local authority.[15] However, approval for these purposes must not be unreasonably withheld and if the authority, within 6 weeks after the submission of plans, fails to notify the applicant of its determination, the plans will be deemed to have been approved. Questions as to the reasonableness of any works that are

---

[12] Under a similarly worded local statute (s.64 Tottenham Urban District Council Act 1900) it was held that where the building land at issue was separated from a watercourse by a strip of land which had been conveyed to another person the building land did not 'abut' a watercourse (*Attorney-General* v *Rowley Brothers and Oxley* (1910) 75 JP 81).

[13] s.262(1) Public Health Act 1936. See also the powers of local authorities to culvert ditches adjoining highways, discussed at 8.2.4 below. On Environment Agency policy on culverting see 4.4.3 above.

[14] s.262(2) to (4) Public Health Act 1936. The offence is punishable by a maximum fine at level 1 on the standard scale, presently £200, and a further fine of £2 per day or each day on which the offence continues after conviction. Note also the discussion of the potential civil liabilities arising from culverting operations at 2.5.3, particularly where subsequent developments in a catchment have the effect of making a culvert inadequate to take the increased flow (considered in *Bybrook Barn Garden Centre Ltd* v *Kent County Council* [2001] Env LR 543).

[15] s.263(1) Public Health Act 1936. Contravention of this requirement is punishable by a maximum fine at level 1 on the standard scale, presently £2000, and a further fine not exceeding £2 for each day on which the offence continues after conviction (s.263(4)).

required by a local authority may, on the application of either party, be determined by a magistrates' court. A local authority may not require an owner to receive, or make provision for, the passage of a greater quantity of water than he is otherwise obliged to receive or to permit to pass. Where, at the request of the local authority, the owner makes provision for a larger quantity of water than he is obliged to permit to pass at the time of commencement of work, any additional cost reasonably incurred by him in complying with the request must be borne by the authority.[16]

The rather anachronistic character of the local authority powers concerning culverting must be noted. In respect of building land, the provisions predate modern planning law and it would now seem to be more appropriate for infilling or culverting conditions to be incorporated within any planning permission which is needed for building or other development. The local authority powers to control culverting of watercourses, and to require culverting of building land, are subject to the proviso that they may not be exercised in respect of any stream, watercourse, ditch or culvert within the jurisdiction of a flood defence authority, except after consultation with that authority.[17] However, it is difficult to see what purpose the requirement of consultation with other flood defence authorities serves when, in effect, internal drainage boards and the Environment Agency are otherwise empowered to determine whether consent should be given for obstructions in watercourses including the installation of culverts.[18] The stipulation that, without local authority funding, a person cannot be required to provide a culvert for a greater quantity of water than he would otherwise be obliged to, seems to beg some weighty questions about the potential civil liability for flooding of those who install culverts. Finally, the relatively low levels of fines which are available in relation to the offences seems to make them less appropriate for a prosecuting authority to pursue than alternative offences arising out of the same situations which are otherwise provided for.[19]

The owner or occupier of land within the district of a local authority will be bound to repair, maintain and cleanse any culvert in, on or under that land. If it appears to the authority that a person has failed to fulfil this

---

[16] s.263(2) and (3) Public Health Act 1936.
[17] s.266(1) Public Health Act 1936.
[18] See s.23 Land Drainage Act 1991, discussed at 4.7.3 above, and s.109 Water Resources Act 1991, discussed at 4.4.1 above.
[19] See 9.3 below on contravention of planning control; s.24 Land Drainage Act 1991, on contravention of prohibitions for obstructions (discussed at 4.4.2 above); s.109(4) Water Resources Act 1991, allowing the removal of obstructions by the Environment Agency (discussed at 4.4.1 above); and Schedule 25 para.5(2)(c) Water Resources Act 1991, concerning the power to make byelaws preventing obstruction of watercourses (discussed at 3.4.10 above).

## Public Health

obligation, the local authority may, by notice, require the person to execute such works as are necessary.[20] Again, it is to be noted that land drainage powers may also be exercised to require works for maintaining the flow of watercourses and these may be exercised by a local authority, internal drainage board or the Environment Agency depending upon the circumstances.[21] However, it is envisaged that a local authority should exercise its public health powers to secure the proper flow of an ordinary watercourse as a priority over the land drainage provisions. That is, the corresponding land drainage provisions may not be exercised by the Agency or an internal drainage board except by agreement with the local authority or where, after reasonable notice, the local authority either fails to exercise its public health powers or exercises them improperly.[22]

### 8.3 HIGHWAY DRAINAGE

#### 8.3.1 Highways and Highway Authorities

As a matter of common law, a 'highway' is construed as a way over which the public has a right to pass freely, without hindrance, at all times. Highways have been created by the owner of land dedicating a public right of passage and public acceptance of that right or by long use by the public as evidence of dedication.[23] For statutory purposes, under the Highways Act 1980, except where the context indicates otherwise, a 'highway' means the whole or part of a highway other than a ferry or waterway and, where a highway passes over a bridge or through a tunnel, that bridge or tunnel is taken to be part of the highway.[24]

Generally, the creation, improvement and maintenance of highways at the public expense is the responsibility of 'highway authorities'. In relation to major roads such as trunk roads and special roads, the 'highway authority' means the Minister with transport responsibilities.[25] Most other roads are the responsibility of the 'local' highway authority which is the county or county borough council, the metropolitan district council, the London

---

[20] s.264 Public Health Act 1936. However, if it thinks fit, a local authority may contribute the whole or a part of the expenses of the execution of works in relation to culverts (under ss.259 to 264) or may, by agreement with any owner or occupier, itself execute any works which he may be required, or is entitled, to execute (s.265).
[21] See s.25 Land Drainage Act 1991, and see also s.107(3) Water Resources Act 1991, in relation to main rivers, discussed at 4.4.5 and 4.71 above.
[22] s.26(2)(b) Land Drainage Act 1991, and see 4.7.1 above.
[23] See s.38 Highways Act 1980 on the power of a highway authority to adopt a highway by agreement. Generally see M. Orlik, *An Introduction to Highway Law* (2nd ed. 2001).
[24] s.328(1) and (2) Highways Act 1980.
[25] That is the Minister for Transport and the National Assembly for Wales: see s.329(1) Highways Act 1980, as amended.

borough council or the Common Council of the City of London.[26] Notably, however, many footpaths and bridleways are maintained by district councils and many private roads and streets are maintained at the expense of their owners.

The general position is that the surface of a highway is maintainable at public expense, together with 'the materials and scrapings of it', and vests in the appropriate highway authority.[27] Where the ownership of the highway has been acquired by the authority by compulsory purchase or agreement, the freehold ownership of the soil beneath the highway will also be owned by the authority. However, where a highway has been created by dedication, as is more commonly the case, ownership of the soil will remain with the owner of the land who originally dedicated it or his successors in title. In this situation, the highway authority will own only so much of the soil beneath the highway as is necessary for its maintenance[28] and vesting does not confer upon an authority any rights in relation to minerals beneath the highway.[29]

### 8.3.2 Highway Drains

In relation to the drainage of highways, a 'drain' includes a ditch, gutter, watercourse, soak-away, bridge, culvert, tunnel and pipe. However, the word 'includes' indicates that the list of possibilities is not exhaustive and other mechanisms for the removal of water from highways may be encompassed.[30] The drains 'belonging to' a road for which the council of the county or metropolitan district are the highway authority vest in the council of the county or district in which the road is situated. Where any other drain or any sewer was at the 'material date' used for any purpose in connection with the drainage of a road, that council will continue to have the right to use the drain for the purpose of draining that road.[31]

---

[26] See s.1 Highways Act 1980, as amended by the Local Government Act 1985 and the Local Government (Wales) Act 1994.
[27] s.263(1) Highways Act 1980.
[28] See *Tithe Redemption Commission* v *Runcorn Urban District Council and Another* [1954] Ch 383 where Denning LJ said (at p.407) that the depth of the highway vested in the authority may be said to be 'the top two spits'.
[29] s.335 Highways Act 1980.
[30] s.100(9) Highways Act 1980.
[31] s.264(1) Highways Act 1980. The 'material date' for this purpose is, in the case of a highway that became maintainable at public expense before the commencement of the Highways Act 1980, the date on which it first became so maintainable or 1 April 1974, whichever is later and, in the case of a highway that became maintainable at the public expense after the commencement of the Highways Act 1980, the date on which it became so maintainable. On drains vesting in the councils of London boroughs and the Common Council of the City of London see s.264(2) Highways Act 1980.

The question of what is to count as a 'drain' for highway drainage purposes has been considered by the courts on many occasions. In the early case of *Croft* v *Rickmansworth Highway Board*[32] the issue arose as to whether the highway authority was acting within its statutory powers to maintain 'drains and watercourses'[33] for highway drainage in relation to use of a 'dumb well' which was located on the claimant's property. The 'dumb well' consisted of a hole in the ground, into which water from the highway was conveyed by a pipe, and from which the water percolated into porous chalk soil. This was held not to be a drain for the reason that a 'drain' should properly be understood as a facility by which the course of water was continuously directed, but this did not arise where water percolated through the soil. The dumb well was, therefore, regarded as no more than a receptacle for water brought by a drain, and the highway authority was not acting within its powers in maintaining it for highway drainage.

In the contrasting decision in *Attorney-General* v *Copeland*[34] the highway authority had maintained a pipe for the discharge of water that collected on a highway. The pipe ran through a hedge alongside the highway into the defendant's adjoining land where there was no defined channel through which the discharge could flow. The defendant stopped up the pipe and claimed that the authority's statutory powers[35] did not authorise the pipe because it was not a 'drain' as it did not discharge into a defined outfall channel.[36] It was held that the pipe fell within the statutory meaning of a 'drain', despite the lack of an outfall channel and, in view of the length of time for which the pipe had been in use, a legal origin ought to be presumed for the right to transmit the water onto the defendant's land.[37]

The line of earlier cases, indicating that a 'drain' would not exist unless a proper outfall was in place, has probably been superseded by the extension of the present statutory wording as compared with previous legislation.

---

[32] (1885) 39 Ch D 272.
[33] Under s.67 Highway Act 1835; now see s.100 Highways Act 1980.
[34] [1902] 1 KB 690.
[35] Under s.67 Highway Act 1835; now see s.100 Highways Act 1980. Similarly, on the presumption that a highway drainage facility has a legal origin, see *The County Council of Kings County and O'Sullivan* v *Kennedy* [1910] 2 IR 544.
[36] See the discussion of the alleged need for a 'proper outfall' in relation to public sewers at 7.4.4 above.
[37] Similar reasoning has been adopted in *Croysdale* v *Sudbury-on-Thames Urban District Council* [1898] 2 Ch 515 (where a disused gravel pit, which received water from a highway through a line of pipes, was held not to be part of the drainage system and into which the highway authority had no right to discharge water) and *Ballard* v *Leek Urban Council* (1917) 87 LJ Ch 146 (where an overflow pipe from a catch pit which received storm water and transmitted it onto the claimant's fields was held not to be a 'gutter or drain' within s.67 Highway Act 1835).

This defines a 'drain' to include a soak-away,[38] which has the consequence that a dumb well of the kind that was disapproved of in the *Croft* case, and other kinds of infiltration drainage system,[39] would now be drainage facilities that a highway authority is entitled to construct and maintain.

Another potential difficulty is the contrast between *highway* drainage and *land* drainage. Although the responsibility for highway drainage lies with highway authorities, the responsibility for land drainage is separately provided for. This contrast is most significant in areas where a two-tier system of local authorities is in place, with the county authority acting as the highway authority and the district authority being primarily concerned with other land drainage matters. In this context, it will be especially important to ascertain whether a particular drain should be classified as a highway or a land drain.

The contrast between highway drainage and land drainage was considered in *Attorney-General* v *St Ives Rural District Council*.[40] The facts concerned two drains on farmland which had not been maintained and were so silted that serious flooding of the land resulted. Although an award under the Enclosure Act 1800 had initially required the drains to be maintained by the surveyor of highways for the parish, this responsibility had passed to different bodies with successive legislation. The question at issue was whether the responsibility for maintaining the drains rested with the county council as the highway authority or whether it remained with the rural district council. This involved interpreting local government legislation which made county councils highway authorities, with functions defined under successive highway Acts, subject to the proviso that rural district councils would retain any functions 'not being functions with respect to highways'.[41] In respect of responsibility for drains, it was found that the purpose served by a particular drain should be the determining factor, rather than its historic origins. Drains that serve only to drain highways should be the responsibility of highway authorities whereas drains that drain agricultural land should not. Where a drain serves both agricultural land and a highway, it is a matter of degree as to whether it is properly regarded as land or road drainage. However, on the facts of the case, the clear purpose of the drains at issue was that of draining agricultural land and, therefore, their maintenance was held not to be the responsibility of the highway authority.

---

[38] Under s.100(9) Highways Act 1980.
[39] See 12.2 below on infiltration drainage.
[40] [1961] 2 WLR 111. See also *Williamson* v *Durham Rural District Council* [1906] 2 KB 65 and *Irving* v *Carlisle Rural District Council* [1907] JP 212.
[41] s.30(1) Local Government Act 1929.

### 8.3.3 Highway Drainage Operations

A highway authority is placed under a general duty to maintain those highways for which it is responsible.[42] However, the general duty must be read subject to the special defence which is provided whereby an authority will not be in breach of the duty where it can show that it had taken all reasonable care to secure that a highway is not dangerous to traffic.[43]

The implications of the general duty to maintain highways were considered in *Goodes* v *East Sussex County Council*[44] where the central question was whether the general duty to 'maintain' encompassed a duty to carry out gritting operations to prevent ice forming so as to keep a road safe for users. Although it was recognised that the duty to 'maintain' was capable of being understood in different senses, it was held that the relevant duty was the same as that which previously applied at common law. This required a narrower construction to be applied, so that it is the physical fabric of the highway that is required to be maintained and this does not include any duty to remove ice or snow. In the context of highway drainage and flooding, this would seem to indicate that a highway authority will generally be required to maintain the structure of highway drainage systems but will not be liable in particular situations, where flood water accumulates on highways, for a failure to secure its removal.

In accordance with the general duty upon highway authorities to maintain those roads for which they are responsible, and to make appropriate provision for surface water to run off through highway drains, powers are provided to allow authorities to undertake specified kinds of drainage operations. Specifically, an authority will be empowered to do the following:

(a) construct or lay, in the highway or in land adjoining or lying near to the highway, such drains as are considered necessary;

(b) erect barriers in the highway or in nearby land to divert surface water into or through any existing drain; and

(c) scour, cleanse and keep open all drains situated in the highway or in nearby land.[45]

Where work within the first two categories is undertaken, the water may

---

[42] s.41 Highways Act 1980 and under s.329(1) 'maintenance' includes repair, and 'maintain' and 'maintainable' are to be construed accordingly.

[43] s.58 Highways Act 1980 and on 'reasonable care' see *Griffiths* v *Liverpool Corporation* [1967] 1 QB 374.

[44] [2000] 3 All ER 603. See the discussion of flood warnings in relation to highways at 11.4.2 below.

[45] s.100(1) Highways Act 1980.

be discharged into or through a drain into any inland waters, whether natural or artificial, or any tidal waters. However, a highway authority will be liable to pay compensation to the owner or occupier of any land who suffers damage by reason of the exercise of the powers,[46] and the exercise of the powers is stated to be without prejudice to any enactment for the purpose of protecting water against pollution.[47] Also, despite the apparent breadth of the operational powers concerning highway drainage, no power is given to a highway authority to interfere with any watercourse (including its banks) or any drainage or other works which are vested in or under the control of the Environment Agency or any other drainage body without the consent of the Agency or body. A consent for these purposes may not be unreasonably withheld and either party may require a question of whether consent has been unreasonably withheld to be referred to an arbitrator or, in the absence of agreement, to the President of the Institution of Civil Engineers.[48]

The general power under (c) above, to scour, cleanse and keep open all drains situated in the highway or in nearby land, allows a highway authority to undertake drainage work on neighbouring land with the owner's consent or on payment of compensation for any loss suffered. However, in *Attorney-General* v *Waring*[49] it was affirmed that it is the common law duty of the owner of land adjoining a highway to scour and cleanse ditches on his land so as to prevent them from causing a nuisance

---

[46] s.299 Highways Act 1980. On provision for compensation, see s. 308 Highways Act 1980. See also *Durrant* v *Branksome Urban District Council* [1897] 2 Ch 291, discussed at 7.7.2 above, concerning the powers of a local authority to discharge sewers into watercourses providing that it does not contain 'sewage or filthy water' (under s.17 Public Health Act 1875) and *British Waterways Board* v *Severn Trent Water Ltd* [2001] Env LR 780 for subsequent interpretation of this. See also the discussion of *Hanscombe* v *Bedfordshire County Council* [1938] Ch 944 at 8.3.8 below, affirming that a highway authority has no right to trespass on adjoining land to culvert a ditch without permission of the owner.

[47] s.100(2), (3) and (8) Highways Act 1980. On criminal liability for water pollution, see Part III Water Resources Act 1991 and particularly s.85 (concerned with offences of polluting controlled waters) and s.89(5) (which provides a defence to a highway authority in relation to discharges from highway drains made in accordance with s.100 Highways Act 1980). Generally, see W. Howarth and D. McGillivray, *Water Pollution and Water Quality Law* (2001) Ch.9.

[48] s.339(1) to (3) Highways Act 1980. 'Other drainage body' means a drainage body within the meaning of the Land Drainage Act 1991. Similarly, insofar as the general highway drainage powers of authorities imply a power to culvert watercourses, they must be read subject to other land drainage provisions which require consent for obstructions in watercourses to be given by an internal drainage board or the Environment Agency. See s.23 Land Drainage Act 1991 (concerning obstructions in ordinary watercourses) discussed at 4.4.2 above, and s.109 Water Resources Act 1991 (concerning obstructions in main rivers) discussed at 4.4.1 above.

[49] (1899) 63 JP 789.

to persons using the highway by flooding. In that case an injunction was awarded against the defendant for causing a nuisance and obstruction of the highway through neglecting to cleanse a ditch on his land. Despite the statutory power of a highway authority to cleanse ditches on land adjoining a highway, the common law power to compel the owner of the ditch to cleanse it might be seen as a preferable alternative from the perspective of a highway authority.

Notwithstanding the duty to compensate landholders who suffer damage, there are limits to the power to construct highway drains and to erect barriers to divert water. In *Thomas v Gower Rural District Council*[50] the power to undertake work on land lying near to a highway had been exercised by the highway authority in constructing a ridge on nearby land to divert water away from the highway. The effect of this was to increase the quantity of water passing to a culvert on the claimant's land and to cause frequent flooding. It was found that although the statutory powers authorised works to be carried out on lands adjoining the highway, they did not authorise the discharge of water from ditches or drains onto such land. Despite the defendant's contention that the claimant's only remedy was a claim for compensation, the court held that an injunction would be allowed to restrain the diversion of the water onto the claimant's land.

The protection of highway drains is provided for in circumstances where a person, without the consent of the highway authority, alters, obstructs or interferes with a drain or barrier which has been constructed, laid or erected by the authority in accordance with the powers to undertake highway drainage operations or which is under the control of a highway authority. In such circumstances, the highway authority may carry out any work of repair or reinstatement necessitated by the interference and may recover the expenses reasonably incurred from the person who is responsible.[51]

The extent of the offence concerning interference with highway drains was considered in *Johnson v Essex County Council*[52] where the defendant was the owner of property adjoining a highway under which there ran a stone culvert which was under the control of the highway authority. The stone culvert connected to a brick culvert located on the defendant's land and

---

[50] [1922] 2 KB 76, concerning s.67 Highway Act 1835; now see s.100 Highways Act 1980. See also *Pearce v Croydon Rural District Council* (1910) 74 JP 429 where a trespass was established where a highway authority had caused surface water to drain from a highway onto private land where no watercourse existed.

[51] s.100(4) Highways Act 1980. Without prejudice to the power to recover expenses, the person responsible will be guilty of an offence and liable, on summary conviction, to a fine not exceeding three times the amount of the expenses.

[52] (1971) 69 LGR 498, concerning s.103(3) Highways Act 1959; now see s.100(4) Highways Act 1980.

which received a flow of water from the stone culvert. In order to prevent flooding of his land, the defendant blocked the brick culvert, which caused the flow of water to be diverted onto the highway. His conviction for obstruction or interference with the highway authority's stone culvert was quashed on the basis that the offence required a direct physical interference with that culvert to be shown. On the facts, the blocking of his own brick culvert did not involve this despite the indirect interference with the flow through the authority's stone culvert that resulted.

Alongside the general power to undertake highway drainage operations, a highway authority may, for the purpose of the drainage of a highway, or proposed highway, exercise particular powers that are otherwise exercisable by a sewerage undertaker. In particular, these concern powers to lay pipes in streets;[53] to lay pipes in other land;[54] to fit stopcocks;[55] to discharge water for works purposes;[56] and to enter land for works purposes.[57] However, where the highway authority is a county council it must give notice of its intention to exercise these powers to the district council and the sewerage undertaker for the area. Where the highway authority is a metropolitan district council it must give such notice to the sewerage undertaker for the relevant area.[58]

A person who is liable to maintain a highway by reason of tenure, enclosure or prescription has, for the purpose of draining it, the same powers as a highway authority to undertake general drainage operations, the same duty to compensate those who suffer damage as a consequence and the same protection is afforded to drains or barriers which are privately constructed or maintained.[59]

A final point in relation to the statutory powers of highway authorities to undertake drainage operations is to emphasise that the various kinds of works which may be undertaken are formulated as *powers* rather than

---

[53] s.158 Water Industry Act 1991.
[54] s.159 Water Industry Act 1991.
[55] s.163 Water Industry Act 1991.
[56] s.165 Water Industry Act 1991. See also s.299 Highways Act 1980 on the power to discharge water.
[57] s.168 Water Industry Act 1991. See also s.291 Highways Act 1980 on powers of entry of a highway authority for the purpose of maintaining certain structures and works.
[58] s.100(5) and (6) Highways Act 1980. In relation to Wales, the 'district council' is to be read as 'the Welsh council' and, where the highway authority is a Welsh council, notice must be given to the sewerage undertaker and, where powers are to be exercised outside a county or county borough, to the Welsh council or district council in whose area the powers are to be exercised (s.100(6A) and (6B) Highways Act 1980, as amended).
[59] s.100(7) Highways Act 1980, that is, s.100(1) to (4) apply equally to private highway drainage.

## Highway Drainage

*duties* upon authorities.[60] This point has already been stressed in relation to a range of other flood defence powers possessed by flood defence operating authorities and the general principles which have been previous outlined[61] apply similarly to highway drainage powers. An illustration of this is to be seen in *Burton v West Suffolk County Council*[62] where, after a highway authority had carried out inadequate drainage work, a road continued to flood and an area of ice formed on the road. The claimant was a motorist who was involved in an accident because of the ice and claimed damages against the highway authority because of the failure to execute adequate drainage works. It was held that the failure to provide adequate drainage was an act of non-feasance for which the highway authority was not liable unless the work had been done negligently or created a new danger.[63]

### 8.3.4 The Power to Fill in Roadside Ditches

If it appears to a highway authority that a ditch or watercourse on land adjoining or lying near to the highway constitutes a danger to users of the highway, the authority has powers to fill it in or to provide an alternative channel for the water.[64] Specifically, the power to fill in a ditch arises if it is considered unnecessary for drainage purposes and any occupier of the land agrees that it is unnecessary. The power of substitution allows the authority to place in the ditch, or in land adjoining or lying near to it, such pipes or culverts as are considered necessary, and thereafter to fill in the

---

[60] Contrast the general *duty* upon highway authorities to maintain highways (under s.41 Highways Act 1980) though this must be read subject to the special defence allowing an authority to show that it had taken all reasonable care to secure that a highway is not dangerous to traffic (under s.58). Also, contrast the potential common law liability of highway authorities in nuisance and see the discussion of *Bybrook Barn Garden Centre Ltd v Kent County Council* [2001] Env LR 543 at 2.5.3 and 2.9 above.

[61] See 4.3.1 above on the powers of flood defence operating authorities.

[62] [1960] 2 QB 72. See also *Masters v Hampshire County Council* (1915) 84 LJ KB 2194 where the failure of a highway authority to prevent road gullies becoming overgrown was found to be a non-feasance for which the authority was not liable. See also 11.4.2 below on the responsibilities of highway authorities to warn highway authorities to warn road users of dangers associated with highway flooding.

[63] Although this decision predates the introduction of a statutory defence to the general maintenance duty upon highway authorities, which arises where an authority has taken all such care as is reasonable to secure that a highway is not dangerous to traffic under s.1 Highways (Miscellaneous Provisions) Act 1961 (now see s.58 Highways Act 1991 and discussion at 11.4.2 above). Arguably, the duty to take reasonably care has now superseded the absence of liability for non-feasance.

[64] See *Tutill v West Ham Local Board of Health* (1873) LR 8 CP 447 where it was found that a local authority power under a local Act allowing it to fill in ditches 'at the sides of roads' and substitute pipes did not allow the authority to fill in a ditch which was in private ownership, and separated from the road by a fence, and an action in trespass could be sustained by the owner of the ditch. Generally see 8.3.8 below on the ownership of roadside ditches.

ditch. However, compensation is payable by the authority to any owner or occupier of any land who suffers damage by reason of the exercise of these powers.[65] Also, despite the apparent breadth of the powers relating to culverting of watercourses, the use or interference with any watercourse or any drainage or other works which are vested in or under the control of the Environment Agency or any other drainage body will require the consent of the Agency or body.[66]

Protection of work which is undertaken in accordance with the powers to fill in ditches and provide a substitute is provided for. Hence, if any person, without the consent of the highway authority, opens up or keeps open any ditch which has been filled in, except where this is necessary for undertaking work on the pipes placed in the ditch, the authority will be entitled to carry out any repair or reinstatement work which is necessitated. Following repair or reinstatement work by the authority, it will be entitled to recover the expenses reasonably incurred. In addition, the person responsible for opening up or keeping open the ditch will commit an offence.[67]

### 8.3.5 Protection of Highways against Hazards of Nature

A highway authority may provide, maintain, alter or remove such barriers or other works as are necessary for the purpose of affording protection against snow, flood, landslide or other hazards of nature. These works may be provided on the highway or on land over which rights have been acquired by the authority in the exercise of land acquisition powers for that purpose. However, a highway authority must pay compensation to any person who suffers damage because of the execution of the works.[68]

---

[65] s.101(1), (2) and (6) Highways Act 1980. For these purposes, s.263 Public Health Act 1936 (prohibiting the culverting of watercourses without approval of the local authority) does not apply, and see 8.2.4 above on this provision (s.100(4) Highways Act 1980). In relation to works which are likely to affect the drainage of land used for a railway or canal undertaking, a requirement to give notice applies and powers must be exercised in accordance with reasonable requirements of the undertakers (s.100(5) Highways Act 1980). See also the discussion of *Hanscombe* v *Bedfordshire County Council* [1938] Ch 944 at 8.3.8 below, affirming that a highway authority has no right to trespass on adjoining land without permission of the owner. See also the discussion of the potential civil liabilities arising from culverting operations at 2.5.3 above.

[66] s.339(1) to (3) Highways Act 1980. 'Other drainage body' means a drainage body within the meaning of the Land Drainage Act 1991. Similarly, the powers must be read subject to other flood defence provisions which require consent for obstructions in watercourses to be given by an internal drainage board or the Environment Agency. See s.23 Land Drainage Act 1991 (concerning obstructions in ordinary watercourses) discussed at 4.4.2 above, and s.109 Water Resources Act 1991 (concerning obstructions in main rivers) discussed at 4.4.1 above.

[67] s.100(3) Highways Act 1980. The offence is punishable by a maximum fine not exceeding three times the amount of the expenses incurred by the authority.

[68] s.102 Highways Act 1980 and see s.250 on highway land acquisition powers.

## Highway Drainage

Further provision is made in relation to the provision of posts to indicate the depth of flood water. In respect of this, it is the duty of a highway authority to provide, in connection with any highway that is subject to flooding to any considerable depth, graduated posts or stones where these are considered necessary or desirable for the purpose of indicating the depth of water covering a highway.[69]

### 8.3.6 Diversion of Watercourses

Various other powers of highway authorities also have implications for highway drainage or land drainage generally. Subject to ministerial authorisation, a highway authority may divert a navigable watercourse if the diversion is necessary or desirable in connection with the construction, improvement or alteration of a highway or other specified matters.[70] However, an order allowing such a diversion will require that any new length of watercourse is reasonably navigable by vessels that would have used the previous watercourse. Also, compensation is provided for persons who suffer damage due to depreciation of any interest in land, and other matters, as a consequence of the replacement except where the land has been acquired compulsorily.[71]

A highway authority may also divert any part of a watercourse, other than a navigable watercourse, and may carry out works on any watercourse if these are necessary or desirable in connection with the construction, improvement or alteration of a highway or other specified matters. However, before carrying out diversion work of this kind, the authority must consult every council in whose area the works are to be carried out. Any person who suffers damage as a consequence of the diversion due to depreciation of any interest in land, and other matters, will be entitled to compensation from the authority except where the land has been acquired compulsorily. Provision is made for notification of owners or occupiers of land that is affected and for objections to be considered by the Minister except where land has been acquired compulsorily or by agreement.[72]

The civil law implications of diverting watercourses are discussed elsewhere in this work,[73] but it may be noted here that the powers of diversion given to highway authorities need to be exercised with some caution to avoid

---

[69] s.103(1) Highways Act 1980.
[70] s.108 Highways Act 1980.
[71] s.109 Highways Act 1980. See also Parts I and III of Schedule 1 which require copies of the order to be served on the Environment Agency and every navigation authority affected by the proposals.
[72] s.110 Highways Act 1980. The 'Minister' means the Minister of Transport or the National Assembly for Wales (see s.329(1) Highways Act 1980. as amended).
[73] Generally see Ch.2 above on civil liability.

unnecessary invasion of the rights of others. A pertinent illustration of this is *Provender Millers (Winchester) Ltd v Southampton County Council*[74] where the highway authority had inserted a new culvert in a stream to give support to a highway passing over it and to prevent the stream flooding. The result of this was to diminish the natural flow of water to the claimants' mill, thereby reducing the power of the mill. It was held that the authority had no defence against a claim that it had altered the bed of the stream to the detriment of the claimants. Moreover, it was stressed that, unless it was not practically feasible to perform statutory obligations in any other way, the authority was not entitled, by virtue of those obligations, to invade the rights of others. The onus of proving that statutory obligations could not be performed in any other way lay upon the authority and, on the facts, it had failed to rebut that presumption.

Despite the apparent extent of the power of a highway authority to divert non-navigable watercourses and conduct works in any watercourse, no power is given to an authority or any other person to use or interfere with any watercourse (including its banks) or any drainage or other works which are vested in or under the control of the Environment Agency or any other drainage body without the consent of the Agency or body.[75]

### 8.3.7 Agreements with Sewerage Undertakers

The Water Industry Act 1991 enables local highway authorities and sewerage undertakers to enter into reciprocal agreements, whereby a highway authority may use any public sewer vested in a sewerage undertaker for the conveyance of surface water from any highway for which it is responsible. Conversely, a sewerage undertaker may enter into an agreement with a highway authority to use any drain vested in the highway authority for the purpose of conveying surface water from premises or streets.[76]

In each case, agreements of this kind may be made on 'such terms as may be agreed' but where a discharge will be made, directly or indirectly, into the sewers or sewage disposal works of another sewerage undertaker, the consent of that undertaker will be required on such terms as it thinks fit.

Moreover, neither a highway authority nor a sewerage undertaker may unreasonably refuse to enter an agreement of this kind or insist upon terms

---

[74] [1940] Ch 131 and see 2.5.3 above on culverts and 2.9 above on civil liability of public bodies.

[75] s.339(1) to (3) Highways Act 1980. 'Other drainage body' means a drainage body within the meaning of the Land Drainage Act 1991.

[76] s.115(1) Water Industry Act 1991. Another possibility is that an agreement of this kind may be entered into between two highway authorities (s.115(6)).

which are unacceptable to the other party. Questions as to whether an authority or undertaker has acted unreasonably must be referred to the Secretary of State for final determination.[77]

### 8.3.8 Responsibilities for Roadside Ditches

A practical problem, which frequently arises in relation to highway drainage, concerns the ownership of, and responsibility for, roadside ditches. As has been noted, highway authorities normally acquire responsibilities for highways by dedication and the extent of their ownership will be determined by the extent of the dedication. Where a ditch runs between the carriageway of a road and adjoining land, a presumption is applied that the ditch does not form a part of the highway.[78] This has the consequence that an authority will not be able to alter or maintain the ditch without the consent of the owner. On the other hand, some roadside ditches have been excavated specifically for the purpose of draining highways and, as such, must be vested in the highway authority. Hence, the general position is that a roadside ditch will be the responsibility of the adjoining landowner, unless it has been specifically constructed to drain the highway or can be shown to be within land owned by the highway authority.

The issue of ownership of a roadside ditch was addressed in *Hanscombe v Bedfordshire County Council*,[79] where a highway authority had placed pipes in a ditch, which adjoined a highway that it maintained, and filled in the ditch. The owner of the adjoining land claimed ownership of the ditch and entitlement to damages in trespass since the authority had no power to fill in the ditch without his permission. On the issue of ownership, it was said,

> 'whether this ditch is vested in [the highway authority] must depend on whether or not it forms part of that which was dedicated to the public. The rights of the public in a high road are to pass and re-pass along it, and their right to use the way for that purpose is not limited to that par-

---

[77] s.115(2) to (5) Water Industry Act 1991. See also s.146(4) which prevents a sewerage undertaker requiring payment to be made by a highway authority in respect of the drainage of any highway or the disposal of the contents of any drain or sewer used for draining a highway.

[78] Generally see *Alan Wibberley Building Ltd v Insley* [1999] 1 WLR 894, where the 'hedge and ditch' presumption was reaffirmed, to the effect that, in the absence of evidence to the contrary, where land which has never been in common ownership is separated by a ditch and hedge it will be presumed that the boundary was drawn before the ditch was dug so that the boundary will be along the top line of the ditch furthest from the hedge.

[79] [1938] Ch 944. Similarly see See *Tutill v West Ham Local Board of Health* (1873) LR 8 CP 447 and *Chippendale v Pontefract Rural District Council* (1907) 71 JP 231. See also *Simcox v Yardley Rural District Council* (1905) 69 JP 66 and *Walmsley v Featherstone Urban District Council* (1909) 73 JP 322.

of the way which is metalled or made up, but extends to the whole highway. When, therefore, the whole portion of a highway which is bounded by a fence or hedge is capable of being used to pass and re-pass, the whole portion is deemed to have been dedicated to the public. When, however, a portion of the whole is a ditch which *prima facie* is not adapted for the exercise by the public of their right to pass and re-pass, the presumption, in my judgment, is that the ditch does not form part of the highway.'[80]

On the facts, the 'extremely strong' presumption against a ditch being part of the highway was not rebutted. Particularly because the ditch served to drain the claimant's land, as well as the highway, it was thought impossible to suppose that any owner, when dedicating the road to public use, could have intended to part with rights in the ditch.

The second question arising in the *Hanscombe* case was whether any powers of the highway authority authorised the culverting and infilling of the ditch that had taken place. On this, the authority claimed to be able to rely on statutory powers to make improvements to highways[81] or powers to maintain ditches adjoining the highway.[82] In neither instance, however, did these powers authorise the highway authority to go upon the land of an adjoining owner to fill in a ditch without that owner's consent.

Having found for the claimant on both counts, however, the court only awarded nominal damages of £2. This was because the pipe which had been laid was found to be as effective as the previous ditch had been in carrying away the surface water and no substantial loss had been suffered.

On the other hand, the presumption that a roadside ditch is excluded from the land dedicated as a highway is capable of rebuttal. In *Chorley Corporation* v *Nightingale*[83] there was evidence that the whole area of a highway between two fences along both sides of a road, and including a ditch, was part of the highway. This conclusion was reached because the ditch had been constructed specifically for the purpose of taking water from the highway. Conversely, evidence in some instances has supported the opposite inference, that a ditch has not been dedicated as part of the highway. Hence in *Simcox* v *Yardley Rural District Council*[84] a road had

---

[80] [1938] Ch 944, per Farwell J at p.949.
[81] s.47 Highway Act 1864; and now see s.72 Highways Act 1980.
[82] s.67 Highway Act 1835; now see s.100 Highways Act 1980, discussed at 8.3.3 above.
[83] [1907] 2 KB 637 and discussed in *Chippendale* v *Pontefract Rural District Council* (1907) 71 JP 231 at p.232.
[84] (1905) 69 JP 66. Similarly, see *Walmsley* v *Featherstone Urban District Council* (1909) 73 JP 322 where evidence from an Inclosure Act was used to establish that a ditch which ran alongside a highway was not within the land dedicated as the highway.

## Highway Drainage

been laid out at precisely the width required by an enclosure award and this excluded the adjoining ditch. This, alongside evidence of maintenance of the ditch undertaken by the claimant who contended that he owned it, confirmed that it was not a part of the highway.

### 8.4 RESERVOIR SAFETY

#### 8.4.1 Introduction

Another important responsibility of local authorities concerns reservoir safety under the Reservoirs Act 1975.[85] Under this Act authorities have extensive registration, inspection and enforcement powers to ensure that dams and similar structures are maintained in a state that does not give rise to a public safety hazard. Although the possibility of an escape of water following the collapse of a dam is a clear example of non-natural flooding, the hazard is no less because of that, since many reservoirs are constructed in uplands of catchments which are extensively developed downstream. In many instances the unanticipated failure of a dam would cause especially destructive inundation of lower land by large amounts of water, often moving at considerable speed and preventing warnings being given or action being taken to avoid danger to persons and property. The 2,500 dams in the United Kingdom that are large enough to fall within the scope of the 1975 Act comprise a large number of earth dams, more than half of which were constructed over a century ago. Whilst there has been no major instance of dam failure in recent years, there is clearly no room for complacency.[86]

Although the impounding of water is subject to a general system of licensing under Chapter II of Part II of the Water Resources Act 1991, impounding activities involving certain reservoirs are subject to further controls where they give rise to a potential flooding hazard. Previous legislation, the Reservoirs (Safety Provisions) Act 1930, was enacted following two tragic incidents of dam failure in 1925, at Skelmorlie in Scotland and Dolgarrog in Wales. Although predating the modern appreciation that a 'precautionary principle'[87] needs to be applied to all areas of environmental management, the legislation concerning reservoir safety is amongst the best examples of a precautionary approach to the avoidance of flooding and illustrates a series of mechanisms designed to anticipate and avert flooding dangers.

---

[85] See W. Howarth, 'Reservoir Safety Reforms' [1986] *Journal of Planning and Environment Law* 578.

[86] Association of British Insurers, *Inland Flooding Risk – Issues Facing the Insurance Industry* (2000) p.8.

[87] See 1.7 above on the precautionary principle.

### 8.4.2 Large Raised Reservoirs

The Reservoirs Act 1975 applies to 'large raised reservoirs'[88] for water. A reservoir is a 'raised reservoir' if it is designed to hold, or capable of holding, water above the natural level of any part of the land adjoining the reservoir. A raised reservoir is a 'large' raised reservoir if it is designed to hold more than 25,000 cubic metres of water above the level of the adjoining land. The provisions made in relation to large raised reservoirs also apply to any place where water is artificially retained to form or enlarge a lake or loch, whether or not use is, or is intended to be, made of the water and whether or not the reservoir has been constructed under statutory powers. Key obligations under the 1975 Act are imposed upon 'undertakers', which means the Environment Agency or a water undertaker in the case of a reservoir that is, when constructed, to be managed by the Agency or an undertaker. In any other case 'undertaker' means, if the reservoir is used or intended to be used for the purposes of any undertaking, the person for the time being carrying on that undertaking or, if the reservoir is not so used, the owners or lessees of the reservoir.[89]

### 8.4.3 Registration of Reservoirs by Local Authorities

Principal duties in relation to the administration and enforcement of the Reservoirs Act 1975 fall to 'local authorities', meaning the councils of counties, metropolitan districts and London boroughs in England and councils of counties and county boroughs in Wales. Hence, it is the duty of each local authority to establish and maintain for their area a register showing the large raised reservoirs situated wholly or partly in that area. The register is to give prescribed information[90] about each reservoir and is to be kept at the principal offices of the local authority where it is to be available for inspection by any person at all reasonable times. As the enforcement authority, it is the duty of the local authority to secure that undertakers comply with the requirements of the 1975 Act.[91]

More specifically, each local authority must, at prescribed intervals, make a report to the Secretary of State giving specified information as to the steps

---

[88] Excluding, canals and inland navigation, and mine and quarry lagoons (under Mines and Quarries (Tips) Act 1929).
[89] s.1(1) to (4) Reservoirs Act 1975. In *Braintree District Council* v *Gosfield Hall Settlement Trustees*, unreported, Chelmsford Crown Court, 13 July 1977, it was held, under the Reservoirs (Safety Provisions) Act 1930, that the Settlement Trustees as owners, and a lessee of a reservoir, were 'undertakers', but an angling association with an under-lease of fishing rights were not 'undertakers' for the purposes of a reservoir safety order under that Act.
[90] See the Reservoirs Act 1975 (Registers, Reports and Records) Regulations 1985, S.I. 1985 No.177, as amended by S.I. 1985 No.548.
[91] s.2 Reservoirs Act 1975.

taken to secure that undertakers comply with the requirements of the Act, or the steps taken by the local authority to comply with those requirements as undertakers for any reservoir. If it appears to the Secretary of State that a local authority has failed to perform its functions under the Act, he may cause a public inquiry to be held, and if the failure to perform any function is established by the inquiry then the Secretary of State may make an order directing the authority to perform its functions in a specified manner.[92]

### 8.4.4 Qualifications of Engineers

For the purposes of the 1975 Act, a panel, or panels, of civil engineers are to be established, and any reference to a 'qualified civil engineer' is a reference to a civil engineer who is a member of the appropriate panel. Any civil engineer may apply to be placed on any panel and if the Secretary of State is satisfied that the applicant is qualified and fit to be placed on the panel the engineer may be appointed to membership.[93] Initially, appointment to the panel is to be for a term of 5 years, with provision for re-appointment, but the Secretary of State may remove an engineer from the panel if, after consultation with the engineer, he is satisfied that the engineer is not fit to remain a member.[94]

### 8.4.5 Certification of Reservoirs

No large raised reservoir may be constructed, whether as a new reservoir or by the alteration of an existing reservoir, or altered so as to increase its capacity, unless a qualified civil engineer, termed the 'construction engineer', is employed to design and supervise its construction or alteration.[95] Where the use of a reservoir has been abandoned and the reservoir is to be brought back into use after being altered so as to increase its capacity, this is to be treated as the construction of a new reservoir. Where a large reservoir is constructed as a new reservoir, or by the alteration of an existing reservoir, it may not be used for the storage of water, or be filled wholly or partially with water, otherwise than in accordance with the certificate of the construction engineer.[96]

---

[92] s.3 Reservoirs Act 1975.
[93] s.4(1) and (2) Reservoirs Act 1975. Detailed provisions relating to panels of civil engineers are prescribed under Reservoirs (Panels of Civil Engineers) (Application and Fees) Regulations 1992, S.I. 1992 No.1527, as amended by S.I. 1998 No.2403.
[94] s.4(3) and (5) Reservoirs Act 1975.
[95] On the potential liability of construction engineers see *Birse Construction Ltd* v *Haiste Ltd (Watson and Others, Third Parties)* [1996] 2 All ER 1 and *Borough of Blaenau Gwent* v *Robinson Jones Design Partnership Ltd and Another* [1997] 53 Con LR 31.
[96] s.6(1), (2) and (3) Reservoirs Act 1975. Provision for preliminary and interim certificates to be issued is provided for under s.7 and see Reservoirs Act 1975 (Certificates, Reports and Prescribed Information) Regulations 1986, S.I. 1986 No.468.

Proceedings may be brought where it appears to the enforcement authority that a large raised reservoir is being constructed, or an existing reservoir altered so as to increase its capacity, and no final certificate has been given for the construction or alteration, and no construction engineer is responsible for the construction or alteration. In these circumstances the authority may serve on the undertakers a notice requiring them, within 28 days, to appoint a qualified civil engineer. An engineer appointed for these purposes must inspect the reservoir and make a report on the construction or alteration, and supervise the reservoir until a final certificate is issued indicating that the engineer is satisfied with the work.[97]

Where the use of a large raised reservoir has been abandoned, the reservoir may not be brought back into use as a reservoir again unless a qualified civil engineer has been employed to inspect the reservoir and report on it, and to supervise work until a final certificate is granted for it. If an abandoned reservoir is brought back into use for the storage of water, or filled wholly or partly with water, it may not be used otherwise than in accordance with the certificate of the engineer. Where a large raised reservoir has been brought back into use after being abandoned without a report being obtained, or a report includes safety recommendations which have not been carried out, the authority may serve notice on the undertakers. Such notice may require the undertaker, within 28 days, to appoint a qualified civil engineer, or require recommendations to be carried out within a period specified in the notice.[98]

### 8.4.6 Periodic Inspections

The undertakers of any large raised reservoir are bound to have the reservoir inspected from time to time by an independent qualified civil engineer and obtain a report of the results of the inspection.[99] Other than where the reservoir is presently under the supervision of a construction engineer, large raised reservoirs must be inspected within the following periods:

(a) within 2 years from the date of any final certificate for the reservoir given by the engineer responsible for the construction or alteration of the reservoir;

---

[97] s.8(1) and (2) Reservoirs Act 1975.
[98] s.9(1), (2) and (7) Reservoirs Act 1975.
[99] 'Independent' means a civil engineer who is not in the employment of the undertakers otherwise than in a consultant capacity, and who was not the engineer responsible for the reservoir or any addition to it as the construction engineer, nor connected with any such engineer as a partner, employer, employee or fellow employee in a civil engineering business (s.10(9) Reservoirs Act 1975).

(b) as soon as practicable after carrying out any alterations to the reservoir which do not increase its capacity but might affect its safety and which have not been designed and supervised by a qualified civil engineer;

(c) at any time when the supervising engineer so recommends; or

(d) within 10 years from the last inspection or within any lesser interval that may have been recommended in the previous report of the inspecting engineer.[100]

As soon as practicable after an inspection, the inspecting engineer is to make a report of the results of the inspection, including any recommendations as to the time of the next inspection and any measures that should be taken in the interests of safety. Where recommendations are included in the report as to measures to be taken in the interests of safety, the undertakers must carry the recommendations into effect as soon as practicable under the supervision of a qualified civil engineer. The engineer must issue a certificate as soon as he is satisfied that the recommendations have been carried into effect. Where it appears to the enforcement authority that an inspection and report have not been made as required, or that the latest report of the inspecting engineer includes a safety recommendation that has not been carried into effect, the authority may serve notice on the undertakers. Such notice may require the undertakers, within 28 days, to appoint an independent civil engineer to carry out an inspection, or require them to carry out the safety recommendation within a time specified in the notice.[101]

For every large raised reservoir, the undertakers are to keep a record in a prescribed form of:

(a) water levels and depth of water, including the flow of water over the waste weir or overflow;

(b) leakages, settlements of walls or other works, and repairs; and

(c) such other matters as may be prescribed.

In order to do this the undertakers must install and maintain such instruments as may be needed to provide the information to be recorded.[102]

---

[100] s.10(1) and (2) Reservoirs Act 1975.
[101] s.10(3), (6) and (7) Reservoirs Act 1975. See *Fyfe Contractors Ltd* v *Scottish Hydro Electric plc*, Scots Court of Session, Outer House, 11 June 1996, on liability arising from dam modification operations.
[102] s.11(1) Reservoirs Act 1975 and see Reservoirs Act 1975 (Registers, Reports and Records) Regulations 1985, S.I. 1985 No.177, as amended by S.I. 1985 No.548.

When a large raised reservoir is not under the supervision of a construction engineer, a 'supervising engineer' is to be engaged. The supervising engineer must advise the undertakers of any matter that might affect the safety of the reservoir and ensure that requirements relating to construction or enlargement, re-use of abandoned reservoirs and periodic inspection are complied with, and draw the attention of the undertakers to any breach of those provisions. It is the duty of the supervising engineer, in respect of matters noted in the final construction certificate, or the latest report of the inspecting engineer, to pay attention to those matters and to give the undertakers a written statement, at least once a year, of the action that has been taken to do so. In addition, the supervising engineer must recommend to the undertakers that the reservoir should be inspected if at any time an inspection is called for. Where it appears to the enforcement authority that a large raised reservoir is not for the time being either under the supervision of a construction engineer or a supervising engineer, the authority may serve notice on the undertakers requiring them, within 28 days from the date when the notice is served, to appoint a supervising engineer.[103]

### 8.4.7 Discontinuance or Abandonment

No large raised reservoir may be altered to render it incapable of holding more than 25,000 cubic metres of water above the natural level of adjoining land, unless a qualified civil engineer is employed to design or approve and to supervise the alteration. The engineer appointed for these purposes must give a certificate as soon as he is satisfied that the alteration has been efficiently executed. When a copy of the certificate is received by the local authority it must remove the reservoir from the register of large raised reservoirs, but until the certificate is received the reservoir will remain a large raised reservoir for the purposes of the Act despite any alterations which have been executed.[104]

Where the use of a large raised reservoir is to be abandoned, the undertakers must obtain a report from a qualified civil engineer as to the measures that ought to be taken in the interests of safety to secure that the reservoir is incapable of filling with water above the natural level of any adjoining land or is only capable of doing so to an extent that does not constitute a risk. Where the report makes any recommendations as to measures to be taken in the interests of safety, the undertakers must, before the use of the reservoir is abandoned, or as soon as practicable afterwards, carry the recommendations into effect. If the report has not been obtained, or it includes a safety recommendation that has not been carried into effect, the

---

[103] s.12 Reservoirs Act 1975.
[104] s.13(1) to (3) Reservoirs Act 1975.

authority may serve on the undertakers a notice requiring them, within 28 days, to appoint a qualified civil engineer or to carry the recommendations into effect within a time specified in the notice.[105]

### 8.4.8 Enforcement Powers

Where undertakers are required by a notice from the enforcement authority to appoint an engineer for any purpose under the 1975 Act, and the undertakers fail to make the appointment, the authority may appoint an engineer for that purpose and the provisions of the Act will apply to that person as if the appointment had been made by the undertakers. Where the undertakers are required by a notice from the enforcement authority to carry a safety recommendation into effect and the undertakers fail to comply with that requirement, the authority may appoint a qualified civil engineer to carry the recommendation into effect. Where the enforcement authority make any appointment of this kind, or exercise powers to carry safety recommendations into effect, the undertakers will be bound to reimburse the authority for expenses that are reasonably incurred.[106]

Where it appears to the enforcement authority that a large raised reservoir is unsafe and that immediate action is needed to protect persons or property against an escape of water from the reservoir, it may take measures to remove or reduce the risk or to mitigate the effects of an escape. Likewise, where a large raised reservoir has been abandoned, but there is an undue accumulation of water and immediate action is needed to protect persons or property against an escape of water, the authority may take measures to remove or reduce the risk, or to mitigate the effects, of an escape. Where an enforcement authority exercises these powers, the undertaker will be bound to reimburse it for expenses reasonably incurred in the exercise of the powers.[107]

A person authorised in writing by an enforcement authority may, at any reasonable time, enter upon land on which a reservoir is situated for any of the following purposes:

(a) to carry out any survey or other operation needed to determine whether a reservoir is a large raised reservoir, or is being constructed or altered so as to become one, whether a large raised reservoir is being altered so as to increase its capacity, or whether a reservoir is or is not in use as such;

---

[105] s.14(1), (2) and (4) Reservoirs Act 1975.
[106] s.15(1), (2) and (5) Reservoirs Act 1975.
[107] s.16(1), (2) and (6) Reservoirs Act 1975.

(b) to carry out any survey or other operation needed to determine whether any recommendation as to safety measures has been carried out, or what period should be specified in a notice requiring the undertakers to carry such a recommendation into effect;

(c) to carry out any inspection of a reservoir under the reserve powers of the authority to appoint an engineer,[108] or any survey or other operation needed to make a report;

(d) to carry into effect any recommendation by the authority[109] as to measures to be taken in the interests of safety; and

(e) to carry out any survey or other operation needed to determine whether measures should be taken in connection with the emergency powers of the authority,[110] or to carry emergency measures into effect.[111]

Compensation is payable by the enforcement authority where, in the exercise of any of the powers of entry, any land on which entry is made and which is not in the occupation of the undertakers is damaged, or any person is disturbed in his enjoyment of that land.[112]

### 8.4.9 Criminal and Civil Liability

If, by the wilful default of an undertaker, any of the main obligations of the 1975 Act are not observed or complied with in relation to a large raised reservoir the undertakers will be guilty of an offence, unless there is reasonable excuse for the default or failure. Similarly, if the undertakers fail to comply with a notice from the enforcement authority an offence will be committed.[113] Lesser offences are also provided for in relation to failure to give notice required under the Act, failure to furnish information, or furnishing false information.[114]

Provision is made for the continuation of civil liability in respect of an escape of water from a reservoir constructed in accordance with previous

---

[108] Under s.15(1) Reservoirs Act 1975.
[109] Under s.15(2) Reservoirs Act 1975.
[110] Under s.16 Reservoirs Act 1975.
[111] s.17(1) Reservoirs Act 1975. Except in respect of exercising a right of entry under (e), in relation to emergency powers, no entry may be demanded unless at least 7 days' notice in writing of the intended entry has been given to the occupier or the entry is authorised by a warrant (s.17(4)). Entry under warrant is provided for by s.17(5).
[112] s.18(1) Reservoirs Act 1975.
[113] s.22(1) Reservoirs Act 1975. Undertakers committing these offences will be liable to a fine, which on summary conviction is not to exceed the 'prescribed sum', presently £5,000.
[114] Provided for under s.22(2) to (4) Reservoirs Act 1975.

or present reservoir safety legislation.[115] Hence, where damage or injury is caused by the escape of water from a reservoir constructed under statutory powers after 1930, the fact that the reservoir was so constructed will not exonerate the persons for the time being having responsibilities for its management and control from any indictment, action or other proceedings to which they would otherwise be liable.[116] In effect, conformity with the 1975 Act or previous legislation will not serve as a defence to civil proceedings arising from an escape of water from a reservoir.[117]

---

[115] Reservoirs (Safety Provisions) Act 1930.
[116] s.28 and Schedule 2 Reservoirs Act 1975.
[117] On civil liability for an escape of water from a reservoir see *Rylands* v *Fletcher* (1868) LR 3 HL 330 and see 2.5.2 above.

# Chapter 9

# PLANNING

## 9.1 INTRODUCTION

The control of land use under town and country planning law is centrally important as a means of implementing flood defence and coast protection policies by preventing developments of a kind which are likely to flood or to cause flooding elsewhere. However, land-use planning law and policy is an area of some intricacy and much of the detail has to be omitted here to emphasise those issues which are of central relevance.[1] Hence, the discussion which follows concentrates upon three key aspects: first, the general role of the planning legislation in requiring development planning and the authorisation of particular development proposals; second, the function of guidance in influencing the content of development plans and the determination of particular applications for planning permission; and, third, the requirements for environmental impact assessment that apply to those projects which are likely to have a significant effect upon the environment.

It is important to emphasise from the outset that the planning system operates *in conjunction with* other systems of land use control. That is, the obtaining of a planning permission for a particular development will not obviate the need for a flood defence or coast protection consent to be obtained if the project is one for which this is required.[2] Also, planning permission for buildings operates in conjunction with the system of building control requirements that relate to the construction specifications of a particular building project.[3] In addition, the fact that a development is authorised by a planning permission is not generally a defence to civil proceedings that arise from the development becoming a nuisance.[4]

---

[1] For a more detailed account of town and country planning law see V. Moore, *A Practical Approach to Planning Law* (7th ed. 2000) and M. Grant, Ed., *Encyclopaedia of Planning Law and Practice* (1976 updated). It is also notable that, at the time of writing, significant changes are in prospect as a consequence of the Government's intention to reform the planning system: see Department of Transport, Local Government and the Regions, *Planning: delivering a fundamental change* (2001).

[2] See 4.4.1 and 4.4.2 above on flood defence authorisations.

[3] See 9.15 below on building control.

[4] Generally see *Hunter and Others* v *Canary Wharf and London Docklands Development Corporation* [1996] 1 All ER 482, but contrast *Gillingham Borough Council* v *Medway (Chatham) Dock Co Ltd* [1993] QB 343. Alternatively, a planning authority will not be liable in negligence where it grants planning permission for a development which subsequently causes a nuisance: see *Lam and Others* v *Brennan and Another* [1997] 3 PLR 22. Generally, in relation to nuisance, see Ch.2 on civil law.

## Introduction

Whether a planning authority can be civilly liable for granting a planning permission which causes other land to be flooded is doubtful. Because authorities are bound to exercise their planning responsibilities as a matter of public duty, and for the general benefit their areas, it almost is inevitable that some planning decisions will adversely affect individual landholders.[5]

### 9.2 THE ADMINISTRATION OF PLANNING LAW

The town and country planning system consists of a range of statutory powers and duties allocated primarily to district or unitary councils, as local planning authorities, but subject to the overall executive control of the Secretary of State.[6] Although practical responsibilities for formulating development plans and determining applications for planning permission are normally allocated to local planning authorities, the Secretary of State has ultimate control over the planning system by means of a range of legislative, administrative and quasi-judicial powers.[7]

In relation to legislative powers, the Secretary of State is provided with extensive powers to secure the implementation of the principal enactment, the Town and Country Planning Act 1990, by making secondary regulations and orders[8] and the practical operation of the land use planning system requires extensive legislative action in this respect.[9] The ministerial responsibilities also encompass wide-ranging powers to issue guidance to local planning authorities to ensure that they act in accordance with general planning policy. Hence, policy control over plans adopted by local

---

[5] *Ryeford Homes Ltd and Another* v *Sevenoaks District Council and Others* [1990] JPL 36. Also see 11.4.1 below concerning flood warning duties of local planning authorities.

[6] That is, the Secretary of State for Transport, Local Government and the Regions; in relation to Wales, the responsibilities are those of the National Assembly for Wales. See 3.2 and 3.3 above on the allocation of ministerial responsibilities.

[7] See *R (on the application of Holding and Barnes plc)* v *Secretary of State for the Environment, Transport and the Regions* [2001] UKHL 3 (joined cases otherwise referred to as the '*Alconbury*' litigation) where issues of compatibility were raised between the power of the Secretary of State to determine planning applications and Schedule 1 Part 1 Article 6 Human Rights Act 1998 (giving effect to Article 6 European Convention on Human Rights) requiring civil rights to be determined by an 'independent and impartial tribunal'. It was held that, although the Secretary of State does not act as an 'independent tribunal', the judicial review procedure met the requirements imposed by the Convention. For a discussion of the case see D. Elvin and J. Maurici, 'The Alconbury Litigation: Principle and Pragmatism' [2001] *Journal of Planning and Environment Law* 883.

[8] s.333 Town and Country Planning Act 1990.

[9] See, for example, Town and Country Planning (Use Classes) Order 1987, S.I. 1987 No.764, Town and Country Planning (General Permitted Development) Order 1995, S.I. 1995 No.418, and Town and Country Planning (General Development Procedure) Order 1995, S.I. 1995 No.419.

authorities is maintained by a requirement that, in formulating a plan, the local authority must have regard to any regional or strategic planning guidance given to assist in the preparation of the plan[10] and, where relevant policy guidance exists, this will be a material consideration in determining any particular planning application.[11] At the judicial level, the Secretary of State has various powers to determine planning appeals, such as appeals against a refusal to grant planning permission or the grant of a permission subject to conditions,[12] and also has the power to 'call in' particular applications for planning permission for his own determination.[13] The allocation of this range of ministerial functions serves to confine the decision-making role of local planning authorities within their statutory powers and to ensure that their discretion does not encroach upon those matters that are subject to the overall control of the Secretary of State.

## 9.3 DEVELOPMENT PLANNING

The central feature of development planning is that a duty is imposed upon local planning authorities to formulate development plans for a range of different purposes.[14] Notably, development plans must include policies for the conservation of the natural beauty and amenity of land, and for the improvement of the physical environment.[15] For many areas, formulation of development plans involves two tiers of planning, with responsibilities allocated at county level for structure plans and at district level for local plans, though in areas where a unitary authority is in existence there will be a unitary development plan divided into two parts encompassing strategic matters in Part I and local matters in Part II. Structure plans provide a broad statement of policies applicable to land use within the area, whereas local plans reinterpret the policies in the structure plan more specifically in relation to particular areas of land.[16]

---

[10] See s.31(6)(a) Town and Country Planning Act 1990, concerning 'structure plans', and see 9.3 below on these plans.
[11] See 9.4 below on development control.
[12] s.78 Town and Country Planning Act 1990.
[13] s.77 Town and Country Planning Act 1990.
[14] Under Part II Town and Country Planning Act 1990. See Town and Country Planning (Development Plan) Regulations 1991, S.I. 1991 No.2794, and, particularly, reg.10 making the Environment Agency a statutory consultee in relation to pre-deposit consultation.
[15] ss.31 and 36 Town and Country Planning Act 1990 and see also Department of the Environment, *Environmental Appraisal of Development Plans: A Good Practice Guide* (1993) and Planning Policy Guidance Note 12, *Development Plans and Regional Planning Guidance* (1992).
[16] See Department of the Environment, Transport and the Regions, Planning Policy Guidance Note 12 *Development Plans* (1999).

## Development Planning 359

Broadly, the functions of development plans are twofold: first, to provide a statement of the manner in which national and local policies are to be applied within the relevant area and, second, to provide a guide to whether particular kinds of development will be allowed in particular locations. Hence, at one level they indicate how strategic objectives for land use, such as the realisation of targets for the provision of housing,[17] are to be realised; at another level they are location-specific in indicating whether a particular kind of development, such as a housing development, is likely to be authorised in a specific location. The location-specific element is never entirely conclusive as to whether a particular development proposal will be given planning permission, but will generally be useful to prospective developers in indicating those areas where specific kinds of development are most likely to secure approval.[18]

The important link, between the content of relevant development plans and the undertaking of a particular development project, is the requirement that 'planning permission is required for the carrying out of any development of land'.[19] Developing land without planning permission is not, by itself, a criminal offence, but unauthorised development will allow the local planning authority to instigate the enforcement machinery relating to planning control.[20] Enforcing planning law is problematic for many local authorities, which may see enforcement proceedings as a costly drain upon scarce resources. However, the procedures provide for the service of an enforcement notice against the person responsible for the unauthorised development that will require an activity to cease or a development to be removed. It is only when the action required by an enforcement notice is not undertaken within the time allowed that a criminal offence is committed.[21] Hence, the fundamental prohibition upon which the planning system rests is that it is unlawful to contravene an enforcement notice. Nevertheless, the undertaking of unauthorised development of land is the first step towards commission of a criminal offence.

The basic requirement that planning permission is required for the development of land allows the granting of particular permissions for development to be related to the content of the relevant development plan.

---

[17] See 9.11 below on housing provision.
[18] See s.54A Town and Country Planning Act 1990.
[19] s.57(1) Town and Country Planning Act 1990.
[20] Under Part VII Town and Country Planning Act 1990 and see Department of the Environment, Circular 10/97, *Enforcing Planning Control: Legislative Provisions and Procedural Requirements* (1997) and *Enforcing Planning Control: Good Practice Code for Local Authorities* (1997).
[21] s.179 Town and Country Planning Act 1990 and generally see Part VII of the Act on enforcement.

This is done by the stipulation that 'where, in making any determination under the planning Acts, regard is to be had to the development plan, the determination shall be made in accordance with the plan unless material considerations indicate otherwise'.[22] The effect of this requirement is to emphasise the importance of the relevant development plan in the determination process by creating a presumption that the plan should be followed where there are no material considerations to the contrary.

Despite the generally 'plan-led' approach, the possibility is left open that other material considerations might be of sufficient weight to justify a departure from the development plan in some circumstances. In essence, the presumption that is applied takes the development plan as a starting point and gives it a weight above that of other factors relevant to the determination. In practice, however, the difficulty will always be that of deciding whether the strength of other material considerations is sufficient to outweigh the presumption in favour of the development plan, or whether not following the plan would cause demonstrable harm to an interest of acknowledged importance.[23]

## 9.4 DEVELOPMENT CONTROL

The requirement that planning permission is required for any development of land leaves a great deal hinging upon the meaning of 'development'. Statutorily, this is defined as 'the carrying out of building, engineering, mining or other operations in, on, over or under land, or the making of any material change in the use of any building or other land'.[24] The caselaw on the interpretation of these words is extensive,[25] but the essential function of the definition is to provide a general and *preliminary* identification of the matters that are to be subject to control. This preliminary identification of regulated kinds of land use is subject to the qualification that 'for the avoidance of doubt' certain matters are declared to constitute development or are stated not to constitute development[26] and detailed secondary legislation is enacted further to indicate what degree of change in land use will be sufficient to constitute a 'material' change of use.[27]

---

[22] s.54A Town and Country Planning Act 1990.
[23] Department of the Environment, Regions and Transport, Planning Policy Guidance 1, *General Policy and Principles* (1997) para.40, and generally see *City of Edinburgh v Secretary of State for Scotland* (1997) 3 PLR 71.
[24] s.55(1) Town and Country Planning Act 1990.
[25] For examples see V. Moore, *A Practical Approach to Planning Law* (2000) Chs.5 and 6.
[26] s.55 Town and Country Planning Act 1990. For example, works by statutory undertakers for the purposes of inspecting, repairing or renewing any sewers, mains or pipes and the use of land for the purposes of agriculture are stated *not* to be development (s.55(2)(c) and (e))
[27] See Town and Country Planning (Use Classes) Order 1987, S.I. 1987 No.764.

To prevent the large number of relatively insignificant changes in land use that are constantly taking place overloading the planning system, a wide range of developments is given deemed planning permission.[28] The effect of this is that specified kinds of minor land use activities are kept within the meaning of 'development', but the need for a formal planning application to be made to a local planning authority is dispensed with. This approach has the advantage that the deemed permission may be withdrawn if the Secretary of State or the local planning authority is satisfied that certain categories of, otherwise, permitted development should be given explicit consideration.[29]

In relation to flood defence activities, the most relevant kinds of permitted development are likely to be the following matters:

(1) excavation or engineering operations necessary for the purposes of agriculture on a unit of 5 hectares or more;

(2) the carrying out of any works for the purpose of inspecting, repairing or renewing any sewer, main, pipe, cable or other apparatus, including breaking open any land for that purpose;

(3) developments by drainage bodies, other than the Environment Agency, in, on or under any watercourse or land drainage works required in connection with the improvement, maintenance or repair of the watercourse or works; and

(4) developments by the Environment Agency in, on or under any watercourse or land drainage works and required in connection with the improvement, management or repair of the watercourse or works.[30]

Notably however, the consent for permitted development which is given in relation to works undertaken by drainage bodies and the Environment Agency, in relation to watercourses and land drainage works, is limited to 'improvement, management and repair', with the

---

[28] See Town and Country Planning (General Permitted Development) Order 1995, S.I. 1995 No.418.

[29] See art.4 Town and Country Planning (General Permitted Development) Order 1995, S.I. 1995 No.418.

[30] art.3(1) and Schedule 2 Town and Country Planning (General Development Procedure) Order 1995, S.I. 1995 No.419. The listed examples fall, respectively, under Part 6 Class A(b), Part 9 Class A, Part 14 Class A and Part 15 Class A(b). On the carrying out of works for the repair of a 'sewer' under (2) above see *Doncaster Borough Council* v *Secretary of State for the Environment* (1996) 74 P&CR 428 where it was held that a drainage ditch came within the meaning of 'sewer' so that explicit planning permission was not required to undertake operations for the removal of silt and vegetation.

implication that substantially new works will not constitute permitted developments.[31]

Where an application is made for planning permission, a range of publicity and consultation requirements apply. Opinions of specified consultees must be sought on applications for particular categories of development and, in determining an application, the local planning authority must take into account representations made by 'statutory' consultees and other representations which have been made.[32] The consultation requirements apply alongside the duty upon local planning authorities generally to publicise planning applications,[33] to ensure that applications are determined on the basis of the fullest practicable input of relevant opinion and expertise. However, the *consultation* obligation remains no stronger than that, and providing that an authority adheres to the procedural requirement that such representations are 'taken into account' there will be no grounds for overturning the grant of a planning permission solely because the opinions of a consultee have not been endorsed in making the eventual determination.[34]

In making the determination as to whether a planning application should be granted, and any conditions to which it is subject, the general obligation upon a local planning authority is that it must have regard to the development plan, so far as material to the application, and to any other material considerations.[35] The test of what is a 'material consideration', both in the preparation of plans and in the control of development, is broadly formulated so that the question is 'whether it serves a planning purpose', that is, 'one which relates to the character and use of the land'.[36] This principle requires planning authorities to take account of a wide range of social and economic factors in exercising planning functions, including matters of specific relevance to flood and coastal defence.

It has long been recognised that it is a material consideration to take account of the risk of flooding, and flooding impacts upon neighbouring land, in granting consent for a development. In a pertinent ministerial

---

[31] Although see 9.14.4 below on environmental impact assessment requirements for land drainage improvement works.
[32] art.10 Town and Country Planning (General Development Procedure) Order 1995, S.I. 1995 No.419.
[33] art.8 Town and Country Planning (General Development Procedure) Order 1995, S.I. 1995 No.419.
[34] See 9.6 below on representations that may be made by the Environment Agency.
[35] s.70(2) Town and Country Planning Act 1990.
[36] Per Lord Scarman in *Great Portland Estates plc* v *Westminster City Council* [1984] All ER 744 at p.750.

planning decision,[37] a planning application for permission to build a residential property, in an unused piece of land in a residential area, was refused due to the proximity of a watercourse and a sewer. In relation to the watercourse, it was found that the proposal involved building closer to a stream than advised by the regional water authority and bank protection works were insufficiently specified to allow the water authority's objection to be overridden. In relation to the sewer, the close proximity of the foundations, and the recognised imprecision of the sewer map,[38] meant that there was a significant risk of damage to the sewer during the construction of the building. Hence, on both grounds, the refusal to grant planning permission was reaffirmed.

In *George Wimpey and Co Ltd* v *Secretary of State for the Environment and Teignbridge District Council*[39] the issue of whether a site, for which planning permission for residential development was sought, would be satisfactorily drained arose in peculiar circumstances. Neighbouring residential development sites had been the subject of negotiations concerning the developers entering into a planning obligation[40] to improve a nearby watercourse, to allow it to take the run-off from the two adjoining sites. Because one of the two intending developers went into liquidation, the remaining developer, the applicant for planning permission, then sought to provide for drainage of its site solely by means of a balancing lagoon. The applicant contended that the balancing lagoon would have been a satisfactory means of drainage, without works being undertaken on the watercourse, since it ensured that the maximum rate of run-off from the site would have been less than the run-off from the land in an undeveloped state. It was held that the Secretary of State had acted wrongly in insisting upon improvements to the watercourse, and the refusal of planning permission would be quashed because he had failed to consider whether the balancing lagoon alone would be satisfactory as a permanent means of draining the site.

Adequate provision for sewage disposal is also a material consideration in a planning application and, where a development is proposed in an area

---

[37] Refusal of planning permission for erection of a dwelling due to proximity of sewer under the land and of adjacent watercourse (Ref.T/APP/y1110/A/86/044187/p3, 8 August 1986) [1987] JPL 217. See also *Bridle* v *Secretary of State for the Environment, Transport and the Regions* (2000) 97(44) LSG 46 where, amongst other grounds, a planning application was refused because of objections raised by the National Rivers Authority that part of the holding lay in a flood plain and, in the absence of information on preventative works, it was found to be unsafe to grant planning permission for residential occupation.

[38] See 7.5 above on sewer maps.

[39] [1978] JPL 776. See also 'Residential development: special requirements as to drainage' (Planning Decision Ref. P291/32, 27 September 1973) [1974] JPL 108.

[40] Now see s.106 Town and Country Planning Act 1990, discussed at 9.5 below.

which is not served by mains sewers, the planning authority must seek to avoid development that places an unacceptable burden on local amenity.[41]

## 9.5 PLANNING CONDITIONS AND OBLIGATIONS

Where a planning permission is granted, it will almost invariably incorporate conditions that govern the characteristics of the development which has been authorised. Hence, a local planning authority may impose such planning conditions 'as it thinks fit' and may impose specific conditions requiring the carrying out of works which are expedient in connection with the development.[42] The scope for imposing conditions is broadly construed to allow these to be imposed for any legitimate planning purpose, which fairly and reasonably relate to the development that is authorised and are not so unreasonable that no local authority could have imposed them.[43] The implication of this is that there is considerable scope for the flooding potential of a development to be reduced, or for the adverse flooding effects upon other properties to be mitigated, by appropriately formulated planning conditions. On the other hand, there may be limitations upon the use of planning conditions insofar as they may not be used to require off-site work to be undertaken as, for example, where downstream flood defence works will be needed as a consequence of a proposed development and the developer has no legal power to undertake such works.[44]

A pertinent example of the use of a planning condition is *W. E. Black Ltd v Secretary of State for the Environment and London Borough of Harrow*[45] where planning permission had been granted for a residential development. This permission was subject to a condition requiring surface water attenuation and/or storage works to be carried out to reduce the risk of flooding in the locality and a further condition was that the development could not be occupied until such works were carried out. The developer maintained that these conditions were invalid because they were inconsistent with provisions under the Water Industry Act 1991 which allowed

---

[41] Department of the Environment, Planning Policy Guidance Note 23, *Planning and Pollution Control* (1994) Annex 3 paras.17–18.

[42] ss.70(1)(a) and 72(1)(a) Town and Country Planning Act 1990. See Department of the Environment, Circular 11/95, *The Use of Conditions in Planning Permissions* (1995); *Pyx Granite Co Ltd v Ministry of Housing and Local Government* [1958] 1 QB 554 and *Tarmac Heavy Building Materials UK Ltd v Secretary of State for the Environment, Transport and the Regions and Buckinghamshire County Council* (1999) 79 P&CR 260.

[43] *Newbury District Council v Secretary of State for the Environment* [1981] AC 578.

[44] Although see *Grampian Regional Council v City of Aberdeen District Council* (1984) 47 P&CR 633 on the use of negatively worded conditions requiring work to be undertaken, such as the provision of flood defence structures, before commencement of a development.

[45] [1997] Env LR 1.

connection to be made with a sewerage undertaker's sewer for the purpose of draining the development site.[46] Although it was accepted that there was a degree of overlap between planning legislation and the 1991 Act, it was found that this did not amount to duplication. Moreover, there was a legitimate planning concern in the avoidance of flooding and its adverse effects upon residential amenities. It was not contrary to these objectives to mitigate pressure on the sewerage system by imposing the planning conditions and their validity was upheld.

Planning conditions are subject to limitations in that they may normally relate only to matters that are within the boundaries of the proposed development.[47] Hence, conditions may not involve monetary payments and may be inappropriate in respect of obligations that require continuing future supervision. However, these limitations may be avoided by a developer entering into an enforceable agreement or undertaking, termed a 'planning obligation', in relation to a proposed development. Planning obligations may be entered into restricting the development or use of land, requiring specified operations or activities to be carried out, requiring the land to be used in a specified way or requiring money to be paid to the local authority. Moreover, legal difficulties involved in enforcing planning conditions against successive landowners do not arise in relation to planning obligations insofar as they will be enforceable against the person entering the obligation *and* against any person deriving title from that person.[48]

Although concern has been expressed about the safeguards against planning obligations being used to 'buy and sell' planning permissions,[49] they have some significant advantages in enabling planning authorities to require developers to meet the broader social costs to communities of major developments. This may be done, for example, by requiring developers to meet the cost of various kinds of improvement in local infrastructure or

---

[46] Under s.106 Water Industry Act 1991 and see 7.2 above on the right to connection
[47] *Ladbrokes Ltd* v *Secretary of State for the Environment* [1981] JPL 427. Although see *Grampian Regional Council* v *City of Aberdeen District Council* (1984) 47 P&CR 633.
[48] s.106(1) and (3) Town and Country Planning Act 1990 and see *Good* v *Epping Forest District Council* [1994] JPL 372.
[49] Nolan Committee on Standards in Public Life, *Third Report* (1997) Recommendation 36 and see T. Cornford, 'The Control of Planning Gain' [1998] *Journal of Planning and Environment Law* 731 and Planning and Environmental Law Reform Working Group of the Society for Advanced Legal Studies, 'Planning Obligations' [1999] *Journal of Planning and Environment Law* 113. Notably also, there is in prospect a significantly new approach to planning obligations, indicated by recent Government proposals for standardised tariffs for such obligations: see Department of Transport, Local Government and the Regions, *Reforming Planning Obligations: a consultation paper* (2001).

providing compensatory environmental benefit to offset the adverse impact of the development. The formal requirement for appropriate use of a planning obligation is that it should meet the following tests:

(1) that it should be necessary;

(2) relevant to planning;

(3) directly related to the proposed development;

(4) fairly and reasonably related in scale and kind to the proposed development; and

(5) reasonable in all other respects.[50]

However, the satisfaction of these criteria, particularly whether a developer's contribution to the improvement of local infrastructure is sufficiently direct in its relationship with the proposed development, may remain a finely balanced issue in many instances. It has been judicially reaffirmed that a test to be applied in determining whether a planning obligation is a material consideration is whether it has some connection with the proposed development which is not *de minimis*.[51]

Official guidance is emphatic that planning obligations should not be used to facilitate unacceptable development, nor required where development would be acceptable in their absence. In theory, these are sound principles, but in practice they are issues on which it might be quite difficult to challenge the exercise of discretion by a local authority or the Secretary of State. Moreover, the official view is that, properly used, planning obligations allow considerable scope to enable environmental impacts of development to be offset by substitution, replacement or regeneration of natural features. Hence, examples are given of the loss of a wetland habitat on a site being offset by the opening up of a culverted stream or river or compensation for a development being provided by action to protect or reduce harm to protected sites or species of acknowledged importance.[52] Whilst some general doubts have been raised as to the extent to which it is genuinely possible to 'substitute' a recreated habitat for one that has been lost as a result of development,[53] there is some evidence that making development

---

[50] Department of the Environment, Circular 1/97, *Planning Obligations* (1997).
[51] *Tesco Stores Ltd v Secretary of State for the Environment and Others* [1995] WLR 759.
[52] Department of the Environment, Circular 1/97, *Planning Obligations* (1997) Annex B.
[53] See S. Whatmore and S. Boucher, 'Bargaining with nature: the discourse and practice of "environmental planning gain"' [1993] *Transactions of the Institute of British Geographers* 166 and C. Brooke, *Natural Conditions – A Review of Planning Conditions and Nature Conservation* (1996) published by the Royal Society for the Protection of Birds.

conditional upon the provision of environmental benefit may be of value in appropriate situations.[54]

In summary, there are various matters that may be provided for in planning conditions or obligations which may have important implications for flood or coastal defence.[55] On-site works are likely to be required under a planning condition to ensure that the site is satisfactorily drained and to ensure that drainage is undertaken without adverse impacts off-site, increasingly, by the use of 'sustainable drainage systems'.[56] Drainage works that are to provide highway drainage will need to be constructed to requirements for adoption by highway authorities.[57] Drainage works that are to be adopted by a sewerage undertaker, as public sewers, will need to be constructed in accordance with the undertaker's adoption specifications.[58] A planning condition may be imposed requiring off-site flood alleviation measures to be conducted before work may commence on the main project for which planning permission is sought.[59] Alternatively, a planning obligation may be entered into, by which the developer agrees to undertake work or to make a contribution to local infrastructure, such as flood or coast defences where improvement is needed in connection with the project.[60] In each instance, the relevant condition or obligation will need to be appropriately worded so that attention is given to both the initial

---

[54] An example is the Barn Elms Reservoirs in south-west London where a 100-acre residential development incorporated a 22-acre wetland area which has proved to be of significant conservation value: see A. Cuthbertson, 'Wasteland to Wetlands', *Planning Week*, 5 September 1996 and R. Desmier, 'To the Waters and the Wild', *Water Magazine*, 31 March 2000.

[55] Generally see the discussion of 'developer contributions' at 9.8.19 below and Environment Agency, *Policy and Practice for the Protection of Floodplains* (1997), discussed at 12.5 below.

[56] See 9.8.6 and 12.2 below on 'sustainable drainage'. For an example of drainage requirements being used as a 'condition precedent' to the commencement of work on a development, see *Tesco Stores Ltd v North Norfolk District Council* (1999) 78 P&CR 359.

[57] See s.38 Highways Act 1980, and see discussion of highway drainage at 8.3 below.

[58] See s.104 Water Industry Act 1991 on adoption and discussion of this at 7.2 above. On 'public sewers' see 7.3 above. Alternatively, a sewer may need to be requisitioned under s.98 Water Industry Act 1991 where drainage of domestic premises is involved.

[59] See *Grampian Regional Council v City of Aberdeen District Council* (1984) 47 P&CR 633.

[60] Under s.106 Town and Country Planning Act 1990. See, for example, *Crest Homes (South West) Ltd v Gloucestershire County Council*, unreported, Court of Appeal, 22 June 1999 where a planning obligation had been entered into requiring a developer to construct a balancing lagoon in accordance with requirements for surface water attenuation works at a site where residential properties were to be constructed. It was held that the imposition of this requirement did not provide a ground for the developer to recover damages against the defendant, who had provided an alternative system of drainage, in accordance with a contractual undertaking, but which was rendered legally unusable because of the planning requirement.

responsibility of the developer and the allocation of continuing responsibility for maintenance of structures where this is needed.

## 9.6 THE PLANNING ROLE OF THE ENVIRONMENT AGENCY

Although the planning system is primarily administered by local planning authorities, subject to the supervisory control of the Secretary of State, the role of the Environment Agency as a consultee in relation to the planning system is of central importance in relation to flood defence and related matters.[61] General ministerial guidance to the Agency indicates that it should become involved in the planning system by,

(1) responding to consultations by local planning authorities in relation to environmental impact assessment;[62]

(2) responding to requests from developers for information;

(3) responding to consultations on planning applications;

(4) responding and providing input to the preparation of development plans;

(5) responding to general enquiries about proposed developments; and

(6) providing technical advice to the Government at regional or national level in response to requests for information about the significance of any likely pollution from a proposed development.

More specifically, in relation to flood defence matters, the Agency should exercise its role as a consultee to consider whether a proposed development plan or an application for planning permission could lead to an increased risk of flooding. The Agency should respond to the planning authority accordingly and should seek to implement the Government's policy of discouraging inappropriate development in areas at risk from flooding or coastal erosion.[63] Understandably, however, the ministerial guidance is stated at a high level of generality and gives little insight into the way in which the Agency should deploy its resources so as to give priority to those planning matters where its input may be most influential and beneficial.

---

[61] Although, remarkably, the statutory water-related functions of the Agency (under s.2(1)(a) Environment Act 1995 and see 3.4 above) make no explicit reference to any function of the Agency in relation to the town and country planning system.
[62] See 9.14 below on environmental impact assessment.
[63] Department of the Environment, Ministry of Agriculture, Fisheries and Food, and Welsh Office, *The Environment Agency and Sustainable Development* (1996) Ch.6 C 'Land Use Planning' pp.26 to 27. See also 9.8 below on Government policy on development and flood risk and 9.9 below on coastal planning.

Various statutory powers and duties are imposed upon local planning authorities to consult the Agency.[64] Hence, in relation to the formulation of development plans, planning authorities are under a duty to consult various statutory bodies including the Agency.[65] This procedure allows the Agency to comment upon the implications of a draft development plan in respect of any function exercised by it, including flood defence. However, it has also been recognised that effective consultation on development planning requires continuing close liaison between the Agency and local planning authorities. In respect of this, a *Memorandum of Understanding* has been established between the Agency and the Local Authorities Association outlining the intentions of the Agency and the Association to build a relationship based on co-operation, openness and the exchange of information to emphasise a common commitment to the protection and enhancement of the environment.[66]

Although the formulation of development plans is primarily a responsibility of local authorities, in accordance with their statutory obligations and policy guidance, the Agency has been increasingly active in seeking to influence local authorities to incorporate environmental policies within development plans. *The Environment Agency and Development Plans*[67] identifies a range of development planning principles that the Agency proposes should be addressed in development plans to secure the protection and enhancement of the environment. Generally, the principles include the need to promote policies that contribute towards sustainable development[68] and to balance the demands of development with the need to protect and enhance the environment. More specifically, in relation to flood defence, the Agency will seek the inclusion of policies within development plans that:

(1) seek to protect flood plains and prevent development which would create an unacceptable increase in the risk of flooding on the site or elsewhere;

---

[64] Other bodies which perform an important role as statutory consultees are the nature conservancy councils (English Nature and the Countryside Council for Wales). Hence, a conservancy council will be a statutory consultee where a planning application relates to a site of special scientific interest (under s.28 Wildlife and Countryside Act 1981, as amended) or an area within 2 km of such a site which has been notified to the planning authority by the relevant council (art.10 Town and Country Planning (General Development Procedure) Order 1995, S.I. 1995 No.419).

[65] s.33 Town and Country Planning Act 1990 and reg.10 Town and Country Planning (Development Plan) Regulations 1991, S.I. 1991 No.2794.

[66] See Environment Agency, *Liaison with Local Planning Authorities* (1997).

[67] Environment Agency (1998). See also Environment Agency, *Policy and Practice for Protection of Floodplains* (1997), discussed at 12.5 below.

[68] See Ch.12 below on sustainable development.

(2) seek to restrict developments which would be subject to unacceptable risk of flooding;

(3) prevent developments which would adversely affect the water environment as a result of an increase in surface water run-off;

(4) protect existing or proposed defences and prevent interference with the ability of the Agency or other bodies to carry out flood control works and maintenance activities;

(5) prevent developments which would require additional public finance for flood defence works; and

(6) prevent developments which would prejudice the capacity of the coast to form a natural sea defence.

In relation to river corridors and coastal margins, the Agency will seek to include policies in development plans that:

(1) protect, enhance and restore, where appropriate, river corridors and coastal margins;

(2) ensure that developments make a positive contribution to the value of these areas in terms of nature conservation, landscape, heritage, fisheries, amenity and recreation;

(3) promote water recreation whilst balancing recreational needs with nature conservation; and

(4) avoid building over or culverting watercourses.[69]

In relation to individual applications for planning permission, as has been noted, local planning authorities are under a duty to notify statutory consultees of certain planning applications. Hence, a planning authority will be bound to consult the Agency in relation to a proposed development which involves the carrying out of works or operations in the bed or on the banks of a river or stream, and other kinds of development which may have an impact upon the aquatic environment. The planning authority will then be bound to take into account any recommendations made by the Agency making the planning determination.[70] Other, non-statutory, obligations to consult the Agency arise in relation to developments that are the subject to particular planning guidance which advises that consultation with the

---

[69] On Environment Agency policy on culverting watercourses see 4.4.3 above.
[70] art.10 Town and Country Planning (General Development Procedure) Order 1995, S.I. 1995 No.419.

Agency should be undertaken.[71] Beyond its formal role as a statutory consultee, the Agency is entitled to make representations in relation to *any* planning application which it considers may have a damaging effect upon the aquatic environment.[72] In practice, the Environment Agency comments on over 100,000 planning applications annually.[73] The basis on which representations are made is set out in the Agency publication *Liaison with Local Planning Authorities*[74] which is a manual to assist local authority planners in their day-to-day dealings with the Agency.

For the Agency, a critical difficulty is that its view as to the undesirability of a particular development is usually only one amongst many material considerations which the local planning authority will have to take into account in determining whether to grant planning permission. An illustration of the difficulties involved in reconciling priorities for the aquatic environment is to be found in *Ynys Mon Borough Council* v *Secretary of State for Wales*[75] which concerned an application for planning permission for a residential development. This proposal was strongly opposed by the National Rivers Authority (the predecessor of the Environment Agency) on environmental grounds since, following construction of the houses, it would have been the statutory right of the developer to make a connection into the local sewerage system,[76] and this was thought to be inadequate to deal with further connections. Notwithstanding the Authority's opposition to all developments involving further connections to the sewerage system until it had been improved, it was held that the 'total embargo' policy adopted by the Authority could not be binding in relation to any particular application for planning permission. Alongside the Authority's policy, other relevant planning considerations needed to be addressed, and the planning authority's overall duty was to give proper consideration and weight to all relevant matters, and this could not be fettered. Taking all the circumstances into account, a planning inspector was entitled to conclude that the Authority's policy could be outweighed by other material planning considerations in favour of the development taking place.

Although the *Ynys Mon* case was primarily concerned with the control of pollution rather than the prevention of flooding, the same approach may be taken to Agency objections based on flood defence grounds. According to

---

[71] See, for examples, the discussion of guidance on development and flood risk at 9.8 below and coastal planning at 9.9 below.
[72] art.19 Town and Country Planning (General Development Procedure) Order 1995, S.I. 1995 No.419.
[73] See Environment Agency, *Annual Report and Accounts 1999–2000* (2000) p.137.
[74] Environment Agency (1997).
[75] [1993] JPL 225.
[76] Under s.98 or s.106 Water Industry Act 1991, and see 7.2 above.

a recent Environment Agency press release,[77] of the 11,432 planning applications considered by the Midlands region of the Agency in the year 2000, 289 gave rise to objections on flood risk grounds. Of those instances where the Agency raised an objection, 45 were 'overruled' by the planning authority. It must be pointed out that these figures relate to a period before new guidance on development and flood risk was introduced,[78] but, nevertheless, they seem to indicate that, in the past at least, there has been quite a widespread willingness on the part of planning authorities not to be bound by flood defence recommendations made by the Agency.

## 9.7 PLANNING GUIDANCE

Although key legal requirements under the Town and Country Planning Act 1990, and their implications for flood and coastal defence, have been discussed, it must be recognised that a large part of the planning system is comprised of ministerial policy guidance which must be followed unless overridden by other material considerations. This guidance includes departmental circulars, particularly where the interpretation of new legislation is involved, and planning policy guidance notes, setting out general principles to be taken into account by local authorities where development plans are being formulated or applications for planning permission are being considered. Also guidance is provided at regional level, in regional planning guidance notes, and in relation to particular sectors, for example, in a series of minerals planning guidance notes.[79] In theory, any of this extensive body of guidance may be important in determining the scope of flood and coastal defence policies in development plans or the outcome of a particular planning application with a flood defence dimension. In practice, however, there are a relatively small number of key documents that are likely to be of central importance and the following discussion focuses upon these.

The discussion that follows, therefore, is necessarily selective. Only limited consideration is given to regional policy, though it is recognised that this might have major implications for some policies and projects.

---

[77] Environment Agency, *Environment Agency acts to prevent development in flood plains*, Press Release, 26 July 2001. See also House of Commons Environment, Transport and Rural Affairs Committee, Second Report Session 2000–01, *Development on, or Affecting the Floodplain* (2000) HC 64-II, *Supplementary Memorandum Submitted by the Environment Agency* p.34, indicating that during the year April 1999 to March 2000, the Agency maintained 818 objections to planning applications on flood risk grounds and 215 of these were granted against the Agency's advice.

[78] See 9.8 below on guidance on development and flood risk.

[79] Generally see Department for Transport, Local Government and the Regions website http://www.detr.gov.uk, under 'planning'.

Also, following the devolution of planning powers to the National Assembly for Wales[80] distinct planning guidance has been issued in relation to Wales which broadly parallels the advice given in planning policy guidance notes applicable to England. To avoid duplication of coverage, the corresponding, *Planning Guidance (Wales): Planning Policy*,[81] and the series of technical advice notes, are not dealt with in detail but reference is made to the broadly corresponding provisions operative in Wales. Hence, the following coverage is primarily concerned with *general* guidance and guidance applicable to *England* alone.

## 9.8 DEVELOPMENT AND FLOOD RISK

Probably the most practically important policy guidance concerning flood defence is the recent Planning Policy Guidance Note 25, *Development and Food Risk*.[82] This guidance underwent especially close parliamentary scrutiny before being adopted, largely because consultation took place at a time when flooding issues were of prominent public concern. As a result, the initial proposal put forward for consultation was superseded by a second draft which sought to strengthen key provisions.[83]

Broadly, the purpose of the guidance on development and flood risk is to:

(1) reaffirm that the susceptibility of land to flooding is a material planning consideration;

(2) emphasise the lead role of the Environment Agency in providing advice on flood issues and in relation to planning applications;

(3) stress the need for development plan policies to give consideration to flood issues, recognising the uncertainties that may be involved;

(4) require planning authorities to apply the precautionary principle and a sequential approach towards flood risk;

---

[80] See 3.3 above on the functions of the National Assembly for Wales.
[81] Welsh Office (1999) First Revision, see particularly section 15.5. For planning guidance relating to Wales, generally see National Assembly for Wales website http://www.wales.gov.uk, under 'planning'.
[82] Planning Policy Guidance Note 25 (hereafter, in this chapter, referred to as 'PPG 25') was published by the Department for Transport, Local Government and the Regions on 17 July 2001 and replaced Department of the Environment Circular 30/92 *Development and Flood Risk* (Ministry of Agriculture, Fisheries and Food Circular FD1/92). In relation to Wales, see Welsh Office, Planning Guidance (Wales), Technical Advice Note 15, *Development and Flood Risk* (1998).
[83] See House of Commons Environment, Transport and Regional Affairs Committee, Second Report Session 2000-01 *Development on, or Affecting, the Flood Plain* (2000) HC 64.

(5) require planning authorities to recognise the importance of flood plains and avoid inappropriate development;

(6) require developers to fund flood defences that are needed because of their developments; and

(7) emphasise that flood risk management needs to be applied on a whole-catchment basis.

### 9.8.1 Sustainable Development and the Precautionary Principle

As guiding principles for development and flood risk, much stress is placed upon the need for sustainable development and the precautionary principle. Although the general implications of these concepts for flood and coastal defence are discussed elsewhere in this work,[84] the precautionary principle is given a relatively specific interpretation in the context of planning guidance. The broad formulation of the principle is that lack of scientific certainty should not be used as a reason for postponing cost-effective measures to prevent serious or irreversible environmental degradation.[85] In the context of planning to minimise flood risk, however, the inherent uncertainty of flooding is translated into relatively specific planning responses associated with land falling within particular risk categories, as described below.

However, any kind of precautionary action is intimately dependent upon the assessment of risk. Whilst an increasing amount of information is becoming available to assist in the assessment of flood risk, the considerable uncertainties that remain must be approached in a precautionary manner. In some respects, the need for a precautionary approach arises from concerns of a global kind, so that planning determinations will need to take account of the latest scientific information on matters such as climate change.[86] In other respects, precaution involves weighing local circumstances into the balance, such as information relating to the flood risks arising in the area where development is proposed or the potential flooding impacts of a development on other land.

Although planning determinations will be made by local planning authorities, in accordance with the precautionary principle, such determinations need to be supported by explicit information. Accordingly, a duty is placed upon developers to provide an assessment of whether any proposed development is likely to be affected by flooding or to increase the

---

[84] See Ch.12 below on sustainable development and 1.7 above on the precautionary principle.
[85] See the discussion of Principle 15 of the Rio Declaration at 1.7 above.
[86] See 1.6 above on climate change.

risk of flooding elsewhere. Hence, developers must satisfy a planning authority that any flood risk will be successfully managed with the minimum adverse environmental impact. In relation to this, fairly detailed guidance is provided as to the manner in which flood risk assessment should be commissioned and undertaken and the minimum requirements for such assessments.[87]

Alongside the responsibilities of developers to provide flood risk assessments, it will be for the local planning authority to evaluate such assessments alongside a range of other relevant information and policy guidance. Of central importance in this respect is information which is provided by the Environment Agency as a consequence of its duty to survey matters relating to flooding,[88] including the identification of areas such as river and coastal flood plains where flooding problems are most likely to arise. The limitations of the *indicative* flood plain maps produced by the Agency are recognised, in that they do not differentiate between defended and undefended areas but, presently, they represent the best available information on the extent of flood risks. The 'indicative' status of the maps, therefore, means that the maps should be used as a basis for consultation and not as the sole basis for planning decisions. By the end of 2002 it is envisaged that the Agency will produce maps for most areas of England showing the likely extent of extreme floods (of 0.1% probability or less[89]) which will allow areas to be identified where major watercourse flooding can be effectively discounted. Nonetheless, it must be recognised that localised flooding may still occur due to intense rainfall exceeding the capacity of particular drainage systems.

### 9.8.2 Flood Risk as a Material Consideration

Given the long-established status of flood risk as a material consideration in planning matters, and the increased frequency and severity of river flooding in recent years, the guidance emphasises a need for a 'step-change' in the responsiveness of the planning system to flood risk management issues. This re-emphasised priority should be applied in the preparation and review of development plans as a means towards achieving greater sustainability and particularly through the avoidance of greater provision of artificial flood defences.

At the level of considering particular applications for planning permission, local planning authorities will need to adhere to increasingly stringent

---

[87] See Appendix F PPG 25 and see 9.8.9 below.
[88] Under s.105(2) Water Resources Act 1991, discussed at 3.4.7 above. See also the discussion of the Environment Agency's flood plain maps at 11.2.3 below.
[89] See 1.5 above on the assessment of flood risk.

principles in assessing flood risk as a material consideration. Permission for most kinds of built development in the flood plain should become wholly exceptional and limited to essential infrastructure that cannot be located elsewhere. Even then, due weight must be given to the need to avoid adding to the risk of flooding or restricting the ability of flood control works to function properly. Moreover, proposals for development should be assessed according to their full life expectancy and the impacts that they will have upon flooding elsewhere during that period. Accordingly, conditions and/or agreements should be attached to planning permissions to ensure that these objectives are fulfilled.[90]

A major innovation provided by the planning guidance on flood risk is the attempt to assess risk more systematically by applying an explicit approach to proposals for development in flood-risk areas. The assessment of risk should take account of the following factors:

(1) the area liable to flooding;

(2) the probability of flooding occurring, both directly and over time;

(3) the extent and standard of existing flood defences and their effectiveness over time;

(4) the likely depth of flooding;

(5) the rates of flow likely to be involved;

(6) the likelihood of impacts to other areas, properties and habitats;

(7) the effects of climate change; and

(8) the nature and expected lifetime of the development proposed and the extent to which it is designed to deal with flood risk.

Hence, in some areas there is a moderately high probability of flooding but this would be likely to be shallow and slow flowing and mitigation measures could be put in place without excessive financial or environmental cost. In such areas raising floor levels and other design features, such as keeping electrical circuits above the level likely to be affected by flooding, might be sufficient in some circumstances to allow buildings better to withstand flooding or to be restored more swiftly after a flood.[91]

However, it is notable that the risk factors that are identified leave considerable discretion to local authorities. Particular difficulties apply in

---

[90] See 9.5 above on planning conditions and obligations.
[91] See 9.15 below on building regulations.

relation to attempts precisely to quantify flood risks. In relation to quantification of risk, flood and coastal defence project appraisal guidance[92] gives indicative standards for protection of existing developments against flooding. Hence, for protection against river flooding, an annual probability of 0.5 to 2.0% is used for intensively developed urban areas and 1.0 to 4.0% for less intensively developed urban areas. For coastal areas, the corresponding indicative standards are 0.3 to 1.0% and 0.5 to 2.0%. Likewise, in relation to areas where development is proposed, it is reasonable to regard an area as being at risk from flooding where the annual risk from river flooding is 1.0% or greater or 0.5% or greater in relation to coastal flooding. Consequently, when formulating development plans or making planning determinations, local planning authorities should have regard to these levels of risk in deciding which areas of land are subject to the specified levels of flood risk.

### 9.8.3 The Sequential Test

Having ascertained whether an area is subject to a specific level of flood risk, discounting any existing provision of flood defences, development plans and planning determinations should apply a 'sequential test' in allocating or allowing sites to be developed. Essentially, the sequential test strives to ensure a prioritisation of development in those locations that have the least risk of river or coastal flooding. This is done by the application of increasing degrees of stringency towards development of sites that are placed in higher categories of flooding risk. For this purpose, three categories of 'flood zone' are identified alongside their appropriate planning responses.

(1) *Zones with little or no risk of flooding (annual probability less than 0.1%):* in these areas there will be no flooding-related constraints upon development other than the general need to secure that development does not significantly increase run-off.

(2) *Zones with low to medium risk of flooding (annual probability between 0.1% and 1.0% for rivers and 0.1% and 0.5% for coastal areas):* these areas are suitable for most development but require an appropriate flood risk assessment to be provided. They may also require flood-resistant construction and suitable flood warning and/ or evacuation procedures to be established. However, these areas are generally not suitable for essential civil infrastructure, such as hospitals, fire stations and emergency depots, but if such infrastructure has to

---

[92] Most recently, see Ministry of Agriculture, Fisheries and Food, *Flood and Coastal Defence Project Appraisal Guidance: Approaches to Risk*, FCDPAG4 (2000) and see 1.5 above on flooding risk.

be within such areas it will require guaranteed access in times of emergency due to flooding.

(3A) *Zones with high risk of flooding (annual probability greater than 1.0% for rivers and 0.5% for coastal areas) which are developed:* these areas may be suitable for residential, commercial and industrial development provided that the appropriate minimum standard of flood defence, and appropriate warning and evacuation procedures, can be maintained for the lifetime of the development. Development will be subject to an appropriate flood risk assessment procedure and guaranteed access for civil infrastructure that has to be located in the zone. Preference will be given to those areas already defended to a satisfactory standard, but development should not be permitted where existing sea or river flood defences will not provide an acceptable standard of safety over the lifetime of the development. Development should also be avoided in areas that have potential for managed coastal realignment or flood plain creation as part of an overall flood defence strategy for coastal cells or river catchments.[93]

(3B) *Zones with high risk of flooding (annual probability greater than 1.0% for rivers and 0.5% for coastal areas) which are undeveloped or sparsely developed:* these areas are generally not suitable for residential, commercial or industrial development unless a particular location is essential for a particular use, such as water-related recreational or transport development, and no lower-risk location is available (subject to appropriate flood risk assessment procedure and guaranteed access for civil infrastructure which has to be located in the zone). Residential use should be limited to job-related accommodation and caravan and camping sites should not be located in these areas. If, exceptionally, development is permitted it should be provided with appropriate flood defence and should not impede flood flows or result in a loss of flood-plain water storage capacity.

(3C) *Zones with high risk of flooding (annual probability greater than 1.0% for rivers and 0.5% for coastal areas) which are in functional flood plains:* these areas may be suitable for some recreation, sport, amenity and conservation uses with adequate flood warning and evacuation procedures (subject to appropriate flood risk assessment procedure). However, built development should be wholly exceptional and limited to essential transport and utilities infrastructure, which has to be within the zone (and guaranteed access provided for civil infrastructure which has to be located in the zone). If, exceptionally,

---

[93] See 12.5 and 12.6 below on managed coastal realignment and flood plain creation.

building development is allowed, it must be designed and constructed so as to remain operational in times of flood; to result in no net loss of flood-plain water storage capacity; not to impede water flows; and not to increase flood risk elsewhere. There will be a presumption against provision of camping and caravan sites in these zones.

Despite the fairly precise planning responses that are indicated towards proposed developments within the defined categories of flood zone, some flexibility may be permitted in exceptional cases. Hence, it is recognised that where extensive areas of land within a locality fall into high risk zones, further development may be needed to avoid social and economic stagnation or blight or to allow existing developments to be adequately protected. For example, in low-lying parts of eastern England there are large areas where alternative sites in lower risk zones are not available. Within these areas, planning authorities will need to give particular attention to design and mitigation issues. Similarly, even in high-risk areas, some land uses which require waterside locations, such as boat-related industries and similar development, will necessarily need to be located in such areas, though ancillary residential accommodation should be limited and designed with flood safety and evacuation considerations in mind.

In addition, there are particular land uses that are recognised to be especially sensitive to flooding. Civil emergency infrastructure, such as hospitals, fire stations and emergency vehicle depots are placed in a special category insofar as these need to be operational, and accessible, in all circumstances. It is emphasised that location of such facilities, even in low-risk flooding areas, could result in their unavailability in a flooding event. However, other kinds of emergency facility such as British Waterways emergency depots, Environment Agency flood control installations and lifeboat stations may, inevitably, need to be located in areas which are exposed to flood risk, though the need to maintain effective access will have to be taken into account in their siting and planning.

### 9.8.4 Previously Developed Land and Housing Provision

Planning policy guidance concerning development and flood risk has clear implications for other areas of policy guidance. Prominent amongst these is the emphasis that has been placed on urban regeneration and the re-use of previously developed land to reduce the need for greenfield site development.[94] A significant difficulty in reconciling regeneration and flood prevention is that much of the land that becomes available for regeneration is located alongside watercourses and is likely to be vulnerable to flooding.

---

[94] See 9.11 below on housing provision.

Proposals for the regeneration of urban land, or the re-use of existing buildings and structures, will need to take account of the risk of flooding and the standards of existing flood defences and should avoid interference with flood plain flows or compromising future shoreline or river management options. A 'balanced flexible approach' is called for in such contexts whereby recognised risks of flooding are mitigated by protecting access, prudent development design and effective public warning mechanisms. For example, sites which are vulnerable to rapid inundation should defences be overtopped or breached are unlikely to be suitable for those of restricted mobility, whether in conventional housing or in institutional accommodation.

### 9.8.5 Integration of Plans

Alongside the statutory development plans that are required under town and country planning legislation, a range of other plans have been developed by other bodies to contribute towards sustainable development, maintaining biodiversity and working with the natural processes that operate within river catchments and coastal areas. These plans may have important land-use implications and it is advised that local planning authorities should be aware of these and take 'due account' of them insofar as they concern land use. Examples of the various kinds of plans that may be relevant for this purpose are listed as the following.[95]

*Shoreline Management Plans*,[96] prepared by coast defence authorities, indicate strategies for sustainable coastal defence within sediment cells, taking account of natural coastal processes and human and other environmental influences and needs, and setting objectives for future management for lengths of shoreline.

*Estuary Management Plans*,[97] arising from an initiative by English Nature, seek to bring together all those with an interest in an estuary to reach a consensus on the sustainable use of that estuary.

*Catchment Flood Management Plans* arise from initiatives by the former Ministry of Agriculture, Fisheries and Food and the Environment Agency to produce plans that allow holistic approaches to be taken towards flood management on a catchment scale.

*Coastal Habitat Management Plans* have been proposed by English Nature and the Environment Agency to assist in the development of

---

[95] See Appendix C PPG 25. Also see the discussion of high level targets at 3.2.12 above on shoreline management, water level management and coastal habitat plans.
[96] See 5.5 above on shoreline management plans.
[97] See English Nature, *Estuary Management Plans: A co-ordinator's guide* (1993).

sustainable coastal defence strategies, and to guide flood defence operating authorities, in those areas where defence measures have implications for internationally important wildlife sites.

*Local Environment Agency Plans* are prepared by the Environment Agency to integrate the range of its functions on a catchment basis and to develop strategies through consultation with local communities and organisations.

*Water Level Management Plans*[98] are prepared by flood defence operating authorities as an integrated means of accommodating the water level requirements for a range of activities in particular areas by adopting a strategic approach to the management of flood defence within a hydrological unit.

*River Basin Management Plans* will be required by the European Community Water Framework Directive[99] from 2009 onwards and will need to establish the environmental objectives for water bodies within river basin districts and to explain how these are to be achieved.

*Community Strategies* are produced by local authorities to promote the economic, environmental and social well-being of their area and the need for community planning partnerships between local bodies on matters which may encompass flood defence.

In addition to these different kinds of plan, other plans which may be relevant to development and flood risk in particular areas are *Heritage Coast Management Plans* (prepared by local authorities, the Countryside Agency and interested bodies); *Biodiversity Action Plans* (published by English Nature to implement United Kingdom Biodiversity Action Plan[100]); *Integrated Coastal Zone Management Plans* (prepared by a number of organisations in 'coastal forums' and intended to encourage sustainable management of human use of the coast); and *Agenda 21 Plans* (prepared by local authorities to promulgate local action in support of the global environment).

### 9.8.6 Sustainable Drainage Systems

Another important innovation in the guidance on flood risk and development is the emphasis that is placed upon addressing flood defence throughout

---

[98] See 10.7 below on water level management plans.
[99] Directive of the European Parliament and of the Council establishing a framework for Community action in the field of water policy (2000/60/EC) and see Department of the Environment, Transport and the Regions, *First consultation paper on the implementation of the EC Water Framework Directive* (2001).
[100] HM Government, *Biodiversity: the UK Action Plan* (1994).

catchments. In respect of this, it is recognised that development at any location within the catchment of a watercourse is capable of having an impact on flooding by increasing the amount of run-off from roofs and paved areas through increasing the impermeable area from which water runs off. The cumulative impact of built development over a significant area is, therefore, to increase and accelerate the flow of water and to exacerbate the risk and severity of downstream flooding. Consequently, flooding issues are not restricted to river and coastal flood plains but need to be considered on a catchment-wide basis and in relation to individual developments that may contribute to floodwater flows.

Addressing flood prevention at the level of individual developments and land uses that exacerbate flooding problems involves a significant change of approach in planning practice. 'Sustainable drainage'[101] involves various kinds of facility which allow rainwater to be controlled as near as possible to the place where it falls, through retention and storage, such as flow limiting devices and sub-surface water storage areas, and the use of infiltration areas of soak-aways where the soil conditions allow this. Additionally, use may be made of 'soft' sustainable drainage systems that seek to follow natural drainage features wherever possible. It is recognised that sustainable drainage features of this kind can contribute effectively to the reduction of peak flows of run-off as well as improving amenity, wildlife conservation and groundwater recharge.

The challenge for the planning system is to ensure that sustainable drainage facilities are as widely used as possible. In relation to this, local planning authorities are encouraged to work closely with the Environment Agency, sewerage undertakers, navigation authorities and prospective developers to see that surface water run-off is managed as near to its source as possible by the use of sustainable drainage systems. In part, this has been facilitated by the amendment of the Building Regulations[102] to encourage the greater use of sustainable drainage in future developments. Additionally, highway authorities and sewerage undertakers are encouraged to make more extensive use of sustainable drainage and to consult with the Environment Agency and navigation authorities in relation to the minimisation of impacts of drainage discharges into watercourses.

### 9.8.7 Regional Planning

Addressing flooding problems at a catchment level may be problematic for many local planning authorities because their administrative boundaries rarely encompass the whole of a river catchment. Because of this, flood

---

[101] See 12.2 below on sustainable drainage systems.
[102] See 9.15 below on building regulations.

management through planning needs to be addressed through regional planning guidance which allows a more comprehensive approach to be taken and allows for the better co-ordination of planning policies and determination of applications between individual planning authorities.

Accordingly, regional planning guidance[103] should identify the principal areas where flooding issues are likely to be of regional significance on the basis of the Environment Agency's indicative flood plain maps. Within such areas regional planning guidance should assess the implications and establish policies that discourage inappropriate development in flood risk areas and otherwise manage flood risk in a safe and sustainable manner. Insofar as it is relevant, regional strategies should reflect the sequential approach to controlling development in flood risk areas previously outlined.

Regional planning strategies should ensure that run-off is managed locally in an economically and environmentally sustainable manner, so that problems are not generated elsewhere in a river catchment. Account should be taken of policies and strategies identified in Local Environment Agency Plans and any catchment flood management plans and relevant Shoreline Management Plans that relate to coastal flooding. This may encompass the safeguarding of areas from development where they are proposed for managed realignment of flood defences.

### 9.8.8 Development Plans

Many of the features of the planning guidance on flood risk have clear implications for the formulation of development plans of various kinds. Clearly, the need for a precautionary and risk-based approach as interpreted through the sequential test will be of considerable importance, as will be the important role of the Environment Agency in providing information about flood risk in particular areas.[104]

Specifically, at the level of structure plans, it is indicated that such plans should seek to establish a strategic approach to flood management and land drainage and in this respect the following issues should be considered:

(1) the record of past flood events and any factors that may have affected the risk of flooding including development or change in land use within a catchment or the carrying out of river or coastal management works;

---

[103] Generally see Department of the Environment, Transport and the Regions, Policy Planning Guidance Note 11, *Regional Planning* (2000), though guidance relevant to particular regions is to be found in the series of Regional Planning Guidance Notes.

[104] See also the role of the Environment Agency in reporting on development plans under high level target 12, discussed at 3.2.12 above.

(2) the need to develop a strategic understanding of the hydrology and drainage of river catchments in consultation with the Environment Agency;

(3) the requirements of Biodiversity Action Plans and the importance of statutory conservation sites in the river and flood plain;[105]

(4) identification, at an appropriate level of detail, of the land most likely to flood, including river and coastal flood plains, taking account of major events of low probability as well as floods that are likely to be of higher frequency; and

(5) whether projected strategic locations for major new developments could exacerbate flood risk downstream.

As a result of considering these matters, and other material considerations, structure plans should establish strategic policies to avoid the threat of flooding where possible, or otherwise to manage it to ensure that future development is adequate protected.

At the level of local plans, the strategic guidance on flood risk will need to be reinterpreted to be applied to local circumstances. Hence, local planning authorities will need to indicate areas of flood risk on local plans or supplementary planning guidance so that sites which are at risk can be identified as precisely as the inherent uncertainties allow. For identified flood risk areas, policies should be applied to manage and minimise the risks in accordance with the sequential test, and reasons for departure from this should be explained. Similarly, authorities should review existing allocations of land for development against the sequential test. In respect of land which is allocated for housing this procedure may be combined with reviews of the sustainability of housing land allocations.[106]

Local plans should also take account of the extent to which an area is actually defended against flood risk and the standard of those defences. Existing defences cannot prevent the possibility of flooding entirely, but only reduce its likelihood. Therefore, the risks involved must be assessed and further development permitted only if those risks are found to be acceptable. This concern is particularly relevant to areas that are protected by sea defences where inundation by the sea may take place rapidly and

---

[105] See Department of the Environment, Policy Planning Guidance Note 9, *Nature Conservation* (1994), discussed at 9.10 below.

[106] See Department of the Environment, Transport and the Regions, Planning Policy Guidance Note 3, *Housing* (2000), paras.30 and 31 of which concern physical and environment constraints upon housing development arising from, amongst other things, flood risk; and see 9.11 below.

## Development and Flood Risk

extend over large areas of land and, in respect of such areas, coast protection authorities should maintain regular contact with the Environment Agency. Given inevitable limitations upon resources for flood protection and the need for these to be used in the most cost-effective manner, the options for low-lying undeveloped areas may include a policy of managed retreat.

Applying the principle that flood risk should be an inherent aspect of any planning determination, local plans should incorporate policies that promote the appropriate use of sustainable drainage systems[107] to prevent development in one part of a catchment increasing run-off and the risk of flooding elsewhere. Hence, the objective is that new development should not increase run-off, as compared with the undeveloped situation, and redevelopment should seek to reduce run-off. The implementation of sustainable drainage requirements should be discussed with the Environment Agency, the sewerage undertaker and relevant waterway navigation authorities during the preparation of local plans.

### 9.8.9 Development Control

In relation to the determination of particular applications for planning permission, the effect of the guidance is to re-emphasise the importance of flood risk as a material consideration. Hence, in relation to any planning application, account must be taken of this risk both in respect of the land which is proposed to be developed and the flooding impacts of the development on other land. Consequently, an applicant for planning permission will be required to provide an assessment of both on-site and off-site flooding risk. Similarly, applications for renewal of a planning permission should be reviewed alongside evidence of flooding risks, should take account of any reviews of development land allocations which have been conducted and should be determined in accordance with the sequential test.

Applications by householders for minor extensions or alterations are unlikely to raise significant flooding concerns unless they have a direct adverse effect on a watercourse or its flood defences or would impede access to flood defence or management facilities. Nonetheless, minor developments should be designed and constructed to conform to flood protection measures already incorporated into the property that is to be extended. In circumstances where an extension which is a permitted development is likely to have a direct and adverse effect on a watercourse or its flood defences, or to impede access, local planning authorities should

---

[107] See 12.2 below on sustainable drainage systems.

consider making a direction requiring full consideration to be given to the flooding impacts of the extension.[108] Local planning authorities must inform applicants for planning permission that the property is within an area of flood risk,[109] identified by the Environment Agency, where an application is made for an extension or alteration of a property. Authorities should also incorporate site-specific flood risk information as a part of their planning search procedures and advise those making searches to consult the Agency for detailed information. Not least significant is the onus placed upon a prospective developer to conduct an appropriate flood-risk assessment that may require detailed hydrological investigation and adoption of appropriate mitigation measures.

### 9.8.10 Developer Contributions

The stress which is placed upon the responsibilities of developers has implications for the contributions that they will be obliged to make to any flood defence works that may be required in relation to a development proposal. Accordingly, local planning authorities and developers are bound to have regard to the following considerations.

(1) Developers cannot normally call on public resources to provide flood defences for their developments unless these resources are already allocated.

(2) Provision of previously allocated public expenditure for flood defence may create opportunities for new development where this does not contribute to flood risk at other locations.

(3) For previously developed land, public expenditure in land remediation and infrastructure may include flood defence and mitigation investment to allow the land to be beneficially used.

(4) Where public expenditure has not been allocated for flood defence or land remediation, other material considerations may be sufficient to outweigh the risk of flooding and allow a proposed development to be permitted. However, flood alleviation works will normally have to be funded by the developer, either in full or proportionately according to the benefit secured for the developer by the development project. To facilitate this, appropriate planning obligations[110] might need to be

---

[108] That is, a direction restricting permitted development, under art.4 Town and Country Planning (General Permitted Development) Order 1995, S.I. 1995 No.418; and see Department of the Environment Circular 9/95, *General Development* (1995) and discussion at 9.4 above.

[109] See also the discussion of warnings of the propensity of land to flood at 11.4.1 below.

[110] See 9.5 above on planning conditions and planning obligations.

## Development and Flood Risk

entered into to ensure that the works are properly carried out and that future maintenance responsibilities are imposed upon the developer. It might be appropriate to vest the resulting defences in the flood defence operating authority with payment of a dedicated commuted sum to cover maintenance costs over a 30-year period, after which it would be reasonable to regard the defences as an asset maintainable at public expense. In addition, it might be appropriate for local planning authorities to consider the imposition of planning conditions preventing a developer from proceeding with a development until the necessary flood defence works have been carried out. Similarly, in relation to the renewal of culverts and the maintenance of unadopted sustainable drainage systems, provision for future maintenance costs would have to be made. One mechanism for securing this objective might be the establishment of a management company entitled to levy service charges on owners and occupiers of properties benefited by flood defence works.

(5) The same requirements, in relation to developers meeting the cost of construction and maintenance of flood defence and mitigation works, apply equally where the works are necessary to prevent consequential flooding risk to other areas and properties.

(6) After considering the preceding matters, the local planning authority will take advice from the Environment Agency and any other relevant operating authorities, and will determine what contribution from the developer is required. Without agreement being reached on the provision of a determined contribution, an application for planning permission should be refused in accordance with the precautionary principle.

### 9.8.11 Application and Consultation Procedures

Applications for planning permission will require particular consideration in respect of flood risk issues in relation to the following areas and project categories:

(1) within a river flood plain shown on the indicative flood plain map prepared by the Environment Agency;

(2) within a coastal flood plain, including that adjacent to the tidal length of a river, shown on the indicative flood plain map prepared by the Environment Agency;

(3) within or adjacent to any watercourse, particularly where there might be potential for flash flooding;

(4) adjacent to or including any flood bank or other flood control structure;

(5) in an area where the Agency has indicated that there may be drainage problems;

(6) areas or projects likely to involve the culverting or diverting of any watercourse; or

(7) projects of such a size or nature relative to the receiving watercourse and/or drainage system that there could be a significant increase in surface water run-off from the area.

On receiving a planning application which raises flooding problems, local planning authorities should undertake internal consultation in relation to their own flood defence responsibilities as well as consulting with the Environment Agency. Although the Agency is a statutory consultee for some categories of development,[111] the need for consultation extends to a much wider range of development proposals where flood risk is involved. Where relevant, local planning authorities should also agree with internal drainage boards on the types of development that are of interest to them and engage in consultation in respect of planning applications that involve these kinds of development. Where run-off considerations are likely to be significant, planning authorities should consult the Agency, the sewerage undertaker and any relevant navigation authority in respect of the capacity of existing drainage systems, the feasibility and desirability of using sustainable drainage systems and the impacts of discharges into watercourses.

It is expected that the Environment Agency will respond to consultation on the flooding aspects of planning applications within 21 days.[112] Because local planning authorities encourage applicants to provide the fullest possible information at the earliest stage, there are benefits in applicants entering into discussion of their proposals with planning authorities and the Agency in advance of an application being submitted. In response to consultation, the Agency, and other operating authorities, must consider the risk of flooding at the proposed site, the impact on flooding elsewhere or the impact of flood alleviation works on other property or nature conservation interests. On the basis of these considerations, the Agency will indicate whether the proposed development is acceptable, or subject to what conditions or modifications it may be acceptable, or seek more information to enable a decision on acceptability to be reached.

---

[111] See 9.6 above on the status of the Environment Agency as a planning consultee.

[112] Although see Environment Agency, *Annual Report and Accounts 2000/01* (2001) p.51, which indicates that in providing advice to local authority planning offices as a consultee on planning applications, the Agency aims to provide advice on 50% of applications within 14 working days; 75% within 21 working days; and 95% within 28 working days.

In a situation where the local planning authority takes the view that other material considerations outweigh any objections raised by the Environment Agency or other consultees on flooding issues, local planning authorities should inform them that they are minded to grant planning permission, and the reasons for doing so, and give the opportunity for further representations to be made. Although consultees may maintain their objections, there may be practicable improvements that could be incorporated which would minimise the perceived impacts.

Consultation arrangements will need to make special provision for particular kinds of development:

(1) where phased or other developments have cumulative effects in reducing the storage capacity of flood plains or significantly increasing run-off and where it is difficult to associate the necessary flood alleviation works with an individual planning application;

(2) where development will obstruct natural or engineered flood flows, leading to higher upstream water levels, flooding or increased erosion;

(3) where there are impacts on statutory nature conservation sites within the flood plain, including the watercourse itself, and areas that may be subject to significant change in surface run-off;

(4) where building works on or near flood defence embankments or other control structures might reduce their effectiveness or seriously impede their maintenance;

(5) where development affects an existing structure, constructed for another purpose, which may incidentally serve as a flood defence, the alteration or removal of which may place a previously protected area at increased risk;

(6) for mineral workings in flood plain areas that could affect water storage and the control of flooding; and

(7) for proposed residential development, particularly for people of impaired mobility, in areas identified through development plan consultation as being susceptible to flooding, whether or not such areas are protected by flood defences.

In addition, for projects which may have a significant effect on the environment, including flood alleviation works, local planning authorities will need to determine whether environmental impact assessment is required and, if so, to follow the appropriate procedures.[113]

---

[113] See 9.14 below on environmental impact assessment.

## 9.9 COASTAL PLANNING

Planning Policy Guidance Note 20, *Coastal Planning*,[114] recognises that the coast is a national environmental, economic and recreational resource of special value, though the subject of increasing concerns about rising sea levels and the need for development to be sustainable. The general role of the planning system in relation to coastal management is to reconcile development requirements with the need to protect, conserve and, where appropriate, improve the landscape, environmental quality, wildlife habitats and recreational opportunities of the coast. These objectives have to be pursued in relation to a coastline that is markedly varied in its topography and includes a wide variety of natural features which are dynamic in character and shaped by powerful natural processes.

Approximately 30% of the coastline in England and Wales is developed, with much of this having taken place before the introduction of planning legislation. However, an increasing proportion of the coast has been specially protected by the planning system and is actively managed by local authorities, landowners and conservation bodies. Hence, special policies will apply to designated areas of high landscape value or of nature conservation or scientific interest, and these will be designated as National Parks, Areas of Outstanding Natural Beauty, Sites of Special Scientific Interest, European Sites, Ramsar Sites, Green Belt Areas and Heritage Coasts.[115] The cumulative effect of this is that 2,000 km of coastline is covered by one or more of these designations, out of an estimated total of 4,400 km of coastline in England and Wales, excluding estuaries.

For planning purposes, the limit of the coastal zone in the seaward direction is mean low-water mark so that local planning authorities have powers to control the development of land only above mean low-water mark, though other agencies have powers to control activities such as dredging for aggregates. Therefore, planning authorities will need to consider how best to define the landward limits of the coastal zone for their planning policies on the basis of local circumstances. These will include the extent of direct maritime influences and key coast-related planning issues such as the needs of areas affected by off-shore or near-shore natural processes, such as areas of potential tidal flooding and erosion.

For planning purposes it is suggested that the coast can be divided into four types:

---

[114] Department of the Environment (1992). In relation to Wales, see Welsh Office, Planning Guidance (Wales), Technical Advice Note 14, *Coastal Planning* (1998). See also National Coasts and Estuaries Advisory Group, *Coastal Planning and Management* (1993).

[115] See 10.2 to 10.4 below on sites of special scientific interest and 10.6 below on European sites.

(1) the undeveloped coast, conserved both for its landscape value and for its nature conservation interest;

(2) other areas of undeveloped or partly developed coast;

(3) the developed coast, usually urbanised but also containing other major developments such as ports and power stations; and

(4) the despoiled coast, damaged by dereliction caused by mining, waste tipping and former industrial uses.

The key policy issues for coastal planning are:

(1) conservation of the natural environment;

(2) development, particularly that which requires a coastal location;

(3) risks, including flooding, erosion and land instability; and

(4) improving the environment, particularly of urbanised or despoiled coastlines.

Most pertinently, the need for policies in relation to 'risks' recognises that coastal geology and landforms in many areas give rise to risks of flooding, erosion by the sea, and land slips and falls of rock. Policies relating to these matters need to be carefully considered to avoid putting further development at risk by minimising development in vulnerable areas. In particular, new development should not generally be permitted in areas which will need expensive engineering works, either to protect developments on land subject to erosion by the sea or to defend land which might be inundated by the sea. There is also a need to consider the possibility of such works causing a transfer of risks to other areas.

Rising sea levels and instances of severe coastal flooding have focused attention on minimising both the risk to life and damage to property. This should be done by identifying areas likely to be at risk from flooding. Moreover, a precautionary approach[116] is required in policies for land affected, or likely to be affected, by erosion or land instability. In the case of receding cliffs, development should not be allowed to take place in areas where erosion is likely to occur during the lifetime of the proposed building and such areas should be clearly identified and shown in development plans.[117]

---

[116] See 1.7 and 9.8.1 above on the precautionary principle.
[117] See also Department of the Environment, Planning Policy Guidance Note 14 on *Development on Unstable Land* (1990) which suggests that local planning authorities should not normally permit built development where there is potential for landslips during the lifetime of the building.

It is recognised that flood defence structures can have a considerable effect on the coastal environment and, whilst improvements to existing sea defence works are not usually subject to control, planning permission is required for new works. The impact on the environment, and on the natural movement of material along the coast, should be taken into account in reaching planning decisions on new flood defence measures and the effects of such measures on economic activity should also be considered. In low-lying, undeveloped coastal areas, options for coastal defence may include a policy of 'managed retreat'.[118] In such areas it should not be presumed that it will be economically justified to maintain existing coastal defences and planning policies should take this into account. It may be appropriate to restrict development in such areas pending decisions on coastal defence, so that future options for managed retreat remain open.

## 9.10 NATURE CONSERVATION

Although not addressing flood defence development directly, Planning Policy Guidance Note 9, *Nature Conservation*,[119] is of considerable importance in determining the planning significance of land that is subject to a nature conservation designation such as a site of special scientific interest or a European site.[120] Given that many flood and coastal defence projects will need to be carried out in areas subject to nature conservation designations, the significance of these designations in planning applications will be a frequent consideration.

Broadly, the approach of the conservation guidance is to affirm that nature conservation is an important material consideration in determining many kinds of planning application, especially in or near sites of special scientific interest, where statutory requirements to consult the relevant nature conservation council will apply.[121] Nonetheless, it is advised that local planning authorities should not refuse planning permission if development can be made subject to conditions that will prevent damaging impacts on wildlife habitats or important physical features, or if other material factors are sufficient to override nature conservation considerations. Clearly, however, the capacity of planning authorities to determine that 'other material factors' override nature conservation considerations will be limited, particularly where European Sites are involved.[122]

---

[118] See discussion of managed retreat at 12.6 below.
[119] Department of the Environment (1994). In relation to Wales, see Welsh Office, Planning Guidance (Wales), Technical Advice Note 5, *Nature Conservation and Planning* (1996).
[120] See 10.2 to 10.4 below on sites of special scientific interest and 10.6 below on European sites.
[121] See 9.4 above and 10.4 below on consultation requirements.
[122] See 10.6 below on the protection given to European sites.

## 9.11 HOUSING

The provision of housing is another matter of general concern with wide-ranging social and economic implications including flood and coastal defence. These concerns are amplified by the predictions of a massive amount of new housing that will need to be built over the next few years. In its policy statement, *Planning for the Communities of the Future*,[123] the Government projected that 4.4 million new households would be established by 2016 and that housing provision would need to be made accordingly.

Planning Policy Guidance Note 3, *Housing*,[124] sets out the general objectives that should be pursued in providing decent housing for all whilst promoting more sustainable patterns of development. Notably, this involves making better use of previously developed land, particularly in existing towns and cities, in preference to the development of greenfield sites. Hence, a national target is reaffirmed that, by 2008, 60% of additional housing should be provided on 'recycled' land and through the conversion of existing buildings.

Although considerable emphasis is placed upon greater exploitation of the capacity for urban regeneration, it is recognised that decisions of planning authorities to allocate land for housing should involve an assessment of the suitability of land for development against clear criteria. The stated criteria include the 'physical and environmental constraints on development' which encompasses an assessment of the level of contamination of land[125] and vulnerability to flood risk, taking into account that such risk may increase as a result of climate change.

The difficulty, from a flood risk perspective, is that many of the urban areas that may be otherwise suitable for housing development are located in identified areas of flooding vulnerability. Moreover, there is a delicate balance to be drawn between redevelopment of areas and the priority that has recently been placed upon avoiding development which is subject to flood risk. In addition, the redevelopment of areas within flood plains may be difficult to reconcile with the need to restore the natural extent of flood plains to a state where they are free from development.[126]

---

[123] Department of the Environment, Transport and the Regions (1998).

[124] Department of the Environment, Transport and the Regions (2000) and see also Circular 9/98, *Affordable Housing*. In relation to Wales, generally see Welsh Office, Planning Guidance (Wales), Technical Advice Notes 1, *Joint Housing and Land Availability Studies* (1997) and 2, *Planning and Affordable Housing* (1996).

[125] See 9.12 above on land contamination.

[126] See Environment Agency, *Policy and Practice for the Protection of Floodplains* (1997) and see 12.5 below.

## 9.12 CONTAMINATED LAND

The need for guidance on contaminated land remediation arises largely through the insertion of Part IIA into the Environmental Protection Act 1990 under the Environment Act 1995. The detail of this regime is beyond the scope of this work,[127] but, broadly, it allows local authorities or the Environment Agency to require polluters or owners of land which is contaminated by past use to secure the remediation of this land to a standard which is suitable for its present or intended future use. The implications of this are particularly significant in relation to extensive areas of, primarily, urban land that have been contaminated by past industrial activities but continue to give rise to pollution problems. The guidance on the operation of Part IIA of the 1990 Act is provided for in a departmental circular which explains the basis upon which remediation requirements for contaminated land are to be applied.[128]

The planning implications are that land contamination or the possibility of it are material considerations needing to be taken into account in development planning and determining individual applications for planning permission. Hence, local planning authorities should satisfy themselves that land contamination issues are properly addressed and, where appropriate, planning permissions should incorporate remediation requirements to ensure that the land is suitable for use for the purpose for which permission is sought. Although present guidance[129] enables local authorities to impose remediation requirements in planning permissions, it is understood that new guidance is in preparation to take greater account of the contaminated land regime in the sphere of planning.

Although the remediation of contaminated land is a matter of general concern, it is an issue that is likely to be of particular significance in relation to urban projects with a flood defence dimension. The contamination of land will be of special importance where developers are seeking to install sustainable drainage systems given the potential capacity of such systems to channel water which has flowed over or through contaminated land into groundwater or surface waters.[130]

---

[127] Generally see S. Tromans and R. Turrall-Clarke, *Contaminated Land: The New Regime* (2000).

[128] Department of the Environment, Transport and the Regions, Circular 02/2000, *Environmental Protection Act 1990: Part IIA, Contaminated Land* (2000). Notably, this guidance applies to England only and separate guidance concerning Wales is understood to be under preparation. See also the Contaminated Land (England) Regulations 2000 (S.I. 2000 No.227) and the Contaminated Land (Wales) Regulations 2001 (S.I. 2001 No.2197 W.157).

[129] See Department of the Environment, Planning Policy Guidance Note 23 *Planning and Pollution Control* (1994) and Department of the Environment, Circular 11/95 *The Use of Conditions in Planning Permissions* (1995).

[130] See 12.3.4 on sustainable drainage systems and groundwater protection.

## 9.13 OTHER PLANNING POLICIES

Although the planning guidance which has been noted is likely to be of most general importance in relation to flood defence, the possibility remains that other guidance will also apply to particular projects. The following Planning Policy Guidance Notes may, therefore, be of special relevance in relation to individual projects.

Planning Policy Guidance Note 2, *Green Belts*;[131]

Planning Policy Guidance Note 7, *The Countryside*;[132]

Planning Policy Guidance Note 14, *Development on Unstable Land*;[133]

Planning Policy Guidance Note 15, *Planning and the Historic Environment*;[134]

Planning Policy Guidance Note 16, *Archaeology and Planning*;[135] and

Planning Policy Guidance Note 17, *Sport and Recreation*.[136]

## 9.14 ENVIRONMENTAL IMPACT ASSESSMENT

'Environmental impact assessment' is a procedure, involving a systematic assessment of the likely significant environmental effects of a project, which must be conducted before it is granted planning permission or other kinds of authorisation. The purpose of this procedure is to ensure that the significance of the predicted effects, and the scope for reducing them, are properly understood by the public and the decision-making authority before a determination of an application is made. Hence, the procedure enables environmental factors to be given due weight, along with economic and social factors, when applications for authorisation are being considered. The cumulative effect of this is to promote a more sustainable pattern of development and land use, and to be of benefit to all who are involved in the planning process.[137]

More specifically, for those flood and coastal defence projects that are

---

[131] Department of the Environment (1995).
[132] Department of the Environment (1997) and, in relation to Wales, see National Assembly for Wales, Planning Guidance (Wales), Technical Advice Note 6, *Agricultural and Rural Planning* (2000).
[133] Department of the Environment (1990).
[134] Department of the Environment (1994).
[135] Department of the Environment (1990).
[136] Department of the Environment (1991) and, in relation to Wales, see Welsh Office, Planning Guidance (Wales), Technical Advice Note 16, *Sport and Recreation* (1998).
[137] Department of the Environment, Transport and the Regions, *Environmental Impact Assessment: A Guide to Procedures* (2001) paras.1 to 2 and see also Department of the Environment, Transport and the Regions, Circular 2/99 *Environmental Impact Assessment* (1999) and Welsh Office Circular 11/99.

likely to have a significant effect upon the environment, the basic requirements of town and country planning law and policy are supplemented by the need for environmental impact assessment to be undertaken before development consent will be given. Given the scale of many structures that serve flood defence purposes, and the ecologically sensitive locations which are often involved, environmental impact assessment is a frequent requirement, alongside the general planning and other controls, to ensure that works are environmentally acceptable.

It must be stressed that environmental impact assessment has a special legal status above the national requirements that are imposed to ensure the environmental and ecological acceptability of flood defence projects. This is because it arises from the need to transpose European Community obligations into national law by transparent legal mechanisms and, as a consequence of this, an extensive body of secondary legislation has been generated. This is for the purpose of incorporating environmental assessment requirements into planning procedures[138] and for adapting other procedures by which authorisations for projects and works are granted, such as authorisation requirements that apply specifically to land drainage improvement works.[139] Nonetheless, in practice, the most common application of the requirement for environmental impact assessment in relation to new flood and coastal defence projects will arise in respect of developments which require planning permission under town and country planning law.

Some points of contrast must be emphasised to distinguish 'environmental impact assessment' from other kinds of environmental procedure that may arise in relation to flood and coastal defence activities. First, local planning authorities have a long-standing power to require applicants for planning permission to provide information about the project for which authorisation is sought.[140] This power is capable of being used to require an applicant to provide additional information about the environmental implications of a project prior to a planning determination being made. Second, the Environment Agency has a general power to do anything which is conducive or incidental to the carrying out of its functions[141] which is so

---

[138] Town and Country Planning (Environmental Impact Assessment) (England and Wales) Regulations 1999, S.I. 1999 No.293.

[139] Environmental Impact Assessment (Land Drainage Improvement Works) Regulations 1999, S.I. 1999 No.1783, discussed at 9.14.4 below.

[140] See reg.4 Town and Country Planning (Applications) Regulations 1988, S.I. 1988 No.1812, which allows a local authority to direct an applicant to supply further information to enable a determination to be made or to provide evidence to verify information that has been provided.

[141] s.37(1)(a) Environment Act 1995.

## Environmental Impact Assessment

broadly formulated that it might reasonably be used to require environmental information to be provided prior to a determination being made of an application for a flood defence consent.[142] Third, environmental 'appraisal' is an integral part of the formulation of an acceptable flood defence or coast protection project in relation to securing central government funding. Hence, whether or not a project requires full environmental impact assessment, to qualify for grant-aid it will need to satisfy environmental appraisal requirements.[143] The point to be stressed is that none of these three kinds of procedure are sufficient to meet the requirements of European Community law insofar as formal environmental impact assessment is required for a particular kind of flood or coastal defence project.

The discussion that follows examines the scope of the European Community obligations concerning environmental impact assessment, and the mechanisms that have been used to transpose these obligations into national law, with specific emphasis upon those features which are likely to have most relevance to flood defence projects.

### 9.14.1 The Environmental Impact Assessment Directive

The European Community Directive on environmental impact assessment[144] requires an assessment procedure to be followed in relation to certain projects, which are deemed, or likely, to have a significant effect upon the environment because of their nature, size, location or for other reasons. Such projects may only be permitted if the authorising body takes into account specified environmental information in making its determination as to whether a project will be authorised and the terms of the authorisation.

The detail of the environmental impact assessment process is quite intricate[145] but, most pertinently, it requires the identification and assessment

---

[142] Under ss.109 and 110 Water Resources Act 1991 and s.23 Land Drainage Act 1991 which also provides similar powers to internal drainage boards; see 4.4.1, 4.4.2 and 4.7.3 above. Also see ss.6 and 7 Environment Act 1995 and ss.61A and 61B Land Drainage Act 1991 concerning the environmental duties of the Environment Agency and internal drainage boards, discussed at 10.2 and 10.3 below.

[143] See Ministry of Agriculture, Fisheries and Food, and Welsh Office, *Code of Practice on Environmental Procedures for Flood Defence Operating Authorities* (1996); Ministry of Agriculture, Fisheries and Food, *Flood and Coastal Defence Project Appraisal Guidance: Environmental Appraisal* (FCDPAG5) (2000); and generally see Ch.6 above on funding.

[144] Directive on the Assessment of the Effects of Certain Public and Private Projects on the Environment, 85/337/EEC (the 'Original' Directive), now amended by Directive 97/11/EC (the 'Amending' Directive).

[145] Generally see W. Sheate, *Making an Impact: A Guide to EIA Law and Policy* (2nd ed. 1994).

of direct and indirect effects of a project upon water and the landscape. This involves consideration of an 'environmental statement' which provides information, specified by Annex III to the Directive, including an account of the project, the aspects of the environment likely to be significantly affected and, where appropriate, an outline of the main alternatives to the proposed development.

For industrial and infrastructure projects listed under Annex I to the Directive, environmental impact assessment is mandatory. None of the categories provided for under Annex I relates specifically to flood defence, land drainage or coast protection, though it is possible that projects in the listed categories will have implications for these matters which need to be considered. For those projects listed in Annex II to the Directive, environmental assessment is necessary 'where their characteristics so require', that is, where a particular project or category of projects is likely to have a significant effect upon the environment. Notably, Annex II encompasses various agricultural operations, such as land drainage projects and reclamation of land from the sea, and infrastructure projects such as canalisation and flood-relief works, and the construction of dams and other installations designed to store water on a long-term basis.

A pertinent illustration of the operation of the Directive, in a flood defence context, is the European Court of Justice decision in the *Kraaijeveld* case[146] where the Court had been asked by the Netherlands Council of State to give a preliminary ruling[147] on questions relating to the interpretation of the Directive in the context of a dyke-reinforcement project. The project included the construction of a replacement dyke that had been approved by the local authority under a modified zoning plan, and approval had been confirmed by the Provincial Executive. However, neither of these approvals had given any consideration of the environmental effects of the project. Although it was clear that the Directive encompassed projects concerned with 'canalisation and flood relief works' where these were likely to have significant effects on the environment, the relevant national requirements excluded the need for environmental impact assessment where a dyke was less than 5 km in length or had a cross-section of less than 250 m. The practical effect of these 'generous' thresholds was to exempt almost all river dyke projects in the Netherlands from any environmental impact assessment requirements.

The Court concluded that the expression 'canalisation and flood-relief works', as used in the Directive, should be interpreted to encompass certain

---

[146] Case C-72/95 *Aannemersbedrijf P.K. Kraaijeveld BV and Others* v *Gedeputeerde Staten van Zuid-Holland Environnement et Consommateurs* [1996] ECR I-5403.

[147] See Art.234 (formerly Art.177) European Community Treaty on preliminary rulings.

types of work on a dyke running alongside a waterway. Moreover, the expression should encompass both the construction of a new dyke and also a modification of an existing dyke which involved its relocation, reinforcement or widening, and it was clear that the replacement of a dyke involved a combination of such works. In respect of the thresholds that had been formulated, it was held that a Member State setting criteria or thresholds at such a high level that, in practice, all projects would be exempted from environmental impact assessment requirements would normally be exceeding the discretion allowed under the Directive. In a situation where the discretion allowed by the Directive had been exceeded by national requirements, it was for the authorities in a Member State to take all measures necessary to ensure that projects were subject to examination to assess whether they were likely to have significant effects upon the environment. Clearly, therefore, excessively generous national exemptions from environmental assessment requirements for flood defence projects may not be used as a justification for failing to implement the substantive requirements of the Directive.

Another pertinent European Court ruling on environmental impact assessment was in proceedings brought by the European Commission against *Ireland*[148] in relation to its failure satisfactorily to implement the Directive in respect of projects involving agricultural intensification, initial afforestation and the extraction of peat (under Annex II). Ireland had established absolute thresholds, respectively of 100 hectares, 70 hectares and 50 hectares for the three kinds of project, so that environmental impact assessment would be required only for projects above those limits. However, the Commission contended that projects having a significant effect upon the environment could be undertaken even where those thresholds were not exceeded. In relation to initial afforestation, there were concerns that the effect of ploughing and land drainage was to bring about a destruction of peatland ecosystems. Similarly, where peat extraction was concerned, the effect of drainage was to lower the water table causing a drying-out process which had significant and irreversible ecological effects.

Despite contested evidence as to whether the alleged environmental damage had actually occurred or not, the Court emphasised that the issue to be decided was whether or not the national thresholds that had been adopted were *capable* of being misused, rather than whether *actual* misuse had taken place. On this, the Court stressed that the Directive required environmental assessment where a project was likely to have significant environmental effects, amongst other things, because of its *nature, size or location*. In effect, by only taking account of the *size* of projects, Ireland

---

[148] Case C-392/96 *Commission v Ireland* [1999] 3 CMLR 727.

had neglected the other criteria in setting its thresholds and so had exceeded the discretion allowed by the Directive. Moreover, the Court found that there had been a failure to ensure that the objectives of the Directive were not circumvented by the splitting of projects into parts which fell below the thresholds. Account, therefore, needed to be taken of the combined effect of projects that fell below a size threshold where the cumulative effect of those projects was likely to have a significant effect upon the environment. Again, therefore, the substantive requirements of the Directive prevailed over inadequate national implementing legislation and emphasised the need for the wording of the Directive to be given precedence over national law.

### 9.14.2 The Amending Directive

Following concerns arising from the unsatisfactory operation of the original Environmental Assessment Directive in different Member States of the European Community, and a need to give effect to international obligations concerning transboundary environmental impacts,[149] the original Directive was modified by the Amending Directive.[150] Amongst other things, the Amending Directive extends the range of projects for which environmental impact assessment is required. Hence, works for the transfer of water resources between river basins, above specified limits, and dams and other water storage installations, above certain capacities, are now included in Annex I. Under Annex II, the range of infrastructure projects now includes coastal works to combat erosion and maritime works capable of altering the coast through the construction, for example, of dykes, moles, jetties and other sea defence works, excluding the maintenance and reconstruction of such works. In respect of Annex II projects, determination of whether environmental assessment is required is to be made either on a case-by-case examination or in accordance with thresholds or criteria set by the Member State, or both of these.

### 9.14.3 The Environmental Impact Assessment Regulations

In relation to those projects that require planning permission under national planning legislation, environmental impact assessment obligations, arising under the original and amending Directives, are now implemented

---

[149] See *Report of the Commission on the Implementations of Directive 85/337/EC on the Assessment of the Effects of Certain Public and Private Projects on the Environment* COM (93) 28 final (The 'Five-year Review Report') and *Convention on Environmental Impact Assessment in a Transboundary Context* (the 'Espoo Convention') signed by European Community, 25 February 1991 (COM (92) 93, as amended by COM (93) 131).

[150] Under Directive 97/11/EC (the 'Amending' Directive).

under the Town and Country Planning (Environmental Impact Assessment) (England and Wales) Regulations 1999.[151] In summary, the Regulations impose procedural requirements in relation to the consideration of planning applications, so that all 'Schedule 1' development (equivalent to projects under Annex I to the Directives) requires environmental impact assessment. For projects under Schedule 2 (equivalent projects under Annex II to the Directives) determination of whether environmental impact assessment is required will be made on a case-by-case basis, but projects will require assessment if they are in an area which is designated as 'sensitive', for ecological, archaeological or landscape reasons, or above specified threshold criteria. Hence, projects for agricultural land drainage will be above the threshold if the area involved exceeds one hectare; all agricultural works involving reclamation of land from the sea are deemed to be above the threshold; canalisation and flood-relief works and construction of dams and other installations for long-term water storage are above the threshold if the works exceed one hectare; and all coastal work to combat erosion and maritime works capable of altering the coast are above the threshold. Extensions of existing Schedule 1 or Schedule 2 projects will also be subject to environmental impact assessment where threshold criteria are exceeded.

For 'environmental impact assessment development', within the Regulations, planning permission may not be granted by the local planning authority or the Secretary of State unless specified environmental information which is reasonably required to assess the environmental effects of a development, has first been taken into account. Notably also, permitted development rights, for projects that would not normally require an application for planning permission, are removed in relation to environmental impact assessment development.[152] The environmental information will include an 'environmental statement' provided by the developer under Schedule 4, and representations made by consulted bodies and representations made by other persons. Detailed 'screening' procedures are provided, under Schedule 3, to determine whether a proposed development requires environmental impact assessment. A developer may also seek a 'scoping' opinion or direction as to the information that should be included in an environmental statement. The local planning authority or the Secretary of State must consult specified bodies with environmental responsibilities before determining the scope of the information that is

---

[151] S.I. 1999 No.293.
[152] Under art.3(10) and (11) Town and Country Planning (General Permitted Development) Order 1995, S.I. 1995 No.418, as modified by reg.35(3) Town and Country Planning (Environmental Impact Assessment) (England and Wales) Regulations 1999 (S.I. 1999 No.293).

required and it may be necessary for these bodies to provide information to the developer in relation to the preparation of the environmental statement.

On the submission of an application for planning permission that is accompanied by an environmental statement, the consultation bodies are to be notified and publicity requirements are to be followed along with copies of the environmental statement being made generally available to the public. Further consultation requirements, between Member States, arise where a project is likely to have significant effects upon the environment of another State. Finally, where an application for planning permission for environmental impact assessment development has been determined, there are publicity requirements to inform the public of the decision and to make available a statement of the main reasons and considerations on which the decision was based and a description of the measures to avoid, reduce or offset the major adverse effects of the development.

### 9.14.4 The Land Drainage Improvement Works Regulations

Although new flood defence projects will generally require planning permission, and therefore will be subject to environmental impact assessment under the Regulations, as previously discussed, an exception to this arises in relation to certain land drainage 'improvement' works for which planning permission is not required. This exception arises because developments by a land drainage body in, on or under any watercourse or any land drainage works will be permitted developments where they involve the improvement, maintenance or repair of the watercourse or works.[153] Therefore, to ensure comprehensive implementation of the Directives, it is necessary that works falling into this category are subject to environmental impact assessment procedures where they are likely to have a significant effect upon the environment.

The Environmental Impact Assessment (Land Drainage Improvement Works) Regulations 1999[154] prohibit land drainage bodies[155] from carrying out certain land drainage improvement works unless specified procedures have been followed. 'Improvement works' encompasses projects to deepen, widen, straighten or otherwise improve any existing watercourse; to remove or alter mill dams, weirs or other obstructions to watercourses; to

---

[153] Schedule 2 Parts 14A and 15A(b) Town and Country Planning (General Permitted Development) Order 1995, S.I. 1995 No.418; and see 9.4 above.
[154] S.I. 1999 No.1783.
[155] That is, the Environment Agency, an internal drainage board and the council of a county, a county borough, a district or London borough and the Common Council of the City of London.

raise, widen or otherwise improve any existing drainage work; and any other permitted developments concerning watercourses or land drainage works. The procedures that are applicable, where works of this kind are envisaged by a drainage body, may require the body to prepare an environmental statement for the purpose of assessing whether the works are likely to have significant effects upon the environment. In certain instances, consent for the works to be undertaken must be given by the 'appropriate Authority', that is, the Secretary of State or the National Assembly for Wales.

Specifically, in relation to any proposed improvement works, the relevant drainage body will be bound to determine whether the works are likely to have significant effects on the environment. In accordance with Schedule 2 to the Regulations, this involves consideration of the 'characteristics' of the works, their 'location' and the 'characteristics of the potential impact'.[156] On the basis of these considerations, if the drainage body concludes that the proposed works are unlikely to have significant effects upon the environment, it must publicise its intention to carry out the works. If no representations that there are likely to be significant environmental effects are received, the drainage body may proceed to undertake the works, but if such representations are received the drainage body must apply to the appropriate Authority for a determination of this issue.

However, if the drainage body concludes that the proposed works are likely to have significant effect upon the environment, but nonetheless, wishes to proceed with the works, it must publicise the works and its intention to prepare an environmental statement. It must also notify consultation bodies, including the appropriate nature conservancy council and any other public authority, statutory body or organisation with an interest in the works. The drainage body may request the appropriate Authority to give an opinion as to the information that needs to be

---

[156] 'Characteristics' encompasses the size, use of natural resources, production of waste, pollution and nuisances, and the risk of accidents arising from the works. 'Location' concerns the environmental sensitivity of the area having regard to the existing land use, natural resources, absorption capacity of the natural environment, and particularly wetlands, coastal zones, mountain and forest areas, and nature reserves and parks, European sites under the Wild Birds Directive (79/409/EEC) or the Habitats Directive (92/43/EEC) (and see 10.5.1 and 10.5.2 below on these Directives), areas in which environmental quality standards under Community legislation have been exceeded, densely populated areas, and landscapes of historical, cultural or archaeological significance. The 'characteristics of the potential impact' refers to the extent of the impact, the transfrontier nature of the impact, the magnitude and complexity of the impact, the probability of the impact and the duration, frequency and reversibility of the impact. See Schedule 2 Environmental Impact Assessment (Land Drainage Improvement Works) Regulations 1999, S.I. 1999 No.1783.

contained in an environmental statement. Information may be required to be provided by any other authority for the purpose of preparing the environmental statement by the drainage body. The statement must be published and copies submitted to the consultation bodies and any other person who requests a copy, and provision is made under Schedule 3 for international consultation in relation to projects having transboundary effects. After expiry of the consultation period, the environmental effects of the proposed works must be assessed in the light of the environmental statement and any representations that have been made. If there are no sustained objections, the drainage body may determine that it will proceed with the works. If there are objections, the proposal must be referred to the appropriate Authority for a determination as to whether consent should be given for the works, and this determination must be publicised along with the reasons and considerations upon which it was based.

Provision is made for the enforcement of the Environmental Impact Assessment (Land Drainage Improvement Works) Regulations 1999 by stipulations that action may be taken if a drainage body carries out works without complying with the Regulations or without the consent of the appropriate Authority, where this is required, or in breach of conditions imposed by the appropriate Authority. In these circumstances, the appropriate Authority may apply for a court order that the drainage body must not proceed with the works, that work that has been carried out must be removed and that the body must reinstate the site. An order of this kind may provide that, in the event of the drainage body failing to remove works or reinstate a site, the work may be undertaken by the appropriate Authority and the reasonable costs of doing so recovered from the drainage body.

### 9.14.5 Strategic Environmental Assessment

The most recent development at European Community level concerning environmental assessment is the adoption of a Directive on Strategic Environmental Assessment.[157] The objectives of this Directive are to provide for a high level of protection of the environment by integrating environmental considerations into the preparation of plans and programmes and by requiring environmental assessment of plans and programmes which are likely to have significant effects on the environment. For this purpose, 'plans and programmes' encompasses policy measures prepared and/or adopted by an authority at national, regional or local level or which are required by legislative, regulatory or administrative provisions. Most pertinently, this requires environmental assessment to be undertaken for

---

[157] Directive of the European Parliament and of the Council on the assessment of the effects of certain plans and programmes on the environment (2001/42/EC).

any plan or programme which is likely to have significant environmental effects in relation to water management, town and country planning and land use. This relates to plans or projects that establish the framework for development consent for categories of project covered by the previous Environmental Impact Assessment Directives. Clearly, therefore, various kinds of plans and programmes that have flood defence or coast protection implications will fall within the scope of the Strategic Environmental Assessment Directive.

Broadly, the requirements concerning strategic environmental assessment are that assessment must be conducted before a relevant plan or programme is adopted and must involve the preparation of an environmental report detailing the likely significant effects on the environment which will result from implementation. The environmental report must be the subject of consultation with designated national authorities and members of the public likely to be affected. Opinions expressed by consultees must be taken into account before final adoption of the plan or programme. Following implementation, Member States must monitor the significant effects of implementation of a plan or programme to identify unforeseen adverse environmental effects and take appropriate remedial action. The requirements concerning strategic environmental assessment are without prejudice to obligations arising under the previous environmental impact assessment Directives. There are also a number of procedural requirements which relate to the exchange of information and communications with the European Commission; and there is a specific requirement that laws, regulations and administrative provisions must be brought into force before 21 July 2004.

At the time of writing, it is difficult to be confident about the full implications of the Strategic Environmental Assessment Directive in the context of national flood and coastal defence, but a wide range of policy documents appear to come within its scope. Various kinds of development plan provided for under town and country planning legislation will clearly require environmental assessment, as will relevant policies adopted by central government. As 'plans or programmes adopted by a national authority', various policies adopted by the Environment Agency appear to fall within the Directive. Moreover, the coverage of measures adopted by an authority at 'local level' would seem to encompass plans of various kinds formulated by internal drainage boards and coast protection authorities insofar as these establish a framework for future authorisations. On first impression, it is difficult to identify any policy measures concerning flood defence or coast protection which, in future, will be excluded from the environmental assessment requirements.

On the other hand, the approaches to policy appraisal that are required by the Strategic Environmental Assessment Directive are not without precedent in national practice. Ministerial guidance has been provided for some years as to the manner in which public bodies should undertake environmental assessment of various kinds of planning exercise.[158] Whilst there can be no doubt that more comprehensive, systematic and explicit practices will need to be adopted to implement the Directive, there are respects in which it represents only a step beyond existing national practice.

## 9.15 BUILDING CONTROL

A final matter which is conveniently considered alongside planning requirements is the system of building controls. Broadly, the Building Act 1984 empowers the Secretary of State[159] to make building regulations with respect to the design and construction of buildings and the provision of services, fittings and equipment in connection with buildings. Pursuant to this, building regulations may be made for the purposes of securing the health, safety, welfare and convenience of persons in relation to buildings and for related matters. Hence, subject to certain exceptions, a person undertaking building work is bound to deposit plans of the work with the local authority. The authority is generally bound to pass the deposited plans unless they are defective or indicate that the proposed work will contravene building regulations, though the authority must satisfy itself of certain matters, such as the provision of adequate drainage, before approval. Further provisions empower an authority to take action where, amongst other things, satisfactory provision for drainage has not been made in relation to any building or where drains and other pipes are defective or prejudicial to health or a nuisance. Local authorities may remedy contravention of requirements under building regulations by executing work or requiring the owner or occupier of a building to execute necessary work.

---

[158] See Department of the Environment, *Policy Appraisal and the Environment* (1991) (providing guidance to public sector bodies involved in policy-making with a significant environmental impact); Department of the Environment, *Environmental Appraisal of Development Plans: A Good Practice Guide* (1993) (setting out a range of environmental techniques and procedures for local authorities in preparing development plans).

[159] In this case the relevant 'Secretary of State' is the Secretary of State for Transport, Local Government and the Regions, in England, or the National Assembly for Wales, in Wales. See 3.2.1 and 3.3 above on ministerial responsibilities. However, the National Assembly for Wales (Transfer of Functions) Order 1999, S.I. 1999 No.672, imposes restrictions upon the transfer of functions to the Welsh Assembly by excluding key provisions under the Building Act 1984 including the power to make Building Regulations (under s.1 Building Act 1984).

The power of the Secretary of State in relation to building regulations has been exercised most recently by the enactment of the Building Regulations 2000 and the Building (Amendment) Regulations 2001.[160] In part, the amending Regulations were made for the purpose of improving provision for sustainable drainage systems.[161] As now provided for, therefore, the amended Building Regulations require that broadly defined kinds of building work must be carried out in accordance with requirements set out in Schedule 1 to the Regulations.

Part H of Schedule 1 to the Building Regulations is specifically concerned with drainage and waste disposal. This requires, in respect of foul water drainage, that an adequate system of drainage to carry foul water from within a building will be required by one of the following means (listed in order of priority): a public sewer; a private sewer communicating with a public sewer; a septic tank incorporating secondary or other wastewater treatment; or a cesspool. In respect of rainwater drainage, adequate provision must be made for rainwater to be carried from the roof of a building and paved areas around a building to enable these areas to be adequately drained. Other than where rainwater is gathered for re-use, rainwater is to be discharged by the following means (listed in order of priority): an adequate soak-away or some other adequate infiltration drainage system; a watercourse; or a sewer. Significantly, the effect of this is to make sustainable drainage systems a priority amongst the options for surface water drainage so that they must be adopted unless it can be shown that an infiltration system is not a reasonably practicable option.

---

[160] S.I. 2000 No.2531 and S.I. 2001 No.3335, with the latter coming into effect on 1 April 2002. See Department of Transport, Local Government and the Regions, *Approved Document H: Drainage and Waste Disposal 2002 Edition* (2001) Ch.3 'Surface Water Drainage' on Departmental website at http://www.safety.dtlr.gov.uk/bregs/brpub/ad/ad-h/index02.htm.

[161] See PPG 25 para.42 and see 9.8.6 above and 12.2 below on sustainable drainage systems.

# Chapter 10

# ENVIRONMENTAL AND ECOLOGICAL IMPACTS

## 10.1 INTRODUCTION

Although flood and coastal defence projects and activities are clearly beneficial in alleviating flood risks to urban areas and improving the productivity of agriculture, they frequently have an environmental or ecological cost which must be carefully weighed into the balance.[1] Projects are often proposed in areas of importance as natural habitats and there is scope for serious adverse impacts upon native species of flora and fauna and the habitats upon which they depend. Likewise, the need for projects to be undertaken in a way which respects landscape, archaeologically and culturally important features, and serves to meet objectives for recreation and amenity, is frequently a factor to be weighed into consideration. In an extreme case, the need to protect features of these kinds may make a flood or coastal defence proposal unacceptable. More commonly, however, there is scope for potential adverse effects to be minimised and for projects to be planned and implemented in a manner that is sensitive to the ecological or other interests involved. In some instances it may even be possible to incorporate features that actually enhance the conservation or other interests involved.

The purpose of this chapter is primarily to consider the environmental and ecological implications of flood and coastal defence projects at an institutional and operational level. Broadly, this involves discussion of the general environmental duties that are imposed upon different flood and coastal defence operating authorities and the interpretation of these obligations in respect of particular projects, especially where these are to take place in areas which are subject to conservation designation. Hence, in relation to areas that are designated for conservation purposes, such as 'sites of special scientific interest' and 'European sites', it is necessary that flood and coastal defence *powers* are exercised consistently with the conservation *duties* that arise. As will be seen, the implications of this involve a sequence of consultative, procedural and substantive requirements

---

[1] Generally see E. C. Penning-Rowsell, D. J. Parker and D. M. Harding, *Floods and Drainage* (1986) Ch.5 on environmental and conservation impacts of flooding policies and see also M. Robins, S. G. F. Davies and R. S. K. Buisson, *An Internationally Important Wetland in Crisis* (1991) published by the Royal Society for the Protection of Birds.

## Introduction

that are intended to secure priority for conservation objectives. Although the cumulative effect of these provisions falls short of 'absolute' protection of any site from the adverse environmental or ecological impacts, for all practical purposes the likelihood of a flood or coastal defence operation being allowed to have such impacts is made quite remote.[2]

Although it is convenient to group together the treatment of environmental and ecological concerns in a single chapter, it should not be overlooked that these matters also feature in discussion elsewhere in this work. Important conservation issues are also raised in procedures relating to funding and planning requirements, particularly where environmental impact assessment is involved, and the discussion which follows should be read alongside the treatment of environmental issues elsewhere.

### 10.2 GENERAL DUTIES OF THE ENVIRONMENT AGENCY

As will be seen, all flood and coastal defence operating authorities are made subject to general environmental and related duties, requiring them to exercise their functions in a way that minimises harm to interests of recognised importance or enhances those interests. Most specifically, general duties upon operating authorities are provided for under the Environment Act 1995 and the Land Drainage Act 1991, as amended. However, these duties have been strengthened by recent amendments to conservation legislation, specifically by the amendment of the Wildlife and Countryside Act 1981 by the Countryside and Rights of Way Act 2000. The effect of the recent amendments is to impose additional conservation duties upon 'public authorities' in relation to sites of special scientific interest[3] and the pre-existing duties must be read subject to these. However, the discussion that follows commences with duties which are formulated most specifically in relation to the flood defence operating authorities and the new duties are dealt with later in the chapter.[4]

General duties are most broadly formulated in respect of the Environment Agency, though the duties upon other operating authorities, to differing degrees, follow the obligations imposed upon the Agency. In respect of the Agency, as has been noted, general duties are imposed in respect of its

---

[2] See also the discussion of environmental impact assessment at 9.14 above and the discussion of environmental considerations in funding applications at 6.2 above.

[3] Generally see 10.4 below on sites of special scientific interest. On the 2000 Act generally see Department of the Environment, Transport and the Regions, *Countryside and Rights of Way Act 2000*, Circular 04/2001 (2001) and S. Payne, 'From Carrots to Sticks – Natural Habitat Protection after the Countryside and Rights of Way Act 2000' [2001] *Environmental Law and Management* 239.

[4] See 10.4.2 below on the conservation duties upon 'public authorities'.

principal aim of contributing towards sustainable development[5] and the need for the Agency to have regard to costs and benefits,[6] and the Environment Agency is subject to a general duty with respect to water resources.[7] More specifically, in relation to conservation, amenity and recreation, the Agency must generally promote:

(a) the conservation and enhancement of the natural beauty and amenity of inland and coastal waters and of land associated with such waters;

(b) the conservation of flora and fauna which are dependent on an aquatic environment;[8] and

(c) the use of such waters and land for recreational purposes.[9]

Characteristically, these general duties are to be adhered to 'to such an extent as it considers desirable', and the discretion given to the Agency to determine what is 'desirable' will need to be exercised within its principal aim, the cost-benefit duty, and alongside other general environmental and recreational duties to which it is subject.[10] The rather diffuse character of legal obligations of this kind will be readily apparent.

Both the Agency, and the Ministers,[11] are subject to broadly formulated obligations which apply in formulating or considering any 'proposal'.[12] When formulating or considering any proposal relating to any of the functions of the Agency, other than its pollution control functions,[13] it is the duty of the Agency, and the Ministers, to exercise their *powers* (though not

---

[5] See s.4 Environment Act 1995 and see the discussion of ministerial guidance at 3.4.2 above.
[6] Under ss.4 and 39 Environment Act 1995 and see the discussion of costs and benefits at 3.4.3 above.
[7] s.6(2) Water Resources Act 1991.
[8] The duty in relation to flora and fauna contrasts with duties imposed elsewhere in the Environment Act 1995 in respect of the environment, meaning the environmental media of air, water and land.
[9] s.6(1) Environment Act 1995. In determining what steps to take in performance of the duty imposed under (c) the Agency must take into account the needs of persons who are chronically sick or disabled. On the meaning of 'chronically sick and disabled', see Chronically Sick and Disabled Persons Act 1970.
[10] See s.7 Environment Act 1995.
[11] See 3.2.1 above on 'the Ministers'.
[12] Significantly perhaps, the meaning of 'proposal', for these purposes, is not defined and this would seem to imply that the provisions are applicable to a broad range of contexts from the widest matters of policy formulation to the narrowest issues involved in determining particular licence and authorisation applications.
[13] By contrast, where the pollution control functions of the Agency are involved, the corresponding duty is 'to have regard to the desirability' of conserving and enhancing natural beauty and conserving flora, fauna and geological or physiographical features of special interest: see s.7(1)(b) Environment Act 1995.

duties) consistently with:

(a) any enactment relating to the functions of the Agency;

(b) the objective of achieving sustainable development (in the case of the Ministers);

(c) ministerial guidance on sustainable development[14] (in the case of the Agency); and

(d) duties with respect to the water industry (in the case of the Secretary of State);[15]

so as to *further* the conservation and enhancement of natural beauty and the conservation of flora, fauna and geological or physiographical features of special interest.[16]

Alongside the general conservation duty, other broadly cultural and social duties are imposed upon the Agency. Hence, in relation to any proposal relating to any of its functions, the Agency is to have regard to, or to take into account:

(a) the desirability of protecting and conserving buildings, sites and objects of archaeological, architectural, engineering or historic interest;

(b) any effect which the proposals would have on the beauty or amenity of any rural or urban area or on any such flora, fauna, features, buildings, sites or objects; and

(c) any effect which the proposals would have on the economic and social well-being of local communities in rural areas.[17]

Subject to these general conservation, cultural and social duties, it is the duty of the Agency and the Ministers, in formulating or considering any proposals relating to any functions of the Agency, to consider specified matters concerning access. Hence regard should be had to, or account taken, of the following matters:

(a) the desirability of preserving for the public any freedom of access to areas of woodland, mountains, moor, heath, down, cliff or foreshore and other places of natural beauty;

---

[14] That is, guidance issued under s.4 Environment Act 1995, and see 3.4.2 above
[15] See s.2 Water Industry Act 1991 on duties of the Secretary of State in relation to the water industry.
[16] s.7(1)(a) Environment Act 1995.
[17] s.7(1)(c) Environment Act 1995.

(b) the desirability of maintaining the availability to the public of any facility for visiting or inspecting any building, site or object of archaeological, architectural, engineering or historic interest;[18] and

(c) any effect which the proposals would have on any such freedom of access or on the availability of any such facility.[19]

The general duties upon the Agency, concerning conservation, the natural and built environment and access, apply so as to impose duties in relation to certain proposals relating to the functions of water and sewerage undertakers in the same way as they apply in relation to the functions of the Agency itself. Hence the general duties upon the Agency will be similarly applicable, in respect of the following matters:

(a) any proposal relating to the functions of a water or sewerage undertaker;

(b) any proposals relating to the management, by a company holding an appointment as a water or sewerage undertaker, of any land held by that company; and

(c) any proposal concerning the disposal of protected land which is treated as a proposal relating to the functions of a water or sewerage undertaker.[20]

In addition, the Agency is subject to a general duty to take reasonably practicable steps for securing that its rights to use water or land are exercised so that these are made available for recreational purposes. In relation to this, the Agency is bound to take into account the needs of persons who are chronically sick or disabled. However, this is not to be construed as requiring recreational facilities to be made available by the Agency free of charge.[21]

### 10.2.1 Duties concerning sites of special interest

The Agency is subject to more specific duties, in addition to those previously described, with regard to sites of special interest. These duties apply where English Nature or the Countryside Council for Wales (termed the 'nature conservancy councils') are of the opinion that any land is of

---

[18] Generally see Ancient Monuments and Archaeological Areas Act 1979 and Planning Policy Guidance Note 16, *Archaeology and Planning* and Welsh Office, *Planning Guidance (Wales): Planning Policy* (1996).
[19] s.7(2) Environment Act 1995.
[20] s.7(3) Environment Act 1995; (c) refers to proposals concerning disposals of protected land under s.156(7) Water Industry Act 1991 which are treated as a proposal relating to the functions of a water or sewerage undertaker under s.3 Water Industry Act 1991.
[21] s.7(4) to (6) Environment Act 1995.

## General Duties of the Environment Agency

special interest by reason of its flora, fauna or geological or physiographical features. Where the relevant nature conservancy council is of this opinion, and the land may at any time be affected by schemes, works, operations or activities of the Agency, or by activities under an authorisation given by the Agency, the nature conservancy council must notify the Agency to that effect.[22] Similarly, where a national park authority or the Broads Authority[23] is of the opinion that any area of land in a national park or in the Broads is land of particular importance,[24] and may at any time be affected by schemes, works, operations or activities of the Agency, or by an authorisation given by the Agency, the authority is bound to notify the Agency of this.[25]

Where the Agency has received a notification from a relevant council or authority with respect to any land, it must consult the notifying body before carrying out or authorising any works, operations or activities which are likely to destroy or damage any of the features by reason of which the land is of special interest, or significantly to prejudice anything of particular importance in relation to the notification of the land. This requirement does not apply in relation to anything done in an emergency where particulars of the emergency and the consequent actions taken are notified to the relevant council or authority as soon as practicable afterwards.[26]

It is notable that the consultation duty upon the Agency in relation to notified land arises both in relation to works conducted by the Agency itself and works which it *authorises* others to undertake. 'Authorisation', for these purposes, includes any 'consent or licence'[27] and is, therefore, capable of encompassing various kinds of authorisation that may be given by the Agency in relation to flood and coastal defence works and activities. Hence, authorisations that are sought by internal drainage boards, local authorities and private individuals may activate the consultation duty on the part of the Agency.[28]

Although changes in the law have since been enacted,[29] the need for

---

[22] s.8(1) Environment Act 1995.
[23] On the 'Broads Authority' see the Norfolk and Suffolk Broads Act 1988.
[24] That is, of 'particular importance' in relation to the duty upon the Agency to promote the conservation of natural beauty and flora and fauna (under s.6(1) Environment Act 1995) or the general environmental and recreational duties upon the Agency (under s.7, other than s.7 (c)(iii) concerned with the effect which proposals would have on the economic and social well-being of communities in rural areas).
[25] s.8(2) Environment Act 1995.
[26] s.8(3) and (4) Environment Act 1995.
[27] s.8(3) Environment Act 1995.
[28] For various examples, see the discussion of the regulatory powers of the Environment Agency at 4.4 above.
[29] See 10.4.2 below on the conservation duties now imposed on public authorities introduced by the Countryside and Rights of Way Act 2000.

consultation where land drainage works are envisaged on land which is of ecological importance is graphically illustrated by *Southern Water Authority* v *Nature Conservancy Council*,[30] where a site of special scientific interest was seriously damaged by a former water authority exercising its land drainage powers.[31] In this case, two farmers, who owned land bordering on a ditch on the site, sought to dredge the ditch to alleviate flooding. The farmers had been notified that dredging was a potentially damaging operation requiring prior notification to the former Nature Conservancy Council (now English Nature). However, the farmers engaged the water authority to undertake the work, which involved entry onto the land and the carrying out of the dredging work which caused extensive damage to the ecological value of the site. The water authority was prosecuted for carrying out a potentially damaging operation on the site without notification. On appeal, it was held that although the water authority had been present at the location for a month, it was not an 'occupier' of the land on which the work took place. This conclusion was reached despite the fact that the authority owned land elsewhere on the site and knew of its designation.

Notably, whilst the *Southern Water* case provides a remarkable illustration of the 'ecological vandalism' that can arise through insensitive flood defence operations, it is unlikely that the same circumstances or legal outcome would be reached today. This is because the events at issue predated the present obligations to consult the relevant nature conservancy council, and to adhere to a code of practice, in relation to works of the kind that were undertaken.[32] Moreover, recent reforms of nature conservation law, brought about by the Countryside and Rights of Way Act 2000, have significantly enhanced the protection of Sites of Special Scientific Interest where flood defence operations are involved.[33]

### 10.2.2 Codes of Practice

The general environmental and recreational duties upon the Environment Agency are provided for at a high level of generality and need to be interpreted more specifically to be applied in particular contexts. To address this, the Ministers have a power to approve any code of practice issued for the purpose of giving practical guidance to the Agency with

---

[30] [1992] 3 All ER 481 and generally see D. Withrington and W. Jones, 'The Enforcement of Conservation Legislation: Protecting Sites of Special Scientific Interest' in W. Howarth and C. Rodgers, Eds., *Agriculture Conservation and Land Use: Law and Policy Issues for Rural Areas* (1992) Ch.5.
[31] Under Land Drainage Act 1976.
[32] Contrast the weaker duty with regard to nature conservation upon the former water authorities under s.22 Water Act 1973.
[33] See 10.4 below on the Countryside and Rights of Way Act 2000.

respect to specified environmental and related duties, and promoting what appear to be desirable practices with respect to those matters.[34] In discharging its responsibilities in relation to the environmental and related duties, the Agency must have regard to any code of practice approved for these purposes.[35] Under previous provisions it was explicitly stated that failure to have regard to such a code of practice would not give rise to any civil or criminal liability on the part of the Agency.[36] However, the omission of this safeguard in relation to the Agency in the present legislation, in theory, leaves that possibility open, though the generality of the provisions in codes that have secured ministerial approval makes this unlikely in practice.

The ministerial powers to approve codes of practice giving practical guidance to the Environment Agency have been exercised most recently by the approval of the *Code of Practice on Conservation, Access and Recreation*.[37] This '*Code of Conservation Practice*' provides guidance to the Environment Agency, and water and sewerage undertakers,[38] on matters concerning conservation, access and recreation that they should take into consideration when discharging their functions. The general responsibilities of the Agency with regard to sustainable development, the pursuit of an integrated approach to the management of the environment and the need for consultation with relevant bodies are reaffirmed. More specifically, in relation to flood and coastal defence and access it is noted that relevant projects may have potential for recreational activities and that this should be incorporated into scheme designs. For example, sailing and

---

[34] The Ministers may not make an order in accordance with these powers unless they have first consulted the Agency, the Countryside Commission, the Nature Conservancy Council for England and the Countryside Council for Wales, the Historic Buildings and Monuments Commission for England, the Sports Council and the Sports Council for Wales and such other persons as he considers it appropriate to consult. The power of the Ministers to make an order of this kind will be exercisable by statutory instrument; subject to the negative resolution procedure. See s.9(3) and (4) Environment Act 1995.

[35] s.9(1) and (2) Environment Act 1995. Notably also, under s.40 Environment Act 1995, the Ministers may give directions to the Agency in respect of its flood defence functions and, in principle, this power might be used to require the Agency to conform to any requirement established under a code of practice.

[36] s.18 Water Resources Act 1991 (now repealed) but see s.61E(2) Land Drainage Act 1991 which retains the exclusion of criminal or civil liability in relation to internal drainage boards and local authorities: see 10.3.2 below.

[37] Department of the Environment, Transport and the Regions, National Assembly for Wales and Ministry of Agriculture, Fisheries and Food (2000) approved by Water and Sewerage (Conservation, Access and Recreation) (Code of Practice) Order 2000, S.I. 2000 No.477.

[38] Corresponding environmental and recreational duties upon water and sewerage undertakers, and provision for approval of codes of practice, are provided for under ss.3 to 5 Water Industry Act 1991.

related activities should be facilitated by preserving adequate channel depths and providing access, launching and mooring sites; similarly, facilities for angling, walking, horse riding and cycling are encouraged, though in all instances it will be necessary to take account of factors such as public safety and disturbance to wildlife.[39] In most respects the matters dealt with by the *Code of Conservation Practice* are stated at a level of some generality and seem unlikely to be decisive of legal obligations but may, nevertheless, be influential in guiding practice on relevant matters.

Another use has been made of the ministerial power to approve codes of practice in the adoption of the *Code of Practice on Environmental Procedures for Flood Defence Operating Authorities*.[40] Whilst the '*Code on Environmental Procedures*' is primarily addressed to the Environment Agency, it is also addressed to internal drainage boards and local authorities in the exercise of their flood defence functions.[41] The Code echoes national policy on flood defence in emphasising that works should be environmentally acceptable as well as technically sound and economically viable. It also emphasises the need for a holistic, long-term and strategic approach to environmental considerations and for enhancement opportunities to be taken in relation to habitat diversity. The importance of strategic planning is stressed in relation to the need for adherence to shoreline management plans, water level management plans and other relevant kinds of plan.[42]

At the project-specific level, the *Code on Environmental Procedures* advocates a procedural progression whereby the urgency of flood defence provision is assessed against the relevant strategic plans. This involves an assessment of likely environmental considerations with specific consideration being given to a 'do nothing' option as a baseline against which other possibilities are assessed. Thereafter, consultation with all the relevant interests is advised, including bodies specifically concerned with nature conservation, to avoid damage to sensitive wildlife features and to

---

[39] Department of the Environment, Transport and the Regions, National Assembly for Wales and Ministry of Agriculture, Fisheries and Food, *Code of Practice on Conservation, Access and Recreation* (2000) paras.5.18 and 5.19.

[40] Ministry of Agriculture, Fisheries and Food, and Welsh Office (1996).

[41] Hence, the *Code on Environmental Procedures* was approved by the Minister of Agriculture, Fisheries and Food and the Secretary of State for Wales under s.9 Environment Act 1995 in respect of the Agency, and under s.61E Land Drainage Act 1991, as amended, in respect of internal drainage boards and local authorities. It is also suggested that the contents of the Code may be equally useful in giving practical advice to local authorities when carrying out coast protection works under the Coast Protection Act 1949 (see Code para.1.4).

[42] See 5.5 above on shoreline management plans and 10.7 below on water level management plans.

examine ways of enhancing wildlife, in appropriate cases, by the creation of new features and habitats. Choice of the preferred option, incorporating formal environmental impact assessment[43] where necessary, should be followed by a design stage which takes account of the need for additional protection, conservation and enhancement including the following matters:

(a) maintenance, improvement and creation of habitats and maintenance of sites of special interest or value;

(b) retention of landscape character, morphological and geological features;

(c) retention of appropriate water supply to adjacent flood plain habitats;

(d) protection of the archaeological, built and cultural heritage;

(e) appropriate timing of works; and

(f) consideration of the effect of future maintenance operations.

At the operational phase, works should be undertaken, in association with appropriate environmental advisers and liaison officers, with properly trained site managers and supervisors with the capacity effectively to implement the environmental requirements of the project. Finally, at the post-project evaluation stage, an audit of the environmental performance of the project should be undertaken and, if original objectives have not been achieved, mitigation action may be required.

Other parts of the *Code on Environmental Procedures* relate to environmental implications of routine maintenance work of various kinds. Hence, it is noted that activities such as dredging, spoil disposal, bank maintenance and weed cutting may impact upon plant diversity. Particularly in watercourses, therefore, dredging should be confined to limited areas at any one time to leave refuges for wildlife and sources of material for recolonisation. Variation in the channel, such as pools and riffles will significantly add to the diversity of habitats in a watercourse and can be introduced without significantly affecting the overall hydraulic performance. Bank maintenance activities should, where possible, be conducted to allow lengths of watercourses to develop a natural meandering form with some eroding and accreting of sections of the waterside. Where erosion control is needed, the use of 'soft' engineering techniques, such as the establishment of willows, should be considered. Likewise, in relation to beach management, all works should take account of the natural

---

[43] See 9.14 above on environmental impact assessment.

structure and sorting processes that occur in an 'active' beach and avoid over-consolidation with material that may change the environmental character and effectiveness of a coastal defence.

Another important document is the *Guide to Good Practice on Coastal Defence and the Environment*,[44] in setting out the range of practical coastal defence techniques and the environmental implications of these. However, this *'Guide'* does not have the status of a statutory code and, insofar as much of the guidance may be directed to coast protection authorities, there is no statutory provision for Ministers to issue a statutory code to these authorities. Nevertheless, since coast protection authorities have recently become subject to a conservation duty imposed upon public authorities generally,[45] the *Guide* may have a greater significance in guiding authorities as to how their functions may be exercised so as to further conservation. Similarly, in relation to the Environment Agency, the *Guide* may be influential in determining how coastal flood defence projects may be undertaken with environmental and ecological sensitivity.

## 10.3 GENERAL DUTIES OF INTERNAL DRAINAGE BOARDS AND LOCAL AUTHORITIES

To a considerable extent, the general environmental duties imposed upon the Environment Agency have been used as the model for duties imposed upon internal drainage boards and local authorities in exercising their flood defence functions. Hence, the Land Drainage Act 1991 was amended by the Land Drainage Act 1994 to interpolate a new Part IVA, on duties with respect to the environment and recreation, largely paralleling the general duties upon the Agency in respect of the natural and built environment and public access.[46] Because of the similarity with provisions that have already been discussed, the general duties upon internal drainage boards and local authorities need only brief consideration.

It is the general duty of an internal drainage board, in formulating or considering any proposals relating to its functions, to observe the following duties:

(a) to further the conservation and enhancement of natural beauty and the

---

[44] Ministry of Agriculture, Fisheries and Food, and Welsh Office, *Coastal Defence and the Environment: A guide to good practice* (1993).
[45] See 10.4.2 below on the conservation duties upon 'public authorities' generally.
[46] Part IVA contains s.61A (duties in relation to drainage boards); s.61B (duties in relation to local authorities); s.61C (duties with respect to sites of special scientific interest); s.61D (ministerial directions to drainage boards); and s.61E (codes of practice).

conservation of flora, fauna and geological or physiographical features of special interest;

(b) to have regard to the desirability of protecting and conserving buildings, sites and objects of archaeological, architectural or historic interest; and

(c) to take account of the effect that proposals will have on the beauty or amenity of any rural or urban area or on flora, fauna features, building sites or objects.[47]

Subject to this general duty concerning conservation and related matters, it is also the duty of an internal drainage board, the Ministers and the Environment Agency, in formulating or considering any proposals relating to any functions of a board,

(a) to have regard to the desirability of preserving for the public freedom of access to areas of woodland, mountains, moor, heath, down, cliff or foreshore and other places of natural beauty;

(b) to have regard to the desirability of maintaining the availability to the public of any facility for visiting or inspecting any building, site or object of archaeological, architectural or historic interest; and

(c) to take into account any effect which the proposals would have on any freedom of access or on the availability of any facility of these kinds.[48]

Essentially the same general duties concerning the natural and built environment and making provision for access are imposed upon local authorities in relation to the exercise of their flood defence functions. Similarly, the Ministers and the Environment Agency will be subject to the same duties in considering any proposals relating to any functions of a local authority under the Land Drainage Act 1991.[49] It may be significant, however, that the general duties only apply to local authorities when exercising functions within the 1991 Act and will not apply, therefore, where coast protection, public health, highways or planning functions are being exercised. Although, as will be seen, general conservation duties

---

[47] s.61A(1) Land Drainage Act 1991. The Secretary of State's general duties with respect to the water industry are provided for under s.2 Water Industry Act 1991.

[48] s.61A(2) Land Drainage Act 1991. See also s.61A(4) concerning the duty to make water or land available for recreational purposes, subject to the consent of any navigation authority, harbour authority or conservancy authority where navigation is obstructed; s.61A(5) requiring account to be taken of the needs of persons who are chronically sick or disabled; and s.61A(6) stipulating that there is no requirement that recreational facilities should be made available free of charge.

[49] s.61B Land Drainage Act 1991.

have been imposed on public authorities under recent amendments to the Wildlife and Countryside Act 1981.[50]

The general duties concerning the natural and built environment and access apply so as to impose duties on internal drainage boards (though not local authorities) in relation to certain proposals of the Environment Agency and water and sewerage undertakers in the same way as they apply in relation to the functions of the board itself. Hence, the general duties of a board will apply in respect of the following matters:

(a) any proposal relating to the functions of the Agency or a water or sewerage undertaker;

(b) any proposals relating to the management, by a company holding an appointment as a water or sewerage undertaker, of any land held by that company; and

(c) any proposal concerning the disposal of 'protected land' that is treated as a proposal relating to the functions of a water or sewerage undertaker.[51]

### 10.3.1 Duties concerning sites of special scientific interest

Where English Nature or the Countryside Council for Wales are of the opinion that an area of land in England or Wales is of special interest because of its flora, fauna or geological or physiographical features, and these features may be affected by works, operations or activities of an internal drainage board or local authority under the Land Drainage Act 1991, the board or authority must be notified of this by the relevant nature conservation body. Similarly, where a national park authority or the Broads Authority is of the opinion that land is of particular importance, and may be affected by works, operations or activities under the 1991 Act, the relevant internal drainage board or local authority must be notified to that effect.[52]

Following notification of this kind, a consultation duty arises.[53] This requires the board or authority to consult the notifying body before carrying out any works, operations or activities which are likely to destroy,

---

[50] See the discussion at 10.4 below.
[51] s.61A(3) Land Drainage Act 1991; (a) refers to proposals concerning disposals of protected land under s.156(7) Water Industry Act 1991 which are treated as a proposal relating to the functions of a water or sewerage undertaker under s.3 Water Industry Act 1991.
[52] s.61C(1) and (2) Land Drainage Act 1991 and see the Norfolk and Suffolk Broads Act 1988 on the 'Broads Authority'.
[53] Note also the further consultation duties that are provided for under conservation, discussed at 10.4.3 below.

damage or significantly prejudice any of the features by reason of which the land is of special interest.[54] However, the consultation duty will not apply in relation to anything done in an emergency, providing the particulars of what has been done and the nature of the emergency are notified to the relevant body as soon as possible after the emergency action has been taken.[55]

### 10.3.2 Ministerial Directions and Codes of Practice

A ministerial direction may be given to an internal drainage board that any works, operations or activities which are being, or are about to be, carried out by the board are likely to destroy or seriously damage things of national or international importance. Hence, where the works are likely to affect any flora or fauna or any geological or physiographical feature of special interest or any building, structure, site or object of archaeological, architectural or historic interest, the Minister may give an appropriate direction to the board. However, except in an emergency, the Minister may not give a direction of this kind to a board unless the board has been consulted. Where a direction has been given by the Minister it will be the duty of the board to comply with it.[56]

The Ministers may approve any code of practice, for the purpose of giving practical guidance to internal drainage boards and local authorities. Specifically, the practical guidance given to boards and authorities is to be in relation to their general environmental and recreational duties and duties concerning sites of special scientific interest,[57] and should promote desirable practices by boards and authorities in relation to those matters.[58] The ministerial power to make an order approving a code must not be exercised unless consultation has taken place with the Environment Agency, the Countryside Agency, English Nature, the Countryside Council for Wales, the Historic Buildings and Monuments Commission for England and such other persons or bodies as are considered appropriate.[59]

---

[54] Although the consultation duty only arises, in the case of local authorities, in relation to works, operations or activities which are undertaken *under the Land Drainage Act 1991*, with the implication that local authority measures undertaken in accordance with other powers, such as those concerning public health and highways, will not be subject to the consultation duty, though consultation may be otherwise provided for in these contexts.
[55] s.61C(3) and (4) Land Drainage Act 1991.
[56] s.61D Land Drainage Act 1991.
[57] That is, matters within the general duties of internal drainage boards under s.61A Land Drainage Act 1991, the general duties of local authorities under s.61B and the common duty with respect to sites of special scientific interest under s.61C, discussed at 10.3.1 above.
[58] s.61E(1) Land Drainage Act 1991.
[59] s.61E(3) and (4) Land Drainage Act 1991.

The contravention of a code of practice is stated not to constitute a contravention of any requirement of the general duties that are imposed upon internal drainage boards or local authorities or to give rise to any criminal or civil liability. However, the Ministers are placed under a duty to take into account whether there has been, or is likely to be, any contravention of this kind in determining when powers under the Land Drainage Act 1991, in relation to boards and authorities, should be exercised.[60] Although not explicit, this raises the implication that the ministerial power to give directions to boards where damage to flora, fauna and other matters of national importance is likely to arise might be appropriately exercised where a contravention of a code of practice has taken place or is in prospect.

The ministerial power to approve codes of practice for internal drainage boards and local authorities has been exercised in the Code of Practice on Environmental Procedures for Flood Defence Operating Authorities (Internal Drainage Boards and Local Authorities) Approval Order 1996.[61] This Order approves the *Code of Practice on Environmental Procedures for Flood Defence Operating Authorities* which has been previously discussed.[62]

## 10.4 DUTIES UNDER NATURE CONSERVATION LEGISLATION

Although important environmental obligations are imposed upon flood defence operating authorities under the Environment Act 1995 and the Land Drainage Act 1991, as amended, these have to be read alongside related obligations that arise under nature conservation legislation. Specifically, Part II of the Wildlife and Countryside Act 1981, as this has been substantially amended by Part III of the Countryside and Rights of Way Act 2000, makes important provision in relation to the protection of species of natural flora and fauna and their habitats. Part I of the 1981 Act, concerned with the direct protection of species, may be of particular importance in relation to flood defence works in locations inhabited by particular protected species.[63] However, Part II of the 1981 Act, concerned with the protection of habitats, is likely to be of greatest importance in practice given the ecological significance of many of the areas in which flood and coast defence works are proposed or undertaken.

---

[60] s.61E(2) Land Drainage Act 1991.
[61] S.I. 1996 No.3062.
[62] See 10.2.2 above.
[63] See also Protection of Badgers Act 1992, creating offences including that of wilfully interfering with a badger sett.

## Duties under Nature Conservation Legislation

Specifically, Part II of the 1981 Act provides for the designation of land as a site of special scientific interest and for a range of protective measures concerning such sites. This has important implications for flood and coastal defence operating authorities: in some cases they may be owners of such sites, in other cases they may need to undertake operations upon them or to authorise others to carry out operations. There is also a possibility that work on other land, which is outside the boundaries of any site of special scientific interest, may have an adverse impact upon such a site. In each instance, the provisions of Part II of the 1981 Act, enforced by English Nature and the Countryside Council for Wales, the 'nature conservancy councils', will be of critical importance.

An indication of the scale of conservation land designation is provided by the *Annual Report* of English Nature,[64] which states that there are presently 4,115 sites of special scientific interest, designated because of their special wildlife or geology, covering over one million hectares and comprising about 7.5% of the area of England. Well over half of this area is of international importance and designated under European Community nature conservation Directives. A large number of sites of special scientific interest are in coastal locations and more than 500 freshwater sites have been identified where water levels are crucial to the survival of wildlife. There can be no doubt about the significance of conservation requirements in relation to many areas in which flood and coastal defence are also a matter of concern.

Although the powers of a nature conservancy council in relation to the control of land for conservation purposes are somewhat intricate, and raise particularly controversial issues of policy where payment of compensation to landholders is involved, the following discussion provides a selective account of the key legal provisions concerning sites of special scientific interest as they are likely to impact most significantly on flood and coastal defence operations.

### 10.4.1 Notification and Protection of sites of special scientific interest

Where the nature conservancy council is of the opinion that any area of land is of special interest by reason of any of its flora, fauna, or geological or physiographical features, it must notify this to the local planning authority for the area, every owner and occupier of any land and the Secretary of State. Notification is also to be published and to specify a time, of not less than 3 months, during which representations or objections may

---

[64] English Nature, *Annual Report: 1 April 2000–31 March 2001* (2001). See also Countryside Council for Wales, *Annual Report 2000–01* (2001).

be made, and the council is bound to consider these. The notification must specify the features that make the land of special interest, the operations which are likely to damage those features and contain a statement of the council's views as to the management of the land. Within 9 months of the initial notification, the council may give further notice either withdrawing or confirming the notification and it will cease to have effect if either withdrawn or on the expiry of the 9-month period.[65]

The owner or occupier of any land within a notified site of special scientific interest must not carry out, or cause or permit to be carried out, any operation specified in the notification unless certain conditions are satisfied. The conditions allow an operation to be carried out where the nature conservancy council has been given notice of the proposal to carry out the operation and has given its consent. Otherwise, the operation may only be carried out in accordance with an agreement or a management scheme or notice.[66]

An owner or occupier who, without reasonable excuse, causes or permits a damaging operation specified in the notification to be carried out is guilty of an offence.[67] Notably, in determining the amount of any fine to be imposed on a person convicted of this offence the court must have regard to any financial benefit which has accrued or appears likely to accrue to that person in consequence of the offence.[68] A 'reasonable excuse' will exist where a person carries out an operation or fails to comply with a notice, if the operation was authorised by a planning permission[69] or is permitted by

---

[65] s.28(1) to (6) Wildlife and Countryside Act 1981. Variation of a notification is provided for under s.28A, notification in relation to additional land under s.28B, enlargement of a site of special scientific interest under s.28C and denotification under s.28D. On 'management schemes' and 'management notices' see 10.4.4 below.

[66] s.28E(1) to (3) Wildlife and Countryside Act 1981. That is, an agreement under s.16 National Parks and Access to the Countryside Act 1949 or s.15 Countryside Act 1968, a management scheme under s.28J or a management notice under s.28K Wildlife and Countryside Act 1981. See also s.28F (concerning appeals in connection with consents) and s.28M(1) (allowing for payments to any owner who suffers loss because of the modification or withdrawal of a consent under s.28E(6)).

[67] s.28P(1) Wildlife and Countryside Act 1981. A person convicted of the offence is liable, on summary conviction, to a fine not exceeding £20,000 or, on conviction on indictment, to a fine. See, for example, English Nature, *Tenant prosecuted for damaging special wildlife site*, Press Release, 23 December 1999, detailing the conviction of a farmer (under previous legislation) though with an absolute discharge, following the deposit of silt and gravel from flood alleviation dredging operations on a site of special scientific interest, without the required notice having been given to English Nature.

[68] s.28P(9) Wildlife and Countryside Act 1981. The same consideration also applies to other offences arising under s.28P.

[69] Under Part III Town and Country Planning Act 1990 and see Ch.9 above on planning law.

a public authority which has acted in accordance with its duty in relation to the authorisation of operations.[70] However, if an operation needs both a planning permission and the permission of a public authority, the authorisation of the activity by a planning permission alone does not constitute a reasonable excuse, since both permissions must be obtained. Alternatively, a reasonable excuse will exist if the operation was an emergency operation, and particulars of it were notified to the nature conservancy council as soon as practicable after the commencement of the operation.[71]

Although the previous offence relates primarily to the activities of owners or occupiers of sites of special scientific interest in carrying out specified operations, the protection of sites is further provided for by an offence that is capable of applying to *any* person other than a 'public authority' exercising its functions.[72] This offence arises where any person who, without reasonable excuse, intentionally or recklessly destroys or damages any of the flora, fauna or geological or physiographical features by reason of which land is of special interest, or intentionally or recklessly disturbs any of those fauna, and who knew that what was destroyed, damaged or disturbed was within a site of special scientific interest. However, as with other offences, a 'reasonable excuse' will exist where the damage was authorised by a planning permission and, where relevant, permitted by a public authority, or where the operation was in an emergency and particulars were notified to the nature conservancy council as soon as practicable.[73]

The flood defence implications of these offences are readily apparent in that owners of sites, excluding flood and coastal defence operating authorities, will need to ensure that operations have the necessary consent from the relevant nature conservancy council. Alternatively, operations may be conducted under a planning permission and a permission from the relevant drainage body but, as will be seen, procedures are required to ensure that these permissions will not be granted unless consultation with the council has taken place and, with relatively narrow exceptions, the advice of the council has been incorporated in the permissions that have been given.[74]

---

[70] That is, the duty under s.28I Wildlife and Countryside Act 1981 (concerning the authorisation of operations by public authorities) and see 10.4.3 below.
[71] s.28P(4) and (5) Wildlife and Countryside Act 1981.
[72] 'Public authority', that is, in the sense used in the discussion at 10.4.2 below.
[73] s.28P(6) and (7) Wildlife and Countryside Act 1981. A person found guilty of this offence is liable, on summary conviction, to a fine not exceeding £20,000 or, on conviction on indictment, to a fine.
[74] See the discussion at 10.4.3 below.

### 10.4.2 Conservation Duties on Public Authorities

A general duty is imposed upon a range of individuals, public bodies and statutory undertakers to exercise their functions, where relevant, so as to further the conservation and enhancement of the flora, fauna or the geological or physiographical features by reason of which a site is of special scientific interest. The 'public authorities'[75] to which this duty applies are the following:

(a) a Minister of the Crown[76] or a Government Department;

(b) the National Assembly for Wales;

(c) a local authority;

(d) a person holding an office under the Crown, an office created or continued by a public general Act of Parliament or an office the remuneration in respect of which is paid out of money provided by Parliament;

(e) a statutory undertaker;[77] and

(f) any other public body of any description.[78]

Notably, in flood and coastal defence contexts, all the key bodies with operational or regulatory responsibilities will be within this list. Whilst there seems to be some overlap or reaffirmation of existing conservation duties upon the Environment Agency and internal drainage boards, the general conservation duty under conservation legislation is significant in extending beyond the flood defence operating authorities. Particularly notable is that the duty will apply to local authorities when exercising functions other than flood defence. Hence, coast protection authorities will be subject to the duty, as will local highway authorities and local authorities generally when acting outside their flood defence functions.

The listed public authorities that are under a duty to exercise their functions

---

[75] For brevity, the range of individuals, bodies and undertakers which are listed here are referred to as 'public authorities' hereafter, though in the terminology of the amended 1981 Act they are referred to as 'section 28G authorities'.

[76] See Ministers of the Crown Act 1975.

[77] A 'statutory undertaker' is defined under s.262(1), (3) and (6) Town and Country Planning Act 1990 to mean persons authorised by any enactment to carry on any railway, light railway, tramway, road transport, water transport, canal, inland navigation, dock, harbour, pier or lighthouse undertaking or any undertaking for the supply of hydraulic power and airport operators (within Part V Airports Act 1986). For particular purposes, a holder of a licence under s.6 Electricity Act 1989 will also be deemed to be a statutory undertaker.

[78] s.28G(1) to (3) Wildlife and Countryside Act 1981.

to further conservation are also placed under a duty to give notice to the relevant nature conservancy council before exercising their functions in certain circumstances. Specifically, the notification duty arises where the exercise of functions by the public authority would be likely to damage any of the flora, fauna or geological or physiographical features by reason of which a site of special scientific interest is of interest. Remarkably, the duty to notify the council applies even if the proposed operations will not take place on land within a site of special scientific interest.[79] Hence, given the capacity of river flood defence works to have impacts on a watercourse for a considerable distance downstream, the possibility is raised of the notification requirement being applicable to works that are to take place at some distance from any site of special scientific interest.

Following notification of an operation which is likely to damage the interest of a site of special scientific interest, the nature conservancy council may notify the public authority that the council does not assent to the operation or that it does assent, with or without conditions. If assent is withheld or the operation is to be conducted otherwise than in accordance with conditions attached to the consent, the public authority may not carry out the operation unless certain 'further conditions' are satisfied and must also comply with 'further requirements'. The 'further conditions' applicable are that the body is to notify the council of the date on which the operation is to commence and how, if at all, it has taken account of any advice which has been given by the council. The 'further requirements' are that the body must carry out the operation so as to cause as little damage as is reasonably practicable to the features of special interest, taking account of advice given by the council, and that the body must restore the site to its former condition so far as reasonably practicable.[80]

A public authority which carries out an operation that damages any of the flora, fauna or geological or physiographical features by which a site is of special interest without first giving notice[81] of a proposed operation to the nature conservacy council commits an offence. Likewise, an offence is committed where a public authority carries out a relevant operation without the consent of the council, or otherwise than in accordance with the terms of the council's assent, and otherwise than in accordance with the conditions and requirements that apply.[82] An exception is allowed for

---

[79] s.28H(1) and (2) Wildlife and Countryside Act 1981.
[80] s.28H(3) to (6) Wildlife and Countryside Act 1981.
[81] 'Notice', that is, as required under s.28H(1) Wildlife and Countryside Act 1981.
[82] That is, the conditions and requirements provided for under s.28H(4) and (5) Wildlife and Countryside Act 1981. An authority committing either of these offences will be liable, on summary conviction, to a fine not exceeding £20,000 or, on conviction on indictment, to a fine (s.28P(2)).

where there is a 'reasonable excuse' for carrying out the operation, and this would allow an operation to be conducted under a planning permission and, where relevant, under a permission by a public authority or in an emergency.[83]

### 10.4.3 Authorisation of Operations by Public Authorities

The duty to avoid damage to sites of special scientific interest, which is imposed upon the 'public authorities' listed above, also extends to situations where the permission of a public authority is needed before an operation may be carried out by another person or body. 'Permission' for these purposes is broadly construed to encompass any authorisation, consent or other type of permit. Previous discussion has provided numerous examples of 'permissions' for flood and coastal defence operations which will come within the scope of this definition.[84] Hence, where a body or individual needs permission from a flood or coastal defence operating authority to conduct an operation, it will fall within the requirements applicable to authorisations of operations by public authorities.

The requirements stipulate that, before permitting the carrying out of any operation likely to damage flora, fauna or geological or physiographical features by reason of which a site is of special scientific interest, the public authority must give notice of the proposed operation to the relevant nature conservancy council. Notably, the duty to notify the council arises even where the operation that is proposed will take place outside the boundaries of any site of special scientific interest that may be affected.[85]

After the nature conservancy council has been notified of the proposed operation, the public body, whose permission for the operation is needed, must wait for 28 days before deciding whether to give its permission. The public body must then take into account any advice received from the council in deciding whether or not to permit the proposed operation and, if the permission is given, in determining any conditions subject to which it is given. If the council advises against permitting the operation, or advises that certain conditions should be attached to a permission, but the public body does not follow that advice, the public body must give the council notice of the terms of the permission and provide a statement of how account has been taken of the council's advice. In these circumstances, the public body must not grant permission for the commencement of the operation to start before 21 days after the council has been notified of the

---

[83] Under s.28P(4) and (5) Wildlife and Countryside Act 1981.
[84] See, for examples, the regulatory powers of the Environment Agency at 4.4 above.
[85] s.28I(1), (3) and (7) Wildlife and Countryside Act 1981.

terms of the permission.[86] The underlying intention is that the further period will allow the council time to discuss ways of mitigating the adverse effects of the operation or to offer a management agreement to the landholder.

### 10.4.4 Management Schemes and Notices

The nature conservancy council may formulate a management scheme for all or part of a site of special scientific interest, that is, a scheme for the conservation and/or restoration of the flora, fauna, geological or physiographical features of special interest. Following prior consultation, the council must serve notice of a proposed management scheme on every owner and occupier of the land to which the scheme relates. A period of 3 months is allowed, from the service of notice, during which time representations or objections concerning the proposed management scheme may be made, and these must be considered by the council. Following the service of notice, a period of 9 months is allowed for a proposed management scheme to be either withdrawn or confirmed, with or without modification, and the scheme will then take effect when notice of this is served upon all the relevant owners or occupiers.[87]

Where it appears that an owner or occupier of land is not giving effect to a provision of a management scheme and, as a result, any flora, fauna or geological or physiographical feature is being inadequately conserved or restored, the nature conservancy council may serve a management notice on that person. However, the council may not serve a management notice unless it is satisfied that it is unable to conclude, on reasonable terms, an agreement with the owner or occupier as to the management of the land in accordance with the management scheme. A management notice will require the owner or occupier to carry out specified work on the land and to do other things within a stated period, where the work and other things are reasonable requirements to ensure the land is managed in accordance with the management scheme.[88]

In the event of the work, or other things required under a management notice, not being done within the period allowed, the council may enter the land and carry out the work and recover from the owner or occupier any

---

[86] s.28I(4) to (6) Wildlife and Countryside Act 1981.
[87] s.28J(1) to (3), (7) and (8) Wildlife and Countryside Act 1981. An agreement relating to a site of special scientific interest, under s.16 National Parks and Access to the Countryside Act 1949 or s.15 Countryside Act 1968 Act, may provide for any matter which could be provided for under a management scheme (s.28J(13) Wildlife and Countryside Act 1981).
[88] s.28K(1) to (4) Wildlife and Countryside Act 1981.

expenses reasonably incurred in carrying out the work.[89] A person who without reasonable excuse fails to comply with a requirement of a management notice will be guilty of an offence.[90]

### 10.4.5 Compulsory Acquisition and Restoration

Under certain circumstances, a nature conservancy council may acquire all or any part of a site of special scientific interest compulsorily. The circumstances arise where the council is satisfied that it is unable to conclude a management agreement with an owner or occupier on reasonable terms, or where an agreement has been entered into but has been breached in such a way that the council is satisfied that the land is not being managed satisfactorily. Where a council acquires land compulsorily, it may manage it itself or dispose of it, or any interest in it, on terms designed to secure that the land is managed satisfactorily.[91]

Another potentially important remedial mechanism is the power of a court to order the restoration of a site of special scientific interest where a person has been convicted of damaging or destroying the site. In these circumstances, in addition to imposing a penalty upon the offender, the court may also order the specified operations to be undertaken for the purpose of restoring a site of special scientific interest to its former state. Notably, an order specifying remediation operations may be made whether the operation involving damage to the special interest of the site took place within or outside the site. The same powers are available in relation to the offences concerning operations by public authorities.[92]

### 10.4.6 Duties concerning Biological Diversity and Ramsar Sites

Although the implications of the designation of land as a site of special scientific interest may have profound implications for flood defence

---

[89] s.28K(7) Wildlife and Countryside Act 1981. Appeals to the Secretary of State against management notices are provided for under s.28L. A council may make one or more payments to any owner or occupier of land in relation to which a management scheme is in force, the amount being determined in accordance with guidance given by the Ministers: s.28M(2) and (3). See also s.50 Wildlife and Countryside Act 1981 which makes provision for payments under s.16 National Parks and Access to the Countryside Act 1949 or s.15 Countryside Act 1968.

[90] s.28P(8) Wildlife and Countryside Act 1981. A person convicted of this offence is liable, on summary conviction, to a fine not exceeding the statutory maximum, presently £5,000, or, on conviction on indictment, to a fine. Proceedings for the offence may not be brought by any person other than the council without the consent of the Director of Public Prosecutions (s.28P(10)).

[91] s.28N(1) and (2) Wildlife and Countryside Act 1981.

[92] s.31(1) Wildlife and Countryside Act 1981, which applies where an offence under s.28P(1) to (3) and (6) has been committed.

operations, there are also other categories of ecologically important site in relation to which special duties exist. Notably, these concern the United Nations Convention on Biological Diversity of 1992[93] and the Ramsar Convention on Wetlands of International Importance especially as Wildfowl Habitats 1971, as amended.[94]

In relation to the Biological Diversity Convention, a duty is imposed upon all Ministers, Government departments and the National Assembly for Wales, insofar as is consistent with the proper exercise of their functions, to have regard to the conservation of biological diversity in accordance with the Convention. For this purpose the Secretary of State and the National Assembly for Wales are, after consultation, to publish lists of species and habitats which are of principal importance in relation to the duty in respect of biological diversity and to take, or promote the taking by others of, reasonably practicable steps to further the conservation of the listed species and habitats.[95]

Where a wetland in Great Britain has been designated under the Ramsar Convention for inclusion in the list of wetlands of international importance, the Secretary of State must notify English Nature or the Countryside Council for Wales, as appropriate. On notification, the relevant nature conservancy council must notify every owner and occupier of the wetland, the Environment Agency and every relevant undertaker[96] and internal drainage board whose works, operations or activities may affect the wetland.[97]

## 10.5 EUROPEAN COMMUNITY CONSERVATION LEGISLATION

As has been seen, European Community legislation concerning environmental impact assessment has important implications for flood and coastal defence operations that are likely to have a significant impact upon the environment and the ecosystems that it supports.[98] However, the most

---

[93] (1992) 31 *International Legal Materials* 818.
[94] (1971) 11 *International Legal Materials* 963.
[95] s.74(1) and (2) Countryside and Rights of Way Act 2000. Generally see *Biodiversity: the UK Action Plan* (1994) Cm. 2428.
[96] 'Relevant undertaker' is to be understood within the meaning of s.4(1) Water Industry Act 1991, which means every water and sewerage undertaker (see s. 219(1)); s.4 requires the relevant nature conservancy council to notify water and sewerage undertakers of land that is of special interest and imposes consultation duties in relation to works, operations and activities of the undertaker which are likely to damage the special interest of the land.
[97] s.37A(1) and (2) Wildlife and Countryside Act 1981.
[98] See 9.14 above on environmental impact assessment.

directly important legislative provisions[99] concerning ecological protection are provided for under the Wild Birds Directive[100] and the Habitats Directive.[101] Hence, the pertinent features of these Directives will be outlined, indicating the national mechanisms that have been established for implementation, with particular emphasis upon provisions for habitat protection and the implications of these for flood and coastal defence projects.

### 10.5.1 The Wild Birds Directive

Alongside measures to prevent the direct destruction of wild birds, the Wild Birds Directive places a general duty upon the Member States of the European Community to maintain the populations of birds. This applies to species of birds naturally occurring in the wild state, and requires 'requisite measures' to maintain populations at a level which corresponds to ecological, scientific and cultural requirements, while taking account of economic and recreational requirements. In particular, this is to be achieved by taking measures to preserve, maintain or re-establish a sufficient diversity and area of habitats for certain species, specifically, by the creation of 'special protected areas' and the general management of habitats. Accordingly, Member States must classify the most suitable sites as special protection areas for the conservation of particular species and take appropriate steps to avoid pollution, deterioration or disturbance of these areas and strive to avoid pollution or deterioration of bird habitats generally.[102]

The implications of the duty with regard to the creation of special protected areas for wild birds are evident from a scan of the relevant caselaw of the European Court of Justice.[103] In relation to the designation of special protection areas, the duty upon a Member State to classify a special protection area must be based on genuine ornithological criteria, and the failure to have regard to this will not provide a justification for non-designation or allowing operations that cause damage to a site that should have been designated. Hence, Spain was found to have been in breach of the Directive where it failed to designate an estuarial site that supported

---

[99] On European Community *policy* concerning wildlife conservation see European Commission Communication, *A European Community Biodiversity Strategy* COM (1998) 42 final, emphasising the Community's obligation to ensure that its policies and instruments contribute to the conservation and sustainable use of biodiversity.
[100] Council Directive on the conservation of wild birds (79/409/EEC) as amended.
[101] Council Directive on the conservation of natural habitats of wild fauna and flora (92/43/EEC) as amended.
[102] Generally see Arts.2 to 4 Wild Birds Directive.
[103] Generally see W. Wils, 'The Birds Directive 15 Years Later' [1994] *Journal of Environmental Law* 219 and D. Freestone, 'The Enforcement of the Wild Birds Directive: A Case Study' in H. Somsen, Ed., *Protecting the European Environment: Enforcing EC Environmental Law* (1996) p.229.

important bird species. It was accepted, in principle, that a range of operations which had been found to damage the site were unlawful; however, operations involving the reclamation of wetlands were excused because, on the evidence, it had to be concluded that these operations had taken place before the Directive came into effect.[104] Notably, Member States are not allowed to take into account economic requirements in deciding to designate areas or determining their boundaries.[105] Accordingly, the United Kingdom was found to have acted unlawfully in excluding an area of mudflats from a special protection area that, under a planning permission, was authorised to be reclaimed from an estuary in order to facilitate the expansion, and enhance the economic viability, of a port.[106]

Where a special protection area has actually been designated, the European Court of Justice has held that the duty to take measures to avoid deterioration or disturbance of bird habitats is to be strictly construed. Hence, in one instance Germany had given approval for a coast defence project which involved the reconstruction of dykes, primarily for the purposes of protecting land from storm tides though, secondarily, for the provision of recreational facilities. It was argued that this constituted a breach of the duties in relation to the special protection area in which the works were undertaken. Specifically, it was observed that the protective duties in relation to special protection areas did not allow Member States to reduce the size of a designated area unless the reduction could be justified on exceptional grounds, that is, where a 'general interest superior to the general interest represented by the ecological objectives of the Directive' was at issue. The need for protection of human life from flooding may have constituted a 'superior interest' to those of the Directive, providing that it was confined to the minimum intrusion that was necessary. Considered alone, however, economic and recreational grounds for the work that had been undertaken could not provide a justification for reducing the size of the special protection area.[107]

---

[104] *European Commission* v *Spain* Case 355/90 [1993] ECR 1-4221 (the *Marismas de Santona* case).

[105] That is, the power to take account of economic and recreational requirements in relation to the 'requisite measures' for the general maintenance of populations of naturally occurring wild birds (under Art. 2 Wild Birds Directive) was not applicable in relation to the designation of special conservation areas (under Art.4(1) and (2)).

[106] *R* v *Secretary of State for the Environment ex parte Royal Society for the Protection of Birds* (the *Lappel Bank* case) [1997] Env LR 442 (European Court of Justice). See also *European Commission* v *French Republic* Case C-166/97 [1999] Env LR 781 (the *Seine Estuary* case).

[107] *European Commission* v *Federal Republic of Germany* Case 57/89 [1991] ECR I-883 (the *Leybucht Dykes* case). However, the circumstances would now be considered under Arts.6 and 7 Habitats Directive, which amends Art.4 Wild Birds Directive, broadly, to apply a test of 'imperative reasons of overriding public interest, including those of a social or economic nature' (see 10.5.2 below).

Although coast protection works undertaken for the purposes of protecting life and property may be justified as 'imperative reasons' for allowing minimal damage or reduction in a special protected area, land drainage operations conducted for other purposes are unlikely to fall within this justification. Hence, in proceedings against France, no justification was accepted where operations involving the systematic drainage of part of a special protection area, to enable intensive cultivation, had resulted in the drying out of the area and a dramatic fall in populations of protected overwintering birds.[108]

### 10.5.2 The Habitats Directive

The Wild Birds Directive is especially concerned with bird habitats, though conservation of such habitats is frequently beneficial to non-bird species. However, the Habitats Directive is more generally concerned with the conservation of natural habitats for *all* species of flora and fauna. Hence, the objective of the Directive is to promote biodiversity, taking into account economic, social, cultural requirements and regional and local characteristics. This is to be done by establishing a coherent European ecological network of sites, termed 'Natura 2000'. This involves each Member State proposing a list of sites indicating which natural habitat types of Community interest[109] and which species of Community interest[110] are native to its territory and to designate 'special areas of conservation' accordingly.[111] Natura 2000, therefore, will consist of the special areas of conservation under the Habitats Directive along with the special protection areas established under the Wild Birds Directive. A detailed procedure is established for the selection of sites involving initial proposals, on the basis of relevant scientific information, by Member States and the transmission of these proposals to the European Commission. On the basis of this information, the Commission must establish a draft list of sites of Community importance in agreement with each Member State.

---

[108] *European Commission* v *France* Case C-96/98 [2000] 2 CMLR 681 (the *Poitevin Marsh* case).

[109] 'Natural habitat types of Community importance' are defined as those sites which are in danger of disappearance in their natural range; or have small natural range following their regression or by reason of their intrinsically restricted area; or present outstanding examples of certain typical characteristics of certain biogeographical regions. These sites are listed in Annex I (Art.1 Habitats Directive).

[110] 'Species of Community interest' is defined, with qualifications, as species which are endangered, vulnerable, rare or endemic and requiring particular attention because of exploitation. The species are listed in Annex II and/or Annex IV or V (Art.1 Habitats Directive).

[111] On the initial selection of sites under the Habitats Directive, see *R* v *Secretary of State for the Environment, Transport and the Regions ex parte First Corporate Shipping Ltd* Case C-371/98 [2001] Env LR 34.

Nevertheless, after consultation, the Commission may forward a proposal, which has not been agreed by a Member State, to the Council for approval.[112]

In relation to special areas of conservation, Member States must establish 'necessary conservation measures' involving appropriate management plans that correspond to the ecological requirements of the habitats and species concerned. In special areas of conservation appropriate steps are to be taken to avoid the deterioration of natural habitats and disturbance of the species for which the areas have been designated. In particular, plans or projects likely to have a significant effect on a site must be subject to an appropriate assessment of their conservation implications. Despite a negative assessment a plan or project must be carried out for 'imperative reasons of overriding public interest', including those of social or economic nature, though compensatory measures may be required to ensure the overall coherence of Natura 2000. Where a site hosts a 'priority' natural habitat type and/or a 'priority' species,[113] the only considerations which may be raised are those relating to human health or safety, beneficial consequences of primary importance to the environment or imperative reasons of overriding public interest identified by the Commission.[114] These requirements apply equally to special protection areas, under the Wild Birds Directive, and special areas of conservation, under the Habitats Directive.[115]

## 10.6 THE HABITATS REGULATIONS 1994

Although the Wildlife and Countryside Act 1981 had been originally enacted to give effect to the Wild Birds Directive, more extensive protection of species and habitats was required under the Habitats Directive, particularly the measures concerning site designation and protection.[116] The principal

---

[112] Generally see Arts.2 to 5 Habitats Directive.
[113] A 'priority natural habitat' means a natural habitat present in the European territory of the Member States which is in danger of disappearance for which the Community has particular responsibility (these habitats are marked with an '*' in Annex I). A 'priority species' means a species for which the Community has a particular responsibility in view of its natural range which falls within the European territory of the Member States (these species are marked with an '*' in Annex II) (Art.1 Habitats Directive).
[114] Art. 6 Habitats Directive and see A. Nollkaemper, 'Habitat Protection in European Community Law: Evolving Concepts of a Balance of Interests' [1997] *Journal of Environmental Law* 271.
[115] Art.7 Habitats Directive.
[116] Under Arts.6 and 7 Habitats Directive. Generally see Ministry of Agriculture, Fisheries and Food, *The EC Habitats Directive: Implications for Flood and Coastal Defence* (1995).

national legislation for implementing the Habitats Directive is the Conservation (Natural Habitats, &c.) Regulations 1994[117] which concern three main areas: the protection of species; the conservation of habitats; and the adaptation of planning and other controls. Although the 1994 Regulations tend to use similar control mechanisms to those originally provided for under the Wildlife and Countryside Act 1981, there are several respects in which the Regulations operate more strictly than the 1981 Act to ensure that obligations under the Habitats Directive are met.

### 10.6.1 General Duties and Powers

For the purpose of implementing the Habitats Directive, the 1994 Regulations impose a general duty upon the Secretary of State, English Nature and the Countryside Council for Wales to exercise their functions under existing legislation (including the Wildlife and Countryside Act 1981) in such a manner as to comply with the requirements of the Directive. In relation to marine areas, any 'competent authority' having functions relevant to marine conservation must exercise those functions so as to secure compliance with the requirements of the Directive.[118] This duty is stated to apply, in particular, to functions under the Water Resources Act 1991 and the Land Drainage Act 1991.[119] More generally, every 'competent authority' is bound to have regard to the requirements of the Directive in so far as they may be affected in the exercise of their functions.[120] For the purposes of the 1994 Regulations, the expression 'competent authority' includes any Minister, government department, public or statutory undertaker, public body of any description or person holding a public office and any person exercising the functions of such authorities.[121]

---

[117] S.I. 1994 No.2716 and see Conservation (Natural Habitats, &c) (Amendment) Regulations 1997, S.I. 1997 No.3055 and S.I. 2000 No.192, hereafter noted as the 'Habitats Regulations'. Generally see C. Rodgers, 'Managing Natura 2000: Priorities for Implementing European Wildlife Law' [2001] *Journal of Planning and Environment* Law 265.

[118] 'Relevant authorities' in relation to a marine area of a European marine site are stated to include local authorities, the Environment Agency, water or sewerage undertakers, and internal drainage boards insofar as they have functions in relation to land or waters within or adjacent to the area or site (reg.5 Habitats Regulations). See also reg.33 requiring the nature conservancy council to advise other relevant authorities of the objectives of a European site and operations which may cause deterioration or disturbance to the site or the species which is hosted. See reg.34 allowing relevant authorities to establish management schemes for European marine sites and reg.35 allowing the relevant Minister to give directions to relevant authorities, amongst other things, requiring conservation measures to be included in a management scheme for a European marine site.

[119] Curiously, there is no reference to the Coast Protection Act 1949.

[120] reg.3(1) to (4) Habitats Regulations.

[121] reg.6(1) Habitats Regulations.

Accordingly, all the public bodies with flood and coastal defence functions will be subject to a duty to exercise those functions to secure compliance with the Directive or, at least, to have regard to the requirements of the Directive.[122]

Specific provision is made by the 1994 Regulations to modify the powers of certain flood defence authorities to allow them to carry out work in relation to European sites where this is in accordance with agreements made with the nature conservancy council. Hence, where an agreement of this kind has been made, by either the Environment Agency or an internal drainage board,[123] it is stipulated that no limitation imposed by law on the capacity of the flood defence authority by virtue of its constitution will operate to prevent the authority carrying out the agreement.[124] Given the broadly formulated environmental duties upon flood defence authorities,[125] it is difficult to envisage circumstances where constitutional limitations might prove problematic; nevertheless, the matter is placed beyond doubt by this stipulation.

### 10.6.2 Site Selection

The main responsibility for initial selection of sites eligible for designation as of 'Community importance' rests with the Secretary of State who must apply specified criteria,[126] on the basis of relevant scientific information, and propose an initial list indicating which priority habitat type is hosted by a site and which priority species are hosted.[127] The final selection of sites of Community interest is undertaken in accordance with a procedure[128] involving adoption by the European Commission and, following this, the Secretary of State must designate such sites as special areas of conservation, as soon as possible, and within 6 years at most.[129]

In the terminology of the 1994 Regulations, a 'European site' means:

---

[122] That is, coast protection authorities would be subject to this obligation.
[123] Notably, no provision seems to be made for agreements with local authorities or coast protection authorities for this purpose.
[124] reg.105 Habitats Regulations.
[125] See 10.2 and 10.3 above on environmental duties on the Environment Agency and internal drainage boards.
[126] Under Annex III Habitats Directive.
[127] reg.7(1) Habitats Regulations. See *R v Secretary of State for the Environment, Transport and the Regions ex parte First Corporate Shipping Ltd* Case C-371/98 [2001] Env LR 34 where it was reaffirmed that ecological criteria must determine the initial site selection.
[128] Under Art.4(2) Habitats Directive, and see Art.5(1) on consultation with the Commission and Art.5(3) on final decisions by the Council.
[129] reg.8(1) Habitats Regulations.

(a) a special area of conservation;

(b) a site of Community importance which has been placed on the list adopted by the Commission;[130]

(c) a site hosting a priority natural habitat type or a priority species in respect of which consultation with the Commission has been initiated, during the consultation period or pending a final decision of the Council; or

(d) an area classified as a special protection area under the Wild Birds Directive[131].[132]

Agreement about the sites to be designated as special areas of conservation should have been reached by June 1998. As at 31 March 2001, 212 candidate sites had been identified in England, and communicated to the European Commission, with a further 17 sites recommended by English Nature; 85 sites have been identified as special protection areas under the Wild Birds Directive;[133] 89 candidate special areas of conservation have been submitted to the Commission for consideration in relation to Wales, along with 13 special protection areas.[134]

The Secretary of State must compile and maintain a register of European sites and must notify the appropriate nature conservancy council as soon as possible after including a site in the register. As soon as practicable after the council receives notification it must give notice to every owner or occupier of land within the site; every local planning authority in whose area the site, or any part of it, is situated; and such other persons or bodies as the Secretary of State may direct.[135]

### 10.6.3 Management of Sites

A nature conservancy council may enter into a management agreement with every owner, lessee and occupier of land forming part of a European site, or land adjacent to it, for the management, conservation, restoration

---

[130] That is, the list provided for in Art.4(2) Habitats Directive.
[131] Under Art.4(1) or (2) Wild Birds Directive.
[132] reg.10 Habitats Regulations. The Conservation (Natural Habitats, &c) (Amendment) Regulations 2000, S.I. 2000 No.192, add a further category to the list of 'European Sites', that is, sites which are included in the list of sites proposed by the Secretary of State and transmitted to the European Commission under reg.7 Habitats Regulations.
[133] English Nature, *Annual Report: 1 April 2000–31 March 2001* (2001).
[134] See Countryside Council for Wales, *Annual Report 2000–01* (2001).
[135] Generally see regs.11 to 13 Habitats Regulations. The planning implications of this are discussed at 10.6.8 below.

or protection of the site, or any part of it. Such agreements may contain provisions concerning the making of payments by the council by way of compensation.[136] Where a council is satisfied that it is unable to conclude a reasonable management agreement, or that a management agreement has been breached, it may acquire an interest in the land compulsorily.[137]

The owner or occupier of any land within a European site may not carry out, or cause or permit to be carried out, on that land any operation specified in a notification unless certain requirements are met. Specifically, the nature conservancy council must be given written notice of a proposed operation and must give its consent. Alternatively, an operation may be carried out in accordance with a management agreement or where 4 months have expired from the giving of notice by the council. Conduct of an operation, otherwise than in accordance with these requirements, is a criminal offence, but exceptions are allowed for emergencies and operations authorised by planning permission. Any person who, without reasonable excuse, contravenes the requirements commits an offence.[138]

Where an application for consent for a notified operation relates to an operation which is not directly necessary to the management of the site and is likely to have significant effect on the site, the nature conservancy council must make an 'appropriate assessment' of the implications for the site and it may only give consent if it has ascertained that the operation will not adversely affect the integrity of the site.[139] Existing consents[140] must be reviewed to ensure compatibility with the conservation objectives of the site and these must be modified or withdrawn accordingly with notice of this being given to every owner or occupier of land within the site.[141]

---

[136] reg.16 Habitats Regulations. Although certain pre-existing agreements may continue in force, see reg.17 Habitats Regulations. Also, notifications of sites of special scientific interest (under s.28 Wildlife and Countryside Act 1981), specifying the features of the site which are of special interest and operations likely to damage the flora and fauna, will have effect under the 1994 Regulations, but notice of any amendment will have to be given to every owner or occupier and the local planning authority (reg.18 Habitats Regulations).

[137] reg.32 Habitats Regulations. On the power to acquire land, and the need for consent of the Secretary of State, see reg.98.

[138] reg.19 Habitats Regulations. A person committing this offence is liable, on summary conviction, to a fine not exceeding level 4 on the standard scale, presently £2,500, though proceedings for the offence may not, without the consent of the Director of Public Prosecutions, be undertaken by a person other than the appropriate nature conservancy council.

[139] reg.20 Habitats Regulations. Contrast the requirements for 'environmental impact assessment', discussed at 9.14 above.

[140] That is, consents under the original s.28(5)(a) or (6)(a) of Wildlife and Countryside Act 1981.

[141] reg.21 Habitats Regulations.

### 10.6.4 Special Nature Conservation Orders

Where there is a danger of a potentially damaging operation being undertaken in a European site without the consent of the nature conservancy council, the Secretary of State may, after consultation with the council, make a 'special nature conservation order' specifying and prohibiting the operations that are likely to damage the flora and fauna of the site.[142] Thereafter, no person may carry out any operation on any European site specified in the order unless the council has been given written notice of a proposal to carry out an operation and the operation is carried out with written consent of the council or in accordance with a management agreement. A criminal offence is provided for, subject to exceptions for emergency operations and operations authorised by planning permission.[143]

As with the general restrictions upon carrying out notified operations on European sites, an application to carry out operations specified in a special nature conservation order requires the nature conservancy council to make an 'appropriate assessment' of the implications of the operation and may only give consent if it is ascertained that the operation will not adversely affect the integrity of the site. However, the owner or occupier may appeal to the Secretary of State. In considering appeals, the Secretary of State may only consent to the operation if he is satisfied that there is no alternative solution and that there are 'imperative reasons of overriding public interest' for allowing the operation to proceed. If the site is not classified as a 'priority habitat' or does not contain 'priority species' then these reasons may include reasons of a social or economic nature. Alternatively, if the site has been classified as deserving priority protection, the only matters that the Secretary of State may have regard to are those relating to public health or public safety and those relating to any beneficial consequences of the operation which are of primary importance to the environment. Also, other reasons that, in the opinion of the European Commission, are imperative reasons of overriding public interest may suffice.[144]

---

[142] reg.22 Habitats Regulations. Where a special nature conservation order is made the council must pay compensation to persons having interest in agricultural land, the value of which is diminished by the order (reg.25). In relation to compensation, where a special nature conservation order has been made, see regs.91 and 92.

[143] reg.23 Habitats Regulations. On summary conviction, the maximum fine for the offence is the statutory maximum, £5,000, and, on conviction on indictment, a fine may be imposed. Where the offence is committed in respect of unauthorised operations contrary to a nature conservation order, a court may order operations to be conducted for the purpose of restoring the land to its former condition (reg.26).

[144] reg.24 Habitats Regulations. However, this does not apply to sites under reg.10(1)(c) (hosting a priority habitat or species).

Pertinently, some of the first uses of special nature conservation orders were in situations where land drainage activities were found to be damaging to European sites. Hence, English Nature was granted the first such order where land in the Peak Moors Special Protection Area had been damaged by an unauthorised drainage system, involving the creation of ditches and the stripping of vegetation.[145] In another early case, a special nature conservation order was made following the conviction of two farmers for unauthorised installation of field drains in grazing land, designated as a site of special scientific interest and subsequently a European site because it provided an important breeding area for moorland birds.[146]

### 10.6.5 Adaptation of Planning and Other Controls

Many of the offences that arise under wildlife conservation legislation admit a defence where the activity or operation is authorised by a planning permission, so it was necessary for the 1994 Regulations to make certain amendments to planning law to secure conformity with the requirements of the Habitats Directive.[147] Three kinds of modification were necessary:

(a) a requirement that all future planning proposals should be assessed to determine whether they will have a significant impact on European sites;

(b) a requirement that a review must be undertaken of previously granted planning permissions, where development has not yet been carried out, and, if appropriate, modify or revoke them to prevent adverse impacts upon European sites; and

(c) the imposition of restrictions upon existing permitted development rights in respect of European sites.

However, the purposes for which planning law needed to be modified have also been similarly applied to 'other controls', which is broadly construed to encompass the functions of 'competent authorities' where, as has been noted, these are the functions of a 'public body of any description'.[148] The effect of this is that flood and coastal defence authorities will be subject to

---

[145] English Nature, Press Release, 6 February 1998, *England's First Special Nature Conservation Order Used to Stop Damage to International Wildlife Site*.

[146] English Nature, Press Release, 24 August 1998, *Owners prosecuted for damage to European wildlife site*. In this instance English Nature obtained an injunction to prevent further drainage work being carried out and the farmers were fined £1,000 with costs.

[147] On the effects of nature conservation implications upon planning policy, see Department of the Environment Planning Policy Guidance Note 9, *Planning Policy Guidance: Nature Conservation* (1994) and Welsh Office Circulars 52/87 and 1/92.

[148] reg.6 Habitats Regulations and see 10.4.2 above.

a range of duties when exercising functions with respect to European sites both in relation to carrying out operations and in authorising others to do so.

### 10.6.6 Assessment of Implications for European Sites

Specifically, a duty arises where a competent authority is deciding whether to undertake a plan or project, or to give consent, permission or other authorisation for another person or body to undertake a plan or project, which is likely to have a significant effect upon a European site, either alone or in combination with other plans or projects. Unless the plan or project is directly connected with or necessary to the management of the site, the authority must make an 'appropriate assessment' of the implications for the conservation objectives of the site. The assessment is to be made on the basis of information provided by the person seeking the consent, consultation with the nature conservancy council and, if appropriate, the opinion of the general public. In the light of the assessment, and any conditions or restrictions that are proposed, the authority must agree to the project if it has been ascertained that it will not adversely affect the integrity of the site.[149]

If a competent authority is satisfied that there are no alternative solutions, and that the plan or project must be carried out for 'imperative reasons of overriding public interest', which may be of a social or economic nature, the competent authority may generally agree to the plan or project notwithstanding a negative assessment of the implications for the site. However, where the site hosts a priority habitat or priority species the reasons for allowing the plan or project must be either reasons relating to human health, public safety or beneficial consequences of primary importance to the environment, or other reasons which, in the opinion of the European Commission, are imperative reasons of overriding public interest.[150]

### 10.6.7 Review of Existing Decisions

Where, before the commencement of the 1994 Regulations, a competent authority decided to undertake, or have given any consent, permission or other authorisation for, a plan or project that would require an appropriate assessment,[151] the authority must review that decision and must affirm,

---

[149] reg.48 Habitats Regulations. However, this does not apply to sites under reg.10(1)(c) (hosting a priority habitat or species).

[150] reg.49 Habitat Regulations, which also provides for the opinion of the Commission to be sought by the Secretary of State and for the Secretary of State to give directions prohibiting an authority from agreeing to a plan or project.

[151] That is, an assessment required under reg.48 Habitats Regulations.

## The Habitats Regulations 1994

modify or revoke it as soon as reasonably practicable. That is, an appropriate assessment must be made of the implications of certain previously approved plans or projects on any European site, along with the necessary consultation.[152] The outcome of such a review may be to confirm that the plan or project may proceed if it has been ascertained that it will not adversely affect the integrity of the site. Otherwise, the same considerations will apply as for new applications for consent: that is, there must normally be no alternative solution and imperative reasons of overriding public interest must be shown before approval will be given.[153]

A potential difficulty arises as to which competent authority should assess or review the implications of a plan or project upon a European site where more than one authority is involved. This may be an issue where the plan or project is undertaken by, or requires the consent, permission or authorisation of, more than one competent authority, or where it is undertaken by one or more competent authorities and requires the consent of another authority, or authorities. The issue of responsibility for assessment or review is addressed by a stipulation that no competent authority is required to assess any implications of a plan or project that would be more appropriately assessed by another competent authority.[154] Although somewhat obscure, this suggests that flood and coastal defence operations and authorisations should be subject to review by the appropriate authority.

Where considerations of overriding public importance are established, and a plan or project is agreed to, notwithstanding a negative assessment of the implications for a European site, the Secretary of State must secure that any necessary compensatory measures are taken to ensure the overall coherence of Natura 2000 is protected. Similarly, despite an adverse assessment, necessary compensatory measures must be taken where a decision, consent, permission or other authorisation is affirmed on review.[155]

### 10.6.8 Planning Permissions: Review, Revocation and Compensation

With some points of contrast, the procedures that have been outlined in relation to 'other controls' are analogously applied in relation to planning permissions.[156] Hence, assessment of implications for European sites[157]

---

[152] reg.50 Habitats Regulations.
[153] reg.51 Habitats Regulations.
[154] reg.52 Habitats Regulations.
[155] reg.53 Habitats Regulations.
[156] Generally see S. Payne, 'Nature Conservation and Development' [1994] *Journal of Planning and Environment Law* 979.
[157] Under reg.48 Habitats Regulations.

and consideration of overriding public interest[158] apply similarly in relation to applications for planning permissions under the Town and Country Planning Act 1990 and other planning legislation. However, where a planning permission is involved, the competent local planning authority may grant planning permission subject to conditions or limitations to avoid effects of the plan or project on the integrity of a European site.[159]

Similarly, the duty upon competent authorities to review previously granted consents[160] applies in relation to any planning permission or deemed planning permission, unless the development which is authorised has actually been completed. However, different requirements apply where a planning permission has been deemed to have been granted by a development order and in relation to specified categories of planning zone or under a public general Act of Parliament.[161] In reviewing any planning permission, the planning authority must consider whether effects upon a European site could be overcome by planning obligations[162] and, if so, invite those concerned to enter into such obligations.[163]

Where the outcome of a review of a planning permission is a decision to revoke that permission, it will be necessary for the planning authority to make an order to that effect under the Town and Country Planning Act 1990.[164] Notably, provision is made under the 1990 Act for the payment of compensation by the local planning authority where an order has been made revoking or modifying a planning permission where work is rendered abortive, or loss or damage has been otherwise sustained, which is directly attributable to the revocation or modification.[165]

---

[158] Under reg.49 Habitats Regulations.
[159] reg.54 Habitats Regulations.
[160] Under regs.50 and 51 Habitats Regulations.
[161] reg.55 Habitats Regulations and see regs.65 to 67 on simplified planning zones and enterprise zones.
[162] Under s.106 Town and Country Planning Act 1990 and see 9.5 above.
[163] reg.56 Habitats Regulations.
[164] reg.57 Habitats Regulations, and see s.97 Town and Country Planning Act 1990 concerning the power to revoke or modify a planning permission and see s.102 concerning orders requiring the discontinuance of use.
[165] s.107 Town and Country Planning Act 1990, though where the Secretary of State decides not to confirm an order under s.97, any claim for compensation under s.107 will be limited to any loss or damage directly attributable to the permission being suspended or temporarily modified for the duration of the period between the making of the order and the Secretary of State determining not to confirm it. Where compensation is payable under s.107, the amount must be determined by the Lands Tribunal unless the Secretary of State indicates that this may be dispensed with (reg.59).

## 10.6.9 General Development Orders

As compared with 'other systems of control', a key point of contrast with the planning system arises because of the need to address developments that may be undertaken, without the need for explicit planning permission to be given, in accordance with general development orders.[166] This is met by a stipulation that any deemed planning permission granted by a general development order will not apply in relation to a development which is likely to have significant effect on a European site and is not directly connected with, or necessary to, the management of the site. Hence, developments of this kind may not commence until the development has actually received written notification of the approval of the local planning authority. Similar requirements apply for developments begun, but not completed, before commencement of the Regulations.[167] Where it is intended to carry out a development of this kind, an application must be made to the nature conservancy council for an opinion as to whether the development is likely to have a significant effect on the European site. The opinion of the council that a development is not likely to have a significant effect upon a site is conclusive for the purpose of reliance upon the planning permission granted by a general development order.[168]

## 10.6.10 Application of Assessment and Review Requirements

Although the theoretical extent of the duties to assess and review various kinds of consents and permission to ensure conformity with the requirements of the Habitats Directive are wide ranging, the practical application of these duties repays consideration. In respect of this, a couple of pertinent examples may be illuminating. Although both examples concern the disposal of spoil from dredging operations undertaken for navigational purposes, the implications for flood and coastal defence operations will be readily apparent.[169]

In the *Harwich Dredging* decision,[170] the Harwich Haven Authority sought

---

[166] See 9.4 above on general development orders.
[167] reg.60 Habitats Regulations. See also reg.62 concerning the procedure applicable for applications of this kind, which involves the local planning authority consulting the nature conservancy council and taking into account any representations made by the council.
[168] reg.61 Habitats Regulations.
[169] Compare the disposal of spoil from flood defence operations, discussed at 4.3.4 and 4.6.2 above.
[170] See Ports Division, Department of the Environment, Transport and the Regions, *Consents to Deposit Dredgings Required under s.34(1) of the Coast Protection Act 1949 and s.13(2) of the Harwich Harbour Act 1974*, 27 October 1998, and see Harwich Haven Authority, Press Release, 27 October 1998, *Harwich Deep Water Channel Deepening*.

permission from the Secretary of State to deepen approach channels to harbours, to accommodate larger container-ships, and to deposit the dredged material at various sites in tidal waters.[171] It was thought likely that the deepening of channels would increase erosion which would have a significant impact on nearby special protection areas under the Wild Birds Directive and the deposit of spoil would have an impact upon sites listed as of international importance under the Ramsar Convention.[172] Hence, both the harbour authority and the Secretary of State were bound to have regard to the requirements of the Habitats Directive in respect of the effects upon the sites.

A mitigation and monitoring package was devised including use of dredged material to recharge inter-tidal mudflats and creation of new inter-tidal habitat. English Nature submitted that if the package was successfully implemented there would be no adverse effect on the integrity of the special protection areas. The Secretary of State consented to the application on the basis that although the activities *would* result in an adverse effect on the special protection areas, this effect would be compensated for by measures outside the site. Moreover, there were no alternative solutions in relation to a project for which there were imperative reasons of overriding public interest given the critically important economic need to accommodate containerised seaborne trade by providing facilities for larger vessels. The Secretary of State was not obliged to seek the opinion of the European Commission because no priority habitats or priority species were involved.

The *Barksore Marshes* determination[173] was concerned with the revocation of a planning permission, following a review of existing permissions that were likely to affect European sites, undertaken in accordance with the 1994 Regulations.[174] The effect of the order, which had been made by a local authority, was to revoke a planning permission insofar as it allowed the reclamation of land for agricultural purposes and the prevention of flooding. This involved the deposit of river dredgings on an area which was

---

[171] Notably, the project was also subject to environmental impact assessment under the Harbour Works (Assessment of Environmental Effects) (No.2) Regulations 1989, S.I. 1989 No.424, as amended by S.I. 1996 No.1946, but now see Harbour Works (Environmental Impact Assessment) (Amendment) Regulations 2000, S.I. 2000 No.2391, and on environmental assessment generally see 9.14 above.

[172] See 10.4.6 above on the Ramsar Convention.

[173] *Application for the confirmation of The Kent County Council (Land at Barksore Marshes, Lower Halstow) Modification Order No.2 of 1997*, Inspector's Report (1998).

[174] Specifically, the proceedings were to consider the confirmation of an Order made by Kent County Council under s.97 Town and Country Planning Act 1990, pursuant to the requirements of reg.50 Habitats Regulations. See 10.6.8 above on the review of planning permissions.

designated as a site of special scientific interest, a special protection area, under the Wild Birds Directive, and as a site designated under the Ramsar Convention.

It was found that the continued deposition of dredgings would have adverse implications for the conservation objectives of the special protection area and to allow this would be contrary to the 1994 Regulations.[175] The Inspector was satisfied that alternative sites existed for the disposal of dredgings, though it was recognised that the use of these would involve higher costs. The Inspector did not accept that there were 'imperative reasons of overriding public interest' for the continued deposit of dredgings at the site so as to maintain navigation in the Port of Medway. It was concluded that an order revoking the planning permission should be confirmed and that decision was confirmed by the Secretary of State.

## 10.7 WATER LEVEL MANAGEMENT PLANS

A principal practical mechanism by which operating authorities are expected to discharge their responsibilities towards sites of special scientific interest and European sites is through the establishment of water level management plans. The basis for water level management plans was initially established under guidance issued in 1994.[176] The purpose of this guidance was to provide a means by which the water level requirements of a range of activities within a particular area, including agriculture, flood defence and conservation, could be balanced and integrated. It was envisaged that, subject to consultation with interested parties, flood defence operating authorities would establish plans for all sites of special scientific interest and European sites by the end of 1998. Although initial progress was unsatisfactory, the matter was made the subject of a high level target requiring plans to be established for such sites by the end of 2000 and programmes of implementation to be put in place by operating authorities by 1 April 2001.[177]

The guidance on water level management plans requires that they should eventually be prepared for all areas which have a conservation interest, and where the control of water levels is important to the maintenance or

---

[175] See reg.48(5) Habitats Regulations.

[176] Ministry of Agriculture, Fisheries and Food, Welsh Office, Association of Drainage Authorities, English Nature and National Rivers Authority, *Water Level Management Plans: a procedural guide for operating authorities* (1994) and see also Ministry of Agriculture, Fisheries and Food, *Water Level Management Plans: Additional Guidance Notes for Operating Authorities* (1999).

[177] See high level target 10 on water level management plans, and see also high level target 11 on coastal habitat management plans, and see 3.2.12 above on high level targets.

rehabilitation of that interest, though sites of special scientific interest and European sites are identified as a priority. Normally, the preparation of plans will be the responsibility of the flood defence operating authority with responsibility for the site; however, ultimate responsibility for sites of special scientific interest and European sites rests with the relevant nature conservancy council (English Nature or the Countryside Council for Wales). As a result of this, it is envisaged that the nature conservancy council will provide a detailed specification of the hydrological regime required for an area by indicating adequate water levels and flows in watercourses, the height of the water table in the growing season, the extent and duration of flooding and watercourse maintenance regimes.[178] Moreover, a plan prepared by an operating authority will not be considered complete until it has been signed by the relevant nature conservancy council to indicate its approval. The significance of that approval is that a plan is thought sufficient to maintain, through water level management, the interest of the area that justified its conservation designation. Similarly, approval by the conservancy council will be taken to show that the operating authority is doing what is necessary to comply with its conservation duties under the Wildlife and Countryside Act 1981, as amended, and the Conservation (Natural Habitats) Regulations 1994 in maintaining sites of special scientific interest and meeting favourable conservation status requirements for European sites. Beyond maintaining the conservation importance of sites, opportunities for enhancement may be provided for in plans, for example, where contributions are to be made towards biodiversity action plans for rare habitats or species.[179]

---

[178] General guidance on water level requirements for a range of wetland species is provided in English Nature, *Water Level Requirements of Selected Plants and Animals* (1997).

[179] See HM Government, *Biodiversity: the UK Action Plan* (1994).

## Chapter 11

# INFORMATION, WARNINGS AND INSURANCE

### 11.1 INTRODUCTION

Information on flooding is of vital importance. Its momentous implications were stressed by the House of Commons Agriculture Committee in 1998:

> 'our view is that much greater emphasis must be placed on the dissemination to the public of locally-appropriate information on the degree of risk to persons and to property presented by . . . natural processes. Our belief is that this is a fundamental component in any national strategy seeking to minimise the hazards posed by flooding and coastal erosion, and we are surprised that more effort in this direction has not been made by the relevant agencies. It is only on this basis that informed judgements can be made by the public as to the risks of development and the most appropriate method for managing flood and erosion risks at the individual level, leading to acceptance of ultimate responsibility for personal actions.'[1]

This chapter considers the role of information of various kinds in relation to flooding. Specifically, it examines the general responsibilities of public bodies to gather and provide information that may be relevant to flooding and, particularly, the role of the Environment Agency in disseminating public information including maps of property vulnerable to flooding and the implications of this. This is followed by discussion of the responsibilities of the Agency in relation to providing flood warnings along with the role of emergency services in responding to flooding incidents. The role of the Agency in relation to issuing flood warnings is contrasted with a range of other situations where a duty to warn against flood hazards is capable of arising. Finally, consideration is given to the general role of insurance in relation to flood damage and particular issues concerning the concept of a 'flood' as it features in insurance law and the significance of information provision in this context.

---

[1] House of Commons Agriculture Committee, Sixth Report Session 1997–98, *Flood and Coastal Defence* (1998) HC 707, para.92.

## 11.2 INFORMATION ACCESS

### 11.2.1 General Provisions

For most purposes concerning flood defence, the most likely source of information will be the Environment Agency. Remarkably, the Environment Agency is not subject to any explicit statutory duty, under the Water Resources Act 1991 or Environment Act 1995 at least, to provide general or particular information to the public about flooding.[2] However, statutory guidance on sustainable development makes it clear that the Agency should strive to provide and promulgate clear and readily accessible advice and information on its work and on best environmental practice.[3]

Nonetheless, the position of the Environment Agency, and other public bodies concerned with flood and coastal defence, must be seen in the light of a succession of generally applicable measures that impose duties to supply environmental and other kinds of information. Hence, access to environmental information, of all kinds, has been significantly enhanced by the European Community Environmental Information Directive.[4] The main object of the Directive is to ensure freedom of access to, and dissemination of, information on the environment held by public authorities and to set out the basic terms and conditions on which such information should be made available. Member States are also placed under a duty to provide general information to the public on the state of the environment by periodic publication of descriptive reports.

The Environmental Information Regulations 1992[5] implement the

---

[2] However, a need to provide certain flood defence information may arise incidentally from the duty upon the Agency to publish an Annual Report, under s.52 Environment Act 1995. See also s.51(1) to (3) requiring the Agency to furnish the appropriate Minister with all information that may reasonably be required. Provision of information may also fall within the incidental general functions of the Agency allowing it to do anything which is calculated to facilitate or is conducive or incidental to the carrying out of its functions (under s.37(1)(a) and see 3.4.12 above).

[3] See Department of the Environment, Ministry of Agriculture, Fisheries and Food and Welsh Office, *The Environment Agency and Sustainable Development* (1996), containing statutory guidance given pursuant to s.4(3) of the Environment Act 1995, and on the Agency's contribution to sustainable development, and see discussion at 3.4.2 above.

[4] Directive 90/313/EEC on freedom of access to information on the environment, see House of Lords Committee on the European Communities, *Freedom of Access to Information on the Environment*, First Report Session 1989–90 (1990) HL Paper 2 and First Report Session 1996–97 (1996) HL Paper 9 and for general discussion see G. Bakkenist, *Environmental Information: Law, Policy and Experience* (1994).

[5] S.I. 1992 No.3240 and see Environmental Information (Amendment) Regulations 1998, S.I. 1998 No.1447, and see Department of the Environment, *Freedom of Access to Information on the Environment: Guidance on the Implementation of the Environmental Information Regulations 1992 in Great Britain* (1992).

Environmental Information Directive by requiring that a 'relevant person', who holds any information which relates to the environment, must make that information available to any person who requests it. 'Relevant persons' are Ministers of the Crown, Government departments, local authorities and other persons carrying out functions of public administration at a national, regional or local level, who have responsibilities in relation to the environment.[6] Also, every Minister, Government department and public body is deemed to have responsibilities relating to the environment in respect of countryside and landscape issues.[7] Hence, a range of bodies likely to possess information relating to flood and coastal defence would be encompassed, including the Department for Environment, Food and Rural Affairs, the National Assembly for Wales, the Environment Agency and other operating authorities. These bodies are subject to a basic obligation to make environmental information available to enquirers, within 2 months, or to state the reasons for refusal to do so. Refusal may be allowed where the request for information is manifestly unreasonable or formulated in too general a manner, otherwise the request will have to fall within specified exceptions.[8] The exceptions apply where information *may* be treated as confidential because, for example, its disclosure would affect national defence or legal proceedings, or for reasons of confidentiality. In other situations certain kinds of information *must* be treated as confidential if, for example, disclosure would contravene a statutory provision, where it is personal information or supplied voluntarily, or where the disclosure would increase the likelihood of damage to the environment to which the information relates.[9]

Alongside the provisions specifically concerning *environmental* information, for the future, access to flood defence information will be covered by the Freedom of Information Act 2000. Broadly, the 2000 Act creates a statutory public right of access to recorded information, of any kind, held by public authorities and specifies the conditions under which

---

[6] regs.2(2), (3) and 3(1) Environmental Information Regulations 1992.
[7] Under s.11 Countryside Act 1968, which provides that, in the exercise of their functions relating to land under any enactment every Minister, government department and public body shall have regard to the desirability of conserving the natural beauty and amenity of the countryside and, for these purposes, a 'public body' is defined to include any local authority or statutory undertaker, and any trustees, commissioners, board or other person, who, as a public body and not for their own profit, act under any enactment for the improvement of any place or the production or supply of any commodity or service (and see Department of the Environment, *Guidance on the Implementation of the Environmental Information Regulations 1992 in Great Britain* (1992) para.11).
[8] reg.3 Environmental Information Regulations 1992.
[9] reg.4 Environmental Information Regulations 1992, as amended by Environmental Information (Amendment) Regulations 1988, S.I. 1998 No.1447.

an authority is obliged to allow access. Generally, public authorities are required to disclose information that is requested, normally within 20 working days, though they will be entitled to charge fees for providing information and must state the basis for refusal of a request where information is not provided. However, in relation to categories of 'exempt information' the disclosure requirements will not apply. A fairly lengthy list of exemptions are provided for in relation to matters concerning national security, defence and international relations, safety of the individual and the public, the integrity of decision-making and policy advice processes, commercial interests, law enforcement and the protection of personal information and information supplied in confidence. The exercise of the right of access to information is regulated by an Information Commissioner and appeals will be possible to an Information Tribunal or to a court where a point of law is at issue. Perhaps most significantly, the 2000 Act creates rights of access to *all kinds of information* held by public authorities and this is not limited to *environmental* information covered by the Environmental Information Regulations.

### 11.2.2 Environment Agency Information

The general provisions on access to information, previously described, may allow an individual to gain access to relatively detailed flood defence information, which is not made generally available. Hence, where a specific request for information is made, the Environment Agency is bound to provide the information unless it falls within the specified categories of exemption. However, most commonly, the information that is likely to be sought is whether a particular property, often the enquirer's home, is vulnerable to flooding. The capacity of the Agency, or any other public body concerned with flood defence, to provide information of this kind is inevitably dictated by whether it actually possesses the information that is being sought.

The duty upon the Environment Agency to *gather* information relating to flood defence arises from a tersely worded statutory requirement that, for the purpose of carrying out its flood defence functions, it must 'from time to time carry out surveys of the areas in relation to which it carries out those functions'.[10] Although concisely expressed, the implications of this duty are far-ranging. Given the duty of the Agency to exercise a general *supervision* of all matters relating to flood defence,[11] its functions would

---

[10] s.105(2) Water Resources Act 1991. See E. C. Penning-Rowsell, D. J. Parker and D. M. Harding, *Floods and Drainage* (1986) p.79 for a discussion of the difficulties that water authorities experienced in producing flooding and land drainage surveys under previous legislation (s.24(5) Water Act 1973). See also P. Bye and M. Horner, *Easter 1998 Floods* (1998) para.4.5.

[11] Under s.6(4) Environment Act 1995 and see 3.4.7 above on this duty.

seem to be exercised in any context where the supervision of flood defence works by a public body or private person is, or might be, involved. Essentially, therefore, the duty applies throughout the area of the Agency and is not restricted to main rivers or locations where the Agency is itself undertaking flood defence operations. However, the obligation to conduct surveys 'from time to time' leaves a great deal of discretion as to the manner in which the duty is exercised, the information which is sought, the frequency with which it is gathered and the form in which it is made available. Nonetheless, information resulting from the surveys that are undertaken will be of critical importance to many property owners, or prospective property purchasers, who may be anxious to know the flood risk associated with a particular location. It is also information which will be of vital importance to local planning authorities in formulating development plans or determining whether a particular application for planning permission will be granted or not.[12]

Information about the propensity of a particular area of land to flood is now available on the Environment Agency's website,[13] where indicative flood plain maps provide an overview of flood risk by showing natural river and coastal flood plains in England and Wales. The river flood plains (coloured blue) include all areas known to face at least a one in one hundred (or 1%) chance of flooding each year and the coastal floodplains (coloured green) show areas facing a one in two hundred (or a 0.5%) chance of flooding each year. The maps can be searched by postcode or grid reference, allowing householders to gain relevant local information about fluvial and sea flooding in their area, but the maps do not distinguish degrees of risk. Moreover, the Agency stresses the limitations of the maps, in that there are significant variable factors which cannot be displayed in the website format, and suggests that enquirers seeking more detailed information should make further enquiries. It is especially important to note that the maps do not indicate those areas in which flood defences are actually provided, and clearly these will give satisfactory protection to properties in many areas that are otherwise vulnerable. On the other hand, it is recognised that the degree of protection will vary because defences have been built to differing standards over time and in view of local circumstances.

Despite all the limitations of indicative flood plain maps, the provision of internet access to information of this kind is of momentous importance.

---

[12] See Ch.9 above on planning law generally.
[13] http://www.environment-agency.gov.uk. Another source of online information about flooding and other adversities to which property may be subject is the Homecheck website provided by Sitescope Ltd: http://www.homecheck.co.uk. On flood plain mapping generally see Association of British Insurers, *Inland Flooding Risk – Issues Facing the Insurance Industry* (2000) Chs.4 and 5.

Although, the fact that a house is liable to flooding is not likely to be information that a person who is trying to sell the house will welcome having publicised, it is information that in the long-term is beneficially placed in the public domain. In the past, pressure for development of unsuitable sites for residential properties may have been fuelled by the confidence of developers that they would have no difficulty in selling the properties to largely unsuspecting buyers. Given the facility for access to critically important information which is now made possible, prospective purchasers are likely to be significantly more circumspect in relation to flooding concerns. The practical effect of highlighting, and perhaps stigmatising, locations that are vulnerable to flooding should be to deter further development in those areas since it will not be in the commercial interests of developers to build houses that few people will wish to buy. Whereas the land-use planning system may have had its limitations in preventing inappropriate development in the past, the property market, furnished with relevant information, now has a clear economic incentive to avoid such development.

Alongside the internet publication of indicative flood plain maps, the Environment Agency has been active in publicising the general problems associated with flooding risk to householders by 'self-help' information and other means. In 1999 the Agency launched a £2 million 'Floodline' campaign, addressed to an estimated 1.3 million householders and others with properties at risk, to raise public awareness of the dangers of flooding and to provide practical advice as to the steps that should be taken to prevent flooding and to reduce threats to persons and property.[14]

## 11.3 ENVIRONMENT AGENCY FLOOD WARNINGS

### 11.3.1 Flood Warning Systems

Along with the general information about the flooding propensities of particular areas of land, the Environment Agency has responsibility for the operation of flood warning systems for the purpose of providing information about imminent flooding incidents. Hence, the Agency is empowered to provide and operate flood warning systems, to provide, install and maintain apparatus required for the purposes of such systems, and to carry out any other engineering or building operations so required.[15] A 'flood warning

---

[14] See Environment Agency, *Floodline* information pack (1999 updated).
[15] s.166(1) Water Resources Act 1991. However, the powers in relation to flood warning systems are not to be construed as authorising any act or omission by the Agency which would be actionable at the suit of any person on any grounds other than a limitation imposed on the capacity of the Agency by its constitution (s.166(2)). Subject to specified conditions, the power to provide, install and maintain apparatus may be exercised by the Agency in Scotland (s.166(3)).

system' is any system for the purpose of providing warning of any danger of flooding, whereby information with respect to:

(a) rainfall, including any fall of snow, hail or sleet, as measured at a particular place within a particular period;

(b) the level of flow of any inland water, or part of an inland water at a particular time; or

(c) other matters appearing to the Agency to be relevant for that purpose,

is obtained and transmitted, whether automatically or otherwise, with or without provision for carrying out calculations based on such information and for transmitting the results of those calculations.[16] Notably, although the statutory provisions seem to place emphasis upon river flooding, they also encompass 'any danger of flooding' and this would seem to encompass flooding from main rivers and ordinary watercourses. Similarly, there is nothing to indicate that flooding from the sea is excluded.

## 11.3.2 The Flood Warning Direction

Two kinds of ministerial direction to the Environment Agency are statutorily provided for. The first of these is a power of the Ministers to give general or specific directions to the Agency with respect to the carrying out of any of its functions, particularly where this is necessary to implement European Community or international obligations. Directions of this kind are binding upon the Agency, but the power to issue such directions, except in an emergency, may only be exercised after consultation with the Agency.[17]

The second kind of ministerial direction is provided for in relation to civil emergencies. Hence, the appropriate Minister, after consultation with the Agency, may give the Agency directions of a general character that are requisite or expedient in the interests of national security or for the purpose of mitigating the effects of any civil emergency which may occur. Similarly, the Minister may direct the Agency to do any particular thing specified in a direction. Where a direction of this kind has been given, the Agency is under a duty to comply with it, notwithstanding any other duty imposed upon it, under the Water Resources Act 1991 or otherwise. For these purposes, any reference to a 'civil emergency' is a reference to any

---

[16] s.148(5) Water Resources Act 1991. 'Inland water' means any of the following in any part of Great Britain: (a) any river, stream or other watercourse, whether natural or artificial and whether tidal or not; (b) any lake or pond, whether natural or artificial, and any reservoir or dock; (c) any channel, creek, bay, estuary or arm of the sea. See 6.3.3 above on ministerial grants towards the cost of flood warning systems.

[17] Under s.40 Environment Act 1995.

natural disaster or other emergency which is likely, in any area, to disrupt water supplies or sewerage services or to involve such destruction of life or damage to property as seriously and adversely to affect a substantial number of the inhabitants of the area whether by depriving them of any of the essentials of life or otherwise.[18] Corresponding powers are given to the Ministers to allow directions to be given to water and sewerage undertakers in the interests of national security or to mitigate a civil emergency.[19]

A direction of the first kind was issued to the former National Rivers Authority in 1996 concerning its general flood defence functions and its power to provide flood warning systems.[20] This required the Authority, and now the Agency, to ensure that area offices maintain a written record of arrangements, circumstances and means by which warnings of the danger of flooding in the area will be transmitted. Pursuant to the establishment of flood warning arrangements, consultation was required with bodies providing emergency services and local authorities in the area. The central, and continuing, obligation under the Direction, however, is that the Agency is bound to take such steps as are reasonable and practicable to provide a warning of any danger of flooding. The effect of this was to transfer obligations to issue flood warnings, previously upon the police, to the Agency, without detracting from the obligation upon other individuals, organisations or authorities to take appropriate actions in respect of flooding or to provide responses in a situation of flooding emergency.[21] Moreover, the Agency is subject to a qualified *duty* to *issue* flood warnings, though this stands awkwardly alongside the permissive *power* of the Agency to *operate* flood warning systems.[22]

---

[18] s.207(1) to (3) and (7) Water Resources Act 1991. Generally see N. Stanley, 'Civil Emergencies and the Water Industry' [1994] *Water Law* 99.
[19] s.208 Water Industry Act 1991; s.152 Water Industry Act 1991 allows the Secretary of State to make grants to water or sewerage undertakers for the purpose of defraying or contributing towards any losses they may sustain by reason of complying with directions of this kind. Curiously, since the repeal of s.150 Water Resources Act 1991 by Schedule 22 para.156 Environment Act 1995, there is now no corresponding provision under the Water Resources Act 1991 allowing grants to be made to the Environment Agency, but it must be assumed that the power to make grants in relation to emergency directions is provided by the general power of the appropriate Minister to make grants to the Agency 'of such amounts, and on such terms, as he thinks fit' (under s.47 Environment Act 1995, and see 6.3.1 above).
[20] Ministry of Agriculture, Fisheries and Food, and Welsh Office, *Water Resources Act 1991, Section 5: Direction to the National Rivers Authority* (signed on behalf of the respective Ministers on 1 and 5 March 1996); s. 5 of the Water Resources Act 1991, now repealed, broadly corresponded to s.40 Environment Act 1995.
[21] See 11.3.4 below in relation to emergency response obligations.
[22] See 11.3.1 above on the power relating to flood warning systems.

### 11.3.3 Environment Agency Flood Warning Practice

Although the issuing of a flood warning by the Environment Agency may be commonly seen as a definitive 'public' event, in reality it is the cumulative act in a sequence of procedures which involve widespread monitoring and gathering of background information, the evaluation of this information, the publication of the warning and the activation of any necessary emergency response. Hence, from the Agency's perspective, a 'flood warning *service*' comprises:

(a) the constant monitoring of weather, catchment and coastal conditions;

(b) the prediction of future river and sea levels;

(c) preparation of warnings for locations at which forecast levels might result in flooding;

(d) dissemination of warnings to those at risk and to operational organisations; and

(e) an emergency response by those organisations, the Agency and the public.[23]

The monitoring process is conducted by a range of remote detection systems that are used to measure rainfall, water level, flow and wind conditions. This information is collected from weather radar and storm tide forecasts provided by the Meteorological Office, weather satellites and various local monitoring systems.

The translation of the diverse body of relevant information into a specific flood warning relies upon a variety of forecasting methods, from simple extrapolation from upstream river levels to sophisticated computer models. However, warnings need to be issued swiftly, since the 'warning lead time' is a significant determinant of how much damage can be avoided. The limitations of the present service provided by the Agency are recognised in that it is restricted to main rivers, estuaries and the coast, and does not generally cover ordinary watercourses and local flooding from sewers, road drainage, overland flow, dam bursts or blockages.[24] In addition, the

---

[23] Generally see Environment Agency, *Flood Warning Service Strategy for England and Wales* (1999) and National Audit Office, *Inland Flood Defence* (2001) HC 299, paras.2.15 to 2.26.

[24] But see 3.4.8 above on 'critical ordinary watercourses'. Notably there was public dissatisfaction because the majority of people affected by the Easter 1998 floods did not receive any form of direct flood warning since their areas had not been identified as high risk locations. However, in those areas that had been identified as 'high risk', flood warnings were issued to 65% of persons at least 2 hours before flooding took place (see P. Bye and M. Horner, *Easter 1998 Floods* (1998) para.5.7(2)).

progressive improvement of the service is dependent upon funding from the Department for the Environment, Food and Rural Affairs and the National Assembly for Wales, though these bodies have recognised that flood warning is the 'highest priority' in relation to funding.[25]

The actual issuing of a flood warning is the responsibility of the Agency, which must alert those at risk of flooding, the emergency services, local authorities and flood defence authorities. This involves a range of direct and indirect methods. Direct methods include automatic voice and fax messaging, warning sirens, public address systems and communications from flood wardens. Indirect methods include bulletins being issued by the media. Clearly, to be effective, it is necessary that flood warnings are readily understood by those to whom they are addressed. With this objective in mind, the Environment Agency has devised a flood warning system which comprises four levels of warning, indicated as follows:[26]

*Flood Watch* – Flooding possible. Be aware! Be prepared! Watch out!

*Flood Warning* – Flooding expected affecting homes, businesses and main roads. Act now!

*Severe Flood Warning* – Severe flooding expected. Imminent danger to life and property. Act now!

*All Clear* – An all clear will be issued when flood watches or warnings are no longer in force.

Co-ordination of the Agency's flood warning service is undertaken by a National Flood Warning Centre, established in 2000, to provide information to the public about flood warnings and related information concerning all aspects of flooding. The Agency's 'Floodline' service[27] provides information on the latest flooding situation in different parts of England and Wales, though summaries of this information are also widely broadcast by the media. However, a more proactive approach is also being taken insofar as the Agency is seeking the permission of householders in some areas to send them flood warning messages through the Agency's 'Automatic Voice Messaging System'. This system communicates flood warnings by making an automatic telephone call to the homes or offices of those registered under the system as soon as a flood warning is issued in their area.[28]

---

[25] See 3.2.6 above on funding priorities.
[26] See Environment Agency website, http://www.environment-agency.gov.uk.
[27] Telephone number: 0845 988 1188.
[28] See Environment Agency Press Release, 22 July 2001, *Environment Agency urges public to sign up to flood warning system now*.

## Environment Agency Flood Warnings

At a strategic level, the Agency has formulated a number of goals for the improvement of flood warning systems which it seeks to secure in the medium and long term. Specifically, the long-term goal is that people living in medium to high flood risk areas will receive a full flood warning service and a 2-hour prior flood warning. In the medium term this will involve progress in implementing automatic warning messages to commercial properties; extending coverage of flood warning services to all medium and high risk areas, completion of planned improvements, and further review of the network of monitoring systems; and the development and implementation of new public alert systems within residential properties.[29] Pursuant to this, specific targets have been set to the effect that 58% of properties in flood risk areas will receive a warning service by 2001, rising to 70% in 2003.[30]

### 11.3.4 Emergency Response Obligations

Clearly, the issue of a flood warning by the Environment Agency is the precursor to a range of preventative actions and operations being taken, by a diverse range of individuals and bodies, to avert loss of life and damage to property from flooding.[31] An emergency operational response to a flood warning involves co-ordinated action by a wide range of bodies including the police service, fire service and local authority services.

Broadly, the police service is responsible for co-ordinating the emergency services at a major flooding incident, establishing cordons to facilitate the work of the other services, and generally protecting the public and assisting flood victims. Local authorities are responsible for co-ordinating emergency plans of other local bodies and providing an immediate response in caring for those affected by a flood. This may involve the provision of food, transport, accommodation and welfare services for persons who have been evacuated; the provision of equipment and material such as sandbags; flood alleviation measures such as the clearing of blocked culverts; and the co-ordination of any voluntary bodies that are involved. The fire service has responsibilities for rescuing trapped persons; containing and extinguishing fires; assisting the ambulance and police services with casualties; and carrying out essential damage control operations such as the pumping out of flood water and salvage works. In addition, responses

---

[29] Environment Agency, *A Framework for Change: Reducing Flood Risk* (2001) p.7. See also Environment Agency, *Environment Agency Response to the Independent Report on the Easter 1998 Floods* (1998).
[30] Environment Agency, *Corporate Plan 2001/2002* (2001) p.49.
[31] Generally see Home Office, *Dealing with Disasters* (3rd ed. 1997); F. Bye and M. Horner, *Easter 1998 Floods* (1998) Ch.5; and Environment Agency, *Flood Defence Emergency Response (FEDR) Project* (1999).

may be required by flood defence authorities to ensure the continuous and effective operation of drainage pumping stations and the inspection of sensitive locations for blockages. Also, public utilities will be required to secure their services and equipment to ensure continuity of supply or to provide alternative means of supply during disruption of services.[32]

The legal context to the range of actions that may be taken in response to a flood warning arises under diverse legislation under which bodies involved in an emergency response operate. Of particular significance is the Local Government Act 1972, which gives important powers to local authorities with respect to emergencies or disasters. Hence, where an emergency or disaster involving destruction of or danger to life or property occurs, or is imminent, or reasonably apprehended, and a principal council is of the opinion that it is likely to affect the whole or part of its area or all or some of its inhabitants, specified actions are allowed. In particular, the council may incur such expenditure as is reasonable in taking action, either alone or jointly with any other person or body either in its area or elsewhere, which is calculated to avert, alleviate or eradicate the effects, or potential effects, of the event. Also, the council may make grants or loans to other persons or bodies on conditions determined by the council in respect of any such action taken by those persons or bodies. With the consent of the Secretary of State, a metropolitan county fire and civil defence authority and the London Fire and Emergency Planning authority may incur expenditure in co-ordinating planning by principal councils in connection with their functions in relation to their emergency or disaster powers.[33]

Where it is appropriate for a principal council to undertake 'contingency planning' to deal with a possible emergency or disaster which would involve destruction of or danger to life or property and would be likely to affect the whole or part of its area, it may incur such expenditure as is necessary on such planning. Expenditure of this kind may relate to a specific kind of emergency or disaster, or generally in relation to possible emergencies and the taking of action accordingly to avert, alleviate or eradicate the effects of the event. For these purposes, 'contingency planning' means the making, keeping under review and revising of plans

---

[32] See Environment Agency, *Flood Warning Service Strategy for England and Wales* (1999) Annex 2 and Environment Agency, *Flood Defence Emergency Response (FEDR) Project* (1999).

[33] s.138(1) and (5) Local Government Act 1972, as amended by s.156 Local Government and Housing Act 1989 and Schedule 29 para.16 Greater London Authority Act 1999. A 'principal council' includes the Common Council of the City of London and, until 1 April 1974, the council of an existing county, county borough or county district (s.138(4)).

for the carrying out of training associated with the plans.[34]

However, it is stipulated that the emergency or disaster and contingency planning powers do not authorise a local authority to take certain actions in relation to flood defence. Specifically, the emergency powers do not allow any drainage works or other works to be undertaken in any part of a main river[35] or a river which is treated as a main river under the Water Resources Act 1991 or any works that local authorities have powers to execute under the Land Drainage Act 1991.[36] Subject to these limitations, however, the emergency and contingency planning powers are stated to be in addition to, and not in derogation from, any power conferred upon a local authority under any other enactment.[37]

Related to the power of local authorities to incur expenditure in respect of emergencies and disasters is the power of the Minister to provide emergency financial assistance to local authorities under the 'Bellwin Scheme'. Hence, in any case where an emergency or disaster occurs, and a local authority incurs expenditure in taking immediate action to safeguard life or property or to prevent suffering or inconvenience, the Minister may establish a scheme for giving financial assistance in respect of that expenditure. Expenditure incurred by the Greater London Authority is similarly treated where it arises from expenditure by the London Fire and Emergency Planning Authority, the Metropolitan Police Authority or Transport for London. Emergency financial assistance of this kind is payable as a grant by the Minister, with the consent of the Treasury, subject to terms and conditions which are appropriate to the circumstances of the emergency and grants may be made conditional upon specified claims being made and other matters.[38]

---

[34] s.138(1A) and (6) Local Government Act 1972, as amended by s.156 Local Government and Housing Act 1989.
[35] See 3.4.8 above on 'main rivers'.
[36] That is, works which may be executed under ss.14 to 17, 62(2) and 66 Land Drainage Act 1991.
[37] s.138(3) Local Government Act 1972, as amended by s.156 Local Government and Housing Act 1989 and Schedule 1 para.22(2) Water Consolidation (Consequential Provisions) Act 1991.
[38] s.155 Local Government and Housing Act 1989, as amended. For these purposes, grants may be made to bodies including county councils, county borough councils, district councils, the Greater London Authority, a London borough council, the Common Council of the City of London, a police authority established under s.3 Police Act 1996 (s.155(4) Local Government and Housing Act 1989, as amended). Presently the operation of the Bellwin Scheme is the subject of consultation: see Department of Transport, Local Government and the Regions, *Bellwin Scheme of Emergency Financial Assistance to Local Authorities: Report of the Review Group* (2001).

At the time of writing, the general provision for emergency planning appears to be on the eve of transition.[39] A Cabinet Office Discussion Document[40] indicates that the Autumn 2000 flooding has prompted a review of emergency planning arrangements, and the Government has concluded that the Civil Defence Act 1948 no longer provides an adequate framework and that new legislation is required. Significant parts of the 1948 Act relate to the protection of the population against a hostile attack, whereas present perceptions of threats, such as that of climate change, are significantly different. The present provision for response arrangements are largely determined at local level and differ significantly between different undertakings. The Discussion Document is, therefore, premised upon the need for greater consistency in the national delivery of emergency services including a new statutory 'leadership' role in emergency planning on the part of local authorities and a duty to share in 'partnership arrangements' by the emergency services and the Environment Agency.

### 11.3.5 Negligence and Flood Warnings

The qualified duty to issue flood warnings upon the Environment Agency is a matter of some gravity. The consequences of failing to issue a flood warning, or excessive delay in issuing a flood warning and, perhaps, even issuing a flood warning where none is needed, are capable of having major consequences for those depending upon the information which is provided, or not provided, as the case may be. Specifically, where a person is not warned of the prospect of a flood which actually occurs, and is thereby prevented from taking measures which would otherwise have been taken to protect persons or property from flooding, the legal issue is whether that failure to warn is capable of constituting negligence on the part of the body that is responsible for giving flood warnings.

Although responsibilities for giving flood warnings are now differently allocated, the facts and reasoning in *Robinson* v *Cardiff City Council*[41] are especially pertinent and illuminating as to the law regarding failures to give appropriate warnings. Here the claimants were the owners of properties that had suffered damage from flooding and who claimed compensation

---

[39] Generally see Civil Defence Act 1948 and Civil Defence in Peacetime Act 1986, and Civil Defence (Grant) Regulations 1953, S.I. 1953 No.1777, as amended, and Civil Defence (General Local Authority Functions) Regulations 1993, S.I. 1993 No.1812.
[40] Cabinet Office, *The Future of Emergency Planning in England and Wales* (2001).
[41] Unreported, 16 October 1987, Cardiff Crown Court. For discussion of the background to this case see D. J. Parker, 'Legal and Administrative Arrangements for Flood Warnings in England and Wales: the Case for Change' (1989) unpublished paper delivered at the World Conference on Water Law and Administration, Alicante, Spain, December 1989 (available from Flood Hazard Research Centre, Middlesex University).

# Environment Agency Flood Warnings 463

for this damage and, in some instances, damages for consequent distress and inconvenience. An action in negligence was brought against three defendants: the Cardiff City Council, the South Glamorgan County Council and the Welsh Water Authority. It was alleged that the claimants had received no warning of the impending invasion of their properties by flood water and were thereby deprived of the opportunity of transferring their movable property to a place where it would be safe from damage. Moreover, the failure of the defendants to issue a timely flood warning constituted a basis for liability in negligence.

The underlying factual situation in the *Robinson* case was somewhat complicated, and disputed between the defendants, since, following a reorganisation of local government and because of other factors, the formal status of a plan governing flood emergency procedures was uncertain. In particular, it was not clear whether the City authority or the County authority was responsible for advising the police that a flood warning should be issued so as to activate emergency procedures, including public warnings. The lack of co-ordination between the City and County authorities had the consequence that a flood warning was not issued until some time after properties had actually been flooded and it was no longer possible for preventative measures to be taken against damage.

On the question of whether the facts constituted negligence, it was necessary to show that the defendants owed a duty to the claimants, that there had been a breach of this duty and that the breach caused, or contributed to, the claimants' loss. On the issue of duty, it was noted that the powers of local authorities with respect to emergencies or disasters allowed a local authority to take actions where an emergency or disaster involving destruction or danger to life or properties occurred, or was reasonably apprehended, and to incur expenditure in taking such action.[42] Also, statutory provision was made for a duty upon the water authority to assist local authorities in taking actions of this kind.[43]

The test that was applied to ascertain whether a duty of care arises on the part of a public body exercising a power to act is whether it is 'fair and reasonable' that such a duty should arise.[44] In determining what was 'fair and reasonable', issues of foreseeability, proximity, public policy and discretion needed to be taken into consideration. In the context that was at

---
[42] s.138 Local Government Act 1972; and see 11.3.4 on emergency response obligations.
[43] Under s.28 Water Act 1973; now see s.207 Water Resources Act 1991, concerning directions to the Environment Agency in the interests of national security, at 11.3.2 above.
[44] Following Lord Morris of Borth-y-Gest in *Home Office* v *Dorset Yacht Co Ltd* [1970] AC 1004 at p.1039.

issue, foreseeability and proximity were not thought to present any obstacle in finding a duty of care, and public policy did not call for any relief of the local authorities from that duty.[45] In respect of the degree of 'discretion' allowed, it was noted that public bodies have such discretion where powers, though not duties, are imposed upon them. However, a contrast of degree should be drawn between policy and operational matters, so that the more 'operational' a power is the more likely it is that a duty of care will arise.[46]

In the circumstances, it was found that there was a duty upon the two local authorities. In effect, this was a twofold duty comprised of a 'prior duty' to take reasonable steps to establish an effective flood warning plan and a 'duty on the day' to take reasonable steps to ensure communication of a public warning to persons in the endangered areas. Moreover, the failure to exercise these duties properly, and particularly the failure to give a timely flood warning, was a sufficiently 'operational' matter to constitute a breach of duty.

On the facts, it was found that the responsibility to issue a flood warning fell upon the City authority, under a flood emergency plan that had never been formally superseded and, therefore, the City authority should bear the greater part of the liability. However, the County authority was also liable because of 'inexcusably insufficient co-operation and co-ordination' through its failure to satisfy itself as to what arrangements were operative in the event of a flooding emergency. Liability was apportioned between these two defendants, with the City authority being found two-thirds liable and the County authority one-third liable. The water authority was found not to be liable because it was found not to be responsible for the issuing of flood warnings or other acts of neglect. Although arguments had been raised that the authority had failed to give sufficiently detailed advice on the effect of tides on flooding, it was found that this advice would not have caused the City authority to have acted any differently, and the argument failed on the issue of causation.

Clearly, the responsibilities for issuing flood warnings are differently allocated today, and a contemporary dispute of this kind would concern the circumstances in which the Environment Agency might be found to have acted negligently in failing to issue a flood warning. As has been seen, there is a general reluctance on the part of the courts to impose liability for

---

[45] Although contrasts were drawn with *Hill* v *Chief Constable of West Yorkshire* [1987] WLR 1126, where the police were held to owe no duty of care towards individual potential victims of crime.

[46] Citing Lord Wilberforce in *Anns* v *Merton London Borough* [1978] AC 728 at p.754.

negligence in circumstances where a public body has failed to exercise a statutory *power*, as opposed to a *duty*, to act. In most instances, liability tends to be restricted to situations where the public body has done something which has actually exacerbated the damage.[47]

In recent decisions concerning the actions of emergency services, this principle has been widely applied, so that, in a situation where the police provided an unsatisfactory response to a '999' telephone call, they were found to owe no specific duty of care towards the individual caller, as opposed to the general duty owed to the public at large.[48] By contrast, an ambulance service has been found to owe a duty to an individual member of the public, which was breached where it failed to provide an agreed response with sufficient expedition, in circumstances where there was no reasonable justification for the delay. These decisions are somewhat difficult to reconcile but, on the face of things, the duty upon the Environment Agency to provide flood warnings seems to be a duty to the public at large, or at least a broad section of the public, rather than a duty to any individual member of the public. Hence, the likelihood of a duty of care arising in relation to individuals who are prevented from taking preventative action through the Agency's negligent failure to issue a flood warning seems remote.

On the other hand, the peculiar legal formulation of the Agency's responsibility to provide flood warnings may be significant. As has been observed,[49] the ministerial Flood Warning Direction given to the Agency is formulated as a *duty*, rather than a *power*, to take reasonable and practicable steps to provide flood warnings. By contrast, the Agency has a *power*, rather than a *duty*, to provide flood warning systems in the first place. Hence, in principle, if the Agency chose not to establish any flood warning systems it would not be liable for that failure, but if it did establish a flood warning system it would be in breach of the duty under the Direction if it failed to issue a particular flood warning where it was reasonably practicable to do so. Perhaps the critical question is as to whom the duty under the Direction is owed. Alternatively, it might be owed to individual members of the public or to the Minister who gave the Direction. On this, a speculative suggestion is that the duty to adhere to the Direction is owed to the Minister, or perhaps to the public at large, but not to any

---

[47] See discussion of *East Suffolk Rivers Catchment Board* v *Kent* [1940] 4 All ER 527, at 4.3.1 above; and see the discussion of liability of statutory bodies at 2.9 above.

[48] *Alexandrou* v *Oxford* [1993] 4 All ER 987. Similarly, see *Capital and Counties plc* v *Hampshire County Council* [1997] 2 All ER 865 (on the extent of the duty upon a fire brigade) and *OLL Ltd* v *Secretary of State for Transport* [1997] 3 All ER 987 (on the duty upon coastguards in making rescues at sea).

[49] See 11.3.2 above on the flood warning direction.

individual member of the public who suffers as a result of a negligent failure on the part of the Agency to issue a particular flood warning.

In the absence of any direct authority, the legal position of the Agency in respect of negligent failure to issue a flood warning seems to be that it would not be liable to an individual as a consequence. It is not possible to affirm this view with complete confidence, but at the very least the decision in the *Robinson* case needs to be read with some caution. Although it provides a unique and pertinent insight into the possibilities for negligence in respect of flood warnings, there are reasons to question whether it would be followed if analogous facts were to arise today.

## 11.4 OTHER KINDS OF FLOOD WARNING

Although there is a tendency to assimilate the term 'flood warning' with the particular function exercised by the Environment Agency in the event of an impending flood, there are actually a range of situations where public bodies or even private individuals may become subject to a duty to warn others of flood-related hazards of various kinds. In most respects, the legal issues fall to be determined as aspects of negligence, but from a factual viewpoint the situations are wide ranging. For example, there may be a duty upon public bodies or private individuals to warn others of the *propensity* of land to flood, rather than about any particular flooding incident. Notably, this duty is capable of arising between those who advise on the flooding potential of land and those who suffer the consequences, or between a seller and buyer in a property transaction involving land that is vulnerable to flooding. Alternatively, there may be situations where public bodies or private individuals have responsibility for, or ownership of, land onto which others have access and where a duty arises to warn those entering the land of a flooding hazard on the land. The range of possibilities in negligence is open-ended, but some examples may illustrate a few of the situations where issues of this kind have arisen in the past.

### 11.4.1 Warnings of the Propensity of Land to Flood

In relation to the public duty to warn of the propensity of land to flood, the decision of the Privy Council in *Christchurch Drainage Board* v *Brown and Others*,[50] on appeal from New Zealand, is instructive. The proceedings, in negligence, were brought by the owners of a property that had been flooded on successive occasions so that they had been obliged to raise the level of the ground floor of the property to prevent the recurrence of flooding. The claimants sought to recover the cost of this work, initially,

---

[50] (1987) *The Times* 14 September.

## Other Kinds of Flood Warning

from the local authority who had given permission for a property, which was 'doomed to be flooded', to be built and from the drainage board which failed to warn that the building was below known flood levels.

On appeal, against a finding that the drainage board was liable for the full amount of damages, it was noted that there were several unsatisfactory procedural aspects of the case. In particular, the drainage board had failed to plead contributory negligence, on the part of the claimants, and the lower court had declined leave to amend the proceedings to allow this, though it was suggested that, had the plea been allowed, the damages would have been reduced by two-thirds. This was because the claimants had been aware of the flood danger and had been 'foolish' not to ask the drainage board to check the flood levels. Similarly, the local authority had been 'foolish' not to refer the application for building permission to the drainage board with an express request to check the flood levels. Likewise, the drainage board had been 'foolish' not to check the application, in accordance with its usual practice, and had submitted an 'uninformative' explanation as to why this had not happened.

Despite the unsatisfactory procedural and evidential features, the question for determination was whether a sufficient degree of proximity existed for the drainage board to owe a duty of care to the claimants. This involved an examination of the local statutory provisions under which the board operated,[51] requiring it to provide and maintain defences against flooding and to research and record flood levels for that purpose. If the drainage board had been expressly requested to check the flood levels in relation to the property, and had given incorrect information that had been relied upon, it was thought that it would have been liable.[52] On the facts, it was 'habitually' the case that the drainage board actually did check flood levels whether or not it received a specific request to do so. Hence, it was reasoned that the liability of the board could not be any less than in circumstances where it had not been expressly asked to check. Accordingly, the finding of liability against the drainage board was affirmed. The Privy Council also felt unable to interfere with the procedural ruling of the lower court, disallowing contributory negligence to be pleaded, though it clearly had some misgivings about the 'foolish' behaviour of the claimants.

Some care has to be exercised in extrapolating from Privy Council decisions to conclusions about national law, particularly where the interpretation of different statutory powers and duties may be involved. Caution is doubly important in the field of negligence, an area which, it was

---

[51] Under the Christchurch District Drainage Act 1951.
[52] Under the principle in *Hedley Byrne and Co Ltd* v *Heller and Partners Ltd* [1964] AC 465.

noted, 'has not ceased to evolve'. A contrasting outcome was reached in *Tidman v Reading Borough Council*[53] where the general issue of liability for a negligent advice given by a public body was considered, after the claimant maintained that a local planning authority had misinformed him of an appropriate procedure to follow, and he claimed to have suffered loss as a consequence of this. It was ruled that the planning authority did not owe a duty of care to the claimant, since the advice had been given voluntarily by the planning authority, which was under a duty to act in the general public interest to an extent which could not be overridden by any duty to advise a particular individual. Moreover, the advice was given informally, over the telephone, in circumstances where there was no reason to think that it would be of critical financial importance to the claimant or, if it was, that he would not be independently advised. Nonetheless, as a general matter, the possibility of liability of this kind was not entirely ruled out providing that the relationship between the parties shows such a high degree of reliance that it is 'equivalent to a contract'.[54] Hence, it was suggested that if a formal approach had been made to a local authority, which was known to have serious financial implications, and the authority chose to respond, this might 'conceivably' generate a duty of care on the part of the authority.

Further grounds for reluctance in allocating liability in negligence to local authorities are to be discerned from the decision in *Ryeford Homes Ltd and Another v Sevenoaks District Council and Others*[55] where it was unsuccessfully argued that an authority was actually responsible for causing flooding through a failure properly to exercise its planning functions. The facts were that the council had granted planning permission for the construction of houses in a development that involved the erection of embankments to block the natural flow of water percolating from higher land owned by the claimants. The effect of this, and the unavailability of adequate sewerage, was to inhibit drainage so that the claimants' land became waterlogged and subject to flooding. The claimants brought proceedings against the council, amongst other things, alleging negligence in authorising the development of the lower land and in failing to ensure that it took place in accordance with the planning permission. It was held that there was insufficient proximity between a council and an individual land owner for the council to owe the landowner a duty of care in deciding whether to grant a planning permission for the development of any land. The council had to act for the benefit of its area as a whole and it was

---

[53] [1994] 3 PLR 72.
[54] See *Spring v Guardian Assurance plc* [1994] 3 WLR 354 and *Henderson v Merrett Syndicates Ltd* [1994] 3 WLR 761.
[55] [1989] 2 EGLR 281.

## Other Kinds of Flood Warning 469

inevitable that some of its decisions would adversely affect some landowners. Even if there had been sufficient proximity it would be contrary to public policy for the council to be liable to an individual landowner in negligence since its duty was to the public as a whole.[56]

In the present context, the task is that of interpreting these decisions in relation to the potential for liability in negligence on the part of the Environment Agency, and perhaps local planning authorities, where reliance has been placed upon information that is provided on the propensity of particular land to flood. Given that the Agency's published flood plain maps are stated to be 'indicative', rather than *definitive*, of areas that are likely to flood, and that the maps are made available to the public in general, it is very unlikely that liability could arise from reliance upon information of this kind. However, the Agency does suggest that enquirers interested in the flooding potential of a particular location should make further enquiries. At this point, information is being given to particular individuals that might reasonably be relied upon, particularly where the purchase of a property is in contemplation. Subject to any explicit exclusions that the Agency may make as to the basis upon which the information is given, the most that can be said is that the possibilities for an action in negligence look stronger.

### 11.4.2 Warnings of Flood Hazards to Highway Users

More generally, a duty to warn of diverse kinds of hazard, which may encompass flooding, also falls upon a range of other bodies where they have public responsibilities in relation to particular land or activities. Duties of these kinds are capable of encompassing a duty to give flood warnings. A good example arises in relation to highway authorities[57] and is illustrated by *Morris* v *Thyssen (GB) Ltd*.[58] The proceedings arose from

---

[56] A contrasting view has been expressed in relation to a situation where development takes place despite sewerage infrastructure being inadequate to accommodate additional development: 'when the local authority themselves do the increased building, or permit it to be done, . . . they are then guilty of nuisance. They know (or ought to know) that the increase in building will cause the existing sewers to overflow, and yet they allow it to go on without enlarging the capacity of the sewerage system. By so doing, they themselves are helping to fill the system beyond its capacity, and are guilty of a nuisance' (per Denning LJ in *Pride of Derby and Derbyshire Angling Association Ltd* v *British Celanese Ltd* [1953] Ch 149 at p.190, citing as authority *Hawthorn Corporation* v *Kannuluik* [1906] AC 105 and *Hanley* v *Edinburgh Corporation* [1913] AC 488).

[57] See 8.3.1 above in relation to highway authorities.

[58] Unreported, Queen's Bench Division, 20 May 1983 and see also *Thoburn* v *Northumberland County Council*, unreported, Court of Appeal, 19 January 1999. On the liability of highway authorities for omissions generally see *Stovin* v *Wise* [1996] 3 All ER 801.

a serious road traffic accident which occurred after a vehicle, driven by one of the claimants, hit a large pool of water in the road whilst overtaking, causing control of the vehicle to be lost. It was alleged that liability for the accident rested with the highway authority on the basis that it knew that water collected at the particular point in the road, no proper steps were taken to clear the water and no adequate warning was given to drivers approaching the hazard. It was found that the highway authority had been informed of flooding on the road and staff had been instructed to do what they could to alleviate the flood and to place warning signs. Authority employees tried, for about 15 minutes, to locate the highway drain in the flooded part of the road, which was thought to be blocked, but were unable to do so. The authority employees then placed flood warning signs alongside the road, at a short distance from the flooded area in both directions. Although there was no evidence that the claimant's vehicle was travelling at excessive speed, he did not see the warning signs that would have deterred him from overtaking as he approached the flooded area.

The general duty of a highway authority to maintain highways in a state which is not dangerous was noted,[59] and it was recognised that a failure to do so will result in liability unless an authority has taken all reasonable care in the circumstances to avoid dangers to *all* road users, and not merely 'model' drivers.[60] On the facts, a breach of this duty was established by the negligent failure of the authority to take action where it knew of the flood and failed to take proper steps to alleviate it. Moreover, having regard to the danger that the flood posed to drivers, the signs that had been placed were found to be an inadequate means of warning of the hazard that lay ahead and amounted to a breach of duty by the highway authority. Nonetheless, the accident had also occurred because of the negligence of the driver in not observing the sign or the flood water and liability was apportioned with two-thirds being allocated to the highway authority and one-third to the driver.

On the other hand, the question of what constitutes 'reasonable care' on the part of a highway authority in ensuring the safety of road users is clearly a matter of degree and account must be taken of all the circumstances including, for example, that the hazard is of an obvious kind.[61] A contrast

---

[59] Under s.44 Highways Act 1959; now see s.41 Highways Act 1980, and see 8.3.3 above.
[60] See *Haydon* v *Kent County Council* [1978] 1 QB 343 and *Rider* v *Rider* [1973] 1 QB 505, but contrast *Goodes* v *East Sussex County Council* [2000] 3 All ER 603, discussed below.
[61] See *Enion* v *Sefton Metropolitan Borough Council*, unreported, Court of Appeal, 9 February 1999.

is provided by the decision in *Pritchard v Clwyd County Council*[62] where the claimant suffered personal injury after falling when crossing a street which was under several inches of flood water which, it was alleged, was due to the failure of the highway authority to maintain the highway drainage system and the failure of the local authority to maintain the sewer under it. In relation to these facts, it was emphasised that the transient presence of flood water following a period of heavy rainfall was, by itself, insufficient to prove a failure to maintain or a neglect to repair the highway.[63] There was no evidence that the system of drainage that had been provided was inadequate and the facts were consistent with the rain carrying recently deposited debris down the highway to cause temporary blockages which neither the highway authority nor the sewerage authority knew about or had any opportunity to remove.

Despite the earlier decisions, the present law on the duty of highway authorities to 'maintain' highways needs to be considered in the light of the decision in *Goodes v East Sussex County Council*[64] where the House of Lords gave specific consideration to the extent of the maintenance duty. Following a motoring accident caused by the accumulation of black ice, which it was alleged that the highway authority was under a duty to prevent by gritting operations, it was concluded that the duty to maintain extended only to the fabric of the road and did not encompass the removal of snow and ice. Extrapolating from this, it would seem that the maintenance duty upon authorities will not require them to remove flood water and no statutory liability will arise from the failure to do so. Possibly, this ruling has the effect of overruling the decision in *Morris v Thyssen*, though this is not altogether clear. Contrasts might be drawn between the absence of a duty on a highway authority to remove flood water and the issue of what warning measures a highway authority is bound to take in circumstances where a flooding hazard has been specifically drawn to its attention. In exceptional circumstances, a failure to take reasonable measures to draw a known hazard to the attention of road users might form the basis of an

---

[62] Unreported, Court of Appeal, 16 June 1992. See also *Burton v West Suffolk County Council* [1960] 2 QB 72, discussed at 8.3.3 above, where the failure to provide adequate drainage was held to be an act of non-feasance for which the highway authority was not liable. In addition, there was held to be no duty to warn a motorist of the hazard of ice on the road.

[63] Following *Burnside v Emerson* [1968] WLR 1490 where Lord Denning noted, at p.1494, 'an occasional flooding, even if it temporarily renders a highway impassable, is not sufficient to sustain an indictment for non-repair', quoting Lindley J in *Burgess v Northwich Local Board* (1880) 50 LJ QB 219.

[64] [2000] 3 All ER 603. Contrast *Rich v Pembrokeshire County Council* [2001] EWCA Civ 410 where it was held that an accumulation of algae on a slipway had become part of the surface of the highway so that the highway authority was liable for personal injury sustained because of a failure to remove the algae.

action in negligence independently of the maintenance duty upon a highway authority. Hence, in *Larner v Solihull Metropolitan Borough Council*[65] it was recognised that a statutory duty to promote road safety did not exclude the possibility of a common law duty towards road users on the part of the local authority. However, a breach of the common law duty to warn road users of a danger would only be found in exceptional circumstances where an authority has acted 'wholly unreasonably' and outside the discretion allowed by the statutory provision.

### 11.4.3 Occupiers' Liability

The need for appropriate flood warnings to be given is not restricted to public bodies discharging their statutory functions and, in some circumstances, duties encompassing the need to give flood warnings may arise upon private individuals. Two pertinent examples of private duties to warn arise in respect of occupiers' liability and the duty of disclosure in relation to property transactions.

The Occupiers' Liability Act 1957 regulates the general duty which an occupier of premises owes to visitors in respect of dangers due to the state of premises and things done or omitted to be done on them. A 'common duty of care' generally owed to visitors is a duty to take such care as is reasonable in all the circumstances to see that the visitor is reasonably safe in using the premises for the purpose for which he is invited or permitted by the occupier to be there. In securing the reasonable safety of visitors, it is recognised that an occupier must be prepared for children to be less careful than adults and that occupiers may expect visitors with special skills to appreciate and guard against special risks ordinarily incident to these.[66]

The common duty of care to visitors may be modified insofar as an occupier is free to extend, restrict or exclude the duty by agreement or otherwise.[67] However, in determining whether an occupier has discharged the duty towards visitors, warning a visitor of a danger is not to be treated, without more, as absolving the occupier from any liability, unless in all the circumstances it is enough for the visitor to be reasonably safe. The duty

---

[65] [2001] RTR 32. Although this case was decided by the Court of Appeal after the decision in *Goodes*, it was primarily concerned with the position of an authority under the Road Traffic Act 1988, s.39 of which imposes duties in relation to road safety and the taking of measures to prevent accidents.

[66] s.2(1) to (3) Occupiers' Liability Act 1957.

[67] Exclusion of liability by notice is restricted by the Unfair Contract Terms Act 1977, but it may be necessary to distinguish exclusion of liability, within the terms allowed by the 1977 Act, from the issue of *adequacy* of a warning notice under the Occupiers' Liability Act 1957.

## Other Kinds of Flood Warning 473

of care does not impose on an occupier any obligation to a visitor in respect of risks willingly accepted by the visitor: that is, the consent of the visitor to a risk may serve as a defence.[68] Hence, where a hazard such as flood water or a flood defence structure is present on land, the occupier of the land must secure the reasonable safety of visitors by taking sufficient steps to ensure this: for example, by warning visitors of any dangers that exist.

Further provision is made under the Occupiers' Liability Act 1984 for liability to entrants 'other than visitors', a term which encompasses trespassers. The duty owed to 'non-visitors' is to take such care as is reasonable in all the circumstances to see that a person does not suffer injury on the premises by reason of a danger of which the occupier is aware, or in the existence of which the occupier had reasonable grounds to believe, and the risk is one 'against which, in all the circumstances, some protection may reasonably be expected to be offered'. A defence is provided whereby an occupier may discharge a duty to non-visitors by taking all reasonable steps to give warning of the danger concerned or to discourage persons from incurring the risk, and no duty applies in relation to risks that are willingly accepted.[69]

The question of an occupier's liability to a trespasser was at issue in *Umek v London Transport Executive*[70] where the 'trespasser' was actually an employee of the defendants. She wished to reach the depot where she worked but was unable to do so because of a flood in a subway that lead to the depot and opted to use another route that involved crossing a railway line. The station foreman had put up a notice on a piece of paper attached to string across the entrance to the subway which stated that a footbridge should be used and that no one should cross the railway line. Other employees had ignored the notice and crossed the railway line, and she did similarly but was killed by a train as she did so. Her personal representatives claimed damages for negligence on the ground that train drivers should have been warned of the potential hazard of station staff walking across the line so that the trains would approach with caution and at a low speed. It was held that, although she had been a trespasser when crossing the line, a common duty of humanity was owed to her by the defendants. The defendants had known of staff crossing the line for more than an hour before the accident and they were negligent in failing to warn drivers of the hazard. Nonetheless, the amount of damages would be reduced by 75% to reflect the degree to which she had been responsible for the accident. Although the flooded subway had constituted only a part of the surrounding

---
[68] s.2(1), (4)(a) and (5) Occupiers' Liability Act 1957.
[69] s.1(3) to (6) Occupiers' Liability Act 1984.
[70] Unreported, Queen's Bench Division, NLJ, 8 June 1984, p.522.

circumstances leading to the accident, it had nonetheless given rise to a duty to warn of other dangers that arose as a consequence.

The general issue of who is an 'occupier' for the purposes of establishing occupier's liability was primarily at issue in *Collier* v *Anglian Water*[71] where the claimant was injured on a seaside promenade when she tripped on a ridge between two large paving slabs, one of which had become displaced. The promenade formed part of the sea defences for which the water authority was responsible, but the local authority owned the land on which the promenade was situated and kept it free from litter. It was concluded that the water authority was an 'occupier' because it was responsible for maintaining and repairing the structure, albeit for sea defence purposes. The water authority knew that the safety of the members of the public who had access to the promenade was dependent upon its state of repair and were therefore liable, despite the ownership of the land by the local authority.

The *Collier* case has quite important implications for the standard of maintenance of some flood and sea defence structures. It was claimed by the water authority that although it had statutory *powers* to maintain the promenade for sea defence purposes, it was under no *duty* to do so. Moreover, the authority was empowered to enforce regional flood defence byelaws[72] that, amongst other things, prohibited any person, without consent, from undertaking any excavation or other operation on any land forming part of a sea defence. As a consequence, it would have been unlawful for the local authority to have undertaken any repair work of a structural kind on the promenade without the consent of the water authority. Clearly, responsibility for the structure of the promenade, including the misplaced paving slab, lay with the water authority and, insofar as it acquiesced to the use of the promenade by the public for recreational purposes, it was bound to take reasonable steps to ensure their safety. It was apparent that the unsatisfactory state of the paving had developed over a substantial period of time and, in doing nothing to rectify this, the water authority was in breach of its duty as occupier under the 1957 Act. Hence,

---

[71] (1983) *The Times* 23 March and contrast the decision in *Hunwick* v *Essex Rivers Catchment Board* [1952] 1 All ER 765 where, before the Occupiers' Liability Act 1957, a catchment board was held not to be in 'occupation' of a sea wall, and see discussion at 5.3 above. Also contrast *Kincaid* v *Hartlepool Borough Council and Northumbrian Water Ltd*, unreported, Court of Appeal, 5 December 2000 (where the claimant suffered personal injury after falling into a 'crevasse', caused by drifting sand covering a surface water drain which ran across a beach, and it was held that no occupiers' liability would arise since it would have been impracticable and disproportionate to have required the area to be fenced and it would have been difficult to place an appropriate warning notice).

[72] Under s.47 Land Drainage Act 1930, and see 3.4.10 above on byelaws.

## Other Kinds of Flood Warning

although it is commonly stated that land drainage bodies have only *powers* in relation to the maintenance of flood defence structures,[73] for public safety reasons, as the decision illustrates, they may also have *duties* to maintain such structures.

Given the present general duty upon flood defence operating authorities to have regard to the desirability of providing recreational facilities for the public,[74] the possibility of excluding public access to flood and sea defence structures is very limited, and it is doubtful whether exclusion of access would be justified solely for the purpose of preventing occupiers' liability arising. The issue was raised in the *Collier* case as to whether imposition of occupiers' liability would throw a great financial burden on sea defence authorities. In the view of O'Connor LJ, a decision that reasonable care should be taken to keep the promenade at a busy seaside resort free from an obvious danger was no authority for assessing what is required of sea defences in other parts of coastline. The implication, therefore, was that such a high standard of repair would not be required of sea defences in remote locations that had relatively few visitors. Second, in the circumstances of the case, the water authority was free to divest itself of any obligation to keep the surface of the promenade in reasonable repair as a promenade rather than a sea defence. This could have been done, at no significant cost to the water authority, simply by giving the local authority permission under the byelaws to do the work necessary to maintain the surface of the promenade in a state that allowed it to be safely used for recreation by visitors.

A contrasting decision, illustrating the circumstances in which a duty to warn visitors of a danger will arise, is *Staples* v *West Dorset District Council*.[75] Here, an adult claimant slipped and fell from a harbour wall, suffering injury, and claimed a breach of the common duty of care under the 1957 Act because of the failure of the defendant local authority to warn of the danger. The harbour wall had been covered in algae and visibly slippery and the claimant was found to have known of the danger that it posed. It was held that, had a warning notice been in place, it would have told the claimant nothing that he did not already know and would probably not have caused him to act any differently in voluntarily accepting the risk of slipping. Hence, in a situation where a risk is obvious there is no obligation upon an occupier to warn of a danger which is known to a visitor

---

[73] See discussion of flood defence powers at 4.3.1 above.
[74] See 10.2 and 10.3 above on general recreational duties.
[75] (1995) 93 LGR 536. Contrast *Rich* v *Pembrokeshire County Council* [2001] EWCA Civ 410 where similar facts gave rise to liability under s.41 Highways Act 1980 and see discussion of *Goodes* v *East Sussex County Council* [2000] 3 All ER 603 at 11.4.2 above.

and, in relation to which, the visitor is free to take appropriate safety precautions.[76]

Clearly, each case where it is claimed that an occupier's 'duty to warn' exists will depend upon its own facts, but in relation to flood water and some kinds of flood defence structure the 'obvious danger' approach is likely to be taken. This has the fortunate practical implication that it will not be generally necessary for flood defence authorities to erect vast numbers of warning signs in the innumerable locations to which the public have access. However, some caution is needed in relation to locations which have proved dangerous on previous occasions or areas which children are likely to enter, given the stricter duty imposed by the 1957 Act in relation to dangers of which they may not be so appreciative as adults.

### 11.4.4 Disclosure in Property Transactions

Another private law instance of a duty to warn of a flooding hazard, or at least a duty not to misrepresent such a hazard, arises in relation to property transactions. Specifically, this is likely to arise where enquiries are made of a seller, by the prospective purchaser of a property, as to the propensity of a property to flood and past experiences of flooding. Normally, where a transaction has been concluded between the parties, the seller's failure to answer questions of this kind truthfully may be pursued as a contractual action, though the basis of the action and the remedies available are primarily determined by the application of the Misrepresentation Act 1967.

A good example of the consequences of inaccurate disclosure of information about past flooding of a property is *Showan* v *Yapp*.[77] The claimants

---

[76] Similarly, see *Cotton* v *Derbyshire Dales District Council* (1994) *The Times* 20 June, where it was held to be unnecessary to warn an adult of sound mind that it was dangerous to go too near the edge of an obvious cliff. See also *Whyte* v *Redland Aggregates Ltd*, unreported, Court of Appeal, 27 November 1997 (where no liability was found for injuries sustained by diving into disused gravel pit and 'danger keep out' signs were sufficient warning); *Darby* v *National Trust* [2001] EWCA Civ 189, discussed in D. Wilkinson, 'Occupier's Liability for Aquatic Risks: Obvious Dangers Excluded?' [2001] *Water Law* 35 (where no liability was found for death following drowning which was found to be an obvious risk in relation to an adult swimming in a pond, and for which warning was not necessary); contrast *Taylor* v *Bath and North East Somerset District Council*, unreported, Queen's Bench Division, 27 January 1999 (where liability was established for injuries sustained after a fall on slippery tiles at the side of a swimming pool and it was found that the occupiers had been negligent in failing to follow a recommended cleaning routine to prevent the tiles becoming slippery).

[77] Unreported, Court of Appeal (Civil Division), 3 November 1998. Contrast *William Sindall plc* v *Cambridgeshire County Council* [1994] 3 All ER 932 where it was held that there was no action in mistake or misrepresentation where, unknown to the vendor, a private sewer was later found to run beneath the land.

maintained that a contract for the purchase of the defendant's house had been induced by misrepresentation and sought damages including the diminution in value of the property attributable to the misrepresentation. The property at issue was a cottage which had a paved garden alongside a stream. Following an offer to buy the cottage, 'subject to contract', the claimants visited the property and a conversation took place in which the seller was asked whether she 'had had any problems with the stream'. The seller replied that the stream 'had flooded part of the lawn'. Whilst this statement was literally correct, it was a misrepresentation in that it conveyed the impression that this was the total extent of the flooding. The truth was that the flood water had entered the house on at least two previous occasions which had been the subject of insurance claims by the defendant. It was not found that the defendant had acted fraudulently in making this statement, though it was suggested that she was 'sailing very close to the wind', since she genuinely believed that she was not bound to divulge the previous flooding of the house. In written answers to questions posed by the claimants' solicitors, it was again stated that the defendant was not aware of any internal flooding attributable to the stream but it was found that this statement had been made by the defendant's mother and not the defendant herself.

Following completion of the sale transferring the property to the claimants, serious flooding occurred on at least three occasions and water containing sewage entered the house to a depth of at least 10 inches. Damage to carpets and furniture was assessed at over £4,000 and additional damages of £2,000 were awarded against the defendant for 'distress and inconvenience' arising from the flooding. However, the principal dispute was about the extent of the defendant's liability for the difference in value between the property as it was claimed to be and as it actually was, that is, with the tendency to flood. On this point, evidence was heard from valuers, representing the parties, who produced widely different estimates of the difference in value. The claimants' valuer estimated that the purchase price of the property, £215,000, should be reduced by £90,000 (about 42%) to reflect its actual value at the time of purchase, whereas the defendant's valuer estimated the reduction at only £12,000 (about 6%). At first instance, the estimate of the defendant's valuer had been accepted as the appropriate amount of damages and this determination was appealed against by the claimants.

On appeal, the Court of Appeal took the view that both valuers' evidence had relied upon 'hunch or gut feeling', which in the case of the defendant's valuer relied upon assumptions about 'minimal water penetration' that were contradicted by the subsequent evidence. In addition, the trial judge had given weight to the anecdotal evidence of another prospective purchaser, and had failed to take sufficient account of the evidence provided by a consultant civil engineer who estimated that flooding would occur, on average, once every 3 to 5 years on the basis of calculations from official rainfall statistics for the immediate locality and expert knowledge of the capacity of the watercourse. Taking account of these factors, the diminution in value of the property was assessed as £40,000 (about 19% of the purchase price).[78]

More generally, the Environment Agency has also expressed concern that, of the 1.25 million property transactions that are conducted annually, only a small proportion of enlightened individuals or solicitors actually enquire about flood risk. The existing voluntary arrangements, agreed between local authorities and the Law Society, based around property search forms, do not encompass information on flooding. The recommendation of the Agency is that the Government should require flood risk information to be provided in future property searches.[79] A similar view was expressed by the House of Commons Agriculture Committee, in 1998, that information of this kind should become part of the property conveyancing process.[80] The Government undertook to pursue the matter with the organisations concerned.[81] However, at the time of writing, it is not apparent what changes are in prospect.

## 11.5 FLOODING INSURANCE

### 11.5.1 General Considerations concerning Insurance

Information about flooding, as has been seen, is important both for the assessment of the propensity of land to flood and in order to take preventative action where a flooding incident is imminent. In the final resort, for many, the potential for damage to be caused by flooding needs to addressed by insurance cover. In the context of insurance, once again, information becomes important for the purpose of assessment of risk and the calculation of premiums.

Two contrasting perspectives upon flood insurance are centrally important:

---

[78] Contrast *Ray v Baker (Valuation Officer)* (1970) 214 EG 1710, Lands Tribunal, where it was held that the rent that could be obtained for a property was not affected by a flood that was unlikely to recur within the foreseeable future.
[79] Environment Agency, *Lessons Learned – Autumn 2000 floods* (2001) p.33.
[80] House of Commons Agriculture Committee, Sixth Report Session 1997–98, *Flood and Coastal Defence* (1998) HC 707, para.92.
[81] House of Commons Agriculture Committee, Fifth Special Report Session 1997–98, *Replies by the Government and the Environment Agency to the Sixth Report from the Agriculture Committee, Session 1997–98, 'Flood and Coastal Defence'* (HC 707) (1998) HC 1117, p.xiv.

# Flooding Insurance 479

first, the recent concerns of the insurance industry about the broader consequences of the range of factors which may be affecting its future liability to meet potentially massive levels of flooding claims; and, second, the narrower issue of when an insurance policy will actually cover losses arising from a 'flood'.[82]

On the broader issue, the insurance industry is becoming increasingly concerned that claims arising from flooding are likely to become more prominent. This is because of the impacts of climate change; the general upward trend in weather-related claims; increasing affluence (leading to a higher level of insurance coverage); pressure for development in the flood plain; and the fact that, in the past, insurance companies have provided insurance cover 'virtually automatically' for homeowners, though it has been suggested that this may not be sustainable in the future.[83]

The concerns of the insurance industry are a reflection of the need for insurers to assess the magnitude of the flooding risks, for which they would have to meet the financial consequences following a catastrophic flooding event, against a background of increasing uncertainty. Hence, past methods of assessing 'risk', by extrapolation from historic levels of claims, may be increasingly inappropriate depending upon the impact of the range of additional factors that now need to be taken into account. As a consequence, increasingly sophisticated risk assessment approaches will be needed to take account of present and future factors relevant to the kinds of hazard involved, the extent of exposure of persons or property to that hazard and the degree of vulnerability of insured assets to the hazard.[84]

Hence, the indicative flood plain maps prepared by the Environment Agency,[85] and similar data provided from other sources, will become of increasing importance to insurers to assess the vulnerability of particular properties to flooding. This data indicates that some 1.2 million properties in Great Britain (excluding Northern Ireland) are at risk from internal flooding, some 4% of the total, and the total insured value of assets within the inland flood plain is approximately £35 billion, equating to an average loss of £28,000 per property. Particularly in relation to properties in the Thames and Trent catchments, constituting about one-third of the overall number of properties at risk, hypothetical 'extreme flooding scenarios'

---

[82] On insurance costs of flooding generally see 1.4 above.
[83] Association of British Insurers, *Inland Flooding Risk – Issues Facing the Insurance Industry* (2000) p.2. See also Association of British Insurers, *Flooding: A Partnership Approach to Protecting People* (2001), discussed at 11.5.4 below.
[84] Association of British Insurers, *Inland Flooding Risk – Issues Facing the Insurance Industry* (2000) p.15, and see 1.4 above on risk.
[85] See the discussion of indicative flood plain maps at 11.2.3 above.

have indicated the potential for losses between £1 billion and £2 billion arising from an extreme incident affecting either catchment. The City of London and its conurbation is placed in a different category as regards flooding potential, in that, though a proportion of the area lies within the flood plain of the Thames, the major threat is posed by tidal surges rather than river flooding. Notwithstanding the Thames Barrier[86] operating to an indicative 1 in 1000 years standard of protection, if flood defences were overtopped the likely losses to properties identified as within tidal flood areas have been estimated to be between £5 billion and £10 billion.[87] Although these alarming 'worst case' scenarios are recognised to be speculative in many respects, they involve assumptions that require increasingly serious consideration by the insurance industry.

### 11.5.2 Legal Aspects of Flood Insurance

It is in the context of insurance law that the narrower but important question of what constitutes a 'flood' has been most intensively scrutinised. In a series of cases the courts have analysed the question of whether or not particular occurrences fall within its meaning for the purpose ascertaining the extent of insurance cover.

In considering flooding insurance cases, however, it is necessary to be appreciative of the legal context in which they are placed. Contracts of insurance have distinct characteristics which set them apart from other kinds of transaction. Basically, such contracts involve one party (the insurer) assuming the risk of the future occurrence of an uncertain event, which is not within the control of the parties, and in which the other party (the insured) has an interest, and in relation to which the insurer is bound to pay money if the specified event occurs. However, this relationship is qualified by specialised principles such as the doctrine of *uberrimae fides* (of the utmost good faith) which requires full disclosure of matters relevant to the risk that is insured against, a strict requirement which is not generally needed in other kinds of contract. Another distinctive aspect of insurance law is the weight that courts have traditionally placed upon the need for certainty and uniformity in the interpretation of words and phrases that commonly feature in contracts of insurance. Because of the tendency to use standard wording in many insurance policies covering the same kinds of risk, any judicial 'reinterpretation' of the meaning of a key word or phrase may have potentially momentous implications for a large number of policy holders. Hence, with an appreciation of the distinctive character of

---

[86] See 3.7.2 above on the Thames Barrier.
[87] Association of British Insurers, *Inland Flooding Risk – Issues Facing the Insurance Industry* (2000) Ch.3.

insurance law, the interpretation of the word 'flood' in contracts of insurance falls to be considered.

### 11.5.3 The Meaning of 'Flood'

The meaning of 'flood' in a contract of insurance appears to have been first directly considered in *Young v Sun Alliance and London Insurance Ltd*.[88] Here, the claimant insured his house under a householder's policy which gave protection against loss, destruction or damage from 'storm, tempest or flood' and 'escape of water from . . . any water, drainage or heating installation'. In the circumstances at issue, water had entered a downstairs lavatory due to the diversion of a natural underground source of water and rose to a depth of 3 inches. The claimant was required to undertake fairly elaborate repairs, involving the installation of a pump, to rectify the problem and claimed an indemnity from the defendants, as insurers, for the cost of the work that had been undertaken, along with redecoration costs, on the basis that the damage which had arisen was due to a 'flood'.

The resolution of the question as to whether the facts involved a 'flood' or not involved careful interpretation of the words 'storm, tempest or flood' as they featured in the policy. On this, it was said,

> '[p]eople often used the word "flood" colloquially to describe an overflow of water in their houses, such as a sink overflowing; but in my judgement it is not what is meant by "flood" in the insurance policy. A "flood" is something large, sudden and temporary, not naturally there, such as a river overflowing its banks. In my judgement the water in the plaintiff's lavatory was not there as a result of a "flood" within the meaning of the policy.'[89]

Notwithstanding the argument that the wording of the policy should be interpreted *contra proferentem* (against the insurers) it was held that the words 'storm, tempest or flood' referred to three related kinds of natural phenomenon: 'storm' meant 'rain accompanied by strong wind'; 'tempest' denoted 'an even more violent storm'; and 'flood' involved 'the overflowing or irruption of a great body of water'. Hence, a 'flood' did not come about by seepage, trickling, dripping or other slow movements of water that could be detected, and in circumstances where the threatened loss could be limited, but only from the abnormal and sudden onset of water where nothing effective could be done to prevent loss. A 'flood', therefore, was construed as 'a natural phenomenon which has some element of violence,

---

[88] [1977] 1 WLR 104.
[89] Per Shaw LJ at p.107, quoting Judge Stockdale in the first instance decision.

suddenness or largeness about it' and the facts that had arisen did not fall within this category.

Similar reasoning was applied to markedly different facts in *Computer and Systems Engineering plc v John Lelliot (Ilford) Ltd and Another*.[90] Here the claimants had engaged the first defendant to undertake work at the claimants' premises. The work was to be undertaken under a standard form building contract of the Joint Contracts Tribunal and involved the installation of steel purlins to support a new ceiling, with this part of the work being subcontracted to the second defendants. Whilst undertaking the work, one of the subcontractors' employees allowed a purlin to fall, and this sheared off part of the sprinkler, fire protection, system with the result that some 1,600 gallons of water were discharged causing extensive damage to the claimants' premises and property.

Although it was clear that the damage had arisen through the negligence of the subcontractors' employee, the issue of liability was dependent upon the wording of the standard form building contract. This provided, in summary, that the building and contents would be at the sole risk of the claimant insofar as loss or damage due to certain 'insured perils' were concerned, and the claimant was bound to maintain insurance in relation to these matters. The 'insured perils' encompassed loss or damage due to 'storm, tempest, flood, bursting or overflowing of water tanks, apparatus or pipes'. The effect of these terms, therefore, was that, despite any negligence on the part of the subcontractors, they would not be liable for losses which fell within the scope of the 'insured perils' since the claimants were bound to take out insurance to cover these matters.

Consequently, the court had to determine whether the damage that had arisen was due to a 'flood' or a 'bursting of an apparatus or pipes' within the meaning of the building contract and consistently with the interpretation the words would be given in any contract of insurance that the claimant was bound to have. On that basis, it was found that the word 'flood' imports,

> 'the invasion of property . . . by a large volume of water caused by a rapid accumulation or sudden release of water from an external source, usually but not necessarily confined to the result of a natural phenomenon such as a storm, tempest or downpour'.

Applying this test, it was found that the events that had occurred were not a 'flood' either in their extent or origin. On the alternative contention, that the events were an insured peril insofar as they involved a 'bursting of an apparatus or pipes' it was found that 'bursting' meant a rupture of a vessel

---

[90] (1990) 54 Build LR 1.

by the exertion of forces, expansion or pressure *from within* that vessel. Hence, the fracturing or severing of the sprinkler system by the falling purlin did not fall within the meaning of 'bursting'. Accordingly, the subcontractors were found liable for the water-related damage which, in insurance terms, did not constitute a 'flood'.

Most recently, the question of what constitutes a 'flood' in relation to a household insurance policy has been revisited in *Rohan Investments Ltd* v *Cunningham and Others*.[91] This case involved an insurance claim for serious damage to a residential property and its contents where water had accumulated on a flat roof and passed into the building during a period when it was unoccupied. The accumulation of water appeared to have arisen from a grating over a downpipe which had become clogged with leaves and twigs and which caused water to reach a depth of 3 to 4 inches on the roof. Over a period of about 10 days, approximately 4 inches of rainfall had been recorded and, in the absence of any satisfactory expert evidence, it was found that the internal damage to the property had been due to an ingress of water over the top of the flashings or through some defect in them.

As in the previous cases, the main issue was whether the facts constituted a 'flood' within the insured perils of 'storm, tempest or flood' covered by the policy. The definition of a 'flood', distilled from the previous cases, was restated as 'an invasion from outside the property by a large volume of water caused by a rapid accumulation from an outside source such as an unusually heavy downpour'. Despite the insurer's claim that this did not encompass a situation where water had *gradually* accumulated on the flat roof, it was found that the preceding days' rainfall had been sufficient to be 'abnormal' and that a relatively large amount of water had entered the building by an ingress that amounted to more than slow seepage or percolation (of the kind considered in the *Young* case). It was concluded, therefore, that the facts constituted a 'flood' within the insured perils.

In reaching this conclusion, Auld LJ offered some illuminating general observations as to the construction of the word 'flood' in insurance contracts, which seem to imply a broadening of its meaning as compared with the previous cases. It was stressed that the overriding consideration is that the word should be given its 'ordinary and natural meaning', so that the factors identified by the *Young* and *Computer Systems* cases were not intended to be applied as rigid 'all-purpose' criteria without reference to the different circumstances that may arise. In particular, the existence of a 'flood' need not depend upon whether the event under consideration was

---

[91] [1999] Lloyd's Rep IR 190.

part of more general flooding of the area since it was recognised that a flood may result from prolonged moderate rainfall and the steady build-up of water which eventually causes damage to property. The need for ingress of a 'large' amount of water should be regarded as a matter of degree in relation to the size of the property that it enters. Also, the need for a flood to arise as a 'natural' phenomenon should be treated with caution since 'a flood is no less a flood, whatever its originating cause' and, for example, the accumulation of debris in the downpipe in the facts under consideration should not prevent the circumstances being categorised as a 'flood'. Finally, there is no need for the flood to arise from circumstances which are so extreme that the householder can do nothing about them, since this requirement confuses the insurable event with the practice of insurers to include conditions that prevent recovery in circumstances where loss has been incurred as a result of negligence on the part of the policy holder.

The cumulative effect of the trio of insurance cases seems to provide some general reassurance to holders of insurance policies which allow recovery in the event of a 'storm, tempest or flood'. Coverage will be construed to encompass most of the flooding hazards which normally arise from external circumstances and the apparent retreat from an overly technical approach to construction seems equitable to address the more unusual circumstances in which flooding may sometimes occur. The coverage of water damage from internal water supply, heating and similar fittings will depend upon the wording of the policy, but a policy restricted to the 'bursting' of pipes, as in the *Computer Systems* case, might be thought inadequate for circumstances where various kinds of accidental damage to pipes might arise. The wording of the policy in the *Young* case, encompassing 'escape of water from . . . any water, drainage or heating installation' is preferable, though it might be better still for a policy to state explicitly whether it covers escapes from washing machines, dishwashers and other domestic appliances that make use of water. In any case, however, it is important to note the distinction between structural damage and damage to contents of a property, since different insurance coverage is likely to be needed depending upon the nature of the damage.

### 11.5.4 Availability of Flood Insurance

Although many owners of residential and business premises may secure an indemnity for flood damage under an appropriately worded insurance policy, the terms, and perhaps availability, of insurance cover of this kind may be greatly dependent upon the circumstances of the property that is to be insured. As has been explained, a distinctive feature of any insurance contract is that the risk that is insured against comprises an inherently

## Flooding Insurance 485

uncertain event[92] and where an event is less than uncertain, in the sense of being to some degree probable, this may raise problems in relation to securing insurance cover. In the present context, this is essentially the difficulty that may be confronted by owners of properties that have been subject to flooding in the past and are likely to flood in the future. Two aspects of this require consideration: first, the duty upon those seeking insurance cover to disclose relevant information and, second, the extent to which insurers are bound to provide insurance coverage for flooding in 'bad risk' cases.

An application for insurance cover which is made fraudulently[93] may be avoided by the insurer and, similarly, may be avoided if a statement of fact is made which is false in a material particular, whether the proposed acted negligently or innocently.[94] Hence, instances of fraud or misrepresentation are, in legal terms, relatively straightforward in their consequences. The greater difficulty arises in relation to the strict duty of disclosure that applies to insurance contracts. This requires the person who seeks to acquire insurance cover to disclose to the insurer, prior to making the contract, all material facts within his or her knowledge which the insurer does not know or is deemed not to know.[95] The effect of a failure to disclose, however innocent this may be, is that the insurer becomes entitled to avoid the contract so that it is deemed never to have existed and no indemnity will be payable under it.[96] The broad effect of the strict disclosure requirement is that a person seeking insurance cover for flooding will be under a positive duty to disclose any past history of flooding of the property, whether or not this is the subject of any question actually posed by the insurer.

In practice, however, the question will invariably be asked by the insurer whether the property for which insurance is being sought has been subject to flooding in the past. If this question is answered in the affirmative, it will probably have implications for the premium that is to be charged under the policy. In an extreme case, the risk of flooding recurring may be regarded as so great that, in principle, the insurer may decline to offer any terms on which the property will be insured. Although insurers in the United

---

[92] In the case of life 'insurance' the fact of a person's death is not uncertain, in the sense that it is bound to happen sooner or later, but the *date* at which it will occur is uncertain. Because of the different kind of uncertainty involved, this type of insurance is sometimes termed 'life *assurance*'.

[93] That is, a statement which is false and which is made without belief in its truth or recklessly as to whether it is true or false: see *Derry v Peek* (1889) 14 App Cas 337.

[94] Although, theoretically, s.2(2) Misrepresentation Act 1967 allows a court to award damages in lieu of avoidance or rescission.

[95] *Carter v Boehm* (1766) 3 Burr 1905.

[96] *Armstrong v Turquand* (1858) 9 ICLR 32 and *Mackender v Felaia* [1967] 2 QB 590.

Kingdom, unlike other countries, have provided flood insurance cover for all homeowners 'virtually automatically', it has been suggested that this practice may not be sustainable and that issues of availability and affordability of flood insurance are likely to become more critical in the future.[97] Essentially, a principle of 'freedom of contract' operates whereby insurers cannot be compelled to provide insurance coverage in circumstances where they conclude that the risk of flooding is excessively high.

The latest indication of future practice in relation to flood insurance cover is provided in a report by the Association of British Insurers, *Flooding: A Partnership Approach to Protecting People*.[98] This Report notes that flood insurance, as a standard feature of household insurance policies in England and Wales, was introduced in the 1960s following government commitments to provide flood defences in areas where risks of coastal or river flooding were high. However, the recent experience of the insurance industry is that flood risk is becoming uninsurable in some areas due to more frequent, heavy rain, poor maintenance of flood defences and inadequate investment in protecting properties in flood risk areas. The insurance industry has given a commitment to maintain availability of flood insurance to existing domestic properties and small business policy holders up to the end of 2002. However, there may be exceptional circumstances where cover may be discontinued where a flood alleviation scheme has been refused by residents on grounds of amenity; where new properties have been built in a flood plain without sustainable defences; or where flood risk has deteriorated to the extent that flooding is inevitable. Beyond the end of 2002, the implication is that availability of affordable flood insurance will be dependent upon action by government in investing in flood defences to a sufficient level to contain insurance costs. It is also recognised that there will be a small number of areas where neither government action nor continued insurance cover is feasible. This may seem very harsh upon the owners of those properties that are likely to become uninsurable, with consequent difficulties in relation to mortgages, but reflects the fact that insurance providers are commercial enterprises that are not legally bound to provide such services on the basis of need alone.

---

[97] Association of British Insurers, *Inland Flooding Risk – Issues Facing the Insurance Industry* (2000) p.2.
[98] Association of British Insurers (2001).

# Chapter 12

# SUSTAINABILITY

## 12.1 INTRODUCTION

This final chapter provides an opportunity for reflection upon the future for flood and coastal defence. A disputatious starting point is to pose the question, whether past approaches have been the 'victims of their own success'? That is, has conventional piped land drainage, concentrating on the accelerated conveyance of water elsewhere, 'solved' the problem of removing excess water from one area of land at the expense of causing lower land to become more susceptible to flooding? Similarly, has increased technical capacity to provide ever higher and more substantial flood and coastal defence structures succeeded in protecting some areas of land from flooding at the expense of contributing to flooding or erosion elsewhere? More generally, have the 'benefits' of flood defence and coast protection been gained at an excessive economic and environmental cost that, in the longer term, may exceed the value of the protection that is being provided? Although questions of this kind tend not to admit categorical answers, they do serve to focus discussion upon some new priorities.

The touchstone of present environmental thinking is the idea of 'sustainable development', which has been popularly defined as 'development which meets the needs of the present without compromising the ability of future generations to meet their own needs'.[1] This rather obscure imperative of national and international environmental policy clearly needs a great deal of interpretation to be applied to particular sectors and activities, but flood and coastal defence is definitely not excluded from its ambit. The new objective must be to progress towards more 'sustainable' approaches which reconcile the traditional objectives of protecting life and property without diminishing future environmental and developmental needs. Notably, as well as being an environmental objective, sustainable development incorporates an inextricable economic dimension which cannot be dissociated from the protection of the environmental media and the ecosystems which they support. The new philosophy, therefore, is to devise approaches to flood and coastal defence that are 'sustainable' by all these measures.

---

[1] World Commission on Environment and Development, *Our Common Future* (1987) (the 'Brundtland Report').

In a general way, the need for sustainable flood and coastal defence has been recognised for some time. Since 1993, Government policy has been to encourage the provision of 'technically, environmentally and economically sound and *sustainable* flood and coastal defence measures'. 'Sustainable schemes' are those which take account of the interrelationships with other defences, developments and processes within a river catchment or coastal sediment cell, and which avoid, as far as possible, tying future generations into inflexible options for flood defence.[2] Increasingly, the need for sustainability has come to incorporate a strategic dimension, whereby flood and coastal defence works should be formulated within a holistic framework which takes fuller account of long-term implications. Hence, particular decisions should be made by reference to catchment-wide local environment agency plans or shoreline management plans, so that account is taken of the capacity of the flood plain to store water and intertidal habitats to absorb energy. In broad terms, it has been recognised that failure to take account of natural river and coastal processes will mean that defences will have to be continually raised and made more substantial to give ever greater protection.[3] The future commitment to maintaining or improving such works cannot be accepted as sustainable.

Although the need for greater sustainability of flood and coastal defence has been generally endorsed at a policy level, more recent developments demonstrate the establishment of particular measures as a means towards this end. Most prominently, as has been seen, recent planning guidance on development and flood risk[4] advocates a significantly greater use of 'sustainable drainage systems' as a step towards greater sustainability in flood defence generally. The thinking behind the new guidance is that development at any location within a catchment of a watercourse is capable of having an impact of downstream flooding by increasing the amount of run-off from roofs and paved areas. All kinds of built developments have the tendency to increase the impermeable area from which water runs off rather than percolating into and through the ground to replenish groundwater resources. The cumulative impact of built development over a significant area is, therefore, to increase and accelerate the flow of water and to exacerbate the risk and severity of downstream flooding. The traditional approach, of seeking to accelerate the conveyance of surface water away

---

[2] Ministry of Agriculture, Fisheries and Food, and Welsh Office, *Strategy for Flood and Coastal Defence in England and Wales* (1993) pp.3 and 36, and see 3.2 above.

[3] Ministry of Agriculture, Fisheries and Food, *Flood and Coastal Defence Project Appraisal Guidance: Environmental Appraisal* (FCDPAG 5) (2000) p.14. See also Institution of Civil Engineers, *Learning to Live with Rivers* (2001) p.38.

[4] Department of Transport, Local Government and the Regions, Planning Policy Guidance Note 25, *Planning and Flood Risk* (2001), discussed at 9.8 above.

## Introduction 489

from the place where it falls or accumulates, needs to be superseded by a new approach of managing surface water as near as possible to its origin by attenuating, rather than accelerating, the downstream flow. Moreover, flooding issues need to be considered on a catchment-wide basis and in relation to a range of land uses which may impact upon floodwater flows.

Although the recent planning guidance for sustainable urban drainage is an important step in a progression towards greater sustainability of flood and coastal defence, it is best regarded as a component element in a wider strategy. Source control for urban water run-off, by itself, is not a solution to problems of flooding of major watercourses receiving substantial flows from non-urban areas, and is largely irrelevant to problems of sea flooding and coastal erosion. Sustainability needs to be addressed across the full spectrum of issues, encompassing land drainage, river flooding, coastal flooding and related erosion and encroachment problems. On this, it is evident that a considerable amount must be done to confront the broader challenges. In 1998, the House of Commons Agriculture Committee reached the conclusion that fundamental changes of approach were needed:

> '[w]e are of the opinion that flood and coastal defence policy cannot be sustained in the long term if it continues to be founded on the practice of substantial human intervention in the natural processes of flooding and erosion. Indeed, it is of great concern to us that the legacy of flooding and erosional problems arising from this practice – and the likely increase in future of climatological and other environmental pressures on the UK's ageing flood and coastal defence infrastructure – might combine to present flood and coastal defence authorities with insuperable difficulties.'[5]

The purpose of this chapter, therefore, is to consider the progress that has been made, or needs to be made, in addressing the challenge of progressing towards greater sustainability in flood and coastal defence. More specifically, the aim is to consider the range of mechanisms that have been devised to enhance sustainability and the legal implications of these.

### 12.2 SUSTAINABLE LAND DRAINAGE

'Sustainable drainage systems' comprise a sequence of management practices and control structures designed to drain surface water in a more

---

[5] House of Commons Agriculture Committee, Sixth Report Session 1997–98, *Flood and Coastal Defence* (1998) HC 707, para.9.

sustainable fashion than conventional techniques.[6] Traditionally, built-up areas have been drained using underground pipe systems that seek to prevent local flooding by conveying water away from the place where it falls or accumulates as swiftly as possible. The affect of this is to prevent natural percolation of water into the ground that, in sustainability terms, is problematic. In addition, the functioning of conventional drainage has become a qualitative concern because of its capacity to convey contaminants from urban areas into other watercourses and groundwater. Also, criticisms have been raised of the failure of traditional drainage systems to recognise amenity needs such as the landscaping and wildlife habitat potentials of drainage facilities. Hence, surface water management systems that seek to deal with run-off as close as possible to its sources and take greater account of quantity, quality and amenity issues have much to commend them in terms of enhancing sustainability.[7]

Although these criticisms of conventional piped drainage systems may be well founded, the important practical question is as to the kinds of drainage facility that will address the shortcomings. On this, it is suggested that there are four methods which may be applied to attenuate the flow of surface water run-off: filter strips and swales; filter drains and permeable surfaces; infiltration devices; and basins and ponds. Briefly, these may be described as follows.[8]

*'Filter strips and swales'* are vegetated surface features that drain

---

[6] In the following discussion some rather speculative observations are made without reference to particular sources. Whilst these are not attributable to any particular individual they draw upon empirical research and discussions engaged in by the author in relation to the following projects: Construction Industry Research and Information Association, CIRIA Research Project 448, *Infiltration Drainage* (see particularly R. Bettess, *Infiltration drainage – Manual of good practice* (1996) Report 156 and W. Howarth and A. Brierley, *Infiltration Drainage – legal aspects* (1995) Project Report 25); CIRIA Research Project 473, *Control of pollution from new and existing highway drainage systems* (see M. Luker and K. Montague, Eds., *Control of pollution from highway drainage discharges* (1994) Report 142 and particularly Ch.3 on 'Standards, Legislation and Practice' by W. Howarth); and CIRIA Research Project 522, *Sustainable Urban Drainage Systems* (see *Sustainable urban drainage systems – design manual for England and Wales* (2000) and P. Martin, *Sustainable Urban Drainage Systems – best practice guide* (2001), particularly Appendix A by W. Howarth).

[7] Construction Industry Research and Information Association, *Sustainable urban drainage systems – design manual for England and Wales* (2000) CIRIA Research Project 522, pp.ix, 1 and 2.

[8] Generally see Construction Industry Research and Information Association, *Sustainable urban drainage systems – design manual for England and Wales* (2000) CIRIA Research Project 522, Ch.2, and Department of Transport, Local Government and the Regions, Planning Policy Guidance Note 25, *Planning and Food Risk* (2001) Appendix E.

water evenly off impermeable areas, particularly small residential developments, parking areas or roads, either from gently sloping areas of ground or by means of long shallow surface channels. The objective of this is to mimic natural drainage patterns, involving shallow ditches or 'dry' watercourses, and to enable surface run-off to pass through vegetation, thereby slowing and filtering the flow and trapping contaminants in the surface soil. Systems of this kind may be integrated into surrounding land uses, such as public open spaces or road verges, and can be enhanced as an amenity or wildlife habitat through the establishment of locally present grass and flower species.

'*Filter drains and permeable surfaces*' comprise a volume of permeable material which is placed below ground and used to retain surface water or to allow the flow of run-off to enter the storage area through a permeable material. Naturally, any vegetated area is permeable to a degree which depends upon the characteristics of the sub-soil, but filter drains and permeable surfaces seek to facilitate or enhance permeability where roads or buildings have obstructed or restricted the natural drainage pattern. Hence, the use of permeable paving blocks, or blocks with interstices filled with gravel or soil which allow permeability, enables the natural drainage pattern to be recreated whilst facilitating access to the land by motor vehicles, for example, where an area is used as a car park.

'*Infiltration devices*' is a term that encompasses a broad range of water management systems by which water is drained directly into the ground either at the source of the run-off or after being conveyed through a pipe or swale. Typically, this category includes underground facilities such as soak-aways, infiltration trenches or basins, but it would also encompass surface facilities such as the filter strips and swales, previously mentioned, and other mechanisms for retaining water such as ponds. Again, the objective of such systems is to utilise and enhance the natural capacity of the ground to absorb and drain water, thereby recharging groundwater and mitigating problems of low flows in rivers and loss of wetland areas.

'*Basins and ponds*' are areas for storage of surface water, either as a periodic flood water containment or attenuation facility, in the case of basins, or for permanent water storage in the case of ponds, though with an increased capacity to accommodate flood water. Generally, basins and ponds should feature at the lower end of the sustainable flood management progression so as to accumulate water that cannot be effectively contained or dispersed by the mechanisms previously described. Clearly, permanent bodies of water have a good amenity and wildlife habitat potential, particularly where wetland areas are incorporated, and basins, when dry, also have potential uses as sports or recreational facilities, providing that this does not involve the construction of buildings or other permanent structures upon them.

The four categories of drainage structure that have been described, in different ways, have many of the characteristics desired of sustainable drainage: they each seek to deal with run-off as close as possible to its source, and take account of quantity, quality and amenity issues. However, the use of these approaches envisages a degree of flexibility in meeting the design criteria for a particular location, including the required flood water storage capacity. Hence, it is recognised that there is no single 'correct' approach to sustainable drainage; the type of sustainable drainage system that is adopted, or more likely the combination of types, is the outcome of a location-specific multidisciplinary process. This involves taking into account the original drainage pattern of the area, the catchment topography and rainfall, the ground conditions, the nature of the development being drained and other factors that may arise such as the need to preserve existing wildlife sites. Notwithstanding the assessment of all these factors, there may be locations where the possibilities for sustainable drainage systems are greatly limited, perhaps because of the contamination of land by past uses or because of the special sensitivity of groundwater to contamination. Not least important, is the fact that any drainage system, sustainable or conventional, can only be expected to function to the limits of its design criteria and can never be expected to provide an 'absolute' guarantee against flooding.[9]

## 12.3 LEGAL IMPLICATIONS OF SUSTAINABLE DRAINAGE

The new philosophy of sustainable drainage has impressive environmental credentials, but raises technical questions as to its practical workability and appropriateness in many locations. Against this, it may be noted that the 'back to nature' approach of sustainable drainage means that much of what is proposed is not so entirely novel that its general workability is placed in doubt. That is, before conventional piped drainage became so commonplace, ponds, ditches and soak-aways were the 'tried and tested' mechanisms for meeting drainage needs. Nonetheless, questions of the workability and appropriateness of sustainable drainage in particular situations are bound to be controversial and, quite likely, drainage engineers and planning authorities will be obliged to concede that conventional piped drainage is

---

[9] Generally see Construction Industry Research and Information Association, *Sustainable urban drainage systems – design manual for England and Wales* (2000) CIRIA Research Project 522, Ch.4.

## Legal Implications of Sustainable Drainage

the only practicable solution in some locations. This conclusion is particularly likely in intensely developed urban areas where the greater space that is needed for sustainable drainage structures may not be readily available.

The shift towards sustainable drainage has been given a significant legal impetus by the recent planning guidance, through the need for development plans to take account of the need for sustainable drainage systems and for developers to incorporate such systems into development proposals. Outside the sphere of planning law, however, there is a range of legal issues arising from the need to accommodate more sustainable drainage systems. Not least, this is because much of the legislation under which flood defence is regulated has been drafted, primarily, with piped drainage systems in mind, and the comprehensive overhaul of this legislation to accommodate the new priorities is not likely in the near future. A brief overview of the issues may be helpful in identifying some of the potentially problematic legal aspects.

### 12.3.1 Categorisation Issues

An initial issue concerns the legal categorisation of a sustainable drainage structure. As has been seen, markedly contrasting drainage rights and duties arise in relation to 'drains', 'sewers' and 'watercourses',[10] and it is, therefore, critical to determine which of the categories a sustainable drainage system falls under, not least, for the purpose of identifying future maintenance requirements. Typically, an issue of this kind might be problematic where it is proposed to incorporate a sustainable drainage system into a major residential development and it is unclear who should be responsible for its future maintenance. Broadly, there seem to be at least four categorisation possibilities:

(1) the structure is a 'public sewer', with responsibility falling to the sewerage undertaker;

(2) the facility is a 'drainage structure' or 'highway drain', for which the local authority has responsibility;

(3) the structure is classified as a 'watercourse' which, though in private ownership, is subject to the supervisory and regulatory jurisdiction of the Environment Agency; or

(4) the structure is a 'private drain' for which the present and future owner, or owners, of the land have responsibility.

---

[10] See the definitions of these terms at 7.3 and notes to 1.1 above.

Although most of the major definitional issues have long been resolved in relation to piped drainage systems, their resolution is not so clear in relation to sustainable drainage facilities and there is scope for dispute and the disclaiming of undesired maintenance responsibilities.

### 12.3.2 Sewerage Adoption Implications

Future maintenance of a sustainable drainage system is clearly of considerable importance. Surface facilities, such as filter strips, swales and basins, will need to have vegetation cut back periodically and underground structures, such as filter drains and infiltration devices, will need to be cleansed from time to time to remove sediment and ensure proper functioning. The practical question is who will be responsible for this kind of work, and this depends upon the legal allocation of continuing responsibility and the issue of whether a facility has been 'adopted' by a particular body.

The first of the four possibilities indicated above concerns the circumstances in which a sustainable drainage facility might be categorised as a 'public sewer'. On this, it should be emphasised that sustainable drainage structures are normally intended to be used for the management of 'clean' surface water run-off. That is, they are not envisaged as mechanisms for dealing with 'foul' water such as domestic or industrial effluent. Nonetheless, as has been seen, the definition of a 'public sewer' encompasses various structures for conveying 'sewage' and this is broadly construed to encompass rain water run-off from built-up areas.[11] Hence, there is no reason, in principle, to exclude a sustainable drainage facility from being a sewer solely on the basis that it is not being used to convey foul effluent.

The legal mechanism for a drainage system being adopted by a sewerage undertaker, as a 'public sewer', usually involves a developer entering into an agreement with a sewerage undertaker concerning the proposed sewer.[12] Such agreements are to the effect that the sewer, if constructed in accordance with agreed specifications, will, on construction, be adopted by the undertaker, so that future responsibility for maintenance will lie with the undertaker. However, the construction standards required for adoption of sewers do not address the possibility of sustainable urban drainage systems being provided. Indeed, the latest edition of *Sewers for Adoption*, the water industry's guide to adoption, states that sewerage undertakers are 'generally constrained to accepting pipe systems for adoption'. Because of uncertainties regarding future ownership and maintenance, and the lack of definitive

---

[11] See the discussion of 'public sewers' at 7.6 above.
[12] See the discussion of adoption by sewerage undertakers at 7.2 above.

guidance, above-ground attenuation facilities and similar sustainable drainage systems will not be adopted by undertakers as a part of the public sewerage system.[13]

The legal basis for excluding sustainable drainage facilities from the categories of public sewer that undertakers are willing to adopt is not clear. Conceivably, the exclusion may be founded upon the legally dubious view that there is a need for a 'proper outfall' for a structure to be classified as a public sewer.[14] Clearly, this is a respect in which statutory definition of 'public sewer' could usefully be clarified to make clear the respective responsibilities of developers and sewerage undertakers. Until clarification is provided, the reluctance on the part of undertakers to accept maintenance undertakings that are perceived to be outside the scope of their legal powers may be understandable.

On the other hand, there are situations where the adoption of sustainable drainage facilities would be significantly beneficial to sewerage undertakers. The present 'right' of developers to make a connection to a public sewer may be exercised to allow connection of surface water discharges to sewers that are likely to become overloaded as a consequence. This is a particular problem where a sewer receives both surface water and foul water, and where the right of connection may still be exercised, unless a separate surface water sewer is provided, despite consequent overloading of the sewer.[15] Clearly, a means of preventing undesirable connections, and preventing consequent flooding from sewers, would be to require a developer to secure site drainage by the provision of sustainable drainage facilities which make connection to a sewer unnecessary. Increasingly, the effect of the new planning guidance and revised building regulations[16] should be to require this.

An instructive example of the difficulties arising from the right of connection is provided by the Office of Water Services ruling in *Rydon Construction Ltd* v *Thames Water Utilities Ltd.*[17] Here, it was concluded that a developer had a right of connection to a sewer where the sewer was intended by the sewerage undertaker to be used only for the collection of foul water and the developer sought connection for the purpose of discharging both foul water and surface water. That is, the power of the undertaker to stipulate that surface water should not be discharged to a foul water sewer was only

---

[13] Water UK and WRc, *Sewers for Adoption* (5th ed. 2001) pp. i and 11.
[14] See 7.4.4 above on the alleged 'proper outfall' requirement.
[15] See 7.2 above on the right of connection to a public sewer, under s.106 Water Industry Act 1991.
[16] See 9.15 above on building regulations.
[17] Office of Water Services, 22 April 1998.

applicable where separate foul and surface water sewers were provided and, on the facts at issue, separate sewers were not provided. In a situation of this kind, it would have been advantageous to the sewerage undertaker to have been able to prevent the entry of surface water to the foul water sewer, and this probably would have been achieved had the developer made use of soak-away surface water drainage. The Director General of Water Services and the sewerage undertaker both thought that, in the situation at issue, soak-away drainage would have been a feasible and preferable alternative to making the mains connection for surface water, but this was of no relevance to the legal provisions which clearly allowed the developer to make the connection that was desired.

The *Rydon* decision provides much food for thought. It is illustrative of a potentially wide range of situations where surface water is logistically, environmentally and, perhaps, economically better dealt with by sustainable drainage facilities rather than by making connection to the sewerage system. Nonetheless, there was no mechanism under the Water Industry Act 1991 by which the installation of soak-away drainage could be compelled. Situations of this kind should, in future, be addressed by the planning guidance requiring sustainable drainage systems to be used in appropriate situations. Nonetheless, the right of connection to sewers under the 1991 Act remains unscathed by the changes in planning policy and practice.[18]

### 12.3.3 Local Authority and Highway Drain Adoption

In relation to adoption by local authorities and internal drainage boards, as has been seen,[19] the general drainage powers under the Land Drainage Act 1991 allow for a potentially wide variety of works to be undertaken for the purpose of securing effective drainage. These powers are fairly broadly and unspecifically formulated and would seem to allow a sustainable drainage system to be constructed for the drainage of land and for continuing responsibility to fall to a local authority. The effect of the recent planning guidance will be to cause local authorities to give primacy to sustainable drainage systems over conventional drainage facilities when determining planning applications. Nonetheless, the wording of the land drainage legislation is regrettably inexplicit in indicating that it was within

---

[18] See also the discussion of *W. E. Black Ltd* v *Secretary of State for the Environment and London Borough of Harrow* [1997] Env LR 1, discussed at 9.5 above (where, despite the developer's right of connection with a public sewer, a planning condition requiring flood attenuation works on site was held to be valid in serving a legitimate planning purpose).

[19] See the discussion of flood defence operations by internal drainage boards and local authorities at 4.6 above.

the powers of local authorities to undertake such works, or to accept future responsibility for such works undertaken by others.

In relation to the use of a sustainable drainage system for the purpose of highway drainage, the developer may enter into an adoption agreement with the highway authority so that the road, including the drainage system, falls to be maintained at public expense provided that it is constructed in accordance with agreed specifications.[20] For these purposes, the definition of 'drain' under the Highways Act 1980 is relatively explicit in including reference to a 'soak-away',[21] making it clear that certain kinds of sustainable drainage system are allowed. Whether or not the other kinds of sustainable drainage system will be construed to come within the meaning of 'soak-away' is not clear. Nonetheless, a highway authority will not be entitled to decline adoption purely on the ground that a non-piped system of drainage has been provided.

### 12.3.4 Environment Agency Involvement

If a sustainable drainage system does not fall within the previous categories, it will be either a private drain or a watercourse and will normally give rise to private responsibilities in respect of maintenance. Despite private ownership, the Environment Agency will be primarily responsible for exercising various supervisory and regulatory responsibilities, particularly where there are 'off-site' implications for other aspects of flood defence or in relation to the aquatic environment more generally. Hence, where a facility for discharging water to another watercourse is involved, this may require authorisation if the structure through which the discharge is made might constitute an 'obstruction' for flood defence purposes.[22]

A particular concern, in relation to certain locations, is that the use of sustainable drainage systems may have adverse effects upon water quality and that these are capable of being more damaging than the use of conventional drainage. Generally, if there is reason to suppose that drainage water discharged from any drainage facility is likely to be of unsatisfactory quality, it will be open to the Agency to impose a discharge consent,[23] though this would not normally be required where surface water has not been contaminated.

---

[20] See the discussion of adoption of highway drains at 8.3.2 above.
[21] s.100(9) Highways Act 1980.
[22] Under s.109 Water Resources Act 1991 and s.23 Land Drainage Act 1991 and see 4.4.1 and 4.4.2 above on the authorisation of obstructions by the Environment Agency. Note also the power of internal drainage boards to authorise certain obstructions under s.23 Land Drainage Act 1991 and see 4.7.3 above.
[23] That is a consent under s.88(1) Water Resources Act 1991, which provides a defence to the principal offences concerning water pollution under s.85.

However, where a sustainable drainage facility is perceived to facilitate the transmission of contaminated surface water into the ground there may be particular reasons for the Agency to take a cautious approach. This might arise, for example, where there is a particular hazard because of the close proximity of groundwater that is used for water supply purposes.[24] Alternatively, the land over, or through, which the surface water flows may have been contaminated by previous industrial uses and the Agency may be concerned to prevent the use of drainage structures that might enable or increase the transmission of contaminants into groundwater, which is especially difficult to de-contaminate. These concerns are reflected in the European Community Groundwater Directive,[25] which is implemented by national legislation including the Groundwater Regulations 1998.[26] The Regulations provide for discharge consents to be imposed upon activities which involve disposal of relevant substances to land, providing that there is no risk of groundwater pollution and, in some instances, discharges will only be allowed where the absence of risk to groundwater has been conclusively established by a 'preliminary assessment' of risks involved.

The extent of these concerns about groundwater contamination, however, is greatly dependent upon the character of the land that is to be drained and the proximity of sensitive aquifers. Surface water run-off channelled into a sustainable drainage system should normally be no more contaminated than rainwater which would naturally pass into the ground, and the capacity of some sustainable drainage systems to filter particulate matter has been noted. Notwithstanding the possibility of concerns about the use of sustainable drainage systems in particular locations, and the corresponding legal powers to address these concerns, it may be noted that the Agency has been generally supportive of the greater use of sustainable drainage systems.[27]

---

[24] See Environment Agency, *Policy and Practice for the Protection of Groundwater* (1998).
[25] 80/68/EEC.
[26] S.I. 1998 No.2746.
[27] See Environment Agency, *The Environment Agency and Development Plans* (1998) under *The Natural and Built Environment: Flood Risk* where it is advised: ' wherever possible surface water should be disposed of as close to the source as possible. Where risks are identified appropriate flow attenuation facilities or mitigation measures may be a prerequisite for development. Consideration should be given to the use of softer engineering structures such as swales, detention ponds, infiltration basins and porous surfaces as alternatives to conventional drainage systems, where appropriate.' Also see House of Commons Environment, Transport and Regional Affairs Committee, Second Report Session 2000–01, *Development on, or Affecting, the Flood Plain* (2000) HC 64-II *Memorandum by the Environment Agency* p.33.

## 12.3.5 Private Responsibilities

Apart from the adoption options previously considered, the responsibility for a sustainable drainage system will fall upon the private owner, or owners, of the land upon which it is situated. For some landowners, this may give rise to concerns about maintenance costs and, potentially, issues of civil liability.

In relation to continuing maintenance costs, whether these need to be met by private owners or statutory bodies, the concern is that maintenance expenditure may be more difficult to ascertain than for conventional piped drainage systems. It is generally recognised that surface infiltration facilities will need to be periodically maintained by the clearing of vegetation and underground facilities will need to be have sediment removed from time to time. However, the relative novelty of sustainable drainage systems may have the consequence that the likely maintenance costs involved are less well established than for the conventional alternatives. With practical experience, knowledge of maintenance costs will improve, but present uncertainties may involve a relatively greater element of unpredictability than conventional drainage.

Alongside the potentially uncertain amount of future costs, there is the question of whom these costs should fall upon in relation to a privately owned sustainable drainage system. This does not present a significant difficulty in relation to a drainage system that is contained entirely within land owned by a single owner. However, in many situations this will not be the case, and potential difficulties may arise as to the distribution and continuity of responsibility for future maintenance. For example, in a residential estate where different houses make use of a common sustainable drainage facility located outside the boundaries of any individual property, it will be necessary to determine what contribution individual homeowners should be making towards the cost of maintaining the communal facility. Moreover, a mechanism will be needed to ensure that, on sale of any property served by the facility, the subsequent owner continues to be bound to contribute an appropriate proportion towards the cost of maintenance.

In law, there are long-standing difficulties in imposing 'burdensome' or 'positive' covenants, involving a duty to maintain a particular structure for example, upon successive property owners. Specifically, it has been held that although a covenant of this kind may be binding upon the initial purchaser of a property, it will not generally bind subsequent purchasers.[28]

---

[28] *Austerberry v Oldham Corporation* (1885) 29 Ch D 750 and *Rhone v Stephens* [1994] AC 310. Contrast *Smith and Snipes Hall Farm Ltd v River Douglas Catchment Board* [1949] 2 KB 500 (on the transmission of a *benefit* of a covenant) and generally see K. Gray and S. F. Gray. *Elements of Land Law* (3rd ed. 2001) Ch.10.

There may be some qualifications to this principle in circumstances where a person who chooses to take the benefit of a communal drainage system may be held to be liable to bear a proportionate part of its cost,[29] but it is uncertain whether this exception would be applicable in the context at issue.

A legal solution to the problem of securing continuing responsibility for a communal drainage facility lies in the use of 'rentcharges' in relation to the properties that are benefited by the system. A rentcharge is an annual or periodic payment charged on or issuing out of land. An 'estate rentcharge' is a rentcharge which is to be performed by the owner of the land and which is enforceable by the person to whom the rentcharge is payable. Specifically, an estate rentcharge may be imposed to ensure contributions are made to the provision of services or the carrying out of maintenance or repairs for the benefit of the land. Essentially, this is a means of coupling an obligation upon a property owner to pay a nominal sum of money with a positive covenant in relation to the maintenance of specified structures. Moreover, an estate rentcharge will be enforceable, by the reservation of a right of entry, despite the general principle with regard to the non-enforceability of burdensome covenants.[30]

Appropriately used, estate rentcharges could be used to compel successive owners of properties on an estate to contribute their proportionate shares towards the maintenance of a communal sustainable drainage facility. This might be done by the developer of the estate transferring the ownership of the drainage facility to a management company, perhaps comprised of the owners of properties served by the facility. The management company would then have the legal powers, arising from the rentcharges, to ensure that each property observed the covenant to pay the appropriate proportion of the expense of maintaining the facility.

The issue of civil liability of private or public owners in relation to sustainable drainage structures might arise, for example, if a pool of temporary or permanent surface water is envisaged for the attenuation of flood water, and there is the question of public access to consider. In respect of this, the possibility of occupiers' liability has been previously

---

[29] See *Halsall* v *Brizell* [1957] Ch 169 and *Thamesmead Town Ltd* v *Allotey* (2000) 79 P&CR 557.

[30] ss.1 and 2 Rentcharges Act 1977 and generally see K. Gray and S. F. Gray, *Elements of Land Law* (3rd ed. 2001) section 5.27. See *Morland* v *Cook* (1868) LR 6 Eq 252, discussed at 2.4.2 above (where an obligation to meet a proportionate cost of repairing a sea wall was enforceable between successors in title to a covenant, despite the positive nature of the covenant and that the defendant had no notice of the liability to contribute).

considered[31] and careful thought needs to be given to the degree of hazard to which such a facility may give rise, particularly in relation to children, and the appropriateness and adequacy of safety or warning measures that are provided. This is not to suggest that sustainable drainage systems are inherently more hazardous than conventional piped approaches, but merely that they may require different considerations to be addressed.

Similarly, in relation to civil flooding potential arising from a sustainable drainage facility which proves to be of inadequate capacity to accommodate flood water, there are important issues to be taken into account but in most respects these are much the same issues as would need to be addressed if a conventional piped drainage system was at issue. Essentially, *any* system of drainage will only function effectively to the limits of its design capacity and negligence is capable of arising in respect of an unsatisfactorily designed, or inadequately maintained, sustainable drainage system to the same extent as any other kind of drainage system.

## 12.4 DRAINAGE OF UNDEVELOPED LAND

An attractive feature of sustainable drainage is that it seeks to address the problem of flooding as near its source as possible. Individual landowners should bear the immediate responsibility for excess water falling on their land and should not be allowed to 'solve' their flooding problem by transferring it elsewhere. However, the various systems that have been identified for sustainable drainage have been proposed as preferable options *for the drainage of urban areas*, and it is notable that they are not envisaged as appropriate for rural or other undeveloped areas of land. Given that the greater part of the land area of England and Wales has not been subject to urban or other development, the question arises as to the extent to which this land is sustainably drained. In respect of land in its 'natural' state, which has not been the subject of any significant human intervention, the issue of sustainability does not arise. In respect of land that is in agricultural or forestry use, however, the question is prompted as to what regulatory response is appropriate to prevent the drainage of such land causing, or contributing to, downstream flooding.

A degree of inseparability has been identified between urban flood alleviation and the drainage of agricultural land. Agricultural productivity is frequently dependent upon adequate field drainage, and this requires adequate discharge capacity into drainage channels and rivers downstream. The receiving watercourses may pass through urban areas and can cause flooding. Hence, given the hydrological interdependence, draining agricultural land may exacerbate urban flooding and complex trade-offs

---

[31] See 11.4.3 above on occupiers' liability.

are involved in allocating gains and losses between rural and urban land uses.[32] However, the control of surface water discharges from agricultural land to prevent downstream flooding is only indirectly addressed in law. Controls applicable to discharges to watercourses[33] apply only for the purpose of controlling discharges that are of unsatisfactory quality. In effect, therefore, farmers have a legally untrammelled right to drain their land and, as riparian owners, to discharge drained water into any available watercourse. Remarkably, the cumulative effect of agricultural drainage of land, potentially over a large proportion of a catchment, and involving a succession of individual discharges into a watercourse, it seems, has yet to be recognised as a matter requiring direct regulatory control.

Planning legislation provides farmers and foresters with a wide dispensation from general controls upon development,[34] and has provided no impediment to major projects involving meadows being ploughed up and extensive land drainage systems being put in place, in some instances with the support of government grants.[35] The general freedom to 'improve' the drainage of agricultural or forestry land seems to be constrained only where the land is of special conservation significance[36] or where the drainage operation is subject to environmental impact assessment.[37]

However, in 2000 the House of Commons Environment, Transport and Regional Affairs Committee stressed the need for environmental impact assessment to be more rigorously applied to agriculture and was critical of the Ministry of Agriculture, Fisheries and Food for having failed to do so. It was observed:

> 'it is salutary that a contributory cause of the recent floods may have been the determination of the MAFF not to implement EIA Directive. This is a grave condemnation of this Ministry. We welcome the statement by the Minister for Agriculture and the Countryside that these regulations will now be issued. This must be done as a matter of urgency.'[38]

---

[32] E. C. Penning-Rowsell, D. J. Parker and D. M. Harding, *Floods and Drainage* (1986) pp.1 and 11.

[33] Under ss.89(1) and 85 Water Resources Act 1991.

[34] See s.55(2)(e) Town and Country Planning Act 1990 and Schedule 2 Parts 6 and 7 Town and Country Planning (General Permitted Development) Order 1995, S.I. 1995 No.418.

[35] See House of Commons Environment, Transport and Regional Affairs Committee, Second Report Session 2000–01, *Development on, or Affecting, the Flood Plain* (2000) HC 64, para.43.

[36] See Ch.10 above on conservation implications.

[37] See 9.14 above on environmental impact assessment.

[38] House of Commons Environment, Transport and Regional Affairs Committee, Second Report Session 2000–01, *Development on, or Affecting, the Flood Plain* (2000) HC 64, para.44.

## Drainage of Undeveloped Land 503

The legislative response to this condemnation was the enactment of the Environmental Impact Assessment (Uncultivated Land and Semi-Natural Areas) (England) Regulations 2001.[39] These Regulations implement the European Community Environmental Impact Assessment Directive[40] in relation to projects on uncultivated land and semi-natural areas by requiring an environmental statement to be provided in relation to certain applications for consent from the Secretary of State for projects that are likely to have significant effects upon the environment. Specifically, this requirement may apply to the execution of construction works or other installations or schemes, or other interventions in the natural surroundings and landscape, which involve the use of uncultivated land or semi-natural land for intensive agricultural purposes. Although the Regulations broadly follow the approach of the Town and Country Planning (Environmental Impact Assessment) (England and Wales) Regulations 1999,[41] projects which constitute a 'development' under the 1999 Regulations are excluded from the ambit of the 2001 Regulations.

The 1999 Regulations require environmental impact assessment to be undertaken where a project is likely to have a significant effect upon the environment by virtue of its nature, size or location. The effect of this is that certain agricultural projects will require planning permission to be carried out, notwithstanding the general exemption of agriculture from planning law. Moreover, an individual assessment of whether environmental impact assessment is required for an agricultural project must be made where it exceeds certain thresholds. Under fairly recent amendments to the law, consideration of environmental impact assessment is explicitly required for projects involving the use of uncultivated land or semi-natural areas for intensive agricultural purposes where the area of the development exceeds 0.5 hectare. Consideration of whether assessment is required is also necessary for agricultural water management projects, including land drainage projects, where the area of the works exceeds 1 hectare.[42] Potentially, therefore, since the imposition of these requirements in 1999, environmental impact assessment could be quite widely used to restrict undesirable agricultural drainage projects.

Despite the eventual application of environmental impact assessment to agricultural land drainage projects, the effect of this will be relatively limited in view of the large area of farmland that has already been drained

---

[39] S.I. 2001 No.3966.
[40] Directive 85/337/EEC, as amended by Directive 97/11/EEC, discussed at 9.14.1 and 9.14.2 above.
[41] S.I. 1999 No.293.
[42] Town and Country Planning (Environmental Impact Assessment) (England and Wales) Regulations 1999 S.I. 1999 No.293, and see 9.14.3 above on these regulations.

to accommodate modern farming practices. The approach advocated by the Environment Committee for the future is the greater use of 'cross-compliance', whereby a condition upon the grant of production subsidies would require adherence to specified environmental standards. Hence, agri-environmental grants could be used to support more sustainable agricultural measures such as the re-creation of wetlands. In addition, it was recommended that cross-compliance measures be introduced to ensure that, where appropriate, farming practices which retain water on the flood plain and slow down run-off from uplands are encouraged.[43]

## 12.5 SUSTAINABLE FLOOD DEFENCE

Insofar as a meaningful contrast can be drawn,[44] 'land drainage' concerns the mechanisms for removing water from land which is normally dry, whereas 'flood defence' is concerned with the containment of water within the banks of watercourses or the sea. Notably, the mechanisms that have been discussed for sustainable urban drainage are primarily concerned with *land drainage* rather than *flood defence* and will probably be of limited assistance in the situation of a major watercourse at risk of bursting its banks in flood conditions. This is not to suggest that sustainable urban drainage is only of local significance, since it is clear that flooding from a watercourse may be reduced by attenuation of flows in any part of its catchment. However, there are inevitable limits to the extent to which urban run-off contributes to the flooding potential of a major river and sustainable urban drainage systems alone may be insufficient to address a problem of this kind.

Traditionally, the problem of river flooding has been addressed by 'hard' engineering approaches involving the construction of flood banks that were sufficiently high and robust to contain flood flows. For economic reasons that have been alluded to, however, considerations of sustainability suggest that there should be greater use of 'soft' engineering solutions. These involve the amelioration of flooding and erosion by the use, and enhancement, of natural defences such as flood plains that allow the storage of flood water and the attenuation of flow. Hence, the House of Commons Agriculture Committee has suggested that,

> 'considerably more could be done to end the reliance on hard engineered flood defences in urban areas, through the provision of source control and washland creation. Source Control seeks to slow the passage of

---

[43] House of Commons Environment, Transport and Regional Affairs Committee, Second Report Session 2000–01, *Development on, or Affecting, the Flood Plain* (2000) HC 64, para. 45.

[44] See the discussion of categorisation at 1.1 above.

water through catchments by introducing water-retaining habitats and features, such as wetland and woodland, into farmed areas. Washlands might include fields which remain in productive agricultural use but where the crop grown would not be harmed by periodic flooding – for example, wet pasture. We are told that both options could assist in lessening the intensity of flash floods, and reduce the impact on downstream flooding.'[45]

At another point in its Report, the Committee proposed that soft engineering solutions might even justify the removal of existing defences:

'[w]herever possible – and providing the fullest possible consideration has been given to the safety or defence implications and the consequences for urban industrial development already there – we believe there is a need to reduce long term downstream flooding and erosion risk through the gradual, phased removal of some hard-engineered constraints on rivers and flood defence now deemed to be obsolete, and their replacement with more environmentally sustainable alternatives, for example washlands and source control measures.'[46]

In its response to the Agriculture Committee, the Government seemed to accept the general argument for greater use of soft engineering solutions in accepting that 'there could be a greater role for less interventionist measures such as . . . realignment of defences, including managed retreat and washland creation, as options for operating authorities to consider within their strategies'. However, it concluded that 'present policies, evolving on the basis of a developing understanding of natural processes, can continue to deliver sustainable flood and coastal defences for the foreseeable future, without the need for the widespread retreat that the [Agriculture Committee Report] envisages'.[47] At another point in its response, the Government seemed to place greater emphasis upon the limitations of soft engineering approaches:

'[a]t the time that a defence reaches the end of its useful life a full range of options, including removal of hard engineered solutions and replacement with control measures, is considered. However, while there will always be cases where the alternative approach is appropriate, existing defences almost always have a significant residual value. It

---

[45] House of Commons Agriculture Committee, Sixth Report Session 1997–98, *Flood and Coastal Defence* (1998) HC 707, para. 105.
[46] House of Commons Agriculture Committee, Sixth Report Session 1997–98, *Flood and Coastal Defence* (1998) HC 707, para. 93.
[47] House of Commons Agriculture Committee, Fifth Special Report Session 1997–98, *Replies by the Government and the Environment Agency to the Sixth Report from the Agriculture Committee, Session 1997–98 'Flood and Coastal Defence' (HC 707)* (1998) HC 1117, p.iv.

may therefore be difficult to justify the cost of constructing something new, on a retired line, compared with the possibly smaller costs of repairing or reinforcing the existing structure. . . . Also, managed realignment is usually the economic best option only when retreat to high ground, or a considerably shorter defence line, is feasible.'[48]

More broadly, the Government emphasised limitations to the more radical approach to sustainability, advocated by the Agriculture Committee, in emphasising that many source control methods work well for moderate events but are often overwhelmed and have little impact on larger floods. Similarly, the management and development of washlands needs to be considered with care because they can exacerbate flooding during larger events.[49]

Despite the apparent disparities of opinion, the difference appears to be a matter of degree rather than one of principle, with the Agriculture Committee being more committed, and the Government more reserved, towards the prospect of replacing hard engineered defences by soft engineered solutions.

In practice, the options for soft engineering solutions, including the retreat of river flood embankments to create flood plains, seem to be clearly envisaged. Hence, ministerial guidance on environmental appraisal of flood defence projects emphasises,

'[w]hen designing schemes to alleviate the effects of river flooding appropriate storage, widening of the available flood waterway, or defence set back options which have environmental benefits should be considered, particularly where such measures have the purpose of protecting or enhancing biodiversity.'[50]

Further insights into the implications of sustainable development for flood defence are provided by the Environment Agency's *Policy and Practice for the Protection of Floodplains*.[51] This document sets out the Agency's

---

[48] House of Commons Agriculture Committee, Fifth Special Report Session 1997–98, *Replies by the Government and the Environment Agency to the Sixth Report from the Agriculture Committee, Session 1997–98 'Flood and Coastal Defence' (HC 707)* (1998) HC 1117, p.xiv.

[49] House of Commons Agriculture Committee, Fifth Special Report Session 1997–98, *Replies by the Government and the Environment Agency to the Sixth Report from the Agriculture Committee, Session 1997–98 'Flood and Coastal Defence' (HC 707)* (1998) HC 1117, p.xiv.

[50] Ministry of Agriculture, Fisheries and Food, *Flood and Coastal Defence Project Appraisal Guidance: Environmental Assessment* (FCDPAG 5) (2000) p.17.

[51] Environment Agency (1997). Notably, this policy document predates Department of Transport, Local Government and the Regions, Planning Policy Guidance Note 25, *Planning and Food Risk* (2001) and may need to be read subject to this on some matters. See also English Nature, *Sustainable Flood Defence – the case for washlands* (2001).

policies in relation to river and coastal flood plains which, overall, are to secure and, where necessary, restore the effectiveness of flood plains for defence and environmental purposes. To some extent, the mechanisms by which the Agency envisages that flood plains may be protected and restored to greater sustainability involve the planning process and these may have been superseded by recent planning guidance.[52] Nonetheless, the Agency will advise local planning authorities to use their powers to ensure that flood plains can fulfil their principal functions while contributing beneficially to the environment. In addition, the Agency will seek to persuade planning authorities to recognise the importance of continuity of flood plains and river corridors for flood defence and environmental purposes and, if appropriate, regenerate flood plains through developed areas. Similarly, in respect of the use of its own powers, the Agency will seek to retain, and where necessary restore, the effective flood flow conveyance and flood water storage capacities of flood plains.

Insofar as these policies involve the objectives of 'restoration' and 'regeneration' of river coastal and flood plains, it is apparent that the Agency sees progress towards sustainable development being made by reinstatement of the natural function of flood plains. How far the 'restorative' part of the policy will be taken is the critical issue, since the loss of developed land for the purpose of re-establishing the natural flood plain of a watercourse is likely to be as controversial as protecting that land by high levels of public expenditure. The argument from sustainable development maintains that future generations should not be saddled with excessive levels of maintenance expenditure for the purpose of retaining inappropriate flood defence structures. That argument may be less readily endorsed by those whose property is to be sacrificed for the purpose of restoring a natural flood plain, and clearly a sensitive balance will need to be drawn.[53]

## 12.6 SUSTAINABLE COAST DEFENCE

Many of the issues that have been raised in relation to sustainable flood defence apply, similarly, to coast defence. To a significant degree the need for economic sustainability to be shown is already addressed by the funding mechanisms that operate to determine which new capital projects are actually undertaken.[54] Also, the wildlife conservation designations that apply to significant areas of coastal land, and the planning implications of these, will restrict coast protection works where they have an unacceptable ecological impact.[55]

---

[52] See 9.8 above on planning and flood risk.
[53] See 12.7 below on the cost of sustainable development.
[54] See 6.6 above on funding of coast protection works.
[55] See Ch.12 above on nature conservation designations.

The more controversial issue lies in the continuing maintenance of some existing coastal defences. On this, planning policy guidance on coastal planning has for some time recognised the potential unsustainability of protecting some areas of coastal land from flooding, erosion and encroachment:

> 'in low lying undeveloped coastal areas, options for coastal defence may include managed retreat. In such areas it should not be presumed that it will be economically justified to maintain existing defences .... It may be appropriate to restrict development in such areas pending decisions on coastal defence so that options remain open.'[56]

Whilst, for planning purposes, it is only necessary to 'keep open' the option of managed retreat, the more critical issue is where that option is actually exercised.

The *Good Practice Guide to Coastal Defence and the Environment,* published in 1995, notes that hard coastal defences, which aim to resist the energy of waves and tides, require constant maintenance and expense because they seek to restrict the natural limits of the coastal zone. Such defences have had a serious effect on many important coastal ecosystems by decreasing the width of the shoreline through a process of 'coastal squeeze'. By contrast, soft engineering aims to work with nature by manipulating natural systems which can dissipate the energy of the waves and tides, and has the potential for achieving economies in coastal defence and reducing environmental impact by comparison with traditional engineering approaches. In particular, managed retreat of the coastline may provide a more extensive natural salt marsh seaward of flood defences which allows such defences to be built to a lesser specification than they would otherwise require. Hence, the good practice guidance emphasises that there is considerable scope for combined use of soft and hard engineering approaches to coastal defence.[57]

By comparison, the House of Commons Agriculture Committee, in 1998, identified a greater potential for managed coastal realignment. Although recognising that there was an 'experimental' aspect to dismantling coastal defences and allowing the sea to encroach to a predetermined 'set back line', the long-term adjustment of the shoreline which this allowed was a means of accommodating sea level rise due to environmental changes.

---

[56] Department of the Environment, Planning Policy Guidance Note 20, *Coastal Planning* (1992) para.2.19. See F. Burd, *Managed Retreat: a practical guide* (1995) published by English Nature.
[57] Ministry of Agriculture, Fisheries and Food, *Coastal Defence and the Environment: A Guide to Good Practice* (1995) pp.48 to 50.

Such an approach might be particularly suitable where the long-term provision of hard defences is economically and/or environmentally unsustainable, and is consistent with the natural cycles of accretion and erosion at the shoreline. More generally, the Committee was of the opinion that coastal defence policy cannot be sustained in the long term if it continues to be founded on the practice of substantial human intervention in the natural processes of flooding and erosion.[58]

More recent statements in project appraisal guidance notes reaffirm the concerns about coastal squeeze due to existing sea walls and the consequent loss of intertidal habitats such as saltmarsh, mudflat and saline lagoons. It is recognised that the only way that new habitats can be created is through the realignment of defences. Ideally, realignment should involve the establishment of a new line of defence on rising ground, but this may not always be practicable and the construction of new walls will be necessary to defend particular assets. Although, in time, old sea walls will breach and new intertidal habitats will be created, operating authorities are encouraged to consider whether breaching such walls should be done purposefully. This will have the environmental advantage of creating new habitats sooner than would otherwise occur and should allow greater control over the process so that public access and safety issues can be more effectively managed and opportunities taken to influence the development of the new habitat. The economic advantages of realigning sea defences is also recognised, in that the set back line is likely to be shorter than the original line and a well-developed saltmarsh will reduce the effect of wave action on a sea wall behind it, so providing further opportunities to reduce construction and maintenance costs.[59]

Managed retreat or realignment of the coast, therefore, seems to be supported by strong sustainability arguments of both an economic and environmental kind. However, there are important contrasts to be emphasised in the alternative ways in which managed retreat may be brought about; first, between not building unsustainable new defences and discontinuing maintenance of existing defences which are unsustainable; and, second, between discontinuing maintenance of existing defences and purposefully breaching those defences. The first contrast arises because existing defences may have given rise to expectations on the part of those who they served to protect, whereas no expectations arise in relation to defences that are not built. The second contrast arises because allowing

---

[58] House of Commons Agriculture Committee, Sixth Report Session 1997–98, *Flood and Coastal Defence* (1998) HC 707, paras.5 and 9.
[59] Ministry of Agriculture, Fisheries and Food, *Flood and Coastal Defence Project Appraisal Guidance: Environmental Assessment* (FCDPAG 5) (2000) p.17.

existing defences to deteriorate will result in the loss of land by the forces of nature whereas, arguably, purposefully breaching those defences involves a loss of land due to human intervention. In the most extreme case, the pursuance of a policy of coastal retreat by a deliberate breaching of a sea defence facility may effectively entail a decision to destroy the property of individual landowners, apparently without compensation. There are, therefore, some profound and controversial issues as to where the costs of greater sustainability in flood and coastal defence must fall.

## 12.7 THE COST OF SUSTAINABILITY

Any change in policy has redistributive effects, benefiting some interests to the detriment of others. Sustainable development seems to place a premium upon future interests in restricting present actions that may impair the capacity of future generations to enjoy a satisfactory environment, insofar as developmental benefits do not compensate for environmental impairment. In the context of flood and coastal defence, this means that the progression towards sustainable development inevitably involves some cost to secure longer-term benefits. Most directly, that cost is likely to be borne by those who suffer as a consequence of policies such as river realignment and managed coastal retreat. For example, where reinstatement of a natural river flood plain involves the loss of land which has previously been defended, or where managed retreat of the coastline involves the abandonment of coast protection measures in relation to land which is subject to erosion, the owners of such land will clearly suffer the consequences.

The *Waverley Report*, into the East Coast floods of 1953, recommended that publicly funded flood defence expenditure should generally be related to the value of properties and land that would be protected. However, the Report recognised that there could be departures from this principle, so that, where 'people living under the protection of defences existing before the flood have developed their property with those defences in view, and . . . *to avoid any breach of public faith* those defences should where practicable, be restored and maintained'.[60] The 'breach of public faith' argument seems to amount to a recognition that there is a moral duty, at least, owed to persons who have acted in reliance upon the public provision of flood defences, so that it would be improper to defeat their reasonable expectations by abandoning flood or coastal defences to the detriment of their properties. As a matter of private law, reasonable reliance is capable of providing a basis for liability to be established in a range of situations.

---

[60] Home Office, Scottish Office, Ministry of Housing and Local Government and Ministry of Agriculture and Fisheries, *Report of the Departmental Committee on Coastal Flooding* (1954) Cmd.9165, para.46 (emphasis added), and see 1.8.1 above for discussion of this Report.

## The Cost of Sustainability 511

The status of reasonable reliance as a ground for liability on the part of a public body, however, is less clear, and in a situation where reliance is apparently unilateral and a considerable amount of publicly funded expenditure is at issue the justification looks particularly weak.

The issue of whether those landowners suffering as a result of river realignment or coastal retreat policies should be compensated for their losses was addressed by the House of Commons Agriculture Committee in 1998. The Committee noted the views of conservation bodies that incentives should be provided to agricultural landowners for managed realignment: 'if in the greater good it... makes sense to retreat someone's land, and in order to facilitate this the farmer receives some form of compensation, it should be perceived as an investment from the national point of view'. More generally, the Committee were 'firmly convinced' of the need to put in place a robust financial mechanism for the reimbursement of property and landowners whose assets are sacrificed for the wider interests of the community. Such a step was regarded as an important mechanism for attaining an economically and environmentally sustainable coastal policy and recognising the important role played by individuals in securing the wider social goal.[61]

The Government was totally unconvinced by this argument. In its response to the Agriculture Committee's Report, it reaffirmed that only in narrowly defined circumstances would a person be entitled to compensation for flooding or erosion.[62] More specifically, compensation would not be payable in situations where it is decided not to defend a particular area, or to undertake managed realignment.[63]

There are situations where it has been legally recognised that environmental costs, incurred for the benefit of the public at large, should not be borne

---

[61] House of Commons Agriculture Committee, Sixth Report Session 1997–98, *Flood and Coastal Defence* (1998) HC 707, para.104.

[62] That is, compensation may be payable where environmental benefit is provided by the creation of additional habitat, so that agri-environmental payments are payable under the countryside stewardship scheme. See the European Community Agri-environmental Regulation (EEC/2078/92) which provides a grant-aid scheme to promote farming practices compatible with the protection and improvement of the environment, and the facility for designation of environmentally sensitive areas and establishment of management schemes under s.18 Agriculture Act 1986. On the effectiveness of these arrangements see English Nature, *The Effectiveness of the Floodplain ESA Schemes in the Maintenance and Enhancement of Biodiversity* (2000) Research Report 364.

[63] House of Commons Agriculture Committee, Fifth Special Report Session 1997–98, *Replies by the Government and the Environment Agency to the Sixth Report from the Agriculture Committee, Session 1997–98 'Flood and Coastal Defence' (HC 707)* (1998) HC 1117, p.vi.

exclusively by private persons. Clearly, compensation which is payable in respect of a compulsory purchase of land for an environmental purpose recognises that a private interest must be respected by payment of a fair market value. On the other hand, there are a range of other environmental restrictions that may be imposed upon land use which fall short of acquisition and, in respect of which, compensation would not generally be payable. The essential difficulty is that of determining what degree of restriction upon land use amounts to 'confiscation' by the State or, in the context of flood and coastal defence, where, if ever, a failure to provide flood or coastal defence effectively involves an 'expropriation' of land.

A revealing illustration from the United States is *Lucas v South Carolina Coastal Council*[64] where a property developer had purchased an area of coastal land, in a location that was recognised to be unstable and ecologically important, with the intention of building luxury sea-front residences. Following the purchase, the State enacted legislation that prevented further development of the land and this had the effect of rendering the land valueless for development purposes. A majority of the Supreme Court held that, whilst it was permissible to impose regulatory controls which are based upon 'existing rules and understandings', where controls upon land use amount to a total prohibition of economically productive or beneficial land use compensation must be paid.

Although the *Lucas* case is properly seen against a background of the constitutional protection of property rights in the United States, the Human Rights Act 1998, incorporating the European Convention on Human rights into national law, provides a counterpart to constitutional protection in the United Kingdom.[65] Most pertinently in this respect, it is provided that,

> '[e]very natural or legal person is entitled to the peaceful enjoyment of his possessions. No one shall be deprived of his possessions except in the public interest and subject to the conditions provided for by law and by the general principles of international law.'[66]

---

[64] (1992) 505 US 1003 and see discussion in K. Gray and S. F. Gray, *Elements of Land Law* (3rd ed. 2001) p.1206.

[65] See the discussion of Human Rights Act 1998 and *Peter Marcic v Thames Water Utilities Ltd* [2001] Env LR 146 and [2002] EWCA 65, 7 February 2002, at 7.9 above.

[66] Protocol I Art.1 European Convention for the Protection of Human Rights and Fundamental Freedoms. See the European Court of Human Rights decision in *Fredin v Sweden (No.1)* (1991) ECHR Series A No.192. In this case, following changes in Swedish nature conservation law, the applicant's licence to extract gravel from his land was revoked. The court rejected the applicant's claim that this action contravened his right to property, under Article 1 of Protocol I of the Convention, on the basis that the Swedish authorities had the legitimate objective of nature conservation as the justification for revoking the licence and the applicant had no legitimate expectation that the right would not be revoked.

Clearly, depriving a person of land without compensation would fall within the scope of this provision. What is less clear is whether the withdrawal of flood or coastal defence protection for the land would constitute a 'depriving' for these purposes and, if it did so, whether it would be justified by the public interest exception. The idea of 'depriving' a person of something assumes that they have that thing in the first place and, in the context of a 'right' to flood or coastal defence, it is far from clear that there is any *right* to publicly funded defence of this kind.[67]

At the time of writing, some of the potential difficulties alluded to are the subject of consultation by the Department for Environment, Food and Rural Affairs.[68] The Ministry's view is that, subject to narrow exceptions,[69] the permissive character of flood and coastal defence legislation is such that no statutory right to protection from flooding or coastal erosion exists. Moreover, no compensation is payable from public funds to those affected by flooding or erosion even where it is decided not to defend a particular area or to undertake managed realignment. By contrast, payment of compensation is possible where quantifiable beneficial land use arises, such as where the land is acquired for the construction or maintenance of defences, where damage arises as a result of such operations, or where land can be shown to contribute to defence.[70] Nonetheless, in relation to the abandonment of flood or coastal defences for which continued funding cannot be justified, it is concluded that no liability could arise in relation to those adversely affected as a consequence of abandonment, providing that reasonable procedures are followed and due notice is given.

Despite the general view that abandonment and retreat policies do not give rise to compensation claims from landowners, the Ministry recognises that human rights legislation needs to be taken into account. Hence, a decision to adopt a particular abandonment policy must be rationally based to ensure that account is taken of the general interest, including economic interests. This is particularly important where the Convention right to

---

[67] Although the human right to protection of property from sewage flooding, which seems to have been recognised in *Peter Marcic* v *Thames Water Utilities Ltd* [2002] EWCA 65, 7 February 2002, may have significant implications in relation to other kinds of flooding: see the speculative discussion at 7.9.8 above.

[68] Department for Environment, Food and Rural Affairs, *Managed Realignment: Land Purchase, Compensation and Payment for Alternative Beneficial Land Use* (2001).

[69] Particularly where land is subject to the requirements of the European Community Habitats Directive (92/43/EEC) and see 10.5.2 above on this Directive.

[70] On compensation generally see 4.3.2 above. See also House of Commons Agriculture Committee, Fifth Special Report Session 1997–98, *Replies by the Government and the Environment Agency to the Sixth Report from the Agriculture Committee, Session 1997–98 'Flood and Coastal Defence'* (HC 707) (1998) HC 1117 on recommendation (g).

peaceful enjoyment of possessions is concerned,[71] where the public interest considerations underlying the adoption of an abandonment policy need to be fully documented. Also of potential relevance is the Convention right to a fair trial[72] which could become relevant where a person seeks to undertake flood or coastal defence works at their own expense, but the necessary consent for the works is unreasonably refused by the relevant operating authority.[73] The infringement of this right could become an issue if some impropriety is alleged for which no satisfactory legal mechanism is provided for challenge and, again, the likelihood of adverse impacts will need to be shown to justify a refusal of consent.

The overall conclusion seems to be that environmental costs arising from the implementation of sustainable development in relation to flood and coastal defence will be left to lie where they fall, on individual landowners. With public provision of defences being withdrawn where expense and sustainability considerations do not justify them, private landowners will be left to fall back upon their private rights to defend their land from flooding and erosion. Worse still perhaps, common law rights of individuals to provide their own flood defence will normally require planning permission and consent from the relevant flood or coastal defence operating authority. It remains to be seen to what extent the planning and operating authorities will decline to give permissions or consents for works which are thought to be unsustainable, but it is likely that there will be some harsh and uncompensated consequences for individual landowners in pursuance of the public objective of securing sustainable flood and coastal defence.

---

[71] Under Protocol I Art.1 European Convention for the Protection of Human Rights and Fundamental Freedoms and 7.9.4 see above.
[72] Under Art.6 European Convention for the Protection of Human Rights and Fundamental Freedoms.
[73] See 4.4.1, 4.4.2 and 5.4.10 above on flood defence and coast protection consents.

# BIBLIOGRAPHY

## BOOKS AND ARTICLES

Anon, 'Thames Water fined £250,000 for pumping toxic waste into homes' (2000) 301 *ENDS Report* 50.

Association of British Insurers, *Inland Flooding Risk – Issues Facing the Insurance Industry* (2000).

Association of British Insurers, *Flooding: A Partnership Approach to Protecting People* (2001).

G. Bakkenist, *Environmental Information: Law, Policy and Experience* (1994).

J. H. Bates, *Water and Drainage Law* (1990 updated).

G. Bennett, 'Bristol Floods 1968: Controlled Survey of Effects on Health of Local Community Disaster' *British Medical Journal*, 22 August 1970, p.454.

R. Bettess, *Infiltration drainage – Manual of good practice* (1996) Construction Industry Research and Information Association Report 156.

J. Bosworth and T. Shellens, 'How the Welsh Assembly will Affect Planning' [1999] *Journal of Planning and Environment Law* 219.

M. Brazier and J. Murphy, *Street on Torts* (17th ed. 1999).

J. Brook, H. Paipai, S. E. Magenis, S. L. Challinor, M. van Zijderveld, J. Gibson and L. Moore, *Guidance on the disposal of dredged material to land* (1996) Construction Industry Research and Information Association Report 157.

C. Brooke, *Natural Conditions – A Review of Planning Conditions and Nature Conservation* (1996) (Royal Society for the Protection of Birds).

F. Burd, *Managed Retreat: a practical guide* (1995) (English Nature).

P. Bye and M. Horner, *Easter 1998 Floods: Preliminary Assessment by the Independent Review Team Report to the Board of the Environment Agency* (1998) (Environment Agency).

P. Bye and M. Horner, *Easter 1998 Floods* (1998) (Environment Agency).

G. Cole, 'Land Drainage in England and Wales' (1976) 30(7) *Journal of the Institution of Water Engineers and Scientists* 345.

Construction Industry Research and Information Association, *Sustainable urban drainage systems – design manual for England and Wales* (2000) CIRIA Research Project 522.

Construction Industry Research and Information Association, *Sustainable Urban Drainage Systems – best practice guide* (2001) CIRIA Research Project 523.

T. Cornford, 'The Control of Planning Gain' [1998] *Journal of Planning and Environment Law* 731.

P. Craig and D. Fairgrieve, '*Barratt*, Negligence and Discretionary Powers' [1999] *Public Law* 626.

A. Cuthbertson, 'Wasteland to Wetlands', *Planning Week*, 5 September 1996.

R. Desmier, 'To the Waters and the Wild', *Water Magazine*, 31 March 2000.

D. Elvin and J. Maurici, 'The Alconbury Litigation: Principle and Pragmatism' [2001] *Journal of Planning and Environment Law* 883.

Environmental Resources Management, *Potential UK Adaptation Strategies for Climate Change* (2001) (Department of the Environment, Transport and the Regions).

E. Fisher, 'Is the Precautionary Principle Justiciable?' [2001] *Journal of Environmental Law* 315.

D. Freestone, 'The Road from Rio: International Environmental Law after the Earth Summit' [1994] *Journal of Environmental Law* 193.

D. Freestone, 'The Enforcement of the Wild Birds Directive: A Case Study' in H. Somsen, Ed., *Protecting the European Environment: Enforcing EC Environmental Law* (1996) p.229.

D. French, '1997 Kyoto Protocol and the 1992 UN Framework Convention on Climate Change' [1998] *Journal of Environmental Law* 227.

J. F. Garner and S. H. Bailey, *The Law of Sewers and Drains* (8th ed. 1995).

M. Grant, Ed., *Encyclopaedia of Planning Law and Practice* (updated 1976).

K. Gray and S. F. Gray, *Elements of Land Law* (3rd ed. 2001).

*Halsbury's Laws of England* (4th ed. reissue, 1997) Vol.49(2) *Water*.

S. R. Hobday, *Coulson and Forbes on Waters* (6th ed. 1952).

D. Howarth, *Textbook on Tort* (1995).

W. Howarth, 'Reservoir Safety Reforms' [1986] *Journal of Planning and Environment Law* 578.

W. Howarth, 'The Doctrine of Accretion: Qualifications, Ancient and Modern' [1986] *Conveyancer and Property Lawyer* 247.

W. Howarth, 'Access to the Foreshore' (1992) *Rights of Way Law Review* 11.

W. Howarth, 'Sewage Flooding and Human Rights' [2001] *Water Law* 169.

W. Howarth, 'Living with Flooding: nuisance liability and cost allocation' [2001] *Environmental Law Review* 282.

W. Howarth and A. Brierley, *Infiltration Drainage – legal aspects* (1995) Construction Industry Research and Information Association Project 448 Report 25.

W. Howarth and D. McGillivray, *Water Pollution and Water Quality Law* (2001).

Institution of Civil Engineers, *Learning to Live with Rivers* (2001).

E. A. G. Johnson, 'Land Drainage in England and Wales' (1954) 3(3) *Proceedings of the Institution of Civil Engineers* 601.

S. Johnson, *The Earth Summit: The United Nations Conference on Environment and Development* (1993).

A.-M. Ketteridge and M. Fordham, 'Planning for Floods: the UK Emergency Planning Picture' (1995) unpublished paper delivered at the International Emergency Planning Conference, Lancaster, July 1995 (Flood Hazard Research Centre, Middlesex University).

R. Kimblin, 'After the Deluge' [2000] *Solicitors Journal* 1092.

R. Lee, 'Devolution and the Environment: Wales' in N. Faris and S. Turner, Eds., *Public Law and the Environment: New Directions?* (1999) p.83.

J. D. Leeson, *Environmental Law* (1995).

A. Longworth, 'Land Drainage Law' [1991] *Water Law* 188.

M. Luker and K. Montague, Eds., *Control of pollution from highway drainage discharges* (1994) Construction Industry Research and Information Association Report 142.

B. Markesinis, J.-B. Auby, D. Coester-Waltjen and S. Deakin, *Tortious Liability of Statutory Bodies: A Comparative and Economic Analysis of Five English Cases* (1999).

R. W. P. May, P. Martin and N. J. Price, *Low-cost Options for Prevention of Flooding from Sewers* (1998) Construction Industry Research and Information Association Report C506.

L. Mayer and D. Nash, Eds., *Catastrophic Flooding* (1987).

V. Moore, *A Practical Approach to Planning Law* (7th ed. 2000).

National Coasts and Estuaries Advisory Group, *Coastal Planning and Management* (1993).

G. Newsom and J. G. Sherratt, *Water Pollution* (1972).

M. D. Newsom, *Flooding and Flood Hazard in the United Kingdom* (1975).

A. Nollkaemper, 'Habitat Protection in European Community Law: Evolving Concepts of a Balance of Interests' [1997] *Journal of Environmental Law* 271.

Office of Water Services, *Flooding from Sewers: a way forward* (2002).

T. O'Riordan and J. Cameron, Eds., *Interpreting the Precautionary Principle* (1994).

M. Orlik, *An Introduction to Highway Law* (2nd ed. 2001).

Oxford Economic Research Associates, *The Flood and Coastal Defence Funding Review: A Discussion of Funding Options* (2001).

D. J. Parker, 'Legal and Administrative Arrangements for Flood Warnings in England and Wales: the Case for Change' (1989) unpublished paper delivered at the World Conference on Water Law and Administration, Alicante, Spain, December 1989 (Flood Hazard Research Centre, Middlesex University).

S. Payne, 'Nature Conservation and Development' [1994] *Journal of Planning and Environment Law* 979.

S. Payne, 'Sewerage Pollution of Beaches – Liability and Clean Up' [1994] *Water Law* 183.

S. Payne, 'From Carrots to Sticks – Natural Habitat Protection after the Countryside and Rights of Way Act 2000' [2001] *Environmental Law and Management* p.239.

E. C. Penning-Rowsell and J. W. Handmer, 'Flood Hazard Management in Britain: A Changing Scene' (1988) 154(2) *Geographical Journal* 209.

E. C. Penning-Rowsell, D. J. Parker and D. M. Harding, *Floods and Drainage* (1986).

Philosophical Transactions of the Royal Society of London, *A Discussion on the Problems Associated with the Subsidence of Southeastern England* (1972).

Planning and Environmental Law Reform Working Group of the Society for Advanced Legal Studies, 'Planning Obligations' [1999] *Journal of Planning and Environment Law* 113.

B. Pontin, 'Beyond nuisance? Enforcing the right to a healthy environment within the framework of the Human Rights Act 1998' [2001] *Environmental Law and Management* 305.

M. Robins, S. G. F. Davies and R. S. K. Buisson, *An Internationally Important Wetland in Crisis* (1991) (Royal Society for the Protection of Birds).

R. J. Roddis, *The Law of Coast Protection* (1950).

C. Rodgers, 'Managing Natura 2000: Priorities for Implementing European Wildlife Law' [2001] *Journal of Planning and Environment Law* 265.

K. T. Salt, 'Problems Arising under the Coast Protection Act, 1949' [1956] *Journal of Planning Law* pp.170 to 177, 247 to 253 and 338 to 340.

W. Sheate, *Making an Impact: A Guide to EIA Law and Policy* (2nd ed. 1994).

J. A. Steers, 'The East Coast Floods, January 31 – February 1 1953' (1953) *Geographical Journal* 280.

H. Stuart Moore, *Coulson and Forbes on Waters and Land Drainage* (5th ed. 1933).

J. Thornton and S. Tromans, 'Incorporating the European Convention on Human Rights: Some Thoughts on the Consequences for UK Environmental Law' (1999) *Journal of Environmental Law* 35.

S. Tromans, *The Environment Acts 1990–1995* (1996).

S. Tromans and R. Turrall-Clarke, *Contaminated Land: The New Regime* (2000).

W. Upton, 'The European Convention on Human Rights and Environmental Law' [1998] *Journal of Planning and Environment Law* 315.

R. Ward, *Floods: A Geographical Perspective* (1978).

Water UK and WRc, *Sewers for Adoption* (5th ed. 2001).

A. Wharam, 'The Prevention of Floods' [1974] *Journal of Planning and Environment Law* 333.

S. Whatmore and S. Boucher, 'Bargaining with nature: the discourse and practice of "environmental planning gain" [1993] *Transactions of the Institute of British Geographers* 166.

J. Wightman, 'Liability for Landslips: Should Landowners be Responsible for the Consequences of Erosion ?' [2000] *Environmental Law Review* 285.

J. L. Wilkins, 'Land drainage legislation and the engineer – a review and discussion paper' (1980) 107 *Chartered Municipal Engineer* pp.123 (Part I) and 147 (Part II).

D. Wilkinson, 'Occupier's Liability for Aquatic Risks: Obvious Dangers Excluded?' [2001] *Water Law* 35.

D. Wilkinson, 'Discharge of Water by Statutory Sewerage Undertaker into Watercourse Owned by Another' [2001] *Water Law* 107.

D. Wilkinson, 'Old Laws Fail to Contain Liability for Sewage Flooding: A Floodgate for Human Rights Claims?' [2002] *Journal of Water Law* 45.

H. W. Wilkinson, 'The Natural Drainage of Land' [1987] *New Law Journal* 867.

W. Wils, 'The Birds Directive 15 Years Later' [1994] *Journal of Environmental Law* 219.

A. S. Wisdom, *Land Drainage* (1966).

D. Withrington and W. Jones, 'The Enforcement of Conservation Legislation: Protecting Sites of Special Scientific Interest' in W. Howarth and C. Rodgers, Eds., *Agriculture Conservation and Land Use: Law and Policy Issues for Rural Areas* (1992) Ch.5.

E. E. Wohl, Ed., *Inland Flood Hazards: Human, riparian and aquatic communities* (2000).

World Commission on Environment and Development, *Our Common Future* (1987) (the 'Brundtland Report').

E. Zebrowski, *Perils of a Restless Planet* (1997).

## OFFICIAL PUBLICATIONS AND PUBLICATIONS BY PUBLIC BODIES

### Government Publications

HM Government, *Financing and Administration of Land Drainage Flood Prevention and Coast Protection in England and Wales* (1985) Cmnd.9449.

HM Government, *Biodiversity: the UK Action Plan* (1994) Cm. 2428.

HM Government, *A Better Quality of Life: A Strategy for Sustainable Development for the UK* (1996) Cm. 4345.

*Royal Commission Report*
Royal Commission on Land Drainage in England and Wales, *Land Drainage in England and Wales* (1927) Cmd.2993.

### Departmental Publications

Cabinet Office, *The Future of Emergency Planning in England and Wales* (2001).

Department of the Environment, Planning Policy Guidance Note 14, *Development on Unstable Land* (1990).

Department of the Environment, Planning Policy Guidance Note 16, *Archaeology and Planning* (1990).

Department of the Environment, Planning Policy Guidance Note 17, *Sport and Recreation* (1991).

Department of the Environment, *Policy Appraisal and the Environment* (1991).

Department of the Environment, Planning Policy Guidance Note 20, *Coastal Planning* (1992).

Department of the Environment, Circular 30/92, *Development and Flood Risk* (1992).

Department of the Environment, *Freedom of Access to Information on the Environment: Guidance on the Implementation of the Environmental Information Regulations 1992 in Great Britain* (1992).

Department of the Environment, Planning Policy Guidance Note 12, *Development Plans and Regional Planning Guidance* (1992).

Department of the Environment, *Environmental Appraisal of Development Plans: A Good Practice Guide* (1993).

Department of the Environment, Planning Policy Guidance Note 9, *Nature Conservation* (1994).

Department of the Environment, Planning Policy Guidance Note 15, *Planning and the Historic Environment* (1994).

Department of the Environment, Planning Policy Guidance Note 23, *Planning and Pollution Control* (1994).

Department of the Environment, Planning Policy Guidance Note 2, *Green Belts* (1995).

Department of the Environment, Circular 9/95, *General Development* (1995).

Department of the Environment, *A Guide to Risk Assessment and Risk Management for Environmental Protection* (1995).

Department of the Environment, Circular 11/95, *The Use of Conditions in Planning Permissions* (1995).

Department of the Environment, *Policy Guidelines for the Coast* (1995).

Department of the Environment, Ministry of Agriculture, Fisheries and Food and Welsh Office, *The Environment Agency Management Statement* (1996).

Department of the Environment, Ministry of Agriculture, Fisheries and Food and Welsh Office, *The Environment Agency and Sustainable Development* (1996).

Department of the Environment, *Enforcing Planning Control: Good Practice Code for Local Authorities* (1997).

Department of the Environment, Circular 1/97, *Planning Obligations* (1997).

Department of the Environment, Circular 10/97, *Enforcing Planning Control: Legislative Provisions and Procedural Requirements* (1997).

Department of the Environment, Planning Policy Guidance Note 1, *General Policy and Principles* (1997).

Department of the Environment, Planning Policy Guidance Note 7, *The Countryside* (1997).

Department for Environment, Food and Rural Affairs, *Consultation on the role of flood and coastal defence in nature conservation in England* (2001).

Department for Environment, Food and Rural Affairs, *Flood and Coastal Defence: The Autumn 2000 Floods* (2001).

Department for Environment, Food and Rural Affairs, HM Treasury, Department for Transport, Local Government and the Regions, National Assembly for Wales and Environment Agency, *The Flood and Coastal Defence Funding Review: Report to Ministers by the Review Steering Group* (2001).

Department for Environment, Food and Rural Affairs, *Managed Realignment: Land Purchase, Compensation and Payment for Alternative Beneficial Land Use* (2001).

Department for Environment, Food and Rural Affairs, *Research and Development Annual Reports* (2001, annual publication).

Department for Environment, Food and Rural Affairs, *Review of Scheme Prioritisation System for DEFRA Grant Aid: Second Consultation* (2001).

Department for Environment, Food and Rural Affairs, *To what degree can the October/November 2000 flood events be attributed to climate change?* (2001).

Department for Environment, Food and Rural Affairs and National Assembly for Wales, *The Flood and Coastal Defence Funding Review: Consultation Document* (2002).

Department of the Environment, Transport and the Regions, Circular 9/98, *Affordable Housing* (1998).

Department of the Environment, Transport and the Regions, *Planning for the Communities of the Future* (1998).

Department of the Environment, Transport and the Regions, Circular 2/99, *Environmental Impact Assessment* (1999).

Department of the Environment, Transport and the Regions, *Countryside and Rights of Way Act 2000*, Circular 04/2001 (2001).

Department of the Environment, Transport and the Regions, *Elaboration of the Environment Agency's Flood Defence Supervisory Duty* (1999).

Department of the Environment, Transport and the Regions, *Indicators of Climate Change in the UK* (1999).

Department of the Environment, Transport and the Regions, Planning Policy Guidance Note 12, *Development Plans* (1999).

Department of the Environment, Transport and the Regions, Circular 02/2000, *Environmental Protection Act 1990: Part IIA, Contaminated Land* (2000).

## Official Publications and Publications by Public Bodies 523

Department of the Environment, Transport and the Regions, *Climate Change: the UK Programme* (2000) Cm. 4913.

Department of the Environment, Transport and the Regions, National Assembly for Wales and Ministry of Agriculture, Fisheries and Food, *Code of Practice on Conservation, Access and Recreation* (2000).

Department of the Environment, Transport and the Regions, Planning Policy Guidance Note 3, *Housing* (2000).

Department of the Environment, Transport and the Regions, Policy Planning Guidance Note 11, *Regional Planning* (2000).

Department of the Environment, Transport and the Regions, *Environmental Impact Assessment: A Guide to Procedures* (2001).

Department of the Environment, Transport and the Regions, *First consultation paper on the implementation of the EC Water Framework Directive* (2001).

Department of Transport, Local Government and the Regions, *Approved Document H: Drainage and Waste Disposal 2002 Edition* (2001).

Department of Transport, Local Government and the Regions, *Planning: delivering a fundamental change* (2001).

Department of Transport, Local Government and the Regions, Planning Policy Guidance Note 25, *Development and Flood Risk* (2001).

Department of Transport, Local Government and the Regions, *Reforming Planning Obligations: a consultation paper* (2001).

Environment Agency, *Review of the Appraisal Framework* (2001).

Home Office, Scottish Office, Ministry of Housing and Local Government and Ministry of Agriculture and Fisheries, *Flood Warning System* (1953) Cmd.8923.

Home Office, Scottish Office, Ministry of Housing and Local Government and Ministry of Agriculture and Fisheries, *Report of the Departmental Committee on Coastal Flooding* (1954) Cmd.9165 (the '*Waverley Report*').

Home Office, *Dealing with Disasters* (3rd ed. 1997).

Ministry of Agriculture, Fisheries and Food, *The East Coast Floods 1953* (1962).

Ministry of Agriculture, Fisheries and Food and Welsh Office, *Coastal Defence and the Environment: A guide to good practice* (1993).

Ministry of Agriculture, Fisheries and Food and Welsh Office, *Strategy for Flood and Coastal Defence* (1993).

Ministry of Agriculture, Fisheries and Food, Welsh Office, Association of Drainage Authorities, English Nature and National Rivers Authority *Water Level Management Plans: A procedural guide for operating authorities* (1994).

Ministry of Agriculture, Fisheries and Food, *Coastal Defence and the Environment: A Guide to Good Practice* (1995).

Ministry of Agriculture, Fisheries and Food, *The EC Habitats Directive: Implications for Flood and Coastal Defence* (1995).

Ministry of Agriculture, Fisheries and Food, Welsh Office, Association of District Councils, English Nature and National Rivers Authority, *Shoreline Management Plans: A Guide for Coastal Defence Authorities* (1995).

Ministry of Agriculture, Fisheries and Food and Welsh Office, *Code of Practice on Environmental Procedures for Flood Defence Operating Authorities* (1996).

Ministry of Agriculture, Fisheries and Food, *Flood and Coastal Defence – Post Project Evaluation Summary Report 1995/96* (1997).

Ministry of Agriculture, Fisheries and Food, *Elaboration of the Environment Agency's Flood Defence Supervisory Duty* (1999).

Ministry of Agriculture, Fisheries and Food, *Flood and Coastal Defence Project Appraisal Guidance: Economic Appraisal* (FCDPAG3) (1999).

Ministry of Agriculture, Fisheries and Food, *Report of the Advisory Committee on Flood and Coastal Defence Research and Development* (1999).

Ministry of Agriculture, Fisheries and Food, *Water Level Management Plans: Additional Guidance Notes for Operating Authorities* (1999).

Ministry of Agriculture, Fisheries and Food, *Flood and Coastal Defence Project Appraisal Guidance: Approaches to Risk* (FCDPAG4) (2000).

Ministry of Agriculture, Fisheries and Food, *Flood and Coastal Defence Project Appraisal Guidance: Environmental Appraisal* (FCDPAG5) (2000).

Ministry of Agriculture, Fisheries and Food, *Consultation on Flood and Coastal Defence Funding Scheme Prioritisation System* (2001).

Ministry of Agriculture, Fisheries and Food, *Flood and Coastal Defence Project Appraisal Guidance: Overview* (FCDPAG1) (2001).

Ministry of Agriculture, Fisheries and Food, *Flood and Coastal Defence Project Appraisal Guidance: Strategic Planning and Appraisal* (FCDPAG2) (2001).

Ministry of Agriculture, Fisheries and Food, *Flood and Coastal Defence Project Appraisal Guidance: Post Project Evaluation* (FCDPAG6) (forthcoming).

Ministry of Health, *Coast Protection Act 1949* (1950) Circular 9/50.

Ministry of Housing and Local Government, *Coast Protection Act, 1949* (1962) Circular 41/62.

Official Publications and Publications by Public Bodies 525

## Welsh Office and National Assembly for Wales Publications

Welsh Office, Planning Guidance (Wales), *Planning Policy* (1999) First Revision.

Welsh Office, Planning Guidance (Wales), Technical Advice Note 1, *Joint Housing and Land Availability Studies* (1997).

Welsh Office, Planning Guidance (Wales), Technical Advice Note 2, *Planning and Affordable Housing* (1996).

Welsh Office, Planning Guidance (Wales), Technical Advice Note 5, *Nature Conservation and Planning* (1996).

Welsh Office, Planning Guidance (Wales), Technical Advice Note 14, *Coastal Planning* (1998).

Welsh Office, Planning Guidance (Wales), Technical Advice Note 15, *Development and Flood Risk* (1998).

Welsh Office, Planning Guidance (Wales), Technical Advice Note 16, *Sport and Recreation* (1998).

National Assembly for Wales, Planning Guidance (Wales), Technical Advice Note 6, *Agricultural and Rural Planning* (2000).

National Assembly for Wales, *High Level Targets for Flood and Coastal Defence and Elaboration of the Environment Agency's Flood Defence Supervisory Duty* (2001).

## Parliamentary Committee Reports

House of Commons Environment Committee, Second Report Session 1991–92, *Coastal Zone Protection and Planning* (1992) HC 17.

House of Commons Environment Committee, First Report Session 1991–92, *The Government's Proposals for an Environment Agency* (1992) HC 55.

House of Commons Committee of Public Accounts, Thirteenth Report Session 1992–93, *Coastal Defences in England* (1992) HC 85.

House of Commons Environment Committee, Session 1995–95, *Environment Bill: Hearings of the Draft Environment Agencies Bill* (1994) HC 40.

House of Commons Agriculture Committee, Sixth Report Session 1997–98, *Flood and Coastal Defence* (1998) HC 707.

House of Commons Agriculture Committee, Fifth Special Report Session 1997–98, *Replies by the Government and the Environment Agency to the Sixth Report from the Agriculture Committee, Session 1997–98, 'Flood and Coastal Defence' (HC 707)* (1998) HC 1117.

House of Commons Environment, Transport and Regional Affairs Committee, Second Report Session 2000–01, *Development on, or Affecting, the Flood Plain* (2000) HC 64.

House of Commons Agriculture Committee, Third Report Session 2000–01, *Flood and Coastal Defence Follow Up* (2001) HC 172.

House of Commons Agriculture Committee, Eighth Special Report Session 1999–2000, *Reply by the Government to the Third Report of the Agriculture Committee, Session 2000–01 'Flood and Coastal Defence Follow Up'* (2001) HC 437.

House of Lords Committee on the European Communities, First Report Session 1989-90, *Freedom of Access to Environmental Information* (1990) HL Paper 2.

House of Lords Committee on the European Communities, First Report Session 1996-97, *Freedom of Access to Environmental Information* (1996) HL Paper 9.

**English Nature and Countryside Council for Wales Publications**

English Nature, *Estuary Management Plans: A co-ordinator's guide* (1993).

English Nature, *Water Level Requirements of Selected Plants and Animals* (1997).

English Nature, *Coastal Habitat Management Plans: An Interim Guide to Content and Structure* (2000).

English Nature, *The Effectiveness of the Floodplain ESA Schemes in the Maintenance and Enhancement of Biodiversity* (2000) Research Report 364.

English Nature, *Annual Report: 1 April 2000–31 March 2001* (2001).

English Nature, *Sustainable Flood Defence – the case for washlands* (2001).

Countryside Council for Wales, *Annual Report 2000–01* (2001).

**Environment Agency Publications**

Environment Agency, *Liaison with Local Planning Authorities* (1997).

Environment Agency, *Policy and Practice for the Protection of Floodplains* (1997).

Environment Agency, *Environment Agency Response to the Independent Report on the Easter 1998 Floods* (1998).

Environment Agency, *Policy and Practice for the Protection of Groundwater* (1998).

Environment Agency, *The Environment Agency and Development Plans* (1998).

Environment Agency, *Annual Report and Accounts 1998/99* (1999).

Environment Agency, *Flood Defence Emergency Response (FEDR) Project* (1999).

Environment Agency, *Flood Warning Service Strategy for England and Wales* (1999).

Environment Agency, *Floodline* information pack (updated 1999).

Environment Agency, *Local Environment Agency Plans* (1999).

Environment Agency, *Policy Regarding Culverts: Technical Guidance on Culverting Proposals* (1999).

Environment Agency, *Policy Regarding Culverts: Explanation of Policy* (1999).

Environment Agency, *Policy Regarding Culverts: Policy Statement* (1999).

Environment Agency, *Sustainable Development: Taking Account of Costs and Benefits* (1999).

Environment Agency, *Annual Report and Accounts 1999–2000* (2000).

Environment Agency, *Corporate Plan 2001/02* (2000).

Environment Agency, *A Framework for Change: Reducing Flood Risk* (2001).

Environment Agency, *Annual Report and Accounts 2000/01* (2001).

Environment Agency, 'Sharp rise in Thames Barrier closures', *Environment Action*, Issue 29, July 2001.

Environment Agency, *Lessons Learned: Autumn 2000 Floods* (2001).

**Miscellaneous Official Publications**

Law Commission, *Report on the Consolidation of the Legislation in Relation to Water* (1991) Law Com. No.198, Cm. 1483.

Nolan Committee on Standards in Public Life, *Third Report* (1997).

National Audit Office, *Inland Flood Defence* (2001) HC 299.

Office of Water Services, *Levels of Service for the Water Industry in England and Wales* (2001).

**European Commission Publications**

European Commission, *Report of the Commission on the Implementation of Directive 85/337/EC on the Assessment of the Effects of Certain Public and Private Projects on the Environment* COM (93)28 final.

European Commission Communication, *A European Community Biodiversity Strategy* COM (1998) 42 final.

European Commission, *Proposal for a European Parliament and Council Recommendation concerning the implementation of Integrated Coastal Zone Management in Europe* COM (2000) 545 final.

European Commission, *Communication from the Commission to the Council and the European Parliament on Integrated Coastal Zone Management: A Strategy for Europe* COM (2000) 547 final.

European Commission, *Communication on the Precautionary Principle* COM (2000) 1.

European Commission, *Decision on the ratification by the EC of the Kyoto Protocol to the United Nations Framework Convention on Climate Change and the joint fulfilment of the commitments thereunder* COM (2001) 579.

# INDEX

'act of God' defence ..................................................................... 72-73
administration
    proposals .................................................................................. 156-58
    responsibilities distribution, assessment ............................... 155-56
adoption
    highway authorities, sustainable drainage systems ............... 496-97
    local authorities, sustainable drainage systems .................... 496-97
    sewerage *see under* sustainable drainage systems
agenda 21 plans .............................................................................. 381
Agricultural Land Tribunal ............................................................ 198
agricultural valuation principles ................................................... 269
agriculture
    drainage and urban flooding ................................................... 501-02
    environmental impact assessment application ...................... 502-04
alleviation of flooding *see* flood alleviation
archaeology, planning guidance .................................................... 395
Autumn Floods (2000) ................................................................ 25-27
    Environment Agency report ...................................................... 26

basins and ponds ....................................................................... 491-92
Bellwin Scheme .............................................................................. 461
biodiversity ..................................................................................... 106
biodiversity action plans ................................................................ 381
biological diversity ................................................................... 430-31
bird habitats ............................................................................... 432-33
building control ........................................................................ 406-07
byelaws ............................................................... 132-34, 145-46, 150

catchment boards ........................................................ 32-33, 128-29
catchment flood management plans ............................................. 380
City of London *see* London
civil emergencies ...................................................................... 455-56
civil rights ................................................................................... 37-39
    *see also* riparian rights
    good neighbourliness .................................................................. 37
    non-feasance and misfeasance ................................................. 305
    public bodies *see* public bodies, civil liability
    sewerage undertakers *see* sewerage undertakers, civil liability
    statutory context ..................................................................... 38-39
climate change ........................................................................... 13-17
    global warming ....................................................................... 13-14
    greenhouse gas emissions ...................................................... 14-15
    guidance from Department for Environment, Food and Rural Affairs ......... 102
    immediate measures ............................................................... 16-17
    Intergovernmental Panel on Climate Change .......................... 102
    Kyoto Protocol ............................................................................ 15
    rainfall predictions ..................................................................... 14
    Rio Earth Summit ....................................................................... 15

530           *Index*

coast defence *see* coastal defence; sustainable coast defence
coast erosion *see* coastal erosion
coast protection ............................................................................................ 204-06
 authorities *see under* Coast Protection Act ................................................ 1949
 boards .......................................................................................................... 213-14
 charges ........................................................................................................ 220-22
 Coast Protection Act 1949 *see* Coast Protection Act
 common law responsibilities .................................................................... 209-13
  Crown duty ............................................................................................ 211
  statutory duties and ............................................................................ 211-13
 compensation ............................................................................................ 225-29
 compulsory acquisition of land ................................................................ 224-25
 consents concerning works ...................................................................... 230-32
 Crown duty .................................................................................................... 211
 default powers of Minister ........................................................................ 235-36
 excavations, prohibition ............................................................................ 232-34
 flood defence distinction .......................................................... 205, 206-09, 237
  artificial nature .................................................................................. 206-07
  coast protection authorities ...................................................................... 206
  legal basis .................................................................................. 206-07, 209
 funding .................................................................................... 205-06, 236-37, 277
 general coast protection work ........................................................................ 218
 grants and contributions towards expenses .............................................. 236-37
 inspections ...................................................................................................... 106
 maintenance and repair ................................................................ 220, 222-24
 notification concerning works .................................................................. 231-32
 policy statement ............................................................................................ 237
 powers of entry .......................................................................................... 234-35
 prohibition of excavations ........................................................................ 232-34
 sale of severed materials .............................................................................. 218
 sea defence commissioners .................................................................... 230 & n
 seashore, definition .................................................................................... 213n
 shoreline management plans ........................................................... 106, 237-38
 subsisting obligations ................................................................................ 229-30
 works schemes .............................................................................. 218-20, 221
Coast Protection Act 1949
 charges ........................................................................................................ 220-22
 coast protection authorities ...................................................................... 213-14
  powers .................................................................................................. 214-17
 coast protection boards ............................................................................ 213-14
 compensation ............................................................................................ 225-29
 compulsory acquisition of land ................................................................ 224-25
 consents concerning works ...................................................................... 230-32
 default powers of Minister ........................................................................ 235-36
 general coast protection work ........................................................................ 218
 grants and contributions towards expenses .............................................. 236-37
 maintenance and repair ................................................................ 220, 222-24
 maritime districts ...................................................................................... 213-14
 notification concerning works .................................................................. 231-32
 powers of entry .......................................................................................... 234-35
 prohibition of excavations ........................................................................ 232-34

## Index 531

*Coast Protection Act 1949 (cont.)*
    sale of severed materials .................................................................218
    sea defence commissioners ......................................................... 230 & n
    seashore, definition .....................................................................213n
    subsisting obligations ................................................................ 229-30
    works schemes .............................................................. 218-20, 221
Coast Protection Act 1949 excavations, prohibition ...................... 232-34
coastal area management plans ................................................................107
coastal defence
    definition ......................................................................... 1-2, 3
    sustainable *see* sustainable coast defence
coastal erosion ........................................................................... 80-81
    development in areas at risk ..............................................................107
    risk assessment ...............................................................................106
coastal planning *see under* planning
commissions of sewers ................................................................ 29-30
community strategies ........................................................................381
compensation, coast protection ................................................... 225-29
compulsory acquisition of land ................................................... 224-25
consents concerning works, for coast protection ........................ 230-32
conservation
    *see also* environmental concerns; public authorities, conservation duties
    planning guidance ...........................................................................392
    special areas of conservation ..................................................... 434-35
contaminated land ..............................................................................394
Crown duty, for coast protection ........................................................211
culverting
    civil liabilities ............................................................................ 71-77
        act of God defence ................................................................ 72-73
        establishing nuisance ............................................................. 74-77
        *Greenock* ruling .............................................................................71
        statutory authority defence ................................................... 73-74
        sufficient capacity obligation .............................................. 71-72
    functional significance ............................................................. 289-90
    local authority powers .............................................................. 331-33
    policy ........................................................................................ 180-81
curtilage ..............................................................................................282

Department for Environment, Food and Rural Affairs
    administrative background ........................................................ 95-97
    biodiversity targets ..........................................................................106
    climate change guidance .................................................................102
    Coast Protection Act 1949 ..............................................................112
    coast protection inspections ...........................................................106
    coastal area management plans .....................................................107
    coastal erosian risk assessment .....................................................106
    development in areas at risk of coastal erosion, identification ......107
    development in areas of flooding, identification ..........................107
    emergency exercises and plans .....................................................105
    encouragement of sound and sustainable measures ................ 98-99
    Environment Act 1995 ............................................................ 108-09
    Environment Agency board members' appointment and ...... 103-04

*Department for Environment, Food and Rural Affairs (cont.)*
    Environment Agency sponsorship .................................................................. 103-04
    environmental guidance ................................................................................. 101-02
    expenditure programmes ..................................................................................... 106
    flood defence inspection .................................................................................... 106
    flood risk assessment ......................................................................................... 106
    flood warning systems ............................................................................... 97, 105
    grant funding priorities guidance ............................................................... 100-101
    high level targets ......................................................................................... 104-05
        biodiversity ................................................................................................ 106
        coast protection inspections ..................................................................... 106
        coastal area management plans ................................................................ 107
        coastal erosian risk assessment ................................................................ 106
        development in areas at risk of coastal erosion, identification ............... 107
        development in areas of flooding, identification ..................................... 107
        emergency exercises and plans ................................................................ 105
        expenditure programmes .......................................................................... 106
        flood defence inspection .......................................................................... 106
        flood risk assessment ............................................................................... 106
        flood warnings, provision ........................................................................ 105
        internal drainage board administration and membership, guidance ....... 107
        National Flood and Coastal Defence Database ....................................... 105
        policy statements ...................................................................................... 105
        shoreline management plans .................................................................... 106
        water level management plans ........................................................... 106-07
    inappropriate development, discouragement ................................................... 103
    indicative standards ................................................................................... 99-100
    internal drainage board administration and membership, guidance ............. 107
    Land Drainage Act 1991 ............................................................................ 110-12
    legal responsibilities ........................................................................................... 96
    National Flood and Coastal Defence Database ............................................... 105
    policy objectives ........................................................................... 97, 105, 248
    research and development ................................................................................ 103
    shoreline management plans ............................................................................ 106
    statutory functions ....................................................................................... 107-08
    technical standards ..................................................................................... 99-100
    water level management plans .................................................................. 106-07
    Water Resources Act 1991 ......................................................................... 109-10
Department for Transport, Local Government and the Regions ......................... 103
development
    in areas at risk of coastal erosion, identification ............................................ 107
    in areas of flooding, identification .................................................................. 107
    developer's flood risk contributions, guidance ........................................ 386-87
development plans *see under* planning
Director General of Water Services, flood alleviation priorities .................. 308-09
disposal of soil ............................................................................... 172-76, 190-91
ditches
    cleansing powers ............................................................................................... 330
    orders requiring cleansing ........................................................................ 197-99
    roadside
        power to fill in ..................................................................................... 341-42
        responsibilities for .............................................................................. 345-47

## Index

drain
  definition .................................................................... 281, 283
  distinct from sewer ............................................................ 282-83
  private ....................................................................................... 493
drainage
  *see also* drain *above*
  agricultural drainage and urban flooding ........................... 501-02
  boards ......................................................................................... 30
  building control ................................................................. 406-07
  charges
    general ............................................................................ 261-63
    special ................................................................................. 263
  definition ................................................................................ 1, 1a
  levies ................................................................................... 265-67
    differential ..................................................................... 271-73
  private ....................................................................................... 493
  rates .................................................................................... 265-67
    appeals ........................................................................... 270-71
    assessment .................................................................... 267-69
    differential ..................................................................... 271-73
    exemption ...................................................................... 273-74
  small areas ................................................................................ 191
  structure ................................................................................... 493
  sustainable systems *see* sustainable drainage systems

East Coast Flood (1953) ............................................................ 19-22
  London and ................................................................................ 22
  Waverly report ................................................................... 20, 510
Easter Floods (1998) ................................................................. 23-25
  Bye report .................................................................................. 23
ecological concerns *see* environmental concerns
emergency response obligations ............................................ 459-62
  Bellwin Scheme ....................................................................... 461
  contingency planning ........................................................ 460-61
  expenditure incurrment ..................................................... 460-61
  financial assistance ................................................................. 461
  fire service ............................................................................... 459
  flood defence authorities ........................................................ 460
  leadership role proposals ....................................................... 462
  local authorities ................................................................ 459-61
  partnership arrangements proposals .................................... 462
  police service .......................................................................... 459
Environment Agency ............................................................. 33, 94
  arrangements with other authorities ............................... 131-32
  board appointments .......................................................... 103-04
  consultee role ..................................................... 368-69, 370-72
  costs and benefits duty ..................................................... 119-20
  Department for Environment, Food and Rural Affairs sponsorship ........ 103-04
  development control ........................................................ 370-72
  development plans, influence on ..................................... 369-70
  environmental duties *see under* environmental concerns *below*
  flood defence byelaws ..................................................... 132-34

*Environment Agency (cont.)*
  flood defence function ................................................................. 124-27
    development planning .......................................................... 126
    flood warnings ....................................................................... 126
    goals and actions .................................................................. 127
    inspection and assessment responsibilities ..................... 125
    overall supervision ............................................................ 124-25
    risk assessment ................................................................. 125-26
  flood warnings *see under* flood warnings
  funding *see under* funding
  incidental functions ................................................................... 135
  indicative flood plain maps ............................... 375, 453-54, 479-80
  information access ................................................................ 452-54
  information gathering role ................................................... 452-53
  local flood defence committees .......................................... 123-24
  main river functions .............................................................. 127-31
  operational powers *see* Environment Agency, operational powers *below*
  organisation ............................................................................ 120-21
  planning authorities, relationship with .................................. 369
  planning role .......................................................................... 368-72
  powers of entry ...................................................................... 134-35
  principal aim .......................................................................... 116-18
  private watercourses, jurisdiction ............................................ 493
  regional flood defence committees ..................................... 121-23
  regulatory powers *see* Environment Agency, regulatory powers *below*
  staffing ..................................................................................... 120-21
  statutory consultee role .......................................... 368-699, 370-72
  statutory functions ................................................................ 114-16
  sustainable development and .................................... 116-18, 119
  sustainable drainage systems involvement *see under* sustainable drainage
    systems
  transfer of functions ............................................................. 131-32
  watercourses, private, jurisdiction ........................................... 493
Environment Agency, operational powers
  agreements with other persons .......................................... 176-77
  compensation ........................................................................ 165-71
    assessment problems ..................................................... 169-71
    betterment offsets .............................................................. 168
    common law claims ........................................................... 166
    statutory liabilities ........................................................... 166-67
  compulsory works orders .................................................... 171-72
  default powers ...................................................................... 177-78
  disposal of soil ...................................................................... 172-76
  general flood defence works ............................................... 160-65
    contractual liabilities ...................................................... 164-65
    permissive character ...................................................... 162-64
    statutory powers ............................................................. 160-62
  schemes for small areas ........................................................ 176
Environment Agency, regulatory powers
  awards variation ................................................................... 186-87
  commutation of landowners' obligations .......................... 185-86
  concurrent with internal drainage boards ....................... 183-84

*Environment Agency, regulatory powers (cont.)*
    controls over structures in main rivers .................................................. 178-79
        determination period ........................................................................ 179
    culverting policy ................................................................................. 180-81
    flood defence authorisations ............................................................. 178-80
    internal drainage boards supervision ................................................ 183
    navigation rights variation ................................................................ 187
    obstructions in ordinary watercourses .............................................. 180
    supervision of local authorities ......................................................... 184-85
    watercourse flow maintenance ......................................................... 182-83
    watercourse repairs ........................................................................... 181-82
environmental concerns
    authorisation requirements ............................................................... 413
    basic issues ........................................................................................ 408-09
    codes of practice ............................................................... 414-18, 421-22
    consultation requirements ................................................................ 413
    Environment Agency ........................................................................ 409-16
        authorisation requirements ......................................................... 413
        basic duties ................................................................................. 409-12
        coastal protection ....................................................................... 418
        codes of practice ......................................................................... 414-18
        consultation requirements .......................................................... 413
        ministerial approval .................................................................... 414-18
        sites of special interest ............................................................... 412-14
    internal drainage boards ................................................................... 418-22
        basic duties ................................................................................. 418-20
        codes of practice ......................................................................... 421-22
        sites of special scientific interest ............................................... 420-21
    local authorities ................................................................................ 418-22
        basic duties ................................................................................. 418-20
        codes of practice ......................................................................... 421-22
        ministerial directions .................................................................. 421-22
        sites of special scientific interest ............................................... 420-21
    ministerial approval .......................................................................... 414-18
    ministerial directions ........................................................................ 421-22
    planning powers ................................................................................ 396-97
    sites of special interest ..................................................................... 412-14
    sites of special scientific interest ...................................................... 420-21
    strategic environment assessment ................................................... 404-06
environmental impact assessment ........................................................... 395-406
    agricultural application .................................................................... 502-04
    basic purpose .................................................................................... 395
    basic requirements ........................................................................... 395-96
    characteristics of potential impact .................................................. 403, 403n
    consultation requirements ................................................. 401-02, 403-04
    EC amending directive ..................................................................... 400
    EC directive ...................................................................................... 397-400
    improvement works and .................................................................. 402-04
        characteristics of potential impact ............................................. 403, 403n
        consultation requirements ......................................................... 403-04
        publicity requirements ............................................................... 403-04

*environmental impact assessment (cont.)*
  land drainage improvement works regulations ........................................ 402-04
  legal status .................................................................................................. 396
  mandatory categories ................................................................................ 398
  procedure .............................................................................................. 397-98
  publicity requirements ................................................................ 402, 403-04
  regulations ......................................................................................... 400-402
  screening procedures ................................................................................. 401
  strategic environment assessment .......................................................... 404-06
  threshold criteria ....................................................................................... 401
estate rentcharge ................................................................................................ 500
estuary management plans ................................................................................ 380
European Community legislation
  basic implications ................................................................................ 431-32
  Environmental Impact Assessment (Amendment) Directive ...................... 400
  Environmental Impact Assessment Directive ................................... 397-400
  Habitats Directive *see* Habitats Directive
  Wild Birds Directive ............................................................................ 432-33
European sites
  adaptation of planning and other controls ........................................... 441-42
  assessment of implications for ................................................................. 442
  assessment and review requirements ................................................... 445-46
  general development orders ...................................................................... 445
  management ......................................................................................... 438-39
  planning permissions, review, revocation and compensation ............... 443-44
  review of existing decisions ................................................................. 442-43
  selection ............................................................................................... 437-38
  special nature conservation orders ....................................................... 440-41
  water level management plans and ...................................................... 447-48
excavations, prohibition for coastal protection ............................................ 232-34
expenses
  coast protection, grants and contributions ........................................... 236-37
  internal drainage boards funding .......................................................... 236-37
extreme flooding events
  Autumn Floods (2000) ........................................................................... 25-27
  East Coast Flood (1953) ......................................................................... 19-22
  Easter Floods (1998) .............................................................................. 23-25

filter drains and permeable surfaces ................................................................ 491
filter strips and swales ............................................................................... 490-91
fire service, emergency response obligations .................................................. 459
flood alleviation
  new requirements ................................................................................ 321-22
  targets ................................................................................................. 308-10
flood and coastal defence
  administration *see* administration
  climate change and ................................................................................ 16-17
  definition ............................................................................................... 1-2, 3
  historical activity ........................................................................................... 6
  legislation in force .................................................................................. 33-34
  legislation principles .............................................................................. 34-35
  policy objectives ..................................................................... 97, 105, 248

Flood Defence Funding Review .................................................................. 245-47
flood hazards *see* flood warnings; hazard
flood insurance
    availability ............................................................................................ 484-86
    claims ........................................................................................................ 8-9
    'flood', meaning of ................................................................................ 481-84
    future practice ........................................................................................... 486
    legal aspects ......................................................................................... 480-81
    risk assessment concerns ...................................................................... 478-80
'flood', meaning in insurance cases ............................................................. 481-84
flood plains, restoration and regeneration .................................................... 506-07
flood warnings ......................................................................................... 97, 105
    civil emergencies .................................................................................. 455-56
    emergency response obligations *see* emergency response obligations
    Environment Agency
        civil emergencies ............................................................................ 455-56
        'Floodline' service ............................................................................... 458
        improvement goals .............................................................................. 459
        liability ........................................................................................... 464-66
        Ministerial directions ..................................................................... 455-56
        National Flood Warning Centre ........................................................... 458
        powers and duties .............................................................. 456, 465-66
        in practice ..................................................................................... 457-59
        propensity of land to flood ............................................................ 466-69
        systems ......................................................................................... 454-55
    'Floodline' service ..................................................................................... 458
    grants for systems ................................................................................. 255-56
    Ministerial directions ............................................................................. 455-56
    National Flood Warning Centre .................................................................. 458
    negligence and ...................................................................................... 462-66
    non-Environment Agency warnings ............................................................. 466
        highway users, flood hazards ......................................................... 469-72
    occupiers' liability *see* occupiers' liability *below*
        propensity of land to flood ............................................................ 466-69
        property transactions, disclosure of hazards .................................... 476-78
    occupiers' liability ............................................................... 472-76, 500-501
        duty of care to visitors ........................................................................ 472
        obvious danger approach ............................................................. 474-746
        trespassers and .................................................................................. 473
    property transactions, disclosure of hazards ............................................ 476-78
flooding
    as adversity ............................................................................................. 6-8
    definition ................................................................................................... 7
    extreme events ...................................................................................... 19-27
    global international agreements and ....................................................... 15-16
    human activities and ................................................................................... 10
    impact ............................................................................................... 7-8, 9
    as natural inundation .......................................................................... 5-6, 7
'Floodline' service ........................................................................................... 458
floodwater, discharge to watercourses .............................................................. 44-46

538  Index

funding
  agricultural valuation principles .................................................................. 269
  annual values
    adjustment ............................................................................................. 269-70
    appeals against determinations ........................................................... 270-71
  arrangements outline ................................................................................. 239-44
  basic principles ............................................................................ 239-43, 251-54
  beneficiary pays principle .......................................................................... 243-45
  borrowing powers ............................................................................................ 275
  central government .................................................................................... 248-51
    consistency of standard .............................................................................. 248
    cost-benefit ........................................................................................... 248, 250
    environment elements ............................................................................ 250-51
    policy objectives ....................................................................... 97, 105, 248
    priorities ................................................................................................. 248-50
    return period specification ......................................................................... 248
  charges .............................................................................................................. 254
  coast protection ........................................................................ 205-06, 236-37, 277
  Coast Protection Act 1949, grants and contributions ............................. 236-37
  cost-benefit ............................................................................................... 248, 250
  costs allocation ........................................................................................... 243-45
  drainage charges, general ........................................................................... 261-63
  drainage charges, special ................................................................................. 263
  drainage levies, differential ....................................................................... 271-73
  drainage rates, differential ......................................................................... 271-73
  drainage rates, appeals .............................................................................. 270-71
  drainage rates, assessment ........................................................................ 267-69
  drainage rates, differential ......................................................................... 271-73
  drainage rates, exemption ......................................................................... 273-74
  Environment Agency
    basic funding ......................................................................................... 251-54
    charges .......................................................................................................... 254
    contributions, from internal drainage boards ..................................... 259-60
    contributions, to internal drainage boards .......................................... 259-60
    contributions, where agency is internal drainage boards .................. 260-61
    drainage charges, general ...................................................................... 261-63
    drainage charges, special ............................................................................. 263
    financial position ......................................................................................... 252
    grants for flood warning systems ......................................................... 255-56
    grants towards expenditure ....................................................... 254-55, 256-57
    levies on local authorities ...................................................................... 257-59
    local powers ............................................................................................ 252-53
    separation of funds ................................................................................ 252-53
    statutory provisions ..................................................................................... 251
  environment elements ............................................................................... 250-51
  Flood Defence Funding Review ................................................................ 245-47
  grants towards expenditure ......................................... 254-55, 256-57, 264-65
  internal drainage boards
    agricultural valuation principles .............................................................. 269
      sub-district division and ..................................................................... 271-73
    annual values, adjustment .................................................................... 269-70

*funding, internal drainage boards (cont.)*
    annual values, appeals against determinations ................................. 270-71
    basic position ........................................................................................... 264
    borrowing powers .................................................................................... 275
    expenses raising ............................................................................... 265-67
    grants towards expenditure ............................................................. 264-65
    hereditaments register ..................................................................... 265-66
    levies .................................................................................................. 265-67
    levies, differential ............................................................................ 271-73
    local authority contributions ........................................................... 275-76
    rates ................................................................................................... 265-67
    rates, appeals ................................................................................... 270-71
    rates, assessment ............................................................................. 267-69
    rates, differential ............................................................................. 271-73
    rates, exemption .............................................................................. 273-74
    special levies .................................................................................... 274-75
  levels ........................................................................................................ 241-43
  levies on local authorities ....................................................................... 257-59
  local authorities
    land drainage finance and .............................................................. 276-77
    levies on .......................................................................................... 257-59
    local powers .................................................................................... 252-53
    outline of arrangements .................................................................. 239-44
    policy objectives ..................................................................... 97, 105, 248
    priorities .......................................................................................... 248-50
    sources ............................................................................................. 241-42
    special levies ................................................................................... 274-75
    statutory provisions ............................................................................. 251

global international agreements and flooding ............................................ 15-16
global warming ............................................................................................. 13-14
good neighbourliness ........................................................................................ 37
green belts, planning guidance ...................................................................... 395
greenhouse gas emissions ........................................................................... 14-15
groundwater
  as buildings support ................................................................................ 77-79
  contamination and sustainable drainage systems ...................................... 498
guidance *see* planning, guidance

Habitats Directive ..................................................................................... 434-35
  Natura 2000 ................................................................................................. 434
  natural habitat types of Community importance ...................................... 434n
  special areas of conservation ............................................................... 434-35
  species of Community interest ................................................................. 434n
Habitats Regulations 1994
  basic legislation ..................................................................................... 435-36
  competent authorities ............................................................... 436-37, 436n
  European sites
    adaptation of planning and other controls ................................... 441-42
    assessment of implications for ............................................................ 442
    assessment and review requirements ............................................ 445-46
    general development orders ............................................................... 445
    management ................................................................................... 438-39

540                                      Index

*Habitats Regulations 1994, European sites (cont.)*
    planning permissions, review, revocation and compensation ........... 443-44
    review of existing decisions .............................................................. 442-43
    selection ................................................................................................ 437-38
    special nature conservation orders .................................................... 440-41
  general duties and powers ........................................................................ 436-37
hazard
  *see also under* flood warnings
  extent .......................................................................................................... 8-10
  potential ..................................................................................................... 9-10
hereditaments
  definition .................................................................................................... 265n
  register ..................................................................................................... 265-66
heritage coast management plans ................................................................ 381
highway authorities ................................................................................... 333-34
  definition ...................................................................................................... 333
  flood hazard warning responsibility ..................................................... 469-72
  maintenance responsibility ................................................... 333-34, 470-72
  sustainable drainage systems adoption ................................................. 496-97
highway drainage
  compensation ......................................................................................... 338-39
  drains, definition ........................................................................ 334-36, 493
    land drainage contrast .......................................................................... 336
    outfall requirement ........................................................................ 335-36
  flood water removal duty .......................................................................... 471
  general maintenance duty ........................................................................ 337
  hazards of nature, protection against ................................................... 342-43
  highway authorities ................................................................................ 333-34
  interference ........................................................................................... 339-40
  land drainage contrast .............................................................................. 336
  operations .............................................................................................. 337-41
    compensation .................................................................................. 338-39
    general maintenance duty ..................................................................... 337
    interference ..................................................................................... 339-40
    powers ............................................................................................. 337-38
    powers distinct from duties ............................................................ 340-41
    sewerage undertakers, notice to ........................................................ 340
  outfall requirement ............................................................................... 335-36
  powers ................................................................................................... 337-38
  roadside ditches
    power to fill in ................................................................................. 341-42
    responsibilities for ........................................................................... 345-47
  sewerage undertakers
    highway authorities, reciprocal agreements with ............................ 344-45
    notice to ............................................................................................... 340
    reciprocal agreements with ............................................................. 344-45
  watercourses diversion .......................................................................... 343-44
historic environment, planning guidance ................................................... 395
historical development of law ..................................................................... 27-28
  early legislation ....................................................................................... 28-30
  land drainage ........................................................................................... 30-32
  modern legislation .................................................................................. 32-34

housing, planning guidance ................................................................. 393
human activities and flooding ............................................................... 10
human rights
    non-sewer flooding .......................................................................... 322
    sewage flooding
        civil liability and ....................................................................... 317-19
        compensation issues ................................................................. 317-21
        Convention rights and .............................................................. 312-14
        justification burden ................................................................. 315-17
    sustainable development costs and ................................................. 512-14

infiltration devices ............................................................................... 491
information access
    basic importance ............................................................................. 449
    confidentiality ................................................................................. 451
    Environment Agency .................................................................. 452-54
    Freedom of Information Act 2000 ............................................... 451-52
    requirements ............................................................................ 450-52
insurance *see* flood insurance
integrated coastal zone management plans ........................................... 381
Intergovernmental Panel on Climate Change ........................................ 102
internal drainage boards .......................................................... 94, 136-38
    administration and membership guidance ........................................ 107
    boundaries ................................................................................ 139-42
    byelaws .................................................................................... 145-46
    composition .............................................................................. 138-39
    concurrent powers .................................................................... 183-84
    constitution .............................................................................. 138-39
    Environment Agency supervision ............................................... 142-44
    environmental concerns *see under* environmental concerns
    funding *see under* funding
    hereditaments register .............................................................. 265-66
    legal functions ............................................................................... 137
    members, appointment and election ................................................ 138
    operational and regulatory powers *see* internal drainage boards, operational
        and regulatory powers *below*
    powers of entry ........................................................................ 146-47
    regulatory powers *see* internal drainage boards, regulatory powers *below*
    relationships with other operating authorities .................................. 144
    reorganisation ........................................................................... 139-42
    supervision of ................................................................................. 183
    supervisory role ............................................................................. 142
internal drainage boards, operational and regulatory powers ................ 188
    disposal of soil ........................................................................... 190-91
    general flood defence works ...................................................... 188-90
        compensation for personal injury ................................................ 189
        outside area ............................................................................... 190
        permissive character .................................................................. 188
    works by arrangement .............................................................. 192-93
internal drainage boards, regulatory powers
    enforcement of repair obligations .............................................. 194-95
    prohibition of obstructions in watercourses ................................. 195-96
    works to maintain watercourses ................................................. 193-94

Kyoto Protocol ............................................................................................................. 15
land
　compulsory acquisition ...................................................................... 224-25
　erosion ....................................................................................................... 79-81
land drainage
　definition ........................................................................................................... 2
　history of legislation .............................................................................. 30-32
land drainage improvement works regulations *see under* environmental impact
　assessment
landowners
　authorisation to carry out works ........................................................ 196-97
　coast protection responsibilities ........................................ 209-13, 229-30
　commutation of obligations ................................................................. 185-86
　ditches, orders requiring cleansing .................................................... 197-99
　duties ................................................................................................................ 95
　maintenance and repair of works ....................................................... 222-24
　rights between in nuisance ..................................................................... 60-62
　　culverting cases .................................................................................. 71-77
　　land drainage rights between ......................................................... 62-66
　　mining cases ........................................................................................ 66-71
　sustainable development costs and .............................................. 511, 513-14
local authorities ................................................................................. 94-95, 148-50
　arrangements with other persons ............................................................. 150
　byelaws ............................................................................................................ 150
　culverting powers .................................................................................. 331-33
　definition ..................................................................................................... 328n
　emergency response obligations ........................................................ 459-61
　environmental concerns *see under* environmental concerns
　highway drainage *see* highway drainage
　internal drainage boards, contributions to ...................................... 275-76
　land drainage finance and ................................................................... 276-77
　levies on ................................................................................................... 257-59
　'local councils', definition ....................................................................... 257n
　operational and regulatory powers *see* local authorities, operational and
　　regulatory powers *below*
　powers of entry ............................................................................................. 150
　public health *see* public health
　regulatory powers *see* local authorities, regulatory powers *below*
　reservoir safety *see* reservoir safety
　statutory powers ................................................................................... 148-49
　supervision of ............................................................................ 149-50, 184-85
　sustainable drainage systems adoption ............................................ 496-97
local authorities, operational and regulatory powers ............................ 188
　disposal of soil ........................................................................................ 190-91
　general flood defence works ............................................................... 188-90
　　compensation for personal injury ...................................................... 189
　　outside area .............................................................................................. 190
　　permissive character .............................................................................. 188
　small area drainage ....................................................................................... 191
　works by arrangement .......................................................................... 192-93

## Index 543

local authorities, regulatory powers
    works to maintain watercourses ............... 193-94
local councils, definition ............... 257n
local environment agency plans ............... 381
local flood defence committees ............... 123-24
local legislation, survival of mandatory duties ............... 199-203
London
    administrative arrangements ............... 150-51
    insurance risk ............... 480
    legislation ............... 150-51
    'London excluded area' ............... 150-51, 154
    Thames Barrier ............... 152-54, 480
        legal basis ............... 152
        legal powers ............... 153-54
        offences ............... 154

main rivers
    controls over structures in ............... 178-79
    designation ............... 127-31
*Marcic* case
    common law claim ............... 310-12
    facts ............... 307-08
    human rights issues ............... 312-14
        compensation ............... 319-21
        Court of Appeal's approach ............... 317-19
        High Court's approach ............... 314-17
    implications ............... 321-22
    priorities for sewerage improvements, determining .. ............... 308-10
maritime districts ............... 213-14
maritime local authorities ... ............... 94-95
mining operations ............... 66-71
Minister
    approval ............... 414-18
    default powers for coast protection ............... 235-36
    directions ............... 421-22
    flood warnings directions ............... 455-56
    general powers ............... 159-60
    planning guidance ............... 372-73
    policy objectives ............... 97, 105, 248

National Assembly for Wales ............... 112-14
National Flood and Coastal Defence Database ............... 105
National Flood Warning Centre ............... 458
National Rivers Authority ... ............... 33-34
Natura 2000 ............... 434
nature conservancy councils ............... 423
    authorisation of operations ............... 428-29
    European sites
        management ............... 438-39
        special nature conservation orders ............... 440-41
    management notices ............... 429-30
    management schemes ............... 429-30
    Ramsar sites duties ............... 431

# 544 Index

nature conservation
  *see also* environmental concerns
  conservation land designation .................................................................... 423
  legislation ............................................................................................... 422-23
  nature conservancy councils *see under* nature conservancy councils *above*
  scale of conservation land designation ...................................................... 423
  sites of special scientific interest, notification and protection ............... 423-25
navigation rights, variation ................................................................................ 187
negligence
  definition ........................................................................................................ 82
  flood warnings and ................................................................................. 462-66
  liability for escape of water ............................................................ 325, 326-27
  nuisance and ............................................................................................ 81-86
  prevention of flooding and ....................................................................... 83-86
Northern Ireland ................................................................................................... 3
notification concerning works, for coastal protection ................................... 231-32
nuisance ............................................................................................................. 38
  actions in ................................................................................................. 62-63
  liability for escape of water ....................................................................... 325
  negligence and ......................................................................................... 81-86
  rights between landowners ....................................................................... 60-62

occupiers' liability *see under* flood warnings
operational powers ........................................................................................... 159
outfall requirement
  highway drainage ................................................................................... 335-36
  public sewer ........................................................................................... 290-93

permeable surfaces .......................................................................................... 491
planning
  administration of law .............................................................................. 357-58
  agenda 21 plans ......................................................................................... 381
  application procedures, flood risk guidance ........................................... 387-89
  archaeology ............................................................................................... 395
  authorities, civil liability .............................................................................. 357
  basic system .......................................................................................... 356-57
  biodiversity action plans ............................................................................ 381
  building control ..................................................................................... 406-07
  catchment flood management plans .......................................................... 380
  coastal .................................................................................................. 390-92
    basic issues ............................................................................................ 391
    types ................................................................................................ 390-91
    zone limits ............................................................................................. 390
  coastal habitat management plans ....................................................... 380-81
  coastal zone limits ..................................................................................... 390
  community strategies ................................................................................. 381
  conditions ............................................................................................. 364-68
    flood alleviation and ............................................................................ 367-68
    initial and maintenance responsibilities .............................................. 367-68
  conservation ............................................................................................... 392
  consultation requirements ......................................................................... 362
    flood risk guidance ............................................................................ 387-89

*planning (cont.)*
   contaminated land ............................................................................................. 394
   developer contributions, flood risk guidance ................................................ 386-87
   development control
      consultation requirements ....................................................................... 362
      development, definition .......................................................................... 360
      flood risk guidance ............................................................................. 385-86
      flooding impacts as material consideration ....................................... 362-63
      permitted developments ...................................................................... 361-62
      sewage disposal as material consideration ........................................ 363-64
   development guidance *see* guidance *below*
   development plans ....................................................................................... 358-60
      Environment Agency influence ........................................................... 369-70
      flood risk guidance ............................................................................. 383-85
      local plans ................................................................................................ 358
      planning permission and .................................................................... 359-60
      structure plans ........................................................................................ 358
      unitary development plans ..................................................................... 358
   Environment Agency role *see under* Environment Agency
   environmental impact assessment *see under* environmental impact assessment
   environmental procedures ......................................................................... 396-97
   estuary management plans ............................................................................ 380
   European sites
      adaptation of planning controls .......................................................... 441-42
      planning permissions, review, revocation and compensation .......... 443-44
   flooding impacts as material consideration ............................................... 362-63
   green belts ..................................................................................................... 395
   guidance .................................................................................................. 372-73
      agenda 21 plans ...................................................................................... 381
      application procedures ....................................................................... 387-89
      archaeology ............................................................................................ 395
      biodiversity action plans ....................................................................... 381
      catchment flood management plans ..................................................... 380
      coastal habitat management plans .................................................. 380-81
      community strategies .............................................................................. 381
      conservation ............................................................................................ 392
      consultation procedures ..................................................................... 387-89
      contaminated land .................................................................................. 394
      developer contributions ..................................................................... 386-87
      development control ........................................................................... 385-86
      development plans ............................................................................. 383-85
      estuary management plans ..................................................................... 380
      flood risk ............................................................................ 373-74, 374-75
      green belts ............................................................................................. 395
      heritage coast management plans ......................................................... 381
      historic environment .............................................................................. 395
      housing ................................................................................................... 393
      housing provision .............................................................................. 379-80
      integrated coastal zone management plans .......................................... 381
      integration of plans ........................................................................... 380-81
      local environment agency plans ............................................................ 381

*planning, guidance (cont.)*
    as material consideration .................................................. 375-77
    precautionary principle and ................................................ 374-75
    previously developed land .................................................. 379-80
    recreation ........................................................................... 395
    regional planning ............................................................... 382-83
    risk assessment .................................................................. 374-75
    river basin management plans ............................................ 381
    sequential test .................................................................... 377-79
    shoreline management plans .............................................. 380
    sport and recreation ........................................................... 395
    sustainable drainage systems ............................................. 381-82
    unstable land, development on .......................................... 395
    water level management plans .......................................... 381
  heritage coast management plans ............................................ 381
  historic environment ............................................................... 395
  housing .................................................................................... 393
  integrated coastal zone management plans .............................. 381
  land use control systems and .................................................. 356
  local environment agency plans .............................................. 381
  local plans ............................................................................... 358
  obligations .............................................................................. 365-68
    environmental benefits ...................................................... 366-67
    flood alleviation and ......................................................... 367-68
    initial and maintenance responsibilities ............................ 367-68
  permitted developments .......................................................... 361-62
  recreation ................................................................................ 395
  regional ................................................................................... 382-83
  river basin management plans ................................................ 381
  sequential test ......................................................................... 377-79
  sewage disposal as material consideration .............................. 363-64
  shoreline management plans ................................................... 380
  sport and recreation, guidance ................................................ 395
  statutory undertaker, definition ............................................... 426n
  strategic environment assessment ........................................... 404-06
  structure plans ........................................................................ 358
  sustainable drainage systems .................................................. 381-82
    contaminated land and ...................................................... 394
  unitary development plans ...................................................... 358
  unstable land, development on ............................................... 395
  water level management plans ............................................... 381
planning development
  definition ................................................................................ 360
  guidance *see under* planning
police service, emergency response obligations ............................ 459
policy objectives ........................................................................... 97, 105, 248
ponds
  cleansing powers .................................................................... 330
  sustainable land drainage and ................................................. 491-92
powers of entry ............................................................................. 146-47, 150
  for coast protection ................................................................. 234-35

precautionary principle ............................................................. 17-19
   aversity to risk ......................................................................... 17-18
   planning development and .................................................... 374-75
   planning guidance and .......................................................... 18-19
   probability standards .................................................................. 18
   reservoir safety and .................................................................. 347
private drain ........................................................................................ 493
private landowners *see* landowners
private law *see* civil law
private and local legislation, survival of mandatory duties ......... 199-203
private watercourses, Environment Agency jurisdiction ................. 493
privatisation ........................................................................................... 33
probability standards ............................................................................ 18
property transactions, disclosure of flooding hazard ................. 476-78
public authorities, conservation duties ......................................... 426-28
   authorisation of operations .................................................. 428-29
   biological diversity ................................................................. 430-31
   compulsory acquisition and restoration ...................................... 430
   definition of public authority .................................................... 426n
   management notices ............................................................... 429-30
   management schemes ............................................................ 429-30
   notification duties ................................................................... 427-28
   Ramsar sites ........................................................................... 430-31
public bodies ................................................................................... 92-95
   civil liability ............................................................................. 86-91
      statutory immunity less likely ............................................. 87-88
      statutory immunity more likely .......................................... 88-89
   responsibilities allocation ....................................................... 92-94
public health
   culverting powers .................................................................. 331-33
   ponds and ditches, cleansing powers ........................................ 330
   statutory nuisances ................................................................ 328-30
public sewer ........................................................................... 283, 493-94
   *see also* sewerage undertakers
   changes in use ....................................................................... 287-89
   culverting, significance ......................................................... 289-90
   customer service standards ................................................... 299-301
   functional definition .................................................................. 284
      changes in use .................................................................. 287-89
      culverting, significance .................................................... 289-90
      purpose of construction .................................................... 284-86
   proper outfall requirement .................................................... 290-93
   purpose of construction ........................................................ 284-86
   right of connection ................................................................ 495-96
   sewer maps ............................................................................ 293-95
      before 1 September 1989 ...................................................... 294
   statutory provisions on flooding ........................................... 299-304
      customer service standards ............................................. 299-301
      discharges from sewers ................................................... 301-03

rainfall predictions ................................................................................ 14
Ramsar sites .................................................................................. 430-31

recreation, planning guidance ................................................................ 395
regional flood defence committees ...................................................... 121-23
regional planning ................................................................................ 382-83
regulatory powers .................................................................................... 159
rentcharge ................................................................................................ 500
reservoir safety
    abandonment ................................................................................ 352-53
    basic responsibilities ......................................................................... 347
    certification of reservoirs ............................................................... 349-50
    civil engineers panel .......................................................................... 349
    civil liability ................................................................................... 354-55
    criminal liability ............................................................................ 354-55
    discontinuance ............................................................................... 352-53
    enforcement authorities ................................................................ 348-49
    enforcement powers ...................................................................... 353-54
    large raised reservoirs ........................................................................ 348
    legislation ............................................................................................ 347
    local authorities registration of reservoirs .................................... 348-49
    periodic inspections ....................................................................... 350-52
    powers of entry .............................................................................. 353-54
    precautionary approach ...................................................................... 347
    qualifications of engineers ................................................................ 349
return period ..................................................................................... 10-12
rights of support ................................................................................ 77-79
Rio Earth Summit .................................................................................... 15
riparian rights and duties .................................................................. 38, 39
    *see also* watercourses
    flowing water ....................................................................................... 41
    ownership ......................................................................................... 39-41
riparian rights and duties, drainage ........................................................ 44
    alleviating flooding from watercourses ........................................ 46-51
        artificial watercourses ............................................................... 50-51
        balancing of interests ................................................................ 47-48
        identifiable flood channel ......................................................... 48-49
        landowner's obligations ............................................................ 49-50
        landowner's power .......................................................................... 49
        other activities ................................................................................. 51
    discharge of floodwater to watercourses ...................................... 44-46
    duty to receive natural flow .......................................................... 45-46
    maintaining channel of watercourse
        easements and ........................................................................... 58-60
        modern approach ...................................................................... 56-58
        powers distinct from duties ..................................................... 52-54
        traditional approach .................................................................. 54-56
    right to natural flow ........................................................................... 44
risk ............................................................................................ 10-13, 17-18
    *see also* precautionary principle
    assessment .......................................................................................... 106
    indicative assessment ..................................................................... 12-13
    return period ................................................................................... 10-12

## Index 549

river basin management plans .................................................................. 381
river boards ................................................................................................ 33
rivers, main *see* main rivers
Royal Commission on Land Drainage ................................................. 30-32

Scotland ....................................................................................................... 3
sea defence commissioners ............................................................ 230 & n
seashore, definition ............................................................................... 213n
sequential test ..................................................................................... 377-79
sewage flooding *see under* human rights; sewerage undertakers
sewer
   *see also* sewerage undertakers *below*
   commissions of sewers ................................................................... 29-30
   definition .......................................................................... 281, 281n, 283
   distinct from drain ....................................................................... 282-83
   public *see* public sewer
sewerage
   *see also* public sewer; sewer; sewerage undertakers
   adoption *see under* sustainable drainage systems
   basic issues .................................................................................. 278-79
   commissions of sewers ................................................................... 29-30
   responsibilities ............................................................................. 279-81
   right of connection ........................................................................... 281
   sewage disposal as material planning consideration ................. 363-64
   sewer maps .................................................................................. 293-95
      before 1 September 1989 .......................................................... 294
   vesting declaration .......................................................................... 280
sewerage undertakers ................................................................... 279-81
   *see also* public sewer
   adoption of system as public drain *see under* sustainable drainage systems
   civil liability .................................................................. 304-06, 310-12
      misfeasance and non-feasance ............................................. 305-06
   flood alleviation
      new requirements .................................................................. 321-22
      priorities .............................................................. 308-10, 316-17
   highway authorities
      notice to ...................................................................................... 340
      reciprocal agreements with ................................................ 344-45
   sewage flooding
      civil liability ............................................................................ 310-12
      flood alleviation, new requirement ....................................... 321-22
      flood alleviation priorities .............................. 308-10, 316-17
      flood alleviation, priorities ............................ 308-10, 316-17
      human rights issues *see* human rights, sewage flooding
      *Marcic* case *see Marcic* case
   vesting in ..................................................................................... 295-99
      historic responsibilities issues ............................................. 298-99
      vesting of sewers in ............................................................. 295-99
shoreline management plans ..................................... 106, 237-38, 380
sites of special interest ............................................................... 412-14

sites of special scientific interest ........................................................... 420-21
    see also under environmental concerns
    authorisation of operations ................................................................ 428-29
    compulsory acquisition and restoration ................................................. 430
    management schemes and notices ...................................................... 429-30
    notification .......................................................................................... 423-25
    offences ............................................................................................... 424-25
    protection ............................................................................................ 423-25
    water level management plans and .................................................... 447-48
small areas
    drainage ..................................................................................................... 191
    schemes .................................................................................................... 176
special areas of conservation ........................................................................ 434-35
sport and recreation, planning guidance ....................................................... 395
statutory undertaker, definition ..................................................................... 426n
'storm, tempest or flood', meaning in insurance cases .................................. 481-84
Storm Tide Warning Service ........................................................................... 97
strategic environment assessment .............................................................. 404-06
structure plans ................................................................................................ 358
surface water management, new approach ..................................................... 488-89
sustainable coast defence .............................................................................. 507-10
    environmental concerns ..................................................................... 507, 509
    managed realignment ............................................................................ 508-10
sustainable development
    basic issues ............................................................................................. 487-89
    compensation ........................................................................................... 511-13
    cost
        compensation ..................................................................................... 511-13
        human rights and ................................................................................ 512-14
        landowners and ......................................................................... 511, 513-14
        reasonable reliance liability ............................................................... 510-11
    definition ...................................................................................................... 487
    human rights and ..................................................................................... 512-14
    reasonable reliance liability ..................................................................... 510-11
    surface water management, new approach ............................................ 488-89
sustainable drainage systems ........................................................... 381-82, 488-89
    agricultural land drainage and urban flooding ....................................... 501-04
    basic approaches ........................................................................... 489-90, 492
    basins and ponds ..................................................................................... 491-92
    contaminated land and ................................................................................ 394
    conventional techniques, criticisms ........................................................ 489-90
    Environment Agency involvement ................................... 116-18, 119, 497-98
        groundwater contamination ................................................................ 498
        water quality effects .............................................................................. 497
    filter drains and permeable surfaces ............................................................ 491
    filter strips and swales ............................................................................ 490-91
    highway authority adoption ..................................................................... 496-97
    infiltration devices ........................................................................................ 491
    legal issues .............................................................................................. 492-93
        categorisation issues .......................................................................... 493-94
        sewerage adoption implications see sewerage adoption implications below

*sustainable drainage systems (cont.)*
  local authority adoption .................................................................. 496-97
  private responsibilities .................................................................. 499-501
    communal drainage .................................................................. 499-500
    estate rentcharge .......................................................................... 500
    hazard considerations .............................................................. 500-501
    maintenance cost, assessment ....................................................... 499
    maintenance cost, distribution ................................................ 499-500
    occupiers' liability .................................................................... 500-501
  sewerage adoption implications .................................................. 494-96
    maintenance responsibilities ........................................................ 494
    public sewer implications .......................................................... 494-95
    right of connection ..................................................................... 495-96
  undeveloped land ........................................................................... 501-04
    urban flooding and drainage of agricultural land .................... 501-04
sustainable flood defence .................................................................. 504-07
  flood plains, restoration and regeneration .................................. 506-07
  soft engineering solutions ............................................................ 504-06
swales ............................................................................................... 490-91

Thames Barrier *see under* London
tidal water ................................................................................................ 43
town and country planning *see* planning

uncertainty *see* risk
undeveloped land, sustainable drainage systems and ..................... 501-04
unitary development plans .................................................................... 358
unstable land, planning guidance .......................................................... 395
urban flooding, agricultural drainage and ..................................... 501-02

warnings *see* flood warnings
warping ..................................................................................................... 1n
water
  authorities .............................................................................................. 33
  quantity distinct from quality .......................................................... 3, 4-5
  supply
    basic issues .............................................................................. 278-79, 322
    civil liability for escape of water ............................................... 325-27
    statutory liability for escape of water ..................................... 323-25
      negligence liability ..................................................................... 325
      nuisance liability ........................................................................ 325
      strict liability ........................................................................ 323-24
water level management plans ........................... 98-99, 106-07, 381, 447-48
watercourses ....................................................................................... 41-44
  *see also* main river, designation
  alleviating flooding from .............................................................. 46-51
  artificially constructed channels ................................................ 42-43
    alleviating flooding from ........................................................... 50-51
  culverting
    local authority powers ............................................................ 331-33
    significance of .......................................................................... 289-90
  definition ..................................................................................... 1n, 41-42

*watercourses (cont.)*
    discharge of floodwater to ........................................................................ 44-46
    flow maintenance powers .................................................................... 182-83
    highway drainage diversion ................................................................ 343-44
    maintaining channel of watercourse
        modern approach ........................................................................ 56-58
        powers distinct from duties ................................................. 52-54, 329-30
        traditional approach ..................................................................... 54-56
    obstructions, prohibition of .................................................................. 195-96
    private, Environment Agency jurisdiction ................................................. 493
    public sewer status ............................................................................. 287-89
    repairs powers ................................................................................... 181-82
    statutory nuisances and ..................................................................... 329-30
    tidal water ................................................................................................ 43
    underground flows ............................................................................... 43-44
    works to maintain .............................................................................. 193-94
Wild Birds Directive ...................................................................................... 432-33